Australian Policing

This edited collection brings together leading academics, researchers, and police personnel to provide a comprehensive body of literature that informs Australian police education, training, research, policy, and practice. There is a strong history and growth in police education, both in Australia and globally. Recognising and reflecting on the Australian and New Zealand Policing Advisory Agency (ANZPAA) education and training framework, the range of chapters within the book address a range of 21st-century issues modern police forces face. This book discusses four key themes:

- **Education, training, and professional practice**: topics include police education, ethics, wellbeing, and leadership
- **Organisational approaches and techniques**: topics include police discretion, use of force, investigative interviewing, and forensic science
- **Operational practices and procedures**: topics include police and the media, emergency management, cybercrime, terrorism, and community management
- **Working with individuals and groups**: topics include mental health, Indigenous communities, young people, hate crime, domestic violence, and working with victims

Australian Policing: Critical Issues in 21st Century Police Practice draws together theoretical and practice debates to ensure this book will be of interest to those who want to join the police, those who are currently training to become a police officer, and those who are currently serving. This book is essential reading for all students, scholars, and researchers engaged with policing and the criminal justice sector.

Philip Birch is Associate Professor of Criminology and Policing in the Centre for Law and Justice at Charles Sturt University, Australia.

Michael Kennedy has been a senior lecturer in the Western Sydney University Bachelor of Policing programme since 2004.

Erin Kruger is a lecturer in criminology and policing at Western Sydney University.

Australian Policing

Critical Issues in 21st Century Police Practice

Edited by

Philip Birch,
Michael Kennedy,
and Erin Kruger

LONDON AND NEW YORK

First published 2021
by Routledge
2 Park Square, Milton Park, Abingdon, Oxon OX14 4RN

and by Routledge
52 Vanderbilt Avenue, New York, NY 10017

Routledge is an imprint of the Taylor & Francis Group, an informa business

© 2021 selection and editorial matter, Philip Birch, Michael Kennedy and Erin Kruger; individual chapters, the contributors

The right of Philip Birch, Michael Kennedy and Erin Kruger to be identified as the authors of the editorial material, and of the authors for their individual chapters, has been asserted in accordance with sections 77 and 78 of the Copyright, Designs and Patents Act 1988.

All rights reserved. No part of this book may be reprinted or reproduced or utilised in any form or by any electronic, mechanical, or other means, now known or hereafter invented, including photocopying and recording, or in any information storage or retrieval system, without permission in writing from the publishers.

Trademark notice: Product or corporate names may be trademarks or registered trademarks, and are used only for identification and explanation without intent to infringe.

British Library Cataloguing-in-Publication Data
A catalogue record for this book is available from the British Library

Library of Congress Cataloging-in-Publication Data
Names: Birch, Philip (Criminologist), editor. | Kennedy, Michael (Criminologist), editor. | Kruger, Erin (Criminologist), editor.
Title: Australian policing : critical issues in 21st century police practice / edited by Philip Birch, Michael Kennedy and Erin Kruger.
Description: Abingdon, Oxon ; New York, NY : Routledge, 2021. | Includes bibliographical references and index.
Identifiers: LCCN 2020037470 | ISBN 9780367464660 (hardback) | ISBN 9781003028918 (ebook)
Subjects: LCSH: Police—Australia.
Classification: LCC HV8280.A2 A953 2021 | DDC 363.20994—dc23
LC record available at https://lccn.loc.gov/2020037470

ISBN: 978-0-367-46466-0 (hbk)
ISBN: 978-0-367-46467-7 (pbk)
ISBN: 978-1-003-02891-8 (ebk)

Typeset in Giovanni, Stone Sans, and Helvetica
by Apex CoVantage, LLC

Philip, Michael, and Erin would like to dedicate this book to all Australian Police Forces and their staff.

Contents

List of figures — xi
List of tables — xiii
About the editors — xv
List of contributors — xvii
Foreword by Michael Fuller — xxxi
Acknowledgements — xxxiii

Examining Australian policing in the 21st century — 1
PHILIP BIRCH, MICHAEL KENNEDY AND ERIN KRUGER

SECTION 1
Education, training, and professional practice — 5

CHAPTER 1 Police education in Australia — 7
COLIN ROGERS AND EMMA WINTLE

CHAPTER 2 Becoming a pracademic: the importance of lifelong learning as a police officer in the 21st century — 23
MELANIE BOURSNELL AND PHILIP BIRCH

CHAPTER 3 Police leadership in the 21st century — 39
GRAHAM SUNDERLAND AND IAN STEWART

CHAPTER 4 The incorporation of multidisciplinary approaches to enhance police communication strategies — 55
KEN WOODEN

| CHAPTER 5 | A critical social justice issue of our time: enabling police wellbeing | 71 |

RHONDA CRAVEN, HERBERT W. MARSH, RICHARD M. RYAN, PAUL W.B. ATKINS, THERESA DICKE, JIESI GUO, PETER GALLAGHER, BROOKE VAN ZANDEN, MICHAEL KENNEDY, AND PHILIP BIRCH

| CHAPTER 6 | Ethics and police practice | 93 |

ALAN BECKLEY AND MICHAEL KENNEDY

SECTION 2
Organisational approaches and techniques — 111

| CHAPTER 7 | Discretion: the elephant in the room | 113 |

MARK FINDLAY

| CHAPTER 8 | Criminal intelligence in Australia | 129 |

TROY WHITFORD AND SHANE LYSONS-SMITH

| CHAPTER 9 | Investigative interviewing and police practice | 145 |

DAREN JAY AND GARY PANKHURST

| CHAPTER 10 | Forensic science in policing | 163 |

GLENN PORTER

| CHAPTER 11 | Police use of force: an examination of Australian policing | 183 |

DRAGANA KESIC AND STUART D.M. THOMAS

| CHAPTER 12 | Working with others: future policing partnerships | 199 |

DOUGLAS E. ABRAHAMSON AND JANE GOODMAN-DELAHUNTY

| CHAPTER 13 | Policing and security: critiquing the privatisation story in Australia | 221 |

RICK SARRE AND TIM PRENZLER

SECTION 3
Operational practices and procedures — 237

| CHAPTER 14 | Police, media, and the digital age in Australia | 239 |

JOHN GAFFEY

CHAPTER 15	Public health and its interface with police practice in the 21st century	253
	STUART D.M. THOMAS	
CHAPTER 16	Emergency management and the role of state police	267
	IAN MANOCK AND SIMON ROBINSON	
CHAPTER 17	Community safety, crime prevention, and 21st century policing	283
	TIM PRENZLER AND RICK SARRE	
CHAPTER 18	Terrorism and the role of state police	299
	NICK KALDAS	
CHAPTER 19	Organised and transnational crime: the impact on Australian police	315
	ANTHONY MORGAN, RICK BROWN, ISABELLA VOCE, AND TIMOTHY CUBITT	
CHAPTER 20	Policing cybercrime: an inside look at private and public cybercrime investigations	333
	ALANA MAURUSHAT AND HADEEL AL-ALOSI	
CHAPTER 21	Australian police officers and international policing practice	349
	KELLY MOYLAN, IRENA VELJANOVA, MICHAEL KENNEDY, AND PHILIP BIRCH	

SECTION 4
Working with individuals and groups — 365

CHAPTER 22	Mental health and the policing context	367
	ERIN KRUGER	
CHAPTER 23	Young people, the police, and policing	383
	PHILIP BIRCH AND LOUISE A. SICARD	
CHAPTER 24	Policing settler colonial societies	397
	AMANDA PORTER AND CHRIS CUNNEEN	
CHAPTER 25	Hate crime: insights into the context, setting, and prevalence	413
	PHILIP BIRCH AND JANE L. IRELAND	

CHAPTER 26	**Policing interpersonal violence**	**429**
	MARK R. KEBBELL AND JANET M. EVANS	
CHAPTER 27	**Policing domestic and family violence**	**443**
	CHRISTOPHER DOWLING, HAYLEY BOXALL, AND ANTHONY MORGAN	
CHAPTER 28	**Police interaction with vulnerable victims**	**461**
	AMBER MCKINLEY	

Index   477

Figures

5.1	SDT Basic Psychological Needs. Psychological Needs Satisfaction and wellbeing stems from the satisfaction of the three basic psychological needs: 1) competence; 2) relatedness; and 3) autonomy	73
5.2	Coping mechanisms employed by members of police organisation	76
5.3	Autonomy support and thwarting across police career stages as measured by percentage of interviews with examples of autonomy support and thwarting coded in text	80
5.4	Competence support and thwarting across police career stages as measured by percentage of interviews with examples of competence support and thwarting coded in text	81
5.5	Relatedness support and thwarting across police career stages as measured by percentage of interviews with examples of relatedness support and thwarting coded in text	81
5.6	Needs support and wellbeing as measured by percentage of interviews classified as "low" or "high" wellbeing.	83
5.7	Needs thwarting and wellbeing as measured by percentage of interviews classified as "low" or "high" wellbeing	83
6.1	Public respect, trust, confidence, and pride in the police force	96
6.2	Results from the quality of service questions in the survey, group *Gender*	103

6.3	Boxplots from the quality of service questions: "Some victims of crime are more deserving of a good service than others" and: "It is a waste of time trying to help some members of the public", in the survey, analysis of group *Gender*	103
6.4	Organisational measures to improve professional standards	104
9.1	Free Recall Model	151
9.2	Conversation Management Framework	152
9.3	Conversation Management Planning Methodology	156
10.1	A theoretical model that consists of three separate elements: process, function, and principles	171
10.2	Mean estimated height of Australian males between 25–34 years	175
12.1	Police-community Continuum of Interaction	207
12.2	Collaborative Policing Framework	209
12.3	Policy Capability Knowledge Barriers	212
12.4	Perceived Impediments to Information and Knowledge Sharing by Police Agency	213
25.1	PRISMA flow chart of included studies	417

Tables

1.1	The process of professionalising the police	15
1.2	Police education and training in Australia	17
5.1	Needs support in the police	79
5.2	Wellbeing program perceived helpfulness	85
10.1	Overview of where forensic science divisions are positioned and their disciplines within forensic practice	165
10.2	Summary of methodologies, including examples of which disciplines are used within those forms of forensic inquiry	172

About the editors

Philip Birch is Associate Professor of Criminology and Policing in the Centre for Law and Justice at Charles Sturt University, Australia. He has previously held posts at the University of Western Sydney, the University of New South Wales, Sydney, Australia, and the University of Huddersfield, in the United Kingdom. Prior to entering academia, Philip worked as a criminologist in the field, holding posts in the UK prison service as well as in the crime and disorder field, which involved managing a specialist crime unit. Philip has published internationally, including books, book chapters, peer reviewed articles, and government reports in his main areas of research: offender management and rehabilitation; police, prisons, and probation practices; and gender symmetry violence, with a particular focus on domestic/family violence and sex work. Philip holds an honorary research fellowship in the School of Psychology, University of Central Lancashire, UK, as well as a Professorial Associate in the Ashworth Research Centre, Mersey Health Care, National Health Services, UK.

Michael Kennedy has been a senior lecturer in the Western Sydney University Bachelor of Policing programme since 2004. Between 1978 and 1996, Michael was a detective in the New South Wales Police. He specialised in organised and major crime investigation and worked at the NSW Crime Commission. Dr Kennedy has also worked with the Brigade de Répression du Proxénétisme and the Brigade du Protection des Mineurs Prefecture, Paris, France. Dr Kennedy worked extensively with the Arabic-speaking community and also specialised in child protection and sexual assault investigations. Between 2013 to 2017 Dr Kennedy was head of the programme ISLES (Security and Law Enforcement) on behalf of Western Sydney University in the Islamic Republic of Maldives.

Erin Kruger is a lecturer in criminology and policing at Western Sydney University. She teaches and researches in the areas of criminology and policing, broadly, and forensics, surveillance, international crime, and high-risk offenders, specifically. Erin has a range of criminal justice employment experience, including working in restorative justice, and as part of a forensic identification unit with a Canadian police agency. She has published in such journals as *Policing and Society*, *Surveillance and Society*, *Body and Society*, *Parallax*, and *Interdisciplinary Science Reviews*. Her 2020 forthcoming works include a sole-authored article, "Covert Positivism in Forensic Domains", in the journal *International Journal for Crime, Justice and Social Democracy*. She also has a sole-authored monograph forthcoming with Routledge's Law, Science and Society series, entitled *The Forensic Image: Scientific Visualization and DNA*.

Contributors

Douglas E. Abrahamson is an adjunct faculty member at Charles Sturt University, a Honorary Research Associate with the Justice Institute of British Columbia (Canada) and an independent consultant who focuses on building public safety and security "good governance" capabilities and capacities around the globe. Over the last 25 years, as a police officer and academic, he has championed improved public safety and security practices at the local, national, and international levels generally and within Canada, United States, Australia, and the United Arab Emirates specifically. Dr Abrahamson currently serves as a peer reviewer for the *Journal of Criminological Research, Policy & Practice, Frontiers in Psychology: Forensic and Legal Psychology* and *Policing & Society: An International Journal of Research and Policy*. His research interests focus on evidence-based policies and practices, organisational information and knowledge sharing, forensic identification science best practices, team (business) coaching, and workplace bullying and harassment prevention.

Hadeel Al-Alosi is a law lecturer at Western Sydney University whose main research interests are related to the legal and societal responses to the abuse of women and children. Hadeel's research is socio-legal and spans across multiple disciplines such as law, criminology, and psychology. Hadeel's doctoral thesis addressed Australia's child abuse material legislation and involved conducting a cross-jurisdictional analysis of the relevant laws in Canada, the United Kingdom, and the United States. It specifically looked at the potential criminalisation of fantasy material, particularly in the form of animations and fictional stories, under current Western laws. These controversial and intriguing issues are discussed in depth in Hadeel's recently published book, *The Criminalisation of Fantasy Material: Law & Sexually Explicit Representations of Fictional Children*.

Paul W.B. Atkins is a facilitator, trainer, executive coach, and researcher. He is a visiting associate professor at the Crawford School of Public Policy, Australian National University. Paul's work has been published in the world's leading management and psychology journals, as well as in two books: *Mindfulness in Organizations* and *Prosocial: Using Evolutionary Science to Build Productive, Equitable, and Collaborative Groups*. Paul is past President of the Australia and New Zealand Association for Contextual Behavioural Science, and has recently been made a Fellow of the international ACBS. He runs a company called The Prosocial Institute that specialises in training facilitators in the Prosocial process to improving teamwork, communication, and conflict resolution.

Alan Beckley served as a police officer in the UK, serving for 30 years in Surrey Police and West Mercia Constabulary. He was then a management consultant for nine years, working in the public sector in the UK and with national police forces in the UK and Europe. The bulk of his work has been focused at the central government level, mainly programme and project management and organisational development. His expertise is in corporate governance and police ethics/human rights issues, risk and contingency planning in the police service, and comparative legal and policing studies. Alan's main work relates to human rights, responses to major and critical incidents, and police ethics. He has taught as a lecturer and visiting fellow at several UK and Australian universities. He is a published author on many police-related subjects and has completed assignments in the police service internationally.

Melanie Boursnell is the Director of Learning Innovation for NSW Police. As an experienced government senior executive, Dr Boursnell has led large-scale organisational transformation and thrives on challenge. Dr Boursnell has held academic positions at the Universities of Newcastle and Sydney whilst concurrently maintaining practice in the areas of mental health and violence, abuse, and neglect, which have also been her research areas. Dr Boursnell is interested in understanding how people engage in learning in the workplace through desire as opposed to direction, in order to continue to evolve and develop their capabilities as a reflection of a flourishing workplace culture.

Hayley Boxall is Principal Research Analyst with the Australian Institute of Criminology's Violence against Women and Children Research Program. Since joining the Institute ten years ago, she has published extensively on domestic and family violence, with a main focus on the criminal careers of domestic and family violence offenders, adolescent family violence, and policing responses to domestic and family violence. Hayley has been the primary investigator on a number of projects aimed at improving current responses to domestic and family violence and victim/survivors, and understanding pathways into domestic and family violence victimisation and offending. Hayley is a PhD candidate at the Australian National University. Her thesis focuses on domestic violence desistance processes.

Rick Brown is the Deputy Director of the Australian Institute of Criminology and a visiting fellow of policing and criminal justice at the University of Derby. He previously ran a crime and justice research consultancy and worked for the Home Office Police Research Group in London. He has published over 60 government reports, book chapters, and journal articles. These have examined a range of issues associated with policing and organised crime, including the financial investigation of organised crime, the use of criminal intelligence, the links between volume crime and organised crime, and the policing of organised vehicle crime.

Rhonda Craven is the inaugural Director of the Institute for Positive Psychology and Education (IPPE), Australian Catholic University (ACU). She is a leading researcher in large-scale education and wellbeing multi-method research. She is an accomplished researcher, having successfully secured over $12 million in nationally competitive funding for 51 large-scale research projects, including 31 prestigious Australian Research Council grants. Her research interests include: educational excellence and innovation; interventions that make a tangible difference in maximising wellbeing and life potential in educational, community, and organisation settings; the structure, measurement, development, and enhancement of wellbeing, self-concept, and key psycho-social drivers of human potential; the impact of enhancing psycho-social drivers on performance, and other desirable outcomes; and the effective teaching of Indigenous studies and Indigenous students.

Timothy Cubitt is Principal Research Analyst for the Australian Institute of Criminology's Serious and Organised Crime Research Laboratory. He previously led professional standards research at the NSW Police Force. His research focuses on misconduct among policing agencies, and using machine learning analytics to develop public policy responses. He has published in the areas of policing and AOD, focusing on prediction and early intervention for police misconduct, substance use among police, and the impact of stress and trauma exposure on police officers.

Chris Cunneen is Professor of Criminology at Jumbunna Institute for Indigenous Education and Research at the University of Technology Sydney. He is a fellow of the Academy of Social Sciences in Australia. Professor Cunneen has worked as a research consultant with a number of Australian Royal Commissions and Inquiries, with the Australian Human Rights Commission, and with state, federal, and local government agencies, and has worked with various non-government Aboriginal and Torres Strait Islander organisations in Australia. He has particular interests in racialisation and criminalisation, Indigenous legal issues, youth justice, justice reinvestment, and penalty. His recent books include (with White and Richards) *Juvenile Justice: Youth and Crime in Australia* (2015, Oxford University Press); (with Brown et al.)

Justice Reinvestment: Winding Back Imprisonment (2016, Palgrave); and (with Tauri) *Indigenous Criminology* (2016, Policy Press).

Theresa Dicke is a senior lecturer at the Institute for Positive Psychology and Education at the Australian Catholic University. Her research interests lie in the realm of organisational, health, and educational psychology. Applying complex quantitative methods, she has extensively studied the roles of (occupational) wellbeing, performance, and their interrelationship in organisations.

Christopher Dowling is Principal Research Analyst with the Australian Institute of Criminology's Serious and Organised Crime Research Lab. He received his PhD in criminology and criminal justice from Griffith University in 2016. He has published empirical research on a variety of topics, including violence, youth offending, organised crime, crime prevention, and policing. He has also undertaken a number of consultancy projects for policing agencies and government stakeholders across Australia.

Janet M. Evans holds a master's degree in investigative psychology and has current experience of law enforcement intelligence collection, analysis, and reporting. She has significant experience in law enforcement practice, criminal intelligence, and system development and implementation, as well as a having a track record of working on nationally significant projects, including updating methodology to ensure processes are consistent with best practice, managing software development teams to move theory into user friendly practice, and delivering training nationally to ensure buy-in and consistency across a wide range of stakeholders. She has held directorship and senior management positions in intelligence in Australia and the UK.

Mark Findlay is Professor of Law at Singapore Management University, and Director of its Centre for AI and Data Governance. In addition, he has honorary Chairs at the Australian National University and the University of New South Wales. Professor Findlay is the author of 29 monographs and collections, and over 150 refereed articles and book chapters. He has held Chairs in Australia, Hong Kong, Singapore, England, and Ireland. At the University of the South Pacific, he was the Foundation Professor of Law and established the Law School in Vanuatu. For over 20 years he was at the University of Sydney as the Chair in Criminal Justice, the Director of the Institute of Criminology and acting Head of School and Pro-Dean. Mark has consulted with the World Bank, the ILO, the UNDP, and many national aid agencies. His main research fields for which he has a global reputation are regulation and governance, international and comparative criminal justice, law's relevance, legal theory, public international law, and cultural criminology.

John Gaffey is a lecturer in criminology and policing in the Centre for Law and Justice at Charles Sturt University. Dr Gaffey is also Justice Studies Discipline Coordinator in the Centre for Law and Justice's Bachelor of Criminal Justice and Bachelor of Public Safety and Security. Dr Gaffey previously taught criminology and sociology at Western Sydney University, and research methods for the University of Tasmania School of Business and Economics. Dr Gaffey is currently researching risk communication in the media, including the reporting of crime and media representation of prison expansion. Dr Gaffey is a member of CSU's Home Affairs, Policing and Security Science (HAPSS) Research Group.

Peter Gallagher was a police officer for 43 years. He variously held the positions of Commander, Employee Management Branch; Human Resources; and Professional Standards Command. He spent two years delivering leadership training programmes to police employees with a view to reducing internal conflict and the stress that results. He was commissioned by the New South Wales Police Minister to report upon sick leave within the Police Force. His report was tabled in the NSW Parliament and resulted in changes to the welfare regime to focus upon early return to work rather than disengagement of officers. He holds a master of leadership and management (policing) and a master of arts (terrorism, safety, and security). He is currently studying for a PhD focused upon preventing officer suicide.

Jane Goodman-Delahunty is Research Professor in Legal and Forensic Psychology at Charles Sturt University and Member of the New South Wales Civil and Administrative Tribunal. She joined academe in 2001. Her empirical legal studies promote evidence-based practices to enhance justice. She is a fellow of the American Psychological Association, a past president of the American Psychology-Law Society and of the Australian and New Zealand Association of Psychiatry, Psychology, and Law, former editor of *Psychology, Public Policy & Law*, and was a NSW Law Reform Commissioner for ten years. She has published over 200 scholarly articles and books including *Evaluating Sexual Harassment: Psychological, Social, and Legal Considerations in Forensic Examinations, 2nd Ed.* (2020, American Psychological Association); *Juries, Science and Popular Culture in the Age of Terror* (2017, Palgrave MacMillan), *Juries and Expert Evidence in Criminal Trials* (2016, Oxford University Press), and *Legal Psychology in Australia* (2015, Thomson Reuters).

Jiesi Guo is a senior lecturer at the Institute for Positive Psychology and Education. He received his PhD in psychology from the Institute for Positive Psychology and Education, Australian Catholic University. His areas of interest include educational and developmental psychology with a particular focus on how multiple systems on the cultural, social, and motivational development of youth shape individual and gender difference in achievement choice.

Jane L. Ireland is a chartered forensic psychologist and chartered scientist. She holds a Professorial Chair at the University of Central Lancashire (UCLan), UK, and is an adjunct professor in the Centre for Law and Justice at Charles Sturt University, Australia. Professor Ireland is the Violence Treatment Lead within High Secure Services, Ashworth Hospital, Mersey Care NHS Trust. Professor Ireland is an elected academy fellow of the Council of the Academy of Social Sciences and fellow of the International Society for Research on Aggression (ISRA). Currently, Professor Ireland is the academic lead for the Ashworth Research Centre (ARC), an NHS centre for research based within Mersey Care NHS Trust. She is also the Research Lead for the School of Psychology, Faculty of Science, UCLan. Professor Ireland formerly worked for HM Prison Service and continues to work for Serco and continues to work for the private prison sector.

Daren Jay is formerly a career investigator of 22 years with the United Kingdom's Royal Military Police Special Investigation Branch. Daren qualified as an Investigative Interview Trainer in 1996 and has been heavily involved in interviewing witnesses, victims, and suspects in connection with a wide range of criminal offences, including sexual offences and other offences against the person. In 2005, Daren qualified with Kent Police (UK) as a UK Home Office Tier 3 video interviewer, enabling him to video interview adults, children, and other vulnerable persons in relation to serious crime offences. Daren joined Charles Sturt University (CSU) as a lecturer in policing in 2008 and currently serves as the lead Investigative Interviewing Trainer at CSU's Australian Graduate School of Policing and Security (AGSPS). Through his role, Daren has designed and delivered investigative interviewing and investigation management short courses to federal and state law-enforcement agencies across Australia and beyond. Daren is Founder and CEO of Interview Management Solutions, the company behind the TILES System®, an investigative interviewing planning and management tool.

Nick Kaldas served for almost 35 years as a NSW Police officer in Sydney, and was Deputy Commissioner for almost a decade. Nick is currently Managing Director of a consulting firm, Kaldas and Associates, in Sydney, providing high-level security, investigative, and governance advice internationally. His career has primarily been in major crime investigations and operations, including counter-terrorism. He was a member of the Australian National Counter-Terrorism Committee for eight years, the peak policy body dealing with counter-terrorism in Australia. Internationally, Nick led the United Nations investigations into the assassination of the Lebanese PM Hariri and 21 related murders in 2009–2010, and the Joint Investigative Mechanism, UN/OPCW investigation into the use of chemical weapons in Syria 2016. He was Deputy Chief Police Adviser with Coalition Forces in Iraq, rebuilding the Iraqi Police in 2004–2005. He serves on a number of bodies internationally. He is an adjunct professor for Western Sydney University and Charles

Sturt University, and is a senior fellow with the Australian Strategic Policy Institute. He holds a master's degree in public policy and administration and received an honorary doctorate of letters from WSU in 2019.

Mark R. Kebbell is Professor of Forensic Psychology at the School of Applied Psychology. His expertise and research are in investigative psychology, particularly with regards the investigation and prosecution of serious crime. His previous work has included writing the guidelines for police officers in England and Wales (with Wagstaff) for assessing witness evidence, and developing risk assessment methods for suspected sex offenders for the Australian Federal Police and the Queensland Police Service. He has worked on more than 70 criminal cases, principally involving murder or serious sexual assault, and has given expert evidence on numerous occasions, including uncontested psychological evidence in an Old Bailey appeal case. He is a registered psychologist in Australia and a chartered forensic psychologist in the United Kingdom.

Dragana Kesic is a clinical and forensic psychologist in private practice in Melbourne and a research fellow at RMIT. Dragana is a co-convenor of the mental health special interest group of the Global Law Enforcement and Public Health Association (GLEPHA). Her research focus is on the matters concerning police interactions with people experiencing mental health issues, in particular the use of force, and examining police responses to this interface.

Shane Lysons-Smith is the Manager for Intelligence and Specialist Capability Development with the Australian Criminal Intelligence Commission. He is a former criminal intelligence analyst with experience working on transnational serious organised crime and national security issues, and leads the development of consistent criminal intelligence practice and tradecraft nationally.

Ian Manock is an emergency-management "pracademic", having over 40 years emergency-management experience. Twenty-five of these years have been involved in front-line emergency management as a member of the military, Royal Hong Kong Police, and Tasmanian State Emergency Service. Since 1999, Ian has coordinated and delivered teaching and education programmes for emergency-management professionals within Charles Sturt University's undergraduate and postgraduate emergency-management programmes. Ian holds both undergraduate and master's degree qualifications in emergency management, has numerous publications to his name, and has spoken at emergency-management conferences and workshops in Australia and overseas. In addition, Ian also conducts training sessions on short courses in policing, law enforcement, and emergency management for organisations in Australia, New Zealand, the Philippines, India, Malaysia, and Canada.

Herbert W. Marsh is a professor of psychology at the Institute for Positive Psychology and Education, Australian Catholic University, Institute for Positive Psychology and Education. He is also Emeritus Professor of Education at Oxford University. He is an "ISI highly cited researcher" (H-index = 179), founded the International SELF Research Centre, and coedits the SELF monograph series. He coined the phrase "substantive-methodological synergy" that underpins his substantive (self-concept, motivation, gender, bullying, educational, developmental, and sport psychology) and methodological (factor analysis, multilevel modelling) research interests.

Alana Maurushat is Professor of Cybersecurity and Behaviour at Western Sydney University. She is the Cyber-Ambassador for the NSW Cybersecurity Innovation Network and Special Advisor for the cybercrime investigation firm, IFW Global. She lectures in cybersecurity, privacy engineering, cybercrime, cyber risk management, usable security, and artificial intelligence across the disciplines of law, criminology and policy, business, political science, and computer science. Alana has done consultancy work on cybersecurity, open data, big data, and civil liberties and technology for both the Canadian and Australian governments, industry and NGOs. She is author of the recently published book, *Ethical Hacking*.

Amber McKinley is a clinical and forensic victimologist and a senior lecturer at Charles Sturt University's (CSU) Australian Graduate School of Policing and Security (AGSPS), based in Barton, ACT. She lectures in theoretical, applied, and forensic victimology. She holds a bachelor of liberal studies, a masters of criminal justice and a doctor of philosophy. She is currently enrolled to study a masters of aging and applied thanatology at the University of Maryland, US. Amber works as a specialist reserve squadron leader in the Royal Australian Air Force and works with the Joint Military Police Unit where she researches and writes reports on topical issues for the Provost Marshal-ADF. Her current research includes the use of forensic taphonomy in solving homicide, the history of serial homicide in Australia from 1820–2019, detection avoidance and homicide solvability, and unreported homicides in Australia.

Anthony Morgan is the Research Manager for the Australian Institute of Criminology's Serious and Organised Crime Research Laboratory, working closely with law enforcement and academia on research to understand and find ways to disrupt organised crime. His own research focuses on the criminal careers of organised crime offenders and outlaw motorcycle gangs. He has published extensively in the area of policing, including policing responses to domestic violence, police investigations and use of technology, police partnerships, and crime analysis to inform policing.

Kelly Moylan is a casual academic at Western Sydney University, where she also completed her PhD. For her thesis, Kelly drew on practice theory and applied ethics to examine the reflections of policing and non-policing participants on the experiences, challenges, and opportunities for ethical practice and human rights in peacekeeping. She has taught widely within the School of Social Sciences, specialising in ethics, with additional teaching experience in policing, sociology, human rights, criminology, and social research methods.

Gary Pankhurst is an investigative interviewing expert with over 30 years' policing experience. Gary is also an accredited counter-fraud specialist who has conducted and managed high-stakes, complex investigations within the UK, Europe, and internationally. Gary has extensive experience working in partnership with public and private sector agencies on confidential and sensitive enquiries with significant public interest issues and impact. He received a Commissioner's Commendation for his work as Interview Adviser on Operation Yewtree, a ground-breaking and award-winning investigation of national importance. He has worked as both a consultant and specialist trainer. Gary has provided bespoke training to various police forces; AXA insurance (Investigators' Unit); International Investigative Interviewing Research Group (iIIRG) Master Class; Royal Air Force Police Special Investigations Unit; Queensland Police (Australia); and Law School, Queen's University Belfast. Gary has an MSc in forensic investigative psychology and has current academic PhD research experience studying information elicitation in investigative interviewing. He is an effective and skilled researcher, and is currently a tutor and visiting teaching fellow at Durham University.

Amanda Porter is a proud descendant of the Brinja clan of the Yuin nation in South Coast New South Wales. She is a senior fellow at Melbourne Law School and an adjunct fellow at Nura Gili at the University of New South Wales Faculty of Law. She has worked as a volunteer for Kinchela Boys Home Aboriginal Corporation, the Redfern Community Legal Centre, the National Centre for Indigenous Excellence, the Shed Suicide Prevention Service, the Redfern Streetbeat, and other Aboriginal community organisations.

Glenn Porter is Associate Professor in Criminology at the University of New England (UNE). He is an experienced forensic criminology practitioner and previously worked with the Australian Federal Police as a forensic imaging specialist. Dr Porter was the founding academic and Head of the Forensic Science degree at Western Sydney University (WSU) and has served as Vice President of the Australian Academy of Forensic Sciences (AAFS). Dr Porter studied photography at the Sydney Institute of Technology, and his postgraduate qualifications include a graduate diploma in science from the University of Sydney, a master of applied science (photography) from RMIT University and a PhD in communication arts from Western Sydney University. Dr Porter has further been awarded the Accredited Senior Imaging Scientist (ASIS) distinction and Fellowship (FRPS) of the Royal Photographic Society. He is an experienced expert witness and his evidence has been heard or presented in various courts and jurisdictions, including the District and Supreme Courts of NSW, Coroners Court of NSW, NSW Court of Criminal Appeal (Sydney), High Court of Australia (Canberra), and the United Nations Human Rights Council (UNHRC) (Geneva). Dr Porter's forensic specialisations include forensic imaging, images as forensic evidence, crime scene investigation, and shoe mark evidence.

Tim Prenzler is Professor of Criminology in the School of Law and Criminology, University of the Sunshine Coast. His teaching and research areas include crime and corruption prevention, policing, the security industry, police and security officer safety, and gender in policing. His books include *Regulating the Security Industry: Global Perspectives* (2018, Routledge, with Mahesh Nalla), *Understanding Crime Prevention: The Case Study Approach* (2017, Australian Academic Press), *Civilian Oversight of Police: Advancing Accountability in Law Enforcement* (2016, Taylor & Francis, with Garth den Heyer), *Policing and Security in Practice: Challenges and Achievements* (2016, Palgrave-Macmillan), *Contemporary Police Practice* (2015, Oxford University Press, with Jacqueline Drew), *Understanding and Preventing Corruption* (2013, Palgrave, with Adam Graycar) and *Ethics and Accountability in Criminal Justice* (2013, Australian Academic Press).

Simon Robinson is a serving police officer with the New South Wales Police Force, having over 30 years of policing, law enforcement, and emergency-management experience. During his career, Simon has served in a wide variety of policing positions, including rescue operations, criminal and coronial investigations, emergency-management training, and staff management/mentoring, with almost 20 years as a general duties supervisor/team leader. In addition to his police duties, Simon also volunteered as a retained fire fighter with Fire and Rescue New South Wales for 15 years. Simon holds both undergraduate and master's degree qualifications in emergency management. Since 2005, Simon has also been a contracted sessional academic within Charles Sturt University's Bachelor of Emergency Management programme, coordinating the teaching of a foundation-level undergraduate emergency-management subject, as well as coordinating the involvement of contracted academic subject support staff.

Colin Rogers is Adjunct Professor of Policing and Law Enforcement at Charles Sturt University, Australia and Professor of Policing and Security at the University of South Wales, UK. A former police practitioner with 30 years' experience, he is a prolific author and researcher having taught police officers at a local, national, and international level. His research revolves around the police organisation, police education, crime prevention, police and technology, and community policing. He is the co-author of *Police and Higher Education: International Perspectives*, published by Policy Press.

Richard M. Ryan is a clinical psychologist and professor at the Institute for Positive Psychology and Education within the Australian Catholic University. He is a co-developer of *Self-Determination Theory*, an internationally recognised theory of human motivation, and the author of over 400 papers and books, including *Self-Determination Theory: Basic Psychological Needs in Motivation Development and Wellness* (2017, Ryan & Deci). Ryan is among the most cited researchers in psychology and social sciences today, and has been recognised as one of the eminent psychologists of the modern era. He has also been honoured with three lifetime achievement awards for his work on motivation, personal meaning, and self and identity, and received an honorary degree from the University of Thessaly and an honorary membership to the German Psychological Society, among other honours.

Rick Sarre is Dean of Law at the School of Law, University of South Australia, having taught law and criminology in Australia, Hong Kong, the United States and Sweden over a 35-year period. He is a fellow of the Australian and New Zealand Society of Criminology (ANZSOC), and its Immediate Past President.

Louise A. Sicard is a lecturer in criminology and policing in the Centre for Law and Justice at Charles Sturt University, Australia. She has previously held posts at the University of Western Sydney, Australia. Louise conducts research within the field of criminology in regards to offender assessment and treatment, as well as the use of music therapy in working with offenders.

Ian Stewart was the 19th Commissioner of the Queensland Police Service from November 2012 until he retired in July 2019, ending a 45-year career in policing. Mr Stewart holds a master of public policy and administration and bachelor of business qualifications. In 2019 he was conferred honorary doctorates from Charles Sturt University and two other universities. He is a fellow of the Institute of Public Administration Australia, a graduate member of the Australian Institute of Company Directors, and the Federal Bureau of Investigation (FBI) National Executive Institute. In 1999, he was awarded an Australian Fulbright Professional Scholarship. In 2020, he was made Officer of the Order of Australia (AO) for his services to policing and the community. His legacy to Queensland includes a flexible and agile policing agency, empowered by world-class technology, capability development, and leadership.

Graham Sunderland specialises in leadership and command, disaster victim identification, and major investigations. He was police officer for over 30 years and a former assistant and acting deputy chief of police in the UK (AC-Crime & Ops). Graham was the lead on behalf of the UK Government for Disaster Victim Identification (DVI) from 2005 to 2011, and was the DVI Advisor at the London bombings. He reviewed the response to the tsunami in 2004 in Thailand on behalf of Interpol, and was the Deputy Chair of the Interpol DVI Standing Committee. As the Course Director of the UK Multi-Agency Strategic Command Course, Graham trained Chief Officers from UK emergency services, government and military. In 2012, he joined Charles Sturt University, Australia. In 2009 Graham was awarded the Queen's Police Medal.

Stuart D.M. Thomas is Professor of Forensic Mental Health at RMIT University in Melbourne Australia; he also holds adjunct positions at Monash University and Swinburne University of Technology. He is an epidemiologist by training and has a background in psychology and law. He is co-convenor of the mental health special interest group of the Global Law Enforcement and Public Health Association, and his research interests focus on policing vulnerable populations, outcome measurement, violent offending, and stigma.

Brooke Van Zanden is Registered Psychologist and Research Associate at the Graduate School of Health, University of Technology (UTS) Sydney. Brooke received her PhD in psychology from the Institute for Positive Psychology and Education, and completed her master's in clinical psychology at the University of Wollongong. At UTS, Brooke's research is focused on the mental health and wellbeing of people living with chronic health conditions.

Irena Veljanova is Senior Lecturer in Sociology at the School of Social Sciences, Western Sydney University. She completed her PhD at WSU in 2011 in the field of human welfare studies and services. Her thesis titled *Identity, Health and Health Capital: The Case of Macedonians in Australia* focused on the complex relationship between ethnocultural identity and health. She has a longstanding research focus upon multicultural health, health ethnographies, critical gerontology, migrant communities, and domestic violence (DV), and actively contributes to professional and academic conversations within these fields. Irena has presented her work at over 40 conferences of international and national standing. Together with Dr Birch, she recently published her work on "Raising awareness, improving victim safety: exploring the efficacy of proactive domestic and family violence prevention measures", in the 2018 *Routledge International Handbook of Human Aggression: Current Issues and Perspectives*, co-edited by Jane L. Ireland, Philip Birch, and Carol A. Ireland.

Isabella Voce is Senior Research Analyst for the Australian Institute of Criminology's Serious and Organised Crime Research Laboratory (SOCR-Lab). Her research focuses include the analysis and disruption of traditional illicit drug markets and darknet crypto-markets, and understanding the recruitment and criminal careers of outlaw motorcycle gang members. She has also published in the areas of policing domestic violence, intimate partner homicide, and evaluations of juvenile justice programmes.

Troy Whitford lectures in intelligence and security studies at the Australian Graduate School of Policing and Security, Charles Sturt University. He is a government-licensed investigator and his research interests include field intelligence, intelligence collection, and analysis.

Emma Wintle is a researcher of policing and law enforcement at Charles Sturt University, Australia. Emma has bachelor in criminology and criminal justice (hons) qualifications from the University of New South Wales, Australia, and is a PhD candidate. Prior to entering academia, she worked in regulatory affairs, analysing policy and lobbying governments for evidence-based practices.

Ken Wooden is a lecturer and academic course advisor for the bachelor of policing programme at Western Sydney University. Prior to his appointment at Western Sydney, he was employed as a senior lecturer within the School of Policing Studies, Charles Sturt University for a period of 12 years and was involved in the delivery of New South Wales Police recruit training. Ken completed his PhD in 2012 through the School of Criminology and Criminal Justice Studies, Griffith University. His area of research dealt with police perceptions of accountability and community policing. Prior to his academic career, Ken worked as a police officer within the New South Wales Police Force for 20 years, performing duties in general duties, anti-theft squad and legal services. Ken's research interests include community policing, ethical orientations of police recruits, and customer service factors impacting upon police work attitudes and motivation.

Foreword

The practice of policing is constantly changing. Birch, Kennedy and Kruger provides a comprehensive, Australian focused, edited collection that offers important and insightful perspectives on policing that support those who are currently employed in policing as well as those who seek to join a policing organisation. An important part of this edited collection is how the text supports current police practitioners, and the police forces that employ them, by providing a platform that informs and recognises the importance of a professionalised model of policing.

This edited collection is split into the four sections: **education, training, and professional practice**, **organisational approaches and techniques**, **operational practices and procedures** and **working with individuals and groups**, and as such the text provides both a rich theoretical lens as well as an applied examination of a range of critical issues policing organisations and their employees face. From individual and internal issues such as the education and training of officers to external community facing issues such as policing violence and domestic related incidents and working with victims.

Australian policing in its various forms deserves an academic text that not only reflects the varied work of police officers but one that can also inform that work. Birch, Kennedy and Kruger provide a well-balanced book in terms of theory and its integration to the real world of policing. This book serves an incredibly important purpose of not only supporting those who work in the field, but by providing academic institutions that teach policing, law enforcement and public safety courses a useful and meaningful text. It is an essential read for anyone involved in or who has an interest in the field of policing, especially in Australia.

Commissioner Michael Fuller APM
New South Wales Police Force, Australia
July 2020

Acknowledgements

Philip, Michael, and Erin would like to acknowledge the kind contribution to this project of all the authors involved who have provided a chapter, reflecting both their expertise and excellent time management skills. It has been a real pleasure working with you, and your diligence and commitment to this project are deeply appreciated.

Philip, Michael, and Erin would also like to extend their acknowledgements to the marvellous team at Routledge, particularly the meticulous and keen eye of Jessica Phillips, along with the support and helpful guidance of Thomas D.M. Sutton.

Examining Australian policing in the 21st century

Philip Birch, Michael Kennedy and Erin Kruger

Contemporary policing requires a labour force that is both educated and skilled, allowing for a flexible and agile approach to work in an ever-changing and dynamic world that police officers are employed to safeguard. In the same way professions such as law, teaching, social work and medicine require a labour force that is able to meet the challenges of a rapidly changing society, those employed in the police profession are no different. Yet police officers are seldom considered peers of lawyers, teachers, social workers and medical doctors; they are measured in their own unique way. It is therefore important to support police forces and the police officers they employ through education and specialised development, enabling police personnel to respond in a flexible and agile manner to the situations they encounter. One way this can be achieved is through a professionalized model of policing which allows individual practitioners to gain educational qualifications and be exposed to continuing professional development with regards to police practice. A strong history and growth in police education along with the recognition of professional development in Australian Policing, as an agency of the state, enables police officers and their employers to be responsible for the conduct, legal liability and, at times, indiscretions they may commit as state agents. More can be done, however, to support police organisations and their personnel in enacting and enhancing a professionalized model of policing.

The following edited collection brings together leading academics, researchers and police personnel to provide a comprehensive body of literature that informs Australian police education, training, research, policy and practice in order to support all police officers and support staff to engage in policing and, more specifically, a professionalized model of policing. Recognising and reflecting on the Australian and New Zealand Policing Advisory Agency (ANZPAA) education and training framework, the following volume addresses a range of 21st-century issues modern day police forces face. Drawing together theoretical and practical debates, this volume of work will be of interest to the policing realm (i.e. students, personnel, academics, researchers and policy makers), as well as those thinking about careers with the police, and those currently training to become a police officer. Split into four sections, the following volume considers Australian police practice within a variety of contexts. In the first section, education, training and professional practice is considered. Here, a range of issues are considered, from police education when first joining the profession, to the continuation of that education and training while in service by becoming a pracademic. Police leaders and police leadership, along with the importance of ethical practice and effective communication, are not overlooked within the context of education and training. Police officer wellbeing is also considered, which is a theme central to emerging police literature and research in recent times. In the absence of a healthy workforce, the role of a police officer is compromised. Consequently, the inclusion of the issue of wellbeing within the first section of this volume, as it relates to education, training and professional development, reinforces the fact that wellbeing in the policing profession has to be paramount from the moment an individual joins the police force throughout their whole career. Section two of this volume shifts the focus of policing onto organisational approaches and techniques. This section is rich in a range of issues that can aid police officers in the successful delivery of police activities, such as the use of criminal intelligence, investigative interviewing and the role of forensic science. This section also reflects on the challenging aspects of police work, for example, the application of police discretion, and the use of force and partnership working. While such issues can provide challenges for police officers and their wider employers if done incorrectly, such approaches can provide much success in the delivery of police work.

Operational practices and procedures are the focus of section three of this volume. There is deep consideration and reflection on a range of issues facing the modern-day police force, including digital media, the interface between public health and police practice and the emergence of cybercrime. In conjunction with these modern-day issues facing the police, further consideration is granted to existing issues such as dealing with emergency-management situations, crime prevention, terrorism, organised and transnational crime, and the international policing roles that states and territory police officers are involved in. The range of issues presented in section three of this volume reinforce the need for a modern-day police force to be engaged, educated, flexible and able to respond to new and emerging issues and trends. At the same time, this section of the book, quite rightly, reminds us of the many traditional aspects of policing which are still very much an important requirement of police work, albeit conjoined with emerging modus operandi, knowledge and practice.

The final section of this body of work speaks to a core component of police work: namely, working with diverse individuals, groups and communities which police officers encounter and serve to regulate and protect. There are many types of issues police officers face when dealing with the community; this final section of the book, arguably, only scratches the surface of the breadth and depth of those issues. Nevertheless, the chapters that form this last section reflect many contemporary issues that, while presented as a single issue in each chapter, in many cases overlap. Mental health, dealing with young people, working with First Nations peoples, responding to hate crime, general violence and domestic and family violence, are all considered in this final section as a means to provide police officers with information and support to both reflect on and inform their practice. This section concludes by considering the victims of crime, who police officers encounter frequently, and support and engage through the activity of policing.

Most existing texts that have focused on the work of police, as well as on police officers themselves, typically capture and reflect a single issue of policing, as illustrated by the work of Grabosky (2009), Marks and Sklansky (2014) and Weber and Bowling (2014). Texts that have sought to capture a wider spectrum of policing, such as Cockcroft (2012), Ortmeier and Davis (2012), Prenzler (2012) and Rogers et al. (2011), do not deal with Australian issues specifically. As such, there is a significant gap in the literature concerning policing and police practice that provides insight into the breadth and depth of police work with regards to Australian policing. It is hoped that the following volume presents a comprehensive Australian-focused resource that few books before it have sought to do. Prior to this volume, arguably, the work of Broadhurst and Davies (2008) and Birch and Herrington (2011) had provided Australian-focused texts that sought to capture a full spectrum of police practice. As these texts become dated, and thus less reflective of the fast-paced, changing nature of police work, the following text seeks to address this gap in the literature and provide Australian police forces with an up-to-date authoritative text for all police officers to use. This volume will also be of primary interest and a welcome resource for academics, researchers and students in criminology, law, sociology, psychology, social policy and related disciplines. It is envisaged that this body of work will also be a key resource for a range of practitioners across the globe working on issues concerning police, policing and the wider criminal justice system.

As the third decade in the 21st century begins, *Australian Policing: Critical Issues in 21st Century Practice* provides a point for all who are involved with Australian policing to pause and assess *where have we come from* and *where are we going*.

REFERENCES

Birch, P., & Herrington, V. (Eds.) (2011). *Policing in Practice*. Palgrave Macmillan, Melbourne, Australia.

Broadhurst, R., & Davies, S. (Eds.) (2008). *Policing in Context: An Introduction to Police Work in Australia*. Oxford University Press, Melbourne, Australia.

Cockcroft, T. (2012). *Police Culture: Themes and Concepts*. Routledge, London.

Grabosky, P. (Ed.) (2009). *Community Policing and Peacekeeping*. CRC Press, Boca Raton, FL.

Marks, M., & Sklansky, D. (Eds.) (2014). *Police Reform from the Bottom Up: Officers and Their Unions as Agents of Change*. Routledge, London.

Ortmeier, P. J., & Davis, J. J. (2012). *Police Administration: A Leadership Approach*. McGraw-Hill, New York.

Prenzler, T. (Ed.) (2012). *Policing and Security in Practice: Challenges and Achievements*. Palgrave Macmillan, New York.

Rogers, C., Lewis, R., John, T., & Read, T. (2011). *Police Work: Principles and Practice*. Willan Publishing, Cullompton.

Weber, L., & Bowling, B. (Eds.) (2014). *Stop and Search: Police Power in Global Context*. Routledge, London.

SECTION 1

Education, training, and professional practice

CHAPTER 1

Police education in Australia

Colin Rogers and Emma Wintle

INTRODUCTION

The type and quality of police officers a society requires often reflects the relationship between the state and its citizens, and this process invariably begins with the education and training of those police officers. This chapter will critically evaluate current police education and training at the state and federal level in Australia. It will consider the way police officers are currently educated in a fast-moving and changing society, and examine whether this is enough for the needs of the community. It will also critically examine future challenges for the police and discuss how prepared police education and training is to meet these at this moment in time. As Dolling (2003) points out, policing does not exist in a vacuum. It is impacted daily and in the long term by changes in the social, political, economic, technological, environmental, and legal structures, in whatever country it is practised. It therefore follows that the education of police officers should be shaped by the future changes within these and other activities.

Policing is also, primarily, a social and information occupation, and is an aspect of the more general concept of social control (Bowling et al, 2019). As such, it involves interaction with people in a wide and diverse range of situations. This interaction involves, on many occasions, obtaining information about a particular community, incident or person, or the use of police intelligence to be found in police data sets (James, 2016). Therefore, those who are responsible for police education in all countries need to clearly understand how society changes, responding to strong currents within a given society. Further, there is a need to understand how information is gathered, exchanged, and utilised, and the consequences of these activities. Globalisation, and the global economy, is now characterised by the almost instantaneous flow and exchange of information, capital, and cultural communication (Castells, 2010). The increasing nature and scope of crime and substantial increases in immigration tend to demonstrate that what happens in one country can have an impact in others. It is in the face of these challenges that the police in Australia need to ensure their training and education provision are part of this process. Understanding the different types of challenges that lie ahead for the police will allow us to critically examine the readiness of training and education in Australia.

FUTURE CHALLENGES

The world's population will reach 8 billion by 2025, up from 6 billion in 2000 (National Intelligence Council, 2008). However, this increase will not occur evenly across all countries. Developed countries will see a decline in population, whilst those of developing countries will increase, particularly in Sub-Saharan Africa and South Asia, which will have extremely youthful populations. Developed countries will witness an aging population rise, coupled with declining fertility rates, leading to less individuals of working age to support the population as a whole. Workers must come from somewhere; consequently, we may witness a large expansion in immigration and shifts in population from one country to another. Such a population shift – which increases both migration and immigration – will bring with it the attendant risk of internal and external change within different societies. For example, the above population shift could bring about an expansion of the "middle classes" across different countries, which could lead to an expansion of the consumerist society already witnessed in most Western countries to the global stage (Spybey, 1996), and wider divisions within society. This in turn could lead to a higher demand from communities for more service-oriented, citizen/consumer-style policing (Clarke et al, 2009), rather than a law enforcement model of policing, as people come to understand their rights as consumers of private and public services.

Urbanisation is set to grow to about 60% in all countries (National Intelligence Council, 2008), which will require not only a concentration of policing services within those areas, but may also elicit a decline in social cohesiveness, which is required to support and promote "self-policing", which reduces demand for formal public police activity. This has been part of a continuing responsibilisation strategy for most democratic governments for some time (Garland, 2001).

There are likely to be rapid political changes, coupled with wider social movements, which might produce serious governance difficulties. There may be wider democratisation, which will lead to greater calls for transparency and accountability in policing agencies across the globe, coupled with greater franchise. This could occur despite the possibility of increased nationalism, and the apparent rise in right-wing politics (Fukuyama, 2018). Clearly, the political landscape will be far more complicated in the future than it hitherto has been.

The biggest area of potential change for Australian policing will be seen in the greater use and expansion of more and more sophisticated technology. Not only will it influence organisational behaviour and crime trends, but it will also impact individual and personal lifestyles.

Developments in technology will further enhance the potential for greater and swifter communication between groups of people who are able to organise themselves for dealing with such activities as political protest, whilst the potential for global crime, such as terrorism, will increase exponentially. Schafer et al (2012) suggest the following major challenges for the police in terms of the current trends in technology:

- New types of crime will come into being;
- Traditional crime will become enhanced by new technologies; and
- There will develop a technology gap, with the police falling further behind the private sector in understanding and acquiring new technologies.

Whilst new technology provides challenges for police, it can also provide benefits. For example, improvements in data analysis tools, biometrics, and less-lethal technologies provide enhancements for police activities.

One cannot ignore the fact that increased problems for policing agencies may occur as a result of environmental and climate change. The recent large-scale bush fires in Australia and long periods of drought may indicate that natural disasters could increase in scale and intensity. Furthermore, the recent COVID-19 pandemic illustrates that increased opportunities for global travel have heightened the possibility of worldwide pandemics. These potential environmental problems and widespread health concerns will, in turn, require different and varied responses at a national and international level, and a greater need and demand for closer cooperation between police agencies with more and wider services across the world.

Possibly, more crime prevention activities will need to be in place, with the greater use of surveillance and situational crime prevention techniques, rather than costly social interventions. The challenge for Australian policing agencies will be that of providing and stimulating a need for greater social cohesion/community involvement (Rogers, 2012; Wedlock, 2006) in the delivery of policing services. This enhanced cooperation and partnership approach with communities will be vital in order to maintain the very legitimacy that allows for policing in democracies.

ORGANISATIONAL CHALLENGES

Like most modern organisations, police agencies in Australia trace their origins to the country's industrial and social evolution. Consequently, their structures are similar, with workers being supervised by an overseer within a hierarchical structure that separates front-line officers from strategic policy-makers (Hebdon & Kirkpatrick, 2006). The hierarchical model of policing does not adapt well to external demands for change or accountability, and there is still a tendency to adhere to historical ideas regarding management practices. Therefore, policing agencies in

Australia may need a "revolution" in their organisation, leadership, and management models in order to deal with the future issues that they will have to face (Batts et al, 2012). The fundamental tool in achieving this will be the education of police officers. The concept of community policing, whether rhetoric or reality, (Greene & Mastrofski, 1988) is an appealing one for countries seeking to legitimise their policing process, especially when tourism or leisure economics are a way of developing growth and security.

Previously, police organisations were considered experts in their field, and were standalone agencies who dealt with all crime-related matters. Over the past decade or so, there has been a drive to involve many other agencies in policing, particularly in the field of crime prevention (Rogers, 2012). This has meant police officers at all levels of the organisation having to become involved in more and complex partnership working arrangements. In particular, police officers now have to work with many other professionals who are, in the main, all degree or higher educationally qualified. The partnership approach to policing means that the police organisation has, in many instances, to improve its performance alongside other professionals. This also encapsulates a different form of thinking about how policing should be carried out with partners. The rise of the Problem Oriented Policing approach (Goldstein, 1990), for example, has introduced sometimes complex theory directly into mainstream policing activities. In support of more focused activities of policing and partnership working, evidence-based policing has gained momentum. Here, the utilisation of information and intelligence to focus police and partner agency resources has meant that a deeper and more scientific understanding of the knowledge gathered by police and other groups is required. In many senses, police officers and staff are becoming knowledge workers, (Gottschalk, 2007), as more complex uses of information and intelligence are developed by the police.

POLICE EDUCATION IN CONTEXT

The earliest stages of police education are generally linked to the work of August Vollmer, who started his University of California at Berkeley police school in 1916. In fact, police higher education was introduced prior to the wider availability of systematic police training (Cordner, 2016). Even at its earliest stages, Vollmer wanted the police to study the social sciences and natural sciences, not just technical police subjects.

Paterson (2011) suggests there have been two distinct models of police education in Australia since the 1990s, one being based upon a traditional method of liberal education with students studying social science subjects, and the other focused upon partnerships between universities and the police. These partnerships invariably involved the police having control and the development of the police discipline. This has been adjudged that this posed a problem for the relationship because the police and university educators have different perceptions about the aims of police education (Mahoney & Prenzler, 1996). However, Wimhurst and Ransley (2007) suggest the incorporation of higher education into police education in Australia has been seen to improve public support for the police and to drive organisational reform into a perceived culture of corruption.

Despite this, for over 20 years, police leaders, ministers, and commissioners have discussed and debated the need to professionalize the police through university education (Trofymowych, 2008). Research into the impact of university education focuses more on police attitudes, as individual performance is often difficult to measure. Whilst most research into higher education and the police proved positive results (see, for example, Shernock, 1992; Terrill & Mastrofski, 2002), there have been a small number of negative impact results, such as greater attrition rates for police with higher degrees (Tronjanowicz & Nicholson, 1976).

A review into police training in Australia in 1986 at the request of the Australian Police Ministers Council (APMC) found that 86% of respondents were in favour of police-oriented university courses for senior police (Rohl & Barnsley, 1995). Following the review, the APMC established the National Police Professional Implementation Advisory Committee (NPPIAC) in 1990. The strategic direction document for this body highlighted, amongst other things, appropriate police training with a national rather than local relevance, as well as tertiary and other courses for police. Trofymowych (2008) states that without exception, all participants in his research agreed in principle that university education is good for the police, as it encourages reflective attributes that become more relevant to the job function.

In some respects, this was surprising. The traditional approach to educating police officers is not without criticism. It has been identified that for most of its history, police recruitment, entry, and training has reflected an apprenticeship model, which was guild-like in operation and form. Members began as recruits to general policing, and normally spent years at this level before becoming, in comparatively limited numbers, specialists of any kind (O'Malley, 2005). Being, by and large, a multifaceted occupation, historically there has been a compromise between what should be included in the training syllabus and what should be left out. Additionally, in terms of training and education to student police officers, the police service still tends to believe that good police practitioners would automatically be good teachers. Whilst there may be some broad merit in that statement, it also reflects in part the closed occupational culture of the police (Reiner, 2000) and may explain why there appears to be some resistance to the use of higher education input delivered by academics. However, the danger of relying upon people from within an organisation to deliver training and education is that of insularity and suspicion of outsiders, and therefore diverse views and wider discussions are discouraged.

There was agreement that police training would benefit from higher education, and not only at the national strategic level. At state level, for example in New South Wales, there was interest for a number of reasons, but primarily to introduce it in order to try and deal with inherent corruption. The Associate Degree in Policing Practice (ADPP) curriculum and mode of delivery employed at the New South Wales Police Force Academy (NSWPF Academy) was introduced as a result of a partnership between Charles Sturt University (CSU) and the NSWPF. This was introduced in line with recommendations outlined in the Wood Royal Commission into corruption in the NSWPF in 1997.

With regard to the education of police officers, the Commission recommended the following:

- There be a restructure of recruit training to introduce a requirement for an entry qualification dependent on an externally acquired tertiary degree or diploma in an approved course followed by skills training delivered at the Police Academy supplemented by field training coordinated and controlled by the Academy (para. 3.151);
- Consideration be given to a scholarship scheme for selected students to assist them to acquire the external academic qualification (para. 3.156);
- Recruitment and remuneration of student police officers be deferred until the skills training phase (para. 3.156); and
- Civilian educators be given a more prominent role in such training (para. 3.154) (Wood, 1997).

It is clear that the Commission believed a tertiary qualification was necessary to broaden trainees' experiences and provide them with the necessary skills and knowledge. This was the formulation of the current ADPP qualification being delivered at present by the NSWPF Academy.

POLICING AS A PROFESSION

The idea of policing as a true profession is one that has generated some debate. Durkheim (1958) believed that what is distinctive about the idea of professional groups is not merely that such groups have high status or high skill, or that those they represent have a politically supported monopoly over certain kinds of work, or that they are a distinctive structure of control over work. More importantly, he argued, such groups infuse their work and collective organisation with moral values; plus, they incorporate the use of sanctions to ensure that these moral values are upheld, which is the challenge of ethical policing.

Professionalism could also be said to be that state of mind, that standard of behaviour, that image of competency and sensitivity, and that constellation of attitudes that one equates with the finest people who follow a calling, who practise the art and science of a vocation and who perform the function of a job. This approach creates in the mind of the public the image of the agency. For example, South Wales Police in the UK currently utilise the phrase, based upon Locard's forensic science principle, that "every contact counts" (Gilbert, 1993) and this translates to how they want their employees to behave when dealing with members of the public.

The professional approach implies that a police officer has reached a level of expertise through

1   Education;
2   Training;
3   Experience.

Importantly, this implies that the professional approach separates him or her from others who are less qualified or less dedicated to public service, whilst also implying that a professional will strive to achieve the highest standards of behaviour and performance. It is this effort that distinguishes the professional from the non-professional, whose attitude is one of getting by with less than optimum standards of ethics, behaviour, and competence. Therefore, if policing is to become professional, the challenge is to develop qualified personnel who are able and willing to assume many awesome responsibilities. In line with many other professions, such as medicine, teaching, etc., a simple knowledge base is insufficient to guarantee effectiveness or customer satisfaction. Rather, there must be an understanding of interaction and communication skills in order to be able to function in an appropriate way.

Despite its public imagery, and also the recruitment literature, the majority of police work does not involve the chasing and arrest of criminals, but rather is about interacting with ordinary members of the public. Traditional training and education methods would appear to be inadequate in providing individuals who meet the demanding criteria for a professional organisation such as the police. Therefore, there must be introduced a vehicle that can move the training and education from being that of the "guild-like craft" towards a true professional status.

FROM CRAFT TO PROFESSION

Stinchcombe (1990) provides a useful understanding of the divisions that exist between "workers" and those considered to be professionals. In his typology, Stinchcombe identifies three distinct types which are useful for our understanding of the movement of the police organisation from being craft-oriented into a professional organisation. These are categorised here.

1   **Craftsmen/women.** This individual learns his/her trade by supervised experience, often on a one-to-one basis. For example, a

student police officer is allocated a tutor officer during their training in order to provide such learning. The individual learns a group of skills that connect practically in a certain job, such as dealing with a shoplifter, which involves dealing with the suspect, taking a witness statement, recovering property, and so on. Training craftsmen is, in the first instance, ensuring they know how to do this in the course of doing the work that the tutor assigns them according to their developing skill. When the individual has learned enough routines involved in the job, their apprenticeship is deemed to be over. For the police officer, this equates the end of their two-year "probationary period" where they are signed off by the training department as being proficient. However, there is nothing intellectual that connects the routines, and the individual then engages in practical work under supervisors who have experience in the application of routines. Consequently, the individual ends up learning a list of routines and knowledge of indicators of when a particular routine should be applied, and the set of routines learned are connected practically to ensure that particular job gets done;

2 **Young professionals**. For Stinchcombe, this category, that of "school"-taught individuals, is perhaps the ideal type in a modern organisation. Here, the individual is taught a set of courses that underpin their work, but these courses include not so much a list of things they ought to know how to do, but more a set of principles they will find useful in doing the various things (which cannot be anticipated) they will have to deal with. If the knowledge of craftsmen is a set of routines unbound by intellectual principles, the knowledge of young professionals is a set of principles they can apply. Young professionals go to work with what "school" has taught them: how to solve problems; and

3 **Senior professionals.** Senior professionals are individuals who have had the "abstract" training of young professionals and the practical experience of many years, so they command the routines of working in a given field. They have the experience of the "craft" and coursework, but they also have the experience of many years of applying abstract principles to various routine situations, and in doing so, have improved the routines by the application of a deep abstract understanding of the objectives and the causal process involved.

The process is illustrated in Table 1.1.

CURRENT PROVISION

This shift to a professionalization of policing has developed throughout many countries, although there is still a reticence in some areas for this to be fully embraced (Green, 2018). There has been a greater move

TABLE 1.1 The process of professionalising the police

	Craftsman	Young professional	Senior professional
Basic training	Supervised experience and minimal input. Learn "bunch" of responses via "apprenticeship"	Taught principles	Own experience analysed in the light of taught principles (reflective practitioner)
Knowledge	List of routines and indicators of when to use routine	Principles without routines; knowledge of what education has taught them	Analysed and reflected routines
Application	Bodies of routines connected "practically" to each other	All areas to which they can apply principles	Creation of new routines, different ways of dealing with routines and higher management
	Traditional police training	Value-added education in police training programme	Professional reflective police practitioner

for degree-educated police officers in countries such as Germany, Norway, the Netherlands, and Sweden, amongst many others (Frevel & Rogers, 2018). This is in recognition that a degree-level education will place officers in the position where they can take personal responsibility for decisions, in often complex and unpredictable environments (College of Policing, 2019). According to the College of Policing in the United Kingdom (UK), one of the fundamental requirements of a profession is the basis on which practitioners are allowed to exercise a high degree of individual autonomy and independence of judgement (College of Policing, 2019). Indeed, police officers are in a unique position in that they often work away from supervision and exercise their authority via discretionary powers. Although there are a range of characteristics related to professional discretion, the core aspects are said to include:

- A specialist knowledge base;
- A distinct ethical dimension;
- Continuing professional development requirements; and
- Standards of education (College of Policing, 2019, p. 1).

A professional framework for the training of police officers has recently been introduced in the UK to ensure a consistent approach to police training across the 43 police forces in England and Wales and to contribute towards the professionalism of the service (College of

Policing, 2019). In what has been referred to as "educating the recruited" and "recruiting the educated" (Ramshaw & Soppit, 2018), the Policing Education Qualifications Framework (PEQF) routes of entry into the police service introduced in 2019 are threefold, namely:

1 **Apprenticeship:** For those without a degree already, this paid position involves three years of on- and off-the-job learning with a degree qualification achieved upon completion;
2 **Degree-holder entry:** Those with a specific police or "other" degree enter into a work-based programme, supported by off-the-job learning. This route takes two years, resulting in a graduate diploma in professional policing practice once probation is completed; and
3 **Pre-join degree:** The third option is to undertake a three-year degree in professional policing at one's own expense, then apply to the force and follow a shorter on-the-job training programme.

In a similar approach, police recruits in Germany require a minimum qualification of a three-year bachelor's degree. Traditionally, the German police had a four-tier career system with a simple middle, upper, and higher career path. New recruits wanting to become a *Polizeimester* (similar to a general duties officer in Australia) received vocational training with the "craft" of policing being taught, under what was deemed the "middle career path" (Frevel, 2018). The "upper career path" was for those jobs that demanded individual responsibility and a broad spectrum of knowledge and skills, often reserved for the ranks of Inspector or Chief Inspector. However, the Keinbaum Report in 1991, which analysed the work of police officers and their competencies and power, concluded that the "middle career path" should be dissolved (Frevel, 2018). Having all police officers in the upper career path is expected to produce:

- Better knowledge about law . . . and social processes in the society;
- Higher policing skills and social competences;
- Better results of policing (less crime, less accidents, better clean up rates, higher satisfaction of citizens with the police, less fear of crime etc.);
- Less misbehaviour of police officers;
- Trustful relationship between public and police; and
- Better, court-proof files leading to efficient trials and fair sentences (Frevel, 2018, p. 202).

Certainly, these factors will contribute towards police legitimacy, as does the accreditation of police training and education (Paterson, 2011). While it is too soon to evaluate the recent amendments in the UK and Germany, in the United States (US) there is a longer history of partnership between higher education and police education. As such, what research has been carried out in the US has indicated police officers with higher-education qualifications are generally more tolerant of minority groups, more prone to problem solve and receive less complaints from the public, and more flexible in their approach to their duties (Lersch & Kunzman, 2001; Roberg & Bonn, 2004; Parker et al, 1976). Therefore, it is proposed that ongoing research and evaluation is required to further inform police training and education and support evidence-based practice.

CURRENT PROVISION IN AUSTRALIA

Table 1.2 summarises the current provisions for police education and training throughout Australia, including minimum entry requirements, qualification, course duration, educators, recruit salary, and the salary of the probationary constable (as of 2020).

The majority of police training in Australia remains at the "craftsman" level. Recruits in Victoria, Queensland, South Australia, Western Australia, the Australian Capital Territory, and the Northern Territory undergo a period of mandatory training at the relevant police academy,

TABLE 1.2 Police education and training in Australia

	Minimum pre-entry qualification	Entry level training/ education	Length of time to complete	Recruit salary	Probationary Constable salary	Educators
NSW	University Certificate in Workforce Essentials (UCWE)	Associate Degree in Policing Practice	One year and 32 weeks (including probation)	N/A	$73,609	Delivered collaboratively by Charles Sturt University and New South Wales Police Force
WA	Completion of Year 10 and Police Entrance Evaluation (PEE)	Diploma Public Safety (Policing)	28 weeks plus probation	$56,329	$74,284	Western Australia Police in alliance with North Metropolitan TAFE and Edith Cowan University
VIC	Victorian Certificate of Education (if under 21) and entrance exam	Diploma of Policing	31 weeks plus probation	$50,834	$69,836	Victoria Police
QLD	Completion of Year 12 or three years full time paid employment and recruiting assessments	Diploma of Policing	25 weeks plus probation	$51,060	$72,944	Queensland Police Service

(Continued)

TABLE 1.2 (Continued)

	Minimum pre-entry qualification	Entry level training/ education	Length of time to complete	Recruit salary	Probationary Constable salary	Educators
SA	Completion of Year 12 desirable and South Australia Police Recruitment Test	Diploma of Public Safety (Policing)	Six months plus probation	$35,000–$58,552	$68,303	South Australia Police
TAS	Completion of Year 10 and Police Entrance Exam	15 units of a 24-unit Degree in Bachelor of Social Science (Police Studies)	29 weeks plus probation	$50,832	$60,470	Delivered collaboratively by Tasmania University and Tasmania Police
NT	Completion of Year 12 or Trade Certificate or considerable employment experience	Diploma of Policing	30 weeks plus probation	$58,930–$62,466	$68,713	Northern Territory Police, Fire and Emergency Services
ACT (AFP)	Completion of Year 10 or Trade Certificate and AFP Entrance Exam	Diploma of Public Safety (Policing)	24 weeks plus probation	$59,252	$61,480	Australian Federal Police

Sources: www.police.nsw.gov.au/recruitment; www.stepforward.wa.gov.au/; www.police.vic.gov.au/police; www.police.qld.gov.au/units/police-recruiting; www.police.sa.gov.au/join-us/achievemore/police-officer-careers/recruitment-process; https://recruitment.police.tas.gov.au; https://pfes.nt.gov.au/careers-policing; www.afp.gov.au/careers/entry-level-recruit-policing-and-protective-service-officer-recruitment

followed by a probationary period in the field. Recruits receive training in areas such as: scenario training, legislation, police policies and procedures, multicultural awareness, prosecutions, crime investigation, traffic, family violence response, firearms, defensive tactics, driver education and "field craft" (Victoria Police, 2020; Queensland Police Service, 2020; Northern Territory Police, n.d.). Consequently, recruit preparation often remains entrenched in the traditional method, fortified by a practitioner-focused skills-based training environment, whereby characteristics of professionalization, including a commitment to higher education, are neglected (Green, 2018), thus limiting the potential of the individual and the police organisation to adapt and respond effectively to complex societal change.

As previously discussed, the Associate Degree in Policing Practice (ADPP) was introduced in New South Wales following the Wood Royal Commission (1997), requiring the highest level of educational attainment for sworn police officers throughout Australia. The curriculum is built on the fundamental principles of communication, ethics, law, and investigation, which develops the "young professional", given that these principles may be applied in variety of circumstances. Notably, the ADPP process involves regular evaluation of their approach to establish the level of preparedness of their constables for duty (Rogers & Wintle, 2019). The ADPP is also unique in offering a distance education mode for initial recruit training, first introduced in recognition of the global demand to provide accessibility to learning and career choices in an increasing number of professions (Davies & Nixon, 2010). The distance mode of delivery has since been extended with the introduction in 2019 of a mixed mode of delivery for Session 1 of the ADPP (New South Wales Police Force and Charles Sturt University, n.d.). The initial eight weeks of training are now delivered via distance education, with the remainder of the session moving into the academy for more practical based learning. It has been argued that the new generation of recruits are likely to be digitally literate; furthermore, police are often faced with large amounts of complex information from a variety of sources, thus, this mode of learning may enhance their abilities as an operational officer (Allan, 2013). As recently observed, this new approach has enabled police training and education to become more flexible, of particular significance when faced with social distancing restrictions due to the COVID-19 pandemic and the continued need to deliver operational police officers to meet current demands.

Tasmania Police also have a slightly different approach than other Australian policing organisations, with their recruits completing units towards a bachelor's degree. Consistent with the ADPP model, recruits are taught by both police practitioners and academics. Providing a collaborative model of training and education for police recruits is not without its challenges, not least of which is the collaboration of two bureaucratic organisations with their own entrenched cultures. Indeed, a prominent theme that arose in a recent study of teaching at the Tasmania Police Academy identified the need for both sides to understand and acknowledge each other's cultures (O'Shea & Bartkowiak-Théron, 2019).

CONCLUSION

The education of Australian police may need to be adjusted to meet the local, national, and international challenges that are likely to occur. An ability to manage change at short notice, coupled with complex skills such as an understanding of research methods, mastering and understanding technological changes and trends will be required. Factors that impact national and international law and an ability to integrate strategy, culture, and political concerns within the organisation will also be required skills. In particular, as a framework surrounding all of these changes and ideas, police leaders of today in Australia need to understand that they were trained in a substantially non-changing, bureaucratic-structured organisation, which has resulted in an organisational culture which sometimes displays fixed attitudes, and that this structure will need to be changed in order to meet the challenges of the future.

REFERENCES

Allan, D. (2013), 'Global Literacies for Australian Police: Thinking Globally, Policing Locally', *Salus Journal*, 1(3), 53–70.

Batts, A.W., Smoot, S.M., & Scrivner, E. (2012), *Police Leadership Challenges in a Changing World*. Retrieved from: www.ncjrs.gov/pdffiles1/nij/238338.pdf.

Bowling, B., Reiner, R., & Sheptycki, J. (2019), *The Politics of the Police*, 5th edition. Oxford: Oxford University Press.

Castells, M. (2010), *The Rise of the Network Society*, 2nd edition. Chichester: Wiley-Blackwell.

Clarke, J., Newman, J., Smith, N., Vidler, E., & Westmarland, L. (2009), *Creating Citizen-consumers: Changing Publics and Changing Public Services*. London: Sage.

College of Policing. (2019), *Policing Educations Qualification Framework (PEQF)*. Retrieved 25/3/2020, from: www.college.police.uk/What-we-do/Learning/Policing-Education-Qualifications-Framework/Pages/Policing-Education-Qualifications-Framework.aspx.

Cordner, G. (2016), 'The Unfortunate Demise of Police Education', *Journal of Criminal Education*, 27(4), 485–496.

Davies, A., & Nixon, J. (2010), 'Making It Real – from the Street to the Online Classroom in Police Education: What Is the Impact on Student Learning?', in S.H.S. Housego (ed.), *Curriculum, Technology & Transformation for an Unknown Future*, pp. 286–291. Retrieved from: http://ascilite.org.au/conferences/sydney10/procs/Davies-full.pdf.

Dolling, D. (2003), *Community Policing: Comparative Aspects of Community Policing Orientated Police Work*. Reiden, Germany: Felix-Varlag.

Durkheim, E. (1958), *Professional Ethics and Civic Morals*. Glencoe: Free Press.

Frevel, B. (2018), 'Starting as a Kommissar/Inspector? – The State's Career System and Higher Education for Police Officers in Germany', in C. Rogers & B. Frevel (eds.), *Higher Education and Police: An International View*. London: Palgrave Macmillan.

Frevel, B., & Rogers, C. (eds.) (2018), *Higher Education and Police: An International View*. London: Palgrave Macmillan.

Fukuyama, F. (2018), *Identity: The Demand for Dignity and the Politics of Resentment*. New York: Farrar, Straus and Giroux.

Garland, D. (2001), *The Culture of Control: Crime and Social Order in Contemporary Society*. Oxford: Oxford University Press.

Gilbert, J.N. (1993), *Criminal Investigation*. New York: Macmillan.

Goldstein, H. (1990), *Problem Oriented Policing*. New York: McGraw-Hill.

Gottschalk, P. (2007), 'Information Systems in Police Knowledge Management', *Electronic Government, An International Journal*, 4(2), 191–203.

Green, T. (2018), 'Down Under: Police Education at the Charles Sturt University, Australia', in C. Rogers & B. Frevel (eds.), *Higher Education and Police: An International View*. London: Palgrave Macmillan.

Greene, J.R., & Mastrofski, S.D. (1988), *Community Policing: Rhetoric or Reality*. New York: Praeger Publishers.

Hebdon, R., & Kirkpatrick, I. (2006), 'Changes in the Organisation of Public Services and Their Effects on Employment Relations', in S. Ackroyd (ed.), *The Oxford Handbook of Work and Organisation*. Oxford: Oxford University Press.

James, A. (2016), *Understanding Police Intelligence Work*. Bristol: Policy Press.

Lersch, K.M., & Kunzman, L.L. (2001), 'Misconduct Allegations and Higher Education in a Southern Sheriff's Department', *American Journal of Criminal, Justice*, 25(2), 161–172.

Mahoney, D., & Prenzler, T. (1996), 'Police Studies, the University and the Police Service: An Australian Study', *Journal of Criminal Justice Education*, 7(2), 283–304.

National Intelligence Council. (2008), *Global Trends 2030*. Retrieved from: https://globaltrends2030.files.wordpress.com/2012/11/global-trends-2030-november2012.pdf.

New South Wales Police Force and Charles Sturt University. (n.d.), *New South Wales Police Recruitment*. Retrieved from: www.police.nsw.gov.au/recruitment/the_training/associate_degree_in_policing_practice/entry_pathways.

Northern Territory Police. (n.d.), *Recruit Constable Information Booklet*. Retrieved from: https://pfes.nt.gov.au/sites/default/files/uploads/files/2020/Constable%20booklet%20ERECRUIT%202020_1.pdf.

O'Malley, P., & Hutchinson, S. (2005), *Converging Corporatisation: Police Management, Police Unionism, and the Transfer of Business Principles*. Paper presented at the Centre for Market and Public Organisation, University of Bristol.

O'Shea, B., & Bartkowiak-Théron, I. (2019), ' "Being a Topic Expert Is Not Sufficient": A Mixed-Method Analysis of Teaching Dynamics at the Tasmania Police Academy', *Police Practice and Research*, 20(3), 288–299.

Parker, L.C., Donnelly, M., Gerwitz, D., Marcus, J., & Kowalewski, V. (1976), 'Higher Education: Its Impact on Police Attitudes', *The Police Chief*, 43(7), 33–35.

Paterson, C. (2011), 'Adding Value? A Review of the International Literature on the Role of Higher Education in Police Training and Education', *Journal of Police Practice and Research*, 12(4), 286–297.

Queensland Police Service. (2020), *Service Training*. Retrieved from: www.police.qld.gov.au/units/police-recruiting/entry-pathways/how-to-apply/service-training.

Ramshaw, P., & Soppitt, S. (2018), 'Educating the Recruited and Recruiting the Educated: Can the New Police Education Qualifications Framework in England and Wales Succeed Where Others Have Faltered', *International Journal of Police Science & Management*, 20(4), 243–250.

Reiner, R. (2000), *The Politics of the Police*, 3rd edition. Oxford: Oxford University Press.

Roberg, R., & Bonn, S. (2004), 'Higher Education and Policing: Where Are We Now?', *Policing: An International Journal of Police Strategies and Management*, 27(4), 469–486.

Rogers, C. (2012), *Crime Reduction Partnerships*. Oxford: Oxford University Press.

Rogers, C., & Wintle, E. (2019), *An Evaluation of the ADPP Curriculum Delivery 2018/2019*, Unpublished report. Manly: Charles Sturt University.

Rohl, T.F., & Barnsley, R.H. (1995), 'The Strategic Transformation of Policing from Occupational to Professional Status', in B. Etter & M. Palmer (eds.), *Police Leadership in Australia*. Sydney: The Federation Press.

Schafer, J.A., Buerger, M.E., Myers, R.W., Jensen, C.J., & Levin, B.H. (2012), *The Future of Policing, a Practical Guide for Police Managers and Leaders*. Boca Raton, FL: CRC Press.

Shernock, S.K. (1992), 'The Effects of College Education on Professional Attitudes among Police', *Journal of Criminal Justice Education*, 3(1), 71–92.

Spybey, T. (1996), *Globalisation and World Society*. Cambridge: Polity Press.

Stinchcombe, A.L. (1990), *Information and Organizations*, Vol. 19. Oxford: University of California Press.

Terrill, W., & Mastrofski, S.D. (2002), 'Situational and Officer-based Determinants of Police Coercion', *Justice Quarterly*, 19(2), 215–248.

Trofymowych, D. (2008), *Police Education Past and Present: Perceptions of Australian Police Managers and Academic*. Retrieved from: https://dspace.flinders.edu.au/xmlui/bitstream/handle/2328/1852/Trofymowych%20jaa.pdf?sequence=4&isAllowed=y.

Trojanowicz, R.C., & Nicholson, T.G. (1976), 'A Comparison of Behavioural Styles of College Graduated Officers vs. Non-college Going Police Officers', *Police Chief*, 43(August), 56–59.

Victoria Police. (2020), *Training at the Academy*. Retrieved from: www.police.vic.gov.au/training-academy.

Wedlock, E. (2006), *Crime and Community Cohesion*. Home Office Report 19. Retrieved from: http://webarchive.nationalarchives.gov.uk/20120919132719/www.communities.gov.uk/documents/communities/pdf/452513.pdf.

Wimshurst, K., & Ransley, J. (2007), 'Police Education and the University Sector: Contrasting Models from the Australian Experience', *Journal of Criminal Justice Education*, 18(1), 106–122.

Wood, J. (1997), *The Royal Commission into the NSW Police Service Final Report*, Vol. 1–Corruption. Sydney: NSW Police Integrity Commission.

CHAPTER 2

Becoming a pracademic
The importance of lifelong learning as a police officer in the 21st century

Melanie Boursnell and Philip Birch

INTRODUCTION

This chapter presents a narrative on the dialogue and considerations concerning the importance of education and training for police. Throughout a career within the police force, an officer will weave through a myriad of requirements, including pre-service education and training, as well as mandatory ongoing professional development. Like many professions that require employees to acquire job-specific skills, the police operate within an evolving complex environment that prioritises public safety. Here, "match fitness" is garnered through lifelong engagement with learning and frequent adaption of practice. This makes the police organisation unique in that they must continually evolve and reflect the rapidly changing landscape around them. Adaptation is therefore important, and so engagement with education, training, and other forms of professional development during an officer's career is imperative. For example, police officers must adapt to the use of technologies used by both the profession and criminals, as well as by identifying and recording actions related to crime. Another factor representing change is that, as policing organisations evolve, millennials will come to dominate the workforce. These emerging professionals will challenge police in new ways, including through their ability to access sophisticated technologies like artificial intelligence and machine learning. Overall, policing faces new challenges that will shape learning expectations, including how learning is facilitated and accessed.

This chapter explores the shifting paradigm of police learning through the consideration of models of policing education. Consideration is also given to how traditional notions of "training", such as on-the job-training, is morphing into incremental, accessible learning formats such as online assessments and workplace simulations, offered not only within the police organisation but in partnership with academic providers. Further, the chapter considers how embracing experts external to the police organisation is of benefit, especially regarding the professionalism of policing. A new identity for police educators thus emerges, one which blends the notion of the police officer with that of the academic. For the purpose of this chapter, this concept and practice will be referred to as the "pracademic". Coined by Posner (2009), the notion is that a *pracademic is a person whose career spans the boundaries of academia and practice*. The notion of pracademic sits well within policing, especially for policing scholars who span both the pragmatic world of policing practice with the ethereal world of academia. The pracademic represents a growing number of police officers who can adopt the principles of professionalism while simultaneously engaging in scholarly activities, extending their capabilities beyond the technical and pragmatic and morphing into this conceptual space which invites their expertise. This is beneficial to both parties and enables mutually constructive discourses to develop, thereby extending previously rigid ideologically driven notions of the career police officer mostly engaged with the tools of his trade. Reflective of the fourth industrial revolution, in which technology is becoming more integrated in our lives, many police officers are engaging in consumption of their intellectual knowledge as it relates to building their profession (Tong, 2017).

There are several concepts associated with learning in police services, often discussed within the vocational field as workplace learning or work-based learning (see the work of Rogers & Frevel, 2018 for an illustration). The interplay of police as "work", as well as the impact of leaders and mentors, all act to influence police in a way that constitutes an ongoing negotiation of identity. That is, police work is not static. Rather, the shifting territory associated with ongoing learning opportunities leads to the development and enhancement of diverse skills within one organisation. The goal is to perpetuate learning opportunities by expanding and developing skills so that officers can build academic credibility whilst concurrently maintaining professional identity. Consequently, this chapter explores several concepts related to the vocational field alongside the emergence of the police "pracademic". These include the principles of lifelong learning, professional development, personal development, and reflective practice. Taken together, these are the cornerstones for all learning and growth. These concepts are framed throughout the subsequent chapter in a way that reflects perceived importance within the organisation. The chapter draws to a conclusion by reflecting on the importance of lifelong learning as a police officer in the 21st century.

CONTEXTUALISING POLICE EDUCATION AND TRAINING

Any consideration of contemporary education and training in democratic policing environments in western democracies, such as Australia, the UK, the US, and Canada, focuses on the tactical, operational, command, and control elements of the profession. These components cannot be removed, as they are essential for officers to meet the obligations of their employment. This tactical element of practice, for example, is conducted primarily through instruction-based activities focused on technical skill with limited learning. This is witnessed in Australian police training, whereby officers incur annual mandatory training that is extensive and an industrial requirement of their employment rather than a driver of a learning organisation (Beighton & Poma, 2015).

Juxtaposed with this mandatory educative component of practice is the notion of professional practice-based education. This refers to the institutional process of systematic learning that develops a sense of judgement and reasoning amongst employees in a range of "technical" skills. There is a focus on the development of critical reflection and analysis abilities, such as learning investigative techniques for those interested in detective work, intelligence, traffic officers, and so forth. There is also an increasing focus on the acquisition of complex cognitive capabilities to build leadership within policing organisations. The focus on leadership links to the overall goal of building authentic organisations supportive of staff who mostly commit the whole of their working lives to the organisation (Roberts, Herrington, Jones, White & Day, 2016). In contrast to professional practice-based education, technical training orientates around learning by doing. The aim of this line of training is improvement of performance, productivity, and competency. Technical programs are designed to achieve competency and reduce risk of dangerous situations and are, therefore, defined by annual skills refreshers and competency assessments as they relate to job-related skills. This technical training ensures police officers can do their jobs efficiently and effectively in utilising their skills, knowledge, and equipment to undertake their duties.

The learning focus in policing is with reference to "on-the-job" skills, with limited opportunities for off-the-job training. Most training is free and paid for by policing organisations, with only those very passionate officers using annual leave for unpaid professional development. Engagement with learning with police organisations in Australia (and overseas) varies from internal short courses, to programs of study and even vocational qualifications provided by external organisations, depending on the contract with the employer and the need for the skill within the organisation.

DEFINING POLICE EDUCATION

By the term education, reference is made to classroom-based instructor-led teaching (ILT) focused on the acquisition of occupational knowledge. This traditional form of education is delivered for both the legislative knowledge-based side of policing, covering the type of events officers will respond to, and the knowledge that is required to deal with the situations effectively. This leads to the intersection of the values, ethics, and beliefs inherent in policing and the general concepts and principles of policing. This "sage on the stage" education, as termed by Basham (2014), is delivered in a lecture-style format to large groups of students and is seen in policing academies globally as the primary educative methodology. This form of education supports the development of a sense of reasoning, understanding, judgement, and intellect in an individual which is often rote learnt, tested through examination and scored to provide a baseline for advancement to operational policing practice. Furthermore, the delivery within a pseudo-police facility commences the enculturation into the organisation, often through wearing of components of the police uniform to support the student in their transition to police officer. As this education progresses, the complexity of the task and the exposure to the "real life" policing environment incrementally increases in preparation for a first field placement.

The lessons learned during this process of education assist new recruits with assimilation and confidence to face future challenges, and prepares them for the diversity of roles of a police officer, combined with the commencement of the ongoing on-the-job training which will last for the entirety of the career. Police learning environments are also evolving to keep pace with the level of skill required in the field. There are numerous examples globally in policing organisations of the incorporation of simulated learning, problem-based learning to support and deepen the classroom-based learning (see Makin, 2016). Emerging new methods are implemented to support the "stickiness" of practical knowledge about the world of policing and common situations that will be faced when they begin the job of policing. It also reflects educators operating as pracademics within policing organisations. In addition, this phase of learning in policing goes beyond stickiness to commence the generation of the relationships that support policing culture and/or organisational enculturation.

Like any other learning, there are various phases of education and levels of learning available within policing which navigate the space of training and education. Qualifications, certificates or professional certifications are awarded to police officers when they achieve a level of education. This is replicated globally in policing education, from commencement as a policing student through to technical experts and pracademics who combine academia and practice.

Key differences between education and training

Most policing organisations have a professional "Education and Training" service who provide a Head of Profession for learning. There are significant differences between training and education. Largely, the difference is understood as such: education is a system of learning that is broad in its scope and is theoretically orientated. In comparison, training is concerned with skill development; it is narrower in its scope and is based on practical application (Surbhi, 2017).

Contemporary policing necessitates a more flexible approach than previously seen in either education or training. Learner-centric models, more commonly known as student-centred learning, for example, required by mobile labour markets and more millennial employees, create an appetite for learning in the same context as other professions such as law, teaching, nursing, and accountancy. Consequently, policing as a profession of choice has entered a professionalization process (in various ways) in countries like in the UK and Australia (over the last 20–25 years). Whilst policing continues to be positioned as a vocation; even in the fluidity of the 21st century it currently remains a lifelong career option for many people (Lumsden, 2017). It is unique that a single institution can provide a range of career pathways and options for its employees who will potentially change the direction of their career many times whilst remaining in the one organisation. Nevertheless, there is a changing of the tides regarding the discourse that the police profession is a cradle-to-grave occupation (Birch, 2018). Some police forces are considering how policing capabilities can be broadened to have relevance in other vocational sectors such as the emergency-management sector. This adoption of capability-based approaches[1] to learning signals an important part of the change process for career police officers, who often identify as specialist officers. For instance, a "Detective" would be good at communication, at influencing and negotiating with people – these skills then become transferrable to other jobs outside of the world of policing, such as policy development and analysis. This approach to utilisation of a whole-of-government capability definition provides a structured vocational framework for education that is comparable and transferrable. Another example of this is the observable shift in the senior officer ranks into government organisations to broaden leadership experience. There are also leadership capabilities emerging within policing organisations. The skills associated with Senior Executive positions blends sworn and unsworn officers' talents in a way that enhances leadership of the policing organisation. Both shifts are emerging, and offer significant opportunities for diversity of professionalization in policing practice.

This discursive shift in policing practice to a professional career increases demand on police standards, training, skills, and expertise. Therefore, the importance of a police officer being engaged in lifelong learning has never been so apparent as it has been in recent times. This is reflected in the increased professionalisation of policing and contemporary policing practice – both positions require an increasing level of operational expertise to effectively work in environments that require the deployment of complex technologies, surveillance, and more sensitive forensic procedures – notwithstanding that crime itself has changed, and this impact has not just a local but a global community impact due to crime spanning national boundaries (cybercrime, child exploitation, and modern slavery are just a few examples). As these traditional notions of policing boundaries are pushed, concurrent to this are shifts in the skill base and capabilities of officers. Accordingly, as explained by Di Nota and Huhta (2019), the requirements of policing now require learning complex cognitive and motor skills. This means traditional police education and training must adapt in areas like the use of force, whilst at a global level it can lead to the enhancement of the sharing of practice and techniques.

The practice of policing is evolving alongside societal technological advancement as it relates to shifting police education. Whilst centralised education remains dominant, meaning the education requirements of a policing organisation are exclusively handled from within the organisation, options to diversify and utilise technologies within police training are increasingly being adopted to support learning opportunities. It is these technological training sessions that support the daily requirements of first-line response and operational policing. Learning at the level of operational policing requires integrating the skills that are practiced with work-integrated learning. This emphasis on embedded education seeks to integrate standards of academic achievement with police practical encounters, as this relationship reveals the nature of the pracademic. For instance, the fundamental cognitive processes underlying motor learning in weapons training, from novel skill acquisition to complex behaviours, require situational awareness, decision-making, and problem solving. The learning of these skills is focused on reducing risk and enhancing safety to ensure officers act appropriately and within organisational bounds. Teaching of these skills in the police curriculum requires ongoing evaluation and incorporation of emerging evidence-based training practices to ensure and enable policing performance. This learning takes into account the physiological responses during high-stress incidents. It also demands police educators be able to meet the benchmarks of educative practice not previously required.

On the other hand, the nature of police work is adaptive, and police practitioners continually engage with a range of traditional and emerging policing roles and a diversity of community values. This requires advanced communication, problem solving, and negotiation skills. The institutional investment in education, training, and developing experienced officers is a considerable financial investment for both parties, and has evolved over time. The initial training or probationary period of two years is the same as it was 30 years ago; however, the content covered in current times is monumentally different. The approach to police education also remains relatively unchanged and requires a contemporary focus to enable timely access to learning.

The development of a professionalized policing model offers benefits to police officers, policing agencies, and state and federal governments. The professionalization of police necessitates ever-changing requirements, evidence, best practice policies, and shared understandings to keep up with the ever-changing rate and pace of globalised crime. Arguably, policing is now comparable to careers such as teaching and nursing, in that they also are seeking to professionalize through the facilitation of university-driven standards. This dialogue is not about centralising policing practice, but about professionalizing the practitioners and those who teach practitioners without losing the "grass roots" nature of the profession. Teaching, nursing and policing professions have all been forced to re-evaluate the means by which to produce "job ready" graduates (Shipton, 2019).

The fluidity of the labour market is just one of many advantages that can be leveraged to the benefit of contemporary policing, whilst concurrently creating space for the pracademic to exist. For instance, attracting recruits with higher levels of qualifications into policing careers may be a short-term strategy to provide them with insider experience before consolidating this into other opportunities within the organisation. In addition, emerging evidence suggests that millennials hungry for a varied career will change notions of a lifelong policing career. Tong (2017) suggests that a portfolio approach to a career is critical to the future of policing. This trend will drive organisations to develop pathways out of the sworn profession into the unsworn policing world to leverage the expertise. The richness of experienced sworn officers transitioning into other roles/careers within the organisation offers great potential.

The evolution of policing as it relates to the role of education and training has future implications. The shift to a capability-based system of professional development is one important signal of the organisation evolving and encouraging its officers to think and behave in a more competitive manner. Here, officers can document through evidence of educational experience why they should be the preferred candidates for promotion, as opposed to the traditional criteria of seniority of service. The rejection of the rote-based learning system, which creates inequity within the organisation, will be replaced with a contemporary egalitarian solution that encourages and increases organisational diversity. For those not wishing to progress in rank, there is still the necessity to garner professional knowledge and skills in this 21st-century context. Regardless of status or ambition, being a lifelong learner is a minimum requirement for being a successful police officer. Well-established policing organisations use a combination of support, engagement, and reflective practice-based learning enabling as these skills translate into operational practice. This is discussed in more depth in the next section.

LIFELONG LEARNING: DEFINITION AND IMPACT

This chapter has recognised the need for lifelong learning in policing organisations as one of the requisite aspects of ongoing professionalism. The need for continual engagement with learning is embedded in notions of professional legitimacy (Thompson & Payne, 2019). As already discussed, policing organisations are experienced with the provision of technical education. To move forwards and create increased legitimacy, there is a requirement for the organisations to evolve their andragogical principles, reflecting the aspiration to create learning organisations. Peter Senge (1990) popularised the notion of the learning organisation. This concept has been developed by many others since it was first introduced. Utilising this lens, the learning organisation is the metaphor and the organisation is the culture. The learning organisation becomes a sub-culture, or a new iteration of the culture (Senge, 1990). The theory of learning organisations suggests that there are incremental steps for organisational transformation until they reach a point of maturity. The application of this theory to understand education within organisations is not unique to policing, but usefully describes the dynamic and constantly changing environment of policing which requires maturity of learning organisations to support ongoing practice development.

Christopher (2015) extends this position, suggesting that police must engage in critical reflective practice, encouraging people to learn throughout their careers. This builds the intrinsic value of learning. To realise this value proposition and generate organisational outcomes, the leadership of the organisation must value education and support the transformational shift to keep policing relevant. This appetite for change and transformation can sometimes result in approaches that can be disruptive to the work of police officers, whilst achieving new and innovative approaches to learning, including flexibility of delivery. This disruption and change enable a learner-centric perspective and can lead to learner empowerment whilst seeking to ensure the organisational needs will be met.

Shipton (2019) has engaged in debate on whether policing organisations are ready to be learner-led or have the staff with skills to adopt a flipped approach to learning, or if this can even be achieved within policing organisations. This is positioned against the tradition of policing education, which is orientated around formal learning based on instructor-led teaching modelling off traditional institutionalised learning approaches. Given the complexification of policing already raised in this chapter, the question of transitioning at least elements of the traditional approach to better serve the police officer and provide skills based on cognitive flexibility and agility required for future policing will need further analysis. Without doubt, evidence suggests that many situations require increasingly complex problem solving and application of information garnered via technology. Technology, in particular, requires application and solutions that learners engage with in educational contexts to lift their skills in a way that is continually evolving at a similar pace to the technology.

Formal education is important for policing, particularly a blend of formal learning and on-the-job learning. This can be accounted for in the 70/20/10 theoretical approach (Clardy, 2018). Formal learning provided by Education and Training Services accounts for the 10%, and the learning provided through localised training for 20%, with the 70% being on-the-job learning through practice under the pupillage or more experienced officers to guide and develop skill mastery (Rabin,

2014). Education can maximise a person's employment opportunities and prospects; however, formal education is only one type of learning. Opportunities to further one's knowledge and develop skills can also be acquired through training opportunities. Regardless of the approach to lifelong learning (formal education and/or training), the essential characteristic relates to the value that is assigned to ongoing learning and skill acquisition to create and maintain a positive attitude to learning towards professional development.

Being a lifelong learner involves having the motivation to learn and develop voluntarily. As such, a lifelong learner seeks to enhance an understanding of the world. This is important for police practice. If this is embedded within the environment of a learning organisation with organisational leadership support, then learning and its value is not questioned. There are two main reasons for lifelong learning: professional development and personal development. Both support personal growth and career opportunities, which can provide leverage within the policing organisation. Learning in whatever context it takes place, whether it be for personal or professional reasons, can boost confidence and self-esteem, provide organisational security and reduce risk by making the organisation more adaptable to change when it happens (important for practice and the policing organisation itself). Developing learning organisations in police contexts forces a shift away from traditional paradigmatic training (technical training relating to "on-the-job" skills) and into learning through facilitation of education.

PROFESSIONAL DEVELOPMENT AND POLICE PRACTICE

Policing organisation professional development is defined as the willingness to learn based on role, rank, and scope of practice. For instance, based on these dynamics, a police officer may have to undertake different annual professional development and/or mandatory training. According to Australia Open Colleges (n.d., para. 3):

> *Professional development consists of education, observation and mentoring that can help to enhance the employees in a workplace. It might include training sessions or graduate classes, spending time with a mentor to observe how others handle conflict or challenges, or mentoring someone else who might be new to the field.*

Professional development builds knowledge and transferable skills and should include reflection of practice for future readiness (e.g. promotion). From a financial point of view, a more highly skilled and knowledgeable workforce is an asset and essential for promotion. Leadership practice requires both ongoing learning and reflection, both of which are known to be key to job satisfaction, and expertise is often a key quality of an effective leader. Engagement in professional development occurs in a myriad of ways within policing organisations, as already discussed in this chapter. The need for professional development is supported within policing. It is the concept of personal development that requires greater enculturation and support, and this is discussed next.

PERSONAL DEVELOPMENT WITHIN THE POLICING CONTEXT

Personal development is a lifelong process reflected in the assessment of skills and qualities, enabling goal setting and supporting realisation of potential. The rationale of learning within policing organisations is often overly practical, and learning through personal development is largely unexplored. As learning organisations are built within the culture of policing, incremental shifts in culture are both explored and realised. Disruption, here, is a positive occurrence that will generate curiosity and enable pracademics to learn beyond their subject matter expertise, enabling active engagement and critical practices.

Focusing on active engagement in learning, this process has learning advantages that foster growth. There are, of course, many reasons why people learn for personal development, including Maslow's (1970) theory of self-actualisation, which purports that individuals have an intrinsic need for personal development. Here, personal development depends on the needs of an individual being met, and as one level of need is satisfied, a higher need can be developed. Maslow outlines five levels in his hierarchy of needs: physiological, safety, love, esteem, and self-actualisation at the highest level.

Translating Maslow's hierarchy of needs within a policing context raises the question of whether the organisational, hierarchal structure is positioned to cater to the intrinsic physiological needs of officers. Specifically, are the basic skills taught to all police officers in their initial training enough to create feelings of operational safety and security in both the physical and economic sense? At a personal level, there are also the questions of whether the needs for love and belonging are satisfied, and whether such needs can be extended to and exercised in a professionalized police context (i.e. through the probationary period through to the progression of a fully sworn police officer).

As discussed, the fourth level of Maslow's hierarchy of needs is self-esteem and self-worth, which brings attention to the facet of empowerment. This relates to police professionalization in that police officers value credibility gained from practice and utilised in developing the space required to become an established pracademic. The fifth level is self-actualisation/the need to understand. Understanding refers to generating abstract ideas, such as curiosity, and searching for meaning/purpose to achieve a deeper understanding. This level relates to acquisition of academic practice and exploring the periphery of practice that is the transition between police officer and academic. At this point there is still the ability to co-exist between worlds; furthermore, there is a continued acceptance of being a police officer as a primary role. The penultimate level relates to aesthetic needs of symmetry and order – where re-identification or transition of identity occurs. At this point, the police officer yields to the pracademic. The police officer and academic can merge, resolving the conflicts between world of practice and academe. Concurrent to this is the confidence and acceptance of their contribution to both worlds, and beyond this is value in both worlds as a chameleon – an interchangeable expert – both police officer and academic. Finally, at the top of Maslow's hierarchy is the need for self-actualisation. This is witnessed in the interchange between the pracademic and the "thought leader" in policing practice as one who instigates learning within the policing organisation.

Utilising Maslow's position enables us to view individuals transitioning into pracademic spaces as having final assimilation and comfort in their place within the policing ecosystem. They emerge into this final stage with specific traits such as competence, autonomy, and limitless potential for growth to achieved through the process of assimilation. Accordingly, self-actualisation leads to self-fulfilment and the opportunity to reach potential as a unique boundary dweller. Maslow's explanation suggests a point of confidence and congruence for pracademics that enables the fulfilment of purpose with that of practice. Within policing, this translates into the ability to be reflective and engage in ongoing educational, professional and personal development.

REFLECTIVE PRACTICE IN POLICING

The critical part of the journey in professional development as it relates to pracademia involves engagement in reflective practice. In its simplest form, this means thinking about and reflecting on actions. At its core, the police force is naturally a critically reflective domain (Christopher, 2015). Reflective practice as a model of professional development links critical reflection to the complexities of policing and aligns learning from or through experience. The difference between casual "thinking" and "reflective practice" is that reflective practice requires conscious effort to consider events and develop insights into them. The habit of reflective practice is useful as a professional and personal tool in policing, acting as a means of enhancing knowledge and skill acquisition.

The skill of reflective practice

There is strong empirical evidence supporting the importance of reflective practice as a learnt behaviour that benefits policing. Reflective practice can be understood as bridging the gap between theory and practice, in the way a pracademic does, supporting practice extension and development of skill. Argyris (2002), who proposed "double-loop learning", suggests that reflection enables distance to observe the single loop of "experience, reflect, conceptualise, apply" before attempting to integrate the second loop, which brings the new paradigm and re-frames ideas. According to Argyris (2002), the second loop enables change and development of practice. The learning extension requires engagement in cognitive practice domains of emotional intelligence, attention, executive, memory, and motor function ability. This assimilation creates space to explore theories and to apply these to experiences in a structured way whilst creating growth and resilience. As a consequence, the skill of reflective practice is important for a police officer as it provides a vehicle for examining the complexities of police practice. Reflective practice relies on the ability to engage in critical, constructive, and creative thinking. Thompson (2015, pp. 238–240), suggests six steps of engagement in reflective practice. In summary, they are:

- **Read** – around the topics you are learning about or want to learn about and develop;
- **Ask** – others about the way they do things and why;
- **Watch** – what is going on around you;
- **Feel** – pay attention to your emotions, what prompts them, and how you deal with negative ones;
- **Talk** – share your views and experiences with others in your organisation;
- **Think** – learn to value time spent thinking about your work.

The discipline of reflective practice involves thinking and developing an understanding of the theory and others' practice. It enables the exploration of ideas with others. Reflective practice should lead to knowledge acquisition, improved working with others and enhanced communication, to name but a few abilities fostered through education and training.

Reflective practice: a consideration of impact

Reflective practice can increase self-awareness making it a key tool to build emotional intelligence. It requires learning through practice, adaption of behaviour and growth of expertise. Reflective practice assists the development of critical thinking encouraging active engagement in work processes a core requirement of contemporary policing, critical thinking can be understood as a way to

> *identify reliable information and make reliable judgements. It encompasses mindset and skills, both of which can be developed through an understanding of key concepts, practice and application* (Monash University, 2020, para. 8).

The crucial policing skill of critical thinking should be built in all officers to reduce risk in the field through constant narrative about practice and improvement for future responses. Dickfos (2019) suggests that pracademic experience is two-way, assisting academics to model, scaffold and coach employability skills to learners with greater exposure to the technical profession they teach.

In policing practice, the regular use of reflective practice supports in-time feedback and discussions, including building meaningful development plans. It provides tangible capability-based examples to use in competency-based situations (for police officers, this becomes critical if they wish to progress in rank). In sum, reflective practice is a tool for improving learning, and therefore acts as a means to build policing organisations. The practice is not widely adopted in policing, probably because it is largely counter-intuitive to an otherwise strong culture of resilience that dominates in policing organisations. Yet, considering the high levels of stress and psychological injuries in policing organisations, reflective practice and critical thinking may be of benefit. It will take time to adopt the technique of reflective practice, although initiating such a move might make relevant the role of the pracademic in that they are able to combine academic pursuits with traditional police duties, all of which could generate intellectual growth and create an innovative and flourishing police culture.

PRACADEMIC – THE FUTURE GEM FOR POLICING?

The importance of learning for policing organisations considered in this chapter has revealed the opportunities possible for the pracademic in policing professions. As noted earlier in the chapter, the term was popularised by Posner (2009), yet it remains an underutilised term. The pracademic typically has significant experience in both academia and practice, allowing them to move between them with ease. Pracademics ensure professionalization and credibility through the facilitation of educational pursuits in a practical context.

The pracademic role can be diverse, according to Volpe and Chandler (2001), who suggest that the pracademic is important for an array of roles, including dispute resolution, procedural justice and supporting universities in research and development. Pracademics serve a role in the policing field, often maintaining "old-school" police styles while supporting the ontological shift toward evidence-based practices. The pracademic is an agent of change, aiming to foster cultural dignity and safety practice, all without scepticism. The pracademic solves problems using academic theory, evidence-based research and years of practical experience in the field of policing. The integration of theory and practice in the context of lifelong learning provides a wealth of potential for pracademics to revolutionise policing.

CONCLUSION

This chapter has considered education and training within the contemporary policing context. The importance of learning amongst the complexities of 21st century policing requires intelligent solutions to meet the ever-changing nature of crime. Policing as a practice has moved from "walking the beat" to a more complex set of practices, which more recently have included adopting emerging technologies and methodologies associated with technology. To be at the forefront of detection, and create safety within societies, the police officer of the future ultimately needs to be a pracademic.

The pracademic has a multipurpose role, enabled through career diversity and professional and personal development, clearing pathways for learning to further create an eminent profession which is both diverse and challenging. To further establish the territory of the pracademic, police education requires disruption in modes of traditional thinking. Rather, a shift is proposed from instructional training (with operational skills on centre stage) towards an emphasis on incremental education (incorporating theory and scientific knowledge). The result of this shift could be beneficial for policing and the advancements of the profession, broadening thinking, generating meaningful research, and further understanding the dynamics of the work of police officers. As such, the outcome is providing a police profession that is fit for the 21st century.

NOTE

1   A focus on what an individual is able to do.

REFERENCES

Argyris, C. (2002). Double-loop learning, teaching, and research. *Academy of Management Learning & Education*, 1(2), 206–218.

Australia Open Colleges. (n.d.). *What Is Professional Development?* Retrieved from: www.opencolleges.edu.au/careers/professional-development

Basham, B. R. (2014). Police instructor or police educator? *Salus Journal*, 2(1), 99–109.

Beighton, C., & Poma, S. (2015). Expanding professional learning: Inside/outside police firearms training. *Studies in Continuing Education*, 37(2), 187–201.

Birch, P. (2018). Higher education and police: An international perspective [book review]. *Policing (Oxford): A Journal of Policy and Practice*, 1–2.

Christopher, S. (2015). The police service can be a critical reflective practice . . . If it wants. *Policing: A Journal of Policy and Practice*, 9(4), 326–339.

Clardy, A. (2018). 70-20-10 and the dominance of informal learning: A fact in search of evidence. *Human Resource Development Review*, 17(2), 153–178.

Dickfos, J. (2019). Academic professional development: Benefits of a pracademic experience. *International Journal of Work-Integrated Learning*, 20(3), 243–255.

Di Nota, P. M., & Huhta, J. M. (2019). Complex motor learning and police training: Applied, cognitive, and clinical perspectives. *Frontiers in Psychology*, 10, 1–20.

Lumsden, K. (2017). 'It's a profession, it isn't a job': Police officers' views on the professionalisation of policing in England. *Sociological Research Online*, 22(3), 4–20.

Makin, D. A. (2016). A descriptive analysis of a problem-based learning police academy. *Interdisciplinary Journal of Problem-Based Learning*, 10(1), 2–17.

Maslow, A. H. (1970). *Motivation and Personality*. New York: Harper & Row.

Monash University. (2020). *Critical Thinking*. Retrieved from: www.monash.edu/rlo/research-writing-assignments/critical-thinking

Posner, P. L. (2009). The pracademic: An agenda for re-engaging practitioners and academics. *Public Budgeting & Finance*, 29(1), 12–26.

Rabin, R. (2014). *Blended Learning for Leadership: The CCL Approach*. Center for Creative Leadership. Retrieved at: www.ccl.org/wp-content/uploads/2015/04/BlendedLearningLeadership.pdf

Roberts, K., Herrington, V., Jones, W., White, J., & Day, D. (2016). Police leadership in 2045: The value of education in developing leadership. *Policing: A Journal of Policy and Practice*, 10(1), 26–33.

Rogers, C., & Frevel, B. (2018). *Higher Education and Police*. London: Palgrave Macmillan.

Senge, P. (1990). *The Fifth Discipline: The Art and Practice of the Learning Organization*. New York: Doubleday.

Shipton, B. L. (2019). Police educators' experiences of teaching and teaching development: Implications for developing police academy staff. *Journal of Criminological Research, Policy and Practice*, 5(2), 95–107.

Surbhi, S. (2017). *Difference Between Training and Education*. Retrieved from: https://keydifferences.com/difference-between-training-and-education.html

Thompson, J., & Payne, B. (2019). Towards professionalism and police legitimacy? An examination of the education and training reforms of the police in the republic of Ireland. *Education Sciences*, 9(3), 241–264.

Thompson, N. (2015). *People skills* (2nd Edition). London: Palgrave Macmillan.

Tong, S. (2017). Professionalising policing: Seeking viable and sustainable approaches to police education and learning. *European Law Enforcement Research Bulletin*, 3, 171–178.

Volpe, M. R., & Chandler, D. (2001). Resolving and managing conflicts in academic communities: The emerging role of the 'pracademic'. *Negotiation Journal*, 17(3), 245–255.

CHAPTER 3

Police leadership in the 21st century

Graham Sunderland and Ian Stewart

INTRODUCTION

There has been so much written about "police leadership" that one may be excused for assuming that leadership within a policing environment is somehow different from other organisations within the public or private sector. Different or not, leadership must be accepted as a crucial aspect of any organisation's ability to operate within Australia in the 21st century (Pearson-Goff & Herrington, 2014). This chapter examines what it means to be a leader within the police service in the 21st century, and focuses on a variety of aspects that impact the reputation of contemporary leaders. For decades, the police have been accused of being resistant to change and their leadership unable to adapt to keep up with societal dynamics. This chapter aims to provide much needed clarity around what a 21st-century leader in the police actually is, what challenges they must meet, and an explanation of the influence they have. Some may argue that the need for change is blatantly obvious, with "armchair critics" often being the first to attack the personality of a senior police officer following an event perhaps not going to plan. This chapter will close the gap between academic conjecture and the reality of leadership within an emergency response agency. It will explore issues around governance and accountability, along with the internal and external influences on leaders within the police service in Australia. This will result in an examination of the leadership appointment process as it exists today and the associated political pressures on a short- to long-term basis.

The ability to foresee challenges the organisation may face is a fundamental competency of any leader; however, to identify the changes required to meet future encounters is vital. The speed of change within society does not necessarily correlate with a need to change the type of leadership. Indeed, it may be argued that a change of leadership will inevitably lead to organisational changes, whether necessary or not. The impact of any changes must be able to be measured to ensure that transformation is not merely a gimmick or a new face. Bearing in mind that this chapter is to examine police leadership and management in the 21st century, it comes with an assumption that these need to be different. Before an assertion can be made that there is a need for the leadership within the police to change, one must firstly determine why, and only then go on to establish what any modification should look like. It is essential to ascertain what success looks like in order to extol the benefits of change. The current leadership within the police may need to be resolute when providing direction for the future of policing in Australia, rather than simply acceding to the capricious suggestions of others who claim to know better. By studying contemporary practices of leadership within the police service in Australia, the chapter will discuss whether any change is necessary. Through the provision of experience-based views, it will indicate what structure and disposition leadership and management within the police should adopt to have the best chance of meeting the challenges of the 21st century.

LEGITIMACY – LEADER AND TEAM

The role of a police leader can only be considered with an appreciation of the complexity of the environment in which they serve. How their legitimacy is established and how it is maintained must include the personal attributes of the individual, but also the team they lead. In this sense the legitimacy of the organisation and the role of police in society is crucial. However, the ideal of legitimacy should not be confused with the notions of authority, responsibility and accountability. While interdependent, these notions can be described as:

- Authority: the ability or permission to make decisions;
- Responsibility: something that it is your job or duty to deal with; and
- Accountability: the way in which we answer for the work we've done or the staff we manage (Oxford Dictionary, 2020).

Legitimacy is linked to the way each of these factors influences behaviours.

Police legitimacy in contemporary Western society can be traced to the advent of the London Metropolitan Police in the 19th century. Much has been said about the "Peelian Principles" originating at the time of the establishment of the London Metropolitan Police, circa 1829, and who "invented" them (Lentz & Chaires, 2007), but there seems little opposition to the notion explored by Reith (1956) that these principles constituted an approach to policing "unique in history and throughout the world, because it derived, not from fear, but almost exclusively from public co-operation with the police, induced by them designedly by behaviour which secures and maintains for them the approval, respect and affection of the public" (p. 140).

Of more recent times in the UK the Home Office (2012) confirmed the application of these principles to modern policing. While there are differences in how policing is practised internationally, Australia is a country which has relied on the "policing by consent" model in general terms over a similar timeframe to that of Britain.

The leaders of policing in Australia today recognise the importance of accountability to the notion of public trust. A common theme surrounding police accountability is the link with "the conduct of police officers with respect to lawful, respectful, and equal treatment of citizens" (Walker, 2006). This of course presents significant complexity, due to the diversity in Australia's contemporary society of cultures, their expectations, and interpretation of the policing models. The complexity is increased by the impact of world events, including terrorism and pandemics, technological change, public order issues, climate change, natural disasters, and social inequality. It would seem logical that the legitimacy of both the broader policing team (or agency), their members and their leaders are linked directly to accountability.

The mechanisms of accountability in Australia for policing include legislation in the forms of criminal, civil and administrative laws, regulatory controls, parliamentary oversight and policy guidance, the judgements of the courts (including administrative tribunals), independent oversight agencies, Oath of Service, internal policies, directions and disciplinary processes, performance monitoring and transparency, independent police statistical bodies, the media (including public reporting using social media), independent complaint systems, unions, and the specific obligations of employment contracts for individual police leaders. All of these mechanisms provide a balance for the significant powers entrusted to police officers generally, and to their leadership more specifically.

Exercising authority under this weight of scrutiny would seem almost impossible for the police leader; however, the context of leadership in policing can provide an insight. As discussed later in this chapter, police are trained leaders from the time of induction until the day they cease their careers. Some progress in the hierarchy of authority (which is traditionally linked to rank progression), while others develop their leadership attributes through action learning and formal training. Formal development, experience, and promotion by merit are key to equipping those who choose the challenge of senior and executive leadership with the capabilities necessary for successful decision-making. Understanding the expectations of all stakeholders is just one of these factors, but it is crucial in ensuring the legitimacy of the team (organisation) and the police leader alike. Who are these stakeholders, and are any of them more important than others? For the police leader, understanding the answers to these questions is crucial.

PROACTIVE LEADERSHIP

Whilst there is an acceptance that there is a marked difference between "leadership" and "management", the associated competencies within each will regularly overlap. Everyone is responsible for what they do, and everyone within the police service has a part to play in leadership, from a front-line Constable to a Chief Officer (Marquet, 2013). Leadership and management may, therefore, be somewhat synonymous yet different, although, without doubt, integral. To explain this incongruity, leadership without management will create an environment of stagnation, whereby ideas will abound without manifestation. Management without leadership, on the other hand, will result in anarchy and "short termism" (sic). The latter leads to a lack of strategic steerage, with little, if any, change. It is therefore crucial that both need to exist in harmony within the police service of Australia to benefit those actually delivering the service and the community receiving it.

The idea of leadership providing the strategy and management dealing with the tactics is quite familiar. The complexity arises when attempting to identify the delineation between the two. The stage where a police leader or manager is entangled in the "stractics" (sic), with a "foot in both camps", must be recognised. That is not say that it should be forbidden because a "manual of guidance" deems it to be erroneous, but acknowledged and accepted due to the experience and training of the leader.

Of course, leaders must set strategic direction for the organisation, and with that obligation comes responsibility to get it right, and accountability should it falter. Leaders within the police service are no exception to this, and therefore it is surely incumbent on stakeholders to trust them to perform this task without undue interference. Only then can the community hold the leadership to account should this undertaking not lead to success. This strategic direction, or organisational planning, has to be the motivation that drives internal change. Planning at this level must take in to account the overall impact on people, both internally and externally, and should not be decided by leaders operating from within a "dark room", devoid of advice or suggestions from all levels of the organisation. Strategic leaders within the police need to be adept at project management and be able to differentiate between short-, medium-, and long-term projects. The aims and objectives of each project require sanctioning at a senior level of leadership with endorsement of the final plan from the same echelon of seniority to exhibit appropriate ownership. The pace of change is not dictated by external sources, other than through due accountability of the strategic leadership to be successful and one has to be cognisant of the saying, "The essence of strategy is choosing what not to do" (Kotter, Porter & Olmsted Teisberg, 2015, p. 1721).

It is crucial for any leader to adequately document their rationale and principles when planning for or implementing organisational change.

INTERNAL AND EXTERNAL INFLUENCES

The complexity of the environment in which Australian police leaders serve is increasing. A range of influences, both internal and external to policing, have required a more coordinated and collaborative approach to issues of crime prevention and enhanced community safety. While not exhaustive, some of these influences are examined both for their impact, outcomes to date and opportunities ahead. No attempt has been made to prioritise the list of influences.

Community diversity

The 2016 Census conducted by the Australian Bureau of Statistics has found that Australia is one of the most culturally diverse nation's on earth. The Census shows that Australia has a higher proportion of overseas-born people (26%) than the United States (14%), Canada (22%), and New Zealand (23%) (Australian Bureau of Statistics, 2016). Unlike many other countries, Australia has been able to celebrate the differences and opportunities provided by the traditions, religious beliefs, social mores and cuisines each of these new groups have shared in their new homeland. While much of the credit for these positive outcomes has been directly attributed to the federal and state policy settings and the support mechanisms available to our new arrivals, the role of policing in these communities has played a significant part in the process of inclusion to the greater Australian community.

Police leaders have been fundamental to these successes. Role models have reached out to the communities, creating trust and confidence in the integrity of policing offering fairness and procedural justice to all, something many new arrivals have never experienced before. It is important to develop relationships and partnerships to enhance communication and information-sharing strategies to address English as a second language, an understanding of Australia's laws and customs, and opportunities for the education of police officers in the cultural norms of the many varied ethnic groups.

Many of these initiatives have been critical in dealing with incidents involving members of different cultural groups who have committed crimes, gang violence, domestic violence or have supported or attempted to undertake terrorist related-incidents. While it is difficult to assess the impact on different ethnic communities where members have been dissuaded from committing offences or from radicalising to terrorist ideologies, anecdotal evidence and the relatively low proportion of crime is a positive indicator.

Other forms of diversity have had significant impacts both on the relationships between policing and these groups but also on the membership of policing agencies themselves. The Lesbian, Gay, Bisexual, Transsexual, Queer, Intersex, and Asexual (LGBTQIA+) community has had a varied experience of policing over many decades in Australia. The positive efforts of police leaders, LGBTQIA advocates and the LBGTQIA community more generally have resulted in greater shared understanding of the challenges faced by individual members of this community and an enhanced confidence in the respect shown to them as citizens. The most notable outcome has been the increase in police members being recruited from the LGBTQIA community and serving members who openly identify as members of that community.

Social disadvantage

Police leaders have long been challenged by social disadvantage within the Australian community. They recognise that some sectors or groups struggle to advance, even with the support of programs and policies that are developed with the best intentions, but fail to reverse issues such as chronic health problems, educational disadvantage, financial dependence on welfare, and disproportionate rates of offending and incarceration, especially amongst young members of these groups. In particular, many Aboriginal and Torres Strait Islander communities and their members suffer these sad outcomes. The historic relationship between police and the Australian Aboriginal community is littered with examples of tragedy, oppression, hostility, and dishonesty but more recently the emergence of mutual respect and friendship. Police leaders have a special role to play in being part of the support mechanisms for these communities, as self-determination and internal leaders emerge to identify and implement pathways to address the disadvantages they suffer.

Aging society

One group which has emerged in recent years that require specific recognition is that of the elderly in society. Australia has a growing proportion of aged citizens who are vulnerable to a range of activities, including crimes such as domestic or institutional violence, theft, fraud, and scams. Protecting and educating this growing population is complicated by such things as access to individuals, mental capacity, cultural norms, and fear of reprisal if a report to authorities is made. The current Royal Commission into Aged Care Quality and Safety in Australia (see www.agedcare.royalcommission.gov.au) is indicative of the challenges for police leaders now and into the future, and for the services they provide to this vulnerable group in our society.

Domestic violence

The tragic impact of domestic violence on the Australian community is well documented, as is the response by governments, agencies like police, and support groups. While much progress has been made, police leaders cannot reduce their focus on this insidious "cancer" within our community which continues to result in the deaths of women and children at an unacceptable level across the nation. New laws, specialist courts, policies, and procedures are but one part of the way forward. The behaviours and conduct of police officers themselves is a major factor for police leaders to consider and shape.

Technology

For the police leader, technology remains a critical influence on both the operational and strategic spheres of law enforcement. But it is a double-edged sword, as criminal elements utilise technology in an attempt to out-manoeuvre policing agencies to commit offences across the globe. Police and academics alike have considered the impact of technology on policing in many contexts, including future predictions (Young & Meli, 2019). Some of the issues to be considered by police leaders are the preparation of their agencies to cope with the vast array of technological innovation, understanding procurement and budgetary implications of the technology lifecycle, data integrity, storage and security, integration, digital transformation, data analysis, and Big Data, and the list goes on. What is certain is that no police leader can ignore the need for technological currency of their agency or workforce, due primarily to its ability to enhance officer and community safety. Clearly, a comprehensive understanding of technology and its evolution is a critical police leader attribute.

Arguably, the list of influences on police agencies and their leaders are endless. A critical factor in the "success" of the police leader is their ability to personally influence, to be "visible" not only at times of crisis, but also to be accessible at other times. In a crowded diary this can be a significant impost for the busy leader.

LEADERSHIP THROUGH CRISIS VS. LEADERSHIP IN CRISIS

A difficulty emerges when one is requested to define the epitome of a good leader. There are too many adjectives that can be associated with quality leadership, but it will be totally dependent on the person being asked. Whether subordinate, a peer or manager, they are likely to have a different view of what they want from a leader, and we haven't even ventured into the area of the describer's motives. There can be little opposition to a leader being willing and able to deal with crisis. To be the "chief problem solver" at a time when people require their problem to be solved has to be one of the key attributes of a leader within the police service. A leader needs to demonstrate the leadership qualities that invite respect from followers or even bystanders. A leader needs to be able to command without arrogance and recognise that they require the authority of those needing assistance to actually lead. By being inclusive and employing the expertise required amongst others, a leader can establish an effective leadership faction. This can only be achieved by a leader who possesses a high degree of emotional intelligence. A "guru" of emotional intelligence, Daniel Goleman (2011), explains the four key tenets:

- Self-awareness;
- Self-regulation;
- Social awareness; and
- Relationship management/empathy.

In essence, therefore, a leader must understand themselves and be able to manage their own feelings, even though the environment may be hostile, before they can understand the plight of others and guide them through to success. Leaders who display a high level of emotional intelligence are likely to be more competent when leading through crisis and achieve it whilst maximising the health and wellbeing of the workforce (Goleman, 2011). The consistent and sincere display of these traits will augment the trust of the community and staff alike, thereby cementing the authority required to lead.

"Most people think of leadership as a position and therefore don't see themselves as leaders" Covey (2006, p. 227).

Of course, within policing, each and every police officer must at times become the leader dealing with crisis. It is, however, understandable and commonplace for "police leadership" to be associated with Chief Officers in a hierarchical structure. It is accepted that every organisation, be it uniformed or not, requires some form of tiered configuration in order to provide order and a separation of strategic decision-making from operational or tactical. In policing, this must be achieved without stifling initiative and by maximising talent through delegation.

Good chiefs need to be inspirational thinkers and to base their strategies on contemporary empirical data. This is not about ego or self-promotion, but is the foundation of what the general community want from their police. The vast majority of the public believe that the police are focused on, indeed exist in order to, apprehend law-breakers and bring them to justice. Unfortunately, there is too much influence and interference from outsiders who claim to know better. Perhaps this is due to there being far too many "police/crime" television programs where the senior police officer is usually portrayed as a "uniform-carrying" jester detached from reality. The "hero" is invariably the officer on the ground, who despite the hindrances of the "boss" still manages to get the job done. There seems to be little cognisance that the senior police officer was once that self-same "hero". This perception may well pave the way for pseudo-experts to make careers of telling police leadership what to do and how to do it. Such an approach does not seem to manifest itself within other public services. It is rare that Chief Fire Officers are told how to put fires out, or Chief Ambulance Officers told how to treat the injured; nevertheless, there is a steady stream of self-appointed connoisseurs, without any experience in fighting crime, who are willing to inculcate their views to Chief Police Officers. What may be classed as criminal, however, is that these Chief Police Officers, who are also the "police leadership", have somehow allowed this to happen. It is not a weakness to rely on over twenty years of experience to stand up for yourself and the organisation you represent, and attest that you just might know best!

The defence forces in Australia, the United Kingdom, the United States, New Zealand, and many other countries are arguably some of the best-educated and trained professionals, through the military researching and analysing their own relevant data to steer leadership decision-making. In order to get to the forefront of the "police and community agenda", police leaders should consider establishing an Australian Police Leadership Academy responsible for providing the real experts in police leadership with the information on which sound decisions can be based. This might be an extension to the remit of the Australian Institute of Police Management. After all, "modern policing revolves primarily around the intelligent management of information" (Broadhurst & Davies, 2008).

One would find it difficult to argue against the police needing to transform the way in which crime is prevented, crimes are investigated and incidents are dealt with, due to the relentless waves of challenge generated by the advancement in technology and globalisation. That does not necessarily mean that the leadership within the police service has to change.

LEADERSHIP THROUGH CHANGE

"Progress is impossible without change, and those who cannot change their minds cannot change anything" (George Bernard Shaw).

With the world changing, seemingly on a daily basis, Shaw's comment speaks both to the "progress" driven by change, and the importance of a leader in modern society adapting to the changes through their role. In the current environment, the responsibilities of a police leader to provide the best possible policing services requires them to also be a change manager. As indicated elsewhere in this chapter, the opportunities for police leaders to shape and reshape their operational models is greater now due to the nature of the influences that impact communities and policing alike.

Fundamental to any change process is the ability to identify the need for change and the benefits of the proposed new process or philosophy, particularly to those whose behaviours are the target of the change being sought. The greater the change, the more important this part of the change management process is. Leading an organisation that is both agile and flexible in the current and future environments is critical to policing, just as much as any other sector. The advent of the COVID-19 pandemic across the world had certainly proven the value of organisations that are accepting of the opportunities change brings. Being able to pivot strategies and resources to take advantage of both planned and unplanned events is a requirement of police leaders rather than a wish. Often, the timing of change depends significantly on the authorising environment, a concept forming part of the seminal studies by Professor Mark Moore of Harvard University on the creation of public value (Moore, 1995, 2007, 2013). The authority and support of government is one of the factors to be considered in this regard.

What then, are some of the attributes of the police leader who accepts the opportunities for change? A comprehensive understanding of the change management process, the nature of risk and considered risk-taking, the processes and pathways to seek support for change, the politics of change, and the benefits of partnerships and alliances. While each topic is a study in its own right, each is critical to the success of a change management initiative.

It is also important to recognise that change driven by a crisis can often be used as a vehicle to achieve outcomes not identified initially. For example, a restructuring of organisational units to align with new government policy and legislation can include the re-balancing of responsibilities for leadership of the organisation. Openness, honesty, and consideration for those affected, including their union representatives, is vital to sustainable change. But a note of caution: even the best intentions and planning for change can be thwarted by those who have values and loyalties that are not aligned to the organisation, but rather to other teams.

The communication of all facets of any proposed change, together with the unequivocal sponsorship and support of police leaders, is crucial. Communication must be honest, authentic, and empathetic, yet confident in better outcomes for all. Explaining the value proposition in ways all stakeholders can understand and accept is a vital responsibility of the primary change leader. Assisting them can be a range of local change champions, those who are passionate for the new outcomes.

Associated with the ongoing nature of change in policing organisations is the concept of change fatigue (Beaudan, 2006). This is not a new phenomenon, and brings into contention the nature of resilience. Like other emergency services and the military in particular, the importance of contingency planning to manage both planned and unplanned prolonged events is a vital role of police leaders. While many examples of organisational resilience exist, there is likely none in recent memory as significant as the response by police and partner agencies to the COVID-19 pandemic of 2020.

A further issue for individual police leaders is the personal impact of leadership itself. The onerous responsibilities which come with the role as a police leader cannot be underestimated in the context of physical, psychological and social wellbeing. For the most senior leaders, consideration of time in role, choosing an exit point, preparing the organisation for leadership renewal and ensuring a seamless transition to the new leader are factors which will add to the legacy of their terms in office. Each must be planned and executed carefully to prevent potential destabilisation.

VISIBLE LEADERSHIP

At the heart of police leadership is the central role individuals play in reassuring the efficacy and integrity of the policing model in their communities. The stakeholders include not only the citizens they serve (including governments), but also the men and women who make up the agencies they lead. Brand management, once the province of private industry, has become a central theme for the public sector (Serrat, 2017). The stature, approachability, and legitimacy of the police leader is a crucial factor in their ability to engage, inspire, motivate, develop, and mentor their community. With a culture steeped in "command and control" leadership (Podhorec, Hriník & Lakoš, 2017) and reputations built during times of crisis (Koehn, 2020), the development and selection of police leaders is fundamental to their success.

Development

There remains significant debate and comment on the topic of leadership development – learned or inherent (Winch, 2015). Ultimately, personality type appears to be a variable in the evolution of an individual to becoming a leader, making styles of leaders and models of leadership important to success.

Police leadership development has been the subject of significant investment by policing agencies, academic institutions, states, and nations around the world. The Australian Institute of Police Management (AIPM), funded primarily by the Australian Government but supported by all Australian jurisdictions, is an example of the importance placed on this topic. Access by jurisdictions and some international participants includes fee-for-service payments for participants with "scholarships" occasionally provided to other jurisdictions, including Pacific Nations.

The benefits of the multi-jurisdictional development opportunities include networking, bench-marking, exchange of operational and strategic initiatives and enhanced understanding of policing at the national and international levels. Many senior leaders have also sought international development through programs recognised and valued by their parent agencies. Some jurisdictions in Australia have supported leadership development through the Pearls Program facilitated by the Netherlands Police (see www.pearlsinpolicing.com). Others have supported programs by other jurisdictions; for example, the US Federal Bureau of Investigation (FBI) LEEDA, NA, and NEI programs (see www.fbi.gov). Access to these international development opportunities are highly sought after and often extremely competitive.

In addition, tertiary qualifications have become the norm for most police leaders in Australia. Merit-based selection processes and the reality of professionalization of policing have driven credentialism.

Models

The emergence of Community Based Policing (Segrave & Ratcliffe, 2004) and Problem Oriented Policing (Mazerolle, Darroch & White, 2013) during the latter years of the 20th century was the beginning of serious debate on the models of policing implemented by police leaders but often at the behest of governments and as a result of official inquiries into policing and or police leadership. Since then, other models have arisen, including Reassurance Policing (Innes, 2005), Harm Reduction models (see www.harmreductionaustralia.org.au), and Evidence Based Policing (Sherman, 2013). All have provided police leaders with opportunities to reshape their organisations, both in front-line policing and support units, in the relentless pursuit of reducing crime and making their communities safer. No Western jurisdiction has yet found the panacea to these goals. One thing is certain: police leaders generally have recognised the need for collaboration in dealing with these complex issues. The various labels and titles given to the many models, ranging from Unit Beat Policing, Neighbourhood Policing, Intelligence Policing, and Proactive Policing, in addition to those mentioned above, should not change the main role and focus of the police, which is public safety.

Selection

The appointment of police leaders in contemporary Australia has almost universally been undertaken through a process of open merit, allowing applicants to self-select their candidacy and then undergo a range of competitive assessments and interviews as a final assessment of their professional fitness for the position. While there are exceptions to this process, the overarching goal has been to select the most meritorious applicant for the position. The relatively high regard generally acknowledged by the community for police leadership in Australia seems to confirm the efficacy and benefits of a rigorous open merit process. It may be argued that a central strategic command program to create a pool of qualified Chief Officers for all States and Territories to select from would be beneficial and assist the cross-fertilisation of initiatives.

Culture

For some time, much has been made of "police culture" (Prenzler, 1997), its existence and its impact. Like any other large and enduring organisation, the traditions and cultures of policing pervade the various work units and the organisation more generally. As a police leader, dealing with the organisation norms and these cultures is always part of the role, particularly in dealing with change. It also means that to undertake the role of the police leader requires an understanding of the unique nature of the Australian police culture.

POLICE LEADERSHIP: IS IT UNIQUE?

Earlier in this chapter, it was suggested that police are trained leaders from the time of induction until they day they cease their careers. This contention is based on the expectations of the community when they request police assistance, often in times of extreme crisis. The attending officers may be seasoned and senior operational leaders, or they may be officers who have only recently emerged from their academy training. The community member has an expectation of leadership, of problem solving, and of support, no matter who attends. While initial police training extends in most Australian jurisdictions beyond the various academy walls, there are many examples of new police officers facing critical life-threatening incidents very early in their operational careers. This is recognised, and subsequently, initial police training in Australia continues to focus on the use of leadership skills to resolve calls for service incidents.

Similarly, the development and assessment of leadership potential continues in all jurisdictions by various means. It is recognised that many leadership skills are provided to members of the police in the context of their personal commitments and affiliations. These may include their activities as a military reservist, a partnership supported by all Australian jurisdictions. Initiatives for developing senior and executive police leaders have been discussed earlier in this chapter. Many are self-initiated.

One of the most important roles of a senior police leader is the development of future leaders. Talent management is described by the Australian Human Resources Institute (2020) as "an overarching term used to describe an organisation's commitment to fostering as well as maximising the potential and performance of their workforce". It has gained favour in describing the systems and process of Australian policing jurisdictions to develop leaders at all levels. Succession planning is also practised, but usually in the context of providing a level playing field for those motivated to apply for development and/or promotional opportunities. Importantly, the notion of personal "fit" for specific roles has gained momentum in the placement of senior/executive leaders to maximise success for both the individual and the organisation generally. Success may include the opportunity to develop a particular skill or enhance the individuals' knowledge of the role allocated.

Key areas of development for future leaders include enhancing political acumen, engagement strategies, representational skills and behaviours, greater understanding of the administration and support functions of police and government organisations, decision-making, and project management. Many future leaders elect to undertake recognised development opportunities, including attainment of credentials such as the courses provided by the Australian Institute of Company Directors (AICD). Many also opt for legal studies, leading to formal admission as solicitors or barristers. While debate still arises over the concept of tertiary qualifications for all police, police leaders generally possess them. Allied to this debate is the concept model of police professionalization in Australia. While there appears to be no disagreement between police jurisdictions and the Police Federation of Australia (see www.pfa.org.au) that policing in Australia is professional, there are differing views on the need for centralised national registration. Until a value proposition is accepted by all, the debate is sure to continue.

A further area of interest for police leadership is the concept of uniqueness. Earlier in this chapter, it has been suggested that the various cultures of policing and police make police leadership unique. Comparing development, promotional opportunities, their status in society, and the critical role they play in times of crisis (locally and nationally) provides some useful insights. In particular, comparisons with military leaders and other emergency services leaders is of interest, due to the opportunities for interoperability and efficiencies that may be achieved through co-development. While there are many similarities of attributes of leaders, and examples of successful joint development with these other agencies, this is only one factor. It is difficult to imagine the legitimacy of leadership being established to an appropriate level (particularly with the membership of a police organisation) should an individual external leader, without a civil policing background, be employed in a senior operational role or in fact take charge of a jurisdiction. This is due in part to the unique role of all sworn police who are conferred the powers and obligations of the "office of constable" throughout their sworn careers. However, other models of police leadership involving non-police leaders do exist in other jurisdictions (for example, see Wood, 2016 on the role of Policing and Crime Commissioners in England and Wales), as does the "direct entry" at senior level.

Perhaps future police leaders in Australia should ensure that they and those that follow, continue to aspire to world class policing for their communities, particularly in the context of the Peelian Principals (see Lentz & Chaires, 2007).

CONCLUSION

This chapter has examined contemporary leadership theory in the context of the policing environment in the 21st century, and has argued that whist police leadership has historically responded to change, the current unprecedented pace of change is not necessarily the reason for them to rethink their role into the future. That does not mean that police leadership should not take a long and critical look at itself to ascertain whether or not it exists for the correct reasons and remains relevant. There is a danger that the police are becoming overwhelmed, being kicked around as a "political football". Perhaps the role of the police should be the same now as it was when first established, and maybe it is time for police leadership to be lobbying for a national review to be undertaken to decide what ancillary tasks should be discarded. As quoted by Nick Ross in his book *Crime*, Chris Sims, the former Chief of West Midlands Police in the UK, says, "The criminal justice system belongs in a domain of serious crime. We do it no favours if we clutter it up with things that are better dealt with by other means" (Ross, 2013),

Police leaders, like new recruits, need to learn to assume nothing, believe nothing, check everything, and then apply professional judgement. By edifying, confirming, and substantiating the views and strategies emerging from Chief's offices whilst simultaneously capturing the views and experience of current and former chief officers, senior politicians, and commissions of inquiry, to name but a few, will equip police leaders in Australia with the credibility to endure in their rightful position through the 21st century.

REFERENCES

Australian Bureau of Statistics. (2016). *2016 Census*. Canberra: ABS.

Australian Human Resources Institute. (2020). *Talent Management*. Accessed at: https://www.ahri.com.au/resources/ahriassist/hr-strategies-and-planning/workforce-planning/talent-management/

Beaudan, E. (2006). Making change last: How to get beyond change fatigue. *Strategic Direction*. Accessed at: www.emerald.com/insight/content/doi/10.1108/sd.2006.05622gad.010/full/html

Broadhurst, R., & Davies, S. (Eds.). (2008). *Australian Policing in Context*. Oxford: Oxford University Press.

Covey, S. (2006). *The 8th Habit Personal Workbook: Strategies to Take You from Effectiveness to Greatness*. New York: Simon and Schuster.

Goleman, D. (2011). *Leadership: The Power of Emotional Intelligence*. Northampton, MA: More Than Sound.

Home Office. (2012). *Definition of Policing by Consent*. London: Home Office.

Innes, M. (2005). Why 'soft' policing is hard: On the curious development of reassurance policing, how it became neighbourhood policing and what this signifies about the politics of police reform. *Journal of Community & Applied Social Psychology*, 15(3), 156–169.

Koehn, N. (2020) Real leaders are forged in crisis. *Harvard Business Review*. Accessed at: https://hbr.org/2020/04/real-leaders-are-forged-in-crisis

Kotter, J. P., Porter, M., & Olmsted Teisberg, E. (2015). Leadership, strategy and innovation. *Harvard Business Review*. Accessed at: https://store.hbr.org/product/leadership-strategy-and-innovation-health-care-collection-8-items/10047

Lentz, S. A., & Chaires, R. H. (2007). The invention of Peel's principles: A study of policing 'textbook' history. *Journal of Criminal Justice*, 35(1), 69–79.

Marquet, L. D. (2013). *Turn the Ship Around!: A True Story of Turning Followers into Leaders*. London: Penguin Random House.

Mazerolle, L., Darroch, S., & White, G. (2013). Leadership in problem-oriented policing. *Policing: An International Journal*, 36(3), 543–560.

Moore, M. H. (1995). *Creating Public Value: Strategic Management in Government*. Cambridge, MA: Harvard University Press.

Moore, M. H. (2007). Recognising public value: The challenge of measuring performance in government. *A Passion for Policy*, 91–116.

Moore, M. H. (2013). *Recognizing Public Value*. Cumberland, RI: Harvard University Press.

Oxford Dictionary. (2020). *Interdependent*. Oxford: Oxford University Press.

Pearson-Goff, M., & Herrington, V. (2014). Police leadership: A systematic review of the literature. *Policing: A Journal of Policy and Practice*, 8(1), 14–26.

Podhorec, M., Hrinĭk, P., & Lakoš, G. (2017). *Leadership in the Process of Command and Control, Place and Role of Commander-Manager*, paper presented at the International Conference of Knowledge-Based Organization, vol. 23, no. 1, pp. 241–245, Sciendo, Berlin.

Prenzler, T. (1997). Is there a police culture? *Australian Journal of Public Administration*, 56(4), 47–56.

Reith, C. (1956). *A New Study of Police History*. London: Oliver & Boyd.

Ross, N. (2013). *Crime: How to Solve It-and Why so Much of What We're Told Is Wrong*. London: Biteback Publishing.

Segrave, M., & Ratcliffe, J. (2004). *Community Policing: A Descriptive Overview*. Canberra: Australian Institute of Criminology.

Serrat, O. (2017). *Knowledge Solutions*. Singapore: Springer Publishing.

Sherman, L. (2013). *The Rise of Evidence-Based Policing: Targeting, Testing, and Tracking*. Chicago: University of Chicago Press.

Walker, S. (2006). *Police Accountability: Current Issues and Research Needs*, paper presented at the National Institute of Justice (NIJ) Policing Research Workshop: Planning for the Future, Washington, DC, 28 November.

Winch, G. (2015). *Can Leadership Be Learned or Are You Born with It?* Accessed at: www.psychologytoday.com/au/blog/the-squeaky-wheel/201502/can-leadership-be-learned-or-are-you-born-it

Wood, D. A. (2016). The importance of liberal values within policing: Police and crime commissioners, police independence and the spectre of illiberal democracy. *Policing and Society*, 26(2), 148–164.

Young, R., & Meli, O. (2019). *Trusted, Ethical, Fast-Moving and Effective: The AFP Investigative Team of 2030*. Accessed at: https://nsc.crawford.anu.edu.au/sites/default/files/publication/nsc_crawford_anu_edu_au/2019-05/afp_investigative_team_of_2030_-_nsc_futures_paper_-_jan_2019.pdf

CHAPTER 4

The incorporation of multidisciplinary approaches to enhance police communication strategies

Ken Wooden

INTRODUCTION

Effective communication skills are an essential tool for the policing practitioner. Policing is a complex profession and, at times, it would appear to consist of competing demands. On one hand, there are organisational requirements for police to provide high levels of customer service in dealing with individuals who can be victims, witnesses or complainants, whilst on the other hand, there is a demand for police to reduce crime and its associated fear. In addition, police also communicate with people of all ages, social classes, and cultural backgrounds on a daily basis. They also need to be effective communicators when appearing in court to give evidence, working with colleagues and supervisors, and liaising with members from other emergency services. It can therefore be argued that effective communication is the most valued skill in policing, as it assists police in keeping the peace, restoring order, and enhancing community cooperation.

Skills in effective communication are essential for all these roles. Therefore, and as evidence suggests, there is a need for the enhancement of police communication skills. This evidence is based on a spiralling trend of customer service complaints against police, as well as difficulties encountered by younger, inexperienced police working within disadvantaged communities and attempting to communicate effectively with community members, particularly youth, during crime reduction strategies. It is contended that contributing factors to these customer service complaints include police not being able to effectively establish rapport, as well as difficulties communicating with young people. This chapter explores enhancements to police communication training in which selected multidisciplinary communication skills from disciplines such as teaching, social work, and medicine are adapted and incorporated into such. Also considered in relation to the policing role is how these disciplines embrace the ethical practice of being a "reflective practitioner", and how this contributes to the enhancement of their communication skills.

EFFECTIVE COMMUNICATION AND ITS RELATIONSHIP WITH CUSTOMER SERVICE OBLIGATIONS

In recent decades, the New South Wales Police Force (NSWPF) has established a firm commitment to strive for increased community satisfaction with the services it provides. The main focus of such has been police and their interactions with community members who are complainants, witnesses or victims. The NSWPF attempt to achieve this community satisfaction through the enhancement of customer service as well as service delivery. Around the time of its commencement in 2009, the then-Assistant Commissioner of the NSWPF, Catherine Burn (2010), acknowledged that the reduction of crime by itself wasn't enough, and that the customer service model of policing would become a "normal" (p. 255), part of the policing role. The subsequent organisational commitment to the customer service model of policing was articulated within the NSWPF Annual Report 2009–2010, which stated, "We promised through the Customer Service Program, to be accessible to those we serve" (NSWPF, 2010, p. 4). Turning to the demands that customer service requirements place upon police, former NSWPF Commissioner Andrew Scipione, in a foreword within the NSWPF Customer Service Charter, declared that the New South Wales community was to receive a high level of customer service. Commissioner Scipione stated, "Ensuring that we maintain quality customer service is one of the highest priorities of every officer. It is what the community demands, deserves and expects" (NSWPF, 2011b, p. 1). In addition to the Customer Service Charter, the NSWPF has produced comprehensive Customer Service Guidelines (2011a) which place numerous obligations upon police concerning their interactions with customers. Examples of such include that police must give witnesses and victims accurate "expectations" concerning the success or otherwise of bail and court outcomes concerning offenders, and that in doing so, "realistic expectations" are facilitated (p. 7). In addition, police are directed to "demonstrate the NSW Police Force's commitment to the victim by your actions; develop their trust" (p. 7). Furthermore, the New South Wales Police Customer Service Guidelines (2011a) stipulate that police in their dealings with victims and witnesses are to, "encourage customer confidence and develop rapport" (p. 7), and that these guidelines are "to be implemented and applied at all times by all staff" (p. 3).

In more recent times, Australian police organisations, including the NSWPF through organisational documents such as its Corporate Plan and Annual Reports, have articulated a commitment to enhance customer service and build relationships with local communities. In fact, a review of the aforementioned organisational documents suggests that customer service has been adopted in police rhetoric and current "management speak". For instance, the NSWPF Corporate Plan (2016–2018) states that "police will work with youth to enhance relationships, prevent and reduce crime and promote a safer community" (p. 2). In addition, the Corporate Plan articulates that police will "provide professional and responsive customer service" (p. 2), and in order to achieve this goal, each member is to act in a manner which "strives for citizen and police personal satisfaction" (p. 2). The NSWPF has also adopted "customer service speak" in their 2018–2019 Annual Report by mentioning that "We focus on increasing community confidence in police. Customer service initiatives and prompt, professional responses to crime and safety issues are meeting community expectations" (2019, p. 20).

There are many benefits of police delivering improved customer service, which include an increase in public confidence, an increase in the willingness of victims of crime and witnesses to cooperate with police investigations, and lower complaint rates from members of the public. In fact, researchers have found that if individuals consider that police have treated them in a fair and respectful manner, they are more likely to be satisfied (Brandl & Horvath, 1991; Sced, 2004). Furthermore, Herbert (2006), Hinds (2007), and Murphy et al. (2008) draw a link between police legitimacy within a community and police using procedural justice during their daily interactions with community members. Procedural justice is related to an individual's perception that they have been dealt with by police in a fair manner which, in turn, enhances an individual's willingness to cooperate with police. Murphy et al. (2008) define procedural justice as the treatment people receive from authority – not just their perception.

In contrast, regarding the impact which poor police customer service such as misconduct and disrespect may have upon local communities, many researchers have recognised the problematic nature of such conduct. As previously mentioned, in order for police to effectively carry out their policing roles, the support of the public must exist. Police misconduct and disrespect diminishes this support, and in some cases, completely removes it. For instance, Weitzer and Tuch (2002) carried out a survey involving 1,864 participants in the United States. The findings indicated that an individuals' negative experience with police, including experiences where police have initiated contact, can adversely impact an individual's attitudes towards police. Survey research conducted by Wu et al. (2009) involving 1,963 residents from 66 neighbourhoods within the United States revealed that not only was an individual's negative experience with police significant in terms of their evaluation of local police, but an individual's evaluation of local police "performance" (p. 150) could also be influenced by the police interactions experienced by an immediate family member. Furthermore, survey and in-depth interview research of 45 participants conducted by Gau and Brunson (2010) highlighted that individuals mistreated by police in previous encounters may, in future encounters, not cooperate with police. Weitzer (2000) reported the results of interviews conducted with 169 residents in three different neighbourhoods in Washington, DC. He found that the way in which police performed their duties and their interactions with the public could be determining factors concerning citizens' opinions of police. The importance of police conduct whilst dealing with members of the public is also supported through research conducted by Reisig and Chandek (2001) in a Midwestern city in the United States. The researchers surveyed 211 citizens who had recent voluntary encounters with police, and 379 respondents whose recent encounters with police were deemed involuntary. They discovered that there was a direct correlation between the level of service an individual received and their satisfaction with that service. Misconduct and disrespect, then, have ripple effects at individual and community levels (Kubrin & Weitzer, 2003).

EFFECTIVE COMMUNICATION AND ITS RELATIONSHIP WITH CRIME REDUCTION STRATEGIES

Effective communication skills are also essential for police when undertaking crime reduction strategies. This is of particular importance, as many disadvantaged communities suffer from high crime rates, and the manner in which police undertake such crime reduction strategies shapes community perceptions and support. Similar to customer service, there is a strong commitment amongst Australian police organisations to reduce crime and its associated fear. For instance, the NSWPF Corporate Plan (2016–2018) articulates that the purpose of NSWPF is to "reduce violence, crime and fear" (p. 1). In addition, the importance of the reduction of crime in high crime areas has been supported by such authors as Reisig and Parks (2004). In order to reduce crime, police are required to target "crime hot spots and repeat offenders" (NSWPF Corporate Plan, 2016, p. 2). Although the measures undertaken by NSWPF such as "stops, searches and move ons" appear to have been successful in reducing crime, they have the potential to create tensions between police and community members. As pointed out by Gau and Brunson (2010), aggressive tactics undertaken by police, such as the widespread use of stop and search powers, "can compromise procedural justice and therefore undermine police legitimacy" (p. 273). For example, a study conducted by Sentas and Pandolfini (2017) examined the experiences of young people targeted by police as part of the Suspect Targeting Management Plan (STMP). This strategy aimed to prevent future crime, but in doing so, young people in particular were subjected to a pattern of confrontation by police. This can have damaging effects on the relationships between young people and the police.

Another problematic issue concerning crime reduction strategies is the age and experience of officers undertaking such. Police in New South Wales for instance, undertake the first three years of their employment as general duties police officers. Due to the nature of their duties, these officers have the most contact with the general public, and in turn are involved with the local area crime reduction strategies. It is contended that many of these typically younger, inexperienced police would benefit from an enhancement of communication training. This is especially so for those undertaking duties within disadvantaged communities where it would appear there is a lack of sufficient communication skills to communicate effectively with community members, particularly youth. As highlighted by Wooden (2017), young, inexperienced police in a particular western Sydney patrol experienced the greatest problems in interacting with the community, and tended to adopt a confrontational approach in their interactions with local youth. Furthermore, research also indicates that young, inexperienced officers are more likely to resort to force in their dealings with community members (Kaminski et al., 2004; Paoline & Terrill, 2007; Terrill & Mastrofski, 2002; Sun et al., 2008). Furthermore, the Crime and Misconduct Commission (2009) also addressed this concern by recommending that programs for police should include effective communication skills in order to better help police in their interactions with young people.

Even though the reduction of crime and its associated fear is an important policing strategy in high-crime areas, the manner in which these strategies are undertaken by police is also important (Reisig & Parks, 2004). It is suggested that crime reduction strategies formulated by police management, in an attempt to reduce the local crime rate, can be conducted in conjunction with effective communication strategies to improve police-community relations. For instance, a study conducted by Davis et al. (2005) found that, during 1994, there was a substantial decrease in civilian complaints within two Bronx precincts, even though there had been an implementation of effective crime reduction strategies within those communities. The crime reduction strategies involved the targeting of drinking in public, fare evasion, vandalism, gun crime, youth violence, and drug offences (Davis et al., 2005, p. 230). The decrease in civilian complaints, which occurred simultaneously with these crime reduction strategies, was achieved through the introduction of a Courtesy, Professionalism, and Respect Policy (CPR). This was delivered via academy and in-service training. This policy addressed the manner in which officers were required to deal with members of the community (Davis et al., 2005), and was supported by disciplinary procedures which dealt with officers who failed to act appropriately.

Similar results have been found in other studies. For instance, Australian research conducted by Mazerolle et al. (2011) reported the results of a Queensland study in which "procedural justice components" (p. 3) were incorporated into the interactions of police conducting random breath tests (RBT) with motorists. 1,645 motorists completed surveys following undertaking an RBT with police, which involved procedural justice elements such as "Neutrality, Trustworthy Motives, Citizen Participation, Dignity and Respect" (Mazerolle et al., 2011, p. 5). A further 1,102 motorists completed surveys after being exposed to routine RBT encounters with police. Mazerolle et al. (2011) reported that there were "significantly stronger perceptions of police fairness, police respect, compliance with police, satisfaction with police, trust in police and confidence in police" (p. 7) amongst those motorists who received procedural justice elements in their RBT encounter with police. As previously noted, procedural justice involves the perception of "fairness" (Murphy et al., 2008, p. 139) which a member of the public holds following their interaction with police. Perceptions of procedural justice held by members of a community increase the legitimacy of police, which enhances community members' willingness to assist police (Murphy et al., 2008).

CUSTOMER SERVICE COMPLAINTS CONCERNING NEW SOUTH WALES POLICE OFFICERS

Although customer service has been articulated as a priority for NSWPF, over a number of years there has been a steady increase in the number of community complaints concerning the quality of such. In fact, complaints against NSWPF officers continue to rise, despite the organisation's commitments to customer service initiatives. For instance, a review of the organisation's annual report for the period 2018–2019 revealed that 2,212 customer service complaints had been lodged against officers. Furthermore, it was reported that the total number of complaints made against police officers were 5,172 and these consisted of 10,142 separate allegations (p. 100). It is noted, though, that the annual report highlighted in these figures could not be compared to that of previous years due to "a change in systems" (p. 100). However, an examination of historical complaints data for NSWPF reveals ongoing increases in customer service complaints. For instance, the annual report for (2016–2017) reveals an increase in customer service complaints during the following periods: 2014–2015 (1,524); 2015–2016 (1,595); 2016–2017 (1,670), being a 4.7% increase for the period 2015–2016 to 2016–2017 (p. 95). Furthermore, the New South Wales Ombudsman's (2017) annual report (2016–2017) stated, "The number of complaints made or notified to our office about police have consistently trended over 3,000 each year for the past 10 years (p. 92). Formal complaints about police received and finalised 2016–17 was 2,992. The number of issues people complained about totalled 9,041 (p. 93). As in previous years, the highest number of complaints related to the general categories of 'misconduct' (2,232) & service delivery (1,525)" (p. 93). These aforementioned figures provide an indication that over the course of a number of years, there has been a spiralling number of complaints made against police, and it is contended that there is a demonstrated need for the enhancement of effective communication strategies focusing upon customer service to address this problematic trend.

STRATEGIES TO ENHANCE POLICE COMMUNICATION SKILLS

At present, gaps exist in the quality of police communication and customer service provision. In searching for strategies to enhance the quality of this communication and customer service provision as well as "stops, searches, and move ons", the discussion turns to the incorporation of multidisciplinary communication skills – such as those skills used in teaching, social work, and medicine. These disciplines specialise in dealing with complex communication issues. It is contended, then, that police communication strategies can benefit from the inclusion of selected specialised communication strategies into the curriculum design, teaching, and assessment of police recruits. Police could also benefit from embracing the professional practice of being "reflective practitioners" from these disciplines into the curriculum.

ENHANCING POLICE TRAINING AND THE ISSUE OF AUTHENTICITY IN COMMUNICATION ROLE PLAYS

Police recruits, as part of their training for the NSWPF, learn and practice communication skills through student-centred learning. This consists of recruits participating in role plays where they are presented with complex interpersonal situations involving role players who are members of staff. Until recently, the students were presented with difficult scenarios in which they were faced with a "member of the public" whose behaviour had been affected by factors such as anger, alcohol and drug abuse, mental illness, and anxiety (Davies & Kelly, 2014). At the completion of the role play, students were provided with feedback concerning the effectiveness of their communication skills, as well as being required to complete a form which entails them to reflect upon their performance. Due to staffing availability, however, this initiative has currently been put on hold with the intention of re-introducing it in the future. Notwithstanding its current suspension, it is acknowledged as a valuable communication learning experience, and it is noted that students still practice communication skills through participation in police practicums.

It can be argued however, there is still a possible disconnect from what is practiced within the learning environment (police academy) and its practical application in the field. In fact, this is not an uncommon problem in other professions which, like policing, strive to prepare their novice learners for the challenges of real-world encounters. For instance, Cahill et al. (2016) reported trainee teachers "lacked skill and confidence about how to communicate with students" (p. 308), whilst Rosenbaum and Axelson (2013) highlighted the views of medical students concerning a disconnect with clinical communication skills delivered pre-clinical learning and those skills utilised during clinical placements. In attempting to enhance trainee teachers' communication skills, Cahill et al. (2016) reported the results of a program in which school students assisted in trainee teacher education. This was facilitated through students providing feedback concerning student-teacher engagement, as well as participating in role plays involving problematic classroom issues. Results from this program highlight the importance of asking the students for feedback, as it showed positive outcomes for both. Specifically, both students and pre-service teachers stated that they experienced an increase in communication skills, self-esteem and confidence.

In reference to the training of medical students, Davies and Lunn (2009) reported benefits to students' communication skills when patients were involved in the formative assessment of such. This assessment process involved a "tripartie" (p. 406) interaction involving the student, tutor, and patient. Student feedback indicated greater confidence in their communication skills following this initiative. The significance of such initiatives to enhance the practical application of communication skills is supported by such authors as Bylund et al. (2008), who contend that the acquisition of relevant communication skills is of the utmost importance, as knowledge by itself is not an indicator of the competent application of such.

In light of research which indicated communication problems encountered by younger inexperienced police (Wooden, 2012), as well as previous research which found that young, inexperienced officers are more likely to resort to force in their dealings with community members (Kaminski et al., 2004; Paoline & Terrill, 2007; Sun et al., 2008; Terrill & Mastrofski, 2002), it is contended that curriculum design for recruit training needs to be enhanced. One possible solution draws upon the aforementioned training programs for trainee teacher and medical students. Central to these initiatives is student learning facilitated through interactions with authentic participants, as opposed to role players. This initiative could be adopted for police training in which community members, and particularly young people, participate in communication and customer service role plays, as well as providing valuable feedback. This would add a significant authentic element to role plays, and would enhance the confidence of police recruits in problem solving and communicating effectively with members of the public from a wide variety of age groups. To further develop this learning experience, role play scripts should be structured around the circumstances and interactions which led to community members lodging customer service complaints against police. Furthermore, scripts should be structured around the circumstances of finalised civil litigation matters in which members of the public have successfully sued the NSWPF following the negligence or unlawful actions of police. These role plays would have dual benefits in providing recruits with real-life problematic situations in which they would be required to use problem-solving skills, as well as providing recruits greater confidence in utilising communication skills to resolve difficult and complex situations.

Another enhancement to police communication training is the acknowledgement within the training context of perceived gaps in knowledge between what is learned in the classroom and that practised in the field. This is especially so for new police who, during their first year as probationary police officers and still undertaking police training, observe that good practice taught during their recruit training is not always replicated by their co-workers in the field. In terms of medical students, Yardley et al. (2013) reported that communication training benefited from educators acknowledging the existence of a gap between communication skills practiced in the classroom and those practically applied in the workplace. The authors argued student perception of such gaps would possibly inhibit effective learning and subsequent adoption of communication skills. They suggested that "constructive comparison" (p. 506) needed to be practised. This involves educators not ignoring such gaps, but rather, addressing these perceived differences in the classroom and encouraging students to think about why such differences may occur. In addition, it was suggested that "mindfulness" (p. 506) could be used in the workplace whereby students, having an awareness of such differences, could incorporate "mindfulness" practices into their reflective practice. In terms of recruit training, this aforementioned approach would be useful in bridging the gap between what is learned at the academy and its practical application in the "real world" of policing on the streets. All too often, probationary police officers commencing duties at a police station are informed that their real learning commences on the job, and what has been learnt at the academy is secondary.

THE USE OF COMMUNICATION SKILLS WHICH BUILD RELATIONSHIPS

The following discussion draws upon the disciplines of social work and teaching to focus upon the use of communication skills to assist in building relationships with community members. As previously mentioned, public confidence in police and their willingness to cooperate are important factors for the effectiveness of the policing role. In turn, good communication and customer service practices are significant features in building these strong relationships with local communities. However, as previously highlighted, young, inexperienced police appear to experience difficulties in communicating with young people, especially those from disadvantaged communities. As a result of these inadequacies, customer service-related matters, as well as "moving on" youths socialising in public spaces, are dealt with by police from a legalistic perspective. This fails to take into account the underlying social factors which, in some cases, influence the behaviour of youth and can consequently lead to confrontational encounters. Turning to the training of recruits, it is argued that training delivered to and used by police consists of a "one size fits all" model which fails to take into account the dynamics of police-community relationships which can vary throughout different patrols. Although recruits are encouraged to build rapport during their interactions with community members, the focus is on the one-off interaction. It is suggested that police need to be taught communication skills in their interactions with youths, similar to those provided to teachers and social workers. These skills assist in the building of professional relationships.

It is instructive to note the research conducted by Rosenbaum and Lawrence (2017) that reported the results of Chicago's Quality Interaction Program (QIP) for police recruits. This training focused on the incorporation of procedural justice, interpersonal communication, decision-making, cultural awareness, and stress management during encounters with the public. This was delivered through case studies involving role plays, as well as feedback to participants. Positive results included an improvement in recruits' decision-making abilities concerning conflict resolution when dealing with troublesome youth. Porter et al. (2011) also highlighted initiatives implemented by Tasmanian Police which led to a decrease in complaints against officers. The authors found that the Tasmanian Police, through placing greater emphasis on a "communication and de-escalation technique" (p. 11) along with "stress inoculation" (p. 10) training, contributed to a decline in citizen complaints. The authors concluded, "Proactive strategies at the recruitment and training phases are likely to have impacted positively on the current workforce" (Porter et al., 2011, p. 18).

Turning to the importance of relationship building, Higham (2020) highlighted the importance of building relationships to enhance communications. The author considered that to build trust with an individual, one's humanity needed to be revealed, and this is achieved through the use of "facial expressions and gestures, tone of voice, and carefully chosen questions to form an effective working relationship with the person" (p. 185).

Similar to policing, learning verbal and non-verbal communication skills is integral to the training programs of social workers, as establishing a positive relationship with the client is essential. Whilst verbal communication can "establish a relationship, convey concern and understanding, and offer support", non-verbal communication "conveys messages through body posture, gestures, and facial expressions" (Higham, 2020, p. 34). Most important are the skills of listening and appropriate pausing which can, at times, gather more information than the posing of rapid-fire questions. The skill of empathic listening is one which needs to be learnt by professionals in all fields, and practice of this skill, together with feedback and experience, assist the relationship to be a helpful versus unhelpful one.

A helpful relationship is non-judgemental and would be especially useful to police when dealing with young people. This non-judgemental approach, vital to social work practice, if taught in police training, would help police de-escalate confrontational situations with youth. It would also have the benefit of building a professional relationship with the individual which would assist the shape and nature of future interactions. It is contended that these relationship-building practices could be incorporated into the curriculum for recruit training, and subsequently used in authentic role plays involving young people and other community members. As highlighted by Higham (2020, p. 34) such relationship-building questions include:

- How are you today? (Invite the person to tell their story);
- That must have been a concern/worrying/upsetting for you. (Share concern, recognise the person's feelings and worries); and
- Last week you mentioned that. . . (Communicate that you remember something of what has been happening).

In a similar way, teacher training in behaviour management of children and young people focuses on avoiding confrontation. Teachers are taught how to ignore low-level, inappropriate or attention-seeking behaviour. Young people, especially, can see teachers as authority figures. Similar to teachers, police need to learn to refuse to enter into arguments due to this low-level behaviour (Cowley, 2014, p. 212). It is therefore important for police training to include communication skills for dealing with aggressive behaviour in young people. Just as teachers learn the theory of behavioural management and hone these skills by experience and feedback, and social workers formalise this by learning to be reflective practitioners, police are required to demonstrate procedural justice – treating young people in a fair and respectful manner.

POLICE EMBRACING THE ETHOS OF THE REFLECTIVE PRACTITIONER

In addition to the incorporation of the aforementioned communication skills, it is also important for police, during their daily duties, to reflect upon the practical application of these and other skills. The purpose of such is to reflect upon the practical application in order to identify what worked and what didn't work, so that improvements can be made in future interactions with the community. As defined by Poulin et al. (2018, p. 114), "Professionalism is possessing competence or expertise expected in one's field". Professionalism is of utmost importance in the relationships health professionals and education professionals establish with young people. Social workers, for example, as part of their professional training, learn the importance of being reflective practitioners. As Higham (2020, p. 190) states, "Developing your communication and interviewing skills is an ongoing task, and your achievement will become evident as you make a determined effort to acquire more knowledge and experience and to think more deeply about how you can improve your practice". Through reflective practice, social workers are able to identify what went well and what did not work. Through various forms of self-reflection and regular supervision, they can improve upon their communication and interviewing skills (Higham, 2020, p. 45).

CONCLUSION

This chapter has explored the importance of customer service and crime reduction strategies to the policing role. The success of these policing strategies, however, hinges upon effective police communication. Evidence gathered through research, and the high rate of customer service complaints, indicate that there are problematic issues with police customer service and crime reduction strategies. This is due to spiralling customer service complaints, as well as research suggesting that younger, inexperienced police experience problems communicating with community members from disadvantaged communities, especially young people. In light of these concerns, it is contended that consideration should be given to the enhancement of communication training of recruits. In particular, benefits could be gained from adapting some of the communication training practices from similar service-oriented professions. Specifically, communication skills taught to recruits could be enhanced through incorporating multidisciplinary communication skills from disciplines such as teaching, social work, and medicine.

In terms of trainee teachers and medical students, enhancements to their communication skills have been achieved through the involvement of students and patients in role plays, assessments, and feedback. Similarly, it is argued that those training initiatives can be adopted and adapted within the training of police recruits. Policing students currently participate in communication role plays during their training, with the role players consisting of other students and members of staff. It is contended that students would benefit from members of the public participating in such role plays. Other realistic components of the curriculum should include cases constructed around authentic customer service complaint matters and completed civil litigation matters brought against NSWPF by members of the public. Another teaching strategy discussed, which was adopted from medicine, was the need for policing educators to acknowledge and address the perceived gap between what is taught in the learning environment and the practical application of such in the field. In addition, drawing upon social work and teaching curricula, the inclusion of communication skills to assist police in building relationships with community members was also discussed. Finally, this chapter explored the benefits of encouraging ongoing reflective practice in everyday police communication and customer service endeavours.

REFERENCES

Brandl, S.G., & Horvath, F. (1991). Crime-victim evaluation of police investigation performance. *Journal of Criminal Justice, 19*, 293–305.

Burn, C. (2010). The New South Wales police force customer service programme. *Policing, 4*(3), 249–257.

Bylund, C.L., Brown, R.F., Ciccone, B.L., Levin, T.T., Gueguen, J, A., Hill, C., & Kissane, D.W. (2008). Training faculty to facilitate communication skills training: Development and evaluation of a workshop. *Patient Education and Counselling, 70*, 430–436.

Cahill, H., Coffey., McLean, L., Davies, J.K., Freeman, E., Acquaro, D., Gowing, A., Duggan, S., & Archdall, V. (2016). Learning with and from: Positioning school students as advisors in pre-service teacher education. *Teacher Development, 20*(3), 295–312.

Cowley, S. (2014). *Getting the Buggers to Behave*. London: Bloomsbury Publishing.

Crime and Misconduct Commission, Queensland. (2009). *Interactions Between Police and Young People*. Brisbane: Crime and Misconduct Commission.

Davies, A., & Kelly, A. (2014). Talking the talk: Developing a student centred approach for teaching communication skills for operational policing. *Salus Journal 2*(3), 1–16.

Davies, C.S., & Lunn, K. (2009). The patient's role in the assessment of students' communication skills. *Nurse Education Today, 29*, 405–412.

Davis, R.C., Mateu-Gelabert, P., & Miller, J. (2005). Can effective policing also be respectful? Two examples in the South Bronx. *Police Quarterly, 8*(2), 229–247.

Gau, J.M., & Brunson, R.K. (2010). Procedural justice and order maintenance policing: A study of inner-city young men's perceptions of police legitimacy. *Justice Quarterly, 27*(2), 255–279.

Herbert, S. (2006). Tangled up in blue: Conflicting paths to police legitimacy. *Theoretical Criminology, 10*(4), 481–504.

Higham, P. (2020). *Communication and Interviewing Skills for Practice in Social Work, Counselling and the Health Professions*. London: Routledge.

Hinds, L. (2007). Building police-youth relationships: The importance of procedural justice. *The National Association for Youth Justice, 7*(3), 195–209.

Kaminski, R.J., Digiovanni, C., & Downs, R. (2004). The use of force between the police and persons with impaired judgment. *Police Quarterly, 7*(3), 311–338.

Kubrin, C.E., & Weitzer, R. (2003). New directions in social disorganization theory. *Journal of Research in Crime and Delinquency, 40*(4), 374–402.

Mazerolle, L., Bennett, S., Antrobus, E., & Eggins, E. (2011). *Key Findings of the Queensland Community Engagement Trial* (Briefing). Brisbane: ARC Centre of Excellence in Policing and Security.

Murphy, K., Hinds, L., & Fleming, J. (2008). Encouraging public cooperation and support for police. *Policing and Society, 18*(2), 136–155.

New South Wales Ombudsman. (2017). *NSW Ombudsman Annual Report 2016–2017*. Retrieved from: www.ombo.nsw.gov.au/news-and-publications/publications/annual-reports/nsw-ombudsman/nsw-ombudsman-annual-report-2016-17

New South Wales Police Force. (2010). *Annual Report 2009–2010*. Retrieved from: www.opengov.nsw.gov.au/publications/11424

New South Wales Police Force. (2011a). *Customer Service Guidelines*. Parramatta: NSW Police Force.

New South Wales Police Force. (2011b). *Customer Service Charter*. Parramatta: NSW Police Force.

New South Wales Police Force. (2016). *Corporate Plan 2016–2018*. Retrieved from: www.police.nsw.gov.au/__data/assets/pdf_file/0008/474830/Corporate_Plan_A3_18_August_2017.pdf

New South Wales Police Force. (2017). *Annual Report 2016–2017*. Retrieved from: www.police.nsw.gov.au/__data/assets/pdf_file/0009/533565/NSW_Police_Force_2016-17_Annual_Report.pdf

New South Wales Police Force. (2019). *Annual Report 2018–2019*. Retrieved from: www.police.nsw.gov.au/__data/assets/pdf_file/0010/658513/NSWPF_2018-19_Annual_Report.pdf

Paoline, E.A., & Terrill, W. (2007). Police education, experience, and the use of force. *Criminal Justice and Behavior, 34*(2), 179–196.

Porter, L.E., Prenzler, T., & Fleming, J. (2011). Complaint reduction in the Tasmania police. *Policing & Society, 1*(22), 1–22.

Poulin, J., Matis, S., & Witt, H. (2018). *The Social Work Field Placement: A Competency-Based Approach*. New York: Springer Publishing Company.

Reisig, M.D., & Chandek, M.S. (2001). The effects of expectancy disconfirmation on outcome satisfaction in police-citizen encounters. *Policing: An International Journal of Police Strategies and Management, 24*(1), 88–99.

Reisig, M.D., & Parks, R.B. (2004). Can community policing help the truly disadvantaged? *Crime & Delinquency, 50*(2), 139–167.

Rosenbaum, D.P., & Lawrence, D.S. (2017). Teaching procedural justice and communication skills during police – community encounters: Results of a randomized control trial with police recruits. *Journal of Experimental Criminology, 13*(3), 293–319.

Rosenbaum, R.A., & Axelson, R. (2013). Curricular disconnects in learning communication skills: What and how students learn about communication during clinical clerkships. *Patient Education and Counseling, 9*, 85–90.

Sced, M. (2004). *Public Satisfaction with Police Contact – Part II: Self-Initiated Contacts*. Payneham, South Australia: Australasian Centre for Policing Research.

Sentas, V., & Pandolfini, C. (2017). *Policing Young People in NSW: A Study of the Suspect Targeting Management Plan. A Report of the Youth Justice Coalition NSW*. Sydney: Youth Justice Coalition NSW.

Sun, I.Y., Payne, B.K., & Wu, Y. (2008). The impact of situational factors, officer characteristics, and neighbourhood context on police behaviour: A multilevel analysis. *Journal of Criminal Justice, 36*, 22–32.

Terrill, W., & Mastrofski, S.D. (2002). Situational and officer-based determinants of police coercion. *Justice Quarterly, 19*(2), 215–248.

Weitzer, R. (2000). Racialized policing: Residents' perceptions in three neighbourhoods. *Law & Society Review, 34*(1), 129–157.

Weitzer, R., & Tuch, S.A. (2002). Perceptions of racial profiling: Race, class and personal experience. *Criminology, 40*(2), 435–456.

Wooden, K.R. (2012). *Have Community Policing Initiatives Changed Police Perceptions of Accountability in Macquarie Fields and Have They Led to Better Police-Community Relations?* [Unpublished doctoral dissertation]. Griffith University.

Wooden, K.R. (2017). The vulnerability of police in policing the vulnerable community of Macquarie fields. In N. Asquith, I. Bartkowiak-Théron & K. Roberts

(Eds.), *Policing Encounters with Vulnerability* (pp. 221–242). London: Palgrave Macmillan.

Wu, Y., Sun, I.Y., & Triplett, R.A. (2009). Race, class or neighborhood context: Which matters more in measuring satisfaction with police? *Justice Quarterly, 26*(1), 125–156.

Yardley, S., Irvine, A.W., & Lefroy, J. (2013). Minding the gap between communication skills simulation and authentic experience. *Medical Education, 47*, 495–510.

CHAPTER 5

A critical social justice issue of our time

Enabling police wellbeing

Rhonda Craven, Herbert W. Marsh, Richard M. Ryan, Paul W.B. Atkins, Theresa Dicke, Jiesi Guo, Peter Gallagher, Brooke Van Zanden, Michael Kennedy, and Philip Birch

INTRODUCTION

> *We see record numbers of officers leaving the . . . Police Force with significant work related injuries, which continue to disable them post-employment and prevent them from ever working in a meaningful way. . .* ***a fresh approach needs to be considered*** *[Emphasis added]* (PANSW, 2011).

> *Without results – results which must be palpable for first responders on the ground – policies risk being just words on paper. Much more needs to be done . . . The human cost of inaction is too great* (Australian Government, 2017, p. xii).

The quotes above emphasise the enduring nature of, and dire need for, fresh approaches to enable police psychological wellbeing. In Australia and globally, there is increasing concern about the serious impact of policing on the psychological health and wellbeing of police officers, their lives, and their families. Police officers are routinely exposed to cumulative stress (e.g. constant risk, surveillance, public dissatisfaction) and critical traumatic incidents (e.g. violent crimes, shootings, deaths). Thus, policing represents a unique and highly emotionally challenging occupation.

The impact of these challenges are reflected in Post-Traumatic Stress Disorder (PTSD) rates that are four to six times higher amongst police officers than the general public (Green, 2004). Police officers are also exposed to more "seemingly" usual, or "normative", workplace stressors (e.g. management, management, structural and law changes; conflicts with the public and within policing organisations; job overload, and multiple demands). All these stressors are contextualised within a command and control structure within which individual autonomy can sometimes be thwarted. Multiple stressors of this complexity and magnitude can also create a fertile ground for interpersonal conflicts and human resource management issues. For example, an Australian Victorian government survey found that nearly a third of police members have witnessed bullying in the workplace, and one-fifth have experienced it first-hand (Cotton et al., 2011, 2016).

In many policing organisations around the world, issues of police suicide, long-term sick leave, management of psychological health issues, medical retirement, and operational deployment capacity have reached a crisis point. This has resulted in significant and unacceptable human costs to the wellbeing of police and their families, including significant loss of police lives due to psychological distress not being addressed. The entrenchment and nature of these enduring issues has also resulted in significant adverse socio-economic costs, including police organisations' capability to protect and serve the community, increased police training costs, and legal costs whereby police organisations have been sued for damages the organisation has caused to employees. These issues have serious consequences for protecting the lives of police officers, the wellbeing and retention of officers and recruits, and, ultimately, the human capability of policing organisations to safeguard the country they serve. Fresh solutions are urgently required to address these complex issues for both the wellbeing of police officers and the citizens they protect.

NEW WAYS FORWARD

Positive psychology

Sweeping psychology is a new emphasis on positive psychology, focused on how individuals can be healthy, productive, and get the most from life. This emphasis highlights the importance of psychosocial factors that are crucial for not only for adjustment, but also engagement and wellbeing. The International Positive Psychology Association (IPPA) posits that "positive psychology is the scientific study of what enables individuals and communities to thrive". As such, positive psychology is a strength-based rather than deficit-based approach. Three elements can be underscored from this definition. Positive psychology focuses on: 1) science, 2) the determinants of thriving, and 3) both individuals and communities. The inclusion of "communities" is especially important, given the role of police organisations in enabling police officers to thrive. The definition also highlights what positive psychology is not: a "rosy" view of life where "wishful thinking" makes things positive, nor is it merely a "pop" psychology. Rather, positive psychology is firmly anchored in a scientific approach to the determinants of being successful and thriving. Further, the perspective does not focus exclusively on strengths, but rather, assesses positive factors within the contextual framework of countervailing challenges. For example, Craven et al. (2016) recently developed a positive psychology approach to Indigenous thriving to propose a fresh approach to address entrenched Indigenous disadvantage. We similarly anticipate that a positive psychology approach to policing can inform fresh ways forward to enable police wellbeing, and advance policing theory and research.

Self-determination theory: psychological needs satisfaction amongst police

Self-Determination Theory (SDT) (Ryan & Deci, 2000; Rigby & Ryan, 2018) is a positive approach particularly relevant to addressing the challenges of enabling police wellbeing in the 21st century. SDT proposes that the motivation, self-regulation, and psychological wellbeing of individuals are influenced by the social context in which they are embedded. Regarding individuals' optimal functioning and overall wellbeing, the theory has identified three basic psychological needs that must be satisfied if an individual is to thrive: 1) autonomy, 2) competence, and 3) relatedness (see Figure 5.1). Critically, SDT proposes that when these psychological needs are met, there will be an enhancement of wellbeing, engagement, and performance. Yet, conversely, when these psychological needs are either not supported or are actively thwarted within a social context, there will be a corresponding deterioration in wellbeing, engagement, and performance.

Within the present research, **autonomy-supporting contexts** were understood as those that allow opportunities for officers to feel a sense of choice and volition in their work and careers, where officers can stand behind and endorse their actions, and/or those in which officers report they are acting in harmony with their personal values and goals. Autonomy is thwarted where they feel no voice, choice, or belief about what is demanded of them. **Competence-supporting contexts** were understood as those that allow officers the opportunity to experience a sense of mastery and control in their day-to-day lives, and to have a sense

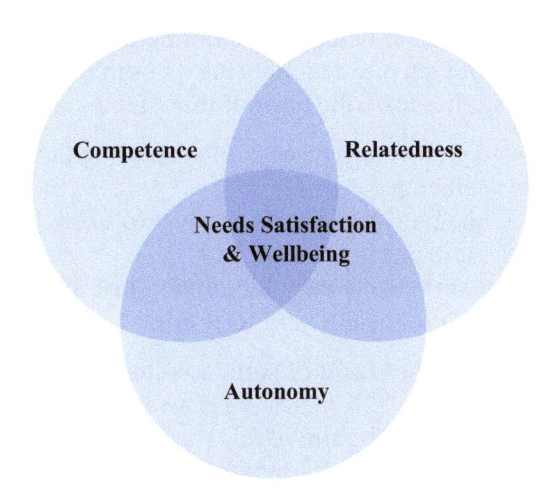

FIGURE 5.1

SDT Basic Psychological Needs. Psychological Needs Satisfaction and wellbeing stems from the satisfaction of the three basic psychological needs:
1) competence;
2) relatedness; and
3) autonomy

of growth and progress in their skills and careers. Finally, **relatedness-supporting contexts** were understood as contexts that allowed individuals to feel a sense of connectedness and belonging with others.

It is important to clarify the specific meaning of autonomy within the context of policing: "According to the SDT formulation, a person is autonomous when his or her behaviour is experienced as willingly enacted and when he or she fully endorses the actions in which he or she is engaged and/or the values expressed by them" (Chirkov, 2003). Importantly, autonomy is not the same as independence, or acting on one's own. Rather, having autonomy means that officers can fully and willingly endorse and follow the rules and demands coming from the police organisation and their superior officers. That is, officers with higher autonomy will report being self-motivated to perform duties and follow orders, with an understanding of how they are aligned with the best interests of the organisation and community.

The three basic psychological needs of competence, relatedness, and autonomy, if satisfied, can contribute to an employee's sense of empowerment and positive adjustment to their job. A primary aim of this study was to explore the ways in which different contexts within a police organisation supported or thwarted these three basic psychological needs.

THE PRESENT INVESTIGATION

The Australian police organisation involved is one of the largest policing organisations in the world. As discussed, policing is complex and difficult work, with well-documented daily stresses (Henry, 2004; Violanti & Paton, 1999; Violanti, 2014). Officers are regularly exposed to trauma and violence, as well as stressors such as shift-work and long hours (Violanti, 2014). What is less understood, however, is the degree to which the working environment of a police organisation can mitigate or exacerbate existing stresses of the job and how to enable police wellbeing. The research described in this report explores this question, utilising both quantitative and qualitative datasets to identify organisational factors associated with understanding and improving wellbeing, functioning, and retention capitalising on both positive psychology and SDT. Three studies form the basis of this chapter:

- **Study 1:** A qualitative interview study exploring factors associated with police wellbeing;
- **Study 2:** A qualitative interview study exploring experiences of needs satisfaction and frustration; and
- **Study 3:** A quantitative survey identifying factors associated with wellbeing, mental-ill health, and retention of officers.

We first summarise the results of Study 1, a study featuring interviews of 40 police participants (26 males, 95% sworn) of varying levels of experience, rank, and age. The aim of this study was to learn more about officer motivations for staying or leaving the police, as well as exploring factors associated with the development of poor mental health amongst staff, and protective factors and coping mechanisms associated with improved wellbeing. Participants were drawn from six Local Area Commands (LACs): three from urban LACs within a metropolitan area, and three from regional/rural areas. The research was further informed by an open-ended survey question completed by 338 officers (out of 1,090 total respondents) across these commands.

Study 2 ($N = 45$) built on the results of Study 1 by exploring officer needs satisfaction and frustration through the lens of SDT. Qualitative data provided numerous accounts of needs satisfaction and frustration. Thematic analysis provided support for the notion that needs satisfaction was associated with accounts of positive subjective wellbeing, whilst needs frustration was associated with reports of poorer wellbeing in interviews. Study 2 results also highlighted differences in wellbeing reported across career stage and position (e.g. new-recruit, 20-year veteran, restricted duties officer, commander). Study 3 utilised quantitative data from police officers ($N = 5,269$) and new recruits ($N = 199$) to identify key factors associated with police wellbeing and mental health.

RESULTS
Study 1: findings and recommendations

Analyses (see Craven et al., 2020) grouped recommendations under the following categories: **Replicating positive command culture and leadership practices.**

Participants reported that they preferred being granted autonomy in their daily work instead of being micro-managed. Participants also commented that clear communication from superiors was helpful in cultivating motivation and purpose within the force. Participants reported that they felt their motivation increased when surrounded by supportive, well-trained colleagues, co-workers, and supervisors.

Further strengthening support for injured officers. Participants reported that they felt the police organisation could provide better support for injured officers. Some officers reported that they felt subject to stigmatisation, did not always feel valued, and often felt isolated from the organisation and colleagues. Furthermore, officer interactions with insurance agencies were often reported as highly stressful. Officers reported a need for follow-up when placed on sick leave; however, they stressed that impersonal follow-up procedures were unhelpful. Some reported that psychological difficulties were still seen to represent weakness amongst officers. Other officers mentioned that the process of applying for stress leave was inherently stressful due to worries of being suspected of "rorting the system".

Enhancing recruitment and early-career training. There was a strong perception amongst officers that many recruits were not suitable for the role. Some officers suggested that better screening processes to identify people at risk of anxiety or depression during the training process may be useful in avoiding psychological harm "down the track". Others commented that they felt current recruitment promotional materials focused too much on the positive, and not enough on the potentially traumatic parts of the job. Some officers believed that this may create unrealistic expectations of policing. Furthermore, some officers suggested training that better prepares for the realities of police work may also assist in managing new recruits" expectations of the job.

Promoting physical wellbeing. Many participants reported that exercise was an excellent way of relieving work-related stress. Some reported that they use exercise to improve sleep quality, improve concentration at work, build up resilience, reduce hypervigilance, and as an alternative to more maladaptive strategies such as the abuse of alcohol for relieving stress. Throughout the interviews, it was clear that the frontline police were aware of the positive benefits of exercise, but felt that the police organisation failed to recognise its importance.

Promoting psychological wellbeing. There was a strong perception among participants that there is a lack of support for frontline officers (77.5% of interview participants and the most mentioned survey response). Participants regularly described the policing profession and PTSD as "going hand in hand". Other mental health difficulties and alcohol abuse were also commonly reported. Many participants felt that the additional burden on their partners around childcare, family events, and the running of the household also meant that it was unfair for them to also share their work experiences at home. Whilst police utilised support networks within the police, these were largely informal (e.g. friends/colleagues at work) because organisational internal support mechanisms were not trusted (see Figure 5.2).

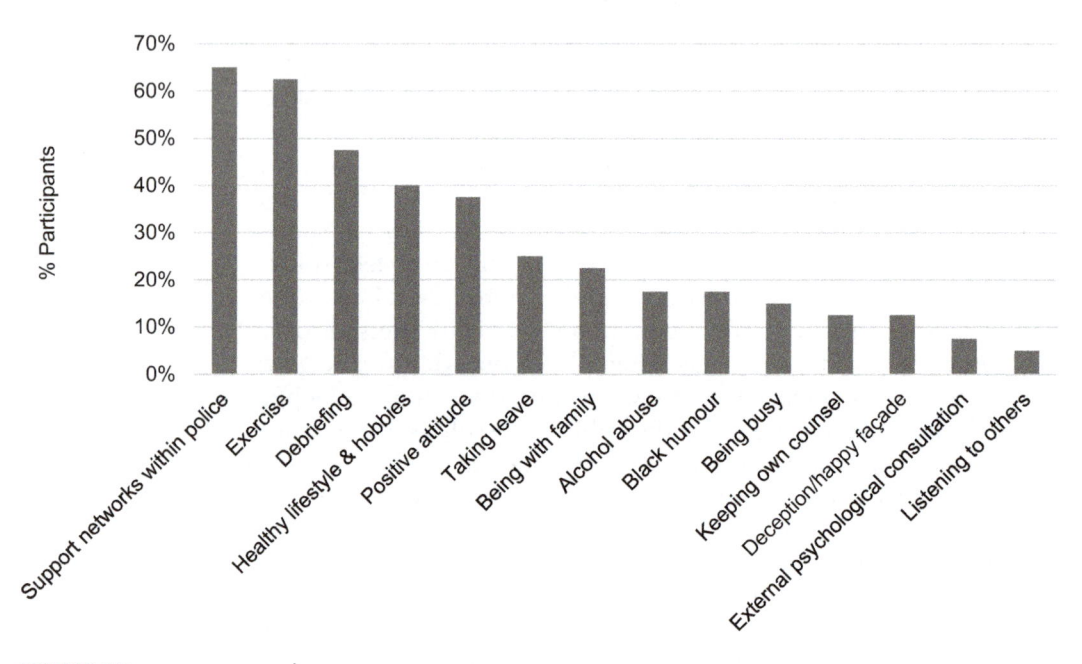

FIGURE 5.2
Coping mechanisms employed by members of police organisation

Managing workload to support wellbeing

In general, shift-work was regarded as an expected part of the job. However, long shifts, along with inconsistent, variable, and short-notice roster changes appear to be a major source of stress for police officers and their families. Data collected in this study reveals that a reluctance to work overtime, diminished social activities, and lack of time to exercise were also attributed to the 12-hour shift. All interview participants mentioned understaffing, especially at the frontline, as an issue, contributing to many problems such as work-related stress and fatigue. The interview data revealed that there appears to be a lack of relief staff for those on maternity, sick, stress, or other leave. The data suggested strongly that a "one size fits all" approach to wellbeing across the organisation may not be appropriate, and that support mechanisms would need flexibility to allow for differences in stressors between commands and units.

The quality of leadership also appears to be highly variable between commands, with significant impact on the wellbeing and motivation of the officers serving at some LACs. Moving from a relatively quiet LAC to a busier and more demanding one, or into a specialist unit, can involve an adjustment to new stressors and workload management, and this emerged as an area in which leadership and management support are important. Officers working in rural towns reported a higher incidence of attending critical incidents involving someone they knew, creating additional anxiety. Finally, a clear division was reported between sworn and unsworn staff, and an almost adversarial division between general duty officers and detectives and senior management.

Refining processes and procedures: Frontline officers reported that they experienced additional occupational stress from the sheer volume of meticulous record-keeping and paperwork required. It is understood that a great deal of work has been undertaken by the police to cut the duplication of detail gathering and to streamline reporting processes; however, from the feedback received throughout the interview process, there is a great deal more to be done. Although complaints of this nature from the public are inherent in the job, participants particularly noted that the stress of external complaints, combined with an unsupportive complaint management process, can create a great deal of stress and personal hardship.

Study 1: summary

Study 1 provided a broad-scope overview of issues concerning police officers; however, questions remained regarding how to best implement change strategies within the organisation to improve current wellbeing. Effective change interventions should be guided by both empirical data and theory. Theory-driven interventions can help organisations provide a model to understand current difficulties, and to anticipate future issues. These models are important because they give organisations a framework that can be consulted when designing new initiatives. Our goal was to identify a theory that police could use to help understand current difficulties, but also utilise and consult when developing new initiatives aimed at improving staff wellbeing. Police officer responses in the current study seemed to reflect three key factors: 1) a desire to increase feelings of support and connectedness, 2) a need for better-trained and more competent officers and organisational procedures, and 3) a preference for officers to maintain some autonomy and control in daily decision-making.

SDT proposes that wellbeing is a function of the degree to which people's needs are fulfilled in the domains of relatedness, competence, and autonomy. Notably, these three psychological needs map well onto concerns spontaneously reported by police in Study 1. As such, the aim of Study 2 was to explore this hypothesis and to begin developing a framework for understanding police wellbeing.

Study 2: findings and recommendations

The goal of Study 2 was to investigate officer experiences of psychological need support and thwarting (as described in SDT) within the context of policing. There is a vast amount of research showing that satisfaction of basic psychological needs not only leads to enhanced wellbeing, it also results in increased engagement with work and enhanced performance (Slemp et al., 2018). This research replicated these findings, clearly showing that those who experienced higher wellbeing and positive work engagement were more likely to have their needs satisfied than those who experienced lower wellbeing. Furthermore, there appears to be an effect across the lifespan of police, whereby those in their first year of the job were much more likely to have their needs satisfied than 20-year veterans. Those on restricted duties (e.g. due to physical or psychological ill health) reported the fewest examples of need support and the most examples of need thwarting relative to the other groups. These results suggest that optimising the contexts in which basic psychological needs are satisfied, and minimising the extent to which they are thwarted, will yield the benefits of a healthier workplace.

Needs support

We aimed to understand the circumstances that supported the needs of autonomy, competence, and relatedness within the NSWPF. We also hoped to better understand the situations in which these needs were thwarted. Themes that emerged from the data are summarised in Table 5.1 (see also Craven et al., 2020 for a detailed presentation of results).

Contexts that support autonomy

We found that strategies that could be more widely implemented to support autonomy include: enabling officers to act with agency by supporting discretion in decision-making in enacting the job and involvement in organisational decision-making processes; providing fair and

TABLE 5.1 Needs support in the police

Needs support in the New South Wales Police Force: what works?

Autonomy supports	• Empowerment to act with agency • Flexibility of work • Internalisation of organisational values and goals
Competence supports	• Competent management • Positive reinforcement and acknowledgement of strengths • Fair and reasonable assessment • Efficient force • Manageable workloads
Relatedness supports	• Supportive and respectful working relationships • Management that cares • Organisational level support • Support from outside the force • Clear and open communication

flexible working arrangements in relation to rosters, recovery time, and transitions back to work; and fostering conversations exploring alignment of organisational values and goals with personal goals. Clearly, good leadership matters and makes a difference to police wellbeing.

Contexts that support competence

Our findings suggest strategies that could support competence needs include: implementing efficient policing strategies that streamline bureaucracy and administrative tasks, providing adequate resources and training, and enabling officers to serve as a member of a high-performing team; providing training at all levels of the NSWPF to acknowledge staff strengths, provide positive feedback, and internalise a personal sense of accomplishment; and implementing best management practice whereby managers are skilled at managing and leading teams, establishing good relationships with colleagues, modelling best practice, and providing a manageable workload with realistic expectations and targets.

Contexts that support relatedness

We found that the following strategies could be implemented to enhance relatedness satisfaction: prioritising supporting and respectful working relationships free from bullying, discrimination, and intimidation; cultivating managers who genuinely care about colleagues, who follow up after critical incidents, and are approachable and compassionate; providing institutional support for wellbeing, including organisational support and due diligence, counselling, access to mental health training and resources, and buddy support systems; reinforcing the importance of taking time out from the job and seeking support from friends, family, and co-workers; and enacting clear and open communication between managers.

Salience of psychological needs across the career

In addition to understanding the degree to which needs were being supported in the participating police organisation, we hoped to understand whether experiences of needs satisfaction and frustration were different for officers at different career stages. To do this, we compared the responses of officers in the earliest stages of their careers (e.g. new recruits at the academy and in the field), officers who were experienced veterans (20-year veterans), officers in senior leadership roles (e.g. commanders), and officers who had been placed on restricted duties. Our goal was to examine the extent to which autonomy, competence, and relatedness needs were supported or thwarted amongst each participant group.

To explore this, we used two methods; first, we examined the proportion of officers in each participant group who reported at least one experience of needs support and thwarting in each category. Secondly, we wanted to understand the extent to which officers discussed experiences of needs support and thwarting. To do this we counted the number of words coded for each sub-theme (e.g. autonomy support) to calculate a proportion of words coded as a sub-theme within each interview.

Autonomy and career stage

Our findings (see Figure 5.3) for autonomy across career stages demonstrated that senior leadership and new recruits in the field had the highest rates of participants (100% and 86% respectively) who reported autonomy-supportive contexts. Restricted duty officers were least likely (50%) to report experiencing autonomy support, and restricted duty officers and 20-year veterans were more likely to report autonomy-thwarting compared to autonomy-supporting experiences. Data regarding the proportion of words in each interview showed a similar pattern. New recruit interviews discussed autonomy support more frequently than all other groups (4% of total interview word count), and discussed autonomy thwarting less than any other group (< 1% of entire interview word count). Hence, overall, early-career officers and trainees

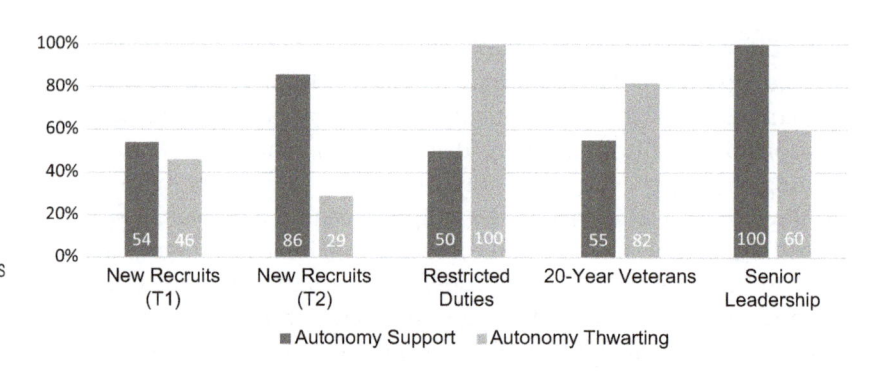

FIGURE 5.3 Autonomy support and thwarting across police career stages as measured by percentage of interviews with examples of autonomy support and thwarting coded in text

exhibited higher levels of autonomy satisfaction, whereas older officers were more likely to report frustration of autonomy needs.

Competence and career stage

Our findings for competence (see Figure 5.4) demonstrated senior leadership and new recruits in the field had the highest rates (100% and 86% respectively) of reporting competence supportive contexts. New recruits at the academy were least likely (38%) to report experiencing competence support. New recruits at the academy, restricted duty officers, and twenty-year veterans were more likely to report competence thwarting compared to competence supporting experiences. This difference was most substantial for restricted duty officers. Data regarding the proportion of words in each interview showed a similar pattern. New recruits discussed competence support more frequently than all other groups (3% of total interview word count). In contrast, 20-year veterans discussed competence thwarting more frequently than any other group (7% of word count). Overall, new recruits in the field exhibited higher levels of competence satisfaction, whereas officers that had served longer in the police were more likely to report frustration of competence needs.

Relatedness and career stage

Our findings for relatedness (see Figure 5.5) demonstrated that senior leadership and new recruits in the field had the highest rates of reporting relatedness supportive contexts (100%). Restricted duties officers

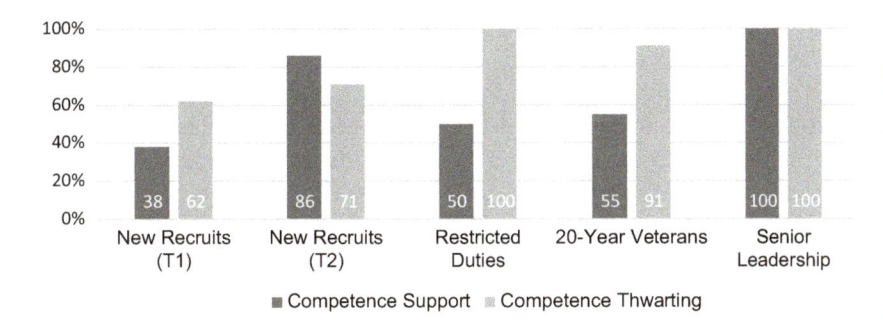

FIGURE 5.4 Competence support and thwarting across police career stages as measured by percentage of interviews with examples of competence support and thwarting coded in text

FIGURE 5.5 Relatedness support and thwarting across police career stages as measured by percentage of interviews with examples of relatedness support and thwarting coded in text

were least likely (75%) to report experiencing relatedness support. Both new recruits at the academy and in the field reported more relatedness supporting experiences compared to relatedness thwarting experiences. Restricted duties officers and 20-year veterans were more likely to report relatedness thwarting compared to relatedness supporting experiences. This difference was most substantial for restricted duties officers. Data regarding the proportion of spoken word in each interview showed a similar pattern. New recruits discussed relatedness support more frequently than all other groups (9% of total interview word count). In contrast, 20-year veterans reported competence thwarting more frequently than any other group (16% of word count). Restricted duties officers also reported very high amounts of relatedness thwarting (11% of word count); and relatedness support and thwarting were more often referred to than any other psychological need. Overall, new recruits in the field exhibited higher levels of relatedness satisfaction, while officers that had served longer were more likely to report frustration of relatedness needs.

These findings suggest that psychological needs are salient across the career span. Successful strategies include the support of autonomy, competence, and relatedness needs for new recruits and early career officers; and targeting autonomy, competence, and relatedness needs could be beneficial for veterans and restricted duties officers.

Psychological needs and wellbeing

A third aim of this project was to explore the relations between needs fulfillment and mental health. Mental health was coded as a dichotomous variable. Participants were classified as having "lower wellbeing" if they reported experiences of mental health difficulties (e.g. depression, anxiety, panic attacks, suicidal ideation, substance use disorder). Participants who did not report mental ill-health were classified into a "higher wellbeing" group. We did not include senior leadership in this analysis as they typically did not explicitly discuss their own mental health (their reflections were predominately focused on their perceptions of the organisation and their leadership roles).

Overall, 9 interviews were classified as reflecting "lower wellbeing", and 23 interviews were classified as "higher wellbeing". All 9 (100%) interviews classified as reflecting lower wellbeing involved stories of exposure to trauma, compared to 43% of interviews classified as higher wellbeing. To explore the relations between wellbeing and psychological needs we compared the proportion of needs supporting (Figure 5.6) and thwarting contexts (Figure 5.7) reported by officers who disclosed mental health difficulties versus those who did not.

There was a consistent pattern demonstrating that officers with lower wellbeing (i.e., more signs of clinically significant psychological distress) were more likely to report need thwarting experiences compared to their peers with higher wellbeing. All officers with lower wellbeing reported experiences of relatedness thwarting.

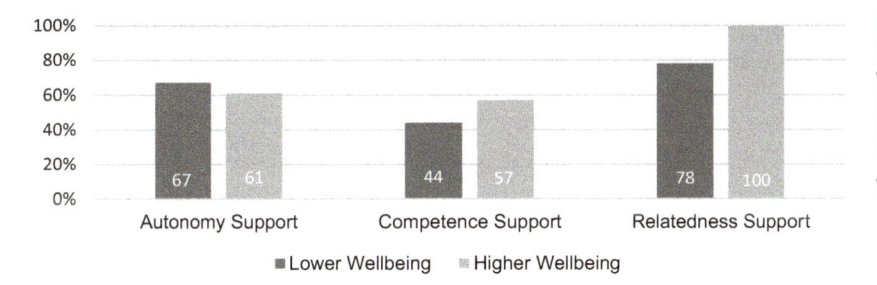

FIGURE 5.6
Needs support and wellbeing as measured by percentage of interviews classified as "low" or "high" wellbeing

Autonomy Support: 67 (Lower Wellbeing), 61 (Higher Wellbeing)
Competence Support: 44 (Lower Wellbeing), 57 (Higher Wellbeing)
Relatedness Support: 78 (Lower Wellbeing), 100 (Higher Wellbeing)

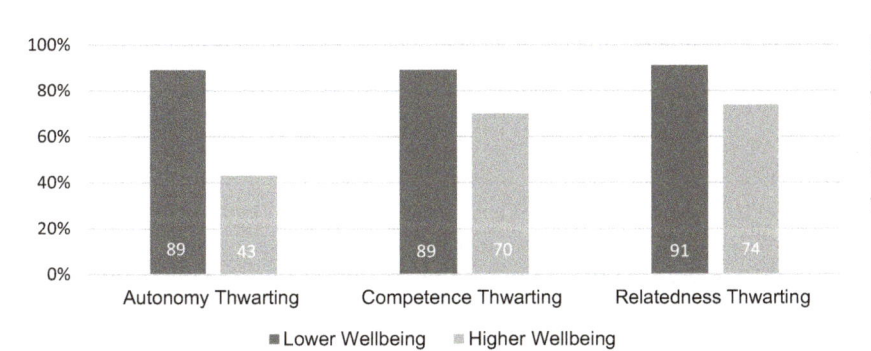

FIGURE 5.7
Needs thwarting and wellbeing as measured by percentage of interviews classified as "low" or "high" wellbeing

Autonomy Thwarting: 89 (Lower Wellbeing), 43 (Higher Wellbeing)
Competence Thwarting: 89 (Lower Wellbeing), 70 (Higher Wellbeing)
Relatedness Thwarting: 91 (Lower Wellbeing), 74 (Higher Wellbeing)

These findings suggest that mental health outcomes are likely to be worse when psychological needs are thwarted. Once again, needs support is likely to lead to better mental health and wellbeing outcomes; and measurement of needs support and thwarting may lead to early indication of mental health concerns.

Study 3: findings and recommendations

Aim

The goal of Study 3 was to investigate factors associated with wellbeing of police. We also aimed to extend on our findings by exploring relations between needs satisfaction and other demographic variables including gender and employment role. Finally, we sought to explore relations between wellbeing variables and key human resource outcomes such as uptake of long-term sick leave and restricted duties.

Method

Study 3 had a high participation rate, with 5269 participants taking part in the online survey. Participants responded to questionnaire items that measured key demographic variables, wellbeing, psychological distress and mental-ill health, alcohol use, psychological needs satisfaction, uptake of sick leave or restricted duties, and physical activity. We predicted that: needs satisfaction would be positively associated with wellbeing and negatively associated with mental-ill health outcomes.

The following results provide a snapshot of key findings (for a detailed presentation of findings see Craven et al., 2020).

Levels of wellbeing and psychological distress

Psychological Distress was measured by the Kessler-6 (K6), a subset of six questions from the Kessler Psychological Distress Scale-10 (K10). Scores range between a minimum possible score of 6, and a maximum possible score of 30. Dichotomous grouping can be used to identify those at risk of serious mental illness: 6–8: *No Probable Serious Mental Illness*, and 19–30: *Probable Serious Mental Illness* (Australian Bureau of Statistics, 2012). Individuals who fall between scores of 8–19 are likely to be experiencing mild-moderate psychological distress (Furukawa et al., 2003). The results reported here are based on the non-imputed dataset so results can be accurately interpreted within provided clinical cut-offs, and as such reflect actual responses of participants who took the survey.

Our results showed that 35% of participants did not report levels of psychological distress that would be consistent with mental ill-health. In contrast, 8% of staff met criteria for "probable serious mental illness", while 57% of staff are likely to be experiencing psychological distress consistent with a mild-moderate mental ill-health.

Wellbeing and life satisfaction

Wellbeing was measured by the Short Warwick Edinburgh Mental Well-Being Scale, a 7-item scale used for monitoring of mental wellbeing among the general population. The average wellbeing scores for police employees (22.36) was only slightly under population averages reported in the United Kingdom (23.61) (Warwick Medical School, n.d.). General Life Satisfaction was measured via a single-item question that asked participants to rate their life satisfaction on a scale from 0–10. Police employees indicated that their life satisfaction was reasonably high, with a mean score of 7.22, although slightly lower than the Australian average of 7.3 (OECD, n.d.).

Alcohol use

Alcohol use was measured by the World Health Organization's Alcohol Use Disorders Identification Test (AUDIT) (Department of Veterans' Affairs, Australian Government, n.d.). We used the three questions that measure alcohol consumption. World Health Organization guidelines state that scores of 6 or more may indicate a risk of alcohol-related harm. Again, the results reported here are based on the non-imputed dataset so results can be accurately interpreted within provided clinical cut-offs. Our results showed that most participants (75.4%) reported that they used alcohol below the cut-off for potential harm whereas almost one quarter (24.6%) reported that they consumed alcohol at risky levels.

Satisfaction and engagement with current NSWPF wellbeing programs

To explore whether officers were satisfied and engaged with current wellbeing initiatives we asked police whether they had participated in any of the available programs, and if so, how helpful they had found the service (Table 5.2). The programs that most employees had accessed were the Employee Assistance Program (Counselling) and Your Health Check (Health Screening Service). Less than 3% of participants had utilised family support services, health and suicide prevention training, and pastoral care services. The Reconditioning (RECON) Program had the highest rates of participant perceived helpfulness, with 78.2% of participants rating the program as extremely helpful. Other programs with very high ratings of perceived helpfulness included: the Peer Support Program, Your Health First, and the Chaplaincy Program. Less people regarded the Employee Assistance Program and the Wellcheck program, as helpful. Not enough people rated the Family Support Coordinator Program to reliability conclude the helpfulness of this program.

Contexts that support need satisfaction and wellbeing

Our qualitative results provided valuable insights regarding the role of psychological need satisfactions and wellbeing, suggesting that satisfaction of autonomy, relatedness, and competence needs is a precursor to positive mental health. We explored this hypothesis by testing the relations between psychological needs satisfaction and wellbeing outcomes.

Autonomy satisfaction had a medium sized positive relation with general life satisfaction ($r = .38$), and a large effect for wellbeing ($r = .54$). Autonomy satisfaction was also negatively related to psychological

TABLE 5.2 Wellbeing program perceived helpfulness

Wellbeing program perceived helpfulness	Not at all helpful	Somewhat helpful	Helpful	Very/extremely helpful
Employee Assistance Program	51 (1.1%)	91 (28.8%)	91 (28.8%)	83 (26.2%)
Peer Support Program	3 (2.9%)	13 (12.5%)	42 (40.4%)	46 (44.3%)
Your Health Check	6 (1.5%)	83 (21.3%)	180 (46.3%)	120 (30.9%)
Reconditioning (RECON) Program	1 (0.9%)	6 (5.5%)	17 (15.5%)	86 (78.2%)
Your Health First	0 (0.0%)	7 (17.5%)	14 (35.0%)	19 (47.5%)
Wellcheck Program	28 (16.2%)	51 (29.5%)	59 (34.1%)	35 (20.2%)
Incident Support	7 (7.5%)	25 (26.9%)	37 (39.8%)	24 (25.8%)
Chaplaincy Program	2 (3.8%)	8 (15.1%)	14 (26.4%)	29 (54.8%)
Family Support Coordinator	2 (20%)	2 (20%)	2 (20%)	4 (40%)

distress (r = -.46) and PTSD symptoms (r = -.45). Relatedness satisfaction had a medium sized relationship with general life satisfaction (r = .39), and a large effect for wellbeing (r = .51). Relatedness satisfaction was negatively related to psychological distress (r = -.44) and PTSD symptoms (r = -.41). Competence satisfaction had a medium sized relation with general life satisfaction (r = .34), and a medium effect for wellbeing (r = .47). Competence satisfaction was negatively related to psychological distress (r = -.44) and PTSD symptoms (r = -.35). These findings demonstrated that, as expected, needs satisfaction is associated with positive mental health and wellbeing, and negatively with measures of mental ill-health (psychological distress and PTSD symptoms).

Gender and needs satisfaction

Compared to female participants, male participants reported higher scores for autonomy and competence satisfaction; however, the size of these differences were small. Interestingly, male participants also reported higher levels of autonomy frustration. Again, this effect was small. In contrast, female participants reported higher scores for competence frustration and relatedness satisfaction.

Gender and wellbeing outcomes

We also explored whether gender was associated with wellbeing outcomes. We report here on correlations that are statistically significant (meaning that the association is greater than chance) and correlations with effect sizes larger than > .10. Results indicated that there were no significant or sizable correlations between gender and any mental health or psychological wellbeing variables, suggesting that male and female police officers report similar levels of distress. There was a small correlation (r = -.21) between gender and alcohol consumption, which indicated that male NSWPF staff may consume alcohol more frequently. There was a small but significant relation between gender and experience of social bullying (r = .10), indicating that being female is more strongly associated with experiences of bullying within social contexts at work. There was no statistically significant difference in reported discriminatory bullying between male and female officers.

Relations between staff roles and needs satisfaction

Unsworn staff reported higher scores for all three need satisfaction measures, and lower scores for all three frustration measures compared to sworn staff. Participants who worked with the public reported higher autonomy and competence frustration than their counterparts who do not work with the public. Most effect sizes between these groups were, however, small in size.

Relations between command type and needs satisfaction

Results indicated that autonomy needs are most satisfied in the Commissioners and Executive Support Offices and Finance and Business

Services. Field Operations (Metropolitan and Country) both reported higher rates of autonomy frustration compared to the surveyed police population. Competence needs appear to be most satisfied in Corporate Services, Finance and Business Services, and Investigation and Counter Terrorism commands. Competence frustration appears to be highest in the Commissioners and Executive Support Offices, and Performance Improvement Planning. Relatedness satisfaction was higher in the following commands: Commissioners and Executive Support Offices, Finance and Business Services, Human Resources Command, and Investigations and Counter Terrorism. Relatedness frustration was higher in the following commands compared to the surveyed police population average: Specialist Operations, Field Operations Country, Professional Standards Command, Performance Improvement and Planning, and Office of the General Counsel.

Needs satisfaction, years in the police force, and rank

Compared to their more experienced counterparts, participants with less than 1 years' experience reported higher autonomy satisfaction and relatedness satisfaction, and lower autonomy frustration. Participants with greater than 31 years' experience also reported higher autonomy satisfaction. Participants who have more than 21 years' experience reported higher autonomy satisfaction and competence satisfaction, and lower competence frustration than their counterparts who have between 1–20 years' experience. These participants also reporter higher relatedness satisfaction and lower scores for relatedness frustration compared to their counterparts who have between 6–20 years' experience. Small correlations existed between rank and psychological needs satisfaction, indicating that higher ranked officers were more likely to report higher levels of autonomy satisfaction ($r = -.10$) and competence satisfaction ($r = -.18$).

Relations between career stage and wellbeing indicators

There was a small correlation between years in the force, PTSD symptoms ($r = .14$) and psychological inflexibility ($r = .10$), suggesting a small but significant relation between length of time served in the force, and the likelihood of experiencing PTSD symptoms, and heightened levels of psychological inflexibility. This makes sense given that psychological inflexibly (e.g. avoidance of difficult thoughts and emotions) is a central feature of PTSD.

A small to moderate correlation ($r = .29$) exists between age and alcohol consumption, indicating that younger officers consume alcohol more frequently. In contrast, a small correlation ($r =.10$) between years in force and alcohol consumption indicates a small relation between length of time served in the force and frequency of drinking. Similarly, rank also exhibited a small correlation with alcohol consumption ($r = .11$), indicating that higher ranked officers were more likely to have higher alcohol consumption.

A small correlation (r = .18) exists between year of birth and physical bullying, indicating that younger age of officers is associated with higher reports of physical bullying victimisation at work. Similarly, lower rank was also associated with higher rates of reported victimisation for verbal bullying (r = .12) and discriminatory bullying (r = .12) indicating that lower ranked officers were more likely to report higher rates of verbal and discriminatory victimisation.

A small correlation (r = -.15) exists between year of birth and having taken long-term leave, suggesting that older police officers were more likely to have taken long-term leave from their duties. Similarly, length of time in the force was associated with having been on restricted duties (r = .11) and long-term leave (r = .21). Older officers and those who have served more time in the force are more likely to report being on long-term leave or on restricted duties. Staff with less than a year, and those with over 31 years of experience reported the highest levels of autonomy satisfaction compared to all other groups.

Other psychological and behavioural factors associated with wellbeing

Burnout was associated with a multitude of negative wellbeing outcomes including PTSD symptoms (r = .61), psychological distress (r = .60), alcohol consumption (r = .12), and reduced wellbeing (r = -.53) and life satisfaction (r = .38). Burnout was also negatively related to psychological need satisfaction (r = -.35 to -.59).

Psychological inflexibility was negatively associated with general life satisfaction (r = -.54), wellbeing (r = -.56), and needs satisfaction (r = -.43 to -.39); but was positively associated with psychological distress (r = .69) and PTSD symptoms (r =.74). Mindfulness was positively associated with general life satisfaction (r = .38), wellbeing (r = -.47), and needs satisfaction (r = .35 to .44). Mindfulness negatively predicted psychological distress (r = -.54) and PTSD symptoms (r =-.56).

Alcohol consumption was primarily associated with PTSD symptoms (r = .18); but did not exhibit any other significant and strong effects with wellbeing outcomes. Physical activity was associated with reduced PTSD symptoms (r = -.10), and higher general life satisfaction (r = .13) and wellbeing (r = .12)

Correlates of restricted duties and long-term sick leave. A final goal of our analyses was to identify factors associated with placement on restricted duties and long-term sick leave. Wellbeing was associated with lower rates of long-term sick leave (r = -.14), and restricted duties placement (r = -.15). Likewise, general life satisfaction was correlated negatively with restricted duties placement and long-term sick leave (both r = -.15). Mindfulness was associated with lower rates of long-term sick leave (r = -.13), and to a lesser degree restricted duties placement (r = -.09). Competence (r = -.10), relatedness (r = -.14), and autonomy satisfaction (r = -.17) were negatively associated with long-term sick leave. Relatedness (r = -.12) and autonomy satisfaction (r = -.17) were negatively associated with restricted duties placement.

PTSD symptoms were the strongest correlates of long-term sick leave (r = .20) and restricted duties (r = .26). Psychological distress was correlated with both long-term sick leave (r = .17) and restricted duties (r = .18). Psychological inflexibility was associated with higher rates of long-term sick leave (r = .18), and restricted duties (r = .21). Burnout was associated with higher rates of long-term sick leave (r = .19), and restricted duties (r = .15). Supervisory and social bullying (both r = .11) were associated with long-term sick leave.

Hence indicators of mental ill-health, burnout, and psychological inflexibility are related to restricted duties and long-term sick leave. Supervisory and social bullying were associated with long-term sick leave. Indicators of wellbeing, mindfulness, and psychological needs satisfaction were all negatively associated with restricted duties and long-term sick leave.

SUMMARY AND CONCLUSIONS

In this report we described research exploring both individual and organisational factors associated with improved wellbeing, functioning, and retention within the police. Results from Study 1 provided valuable insights into the wellbeing of NSWPF staff; allowing the identification of specific coping strategies and protective factors associated with improved wellbeing.

Results from Study 2 provided support for the notion that basic psychological need satisfaction is strongly linked to wellbeing and mental health amongst officers. Responses indicated that officers who experienced mental health difficulties were more likely to report instances of needs frustration compared to those who did not report experiences of mental ill health. Results suggest that autonomy satisfaction can be supported by helping to empower officers by allowing them opportunities to contribute to decision-making; allowing greater flexibility of work; and assisting officers to internalise organisation values and goals. Officer responses indicated that competence can be supported via: enhancing competency of management; reinforcing officer successes and strengths through more positive feedback; fostering efficiency through adequate provision of resources and reduction of paperwork; fair distribution of workloads; and provision of fair and reasonable assessment (particularly with regard to current promotional and complaints systems). Responses regarding relatedness indicated that officers desire supportive and respectful working relationships, whereas discrimination, stigma, and favouritism makes it hard for officers to feel connected. Officers also expressed preferences for managers that display genuine care, more effective organisational level supports, and support from people outside of the force. Clear and open communication was valued not only between colleagues but also between management and frontline troops.

Study 3 provided quantitative results showing that basic psychological needs satisfactions represent a crucial factor that is closely related to psychological distress, PTSD symptoms, wellbeing, and general life satisfaction. Need satisfactions, alongside individual factors (e.g. mindfulness, psychological flexibility) and other contextual factors (e.g. bullying) were also related to long-term sick leave and placement on restricted duties. Although large numbers of police appear to report levels of psychological distress consistent with mental ill-health, there appears to be a smaller proportion of individuals who engage in help-seeking via wellbeing programs. This signals a need for police to develop strategies to better understand the needs of staff, but also develop work policies and support services that staff believe to be useful and effective in promoting psychological health, while also being non-stigmatising.

Given the high prevalence of anxiety, mood, and personality difficulties within the police, it may be helpful to focus on normalising anxiety as a human response to difficult or challenging situations. Normalising difficult feelings and emotions may help to reduce stigma while increasing help-seeking behaviours. This strategy is consistent with acceptance approaches to mental health difficulties, where emphasis is placed on accepting difficult emotional states rather than trying to avoid or reject internal experiences.

Our results suggest that the wellbeing of our participants was often highest during early career stages, whereas more experienced officers tended to exhibit some decreases in needs satisfaction and wellbeing over the course of their career (although it is worth noting that slight increases in needs satisfaction were observed for officers with the highest ranks and longest tenures). Interview data showed that commanders and senior leadership staff were more likely to have positive perceptions of the police environment. This perhaps reflects their role (which may allow for greater autonomy) and the impacts of successful career progression on officers' sense of self. It is possible that feelings of competence and accomplishment are internalised by those who climb the ranks of the police.

We found that needs satisfaction is associated with mental health and wellbeing of both police and new recruits. Hence policing organisations should endeavour to develop working environments that better support autonomy, relatedness, and competence. The qualitative study of this report provides specific recommendations based on officers' lived experience that may assist in meeting this goal. Evidence-based interventions developed within SDT may be useful in advancing this aim (Ryan & Deci, 2017). Quantitative data suggests that psychological factors such as mindfulness and psychological flexibility are associated with wellbeing. Psychological interventions can assist individuals in developing these skills. Acceptance based approaches may be particularly helpful for police experiencing psychological distress (e.g. Acceptance and Commitment Therapy, Mindfulness, and Self-Compassion).

Police wellbeing and needs satisfaction appears to be lower amongst longer-serving staff compared to new trainees (with some exceptions to individuals with the longest tenures and highest ranks, who appear to show increases in needs satisfaction and wellbeing). Although new recruits report better mental health compared to their more experienced counterparts, over half of new recruits still report psychological distress consistent with a mild-moderate mental health disorder. These results imply early intervention would be beneficial.

Mental ill-health, burnout, and psychological inflexibility are associated with restricted duties and long-term sick leave. Supervisory and social bullying are associated with long-term sick leave. Improving early intervention initiatives regarding mental health support may be of benefit in reducing uptake of restricted duties and long-term sick leave.

Staff support services appear to have much lower rates of participation compared to rates of psychological distress. Increasing awareness of services and modifying support in line with staff feedback may be helpful in reducing this gap between distress and uptake of service.

This report synthesises the results from the above research, and provides evidence-based, theory-driven recommendations to inform enabling police wellbeing. Results suggest that optimising the contexts in which basic psychological needs are satisfied and minimising the extent to which they are thwarted, will yield the benefits of a healthier workplace, and enable police wellbeing. The results also imply that Self-Determination Theory offers an influential platform from which to move research and practice towards a positive psychology of policing that enables police wellbeing.

REFERENCES

Australian Bureau of Statistics. (2012). *Information Paper: Use of the Kessler Psychological Distress Scale in the ABS Health Surveys, Australia, 2007–08*. Retrieved from: www.abs.gov.au/ausstats/abs@.nsf/lookup/4817.0.55.001Chapter92007-08

Australian Government. (2017). *Commonwealth of Australia: The Senate. Education and Employment References Committee*. Canberra: Australian Commonwealth Government.

Chirkov, V., Ryan, R. M., Kim, Y., & Kaplan, U. (2003). Differentiating autonomy from individualism and independence: A self-determination theory perspective on internalization of cultural orientations and well-being. *Journal of Personality and Social Psychology*, 84(1), 97–110.

Cotton, P. et al. (2011). *Research Summary: Bullying Behaviours in the Public Sector*. Retrieved from: www.comcare.gov.au/psychological-injury-portal

Cotton, P., Hogan, N., Bull, P., & Lynch, M. (2016). *Victoria Police Mental Health Review: An Independent Review into the Mental Health and Wellbeing of Victoria Police Employees*. Melbourne: Victoria Police.

Craven, R. G., Atkins, P. W., Van Zanden, B. E., See, S., Ko, H., Marsh, H. W., Parker, P. D., Dicke, T., & Ryan, R. M. (2020). *From Strength to Strength: Furthering Fresh*

Futures for NSW Police, Psychological Strengths, Wellbeing and Retention (IPPE Report). (ISBN:978-1-922097-91-0). Sydney: Institute for Positive Psychology and Education, Australian Catholic University.

Craven, R. G., Ryan, R. M., Mooney, J., Vallerand, R. J., Dillon, A., Blacklock, F., & Magson, N. (2016). Toward a positive psychology of indigenous thriving and reciprocal research partnership model. *Contemporary Educational Psychology*, 47, 32–43.

Department of Veterans' Affairs, Australian Government. (n.d.). *Alcohol Screen (AUDIT)*. Retrieved from: http://nceta.flinders.edu.au/files/3314/2257/4957/Right_Mix_3.pdf

Furukawa, T. A., Kessler, R. C., Slade, T., & Andrews, G. (2003). The performance of the K6 and K10 screening scales for psychological distress in the Australian national survey of mental health and well-being. *Psychological Medicine*, 33(2), 357–362.

Green, B. (2004). Post-traumatic stress disorder in UK police officers. *Current Medical Research and Opinion*, 20(1), 101–105.

Henry, V. E. (2004). *Death Work: Police, Trauma, and the Psychology of Survival*. Oxford: Oxford University Press.

OECD. (n.d.). *OECD Better Life Index: Life Satisfaction*. Retrieved from: www.oecdbetterlifeindex.org/topics/life-satisfaction/

PANSW (Police Association of New South Wales). (2011). *Letter to the NSPWF Review Team*. Internal Document. Sydney: PANSW.

Rigby, C. S., & Ryan, R. M. (2018). Self-determination theory in human resource development: New directions and practical considerations. *Advances in Developing Human Resources*, 20(2), 133–147.

Ryan, R. M., & Deci, E. L. (2000). Self-determination theory and the facilitation of intrinsic motivation, social development, and well-being. *American Psychologist*, 55(1), 68–78.

Ryan, R. M., & Deci, E. L. (2017). *Self-Determination Theory: Basic Psychological Needs in Motivation, Development, and Wellness*. New York: Guilford Press.

Slemp, G. R., Kern, M. L., Patrick, K. J., & Ryan, R. M. (2018). Leader autonomy support in the workplace: A meta-analytic review. *Motivation and Emotion*, 42(5), 706–724.

Violanti, J. M. (2014). *Dying for the Job: Police Work Exposure and Health*. Springfield, IL: Charles C. Thomas Publisher.

Violanti, J. M., & Paton, D. (1999). *Police Trauma: Psychological Aftermath of Civilian Combat*. Springfield, IL: Charles C. Thomas Publisher.

Warwick Medical School. (n.d.). *Collect, Score, Analyse and Interpret WEMBWS*. Retrieved from: https://warwick.ac.uk/fac/sci/med/research/platform/wemwbs/using/howto

CHAPTER 6

Ethics and police practice

Alan Beckley and Michael Kennedy

INTRODUCTION

This chapter will explain why ethical practice is so important for law-enforcement practitioners and citizens alike. Within the context of policing practice located in liberal democracies, the rule of law is a foundational tenet of the practitioner approach that is linked to the "social contract" that exists in contemporary democracies and is reinforced by respect for the dignity and human rights of individuals. This discussion on policing culture at an agency and structural level underlines the importance of codes of conduct and ethics at the institutional level along with individual agency and accountability of all law-enforcement practitioners. This discussion takes place within a law enforcement and governance framework and includes the legitimacy of practitioners calibrating the consequent trust and confidence in law enforcement from the various communities they serve. The chapter ends with a description of methods for enhancing practitioner ethics and more effectively managing misconduct and criminal behaviour.

DEMOCRATIC POLICING SYSTEMS

Liberal Democracies in Australia, the UK, Canada, and the US practice *democratic policing*, which recognises individual rights. Democratic policing is described as "the most legitimate form of policing" (Prenzler, 2016:52). The various parts are defined as follows:

1. Police must be accountable to law rather than to Government;
2. Police must protect human rights, especially those rights that are required for the sort of political activity that is the hallmark of democracy;
3. Police must be accountable to people outside their organization who are specifically designated and empowered to regulate their police activity; and
4. Police must give top operational priority to servicing the needs of individual citizens and private groups (Bayley, 2006:19).

This definition is further developed by capacity-building organisations (Beckley, 2012) such as the Organization for Security and Cooperation in Europe (OSCE), which lists the "key principles of democratic policing" as: "(i) Objectives of democratic policing; (ii) upholding the rule of law; (iii) police ethics and human rights; (iv) police accountability and transparency; (v) police organization and management issues" (OSCE, 2008:9–10). In this chapter, the constituent parts of democratic policing are discussed in terms of: rule of law, police ethics (police culture), human rights, legitimacy of police, and governance of police.

RULE OF LAW

The term rule of law was used in history by Aristotle; subsequently its three characteristics were defined by A.V. Dicey (1835–1922) as: (i) The law applies equally to all in society; nobody is above the law; (ii) Nobody is subject to punishment except for a definite breach of the law as determined by the courts; and (iii) The courts are independent and not subject to political interference or control in making their decisions (Taylor, 2019). As discussed earlier, democratic policing systems must be "accountable to law rather than to government" (Bayley, 2006:19) in that they should be operationally independent and not, within the law, directed by politics or politicians. However, the police must be publicly accountable, which highlights the importance of deontological ethics and the rule of law, whereby the ends can never justify the means.

POLICE CULTURE AND ASSOCIATED ISSUES

Police culture is very topical in corruption inquiries and commissions oversighting bad practice and misconduct, but so often the focus is on agency and there is little emphasis on police work and police culture being intrinsically linked to stress and anxiety (Paoline, 2003:201). A positive aspect of practitioner culture is the camaraderie between colleagues and the esprit de corps required for teamwork when dealing with critical incidents (Beckley, 1997). Camaraderie is described as: "the sense of friendship, mutual support, and shared understanding that helped officers cope with and survive in an occupation that is dangerous, unpredictable, and unpleasant" (Chan et al, 2003:250). The negative aspects of the same camaraderie are seen in the "blue wall of silence" that is identified when police officers refuse to report misconduct of their colleagues and thus do not cooperate with inquiries into police misconduct and corruption (Wood, 1997:134). But are police any different than other vocations in the criminal justice system? Chan lists the negative aspects of police culture: "the readiness to stereotype, the paranoia and cynicism, and the cover up of misconduct" (Chan et al, 2003:252). Ironically Chan also noted positive changes from before the Wood Commission: "pre-Royal Commission culture of heavy drinking and criminal cover up was no longer as prevalent" (Chan et al., 2003:266). Academic researchers have mostly focused on the negative culture characteristics, whereas practitioners argue their "dirty hands" vocation contributes to society wellbeing, notwithstanding this can revert to cynicism if efforts are not recognised (Beckley, 2014).

Structural racism is another concern regarding policing culture. MacPherson (1999) explains this discrimination by police officers as targeting or offering a reduced police service in minority groups. Examples of this phenomenon also exist in Australia and the US. In Australia, Indigenous people are overrepresented in all aspects of the criminal justice system, the NSW Ombudsman (2013) arguing that, with respect to this issue, police powers were used in a discriminatory way.

ORGANISATIONAL POLICE CULTURE

Organisational ethics are the applied values, standards, principles, rules, and strategies associated with institutional culture (Letendre, 2019:1). The holistic culture sets expectations of the practitioners and shapes individual agency. This culture is organisational and determines institutional governance as "encompassing the procedures and methods aimed at ensuring the efficient discharge of the policing function" (Walsh and Conway, 2011:62). Although values and standards are articulated in organisational policy, the actual day-to-day practice can be markedly different than policy expectations. The complexity and sophistication of law-enforcement practice is changing at an ever-increasing pace and policy expectations can have difficulty keeping pace with first responder practice.

Democratic policing systems rely on the support and trust of the community where they operate, which is "policing by consent" within a Robert Peel-based model arising from the 19th century. Referred to as police legitimacy by (Rochel, 2011), it is also defined as: "the right to rule and the recognition by the ruled of the right" (Hough et al, 2013:147). The foundation of this concept being the practitioner's ethics:

> *Members of the public are the key constituency of police, and their perception of police integrity are an extremely important test of the ethical standing of police. Corruption in a police force can be widely known, and this is often reflected in low levels of public confidence* (Prenzler, 2009:56).

The words *confidence* and *trust* are generally regarded by practitioners as being interchangeable, but when the public are made aware of corruption or misconduct, trust can be diminished (Prenzler et al, 2013). When negative incidents occur, police institutions have to work hard to restore confidence, otherwise community assistance becomes problematic and may lead to conflict and public unrest, particularly where practitioners appear to have used excessive force. Rank-and-file police need to understand the media is not their friend and that citizens accept that reasonable and even assertive force can be necessary to resolve conflict (Gerber and Jackson, 2016). In support of this assertion, a recent research study supported citizen support of the police when it found that:

> When citizens perceive police officers to be treating them with dignity and respect, making clear and fair decisions, explaining the reasons for every decision, listening to what they have to say, both the belief that the police are trustworthy and public judgements about the legitimacy of the police increase (Oliveira et al, 2019:14).

Both authors of this chapter (Michael Kennedy and Alan Beckley) served police in NSW and Britain for over 50 years between them and both agree that many police underestimate the level of public respect and confidence in the police. The graph shown here (see Figure 6.1) shows respect for police officers in their own opinion and compares it with external criminal justice practitioners (CJP).

What has had a negative impact on police legitimacy in recent years is that there has been an approach to operational policing often referred to as "militarization", particularly in the United States. Police officers attended incidents of public disorder dressed in combat-style military uniforms with military weapons (Sheptycki, 2013). Police in Ferguson, Missouri, US. for example, were deployed in combat-style uniforms following the police shooting of a black teenager. The community rejected the agency of these police as unacceptable (Evans, 2014). It was suggested that police had escalated this conflict rather than attempting to de-escalate the incidents and work with the community.

Academic theories of procedural justice and organisational justice link police legitimacy to trust and confidence in the police, which was described in the preceding paragraphs. Procedural justice has been studied in detail and is described as how the agency of police is better

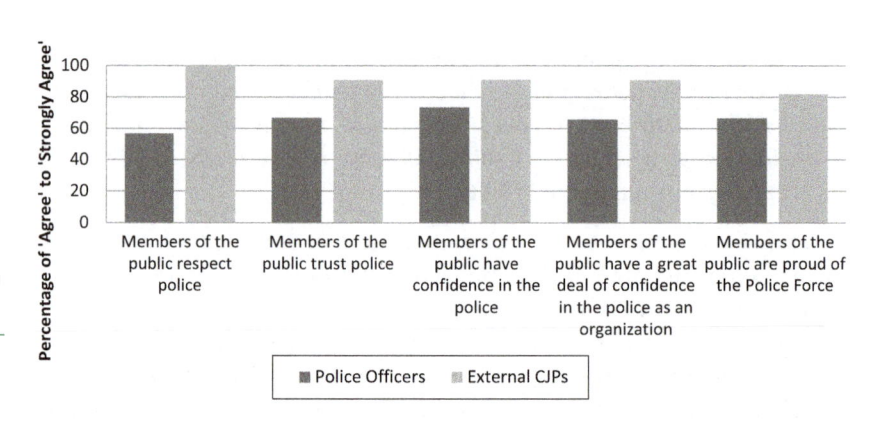

FIGURE 6.1
Public respect, trust, confidence, and pride in the police force

Source: Beckley, 2019a.

received when members of the community are treated fairly and justly in everyday interactions, even when placing persons in custody (Tyler, 1989). There are significant incidents in the public arena of procedural justice issues where police officers interact with the public in an arrogant and discriminatory manner. Organisational justice theory explains how practitioners are managed by their own organisation, which in turn demonstrates how they perceive loyalty towards the institution they work for. Disgruntled employees will generally not perform well and may even sabotage efforts to reinforce organisational goals (Beckley, 2014). An area of concern for practitioners illustrated in the previously mentioned survey was that mental health issues were not effectively supported by their institutions when they had to deal with traumatic incidents (Beckley, 2019a). Birch et al (2017) explain that despite this concern being recognised for decades, many institutions failed in their duty of care for practitioners, with the result that many police practitioners or ex-practitioners suffer from post-traumatic stress disorder (PTSD). Police organisations, however, failed to put in place systems to recognise that or to provide adequate support to alleviate or prevent it from happening. Moving from police organisational culture, a related factor to the subject of police ethics is accountability.

POLICE ACCOUNTABILITY

Policing institutions and practitioners are held publicly accountable through numerous checks and balances. First and foremost, the work of the police is governed by statute and the criminal justice system. Mass media, television, and social media are a universal factor in police accountability and public protests. A dominant factor in police accountability is the body-worn cameras that police officers are increasingly carrying to record first response incidents (Beckley, 2019b). When allegations are made regarding practitioner conduct, numerous internal policies and procedures generally are instituted.

POLICE ETHICS

Police ethics are the expected standards of behaviour of individual practitioners that are written codes of conduct and often linked to a statement of values. Ethical codes for practitioners describe the standards of behaviour for practitioners to comply with. Goodman-Delahunty et al (2014) explain that in the case of misconduct, the actions that police officers take when both on and off duty can be assessed by the behavioural descriptors within those codes to establish whether they are ethically acceptable or unethical and therefore unacceptable behaviour.

Historically, ethical codes were written and applied to professions such as the legal and medical professions to ensure high levels of conduct: "An ethical code is a publicly expressed set of principles, by considering which a practitioner of the profession in question may decide upon the right course of action" (Villiers, 1997:107). This relates to the professionalization of the police service, which is discussed later in this chapter. However, it is important to understand that there are many conflicts of interest and *ethical dilemmas* in police work which raise personal issues. Ethics may dictate one solution, whereas private concerns or morals of police officers may suggest another answer. For example, an individual police officer's private concerns or moral beliefs might conflict with their public duty in relation to religious or political matters when dealing with public protests. Two examples of police codes of ethics are that of New South Wales Police Force (NSWPF) and the Police Service of Northern Ireland (PSNI), which illustrate different approaches.

First, the NSWPF Code of Conduct and Ethics (NSWPF, 2008) was designed by the Wood Royal Commission but was only ever applied to police practitioners (Wood, 1997). Point 10 of this Code indicates it is the duty of all employees to: "report misconduct of other NSW Police Force employees". In a recently reported survey of police officers in NSWPF (Beckley, 2019a), participants stated they would be willing to report incidents depicted in realistic scenarios of police misconduct used internationally (Ivković and Haberfeld, 2015), at a higher level than their colleagues, although the report would be made to a police supervisor or manager who might or might not take action. Anecdotally, police officer participants stated they were concerned about ostracism or harassment from workmates if they reported incidents of police misconduct. We should not be surprised that few whistle-blowers exit their experience better than they entered (Beckley, 2019a:151). All respondents who answered the survey question stated that they gave their honest opinion in the survey, but over 25% of participants did not answer this question. When asked whether they thought most police officers would give an honest opinion, the results showed 13.9% of officers would *not* give an honest opinion.

The second example is taken from the Police Service of Northern Ireland (PSNI) Code of Ethics 2008 (NIPB, 2008), which includes reference and linkages to the European Convention of Human Rights and the Universal Declaration of Human Rights (UN, 1948). This code of ethics is intended: "1. To lay down standards of conduct and practice for police officers; and 2. To make police officers aware of their rights and obligations under the Human Rights Act 1998 and the European Convention on Human Rights" (NIPB, 2008:6). Indeed, the Oath of Office for Police Service Attestation refers specifically[1] to "upholding fundamental human rights" in Northern Ireland. Also differing from the NSW document, the PSNI Code of Ethics firmly places the responsibility to "secure, promote and maintain professional standards and integrity" on police supervisors (Article 10).

Ethical dilemmas arise during policing operations when operatives do not know the right course of action, have difficulty deciding what is right (or ethical), and find an unethical option very tempting to use to resolve the situation. In other words, policing is a "dirty hands" vocation (Kennedy and Birch, 2018). Examples of ethical dilemmas can be present every day in police work in the use of police discretion, police duty, honesty or integrity, and loyalty to the organisation or colleagues. These policing situations are very practical occurrences, although readers should consider the theory behind the principles of ethics. At the same time, readers should understand that theoretical principles might lack realistic application in a dynamic modern setting.

The concept of ethics originates from Greek philosophers when Plato (428–348 BC) argued that ethical decisions should reflect "the good" in society. Aristotle (384–322 BC), however, through the "doctrine of the mean", believed that each decision should be judged on its own merits and that ethics is therefore relativistic in that the path to virtue lies between the extremes of excess and defect (i.e. too much or too little). Later, Immanuel Kant (1724–1804) suggested that doing the right thing was a duty to act in a deontological manner, whereby the ends can never justify the means. At about the same time, Jeremy Bentham (1748–1832) suggested the correct ethical way to decide was based on the teleological solution, which creates the most good for the most people. The current major ethical theories are ethical formalism, utilitarianism, religion, natural law, ethics of virtue, ethics of care, and egoism (Pollock, 1998). However, what is clear is that the theories of ethics listed here are irreconcilable. Thinking of practical examples, one cannot arrive at a decision that achieves the best solution for all parties while acknowledging infringement of the rights of individuals; decision-making then becomes mechanical and bureaucratic rather than meaningful, fair, and just. Much of the "dirty work" of policing enforcement can be lawful, but by applied ethical standards of not increasing individual suffering, regardless of who the sufferer is, the policing practice lies somewhere between ethical and unethical. The dilemma for the police practitioner is to ensure their action is lawful – and just as important – that it is not unethical. The taking of a life is clearly unlawful in most circumstances for most people. For police practitioners, it needs to be lawful, but also it cannot be seen to be unethical. Yet how can the taking of a life, regardless of the circumstances, be deemed ethical? So much of policing practice can be seen to be contradictory with regards applied ethical principles.

The concept that illustrates this paradox is that of *noble cause corruption*, a phenomenon recognised in several police corruption investigations and defined as "a mindset or sub-culture which fosters a belief that the ends justify the means" (Rothlein, 2008:1). Noble cause corruption in popular fiction is depicted in films as the *Dirty Harry* syndrome (Klockars, 1980). Four circumstances herald the *Dirty Harry* ethical dilemma in police work as:

1 They have the opportunity to achieve some morally good end or outcome, and they aim to do so;
2 The means they use to achieve this good end are normally morally wrong (they are dirty);

3   The use of these means is the best or perhaps the only practicable way of ensuring that this good end is realised; and
4   The good likely to be achieved by using the dirty means far outweighs the evil likely to follow from their use.

(Dunnighan, 1999)

Practitioners can be convinced of the guilt of criminals for a variety of reasons. Those engaging in noble cause corruption provide or omit evidence to secure a conviction. Kennedy (2001) explains that a hierarchy of a "managerial" and/or "performance culture" such as NYPD Compstat[2] is designed to achieve "key performance indicators", at any cost, resulting in noble cause corruption.

IMPORTANCE OF HUMAN RIGHTS IN POLICING

Earlier in this chapter the subject of rule of law was described in terms of its importance to democratic policing systems and its links to police ethics and human rights (OSCE, 2008:6). The law on human rights is recognised in most countries with democratic policing systems, but in Australia only the state of Victoria and the territory of Australian Capital Territory (ACT) have specifically adopted human rights legislation. Australia as a country has ratified specific international human rights treaties such as the United Nations *Universal Declaration of Human Rights* (UN, 1948). In practice, all courts in Australia purport to adopt human rights principles, but Australia is a Federation of States and as such these treaties are not legally enforceable in all states and territories.

It is unfortunate that police officers are not held to account against specific laws and fundamental freedoms linked to human rights law as is the practice in most other countries incorporating democratic policing systems. A human rights law quiz (Beckley, 2019a) held in New South Wales saw police officers' knowledge and understanding of human rights principles lacking. Most policing activities which infringe upon citizens' rights relate directly to fundamental freedoms and human rights; that is, police powers of stop, search, seizure and arrest and the application of coercive powers such as use of force which all should be used with proportionality and only where absolutely necessary. However, there are instruments to protect the human rights of witnesses, victims, and community members in documents such as the NSWPF Customer Service Charter, which undertakes to "be accessible to all persons regardless of their culture, language, age, sexuality, physical and mental ability, locality and socio-economic background", and to treat customers "fairly and with respect" (NSWPF, 2009) – all of which may lead to complaints against police.

COMPLAINTS AGAINST POLICE (PROFESSIONAL STANDARDS)

In countries with democratic policing systems, to build police legitimacy it is essential for citizens to have access to a rigorous, robust, and user-friendly avenue of redress when police officers have overstepped their legitimate powers or been over-zealous or neglectful in their duty. Within police organisations there is a department entitled "internal affairs" or more recently "professional standards department (command)". This office is responsible for accepting, triaging, and investigating complaints against police as well as liaising with senior police managers to investigate disciplinary matters within the police organisation. Investigations may be undertaken by the professional standards department or, depending on the severity and timeliness, delegated to a more local senior police officer to investigate. In relation to more serious complaints and incidents where death or serious injuries occur to citizens, there may also be involvement from independent oversight bodies, and a critical incident investigation may be commenced.

Experience from the many official inquiries into serious misconduct and corruption in police forces reveals that professional standards departments target vulnerable and high-risk areas of police work which have provided most examples of wrongful behaviour. Vulnerable areas of police work relate to access to private information and criminal intelligence, inadequate supervision, relationships with police informants (or covert human intelligence sources), targeting of police officers by criminals, and non-organisational factors. The non-organisational factors are police officers who are suffering from domestic and personal problems, relationship problems, drug and alcohol problems, financial difficulties, relationships with criminals, and other adverse long-standing relationships. As such, the high-risk areas of police work to be targeted are: criminal investigation department and poor process activities (such as "planting" evidence); traffic patrol and opportunistic bribes; unethical behaviour in custody suites or police cells and assaults or deaths in custody; motor vehicle patrols and dangerous high-speed pursuits; special tactics units and excessive force in raids and sieges; drug squads and on-selling of drugs or shakedowns of dealers; and illicit access to and misuse of confidential information. Investigators working in the professional standards department will target investigations into these areas and possibly implement some "integrity testing" for police officers working in vulnerable or high-risk areas.

EXTERNAL OVERSIGHT OF INVESTIGATIONS INTO POLICE MISCONDUCT OR CORRUPTION

Policing is one of many activities that are prone to corruption, but additionally it has a further myriad of opportunities, pressures, and temptations that can lead to deviance. The "importance of police accountability can hardly be overstated. It is a corner stone of democracy and the rule of law" (Prenzler, 2004:6) which is of fundamental importance to democratic societies. Scrutiny of the police organisation must be external to the organisation itself to ensure independence, accountability, and integrity (den Heyer and Beckley, 2016). The blunt conclusion of the many multinational high-level inquiries into police corruption is that police cannot be trusted to investigate their own misconduct; therefore, there must be powerful and robust independent oversight of the police.

Because of this, rigorous and robust independent oversight organisations with strong legal powers have been introduced in most countries which have democratic policing systems. Researchers have identified the history and the many varieties, properties, terms of reference, and powers of these organisations (den Heyer and Beckley, 2016; Prenzler, 2009). Evidence from police misconduct reform has found that action by external oversight bodies will affect the careers and behaviour of individual police officers to ensure greater integrity and more ethical behaviour (Long, 2019). However, although most independent oversight bodies have robust and rigorous powers, many have insufficient resources and direction to ensure accountability of the police force or public service organisations they scrutinise (Holmberg, 2019).

POLICE INTEGRITY – THE CURRENT SITUATION

In the last several years, there have been international efforts to identify, understand, and recommend ways to address and reduce police misconduct and corruption. For example, in New South Wales (NSW), Australia, four research studies into police integrity were completed (Beckley, 2019a) and, using similar research methodology, the level of police integrity has been measured and compared across many countries in the world (Ivković and Haberfeld, 2015). The findings from the study carried out by the author revealed that the level of police integrity in NSW had not significantly changed between 1995 and 2016. Therefore, the level of integrity had not diminished, but it also had not improved. In contrast to this, studies conducted in Croatia, first in 1996 and then in 2016, found "that respondents in the 2016 sample evaluated scenarios as more serious, thought that harsher discipline would be appropriate, and stated that they would be more likely to report misconduct", thereby indicating a higher level of integrity in the country (Ivković et al, 2019:1).

Research shows that gender equality in police organisations can positively affect the level of police integrity. For example, a study in Slovenia, in surveys using the results of theoretical scenarios similar to those used in NSW, found that police brutality and preferential treatment was apparently more acceptable to male police officers. Also, female officers "paid less attention to social clues in deciding whether to report police misconduct or not than did males" (Pagon and Lobnikar, 2004:1). Male police officers had a higher level of trust in their colleagues' moral standards than female officers (Pagon and Lobnikar, 2004). In the author's (Beckley) research in NSW, there were some striking differences between the responses of male police officers and female officers in empathy with victims (see Figures 6.2 and 6.3). For example, in the first question in Figure 6.2, a greater percentage of female police officers did not agree with the statement "Some victims of crime are more deserving of a good service than others."

Respondents were asked the three questions on the left-hand side of Figure 6.2 and asked to grade their answers from "strongly agree = 1" to "strongly disagree = 7", thereby measuring their agreement with quality of police service factors in policing. The results showed significant differences in the mean and standard deviation. The differences in the results are easy to see in the box plot in Figure 6.3.

Survey questions: QUALITY OF SERVICE	Gender	Mean	Std. Dev	Std. Error
Some victims of crime are more deserving of a good service than others.	Male	3.46	1.967	.178
	Female	4.56	2.237	.349
It is a waste of time trying to help some members of the public.	Male	3.37	1.938	.175
	Female	3.98	2.092	.327
Some people do little to earn the respect of the police.	Male	2.18	1.408	.128
	Female	2.56	1.598	.250

FIGURE 6.2
Results from the quality of service questions in the survey, group *Gender*

Source: Beckley, 2019a.

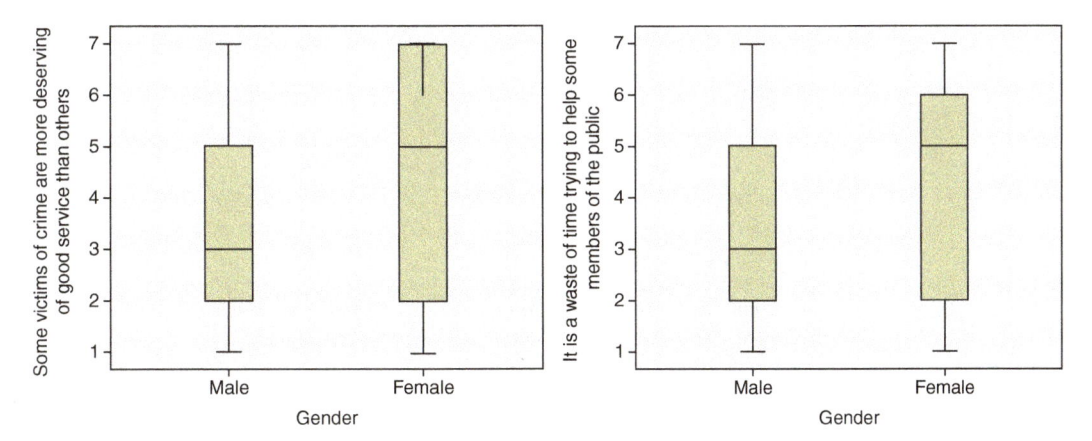

FIGURE 6.3
Boxplots from the quality of service questions: "Some victims of crime are more deserving of a good service than others" and: "It is a waste of time trying to help some members of the public", in the survey, analysis of group *Gender*

Source: Beckley, 2019a.

In another section, the Quality of Service aspect of the survey (Beckley, 2019a), police officers were asked nine human rights questions taken from Legal Studies examination papers on human rights law at Higher School Certificate (year 12) level. The knowledge and understanding of this subject was a disappointment in all participating police officers when male officers scored an average of 40% correct answers and female officers scored 44.6% average.

WAYS TO ADDRESS POLICE MISCONDUCT AND ENHANCE POLICE ETHICS

The authors teach a unit in a policing degree at Western Sydney University where the ways to address police misconduct and enhance police ethics are discussed (Beckley and Kennedy, 2019). Figure 6.4 shows a slide from the course that sets out measures that can be taken to improve professional standards.

Firstly, the right culture and values must be instilled into the organisation through capacity-building programs (Beckley, 2012) while removing deleterious factors such as systemic misconduct and corruption. Secondly, human resources in the recruitment, selection, and evaluation procedures must be rigorous to only select positive, non-discriminatory personnel with high levels of honesty, personal integrity, and courage. Supervisors and managers must be good role models to give a good example of ethical behavior and high integrity, and they should only have been promoted to supervisory and management positions after exhibiting and demonstrating those behaviours. The policing organisation should operate with maximum openness and transparency, with good communication both within the organisation and externally. There should be good control and management in the organisation and an effective

FIGURE 6.4
Organisational measures to improve professional standards

Source: Beckley and Kennedy, 2019.

- **Structures** – Management organisations best fit the role
- **Management of human resources:**
  - **Recruiting** – the need for the whole community to be included, especially minorities
  - **Selection** – type – open and transparent
  - **Evaluation** – fair – based on agreed parameters that reflects the job skills
  - **Promotion systems** – linked to evaluation
  - **Leadership styles**
- **Transparency and accountability** – an ongoing theme from personal to organisational development
- **Control and measure of security** – internal structures (internal affairs/discipline) to maintain effectiveness and efficiency of individuals in the organisation
- **Communication** – internally and with the community being served.

professional standards department to maintain high integrity standards and tight security of data protection and criminal intelligence. Finally, the high ethical standards and integrity should be included in all police training so that all police officers clearly understand the requirements of the organisation. This list is not exhaustive and is not easy to achieve, as it will require considerable change in most police organisations.

Another method of instilling improved integrity and ethics within the organisation is to professionalize the police service; this has been attempted in other countries such as the UK, but Australia is still going through a transformation towards this objective.

PROFESSIONALIZATION OF THE POLICE

An observation of the current situation of the police service in Australia would reveal that there is a long way to go before ethical standards can be achieved, as there are few characteristics of professionalization in place currently. It should be remembered that professions such as the law and medicine have taken many centuries to arrive at their present status. MacVean and Neyroud (2012:30) list the characteristics of a profession as:

> *(1) A body of knowledge and higher-level theory underpinning the practice of the profession; (2) control or regulation on entry to the profession by a professional association; (3) autonomy, discretion and a degree of self-regulation normally exercised by the professional association; (4) the profession is underpinned by vocational practice, and; (5) the profession has a code of ethics.*

The police forces in Australia do not have many of the characteristics of a professional organisation at present. Out of the five characteristics, the police service in Australia can claim it has incorporated only points 4 and 5. However, transformative work is being undertaken currently by the Association for Australia New Zealand Council of Police Professionalization (ANZCoPP) which holds the brief to:

1. Advance, lead and advocate for professionalization of policing in Australia and New Zealand;
2. Develop, establish, maintain and approve police practice standards for education and training;
3. Develop, establish, maintain and approve standards for policing practice; and
4. Progress the development of the policing profession in Australia and New Zealand (ANZCoPP, n.d.).

The Australian and New Zealand communities should watch the development of professionalization of the police with interest and patience, as it will take some time to implement the suggested changes with respect to the strategy, mission, vision, and values of the police organisations and their culture. Change programs of this ilk are notoriously difficult to implement and are faced with a myriad of problems, as the recommendations from the Wood Royal Commission illustrated (Chan and Dixon, 2007). Guidebooks on change management emphasize that many change management programs fail for different reasons and fall by the wayside due to resistance to change or lack of energy in the organisation (Speculand, 2005:1), but they can succeed with perseverance, tenacity, tact, and diplomacy (Beckley, 2012:269). The move to centralized policing in Scotland indicates that members of the public need to be included in change management programs (Henry et al, 2019).

CONCLUSION

Policing is a difficult, risky, and highly stressful occupation which one day might be recognised as a profession. It requires expertise, tactfulness, fairness, experience, and extreme responsibility to serve and protect citizens in society. Above all, its observance of integrity and high ethical standards is of supreme importance.

NOTES

1 *Police (Northern Ireland) Act 2000*, Section 38 (1).
2 Compstat is a crime reduction management tool using computer-generated crime statistics first used in the New York Police Department. It was subsequently criticised for creating undue emphasis on crime reduction to the neglect of quality and integrity of policing operations.

REFERENCES

ANZCoPP. (n.d.). *Rules of association for Australia New Zealand council of police professionalisation*. Sydney: Australia New Zealand Council of Police Professionalisation Inc.

Bayley, D.H. (2006). *Changing the guard: Developing democratic police abroad*. New York: Oxford University Press.

Beckley, A. (1997). *Operational policing: Liabilities & entitlements*. London: Police Review Publishing Company Ltd.

Beckley, A. (2012). Capacity building. Chapter 8, in Aepli, P. (ed.), *Toolkit on police integrity*. Geneva: Geneva Centre for the Democratic Control of Armed Forces (DCAF). 249–286.

Beckley, A. (2014). Organizational justice: Is the police service ready for it? *Journal of Policing, Intelligence and Counter Terrorism*, vol. 9, no. 2, 176–190.

Beckley, A. (2019a). *Examining human rights and ethical practice in Australian policing: A New South Wales case study*. PhD Thesis. Sydney: Western Sydney University.

Beckley, A. (2019b). Literature review: What the research reveals about the effectiveness of body worn cameras. *Policing Insight*, July 22. Retrieved from: https://policinginsight.com/analysis/literature-review-what-the-research-reveals-about-the-effectiveness-of-body-worn-cameras/

Beckley, A. and Kennedy, M. (2019). *Governance in policing*. Unit 102169. Sydney: Western Sydney University.

Birch, P., Vickers, M., Kennedy, M. and Galovic, S. (2017). Wellbeing, occupational justice and police practice: An "affirming environment"? *Police Practice and Research*, vol. 18, no. 1, 26–36.

Chan, J.B.L., Devery, C. and Doran, S. (2003). *Fair cop: Learning the art of policing*. Toronto: University of Toronto Press.

Chan, J.B.L. and Dixon, D. (2007). The politics of police reform: Ten years after the royal commission into the New South Wales police service. *Criminology and Criminal Justice*, vol. 7, no. 4, 443–468.

den Heyer, G. and Beckley, A. (2016). Police independent oversight in Australia and New Zealand. Chapter 10, in Prenzler, T. and den Heyer, G. (eds.), *Civilian oversight of police: Advancing accountability on law enforcement*. Brisbane: CRC Press. 205–228.

Dunnighan, C. (1999). *Certificate in professional policing ethics (Course material)*. Middlesbrough: University of Teesside.

Evans, Z. (2014). Excuses for police militarisation: "You can't put a price tag on keeping someone safe". *Reason*, July 25. Retrieved 2014, July 25 from: http://reason.com/blog/2014/07/25/excuses-for-police-militarisation-you-ca

Gerber, M.M. and Jackson, J. (2016). Justifying violence: Legitimacy, ideology and public support for police use of force. *Psychology, Crime and Law*. Retrieved 2016, July 25 from: http://ssrn.com/abstract=2710103 or http://dx.doi.org/10.2139/ssrn.2710103

Goodman-Delahunty, J., Beckley, A. and Martin, M. (2014). Complaints against the New South Wales police force: Analysis of risks and rights in reported police conduct. *Australian Journal of Human Rights*, vol. 20, no. 2, 81–105.

Henry, A., Malik, A. and Aydin-Aitchison, A. (2019). Local governance in the new police Scotland: Renegotiating power, recognition and responsiveness. *European Journal of Criminology*. doi:10.1177/1477370819855652

Holmberg, L. (2019). In service of the truth? An evaluation of the Danish independent police complaints authority. *European Journal of Criminology*. doi:10.1177/1477370819856514

Hough, M., Jackson, J. and Bradford, B. (2013). The drivers of police legitimacy: Some European research. *Journal of Policing, Intelligence and Counter Terrorism*, vol. 8, no. 2, 144–165. doi:10.1080/18335330.2013.821735

Ivković, S.K. and Haberfeld, M.R. (eds.). (2015). *Measuring police integrity across the world: Studies from established democracies and countries in transition*. New York: Springer.

Ivković, S.K., Mraović, I.C. and Sudar, D. (2019). The speed of progress: Comparing citizen perceptions of police corruption in Croatia over time. Chapter 10, in Ivković, S.K. and Haberfeld, M. (eds.), *Exploring police integrity*. Cham: Springer. 341–364.

Kennedy, M. (2001). *Zero tolerance policing and Arabic speaking young people*. Sydney: NSW Council for Civil Liberties. Retrieved from: www.nswccl.org.au

Kennedy, M. and Birch, P. (2018). Changing the perception of police culture: Recognising masculinity diversity and difference in a "dirty hands" approach. *Journal of Forensic Practice*, vol. 20, no. 1, 54–57.

Klockars, C.B. (1980). The dirty Harry problem. *Annals of the American Academy of Political and Social Science: The Police and Violence*, vol. 452, November, 33–47.

Letendre, M.C. (2019). *Organizational ethics*. New York: Marymount International, Bioethics International.

Long, W. (2019). How does oversight affect police? Evidence from the police misconduct reform. *Journal of Economic Behavior and Organization*. https://doi.org/10.1016/j.jebo.2019.10.003.

MacPherson, W. (1999). *The Stephen Lawrence inquiry*. Report of an Inquiry by Sir William Macpherson of Cluny presented to parliament by the Home Secretary. Cm. 4262-1, February. London: HMSO.

MacVean, A. and Neyroud, P. (2012). *Police ethics and values*. London: Sage Publications.

NIPB. (2008). *Police service of Northern Ireland code of ethics 2008*. Belfast: Northern Ireland Policing Board. Retrieved from: www.nipolicingboard.org.uk/sites/nipb/files/publications/code-of-ethics.pdf

NSW Ombudsman. (2013). *Consorting issues paper – review of the use of the consorting provisions by the NSW police force*. Sydney: NSW Ombudsman.

NSWPF. (2008). *Code of conduct and ethics and statement of values*. Sydney: New South Wales Police Force. Retrieved 2017, July 1 from: www.police.nsw.gov.au/__data/assets/pdf_file/0009/87993/SPC_Conduct_2008_INTRANET_230608.pdf

NSWPF. (2009). *Customer service charter*. Retrieved 2018, January 4 from: www.police.nsw.gov.au/__data/assets/pdf_file/0016/150127/Customer_Service_Charter.pdf

Oliveira, T.R., Jackson, J., Murphy, K. and Bradford, B. (2019). *Do trust and legitimacy 'arrive on foot' and 'leave on horseback'? A longitudinal test of the asymmetry thesis of police-citizen contact*. Retrieved from: www.academia.edu/40928279

OSCE. (2008). *Guidebook on democratic policing* (2nd edition). Vienna: Organization for Security and Co-Operation in Europe.

Pagon, M. and Lobnikar, B. (2004). Gender differences in leniency towards police misconduct. *Safety and Security in Local Communities (2015–2018)*. Retrieved from: www.researchgate.net/publication/242359338

Paoline, E.A. (2003). Taking stock: Towards a richer understanding of police culture. *Journal of Criminal Justice*, 31, 199–214.

Pollock, J.M. (1998). *Ethics in crime and justice*. Belmont: Wadsworth.

Prenzler, T. (2004). Stakeholder perspectives on police complaints and discipline: Towards a civilian control model. *Australian & New Zealand Journal of Criminology*, vol. 37, no. 1, 85–113.

Prenzler, T. (2009). *Police corruption: Preventing misconduct and maintaining integrity*. Boca Raton, FL: CRC Press.

Prenzler, T. (2016). Democratic policing, public opinion, and external oversight. Chapter 3 in Prenzler, T. and den Heyer, G. (eds.), *Civilian oversight of police: Advancing accountability in law enforcement*. Boca Raton, FL: CRC Press. 51–72.

Prenzler, T., Beckley, A. and Bronitt, S. (2013). Police gifts and benefits scandals: Addressing deficits in policy, leadership and enforcement. *International Journal of Police Science and Management*, vol. 15, no. 4, 294–304.

Rochel, T.R. (2011). Can police legitimacy promote collective efficacy? *Justice Quarterly*, vol. 29, no. 3, 384–419.

Rothlein, S. (2008). *Noble cause corruption*. Public Agency Training Council, E-Newsletter. Retrieved 2018, January 4 from: www.patc.com/weeklyarticles/noble-cause-corruption.shtml

Sheptycki, J. (2013). *Global policing*. Human Rights and Policing Conference, ARC Centre for Excellence in Policing and Security (CEPS), April 16–18. The Rex Hotel, Canberra.

Speculand, R. (2005). *Bricks to bridges: Make your strategy come alive*. Singapore: Bridges Business Consultancy.

Taylor, V.L. (2019). The mythology of (rule of) law (essay). *Hague Journal on the Rule of Law*, vol. 11, 331–339. doi.org/10.1007/s40803-019-00123-0

Tyler, T.R. (1989). The psychology of procedural justice: A test of the group-value model. *Journal of Personality and Social Psychology*, vol. 57(5), November, 830–838.

United Nations. (1948). *Universal declaration of human rights*, December 10. Document 217A (III). Retrieved 2018, January 4 from: www.refworld.org/docid/3ae6b3712c.html

Villiers, P. (1997). *Better police ethics: A practical guide*. London: Kogan Page.

Walsh, P.J. and Conway, V. (2011). Police governance and accountability: Overview of current issues. *Crime Law Social Change*, vol. 55, 61–86.

Wood, J.R.T. (1997). *Royal commission into the New South Wales police service: Final report, volume II: Reform*. Sydney: New South Wales Government.

SECTION 2

Organisational approaches and techniques

CHAPTER 7

Discretion
The elephant in the room

Mark Findlay

INTRODUCTION

It is not so much the extent and intrusiveness of legislative provision which create the opportunity and perpetuate the potential for abusive policing powers.[1] The abuse of policing powers involves what Rosa Luxemburg referred to in another context as:

> *The invidious disfiguring, dismembering and dis-remembering of significant historical experiences that do not have powerful enough (counter) lobbies in the present and therefore merit dismissal or belittlement* (Nixon, 2018, p. 99).

In his analysis of power, Badiou argues it resides with those who *claim to have the monopoly of possibilities*: what pronounces that which is possible and impossible (Nixon, 2018, p. 109). Regarding policing power, it is discretionary decision-making, regularly unbounded by restrictions on what is possible, that enables police in so many citizen encounters to monopolise and control the possible and demark the limits of impossibility. Discretion (individual, operational, and institutional) makes the legislative and administrative power forms conditional on the perception of those against whom they are directed.

This chapter spends no intellectual energy on the explosion of policing powers as a consequence of globalised and nationalised securitisation (Findlay et al, 2014). Though somewhat out of date now, thematically the "powers" given to police are described sufficiently in *Australian Criminal Justice*. Magnify these tenfold in the context of "terrorism prevention" and you have the substantive context of policing powers in Australia. Add to this the populist policing powers *knee-jerks* in response to criminal associations, and more recently public protest, and you have the explanation for why Australian police forces now prowl city streets as armed paramilitaries – no longer community protectors and moralisers (if that they ever truly were).

Of more interest to me is the contemporary policing powers' abusive phenomenon, where authorised power to counter popular resistance provides the situation and scenario for police to use criminal force against communities in protest. If such had eventuated as the central empirical focus for this chapter, it would have discussed the recent travesties of human rights and civilised discipline perpetuated to shocking degrees by the Hong Kong Police (Amnesty International, 2019). However, finding it personally impossible not to be intellectually and actively complicit on one side of the riot barriers in this historical epoch of resistance, the discussion of resistance which proceeds from this introduction is intended to challenge the misconception that the sharp edge of policing power can be understood by reviewing written rules, laws, and guidelines alone. The argument will have an early grounding in contexts of resistance and move in later sections to consider how discretion in police decision-making reveals exacerbated abusive potentials as operational biases are magnified via the introduction of artificial intelligence (AI)-assisted data management into police/civilian encounters.

It is the purpose of the body of the chapter to reveal how, through largely ungoverned discretionary decision-making, policing powers are manifest often in lawless ecosystems, whether these be clashes with protesters, or through more private, individualist, but no less invasive exercises of police profiling. Through a brief analysis of the manner in which AI-assisted information technologies risk aggravating "lawless" discretionary decision-making, the reader is forewarned that efforts to constrain abusive policing power are fought not only on the floor of Parliament or in challenging the commissioner's administrative directives but by appreciating, exposing, and neutralising the biased reasoning – and now the perverted data injection – which fuels and justifies abusive discretionary applications when police and citizens interact.

This analysis of the enabling potential of discretion – when policing power removes itself beyond any substantive, if questionable, legitimacy – is based on two simple but profound realisations:

- In the minds of many policing operatives, the primary purpose in exercising power is to engender and maintain respect for police authority. The consequences of any perceived challenge to respect are very likely to be abusive; and
- Neither the police nor the citizen knows the limits of substantive policing power, particularly in confrontational encounters. Therefore, understanding policing powers and the role of discretion in their manifestation is an exercise in reading perceptions.

These realisations assume a disproportionate power dispersal in citizen encounters on which the exercise of policing power is premised. Force and violent repression are always in the wings of a policing encounter. Even if things progress without confrontation, the unspoken message in policing is a relationship of incipient oppression. Put so clearly by Paulo Freire in his enlightening encounter of power transactions and the enslaving role of perception:

> *The oppressed, having internalised the image of the oppressor and adopted his guidelines, are fearful of freedom. Freedom would require that they reject this image and replace it with autonomy and responsibility. Freedom is acquired by conquest, not by gift . . . the oppressed who have adapted to the structure of domination in which they are immersed, and have become resigned to it, are inhibited from waging a struggle for freedom so long as they feel incapable of running the risks it requires, . . . The oppressed suffer from a duality which has established itself in their innermost being. They discover without freedom they cannot exist authentically. Yet although they desire authentic existence, they fear it. They are at one and the same time themselves and the oppressor whose consciousness they have internalised* (Freire, 2000, pp. 47–48).

THE DISSENT TRIGGER

In the critical literature on dissent, concepts of safe space within communities for the healthy and responsible exercise of dissent are redolent (Fernandez, 2008). As Teubner demands, space where dissent can flourish and where there is legitimate collective room for a conflict of ideas that doesn't lead to physical violence is what determines civilized community (Findlay, 2018) As has been so painfully played out in the exercise of violent repression by the police in Hong Kong from 2019, the mass withdrawal of consensus and respect by the majority has made policing power an uncivilising force (Rogers, 2019).

Discretion is too often exercised by police in states of anger, frustration, and fear when civilian encounters do not go in their favour. In these situations, the anger generated on both sides could be said to be unproductive, and can result in discretionary powers becoming abusive.

Anxiety over the loss of consensus and respect, igniting anger about the advance of the new community consciousness released from perceptions of obedience via oppression, and a *new freedom* through the denial of compliance and the withdrawal of respect that slates the police's earlier unquestioned expectations of community compliance, should logically be met by interrogating what spoiled the old and took the new beyond reach. This is not how general abuse of policing power discourse progresses because it does not sufficiently factor in languages of anxiety and fear on both sides of the barricades and ignores personal and collective considerations of anxiety reduction beyond misplaced hope in disciplinary procedures, legal remedies, and emergent conciliation.

Word limits do not allow here for developing a convincing (and distinctly inevitable) connection between neoliberal policing in decay and spontaneous millennial urban resistance (LaVenia, 2015) beyond identifying lines of battle which the police individually and organisationally do not recognise for what they are. A primary justification for the creation of the Peel Police in London was a need to control an unruly and often resistant labour force. This connection was even more apparent with US city policing in the late 1800s (LaVenia, 2015; Bowden, 1978). Historically and in the present, state policing is the strong-arm of capitalist labour ordering. Today this has morphed into another equally violent defensive role for policing power where it reinforces the exclusionist property interests of neoliberal market stakeholders against a mass of dispossessed and disaffected youth for whom the espoused benefits of neoliberal wealth generation will never be realised – the old is dying and the new cannot be born without violent resistance.

Discretion behind the exercise of policing power to determine the accessibility of space for dissent and peaceful resistance is determined and contested by the police and the protesters in terms of the:

- Importance of space (identifying with, claiming, and defending);
- Importance of safe space (location for legitimate protest and dissent – wherein to negotiate peace and violence);
- Importance of symbolism in space (riot gear, umbrellas, masks);
- Importance of virtual space (social media call-to-arms, digital communities, being "like water");
- Importance of vocalising space ("Glorious Hong Kong" vs police loud-hailers);
- Importance of constiutionalising space (one country/two systems, defending the motherland); and
- Social bonding in space through dissent and resistance (comradery in violence).

The recent social ecology of public dissent and policing power abuse in Hong Kong is the clash of two visions on how space is to be understood and enjoyed, two visions of how decisions about space need to be activated, and two visions of the legitimacy of police discretion determining policing power. One vision grows from desires for self-determination, inclusion, dignity, and democratic liberties, now tempered by an aggressive reaction to the incursion of external authority. The other requires obedience, demands authority endorsed through force, and celebrates private property and clear demarcations of power whereby space can be alienated and access awarded only externally through rules and recognition. The one thing that has in the past bound these visions in a tense, but non-violent alliance is respect for their different claims to integrity and the compromise of social order. Social order is now long lost. Once this respect vanished, the discretion to invoke abusive policing powers was unleashed from the moderation on power which the respect balance required.

DISCRETION WITH AND WITHOUT MODERATION

Discretion can be viewed as the context in which both legitimate and illegitimate policing and lawful or abusive policing power occur. As a mechanism for exercising power, it is any and all of the following:

- Individual decisions;
- Decision-making;
- The process through which decisions are made.

Policing power is activated through discretion. As touched upon in the preceding section, when looking at how policing power materializes, it is essential to consider the internal and external influences that operate on discretion where police have significant control over their decision-making and consequent daily encounters with individual members of the community.

Davis saw discretion for policing "as a tool indispensable for the individualisation of justice". He talked of discretion enabling "governments of law and of men, where rules alone cannot cope with the complexity of modern government" (Davis, 1975, 1976). This *inevitability approach* in operationalising criminal justice runs counter to *rule of law* foundations underpinning the exercise of formidable administrative powers that can define and construct any enjoyment of civil rights (Tamanaha, 2008). It also jeopardizes justifications for police independence if justifications do not remain under the law (Chakrabati, 2008).

Viewed positively, discretion provides a source of creativeness subjectifying the administration of law and is essential for selective law enforcement from a police perspective. If discretion begins where rule-based certainty ends, then its exercise may mean beneficence or tyranny, justice or injustice, reasonableness or arbitrariness.

Bottomley argued that the meaning of law and law enforcement is essentially transferred through the exercise of discretion (Bottomley, 1973). As such, discretion is crucially influenced by the characteristics of the parties to the process.

At an operational level, police discretion may be regulated by:

- Perceptions of how policing agencies will and should function, whether these come from within the system or are represented from community and media interests;
- Internal bureaucratic constraints such as the structures of a disciplined service;
- Interpretations of the law where its substance and application depend on the decisions of individuals;
- Professional standards and job satisfaction;
- Pressures from other agencies, whether direct, or indirect, where the operation of one component of the criminal justice system impacts on the potential of another; and
- Occupational solidarity, which is an isolating and consolidating factor of all criminal justice agencies.

POLICING POWER AND DISCRETION

The preconditions for the exercise of police discretion in many respects influence the nature and functions of policing power. Policing power in its various forms relies on discretion both in form and application; therefore, the nature of policing power and its situational impact is only to be fully understood against the context of opportunities for discretion.

One way of seeing the nexus between policing power and discretion is as a continuum from substantive legal entitlement to unfounded personal perceptions of empowerment. Somewhere between these poles we can position individual policing operatives (and in a three-dimensional consideration, the policing styles which they practise and the job they perform) as discretion is used against a specific policing power context. Such an understanding of discretion and policing power is cyclical in that discretion activates power and appreciations of power stimulate discretion.

It would be cavalier to rely on police discretion alone as the way of resolving conflicting expectations for policing power and creating the necessary balance between competing interests within the community. The police are too close to the exercise of their powers, and in democratic government the responsibility for determining the appropriate regulation of policing power should rest with those more directly accountable to the community at large. In the practice of discretion, this accountability chain should not be assumed.

The push/pull of consensus and resistance is the inevitable tension within which discretion is played out in police/community interactions. Policing by consent has been the historical inevitability where policing power is neither draconian nor resource rich. If and when the police lose public support and goodwill to any significant degree, or at the very least see a shift in ambivalence towards policing into outright opposition, it would become clear that the traditional consensual character of policing authority would revert to force and fear (Critchley, 1978).

As consent and consensus degenerates into ambivalence for significant sections of the community towards the exercise of policing power, discretionary decision-making, and even police presence, may be met with hostility. Policing under community challenge will substantially influence the police perception of their role and the development and exercise of policing power. The community's ambivalent attitude towards the police may reflect a wider alienation from all aspects of the justice process, with police encounters as the initial and governing impression of justice in action. The exercise of policing power is more apparent and regularly more confrontational than is the case with other justice agencies, and therefore public challenges to consent will significantly influence the exercise of police discretion.

Demands for increased policing power are predictably directed against those elements in society traditionally seen by the police as a challenge to their authority and therefore a threat to public order. Calls for greater powers also connect with calls to increase conviction rates, to make more aggressive the prosecution of criminal offences and to sentence longer, harsher, and more automatically. In this punitive discourse, judicial discretion is denigrated, while police discretion, if producing extrajudicial, retaliatory, or even vindictive responses, is applauded. The clip under the ears instead of the caution is preferred as deterrent rather than reintegrative police engagement.

Essential for understanding policing power as an instrument of popular governance is the influence of law-and-order politics. The police themselves play a vital role in the expansion of policing power and the entrenchment of discretion by supporting regular and constant demands for the expansion of discretionary authority and thereby of policing power. In an atmosphere where law-and-order politics prefers mandatory law enforcement and sentencing, in particular, reintegrative police discretion may provide a counterpoint to conservative arguments about severity and certainty.

CONTEXT-SPECIFIC DISCRETIONARY POWER

The institutional and community contexts in which discretion is exercised determine a particular policing style. As mentioned previously, the ideology of independence and the original powers doctrine (Carabetta, 2003) play a central role in the logic of discretion as an individualising mechanism for police powers.

For police officers, discretion and its prevalence are dependent on:

- Legal limits such as the definition of an offence;
- The visibility of its exercise, and the context in which discretionary encounters occur;
- Accountability for its exercise, both formal and informal;
- The demeanour of those encountered by police and the respect or otherwise that they demonstrate; and
- General public expectations of the exercise of police powers.

Predeterminants for the exercise of police discretion at both individual and organisational levels are formed by police and public perceptions of policing power, and these depend on the ways police interpret challenges and resistance to their function, or situations in which the law and the legal process stand in the way of what they consider to be their preferred outcome. Reduced to a battle over respect, mentioned above, perceptions of necessity, authenticity, and tolerance will determine how far policing power is pushed and how vigorously it is confronted.

Skolnick (2011) proposed policing as an exercise in balancing the tension between legal regulation and crime-control imperatives – some might say a problematic duality if self-interest and perverse job satisfactions are removed from the equation. In this, he argued that the police use discretion to bring about what they and the proponents of law-and-order politics believe to be just outcomes which would otherwise be modified by due process (Skolnick, 2011). Doreen McBarnet (1978, 1979) countered that the manner in which the law creates police powers tends to institutionalise the opportunity for the police to use discretion to interpret justice as they see fit. For her, the dichotomy suggested by Skolnick is false, rather revealing policing power as a function favouring certain class interests in society and ensuring applications of its laws to the serial disadvantage of other class interests. McBarnet dismisses the notion that the fairness and efficiency of criminal justice rests on the exercise of discretion and would be challenged through a stricter adherence to existing law. For her, law enforcement in practice, particularly as interpreted by police, does not conform to the ideology of legality. In both its substantive and procedural content, the law positively contradicts the precepts of due process, so consequently there is no fundamental conflict between the formal system of law and the informal and sometimes seemingly aberrant practices of agencies such as the police and the courts. Police discretion, the potential for selectivity, discrimination, and other discriminators usually labelled as abuses or informal accommodations to conflicting demands, are shown to be positively confirmed by, and affirmed through, law's language and application (McBarnet, 1978, 1979).

MEASURING DISCRETION'S IMPACT

A significant difficulty in analysing or evaluating the abusive impact of police discretion is that police operatives themselves diminish or misunderstand its place in their work. I previously emphasised the importance of recognising police discretion when distinguishing police work and policing styles. The corollary to this is that police work and different policing styles will in turn influence the exercise of discretion. Take, for example, policing traffic encounters. Traffic police regulate in a largely reactive/punitive environment and as such they anticipate that their encounters with civilians likely will be negative and often, hostile. As a result, traffic police are particularly susceptible to the demeanour of those they pull over on the roadside and tailor their discretion accordingly. So often, as one-on-one policing interventions, discretion in traffic situations is applied in the exercise of policing power with little concern for the limits of the law and the accountability requirements these limits might theoretically demand. The isolation of certain policing styles, work designations within community interactions, and the almost anonymous individuality of discretion, exacerbates the problems of recognition and control as they relate to discretion, leading to abusive policing powers.

Add to contextual variables the necessary ambiguity involved in the language of rules and laws governing policing, and as a regulator of excessive power the law can only be looked to for general guidance. More significantly, subjective interpretations of rules and laws by police means that the factors weighing on individual judgement, even more than administrative guidance from within the police organisation, will prove essential determinants of the directions for discretion. If there is a predisposition in any policing style or any work field to stretch or even disregard legal parameters, then the anomie of discretion, bounded only by bias and prejudice, fuels abusive power.

When talking about the exercise of police function, I have referred to the political and organisational basis of police discretion (Eggar and Findlay, 1988). The gulf between policing powers in principle and in practice is often concealed by the ideology of police independence and impartiality. Political, organisational, and industrial determinants of discretion generally are not recognised, articulated, or regulated in the operation of police powers, nor are even these documented variables interrogated when examining how discretionary decision-making can reflect preferencing and bias. In later sections of this chapter I suggest that the introduction of AI technologies into policing not only presents a challenge in exacerbating bias, but offers opportunities for its more empirical identification and charting as well.

The regularity of discretionary decision-making in the face of a lack of its recognition can be explained by often unarticulated policing policies (such as those relating to the maintenance of respect and discretionary reactions to suspects), the occupational culture of policing, and the institutional values of the organisation which may compete with laws and rules (such as loyalty over legality).

Police are unique among most bureaucratic agencies in that the degree of discretion which they exercise increases as one moves down the line of managerial responsibility. Also, the extent of discretion as a feature of police work is often inversely proportional to the visibility of a police/citizen encounter. As a consequence, it is police officers, who are inexperienced, less resilient, and often the most vulnerable to the negative impacts of social isolation, that are offered wide-ranging opportunities for discretion without the reassurance and governance of accountability to more senior personnel better placed to foresee the dangers associated with abusive action and reaction.

Law enforcement is recognised as an imprecise and consciously selective enterprise, and the tensions within the exercise of police discretion as a technique for utilising and activating policing powers are constantly shifting between action and inaction. It is common knowledge that the vast majority of behaviours and community contexts which could be deemed "criminal" do not come to police attention, and of those that do, most progress no further into the system. In fact, the significance of police discretion in no small part rests on its fundamental connection with the selective activation of significant police powers and the individual interpretation of when to enforce the law and when to go beyond it.

The sections that follow develop two themes discussed so far, in the emerging context of AI-assisted police decision-making:

- When the exercise of policing powers is influenced by bias, the resultant occasions of police public interaction may feature more abuse of police power; and
- If bias and its potential influence over police discretion is identified and understood, resultant power abuses may be minimised through introducing countermeasures in data analysis and decision-making.

AI POLICING TOOLS[2]

For the purposes of enhancing policing power, AI can be broadly defined as "a machine-based system designed to operate with varying levels of autonomy that can, for a given set of human-defined objectives, make predictions, recommendations, or decisions influencing real or virtual environments" (OECD Legal Instruments, 2019, para. 12). Policing is an ideal power frame for AI adoption due to a large portion of policing activities being information based and data producing, requiring routine and systematic analysis before informing police decision-making and consequent action. In addition, information management is a primary job in policing, and while police may not cherish being seen as data-crunchers, data sets such as crime intelligence are treated as essential components in the predictive and investigative policing styles.

Currently, and generally, AI tools created and employed to enhance police discretion take two forms. The first is predictive and proactive (Freilich and Newman, 2017),[3] applying machine learning and data analytics to information collected, classified, and stored by police departments in an effort to forecast when and where crime is most likely to occur and what offences types are most likely (McCarthy, 2019). As a consequence of most police data being generated from civilian encounters in public places, the pathways of prediction are likely to be skewed towards offenders and offences in public spaces. Besides generating analytical options that could predict potential crime events or criminal behaviours prioritised by police as worthy of AI application, predictive algorithms are also used to identify suspects who might be at a high risk of deviant activities (Faggella, 2019). Additionally, there are tools that offer a *solvability analysis* said to help police identify which crimes are more likely to be cleared up and as such should be investigated further (Howgego, 2019). The policing power-enhancing expectations surrounding the use of these prediction tools assume that crimes to which they're directed are foreseeable and that patterns can be recognised by AI algorithms analysing large volumes of data. This assumption, in turn, focuses the AI/policing alliance on "street crime" and thereby reflects and exacerbates discretionary biases regarding policing power priorities and reinforces predictive data biases (Brown, 2001).

The second AI-information management tool for augmenting policing discretion offers crime detection analysis through *smart technology* devices for surveillance, scanning devices, facial and text recognition, auto patrol, and crime incident detection (Carnegie Endowment for International Peace, 2017). In these applications, AI text and image recognition technologies provide the police with information such as license plate numbers, physical identifiers, and the timing of gunshot occurrences (ShotSpotter, 2019). Police possessing such technological data facilitation widens the scope of surveillance capacity, anticipating more targeted and timely response rates. Again, however, the street crime context towards which these tools are directed leaves out serious crime threats in the private, commercial, and domestic spaces and generates the criminogenic biases that obviously correspond. It is argued for crimes in public domains that commonly are under-reported, enhanced surveillance offers an answer. However, the continued over-representation of policing interest in public spaces and citizen encounters where predatory policing is active (Carbado, 2006–2007) skews arrest rates, creating further bias problems in the data sets fed into these AI applications.

GARBAGE IN – GARBAGE OUT!

Concerns about the potential for AI-assisted data management and analysis technologies in policing to exacerbate pre-existing individual and institutional biases have found evidence in a number of high-visibility racial profiling cases, especially in the US.[4] Research is underway to better appreciate and find ways to counteract bias distortion through higher predictive capacity (Vera Institute of Justice, 2018).

It is important to remember that AI technologies do not create policing bias. It is the data which feeds these technologies, almost all of it produced by human police/citizen interaction which may magnify bias in the conflation of data sets and the speed and assumed accuracy of the analysis it can produce. In the US, the most fundamental variable for policing bias and its impact on the exercise of policing discretion is race. Racial stereotyping has always featured in American policing. That AI can apparently confirm and even validate this bias makes the misuse of data sets and populations so much more dangerous as an influence in abusive police/citizen encounters through discretionary analytical preferencing.

Police regulators and accountability authorities can utilise AI analytics and can audit algorithm applications with their own AI-assisted information management tools to uncover operation bias and then to authenticate their suspicions that bias influences police discretion. Along with this empirical capacity comes the potential to map bias across policing styles and job types right down to police/civilian encounter modelling. AI can articulate operational and cultural biases located in specific policing functions, converting sixth sense into tangible data and even plotting the magnification of the biases once attention is drawn to them.

The historical moulding of policing patterns through bias, and the conversion of bias into policing common sense, by AI's quantifying and articulating of these blind spots, allows for a much more targeted decoding of what information sources and forms are most likely to transform contaminated data into perverse decision-making processes and abusive encounters. Algorithms, as much as discriminating in employment decisions, could also reveal biases in the policing organisation itself when hiring and firing officers. The more the various sources of bias are exposed, the more awareness the police can have on their own actions. Reducing perceptions and actual biased policing is a key element that will increase the public's trust in the police and contribute to the preservation of respect.

DISCRETION OR NO DISCRETION?

There can be little doubt that discretion is necessary for abusive policing powers. This truism raises the simple causal conclusion that less discretion equals less abuse. Specifically with routine policing encounters, a greater role can be played by AI to eliminate the opportunity for police to exercise individual discretion and thereby personalise bias. Routine policing such as traffic enforcement can be more discretionary than complex, team-based crime investigation, and external factors such as resource constraints, rostering, clear-up targets, and policies of situational crime prevention may result in targeted communities being over-policed compared to others. In every city, there are inevitably areas where police patrolling is more concentrated. In routine policing, violations of law are administrative and rarely involve multifaceted disputation over facts, AI can automatically enforce the law regardless of neighbourhood, the characteristics of the suspect, and whether violations have taken place on the back of situational bias. Speed cameras regulating traffic flow are an example of automated full enforcement (Darke, 2019). The limitation on police discretion has also been recognised in domestic violence encounters. For example in some Australian jurisdictions recognise the operational bias of police against intervention in the domestic setting, legislation makes arrest compulsory once certain offence and safety issues are met (Cretney and Davis, 1997).

Introducing AI into policing as a way of minimising human intervention has its risks, particularly if it were to lead to perceptions of over-surveillance. For instance, AI usage in Shenzhen, China, where facial recognition technology was recently implemented by the traffic police to publicly shame jaywalkers (Baynes, 2018), has profound implications for civil rights and the risks in secondary data bleeding (NYT, 2018). Shaming was achieved by an AI firm that provided technology to display jaywalkers' faces on large LED screens at the intersections. This AI firm is reported to be further exploring ways to notify the jaywalker of their wrongdoing via instant messaging as well as sending them an instant fine digitally (Tao, 2018). The instant messaging and fine would be enabled through partnerships with local phone carriers and social media platforms such as WeChat (Tao, 2018). It is important that when AI is used as a law-enforcement tool, representing zero-tolerance policy, friction points between the police and the public must be identified or AI will become another reason for the withdrawal of community consent. Even though it could be claimed that blanket surveillance policing administered through AI technologies may eliminate abuse issues such as racial bias, the potential for the technology to expand policing power itself may be seen as abusive in a rights context.

To summarise, AI's unparalleled capabilities to accumulate and analyse unprecedented amounts of data present opportunities and challenges for discretion and policing power. AI-assisted data management can streamline mundane information processing while either exacerbating or exposing and red-flagging individual, cultural, and institutional bias. Image and text recognition capabilities can revolutionise criminal investigation practice, but the dangers posed through race profiling are equally expansive. In whatever job or policing style it is employed, AI enables the police to surface patterns in their decision-making and thereby promote higher accountability expectations. The other side of the coin is that if police are comfortable with biased decision-making or ill-disposed to the harsh light of day as a first step to remedy, AI can efficiently cover up or ignore the offending data analysis.

CONCLUSION – HISTORICAL RACISM IN POLICING ABORIGINAL IDENTITY

Bias in the exercise of policing power through discretionary decision-making is not a product of applying artificial intelligence technologies. In large measure, discretionary bias is only exacerbated by the exponential capacities of AI to speed up and vastly expand policing's predictive and profiling capacities.

If the US experience in the application of AI to policing power is anything to go by, race as a factor of biased decision-making is the dominant influence in the distortions and abuse that can flow from particular data set sharing (Buranyi, 2017). The history of policing in Australia is a tragic litany of applying discretion in exercise power to the degradation and destruction of indigenous peoples (Cunneen, 2006). In significant measure, this discrimination has been legitimated through the racist profiling of indigenous people, and AI now offers an as yet unimagined possibility for that subversion of legitimacy to propagate.

There is neither the time nor sufficient available data at this point of the chapter to confirm the potentially dangerous relationship between the AI technologising of the discretion trigger in policing powers, and the further subjugation of Indigenous citizens in policing encounters. That said, it would be irresponsible not to raise a red flag, the warning resting on generations of shameful abuse in the exercise of policing powers as a defining feature of Australian policing. To offer this predisposition in policing powers the scientific stamp of objectivity with which AI is misguidedly assumed to imbue decision-making is an even greater danger than the mechanics of mass profiling and prediction. As noted through Greene:

> [P]redictive policing systems are built with "dirty data" compiled over decades of police misconduct, and . . . there's no current method by which this can be resolved with technology. . . . Left unchecked, the proliferation of predictive policing risks replicating and amplifying patterns of corrupt, illegal, and unethical conduct linked to legacies of discrimination that plague law enforcement agencies across the globe. . . . Ultimately, predictive policing systems and the data they process are the offspring of an unjust world. While the United States' criminal justice system is a vestige of slavery and centuries of racism against Black and Brown people, discriminatory policing is endemic across the globe, including in Europe. (2020, para. 8)

This sentiment is arguably applicable in Australia and for Australian policing powers, but perhaps even more to be feared in the context of discriminatory policing Indigenous identity.

NOTES

1 I employ this phrase rather than police powers to avoid limiting its interpretation to a more static institutional context. In the analysis to follow, power is considered as active, dynamic, relational, and transformative. It is not to be circumscribed by its sources, processes, or outcomes but rather provides the decision-making momentum that brings policing into the citizen's life-space.

2 The descriptive resources used in the remaining analysis of policing and AI has been assisted by the work of Jewel Seo in her research paper (2019), "Examining the Impact of Artificial Intelligence on Policing Legitimacy: Analysing the pessimistic and optimistic potentials".

3 This is similar to the thinking underpinning situational crime prevention, which seeks to find intervention strategies by analysing specific crime types to uncover the environmental and contextual factors that facilitate their commission.

4 A 2016 case in Tulsa, OK, US, where a police officer shot an unarmed black man, Terence Crutcher, and the 2014 case in Ferguson, MO, US, involving the shooting of Michael Brown.

REFERENCES

Amnesty International. (2019). 'Arbitrary Arrests, Brutal Beatings and Torture in Police Detention Revealed'. Retrieved from: www.amnesty.org/en/latest/news/2019/09/hong-kong-arbitrary-arrests-brutal-beatings-and-torture-in-police-detention-revealed/

Baynes, C. (2018). 'Chinese Police to Use Facial Recognition Technology to Send Jaywalkers Instant Fines by Text', (29 March 2018). Retrieved from: www.independent.co.uk/news/world/asia/china-police-facial-recognition-technology-aijaywalkers-fines-text-wechat-weibo-cctv-a8279531.html

Bottomley, K. (1973). *Decisions in the Penal Process*. Oxford: Martin Robertson.

Bowden, T. (1978). *Policing the Limits of the Law: A Comparative Study of the Police in Crisis Politics*. London: Pelican.

Brown, D. (2001). 'Street Crime, Corporate Crime and the Contingency of Criminal Liability', *University of Pennsylvania Law Review* 149(5): 1295–1360.

Buranyi, S. (2017). 'Rise of the Racist Robots – How AI Is Learning Our Worst Impulses', (8 August 2017). Retrieved from: www.theguardian.com/inequality/2017/aug/08/rise-of-the-racist-robots-how-ai-is-learning-all-our-worst-impulses

Carabetta, J. (2003). 'Employment Status of Police in Australia', *Melbourne University Law Review* 27(1): 1–32.

Carbado, D. (2006–2007). 'Predatory Policing', *UMKC Law Review* 85: 545–573.

Carnegie Endowment for International Peace. (2017). 'Global Expansion of AI Surveillance'. Retrieved from: https://carnegieendowment.org/2019/09/17/globalexpansion-of-ai-surveillance-pub-79847

Chakrabati, S. (2008). 'A Thinning Blue Line? Police Independence and the Rule of Law', *Policing: A Journal of Policy and Practice* 2(3): 367–374.

Cretney, A. and Davis, G. (1997). 'The Significance of Compellability in the Prosecution of Domestic Assault', *British Journal of Criminology* 37(1): 75–89.

Critchley, T.A. (1978). *A History of the Police in England and Wales*. London: Constable.

Cunneen, C. (2006). 'Racism, Discrimination and the Over-Representation of Indigenous People in the Criminal Justice System', *Current Issues in Criminal Justice*, 17(3): 329–346.

Darke, A. (2019). 'The New Tech Driving Traffic on Singapore's Roads', (13 June 2019). Retrieved from: www.channelnewsasia.com/news/singapore/new-technology-driving-traffic-singapore-roads-11688500

Davis, K. (1975). *Police Discretion*. St Paul: West Publishing.

Davis, K. (1976). *Discretionary Justice: A Preliminary Enquiry*. Urbana: University of Illinois Press.

Eggar, S. and Findlay, M. (1988). 'The Politics of Police Discretion', in M. Findlay and R. Hogg (eds.) *Understanding Criminal Justice* (pp. 209–233). Sydney: Law Book Company.

Faggella, D. (2019). 'AI for Crime Prevention and Detection – 5 Current Applications'. Retrieved from: https://emerj.com/ai-sectoroverviews/ai-crime-prevention-5-current-applications/

Fernandez, L. (2008). *Policing Dissent: Social Control and the Anti-Globalization Movement*. New Brunswick: Rutgers University Press.

Findlay, M. (2018). *Law's Regulatory Relevance: Property, Power and Market Economies*. Cheltenham: Edward Elgar.

Findlay, M., Odgers, S. and Yeo, S. (2014). *Australian Criminal Justice* (5th edn.). Melbourne: Oxford University Press.

Freilich, J.D. and Newman, G.R. (2017). 'Situational Crime Prevention'. Retrieved from: https://oxfordre.com/criminology/criminology/view/10.1093/acrefore/9780190264079.001.0001/acrefore-9780190264079-e-3

Freire, P. (2000). *The Pedagogy of the Oppressed*. London: Bloomsbury Publishing.

Greene, T. (2020). 'AI Now: Predictive Policing Systems Are Flawed Because They Replicate and Amplify Racism'. Retrieved from: https://thenextweb.com/neural/2020/02/20/ai-now-predictive-policing-systems-are-racist-because-corrupt-cops-produce-dirty-data/

Howgego, J. (2019). 'A UK Police Force Is Dropping Tricky Cases on Advice of an Algorithm', (8 January 2019). Retrieved from: www.newscientist.com/article/2189986-a-uk-police-force-is-dropping-tricky-cases-on-advice-of-analgorithm/

LaVenia, P. (2015). 'Police Behaviour and Neoliberalism'. Retrieved from: www.counterpunch.org/2015/01/16/police-behavior-and-neoliberalism/

McBarnet, D. (1978). 'False Dichotomies in Criminal Justice Research', in J. Baldwin and K. Bottomley (eds.) *Criminal Justice*. Oxford: Martin Robertson.

McBarnet, D. (1979). 'Arrest: The Legal Context of Policing', in S. Holdaway (ed.) *The British Police*. London: Edward Arnold.

McCarthy, O.J. (2019). 'AI & Global Governance: Turning the Tide on Crime with Predictive Policing'. Retrieved from: https://cpr.unu.edu/ai-global-governance-turning-the-tide-on-crime-with-predictive-policing.html

New York Times (NYT). (2018). 'Inside China's Dystopian Dreams: AI, Shame and Lots of Cameras', (8 July 2018). Retrieved from: www.nytimes.com/2018/07/08/business/china-surveillance-technology.html

Nixon, J. (2018). *Rosa Luxemburg and the Struggle for Democratic Renewal*. London: Pluto Press.

OECD Legal Instruments. (2019). 'Recommendation of the Council on Artificial Intelligence'. Retrieved from: https://legalinstruments.oecd.org/en/instruments/OECD-LEGAL-0449

Rogers, B. (2019). 'Thuggery and Terror: How Police Violence Fueled the Hong Kong Crisis'. Retrieved from: www.hongkongfp.com/2019/11/24/thuggery-terror-police-violence-fuelled-hong-kong-crisis/

ShotSpotter. (2019). 'How ShotSpotter Works'. Retrieved from: www.shotspotter.com/

Skolnick, J. (2011). *Justice Without Trial: Law Enforcement in Democratic Society*. New York: Wiley.

Tamanaha, B. (2008). *On the Rule of Law: History, Politics, Theory*. Cambridge: Cambridge University Press.

Tao, L. (2018). 'Jaywalkers Under Surveillance in Shenzhen Soon to Be Punished Via Text Messages', (27 March 2018). Retrieved from: www.scmp.com/tech/china-tech/article/2138960/jaywalkers-under-surveillance-shenzhen-soon-bepunished-text

Vera Institute of Justice. (2018). 'Bias in Crime Assessment: A Tool and Guidelines for Law Enforcement and Concerned Communities'. Retrieved from: www.ncjrs.gov/pdffiles1/nij/grants/252011.pdf

CHAPTER 8

Criminal intelligence in Australia

Troy Whitford and Shane Lysons-Smith

INTRODUCTION

Criminal intelligence is the collection and analysis of information from various sources to detect, deter, and disrupt criminal activity. It is an essential component of wise decision-making in law-enforcement agencies. Australian criminal intelligence in the 21st century has undergone some significant changes at the operational and strategic level. The implementation of intelligence-led policing, the National Criminal Intelligence model, and the introduction of the National Criminal Intelligence System are just some of the approaches being undertaken by various law-enforcement and intelligence agencies to better integrate and share criminal intelligence across jurisdictions and agencies in Australia. Underpinning these changes are a range of Government inquiries and legislation designed to assist in the collection and analysis of criminal intelligence. Predominately, emphasis has been placed on emerging technologies and how to capture data. But there is also a renewed interest in the importance of human intelligence collection. This chapter focuses on the models and factors driving the way police collect, analyse, and share data in an intelligence context. This chapter also examines some cultural issues within the intelligence community. These cultural issues are specific to criminal intelligence and include issues such as the institutional view of intelligence within the police force, a lack of awareness of the possibilities intelligence can offer investigations, and differences between intelligence and evidence.

Prior to examining the role of intelligence in Australian law enforcement, some explanation of the types of intelligence used is required. Broadly, there are four kinds of intelligence: basic, tactical, operational, and strategic. Each produces different types of intelligence products. Basic intelligence often provides background or facts and figures that can be used as the basis for further research or data collection. Tactical intelligence provides insight to assist an operation. It is focused on current unfolding events as they are happening and orientated to a specific individual or activity. Tactical intelligence will produce products such as crime charts, crime trends, or target profiles. Operational intelligence plays a vital role in supporting policing operations focused on the arrest and prosecution of offenders or disruption of criminal activity. In the Australian context, operational intelligence aims to inform and influence decision-makers in regards to the broader operating environment, often focused on serious organised crime. Operational intelligence is typically information-rich and comprises multiple and varied sources of information. Output may encompass knowledge products (i.e. environmental scans), tactical intelligence (i.e. profiles), or insight products (i.e. new or emerging issues). Strategic intelligence provides a comprehensive view of a target or activity. It is designed to advise policy development. Strategic intelligence products will be more detailed in content and also provide some predictive analysis (Prunckun 2019).

SOME CULTURAL PROBLEMS IN POLICE INTELLIGENCE

Traditionally, criminal intelligence in Australia is impacted by a range of problems that are institutional or culturally based, such as sharing information interstate and between states and federal law enforcement. Police culture is traditionally viewed as investigative and evidentiary based, with success measured in terms of arrests and convictions. The role of intelligence was viewed as incompatible with that culture unless it directly led to evidence or arrests. Subsequently, the professionalization and recognition of the contribution criminal intelligence makes to law enforcement has been undervalued. The difficulty in implementing and addressing these problems within law enforcement require cultural and institutional change (Ransley & Mazerolle 2009), much of which may be incidentally addressed by cultural reforms underway in many jurisdictions. Within law enforcement there is a perception that intelligence units are comprised of police lacking in investigative or frontline policing skills. In addition, many intelligence units or commands are made up of civilian analysts who may not have an operational policing background. This often causes a "clash of cultures" whereby intelligence is perceived to lack credibility or is seen to challenge the role of police officers as crime experts (Cope 2004) Unsworn civilian analysts and civilian field officers providing intelligence are perceived by the wider police community as outsiders without operational experience. Their presence and contribution to law enforcement challenges the notion that it is only sworn officers who have the knowledge and skills to prevent crime.

There is a lack of appreciation by police officers for the contribution intelligence can make to policing. In part, the perception that intelligence has little to offer policing comes from a traditional cultural approach to policing. The traditional cultural approach to policing has been reactive. Police traditionally have been concerned with responding to requests for assistance from individuals, communities, or victims of crime. Successful law enforcement was based on arrests and convictions rather than more contemporary models, which also emphasise predictive policing and disruption of criminal activities. Predictive policing is the use of intelligence analysis (such as crime trends and hotspot mapping) to predetermine likely criminal activity. But traditional approaches to investigations focus on the need to gather evidence. Unless intelligence could lead to evidence collection, it was seen as having little value to investigative work. Finally, there is a lack of understanding from police commanders about what products intelligence units can provide and what information can be requested. In some instances, intelligence units are simply used to gather crime statistics to contribute to reports. In other Local Area Commands, intelligence units may provide predictive policing support through hotspot mapping or other analytical techniques. Essentially, it depends on the Commander's understanding of intelligence and the abilities of the intelligence unit. Efforts to change the cultural perception of intelligence in law enforcement have manifested through the introduction of intelligence-led policing. A renewed focus on education and training (for both the analyst and consumer) through the Australian Criminal Intelligence Commission's (ACIC) education and training continuum and tertiary recognised qualifications in the field of intelligence studies are making a difference in the role and professionalization of criminal intelligence. Further, the Australian Criminal Intelligence Model and rise in use of technologies such as social media for preventive policing are giving intelligence collection and analysis greater recognition and purpose.

An ongoing challenge for criminal intelligence is operating in an information-rich, all-source environment. Analysts must be adept at manipulating and analysing large quantities of data to derive meaning. Their utility is in the *value-add* they provide for decision-makers and intelligence consumers. *Value-adding* to intelligence products means providing intelligence that enhances the understanding of a situation in a manner that may not have been thought by intelligence consumer or decision-maker requesting the intelligence product. Culturally, though, there persists a desire amongst operational police and investigators for an information-heavy intelligence product (Cope 2004). Information-heavy products tend to provide figures, data, and background without analysis of meaning and significance. Many analysts continue to grapple with providing products which meet the needs of the intelligence consumer, on one hand, while still providing products that have been analysed and are predictive in nature or provides insight, on the other hand. However, improved education and training, specifically focused on those that manage intelligence staff, as well as those that use or consume intelligence products, continues to address this issue.

In practice, the shift toward *value-adding* and moving beyond information-heavy products involves adapting predictive analysis in intelligence products. Within the traditional information-heavy approach, the emphasis was on what can be termed basic intelligence – intelligence that is predominately historically based and an "encyclopaedia-like compilation of facts and figures" (Prunckun 2019, 17). At the tactical and operational level, intelligence products are more concerned with the present, the day-to-day updates or operational activities that provide a broader perspective (Prunckun 2019). Traditionally, it has only been at the strategic intelligence level that predictive analysis it adopted. Introducing elements of strategic intelligence into other intelligence products, such as advice on threats, risks, warnings, and advice for planning (Prunckun 2019), are all *value-adds* to the intelligence product.

INTELLIGENCE-LED POLICING

Intelligence-led policing originated in the United Kingdom in the late 1990s. It aimed to move policing practice from a reactive position to one that was actively inhibiting crime through proactive means (i.e. overt and covert techniques) (Ratcliffe 2003). The driving force toward intelligence-led policing was as a result of previous failures to address the sources and patterns of crime (Tilley 2008). Intelligence is used to target groups, individuals, or crime hotspots. Intelligence-led policing interprets the criminal environment police are operating within through a range of collection and analytical techniques (tradecraft) from both human and technological sources. The process also adopts the intelligence cycle of tasking, data collection, analysis, dissemination, and feedback as a means to organise the process. The interpretations made through the intelligence process are designed to influence the decision-maker. The intelligence process provides information that can be used to implement approaches to counter crime. It allows the decision-maker to impact the criminal environment (Ratcliffe 2003).

Most state and territory police and the Australian Federal Police acknowledge the importance of intelligence-led policing, which is generally accepted as part of the law-enforcement lexicon. However, there are some concerns that intelligence-led policing's meaning and purpose lack definition and direction (Ratcliffe 2014). It appears to have broad and subjective meanings. In some instances, intelligence-led policing is viewed as a covert activity pertaining to shaping operations or activities designed to disrupt organised criminal activities. Other interpretations are more akin to predictive policing – using data to make predictions on future crime or criminal behaviours. Overall, the role of intelligence-led policing and criminal intelligence is based on the interpretation made by senior decision-makers. A study conducted in 2004 showed that NSW Local Area Commanders interviewed had different opinions of intelligence units under their supervision. Some stated that intelligence was proactive in developing intelligence products which highlight hotspots and trends. Other Local Area Commanders believed the intelligence units had to be pushed to conduct basic intelligence analysis (Ure

2005). These varied opinions led to a lack of uniformity with respect to intelligence practice and products.

While the term intelligence-led policing has widespread currency in Australian law enforcement, it remains unclear if there is a standard practising definition. In the United Kingdom, the development of the National Intelligence Model has successfully unified the role of intelligence and intelligence products (John & Maguire 2006) and provides a clear role for criminal intelligence. Through the National Intelligence Model, an interpretation of the criminal environment is made by criminal intelligence analysis. The analysis influences the decision-maker who is then able to make an impact on the criminal environment. In the United Kingdom, there are nationwide agreements on terminology, roles, and responsibilities of intelligence collection and analysis. It has essentially operationalised intelligence-led policing. Efforts to emulate the National Intelligence Model in Australia can be identified in the Australian Criminal Intelligence Model and the Australian Criminal Intelligence Strategy; however, Australia's jurisdictional model has provided a number of challenges in regards to standardisation and consistency.

THE AUSTRALIAN CRIMINAL INTELLIGENCE MODEL

The Australian Criminal Intelligence Model is an approach to coordinate intelligence partnerships with state and federal law-enforcement agencies. It has five major strategic objectives:

1. Ensure quality intelligence supports tactical, operational and strategic decision-making, via common standards processes and protocols;
2. Inculcate a culture where security requirements are balanced and information generated and held by individual jurisdictions and the Commonwealth is valued as a national asset for all;
3. Professionalise the intelligence discipline through development of national standards for intelligence practitioners and analysts;
4. Maintain an agreed national threat, harm and risk assessment methodology; and
5. Pursue common technical and security architectures for data, information and intelligence holdings (ACIC 2017).

The key themes in the objectives are greater coordination between law-enforcement and government agencies, uniformed intelligence products, and the professionalization and standardisation of training. Commonly identified problems within the Australian law-enforcement community are lack of uniform training and sharing of information. The cultural problems outlined previously are being addressed in the strategic goals pursed in the Australian Criminal Intelligence Model.

Of particular note is the problem of intelligence training. Greater acceptance of the role of intelligence in law enforcement rests heavily on education and training. Uniform fundamental intelligence training across the criminal intelligence community has great benefits for intelligence practitioners and clients of intelligence products. It standardises intelligence products across law-enforcement agencies, encourages greater sharing of intelligence, and gives the role of intelligence greater professionalization. The Australian Criminal Intelligence Commission (ACIC) has taken a lead role in developing a uniform industry-based continuum of training. In collaboration with the ACIC, Australian Federal Police (AFP) and state law enforcement have developed the Australian Criminal Intel Training and Development Continuum (CITDC). The principles of the CITDC include integrated and sequential training rather than a range of different courses with no clear link, assessments that are linked to clear learning outcomes, provision of a clear pathway for professional development that articulates with tertiary education, and establishment of a standardised tradecraft curriculum (Harrison et al 2018). Those principles which underpin the continuum are widely accepted, though agencies have adopted various components dependent on their own training needs. The continuum is described as:

> *an end-to-end continuing professional development framework for criminal intelligence analysts and field intelligence officers that monitor proficiency, competence, and knowledge achievement through pre-entry aptitude testing, rigorous class room, and workplace mentoring. The continuum is designed at the post-graduate level and articulates with Charles Sturt University's Master of Intelligence Analysis* (Harrison et al 2018, 1).

The continuum represents a number of important new opportunities in training and professional development which over the long term will instigate the much-needed cultural reform in criminal intelligence practice. Through a universal training model, intelligence products such as target assessments, situational reports, and briefings can move towards standardisation, providing clear expectations and guidelines for intelligence practitioners and greater clarity of what to expect for intelligence consumers. Greater professionalization of the intelligence profession is also an important product from the continuum. Providing opportunity for the intelligence profession to acquire tertiary qualifications allows for and encourages further research in the field of intelligence studies and lifelong learning. Perhaps the greatest opportunity for cultural change brought about by the learning continuum is breaking down "silos" between agencies and even within agencies. Encouraging greater sharing of intelligence – through illustrating its benefits within the curriculum – will provide additional opportunities and a greater interest in sharing information.

THE AUSTRALIAN CRIMINAL INTELLIGENCE STRATEGY

The Australian Criminal Intelligence Strategy sets the agenda for criminal intelligence on a national level. It was developed and endorsed by the National Criminal Intelligence Capability Committee (NCICC), comprising the heads of intelligence from state and territory police, commonwealth criminal intelligence, and law-enforcement agencies. The main objectives of the strategy are centred on targeting transnational serious organised crime impacting Australia and building greater national and international networks in order to leverage capability (ACIC 2018a). It also seeks to identify the greatest criminal threats and/or harms to Australia and provide broad environmental scans of major crime issues. The strategic objective to discover and disrupt targets is realised through the ACIC Australian Priority Organisation Target list, focusing on significant offshore targets impacting Australia (ACIC 2018b) and the National Target System which ACIC describes as a "secure online data repository containing information on nationally significant organised crime groups" (ACIC 2018c, National Target System section para 16). Finally, national criminal targeting lists and gang lists also contribute to part of the targeting strategic objective. The gang list is developed and maintained by the Gangs Intelligence Hub and includes information about gang activity in Australia and overseas that is accessible by Commonwealth and state law-enforcement agencies (ACIC 2018d).

A continued focus on sharing intelligence and information as part of the Australian Criminal Intelligence Strategy is also evident in the development of a near real-time intelligence sharing system. In 2020, the National Criminal Intelligence System was introduced to replace the ageing Australian Criminal Intelligence Database. The new system provides a national, unified picture of criminal activity to assist law-enforcement agencies to avoid duplicating investigations. It provides real-time interconnectivity between federal and state law-enforcement agencies, bringing together state and federal data bases such a PROMIS, COPS, and LEAP (Hendry 2019).

A further program to better integrate intelligence and information between Commonwealth and state law enforcement is the National Police Reference System (NPRS). The merging of the Australian Crime Commission and CrimTRAC in 2016 further strengthened the ability to integrate and share data through various national police information systems. NPRS is available to more than 75,000 police officers across Australia. It includes access to more than 11 million records and 10 million photographs, and it records core data related to offenders, including:

- name;
- identity information and photographs;

- information on warnings, warrants, and wanted persons;
- offence history;
- protection and violence orders;
- firearms involvements;
- information relating to the child protection register; and
- information on missing persons, unidentified persons and bodies, and escapees (ACIC 2019a, National Police Reference System para 4).

CHANGES IN STRATEGIC INTELLIGENCE

Strategic intelligence is the collection, analysis, and dissemination of intelligence to advise policy. In law enforcement, it informs high-level decision-making, aiming to tackle serious long-term issues to support policing in its efforts to be proactive. It is typically problem-orientated in contrast to tactical and operational intelligence, which are usually target-focused (Ratcliffe 2009). Much has been written about intelligence failures and the role that strategic intelligence could have played in providing forewarning and avoiding surprise, though research has typically focused on failures concerning national security (Coyne & Bell 2011). When considered in the law-enforcement context, strategic intelligence plays a similarly vital role, though it is heavily reliant on being understood (as a function) and applied correctly to policy and planning. An issue for police commanders is the difficulty in measuring the impact of strategic intelligence. While operational outcomes (and to a lesser extent tactical intelligence) can be more easily measured (arrests, drug seizures, and successful prosecutions), strategic intelligence may have influenced initial planning or strategy, though it is often overlooked and gains little recognition when operational success is finally realised.

Within Australian law enforcement, strategic intelligence has often struggled to cement its place and gain long-term acceptance. Over the past 30 years, strategic intelligence has often vacillated between being too operationally focused or being too academic, thus struggling to find a balance. In part, this confusion can largely be traced back to the establishment of the Australian Bureau of Criminal Intelligence, the National Crime Authority, and the Office of Strategic Crime Assessments in the 1980s and 1990s. While these agencies grappled with strategic criminal intelligence as a process and product, difficulties were further compounded because the agencies mostly recruited or seconded current or ex-police officers with little or no training as strategic analysts (Ratcliffe 2009). These agencies have now been superseded by the Australian Criminal Intelligence Commission, though similar challenges continue to plague most Australian police forces.

Following the widespread adoption of intelligence-led policing in the late-1990s, a subtle shift took place when strategic intelligence began to be considered essential to operational policing as well as a tool that could be used to inform or shape public policy. As this was occurring, however, strategic intelligence slowly became more academic, largely as a result of recruitment practices which targeted researchers or those with an academic background. Subsequently, the rigour used to draft strategic intelligence products tended to resemble academic papers rather than indicators and predictors of criminal targets or activities. Strategic intelligence was then perceived to suffer from a disconnect between strategic analysts and operational areas, which contributed to organisational misunderstanding of the role, potential, and benefits that strategic intelligence can offer (Cope 2004). However, regardless of the educational or vocational background of the individual analyst, operational and strategic intelligence share a symbiotic relationship. Without operational data and intelligence, strategic intelligence is "flying blind" and would be unable to identify emerging trends or make predictive analysis. While strategic intelligence provides operational areas context of the operating environment, it can also identify priorities and allow police commanders to more effectively direct police resources.

Strategic intelligence products are predictive in nature and seek to anticipate and plan for change. Over recent years there has been a shift toward short reports, the use of infographics to more simply convey complex data and the production of "just-in-time" products to influence short-term decision-making. In addition, in the national context, strategic intelligence has shifted to ensure it is more useable and digestible by government, as well as suitable for informing and shaping public policy – that is, not limited to criminal justice issues. An example of this is the National Wastewater Drug Monitoring Program run by the ACIC. This program monitors and assesses the use of illicit and licit drug use across the country to provide a national picture to government and the Australian public (ACIC 2019b). While the data from this program can be used for operational-level responses and influence the allocation of police resources, health departments and social services can use the data to inform their development of social policy and harm-reduction strategies.

CHANGES IN OPERATIONAL INTELLIGENCE

Operational intelligence within Australian law enforcement has changed considerably over the past 10 to 15 years. While work to professionalize criminal intelligence has been a contributing factor, these changes have largely been a result of a rapidly changing criminal landscape. The introduction of encrypted communications, a globalised and digital world, and an increasing quantity of available data has challenged operational intelligence. The widespread uptake of mobile phones in the early 2000s provided law enforcement with an unprecedented access to data. In the space of a decade, telecommunications data grew to be an essential tool in relation to identifying networks, placing individuals at crime locations, and analysing their life pattern (Branch 2014). Conversely, traditional law-enforcement tradecraft, specifically the use of human intelligence, became less crucial. However, the rapid uptake of encrypted communication platforms has reinvigorated and increased the focus on human intelligence. In some jurisdictions, this has included embedding intelligence analysts in covert human intelligence units to validate reporting, assess potential opportunities, and guide human source recruitment.

Analysis of social media has provided additional collection opportunities not previously available to criminal intelligence analysts. From identifying individuals and associates to mapping networks, detecting extremist ideology, or understanding changes in public sentiment, social media has added a human behavioural element for operational analysts to consider (Walsh & O'Connor 2019). While interpreting behaviour and motivation was once the domain of criminal profilers or psychologists, the increased reliance on social media data has required analysts to develop these capabilities as a core skill. While not removing the need for highly skilled operational psychologists or criminal profilers, it has allowed intelligence analysts to integrate offender behaviour as part of their day-to-day analysis.

Quantity of data is an additional challenge being faced in the operational intelligence space. However, with increasingly sophisticated databases and analytical platforms, the quantity of data alone is not the greatest challenge. Instead, it is the complexity of data being received. Traditional data such as travel movements, financial data, and telecommunication metadata continue to be the mainstay for operational analysis. However, in an increasingly digital world whereby most business is transacted online (including criminal activity), its unstructured nature significantly makes data more complex to organise and analyse. The complexity inherent in data has resulted in the establishment of multidisciplinary teams which include intelligence analysts, data scientists, and programmers to manage and interpret unstructured data and conduct bulk data matching and analysis. However, in an information-rich environment, analysts continue to grapple with delivering products which may satisfy the investigator consumer but fail to deliver the value-add which operational commanders and senior decision makers are seeking.

CRIMINAL INTELLIGENCE AND CORRECTIONS

Criminal intelligence extends into the corrections system. An inclusive approach to criminal intelligence necessitates coordination between law-enforcement agencies and the corrections system. It's widely recognised that criminal activity does not stop once someone enters prison, and criminal activity within the walls of a prison often has a nexus to offending in the community. Given this, the collection and analysis of data related to criminal activity should not stop at the gates of corrections facilities or the doors of community corrections offices. Subsequently, it is important to include some of the trends and changes taking place in corrections intelligence.

Similar to the history of intelligence in policing whereby investigators and police officers informally collected and analysed their own intelligence, corrections in Australia has long performed an intelligence function internally through similar informal arrangements (United Nations 2016). However, as with their policing counterparts, there has been growing recognition of the role that intelligence can play within a corrections environment. While the pace of this change has been considerably slower, global and regional events have largely shaped this, including the rise in terrorism and the increased national focus on gangs.

Broadly, intelligence in corrections aims to mitigate risk, anticipate potential threats, and contribute to the safety and security of the corrections environment. It does this through providing tactical, operational, and strategic intelligence to inform and influence decision-making (ACTCS 2018). The intelligence models used by the different jurisdictions vary; however, all generally follow from the traditional intelligence cycle in regards to the process they apply. Some jurisdictions have also incorporated their internal corruption/integrity function as part of their intelligence operating framework. In practice, this may present some issues, especially the sensitivity of some data (specifically that which relates to staff) and the relatively small size of corrections agencies (in comparison to police agencies). However, its benefits are realised with the ability of the intelligence analyst to integrate or overlay integrity or corruption-related data with other information to identify trends or common themes. Notably, integrated units are in contrast to police and law-enforcement agencies which almost always separate their intelligence and integrity functions.

The relationship between corrections and police can be a challenging one. The perception of prison officers and corrections staff is often compounded by entrenched stereotypes. While the corrections environment offers an abundance of intelligence collection opportunities, and corrections agencies are increasingly sharing this intelligence with partner agencies, on occasion there is a reticence amongst police to share their information with corrections (Walsh 2011). This may be because of legislative restrictions, or because of distrust between corrections and police agencies. However, regardless of the reasons, without open channels of communication and a "joined up" collaborative approach, corrections intelligence will struggle to integrate external information (and sometimes external threats) with the intelligence picture they may have generated.

Intelligence in corrections must also overcome institutional cultural issues. Many staff, both new and experienced, fail to appreciate the value that intelligence can provide. Oftentimes, this is as a result of the importance (or lack thereof) that agencies, individual prisons, or probation and parole offices have placed on intelligence. For example, in some jurisdictions, intelligence in prisons is the responsibility of prison officers on a part-time or rotational basis, or in addition to other duties (Walsh 2011). This means that intelligence is ad hoc at best, and at worst non-existent. Similar to policing, corrections has traditionally been response-orientated, with success measured by tangible results (i.e. the number of searches conducted or contraband items seized). Being intelligence-led challenges the traditional success paradigm, which is largely based on quantitative date or observable, measurable events. It requires proactive action, but how that leads to measuring success is problematic. Acting on intelligence may require senior executives to further deprive a person of their rights in custody or else act on information which may return someone to custody from the community. In both instances, there is the possibility of disclosing intelligence capability. The further deprivation of a person's rights in custody leads to human rights compliance processes that may expose the source of intelligence. A re-incarceration of an individual has the potential requirement to release the information to an offender or their lawyer, disclosing intelligence capability or the source of information.

Similar to law enforcement, an ongoing issue in corrections is education and training – both staff involved in intelligence as well as consumers of intelligence. While some agencies have developed their own internal training programs and nationally recognised qualifications, others rely on external partner agencies or third-party providers to deliver the bulk of their training (Queensland Corrective Services 2016). This has led to little national consistency, different standards, and a lack of appreciation, particularly at the senior executive level, of the benefits that intelligence can provide.

POLITICS AND POLICE USING DATA

Since 9/11, there has been near political bipartisanship in attempts to give law enforcement and national security agencies greater powers in collecting intelligence. There has been little effective opposition to increases in policing powers, and subsequently, much of the legislation enacted at a state and Commonwealth level has supported the provision of greater powers. The introduction of data retention laws through amendments to the Telecommunications (Intercept and Access) Act 1979 and the Assistance and Access Act 2018 are indicative of government support for law enforcement using data for intelligence and evidentiary purposes. For law enforcement, the political environment is generally supportive.

While law enforcement enjoys political support, keeping legislation up to date with technological progress is a challenge. Within the last five years, technology has advanced at a pace greater than legislation. Police using data for intelligence purposes are confronted with new challenges and opportunities to collect and analyse vast amounts of data generated from social media, online sites, financial transactions, and mobile telephones. Relevant legislation and government inquiries are working through the legal and ethical aspects, but these lag behind technological developments. For example, the technology for matching faces against a database of facial images has been developing since the late 1980s. By 2017, such technology was being used by frontline police in the United States, and variations of facial recognition software were also used by Australian state and territory police in 2018. However, broad legislative requirements allowing the use of the technology didn't emerge in Australia until the introduction of the Identity Matching Services Bill in July 2019 and the Australian Passport Amendment Bill in 2018. Australian State Governments have begun making progress toward linking facial recognition software with state driver's licenses. It is expected that all Australian states and territories will have uploaded their data to the National Driver Licence Facial Recognition Solution (NDLFRS) database by September 2021 (Hendry 2019).

Social media is a further example of technology outpacing legislative change and ethical deliberations. Social media platforms such as Facebook, Twitter, and Instagram provide an opportunity for mass surveillance and enhance the opportunity for intelligence-led policing (Walsh & O'Connor 2019). Monitoring social media using Machine Learning or Artificial Intelligence to find key words or expressions is a common tool of both the corporate and law-enforcement sectors. The Commissioner for Law Enforcement Data Security in its report on social media and law enforcement stated the Victorian Police State Intelligence Division is using social network analysis software to analyse friendship networks to ascertain any possible criminal associations. It also aims in the future to develop capabilities to measure the strengths of relationships and public sentiment (Commissioner for Law Enforcement Data Security 2013). There appears to be little to no legislation protecting the privacy of individuals posting content online that may in turn be used as intelligence for law enforcement; however, it could be argued that individuals who post content in the public domain have provided their (implied) consent. The technology has already enabled the collection of data from social media. The technologies being adopted are outpacing ethical debate or privacy concerns. The slow pace of legislative change places the emphasis back with individual agencies and the law-enforcement community to effectively police themselves in regards to privacy and ethics. However, in the thirst for information and knowledge, it's unknown how effective self-regulation will be, or if internal policy and procedures will ever be congruent with public sentiment.

CONCLUSION

Criminal intelligence in Australian law enforcement has undergone a number of substantial changes over the past decade. An increased acceptance of intelligence within police forces, an increased focus on professionalizing intelligence as a discipline, and broad agreement across jurisdictions and agencies of the need to better integrate and share intelligence has contributed to rapid change. Despite this, there are still challenges. Cultural reforms are underway in many police forces. There continue to be cultural differences between intelligence units and investigators,. This is in large part due to intelligence being largely made up of civilian staff who may not have an operational policing background. Technological development continues to outpace legislative change, increasing the risk that police and intelligence will operate in an ethical and legal "grey area". This is especially the case with social media. There has already been a significant uptake and reliance on the collection of social media intelligence to understand and map criminal networks or understand public sentiment. While legislative change has not kept pace, police and intelligence are reliant on their own judgement of what is and what is not acceptable within their own ethical framework.

There has been significant change in regards to the use of both operational and strategic intelligence. The increased quantities of data have led to the establishment of multidisciplinary teams, and the return to human intelligence as a primary source of information has changed the dynamic between analysts and covert policing units. The changes have required closer collaboration and understanding of function between analysis and covert policing units. Strategic intelligence continues to grapple with its role and place in law enforcement. It continues to strive for acceptance as an operational enabler, not just for senior decision makers but for community police and investigators as well. However, progress continues to be made, especially in regards to the opportunity for short, succinct strategic products to inform and influence government and policy development, which is no different from counterparts in the national security space.

The changes taking place in criminal intelligence in Australia reflect an awareness and desire on behalf of law enforcement to embrace the possibilities that intelligence can offer in preventing and solving crime. Enhanced and uniformed training of intelligence professionals will not only standardize products and customer expectations but will increase criminal intelligence's standing in law enforcement. The reorientating of intelligence within law enforcement and the professionalization of the field means criminal intelligence will no longer be the "poor cousin" of police investigative practices.

REFERENCES

ACT Corrective Services (2018). *Corrections Management (Intelligence Framework) Policy*. Retrieved from www.legislation.act.gov.au

Australian Criminal Intelligence Commission (ACIC) (2017). *Australian Criminal Intelligence Management Strategy 2017–20*. Retrieved from www.afp.gov.au/sites/default/files/PDF/ACIM-strategy-2017-20.pdf

Australian Criminal Intelligence Commission (2018a). *Criminal Intelligence Systems and Databases, ACIC Annual Report 2016–2017*. Retrieved from www.acic.gov.au/criminal-intelligence-systems-and-databases

Australian Criminal Intelligence Commission (2018b). *Strategic Intelligence, ACIC Annual Report 2017–2018*. Retrieved from www.acic.gov.au/22-strategic-intelligence-0

Australian Criminal Intelligence Commission (2018c). *Strategic Plan 2018–23*. Retrieved from www.acic.gov.au/sites/default/files/2018/07/australian_criminal_intelligence_commission_strategic_plan_2018-23.pdf?v=1564628108

Australian Criminal Intelligence Commission (2018d). *Criminal Intelligence Systems and Databases, ACIC Annual Report 2016–2017*. Retrieved from www.acic.gov.au/criminal-intelligence-systems-and-databases

Australian Criminal Intelligence Commission (2019a). *National Police Reference System*. Retrieved from www.acic.gov.au/our-services/national-police-reference-system

Australian Criminal Intelligence Commission (2019b). *National Wastewater Drug Monitoring Program*. Retrieved from https://www.acic.gov.au/sites/default/files/national_wastewater_drug_monitoring_program_report_8_2019_pdf.pdf?v=1571983781

Branch, P. (2014). Surveillance by Metadata. *Issues, 109*, 10–13. Retrieved from www.issuesmagazine.com.au/article/issue-december-2014/surveillance-metadata.html

Commissioner for Law Enforcement Data Security (2013). *Social Media and Law Enforcement Report, Victorian Government*. Retrieved from www.parliament.vic.gov.au/file_uploads/Commissioner_for_Law_Enforcement_and_Data_Security_Report_2013-14__0fDYsRCs.pdf

Cope, N. (2004). Intelligence Led Policing or Policing Led Intelligence? *The British Journal of Criminology, 44*(2), 188–203.

Coyne, J. W., & Bell, P. (2011). Strategic Intelligence in Law Enforcement: A Review. *Journal of Policing, Intelligence and Counter Terrorism, 6*(1), 23–39.

Harrison, M., Walsh, P. F., Lysons-Smith, S., Truong, D., Horan, C., & Jabbour, R. (2018). Tradecraft to Standards: Moving Criminal Intelligence Practice to a Profession Through the Development of a Criminal Intelligence Training and Development Continuum. *Policing (Oxford): A Journal of Policy and Practice*, 1–13.

Hendry, J. (2019). National Real-Time Intelligence System Quietly Gets Another $59m. *IT News*, January 19. Retrieved from www.itnews.com.au/news/national-real-time-intelligence-system-quietly-gets-another-59m-517833

John, T., & Maguire, M. (2006). *The National Intelligence Model: Key Lessons from Early Research*. Retrieved from www.researchgate.net/publication/242484328_

Prunckun, H. (2019). *Methods of Inquiry for Intelligence Analysis*, 3rd ed. New York, Rowman & Littlefield.

Queensland Corrective Services (2016). *Corrections News*. Retrieved from https://corrections.qld.gov.au/wp-content/uploads/2018/07/Corrections-News-August-2016.pdf

Ransley, J., & Mazerolle, L. (2009). Policing in an Era of Uncertainty. *Police Practice and Research: An International Journal, 10*(4), 365–381.

Ratcliffe, J. (2003). *Intelligence-Led Policing Trends & Issues in Crime and Criminal Justice, Australian Institute of Criminology*. Retrieved from https://aic.gov.au/publications/tandi/tandi248

Ratcliffe, J. (Ed.). (2009). *Strategic Thinking in Criminal Intelligence*. Sydney, Sydney Federation Press.

Ratcliffe, J. (2014). *Intelligence Led Policing*. New York, Routledge.

Tilley, N. (2008). Modern Approaches to Policing: Community, Problem-Oriented and Intelligence-Led. In *Handbook of Policing*, ed. N. Tim, 2nd ed. London, Routledge.

Ure, J. (2005). Preventing Crime Through Intelligence-Led Policing: Are We There Yet? *Journal of the Australian Institute of Professional Intelligence Officers*, 14(1), 27–44 [online].

United Nations (2016). *Handbook on Dynamic Security and Prison Intelligence*. Retrieved from www.unodc.org/documents/justice-and-prison-reform/UNODC_Handbook_on_Dynamic_Security_and_Prison_Intelligence.pdf

Walsh, J., & O'Connor, C. (2019). Social Media and Policing: A Review of Recent Research. *Sociology Compass*, 13(1), e12648.

Walsh, P. F. (2011). *Intelligence and Intelligence Analysis*. London, Routledge.

CHAPTER 9

Investigative interviewing and police practice

Daren Jay and Gary Pankhurst

INTRODUCTION

In the 1990s, Investigative Interviewing was adopted as a specialisation by law-enforcement agencies in Australia that imported theory and practice from several international jurisdictions. Whilst agencies continue to administer basic and intermediate level trainings to police officers, not all agencies engage in advanced interviewing and interview management training initiatives common in overseas jurisdictions (Norway, United Kingdom, Canada). Observations from tertiary education environments and recent operational evidence indicate that interviewing practice across the diverse policing landscape of Australia may be suffering some level of deterioration; with variations to best practice emerging, particularly around the structure and planning of interviews. This chapter will examine the investigative interviewing context here in Australia and seek to draw on the operational and training experience of the authors to offer academics and practitioners a clarity of understanding in respect of the "Free Recall" (FR) and "Conversation Management" (CM) frameworks used for witness and suspect interviews. The chapter will then look briefly to the future and consider whether technological advances, particularly around eLearning content and scalable online training, may represent an opportunity to address some of the key issues impacting investigative interviewing in Australia.

BACKGROUND TO INVESTIGATIVE INTERVIEWING IN AUSTRALIA

Criminal justice processes in Australia are rooted in the tradition of English common law, and there remain many similarities within both countries given their historic ties (Findlay, Odgers, & Yeo, 2009). Common law justice systems operate an adversarial trial process where partial lawyers present opposing arguments before a legal decision-maker. A guiding principle of Australian Law is procedural fairness. Legal protections afforded to a person accused of a crime during an investigation are of the utmost importance, including the principles of the presumption of innocence and the right not to self-incriminate. The role of police investigators is to act lawfully and impartially in pursuing evidence. A crucial procedure within any investigation is the interviewing of relevant parties. Criticisms of police interview practice have acted as a research catalyst and driven reform in many countries. As we shall see, the rate of progressive change in interviewing in Australia is a mixed picture.

Australian policing has continued to develop interview practices over the last decade, although the speed and structure of reforms vary between jurisdictions (Adam & van Golde, 2020). There has been pressure to reform on some agencies due to miscarriages of justice. However, there is also a motivation to seek out best practice from the experience of other countries. Increasingly, Australian jurisdictions are adopting the investigative interviewing framework, known as the "PEACE" model, developed and used throughout England and Wales. Historically, police officers learnt by shadowing their experienced colleagues, since no formal interview training was available (Moston & Engelberg, 1993; Norfolk, 1997). Interviewers were considered to be effective if they could obtain a confession. Officers often used psychological manipulation, including social persuasion and coercion to secure a confession from the interviewee (Blair, 2005), (Kassin & Gudjonsson, 2004). This could be termed Investigative Interviewing 1.0 and had remained unchanged for many decades. Such techniques have received considerable scrutiny and criticism from both the courts and academics (ibid; Leo, 2008). The use of such coercive and manipulative techniques has been shown capable of eliciting false confessions (Gudjonsson, 2003), (Kassin, 1997). An accusatory, confession-seeking interview is unlikely to be compatible with the principle of procedural fairness and has been shown to be less effective at gathering information.

This was a conclusion reached in the UK when fundamental reforms followed from prominent miscarriages of justice involving confession and interview evidence issues. This included the audio recording of all interviews with suspects, previously a contemporaneous written record. This development contributed to a transparent, accurate, and ethical approach to investigative interviewing and allowed researchers access to the interview process. (Baldwin, 1992) described the continued importance police placed on the suspect interview and how seeking a confession was still regarded as highly significant. A further major development was the national introduction of interview training. It marked a transition away from confession-focused interview objectives to questioning to elicit accurate and comprehensive accounts generating information (Clarke, Milne, & Bull, 2011). The PEACE acronym represents a five-stage interview structure; **P**lanning and preparation, **E**ngage and explain, **A**ccount, **C**losure and **E**valuation. Supporting the interviewer to obtain and verify the accuracy of the interviewee's account, identify and test lines of enquiry and clarify and confirm the account details. This was rolled out in a national training programme in the 1990s. The measures of legislative guidance, recording of interviews and a simple, trained framework have proven effective in reducing misconduct within the interview process. Significant improvements in interviewing skills and knowledge resulted after training in the PEACE model, given that this was the first formal training (McGurk, Carr, & McGurk, 1993). Investigative Interviewing 2.0 had been launched. Clarke, Milne, and Bull (2011) observed that although the skills had improved since the implementation of PEACE, more complex social and communication skills remained elusive and difficult to maintain post-training. Variations on the PEACE framework of investigative interviewing have been adopted in many developed countries, including some jurisdictions, such as Queensland and NSW, within Australia.

CURRENT ISSUES IN AUSTRALIA

With a diverse population of approximately 25 million across 7.6 million sq. km, Australia represents a dynamic and complex jurisdiction that comprises the six state police agencies (New South Wales Police Force, Northern Territory Police, Queensland Police, South Australia Police, Tasmania Police, and Victoria Police); two territories (Northern Territories Police and Australian Capital Territory), the Australian Federal Police and Australian Border Force. Each jurisdiction faces unique challenges, from big city areas to the bush, with the operational demands of vast distances, harsh environments, and variations in local infrastructure and approach at a local and state level.

This lack of standardisation is concerning when considering the fundamental task of interviewing. Australia lacks a cohesive and national approach to the training and conducting of investigative interviews. By comparison, in the UK, each agency appoints an Investigative Interviewing Force Champion who reports to a National Interview Advisor (National Crime Agency). A national strategic steering group chaired by a Senior Officer has oversight responsibility for the national programme. Academics and practitioners from across the criminal justice system sit on the National Steering Committee. This structure ensures that research developments, best practice, emerging issues, and improvement opportunities are identified. Information can be disseminated rapidly between areas that forms an interviewing ecosystem of development, management, and supervision.

Since the introduction of Investigative Interviewing into Australia, research involving police agencies has been held back by what Moston refers to as a "deep-seated mistrust (in both directions) between academics and police officers" (Moston, 2009). This reflects the experience of other countries and the importance of embedding a culture of mutual respect between practitioner and academic leading to research driven, evidence-based practice. This culture is developed by visible and clear organisational support. The need for development and reform in interviewing was underlined by a review of Investigative Interviewing in Australia (Green, 2012) that highlights a number of high-profile cases which have received widespread media attention where significant shortfalls in investigative interviewing standards were identified (Haneef, 2007; Mallard, 1994; Evans, 2009).

The Supreme Court of Queensland overturned a conviction for child sexual offences on the basis of leading and inappropriate questioning in eliciting the 15-year-old complainant's account (*R v Lawton*, 2010).

Gene Gibson had his 2014 manslaughter conviction quashed by the Western Australia Supreme Court of Appeal on the basis that at the time of his police interviews he had not been afforded an interpreter. His capacity to understand English was further undermined through his status as a vulnerable individual possessed of "significant and pervasive" cognitive impairments (*R v Gibson*, 2017; Tulich, Blagg, & Hill-De Monchaux, 2017).

The Supreme Court of Queensland ruled at a pretrial hearing that a suspect's interview record should be excluded on the grounds that questioning of an 18-year-old murder suspect had continued in absence of legal advice despite the suspect asking to be granted access to a lawyer. The ruling highlighted that police conduct had been "deliberate and was a flagrant disregard of the [suspect's] rights" (*R v Bennetts*, 2017).

Most recently, in April 2020, a former Senior Detective in NSW was convicted and fined $10,000 for having illegally recorded four investigative interviews with a person of interest in a high-profile homicide inquiry (Mitchell, 2020). The case in question concerned the disappearance of 3-year-old William Tyrrell in 2014, which in May 2020 remains unsolved.

Whilst the William Tyrrell case remains an investigation of national significance, it is argued that each of the cases highlighted concern procedural breaches of investigative interviewing standards, policies, and in some cases, law. This can arise from a task-focused approach by investigators acting in pursuance of their role, that is, acting to get what they need to prove or disprove a case, secure a criminal charge, and potentially put an offender before the courts. It is difficult to determine whether the individuals involved were guilty of deliberate malfeasance or made mistakes through poor understanding or training. It is clear that issues are not only at the strategic level but also in the behaviour and decisions made by individuals.

From an international perspective, history teaches us that in high-stakes investigations, pressure to resolve an investigation can force investigators to lose objectivity and suffer confirmation or investigative bias. This task-focused approach has the potential to impact decision-making and thus thwart the open-mindedness of investigative teams, leading to errors and potential miscarriages of justice.

THE INTERVIEWEE-CENTERED APPROACH

The absence of research into investigative interviewing in Australia makes it difficult to draw conclusions about whether issues may be caused by individual malpractice or whether they are indicative of wider issues of interview training, supervision, and management at an operational level. What can be ascertained, however, is that such deviations from best practice can all be mapped back to a task-focused approach to interviewing and an absence of an interviewee-focused mindset and approach.

A key skill within investigative interviewing is the building and maintenance of rapport, associated with increased accuracy of information provided by adult witnesses (Kieckhaefer, Vallano, & Compo, 2013) and increased trust and cooperation (Abbe & Brandon, 2013). The significance of rapport has been seen in its inclusion within several interviewing protocols, including the PEACE model (UK), KREATIVE (Norway), and the National Institute of Child Health and Human Development (NICHD) (US). Procedural fairness within interviewing is achieved through openness, transparency, and impartiality, key behaviours for establishing trust and rapport.

Current planning methodologies, where planning does occur, seem to be task-focused on accounts, required evidence, and points to prove or "proofs". This approach can be refocused to an interviewee-centric approach, as in therapeutic settings as part of a "working alliance". The working alliance is formed when there is an alignment between interviewee cooperation and interviewer intent. The working alliance has been mapped and evidenced to successful outcomes, achieved through focus and agreement on three key elements: the agreement on goals, the assignment of tasks, and the development of bonds (Bordin, 1979).

Whilst rapport is widely understood to be an essential ingredient in investigative interviews, it is considered that an interviewee-centric approach to planning interviews, in a similar way to counselling sessions in a therapeutic practice, may have application within the forensic context. If the interviewer can build rapport and trust into the interview as a main theme, and plan to do so even from the planning stage at the outset, the interview will more closely align with the PEACE model framework.

Free Recall (FR) is used as an information gathering approach within the PEACE model framework because it remains an effective method in terms of memory performance. The FR model reduces suggestibility issues during the retrieval process and minimises the number of direct questions required, instead drawing on the narrative responses from the interviewee, without contamination and suggestion.

Similarly, the Conversation Management (CM) framework provides a structure for the interview in which the interviewee has opportunities to provide a full account uninterrupted and the interviewer can properly explore all alternative hypotheses prior to presenting evidence. An interviewer may robustly challenge discrepancies in an interviewee's account, but without breaching the trust developed between the interviewer and the interviewee. The CM framework facilitates what is known as the Strategic Use of Evidence (SUE), enabling interviewee accounts to be challenged, where required, professionally and respectfully, in a way which does not leave the interviewee aggrieved or unheard.

Significantly, both the FR model and the CM framework are structures that offer interviewers a form of cognitive governance support, which should limit the potential for interviewers to succumb to confirmation bias; the natural propensity to seek out and interpret evidence, intelligence, or information to align with preformed beliefs, expectations, or hypotheses (Nickerson, 1998).

THE INTERVIEW MODELS – AN INTRODUCTION

Taking a closer look at the FR model and the CM framework, each can be used to structure conversations with all types of interviewees, including witnesses and suspects or "persons of interest". Before looking at each in depth, we will first introduce the concepts of FR and CM, consider their relationship as interchangeable models, and examine how each can be applied.

The term "Free Recall" refers to an interviewing model designed to enable a cooperative interviewer to secure an accurate and reliable account from an interviewee who may have witnessed an episodic event. The model promotes the opportunity for an interviewee to explain their recollection of an event without influence from an interviewer and is derived from the PEACE model Cognitive Interview (PEACE CI) (see Dando, Wilcock, & Milne, 2008 for an explanation of PEACE CI). FR is distilled from the PEACE CI, but deficient of reverse recall and change perspective instructions which have been found to be cumbersome to use operationally (Fisher & Geiselman, 2019). The event of investigative focus might become the subject of a full interview, or it could relate to just one topic, forming part of a broader conversation. The FR model discussed herein is set out in such a way as to give practitioners a clarity of understanding of how the components of FR can be assembled and practically applied.

The theory behind FR is drawn from memory research that indicates that it can be useful for an interviewee to recreate the context that existed at the time of the event to be remembered (Tulving & Thomson, 1973). Once context reinstatement has occurred, the interviewee can be encouraged to mentally "relive" the incident and report detail while "watching" and "listening" to the event unfold again in their "mind's eye". Research indicates context reinstatement is a powerful memory recall tool, capable of increasing the amount of information retrieved by up to 47% (Fisher, Geiselman, & Amador, 1989).

The following graphic (see Figure 9.1) seeks to demonstrate the component stages to Free Recall.

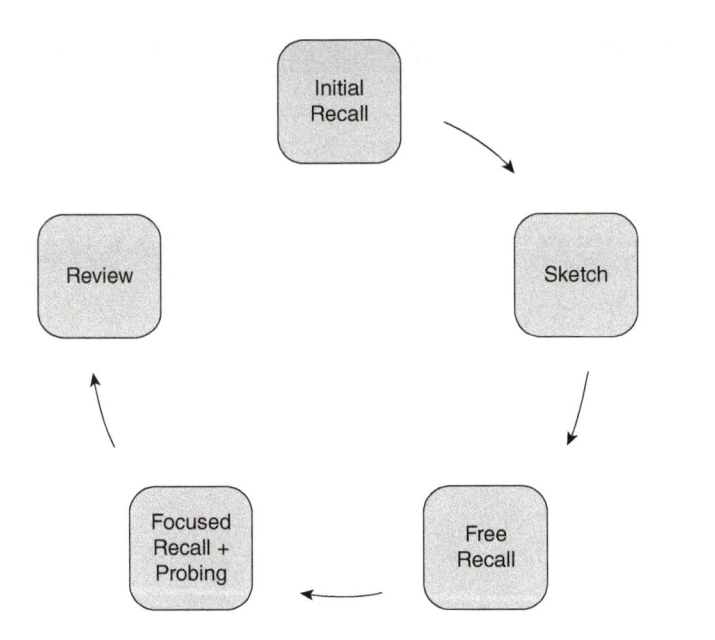

FIGURE 9.1
Free Recall Model

We will come back to examine each of the components of "Initial Recall", "Sketch", "Free Recall", "Focused Recall + Probing", and "Review". For now, we highlight only that the model can be used to navigate an account provided by a witness to an episodic event.

The CM framework represents a three-phased approach to an investigative interview with an interviewee who may be more resistant (Milne, Griffiths, Clarke, & Dando, 2019). The CM framework discussed here comprises three phases or "Agendas", known as the "Interviewee Agenda", the "Investigative Agenda", and the "Compare and Contrast Agenda". The framework is based upon the research-accepted practice of "Account and Clarification"; comprising obtaining an interviewee's account before clarifying and challenging, if required. (See Griffiths & Milne, 2006 for broader discussion on the framework.)

The following graphic (see Figure 9.2) offers a visual representation of the CM framework.

Topics in Figure 9.2 are numbered to indicate the progressive flow of conversation through the framework. We should consider, however, that during an interview, both FR and CM may be used depending on the topic of discussion and interviewee's level of cooperation. Each Agenda may comprise a greater number of topic areas than depicted here for explanatory purposes.

FREE RECALL

The FR model is designed to elicit a comprehensive narrative account of an event or incident and aligns with research theory on memory and recall. Cognitive interviewing incorporates the use of free recall

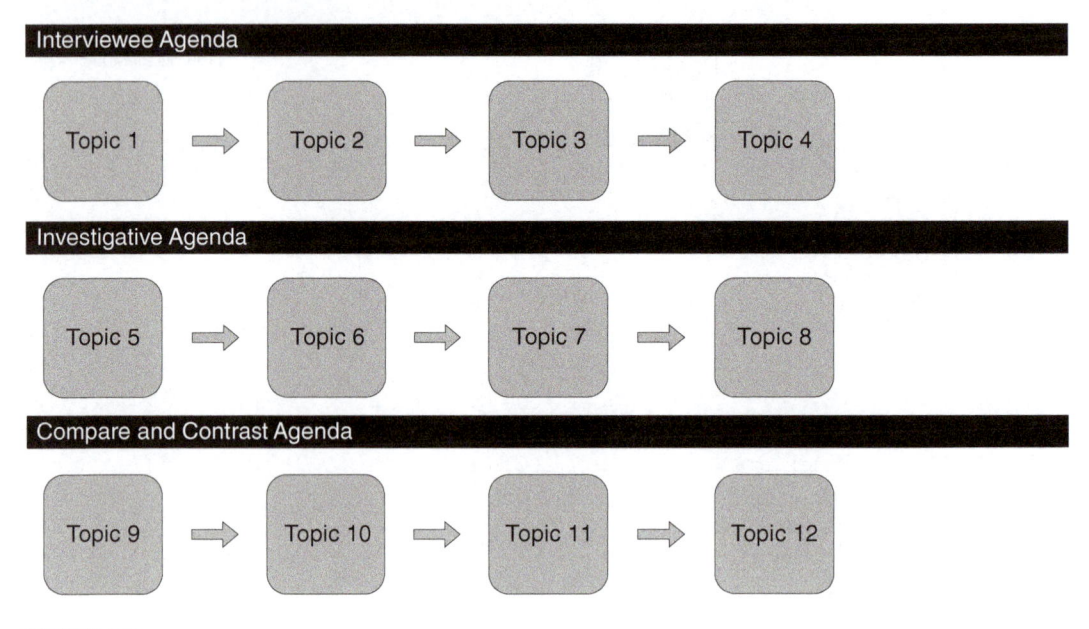

FIGURE 9.2
Conversation Management Framework

to facilitate memory and obtain a full and accurate account from an interview.

When conducting an interview, having established rapport and explained the nature and purpose of the interview, there comes a point when the interviewer needs to initiate conversation about the actual incident. The FR model commences with an Initial Recall which should be triggered by a carefully worded explicit instruction, such as, "Tell me what you can about what you witnessed this morning". The resultant account may see the interviewee providing a summary of what occurred, relying upon only three to four sentences to do so. Upon receipt of the initial recall, and once satisfied the response is relevant and of investigative interest, the interviewer should set about asking open questions designed to learn only about the interviewee's immediate context at the time the event occurred. Specific details, such as the date, time, and place of the incident and the interviewee's exact location should be covered. Additional situational details specific to the interviewee at the time of the event (what they were doing, how they were feeling, what they were thinking, etc.) can also be covered. The objective is to secure a variety of self-generated cues from the interviewee, which the interviewer can deploy to help facilitate further recall.

Having secured the initial recall and self-generated memory cues, the interviewer should then invite the interviewee to compile a Sketch Plan of the place that the event or incident occurred. The sketch should be drawn by the interviewee, and they should be licensed to draw or annotate the sketch with any information they deem relevant. The reasons for the introduction of the sketch plan and its timing are twofold. First, the sketch plan serves to facilitate communication between the interviewee and the interviewer, allowing the locus of control to pass to the interviewee. Second, the sketch plan will assist the interviewee to recreate the event or incident in their mind. Crucially, these self-generated cues are less likely to contain confabulation (Dando, Wilcock, & Milne, 2009). Interviewee will often offer a commentary while drawing the sketch to aid understanding.

To this point, interviewees have provided partial accounts when asked to recall the event, however, for the full free recall, the interviewer invites a comprehensive narrative of the incident by encouraging the interviewee to fully "relive" the event from start to finish, without interruption. To initiate such a narrative, the interviewer will provide the interviewee with clear instructions about the purpose of the account and the level of detail needed. The use of a model statement as part of the instructions, in which the interviewer provides an example of a short narrative containing detailed information about a neutral topic, should be delivered. The model statement has been proven to enhance the yield of accurate and reliable information provided by an interviewee, who becomes aware of how much detail is required (Vrij, Hope, & Fisher, 2014). The interviewer should explain that this free recall of the event(s) will require a high level of concentration and provide the interviewee with any ground rules deemed relevant (report everything; don't guess; take your time). Immediately before commencing the free recall narrative, the interviewer might choose to repeat any instructions, especially to mentally relive the event as if it were happening now and may include specific instructions such as, "Take your time. . ., in as much detail as you can. . ., can you tell me what happened?". The interviewer may support any resultant free-flowing commentary with silence and active listening until the narrative report is exhausted.

The next stage of the model involves moving into a period of Focused Recall and Probing whilst the interviewee is still considering, and indeed reliving, the event(s) in question. During this stage, the interviewer can systematically move the interviewee's focus through various topics of interest within the account. The interviewer may make use of open questions, then closed probing questions, eliciting further information and fine-grained detail from the interviewee. If possible, the interviewer can make efforts to leave the interviewee "in context", allowing the interviewee to retrieve and report information from their "mind's eye", as though still back at the scene.

Once the interviewer has developed a narrative and obtained sufficient detail, the final stage of Review may be administered. This will involve the interviewer making a summary of the salient points of the interview so that the interviewee may edit, accept, or clarify information provided. The Review will also aid the interviewer in checking their understanding of what the interviewee has said. Post-review, the interviewer can now determine whether or not it is necessary to compile a written statement.

The critical point to note in respect of FR is that the model is a guide. Operationally, it will not always be possible to apply each phase of the model due to time constraints or other pressures. In such cases, the interviewer is free to use the model in "lite-mode" to secure the best account possible in the circumstances. Arriving at a crime scene where a suspect has recently fled, FR may just involve the "interviewer" asking a couple of open questions regarding a potential suspect's description. The ethos of FR involves securing as much information as possible, through the fewest number of questions. By investing in rapport, providing clear instructions, and obtaining self-generated memory cues, the FR model represents an effective and efficient way to secure accurate and reliable information from an interviewee. The use of open questions in search of narrative responses also serves to reduce the risks associated with contamination of the interviewee's account through the careless use of poorly framed questions.

CONVERSATION MANAGEMENT

The CM framework offers investigators a structure within which to plan and conduct investigative interviews with all interviewees but particularly with those interviewees who may be inclined to limit their cooperation in an investigation or provide false or misleading information in response to questioning.

The CM framework planning methodology delivers an interview plan which is strategically fit for purpose and facilitates SUE (Granhag & Hartwig, 2015). Before examining the three Agendas which form the CM framework, there are three underpinning principles to consider. First, an interviewee should be allowed to provide their uninterrupted response to questions regarding their involvement (or otherwise) in any matter under investigation through the use of open questions. The use of open questions serves to control information which may be inadvertently passed to the interviewee (Mosser & Evans, 2019) which could contaminate or confuse the interviewee's account. Best practice requires that an interviewer should invite the interviewee to provide their response in full before the investigator pursues their questioning Agenda.

The second theoretical principle tells us that by introducing evidence that tends to indicate guilt or some level of involvement, an interviewee may adapt their version to suit the evidence which is disclosed. To avoid the strength of inculpatory evidence being undermined in this way, the interviewee should be given every opportunity to raise relevant defences, *before* being made aware of the weight of evidence (see Hartwig, Granhag, Strömwall, & Kronkvist, 2006 for a comprehensive review of SUE methodologies). The critical point of such an exploration of potential defences is that it should be undertaken without disclosing to the interviewee that the evidence exists. By way of example, before introducing the fact that a fingerprint matching the suspect had been recovered from within a burglary victim's home, the investigator would explore potential defences related to the existence of that evidence, without disclosing to the interviewee that the fingerprint was available. Questions such as, "Can you tell me about any occasions on which you have been to that property?" or "Can you tell me about the people who live at that house?" would be designed to prompt an innocent explanation from an interviewee, which might reasonably account for the existence of the inculpatory evidence.

The third principle underpinning CM requires that challenges to an interviewee's account should be left until the end of the interview. Delaying challenges allows an interviewer to maintain rapport with an interviewee for as long as possible, reducing the risk of a loss of information caused by a "no comment" reply in response to a challenge.

The first stage of the CM framework is the Interviewee Agenda where the interviewee is invited to provide their account. This is an opportunity for the interviewee to provide their version or account. In the second phase of the interview, we have the Investigative Agenda; this is where the interviewer should cover investigative topics of interest, including any topics not raised by the interviewee in the Interviewee Agenda. In the Investigative Agenda, a key focus should be placed on exploring potential defences to inculpatory evidence. The final phase of the interview is the Compare and Contrast Agenda; where the interviewer will potentially challenge aspects of an interviewee's account through a process of compare and contrast. If no anomalies exist at the end of the Investigative Agenda, that is, potential defences have been explored for each piece of inculpatory evidence, and the evidence is adequately accounted for, the Compare and Contrast Agenda is rendered redundant.

CONVERSATION MANAGEMENT – PLANNING FOR THE INTERVIEW

In planning for a CM interview, it can be useful to adopt a "reverse-engineering" methodology to think about what will be discussed, when, and how. While a questioning strategy will need consideration, planning should be restricted to a macro-level (structure, topics, strategy) as opposed to drawing up an exhaustive list of questions.

For ease of reference, Figure 9.3 sets out a series of numbered topics, which will be referred to here to explain the "reverse-engineering" planning methodology.

For the purposes of this explanation, we will examine an investigative interview where there are four outstanding pieces of inculpatory evidence which tend to indicate the interviewee may be responsible for, or otherwise involved in, the matter under investigation.

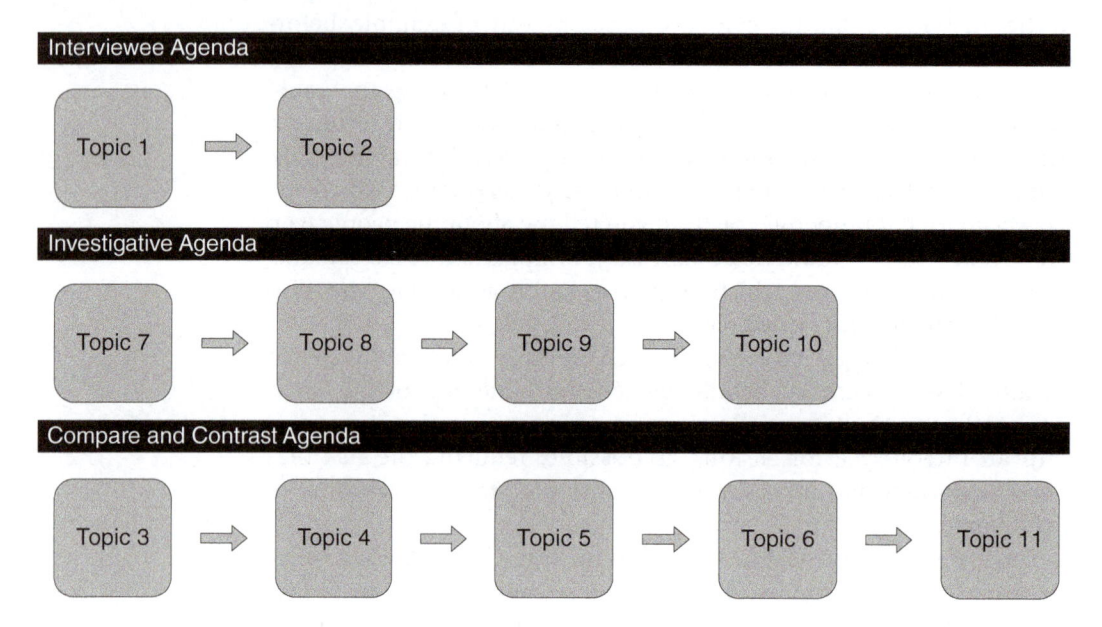

FIGURE 9.3
Conversation Management Planning Methodology

The planning regime commences with Topic 1, which should contain all topic areas designed to Engage and Explain (see Scott, Tudor-Owen, Pedretti, & Bull 2014 for a discussion on Engage and Explain and its phase within the broader PEACE model framework). Areas to cover at the Engage and Explain stage may involve setting out introductions, roles, responsibilities, cautions, warnings, and ground rules, each delivered in a manner conducive with rapport-building. Each of these areas should be set out in advance, enabling the interviewer to ensure the interviewee develops a clear understanding of their rights and the purpose of the interview, removing anxiety from the outset.

The next planning task (Topic 2) should involve the interviewer setting an open question or explicit instruction designed to trigger the interviewee's account. The interviewer should be direct here; "Tell me about your involvement in those matters?" In anticipation of a denial or refusal to respond, a supplementary question should be prepared, for example, "Okay. If it wasn't you, tell me more about your movements between 9.00 pm last night and 6.30 am this morning?" We can anticipate potential responses as part of our broader interview plan, but it may not be possible to plan any further in respect of the topics the interviewee may raise in response.

Aside from considering the content of any significant statements made by the interviewee prior to the interview, planning for the remainder of the interviewee agenda may be difficult. As a result, flexibility of the interviewer in managing the unfolding interviewee agenda in real time will be paramount.

Back to our remaining planning methodology, the natural step might be to step down to the Investigative Agenda and begin planning the topics of discussion we may wish to raise once the Interviewee's Agenda has been probed. Instead, it is recommended the next stage of planning to be addressed is the Compare and Contrast Agenda. The reason for doing so is that the Investigative Agenda will, in the main, be "reverse-engineered" from the Compare and Contrast Agenda.

Planning for the Compare and Contrast Agenda should involve setting out each of the inculpatory pieces of evidence that tend to point to the interviewee's involvement (CCTV, documentary records, forensic evidence, etc.). Each piece of evidence should form a single topic (see Topics 3–6 in Figure 9.3), and the interviewer should understand what the evidence is, and consider, from a factual perspective, what it tends to indicate. For example, the victim's DNA inside the suspect's vehicle might indicate (1) the victim or something related to the victim has been in the vehicle; (2) the suspect (or some other person) has had contact with the victim, or something related to the victim and accessed into, or traveled in, the vehicle at some point. After setting out the inculpatory evidence topics, the interviewer can think carefully about the topic order and how each topic will be introduced, having regard to both strategic and tactical opportunities that may be available.

Planning for the Investigative Agenda, the interviewer is now in a position to use each topic within the Compare and Contrast Agenda to "reverse-engineer" corresponding topics within the Investigative Agenda. If we use the example of CCTV (being Topic 3, see Figure 9.3), which places the interviewee at the crime scene, a related topic to be covered in the Investigative Agenda might be positioned at Topic 7 (see Figure 9.3), with an objective to explore potential defences to the interviewee being at the relevant place at the material time. At Topic 7, without making any reference to the existence of the CCTV, the interviewer might ask a series of questions designed to explore potential defences which the interviewee could rely upon when later told of the existence of the CCTV. Could the interviewee have been at that place at that time for any reason? When was the last time the interviewee was actually at that place? Can the interviewee confirm, "to the negative", that they did not go there that day? Can they confirm (again, if necessary) what they were wearing on the day? These questions are designed to explore and potentially close down any opportunity the interviewee may have to construct a fabrication in response to seeing the CCTV and realising they need to account for their presence at the scene. Defences such as, "Yes, that's me, but I wasn't stabbing him – I leaned in to buy drugs, he's my dealer" can hastily be constructed by a creative interviewee. The Investigative Agenda should be used to explore and close down all opportunities for such creativity. To do so requires critical consideration to be given to the inculpatory evidence, and this is achieved with a particular focus on the concept of "think defence". The process in executing the Investigative Agenda in this manner also provides a truth-telling interviewee an opportunity to offer a narrative version which may innocently account for what appeared to be inculpatory evidence.

The final planning activity for the CM framework is to set the strategy for the closure of the interview; in this case, at Topic 11 (see Figure 9.3), a final topic is added representing areas to be considered prior to closing the interview. Such areas could include salient points to be summarised, contact details, next steps, etc. and should be built around an effort to restore rapport levels between the interviewer and interviewee.

EXECUTING THE PLAN

Once the interview has commenced, any topics raised in the Interviewee Agenda can be covered, either in order of significance or in the order by which they were raised by the interviewee. Once the Interviewee Agenda is complete, the interviewer should have developed the interviewee's account, so they have come to understand as much detail as possible about what the interviewee is prepared to volunteer. In the Investigative Agenda, the interviewer should have explored all available potential defences to the inculpatory evidence and also covered all other investigative topics which had not been raised by the interviewee in the Interviewee Agenda. Crucially, by the conclusion of the Investigative Agenda, the status will be that, (1) the interviewer should know everything there is to know about the relevant information the interviewee has been prepared to share; (2) No challenges to the interviewee's account will have been made; thus, rapport should still be intact; (3) The interviewee will have no understanding of the extent, or otherwise, of the evidence against them; and (4) All potential defences to inculpatory evidence will have been explored and thus negated.

The final stage of the CM framework involves dealing with the inculpatory evidence. The relevant fact in issue will be introduced and through a process of compare and contrast, the interviewee will be invited to account for the discrepancy between what they have said and what the evidence tends to indicate.

It should be noted that in relation to FR, any of the topics within the Interviewee Agenda or the Investigative Agenda could technically relate to an episodic event that we might want the interviewee to recount as a free recall narrative. Even an investigation subject may be cooperative enough to engage with a free recall and if the interviewer felt that a full cognitive report of the event would be valuable, a FR approach should be considered. As stated, the CM framework and FR model can be used together; their use will depend on the topic of conversation and the level of cooperation being experienced from the interviewee.

CONCLUSION

Australia is entering an exciting period in which there may be a requirement, and indeed an opportunity, to reconfigure investigative interviewing training and practice for the future. The complexities of the policing landscape in Australia are evidently posing many challenges for investigative interviewing in the region. The remoteness of investigation teams who are required to operate autonomously and conduct increasingly complex investigations offers an opportunity to reengineer the manner in which investigative interviewing is trained and also the way that operational practice is conducted.

The FR model and CM framework presented within this chapter give trainers and practitioners a way to standardise the training methodology and operational application of the interview methodologies. It is recognised that an extensive amount of underlying theory relates to FR and CM, yet the simplistic way in which each is introduced and explained here may be replicable and result in a consistency of training and operational practice being achieved. Each of the frameworks has the potential to ring-fence interviewers more robustly into an interviewee-centric approach to interviewing. The standardisation of each approach has already enabled academics and private practice to develop scalable online investigative interviewing training resources and interview management software, heralding an era in which a digital, Investigative Interviewing 3.0 is now a reality.

REFERENCES

Abbe, A., & Brandon, S. E. (2013). Building and maintaining rapport in investigative interviews. *Police Practice and Research*, *15*(3), 207–220. https://doi.org/10.1080/15614263.2013.827835.

Adam, L., & van Golde, C. (2020). Police practice and false confessions: A search for the implementation of investigative interviewing in Australia. *Alternative Law Journal*, *45*(1), 52–59. https://doi.org/10.1177/1037969X19874415.

Baldwin, J. (1992). *Video taping police interviews with suspects: An evaluation*. London: Home Office.

Blair, J. P. (2005). What do we know about interrogation in the United States? *Journal of Police and Criminal Psychology*, *20*(2), 44–57. https://doi.org/10.1007/bf02852652

Bordin, E. S. (1979). The generalizability of the psychoanalytic concept of the working alliance. *Psychotherapy: Theory, Research & Practice*, *16*(3), 252–260. https://doi.org/10.1037/h0085885

Clarke, C., Milne, R., & Bull, R. (2011). Interviewing suspects of crime: The impact of PEACE training, supervision and the presence of a legal advisor. *Journal of Investigative Psychology and Offender Profiling*, *8*(2), 149–162. https://doi.org/10.1002/jip.144

Dando, C., Wilcock, R., & Milne, R. (2008). The cognitive interview: Inexperienced police officers' perceptions of their witness/victim interviewing practices. *Legal and Criminological Psychology*, *13*(1), 59–70. https://doi.org/10.1348/135532506x162498

Dando, C., Wilcock, R., & Milne, R. (2009). The cognitive interview: The efficacy of a modified mental reinstatement of context procedure for frontline police investigators. *Applied Cognitive Psychology*, *23*(1), 138–147. https://doi.org/10.1002/acp.1451

Findlay, M., Odgers, S., & Yeo, S. (2009). *Australian criminal justice*. Oxford: Oxford University Press.

Fisher, R. P., & Geiselman, R. E. (2019). Expanding the cognitive interview to non-criminal investigations. In J. J. Dickinson, N. S. Compo, R. Carol, B. L. Schwartz, & M. McCauley (Eds.), *Evidence-based investigative interviewing: Applying cognitive principles*. London: Routledge.

Fisher, R. P., Geiselman, R. E., & Amador, M. (1989). Field test of the cognitive interview: Enhancing the recollection of actual victims and witnesses of crime. *Journal of Applied Psychology*, 74(5), 722–727. https://doi.org/10.1037/0021-9010.74.5.722

Granhag, P. A., & Hartwig, M. (2015). The strategic use of evidence (SUE) technique: A conceptual overview. In P. A. Granhag, A. Vrij, & B. Verschuere (Eds.), *Detecting deception: Current challenges and cognitive approaches*. London: Wiley-Blackwell.

Green, T. (2012). The future of investigative interviewing: Lessons for Australia. *Australian Journal of Forensic Sciences*, 44(1), 31–43. https://doi.org/10.1080/00450618.2011.581248

Griffiths, L., & Milne, B. (2006). Will it end in tiers? Police interviews with suspects in Britain. In T. Williamson (Ed.), *Investigative interviewing: Rights, research, regulation* (pp. 167–189). Cullompton: Willan Publishing.

Gudjonsson, G. H. (2003). *The psychology of interrogations and confessions: A handbook*. London: John Wiley & Sons.

Hartwig, M., Granhag, P. A., Strömwall, L. A., & Kronkvist, O. (2006). Strategic use of evidence during police interviews: When training to detect deception works. *Law and Human Behavior*, 30(5), 603–619. https://doi.org/10.1007/s10979-006-9053-9

Kassin, S. M. (1997). The psychology of confession evidence. *American Psychologist*, 52(3), 221–233. https://doi.org/10.1037/0003-066x.52.3.221

Kassin, S. M., & Gudjonsson, G. H. (2004). The psychology of confessions: A review of the literature and issues. *Psychological Science in the Public Interest*, 5(2), 33–67. https://doi.org/10.1111/j.1529-1006.2004.00016.x

Kieckhaefer, J. M., Vallano, J. P., & Schreiber Compo, N. (2013). Examining the positive effects of rapport building: When and why does rapport building benefit adult eyewitness memory? *Memory*, 22(8), 1010–1023. https://doi.org/10.1080/09658211.2013.864313

Leo, R. A. (2008). *Police interrogation and American justice*. Cambridge, MA: Harvard University Press.

McGurk, B. J., Carr, M. J., & McGurk, D. (1993). *Investigative interviewing courses for police officers: An evaluation*. London: Home Office.

Milne, R., Griffiths, A., Clarke, C., & Dando, C. (2019). The cognitive interview. In N. S. J. J. Dickinson (Ed.), *Evidence-based investigative interviewing*. London: Routledge.

Mitchell, G. (2020, April 8). Jubelin convicted and fined $10,000 over illegal recordings during Tyrrell case. *The Sydney Morning Herald*. www.smh.com.au/national/nsw/one-of-their-best-jubelin-praised-ahead-of-sentencing-over-illegal-recordings-20200408-p54i1a.html

Mosser, A. E., & Evans, J. R. (2019). From the police station to the hospital bed: Using the cognitive interview to enhance epidemiologic interviewing. In J. J. Dickinson, N. S. Compo, R. N. Carol, B. L. Schwartz, & M. R. McCauley (Eds.), *Evidence-based investigative interviewing*. London: Routledge.

Moston, S. (2009). Investigative interviewing of suspects in Australia. In T. Williamson, B. Milne, & S. P. Savage (Eds.), *International developments in investigative interviewing*. Cullompton: Willan Publishing.

Moston, S., & Engelberg, T. (1993). Police questioning techniques in tape recorded interviews with criminal suspects. *Policing and Society*, *3*(3), 223–237. https://doi.org/10.1080/10439463.1993.9964670

Nickerson, R. S. (1998). Confirmation bias: A ubiquitous phenomenon in many guises. *Review of General Psychology*, *2*(2), 175–220. https://doi.org/10.1037/1089-2680.2.2.175

Norfolk, G. A. (1997). *Fit to be interviewed by the police*. Harrogate: Association of Police Surgeons.

R v Bennetts (2017) QSPCR 3.

R v Gibson (2017) WASCA 141.

R v Lawton (2010) QCA 353.

Scott, A. J., Tudor-Owen, J., Pedretti, P., & Bull, R. (2014). How intuitive is PEACE? Newly recruited police officers' plans, interviews and self-evaluations. *Psychiatry, Psychology and Law*, *22*(3), 355–367. https://doi.org/10.1080/13218719.2014.949397

Tulich, T., Blagg, H., & Hill-De Monchaux, A. (2017). Miscarriage of justice in Western Australia: The case of Gene Gibson. *Griffith Journal of Law & Human Dignity*, *5*(2), 118–142.

Tulving, E., & Thomson, D. M. (1973). Encoding specificity and retrieval processes in episodic memory. *Psychological Review*, *80*(5), 352–373. https://doi.org/10.1037/h0020071

Vrij, A., Hope, L., & Fisher, R. P. (2014). Eliciting reliable information in investigative interviews. *Policy Insights from the Behavioral and Brain Sciences*, *1*(1), 129–136. https://doi.org/10.1177/2372732214548592

CHAPTER 10

Forensic science in policing

Glenn Porter

INTRODUCTION

Science and mathematics have inarguably shaped our modern world in almost every aspect of our lives. This level of impact has also had significant influences in the way our contemporary justice system operates. Williams (2015) suggests that science has become the dominant form of knowledge which replaced metaphysics, ethics, and political philosophy. The greatest advantage scientific reasoning has over other forms of knowledge is the need for its practitioners to be disinterested in the results and operate objectively (Williams, 2015).

While the concept of science as a source of knowledge has been around since the Ancient Greeks, the term *science* is a relatively new concept. *Science* was previously referred to as *natural philosophy* and from an Aristotelian perspective meant developing knowledge from observing the natural elements of the world or nature itself. Williams (2015) suggests "Today's forensic scientists make great use of the knowledge generated by the last 500 years of investigation undertaken by natural philosophers" (p. 35).

There were two major spikes in the develop of scientific reasoning and understanding natural phenomena, including (1) the Renaissance period (14th–17th century) and (2) the Enlightenment (1685–1815). The Renaissance took civilisation out of the Dark Ages and witnessed tremendous intellectual development in the arts, culture, and natural philosophy, as it relates to science. Great advancements in knowledge were experienced in chemistry, mathematics, physics, anatomy, geography, astronomy, and engineering.

The age of reason or more simply known as the Enlightenment had three distinctive periods. A key precursor for the Enlightenment and advancement of scientific knowledge was Newton's publication titled *Principia Mathematica* (1687) and later *Optiks* (1704). The resulting discoveries and development of science during this period is often referred to as the *scientific revolution*. Experimental science was being developed within a framework called the *scientific method*, in addition to expanding the thinking of science beyond observations of natural phenomenon to include the classification of the natural world by taxonomic descriptions and the understanding of how the human mind functions. How scientific reasoning operates was also an area of interest for philosophers such as Francis Bacon (1561–1626), Robert Boyle (1627–1691), Marquis de Condorcet (1743–1794), John Stuart Mill (1806–1873), and William Whewell (1794–1866). They challenged theories relating to whether science uses deductive or inductive reasoning for sourcing new knowledge (Williams, 2015) and what defines science and its practices.

Today most people likely believe they know what the concept of science is about, despite the philosophical challenges and complexities this topic presents. The term "science" has become popularised in popular culture and in the media. The influence of this notion caught the attention of the media when the popularity of the television drama *CSI* was at its peak. There were suggestions that the influence of such television dramas would impact the decision-makers within the justice system. Characterised by the media as "the CSI effect", further research into its influence has indicated that there is not the effect the media feared (Cole & Porter, 2018).

FORENSIC SCIENCE DIVISIONS AND DISCIPLINES

Forensic science departments became synonymous with law-enforcement agencies not long after their inception in the 19th century. The application of forensic science within law-enforcement agencies varies with each jurisdiction, but broadly speaking there are three separate forensic divisions that reside in different Government agencies and include (1) police agencies, (2) state laboratories, and (3) medical institutions.

There are obvious overlaps of responsibility between jurisdictions, and some law-enforcement agencies have greater laboratory capacity within the chemistry and molecular biology disciplines, while others rely more on the State-operated laboratories outside of policing institutions. Table 10.1 provides an overview of where forensic science divisions are positioned and their disciplines within forensic practice.

The divisions arise from the differences in practical expertise, the cost of staffing and equipping laboratories, and how legislation may affect forensic practice. Forensic science practices within policing are primarily based around crime scene investigation and physical evidence examination. Practitioners are predominantly trained internally or on the job on skills relating directly to their role, and while science qualifications may be common, they are not mandatory nor a requirement in many police forensic functions. Training to a high level of expertise is the central priority within a majority of forensic science disciplines within policing institutions.

TABLE 10.1 Overview of where forensic science divisions are positioned and their disciplines within forensic practice

Forensic division	Forensic discipline
Police	Crime scene investigation
	Physical evidence (shoe mark, physical fits, tyre impressions, toolmarks, vehicle examination etc)
	Fingerprints
	DVI (Disaster Victim Identification)
	Firearm identification
	Forensic photography
	Face identification
	Forensic computing
	DNA identification
	Accident reconstruction
	Bloodstain Pattern Analysis (BPA)
	Shooting reconstruction
	Forensic artists
	Document examination
	Fire investigation
	Hairs and fibre comparison
Laboratory	Chemical analysis
	Drug identification
	Molecular biology (including DNA)
	Biochemistry
	Botany
	Explosive and gunshot residue
	Pathogen identification (e.g. anthrax)
Medical	Pathology specialists (cause and time of death)
	Forensic medical clinicians
	Sexual assault examinations
	DVI (Disaster Victim Identification)
	Forensic anthropology
	Forensic odontology
	Forensic toxicology
	Serology
	Forensic radiology
	Forensic psychiatry
	Forensic entomology
	Grievance counselling

Laboratory-based forensic science largely resides in State-operated laboratories, but several law-enforcement agencies do also provide some limited services, especially in DNA analysis. A science qualification is a necessity for forensic disciplines operating within science laboratories, in addition to specialised training. Laboratory-based scientists are often considered as the hard-science operators within the forensic science domain, and DNA analysis is often referred to, and some would say controversially, as the gold standard within forensic science.

The medical division of forensic science also plays a pivotal role within the justice system. Forensic medicine operates from either separate forensic medicine institutions, pathology institutions aligned with Coroners or departments within public hospitals. They provide a variety of functions and include medically qualified personnel, including specialists and medical science qualified scientists. In lay terms, this difference consists of doctors (medicos) and medical scientists. Medical specialisations include forensic pathology, forensic clinicians, forensic psychiatry, sexual assault specialists, and forensic odontologists (dentistry), while the medical scientists perform examinations such as forensic toxicology, entomology, serology and anthropology, etc.

Medical practitioners are also essential when obtaining what are defined as "intimate" samples from victims or suspects. Legislation like the *Forensic Procedures Act [2000]* requires registered medical practitioners to collect intimate samples including sexual assault examinations. Often these procedures require internal examinations of intimate areas of the body and medical staff are more suited for this type of examination. There is some consideration for nurse practitioners or forensic nurses to conduct this type of procedure, but this varies between jurisdictions.

Forensic psychiatrists are another area of forensic medicine, and their role includes providing expert reports regarding the psychological condition of the accused or the impact traumatic experiences has had on victims. Forensic psychiatrists also provide services within Corrective Services to assist in the rehabilitation and wellbeing of inmates with mental health conditions.

A key principle for all forensic science practices is to examine items, people, or places for the purpose of obtaining evidence or intelligence. Particularly in policing, the role of forensic personnel was mostly a reactionary one, that is, when a criminal incident occurred, forensic staff would respond and investigate. Responding or reacting to an event was the large majority of the forensic science department remit. However, there has been a significant shift in recent times and investigating matters for the purpose of obtaining forensic intelligence has become an equally central responsibility of forensics.

Raymond and Julian (2015) reported on a workshop held with key policing stakeholders in 2011 that addressed the need to develop the level of forensic intelligence to support a paradigm shift in policing practice involving intelligence-led policing. Raymond and Julian (2015) suggested that forensic intelligence is critical support for the strategic shift in policing practice. They define intelligence-led police as "intelligence-led policing in its broader sense is the reduction of crime through suspect targeting, understanding of cause and effect of policing initiatives and the analysis of crime trends" (Raymond & Julian,

2015, p. 373). Their report indicated that forensic science within law-enforcement agencies needed to integrate forensic intelligence operations within their support services and shift from the exclusive function of obtaining evidence for prosecutorial outcomes and incorporate support for other strategic policing initiatives such as crime prevention, crime reduction, and suspect targeting. This outcome has now become an increasing reality and forensic science plays an important role in intelligence-led policing practices.

Within the context of providing evidence to a court of law, forensic practitioners often hold a distinctive privilege within court hearings. Due to the nature of the type of evidence and information forensic practitioners are providing the court, they are afforded an exemption to the rule that does not permit opinion-based evidence. Witnesses that can provide a level of specialised knowledge are considered as *expert witnesses*. To become considered as an *expert witness*, the court has to be satisfied the person has a certain level of specialised knowledge based on their training, study, or experience, and that the evidence they are providing is wholly or substantially based on that knowledge. If the court accepts the person as an expert, then they are permitted to provide an opinion with respect to their examination.

Expert witnesses are bound to a code of conduct that the court insists on and is based on a set of professional values. A key value is that they are non-partisan to any side of the juridical system (prosecution or defence, complainant or plaintiff) and they are disinterested witnesses. By being disinterested, this is not to show a lack of interest in the knowledge behind their type of evidence; it means they are disinterested in the result, the evidence findings or court outcome. They provide evidence that is examined more objectively without emotion and unsentimentally, regardless of the effect the findings may have on any particular side.

THE DEVELOPMENT OF FORENSIC IDENTIFICATION

Establishing when forensic practice was first developed within law-enforcement agencies is difficult to pinpoint because it was developed gradually over a period of time. When Robert Peel (1788–1850) successfully petitioned in the British Parliament for the *Metropolitan Police Act* in 1829, the first official Police Force was established. Interestingly, photography was invented around the same time, in 1826, and early police investigators would often commission local photographers to document the evidence of serious crime *in situ*. Medical doctors working on behalf of the Coroner's Office would also attend crime scenes involving death for the purpose of establishing the cause and time of death. Excluding the investigating police, pathologists and photographers became the first specialists to attend scenes and formally apply their skills to obtain crime scene evidence.

The Industrial Revolution brought a significant cultural shift from an agrarian and cottage industry society into a highly industrial one with mass manufacturing. During this period, the population began to relocate into urban environments seeking employment in factories. Cole suggests that as the population of cities began to grow and as cities increased in population density, "the informal system of personal acquaintances and collective memory began to collapse" (Cole, 2001, p. 8). The rapid population growth of urban areas resulting from the industrialisation, combined with substantial law reforms offering first offenders more lenient sentencing, led to the imperative necessity for a scientific method that could identify individuals and be based within the newly formed police institutions. As police forces were being established around the globe, the issue of identification remained a problem until a French police clerk named Alphonse Bertillon (1853–1914) developed an identification system and database using a biometric system comprising the anthropometric measurement of 11 parts of the body. This system gained its first positive identification in Paris in February 1883 and quickly became a global method of determining a person's identity (Cole, 2001). Bertillonage developed a database that could compare any unknown person of interest with previous data sourced from individuals. Bertillon also developed an ingenious card database system for the rapid retrieval of information and conceptualised the mug shot which consists of facial photographs using both front and side views.

Around the same time as Bertillonage was developed, the ability to identify people from the pattern of their finger's friction ridges was also being conceived. While several people contributed to the development of fingerprinting, it was in 1892 that statistician Francis Galton (1822–1911) published his book *Finger Prints*, which formalised this form of identification within law enforcement (Nickell & Fischer, 1999). Fingerprints had several advantages over the biometric system of Bertillonage, particularly with measurement error being less of a problem because the identification method relied on the structure of the friction ridge pattern as opposed to physical measurements of the body. The other advantage fingerprinting offered was the ability to detect fingerprints as trace evidence at a scene or on objects, which meant identifications can be made employing a search of the database without having to take a direct sample from the person.

Unlike Bertillonage, fingerprint identification remains a significant form of identification within police institutions and was the dominant method of identification for more than a century. It was a British geneticists Alec Jeffreys who developed an innovative method of identification with the first DNA profile used in a British case in 1984 (Nickell & Fischer, 1999). DNA took trace identification evidence into the molecular dimensions and further advancements in rapidly multiplying the DNA using polymerase chain reactions (PCR) increased the level of sensitivity to biological features. Databases of fingerprints and DNA have been well established within law-enforcement agencies. Searches are now conducted using computerised database systems or taking exemplar samples directly from the suspect.

Recently a third form of forensic identification has been developed and is emerging as a key milestone in forensic advancement. Due to the proliferation of surveillance cameras and incorporating cameras into mobile phones, criminal activities are now more regularly captured by cameras (Evison, 2015; Porter, 2009). Capturing people in the commission of a crime is more like a secondary source of trace evidence, in comparison to a fingerprint or DNA sample where the trace element is primarily sourced directly from the body. The image, whilst made directly from the source, isn't a biological object in its own right but nevertheless is a representation of anatomy which can be considered as biological. Evison describes this new identification method as *"the third forensics"* suggesting the first two principal forensics are fingerprint and DNA identification (Evison, 2015). Facial identification is at the time of writing being developed as a forensic specialisation by several police agencies in Australia and overseas. Facial identification methods employ a comparison of anatomical structures of the face (Porter & Doran, 2000; Edmond et al, 2009) between the unknown captured image and an exemplar image. Facial recognition software is incorporated within the examination process, but the actual identification is performed using different criteria than the software and completed by a forensic expert in a system similar to fingerprinting. Recognition software does, however, provide assistance in the database search capacity of unknown persons of interest. State organisations outside police institutions like road and traffic authorities and the passport office have been collecting biometric data from facial photographs used within the authority's documents (driver's licenses, passports, etc) for decades. Police organisations have also been accumulating images of faces for more than a century due to Bertillon's concept of the *mug shot* remaining an essential identification process during the charging of individuals.

At the time of writing, Australia has not yet established a national database of facial images and their biometric data associated with the face, unlike the current national fingerprint and DNA databases. However, there are currently considerations within the Federal Government advocating for the development of a National database which would incorporate all previous sources of facial biometric data including driver's licenses and passports. A significant difference in the current biometric databases of fingerprints and DNA is that these two databases have been created using information obtained from individuals who have been charged for offences. While the police arrest photographs are consistent with this data collection practice, biometric data from driver's licenses and passports present a different level of collection principle and would incorporate a large percentage of the adult population that has never being charged with any offence. This may become quite a controversial issue in the years to come and notwithstanding DNA databases are not without their controversary. For example, with regards to familiar matching of DNA using DNA databases from privately owned genealogy companies. An interesting aspect of the new or third forensics of identification using facial identification is that while the methods do not incorporate completely an anthropometric approach, the use of human anatomy is making a comeback after Bertillonage was abandoned in the early 20th century.

THE PRACTICE OF FORENSIC SCIENCE IN POLICING

Several disciplines or specialisations in forensic science within policing institutions have been developed. Staff are trained as either experts or technicians within a field of specialisation and can be sworn or unsworn members of the police service. Developing staff expertise within narrow areas of specialisation has been a training strategy for several decades based on the notion that specialisation, rather than multi-skilling, establishes a more robust level of expertise within the workforce.

Despite the prevalence of separate forensic disciplines within policing, the majority of specialisations have a common function – identification! The identification of individuals or the source of marks or patterns made by objects, or illicit material like prohibited drugs, all have the common objective of identification. The objective of fingerprint examination, DNA analysis, and facial recognition is to identify individuals who leave biological trace evidence at the scene or on objects or who are captured by cameras like CCTV. The identification of the source of marks like shoe prints, tyre impressions, tool marks, rifling marks on bullet projectiles, glass fragments matching in refractive index is intended to determine whether a certain object can be identified as the sole source of the marks. Material sampled from a suspect's hands that is not visible to the naked eye and is identified as gunshot residue or a white powdered substance that is identified as cocaine are examples of the common objective of identification. These functions do, however, operate using different examination methods, and training requires experts to understand the scientific nature, dynamics, and nuances of their area of expertise.

The objective of the identification of a person or object as described here may be considered as a forensic priority in most situations. However, there is also an opposing priority based on the same principle. The opposite of a positive identification is a non-identification. Non-identification results, referred to as eliminations, are not always considered as failed identifications – in fact, non-identifications also form a critical function of forensic science. Eliminating suspects of criminal events swiftly is a moral and ethical responsibility of policing, and it presents several benefits in maintaining a respectable social contract with the community. By the process of eliminating suspects from a forensic intelligence perspective, resources are not tied up and the investigation can become more effective and resolve the matter in a timelier manner. Another important advantage of eliminating suspects quickly is the reduction of personal stress caused on the individuals when they are the subject of an investigation. When people become suspects of serious crime, especially crimes involving violence or sexual deviancy, and especially when involving other family members, these individuals undergo enormous levels of stress even when they are completely innocent of any wrongdoing. Suspects of serious crime can often lose their jobs and financial security, be ostracised by family and friends, and be publicly humiliated by the media. Eliminating suspects early can prevent this type of personal anxiety and loss and can prevent any possible deterioration of their mental health. Forensic identifications that eliminate suspects is a positive outcome for policing institutions as a whole.

When considering how forensic science functions within law-enforcement agencies and within the realm of scientific investigation, a theoretical model has been developed that consists of three separate elements (see Figure 10.1). The purpose of this model is to view the entire forensic investigation holistically and ensure that consistency of the forensic evidence remains paramount. The three elements consist of process, function, and principles. The first element in the model is *process*, which is the sequence of the scientific investigation starting from the collection and detection of evidence at scenes of crime, continuing to the forensic examination of the items, and finally ending in the reporting (Porter, 2011). Throughout the entire process it is critical that operators follow standard operating procedures (SOP) developed internally by the police agency; maintain a high level of evidence integrity, including the chain of custody and evidence storage; use reliable examination methods; and report in the required format. Process is critical during the entire investigation and if not followed correctly may lead to evidence not being accepted by court authorities.

The second element, *function*, describes the methodological approach used during the forensic examination. There are various methodological approaches that describe the form of inquiry imposed on most forensic examinations. There are no hierarchical elements to these methods, but some would argue they may present a greater or lesser application

PROCESS + FUNCTION + PRINCIPLES

The sequence of the scientific investigation | The examination methodology | The significance of the evidence

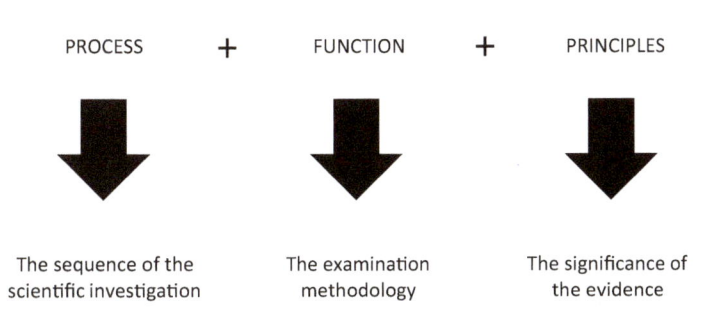

FIGURE 10.1
A theoretical model that consists of three separate elements: process, function, and principles

of actual science. The four methodological approaches include *empirical analysis, comparative analysis, interpretative analysis,* and *observation*. Table 10.2 provides a summary of each method, including examples of which disciplines are used within those forms of forensic inquiry.

Empirical analysis of physical evidence is described as "a method that relies on scientific instrumentation to provide quantitative data that can mathematically represent results" (Porter, 2011, p. 34). An example of this form of scientific inquiry is the chemical analysis of illicit drugs. Various chemistry instrumentation can provide a spectrometric analysis of the specimen in determining its composition, purity, quantity, and identification. There often remains some degree of interpretation of the results, but this level of interpretation of the data is produced by an analytical and scientific instrument rather than the item or material itself, and the findings can be supported by statistical representation (Porter, 2011). Empirical analysis is at the heart of a positivist approach

TABLE 10.2 Summary of methodologies, including examples of which disciplines are used within those forms of forensic inquiry

Methodology	Method description	Typical forensic disciplines
Empirical analysis	Applies scientific instrumentation with mathematical output of data	Chemical analysis Toxicology Drug identification DNA analysis Gunshot residue analysis (GSR)
Comparative analysis	Compares a known exemplar specimen to an unknown specimen or sample	Shoe mark identification Fingerprinting Tyre impressions Toolmarks Firearm identification Hairs and fibres Handwriting analysis
Interpretative analysis	The application of heuristic and intuitive skills to interpret visual clues or evidence	Cause of death (pathology) Crime scene investigation Bloodstain pattern analysis (BPA) Forensic radiology Shooting reconstruction Fire investigation Accident investigation CCTV interpretation Physical fit evidence
Observation	General observation of items and evidence	Eye witnesses Detection of items/evidence *in situ* Suspect's clothing at time of event Eyewitness photographs or footage

to scientific investigation, and the quantification of forensic data, even visual material, can provide several benefits within the context of producing stronger science-based outcomes (Humphreys et al, 2008; Vanderwee et al, 2011).

Comparative analysis is considered as the hallmark of police forensics practice and defined as "a method that involves the comparison of an item of evidence of *unknown* source against an item of *known* source or origin" (Porter, 2011, p. 35). An example of the comparative analysis method is in shoe mark identification. The objective of shoe mark examinations is to identify the source outer sole of the shoe which made the mark at the scene, or alternatively, to eliminate the suspect shoe as not making the impression. Shoe mark examinations are made by comparing images made of the shoe impression at the scene with exemplar impression images made from a suspect shoe. A key examination value in the comparative analysis method is the comparison between the unknown and the known or exemplar material; they are matched in composition for a like-for-like comparison.

Interpretative analysis consists of valued judgements made by experienced and trained forensic practitioners. According to Porter, "[I]nterpretative examinations provide evidence usually gained by the reconstruction of visual clues left at the scene. This form of physical evidence uses interpretation that is more heuristic and requires intuitive skills developed in trained and experienced practitioners" (Porter, 2011, p. 35). The cause and origin of a fire by crime scene investigators is an example of this type of forensic method. A hypothesis is established using deductive reasoning and based on the clues presented to the examiner's trained eye. Subjectivity and contextual bias can become problematic when using this type of forensic examination method. An alternative application of interpretative analysis is the reconstruction of events and testing various possibilities during the reconstruction.

Observation is a simple method that involves observing evidence *in situ* or describing situations experienced when at the scene (Porter, 2011). This form of examination is akin to eyewitness evidence. For example, if the crime scene investigator noted the front door of a premises was damaged, then the observation becomes a simple fact that the door was damaged. It does not speculate how the door was damaged or that a particular tool was the source of the damage, or who damaged the door. It is just a simple observation that could nevertheless result in valuable evidence within the circumstances of a case.

The third element of the proposed theoretical model (Figure 10.1) is *principles*, which relate to the examination findings and explain how effective the evidence results may be or how they should be considered. Several forensic science principles have been established over the years, including *Locard's Exchange Principle* and Paul Kirk's principle of *individualisation*; these concepts will be discussed in more detail in the following section. However, within the construct of this theoretical model, principles facilitate how the evidence findings of the examination may be considered by the decision-makers.

An example of how principles operate within this framework is the photogrammetric examination of a person of interest's (POI) height when depicted on CCTV. Determining the height of a POI has more application from a forensic intelligence perspective or in the elimination of suspects and only moderate probative value from a prosecutorial perspective, which at best may be circumstantial-based evidence. What is important, however, is how this type of forensic evidence is presented to the decision-makers. Unfortunately, previous casework has emphasised the correlation between the height of the POI and the accused as an ad hoc method of identification, suggesting the heights "match". This is an inappropriate depiction of the findings, and greater explanation regarding the principles of the evidence is required to allow greater accuracy when the decision-makers are considering the height as evidence.

The matching of heights obviously does not provide identification at an individual level, but providing further clarity regarding the significance or insignificance of this evidence is important and relates to the evidence principles and as a consequence should be included in the reporting. For example, if the suspect is male, aged 27 years, and 178 cm tall, and the photogrammetry measured the POI at 178 cm with a ±3.4 cm error rate, the conclusion is the suspect and POI depicted on the CCTV match in height. However, if the error rate is incorporated into the POI height, as it should be, then what we can conclude from the ABS database (see Figure 10.2) is that the POI height (between 174.6 to 181.4 cm) also corresponds with 72% of the male population for that age group and within the height classifications of the dataset. It is not a conclusive result by far, and even when considering just the 178 cm height, this range still represents 29% of the population category. The critical point here is if the expert is suggesting that the heights of the suspect and POI *match*, with the inference that they are then the same person, this becomes a false supposition hidden within the details of the results and without the proper context or evidence principles. Equally disingenuous is the notion that the suspect *could not be eliminated* based on the analysis of height, which is another way of inferring it must therefore be the same person. This is a highly problematic conclusion at times exploited by some forensic experts.

Alternatively, if the height of the POI and suspect have a corresponding height that is two or maybe three standard deviations from the norm (e.g. 210 cm) then a more significant result may be applicable and greater evidential emphasis applied. Principles provide the decision-makers with context in relation to the evidence so they are able to place an appropriate weighting of that particular evidence rather than just providing the results of the examination (i.e. a match in height). Other types of evidence principles may consist of the location of fingerprints or whether the suspect had access to the location or item, statistical inferences in DNA identification with likelihood ratios to determine

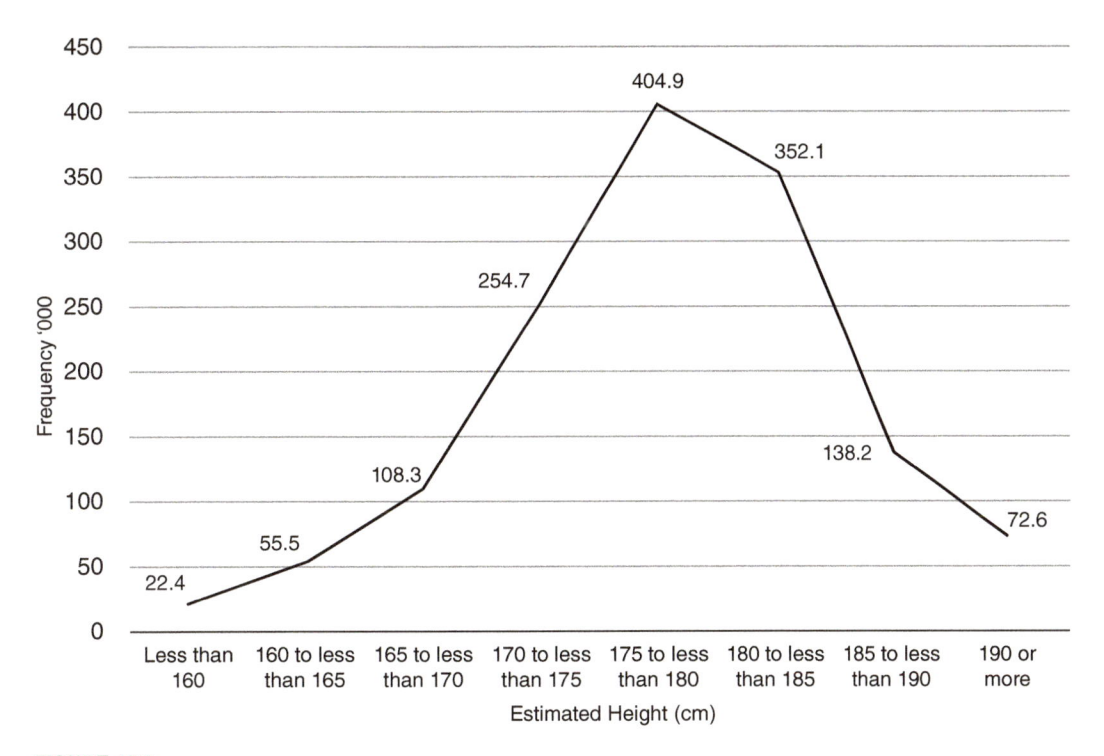

FIGURE 10.2
Mean estimated height of Australian males between 25–34 years

Source: Australian Bureau of Statistics 2012 (mean = 178, median = 178).

the probability of another person having the same DNA profile, or Bayesian probability of the evidence as a single source.

FORENSIC SCIENCE THEORETICAL FOUNDATIONS

The development of forensic science has witnessed tremendous advancements in science and technology in recent times, especially the miniaturisation of scientific equipment and its potential to be used in the field and link remotely with databases. Conceptual development and understanding how forensic science works have also been an area of intellectual inquiry, with several theories or principles being established. Bertillon's development of a systematic method of establishing the identity of individuals was certainly a landmark moment for forensic policing as was the development of fingerprinting and DNA identification methods.

A notable conceptual development was established in 1920 by Edmond Locard (1877–1966) who described the transference of material for trace evidence and is referred to as "Locard's Exchange Principle" (Nickell & Fischer, 1999). Locard (1920) explained that during the commission of a crime, due to the actual presence of the person committing the crime, trace material is left behind that is linked to them and by the inverse action, they take material from the scene or victim with them (Locard, 1920). This explanation of trace material transference has become symbolically expressed as "every contact leaves a trace", a phrase attributed to Locard despite the fact that he never actually explained it that way. Locard's Exchange Principle remains a key forensic concept today to establish a link between scenes, items, victims, or suspects. Based on Locard's theory, various trace evidence is examined, including hair, fibres, fingerprints, material containing DNA, glass fragments, gunshot residue, explosive material, botanical seeds or pollen, diatoms found in water and soil, and several others.

Biochemist Paul Kirk (1902–1970) made several contributions regarding the conceptual development of forensic science. He is believed to have been the first to describe the discipline of forensic science as *criminalistics*. He developed courses at the University of California's School of Criminology, at which he became Head of the Criminalistics Department (Nickell & Fischer, 1999). Kirk's most significant forensic science contribution with regards to conceptual development was the notion of *individualisation* which was featured in his paper, "The Ontogeny of Criminalistics". In that paper, Kirk explained: "Identity is defined by all philosophical authorities as uniqueness. A thing can be identical only with itself, never with any other object, since all objects in the universe are unique" (Kirk, 1963, p. 236).

Kirk established a working principle in forensic identification that everything was unique to itself; therefore, the identification method involved distinguishing what features are considered as individual characteristics that may only exist between the trace and the source. Examples are a shoe mark left at the scene identified with the outer sole of a particular shoe and a fingerprint impression left on an object with the friction ridge pattern of a person's finger. While the concept of individualisation in forensic science is attributed to Kirk, the concept of uniqueness, however, had been developed in the 17th century by German philosopher Gottfried Leibniz (1646–1716). This concept is known as *Leibniz's Law*, and the concept involves the identity of indiscernibles (Saks & Koehler, 2008).

The notion of individualisation is primarily statistically based on the product rule and became a standard in the forensic identification sciences. However, in 2008 Kirk's concept was challenged by Michael Saks and Jonathan Koehler in their paper "The Individualization Fallacy in Forensic Science Evidence". Saks and Koehler (2008) argued that the concept of individualisation is a metaphysical idea, and there is no scientific basis to prove anything is unique. They claim that uniqueness is unprovable within the realms of scientific validation and question whether this type of metaphysics has any place in forensic identification sciences. Saks and Koehler (2008) dismiss the concept of individualisation by suggesting the capabilities indicated by this conventional wisdom does not hold any scientific basis and its notion is therefore a fallacy (Saks & Koehler, 2008). Saks and Koehler's paper had an enormous impact on police forensic science due to the possibility that their rational idea may become the basis for challenging identification methods in court. To this day, the words *unique*, *uniqueness*, and *individualisation* have been banished from the forensic science vocabulary.

QUESTIONING RELIABILITY

Several questions have been imposed externally onto forensic science, including (1) whether forensic science evidence is reliable, (2) whether the forensic experts can actually do what they claim they can do, and (3) whether forensic science is actually science? The reasons why the reliability of forensic science became a focus may have several origins, but the main catalyst is due to the effect the *Innocence Project* was having in the United States, where several hundred wrongfully convicted people serving long prison sentences were proven to be innocent. Ironically, it was also forensic science that provided the evidence that supported the proof of innocence. DNA examinations of previously used physical evidence exposed a number of wrongfully convicted cases. The Innocence Project brought serious questions to bear regarding the United States criminal justice system, including forensic science.

The questioning of the reliability of forensic science came from several directions, including the justice system itself, academic research, and governmental inquiries. Two major inquiries were held in the United States by the National Research Council (NRC) of the US National Academy of Sciences (NAS) and the US President's Council of Advisors on Science and Technology (PCAST). While these extensive inquiries were both held in the United States, their findings were considered more as a global critique of forensic science. The NRC inquiry was established as a directive from the US Senate and the report "Strengthening Forensic Science in the United States: A Pathway Forward" was published in 2009.

The NCR (2009) report found a range of crucial issues associated with several forensic science disciplines and made a number of recommendations, including the need for further research and scientific validation of forensic practices. The PCAST report followed in 2016 on the request of President Obama to follow up on the progress and implementation of the NCR recommendations. Obama requested the committee examine whether there were any additional steps with respect to improving the scientific application of the disciplines the NCR criticised and whether improvements could ensure the validity of forensic evidence within the nation's legal system (PCAST, 2016; Edmond & Martire, 2017). The PCAST committee aims were to close the gaps on a number of feature-comparison methods and specifically examine the validity of forensic disciplines such as DNA, bitemarks, fingerprints, firearm marks, shoe mark impressions, and hair (PCAST, 2016). The report summarises the NCR's initial findings as follows:

> *The 2009 report described a disturbing pattern of deficiencies common to many of the forensic methods routinely used in the criminal justice system, most importantly a lack of rigorous and appropriate studies establishing their scientific validity, concluding that "much forensic evidence – including, for example, bitemarks and firearm and toolmark identifications – is introduced in criminal trials without any meaningful scientific validation, determination of error rates, or reliability testing to explain the limits of the discipline"* (PCAST, 2016, p. 4).

The PCAST committee concluded that "there are two important remaining gaps; i) the need for clarity about the scientific standards for the validity and reliability of forensic methods and ii) the need to evaluate specific forensic methods to determine whether they have been scientifically established to be valid and reliable" (PCAST, 2016, p. x). The committee indicated there were concerns regarding the "foundational validity" of the methods examined and their "validity as applied" within their practice in courts (PCAST, 2016). It is difficult to summarise the extensive findings of both the NCR (2009) and PCAST (2016) reports without risking oversimplification and diluting their significance. Nevertheless, the committees found the need for there to be a better alignment with science-based practices; further research, testing, and validation of current forensic comparison methods; greater training and education of practitioners; and a review of procedures.

Due to the highly critical nature of the findings and the level of inquiry both studies undertook, and for the highest US authorities, one would think the ominous findings would have a major impact on the forensic science industry, especially within police forensic science, which relies on more subjective comparative analysis methods. One would think the general acceptability within the justice system of forensic science would have suffered. Surprisingly, though, with the exception of some academic research and moderate changes to SOPs, very little impact or disruptions to forensic science has resulted from the reports. Shortly after the 2016 PCAST report, the Council of the Australian and New Zealand Forensic Science Society (ANZFSS) posted a statement on their website that indicated while they accept the concerns proffered by the PCAST report, they distanced its findings by suggesting it is solely a US-based issue and not consistent with Australian practice, while also suggesting the report "portrays forensic science in an overly simplistic manner and has too narrow a view" (Edmond & Martire, 2017, p. 142). Edmond and Martire (2017) are highly critical of the ANZFSS response and stated: "The review undertaken by PCAST is one of the first serious independent attempts to assess a range of feature-comparison methods using scientific rather than legal criteria" (p. 149). Nevertheless, the impact of both reports has been modest at best and completely ignored at worst.

The question of how the judiciary deals with forensic science evidence has also been challenging for many years, which PCAST also attempted to resolve. Within an adversarial judicial framework, forensic evidence is often presented to the court by the prosecution, while the defence may offer an alternative forensic expert that explains any difficulties of the evidence or method and may possibly present an opposing finding. While this may add confusion and difficulties for the court actors to comprehend, this is the nature of the adversarial system. For forensic evidence to be admitted into court, the submitted evidence has to conform to certain rules of evidence that deal with a range of considerations, including that the evidence must be lawfully obtained, that the court has to accept the expert as having the necessary specialised knowledge, and that the evidence must conform with any relevant standards. Forensic evidence is accepted by the court based on its admissibility as indicated by the rules of evidence and legislation such as the *Uniform Evidence Act*. What remains deficient within the admissibility standard is the actual reliability of forensic evidence, which the adversarial system is in part has the responsibility to establish. Notwithstanding these facts, it is advantageous for courts to dismiss any evidence that may be known to be unreliable.

The question is "How do courts consider reliability as an evidence admission standard?" In 1993, the US Supreme Court in the matter of *Daubert v Merrell Dow Pharmaceuticals [1993]* established five standards that could be considered when expert evidence is presented to the court. This standard, known as the *Daubert Standard*, is a guideline for court officers to use when considering the admissibility of scientific evidence. The five elements are:

- Whether the theory or technique in question can be and has been tested;
- Whether it has been subjected to peer review and publication;
- Its known or potential error rate;
- The existence and maintenance of standards controlling its operation; and
- Whether it has attracted widespread acceptance within a relevant scientific community.

While the Daubert Standard applies only in jurisdictions in the US, and a motion to challenge the evidence using the standard must be raised, *Daubert* is often cited in Australian cases involving difficulties with forensic evidence. It also provides a robust foundation when considering establishing forensic procedures and practices which include the concepts of testing, establishing error rates, acceptance in the forensic science literature, and transparency with regard to methods and procedures. All of these items are important elements to consider and are highlighted by the NRC and PCAST reports.

Another recent challenge to the legitimacy of forensic science arose from cognitive psychology research by Itiel Dror et al. published in

2006. Dror conducted an experiment with experienced fingerprint experts that examined "whether experts can objectively focus on feature information in fingerprints without being misled by extraneous information, such as context" (Dror et al, 2006, p. 74). Testing the accuracy of fingerprint laboratories was motivated by the then recent misidentification (false positive error) by the Federal Bureau of Investigation (FBI) of an American citizen for the Madrid bombing in 2004 from supplied crime scene fingerprints from Interpol.

The experiment involved testing five experienced fingerprint experts by providing them with pairs of fingerprints from a previous case they had correctly identified as a positive match (the prints were verified as a match). Without the participants knowing they had previously identified a match under normal case conditions, each participant was provided with the same pair of fingerprints in their original format. The testing occurred during their normal work duties and without knowing they were conducting the test (a condition agreed to by the participants), so the environmental conditions were consistent with their practice (Dror et al, 2006).

Participants were prescreened so that they had not seen the misidentified Madrid bombing fingerprint sample. A colleague gave each participant their original crime scene and exemplar fingerprints from a previous case that had made a match. However, a condition of the experiment was to also provide them with further context. The colleague instructed them to examine the prints and determine whether there is enough detail to make a definite and sound decision, and to confirm either a match or non-match. The context provided to the expert was a critical component of the experiment. Dror et al (2006) explains: "They were told that the pair of prints was the one that was erroneously matched by the FBI as the Madrid bomber, thus creating an extraneous context that the prints were a non-match" (2006, p. 76).

The results of this experiment concluded that four out of the five experts changed their original correct decision on the basis of the extraneous and incorrect contextual information. Three experts changed their result to a non-match, one changed to an inconclusive result, while only a single expert remained with the correct match finding (Dror et al, 2006). Due to the complexity and natural conditions of the experiment, a low sample size is evident. Nevertheless, an 80% rate of change of decision due to false contextual information certainly had an impact on the forensic science community. Combined with the embarrassment of the FBI's misidentification on such a high-profile international case, the fingerprint and other police forensic practices began to consider the imperatives of contextual bias within their practices, especially disciplines that use comparative and interpretative analysis methods. Contextual bias also confirms the importance of developing well-considered SOPs within the process phase of the previously described theoretical framework.

REFERENCES

Cole S.A., (2001) *Suspect Identities: A History of Fingerprinting and Criminal Identification*, Cambridge, MA: Harvard University Press.

Cole S.A., Porter G., (2018) The CSI Effect, chapter found in Rossy Q., Décary-Hétu D., Delémont O., Massimiliano M., eds., *The Routledge International Handbook of Forensic Intelligence and Criminology* (pp. 112–124), London: Routledge.

Dror I.E., Charlton D., Péron A.E., (2006) Contextual Information Renders Experts Vulnerable to Making Erroneous Identifications, *Forensic Science International*, 156, 74–78.

Edmond G., Biber K., Kemp R., Porter G., (2009) Laws Looking Glass: Expert Identification Evidence Derived from Photographic and Video Images, *Current Issues in Criminal Justice*, 20:3, 337–377.

Edmond G., Martire K.A., (2017) Antipodean Forensics: A Comment on ANZFSS's Response to PCAST, *Australian Journal of Forensic Science*, 50:2, 140–151.

Evison M.P., (2015) The Third Forensics: Images and Allusions, *Policing and Society*, 25:5, 521–539.

Humphreys J.D., Porter G., Bell M., (2008) The Quantification of Fingerprint Quality Using a Relative Contrast Index, *Forensic Science International*, 178(1), 46–53.

Kirk P.L., (1963) The Ontogeny of Criminalistics, *Journal of Criminal Law and Criminology*, 54(2), 235–238.

Locard E., (1920) *The Criminal Investigation and Scientific Methods*, Paris: Aufl. Flammarion.

National Research Council (2009) *Strengthening Forensic Science in the United States: A Path Forward*, Washington, DC: National Academies Press.

Nickell J., Fischer J.F., (1999) *Crime Science: Methods of Forensic Detection*, Lexington, University of Kentucky Press.

Porter G., (2009) CCTV Images as Evidence, *Australian Journal of Forensic Sciences*, 41:1, 11–25.

Porter G., (2011) A New Theoretical Framework Regarding the Application and Reliability of Photographic Evidence, *International Journal of Evidence & Proof*, 15:1, 26–61.

Porter G., Doran G., (2000) An Anatomical and Photographic Technique for Forensic Facial Identification, *Forensic Science International*, 114, 97–105.

President's Council of Advisors on Science and Technology (US) (2016) *Report to the President, Forensic Science in Criminal Courts: Ensuring Scientific Validity of Feature-Comparison Methods*, New York: Executive Office of the President of the United States, President's Council of Advisors on Science and Technology.

Raymond T., Julian R., (2015) Forensic Intelligence in Policing: Organisational and Cultural Change, *Australian Journal of Forensic Sciences*, 47:4, 371–385.

Saks M.J., Koehler J.J., (2008) The Individualisation Fallacy in Forensic Science, *Vanderbilt Law Review*, 61:1, 199–219.

Vanderwee J., Porter G., Renshaw A., Bell M., (2011) The Investigation of a Relative Contrast Index Model for Fingerprint Quantification, *Forensic Science International*, 204, 74–79.

Williams A., (2015) *Forensic Criminology*, London: Routledge.

CHAPTER 11

Police use of force
An examination of Australian policing

Dragana Kesic and Stuart D.M. Thomas

INTRODUCTION

In the role of serving and protecting the public, and enforcing the law, police are given broad legal powers. Perhaps the most contentious of these are their right to use physical force to effect cooperation from the public and their right to use lethal force to protect their or another's life. This chapter will provide a brief summary of the police use of force research, with specific focus on the state of the research and practice in Australia. Particular focus will be on the issues of use of force on people experiencing mental health issues[1] and the widespread dissemination of the Conducted Energy Devices, commonly known as Tasers.

FATAL POLICE USE OF FORCE INTERNATIONALLY

Examinations of the appropriateness and the dynamics of police use of force on citizens have been ongoing for more than 60 years; despite this, there has been little consistency in conceptualising and measuring use of force (Khalm IV, Frank, & Liederbach, 2014). Research on police use of force has largely been conducted in the United States of America (USA) and originally tended to concentrate more on fatal force encounters than non-fatal force encounters, thus resulting in limited understanding about the latter (Hickman, Piquero, & Garner, 2008). However, other researchers have suggested that due to the rarity of fatal force events and issues such as limited access to data that allows empirical analysis of deadly encounters, our understanding of fatal police encounters also remains limited (McElvain & Kposowa, 2008).

Police use of fatal force is, fortunately, a very rare occurrence. Nevertheless, many countries including the USA, do not report reliable national statistics on how frequently it occurs. The majority of the published studies of fatal use of force were conducted in the USA in the 1970s and 1980s (McElvain & Kposowa, 2008). While these early studies tended to examine the influence of sociological theories of crime and control, more recent research has moved to understanding fatal use of force as a complex phenomenon that is affected by an interplay between external environment (e.g. laws, community demographics), internal environment (e.g. police training and policy), and situational factors (individual officers', citizens' and situational characteristics). However, some of the extant research has produced mixed findings; for instance, despite numerous years and many studies, Hollis and Jennings' (2018) narrative meta-analysis found that the relationship between police use of force and race "remains unclear". On the other hand, research has very consistently found that males are more likely to be the fatalities (Gill & Pasquale-Styles, 2009; Mumola, 2007) and that it is male police officers who are involved in these shootings (e.g. McElvain & Kposowa, 2008). Most importantly, the extant research shows that the vast majority of decedents had been armed with a weapon at the time of the incident and exhibited a high degree of aggressive and threatening behaviour towards police, which likely impacted on risk perceptions (Gill & Pasquale-Styles, 2009; Mumola, 2007).

NON-FATAL POLICE USE OF FORCE INTERNATIONALLY

Extant research findings indicate that non-lethal force is a very rare occurrence in general interactions between the police and the public. US studies estimate police use of force to occur anywhere from 0.03% of all police service calls (IACP, 2001) to 58.4% of police–suspect encounters (Terrill & Mastrofski, 2002); this very large discrepancy is mainly attributable to the very disparate methodologies used, including different use of force measurements (e.g. dichotomous force, continuum force, force factor, etc.) and the use of a wide range of "data" (e.g. arrest reports, official use of force reports, citizen complaints, suspect surveys).

Including situational characteristics in examination of use of force has significantly increased understanding of this phenomenon and arguably led to more robust and consistent findings. Indeed, Bolger's recent meta-analysis indicates that the strongest predictors of police use of force are suspects' resistance and demeanour (Bolger, 2015).

Klahm IV and Tillyer (2010) criticised the available studies on police use of non-lethal force for their failure to properly operationalise the definition of force and for a lack of sophisticated statistical analyses. More recently, the authors conducted a meta-analysis, highlighting the many inconsistent and conflicting findings and renewing decade-old criticisms, which perhaps suggest that little has been done to improve this research (Khalm IV et al., 2014).

MENTAL HEALTH ISSUES AND POLICE USE OF FORCE

Dealings with persons with mental health issues is perceived as a distinct challenge for the police. Their contact can occur in a wide variety of contexts, including being witnesses of crimes, victims of crime, alleged offenders, or persons in need of assistance. Following the deinstitutionalization of mental health, there has been continued and widespread criticism internationally and in Australia that services are incapable of providing adequate community-based mental health services to people with mental health issues (e.g. Senate Select Committee on Mental Health, 2006). It has been claimed that as a result of the shortage of appropriate community care, the police, as the only 24-hour emergency service, have had to increasingly take on the responsibility of providing regular assistance to persons experiencing mental health issues (Carroll, 2005). Indeed, research findings indicate that these encounters are commonplace in many countries around the world, including in Australia (Fry, O'Riordan, & Geanellos, 2002). Given this, it is not surprising that the police are their primary referral sources to emergency departments, both internationally (Klein, 2010) and in Australia (Knott, Pleban, Taylor, & Castle, 2007).

Broadly speaking, this research has measured the presence of mental health issues through: (1) simply specifying that the person was diagnosed with mental illness/disorder; (2) examining whether the person had a history of mental health treatment; (3) seeking police officer's *perceptions* of whether the person is exhibiting signs of mental health issues through such constructs as their appearing "emotionally disturbed", "mentally unsound", or other; or (4) examining whether the person was a mental health patient under a Mental Health Act or was transported by the police under a Mental Health Act.

The international studies have reported a high incidence of people with mental health issues in fatal force incidents. Mental health issues have most commonly been examined in a subset of police fatalities historically commonly referred to as "suicide-by-police" events. Although there are a number of operationalised definitions of this phenomenon, in short, it refers to situations where individuals who are intent on death by suicide to do so by provoking the police to shoot them. The differences between the various definitions of suicide by police seem to centre on how specifically, and conversely, how broadly, the phenomenon is defined. Consequently, estimates of how frequently this phenomenon is potentially encountered in all incidents of police shootings differ accordingly, with extant research estimates of between 10% and 50% being reported (e.g. Best, Quigley, & Bailey, 2004; Mohandie, Meloy, & Collins, 2009). McKenzie (2006) criticized the extant research for the lack of scientific rigor and consistency. He proposed that there is a difference between those individuals who may have been indifferent as to whether they live or die and those who intended to die by suicide and suggested that in the absence of clear and reliable evidence that the person wanted to die, a "behavioural chain of events" ought to be examined.

Due in part to diverse methodologies used by researchers noted earlier, the existing evidence base regarding non-fatal force remains equivocal. Some studies have found that police are no more likely to use force on people whom they perceive to be experiencing mental illness in samples of arrestees (Johnson, 2011; Kaminski, DiGiovanni, & Downs, 2004) and in police–suspect encounters (Terrill & Mastrofski, 2002). Johnson (2011) found that police reported using more severe levels of force on suspects who appeared "mentally unstable"; however, this relationship was not statistically significant after taking into account other pertinent factors, including suspect violent behavior and possession of weapons. Conversely, Lawton (2007) found that police were more likely to use force on those who appeared "mentally unsound" even after taking into account other risk factors, including their demeanor and substance intoxication.

POLICE USE OF FORCE IN AUSTRALIA

Each state and territory in Australia has their own legislation governing police use of force that appears in line with the Commonwealth Act (Crimes Act 1914 (Cth) s3ZC). Additionally, all Australian police forces adhere to the set national guidelines on the use of force. The Australian and New Zealand Policing Advisory Agency (ANZPAA) provides these national guidelines. ANZPAA defines the use of force as "any situation where, in the execution of their duty, police use physical force or other techniques, including a weapon, instrument or implement to respond to an actual or perceived threat" and provides a set of guiding principles for the states in implementation of policies and procedures related to this area (ANZPAA, 2014, p. 1). ANZPAA further specifies appropriate police use of force as being "reasonable, necessary, proportionate and appropriate to the circumstances" where "no more force than is reasonably necessary for the safe and effective performance of their duties" should be used (2014, p. 1).

The guideline proposes that Australian jurisdictions should adopt situational or tactical options models of force to guide officers in deciding which level of force is appropriate in a given situation. These models – and each state has their own adaptation – are depicted as a circular configuration, with certain guiding principles at their centre and different tactical options surrounding the circle. For instance, the most recent Victoria Police model has centred the principles of "safety first" and "assess and reassess", followed by "communication skills", from which all other police options extend, including police presence and the use of different weapon-less and weapons tactics. Based on an officer's risk assessment, they may escalate or deescalate their response to the situation by choosing from the various tactics whilst ensuring that they continually assess the situation, communicate with the citizen, and ensure the safety of all (Tuckey, 2004).

The ANZPAA guidelines specify that police organisations need to collect data on use of force encounters (2014). Until very recently, Victoria Police's Use of Force Register, established in 1995, was the only comprehensive recording method of use of physical force by officers in response to threat or use of physical force by the public (Victoria Police, 2004). When force incidents occur, involved officers fill out a "Use of Force Form" entering details about incident type and location, environmental factors, personal characteristics of citizens, force type used by police and citizens, outcomes, and injuries. It has previously been estimated that underreporting on the Use of Force Register is anywhere between 20% and 70% (Strong, 2009).

In other states, the situation with regard to when and what force is recorded varies somewhat, however due to the lack of published information and no current national recording/reporting mandate, there is a significant gap in our knowledge about what actually occurs nationally. Similar to Victoria Police, Australian Capital Territory police must also complete and submit a detailed "Use of Force Report" in all instances where they have used or threatened to use force, excluding verbal threats/commands (ACT Annual Report, 2016/17). In Queensland, use of force reporting captures a more limited range of force options: officers are only required to report when they deploy or present a Firearm, Taser, and Oleoresin Capsicum (OC) Spray; are involved in a pursuit; or cause an injury requiring first aid or medical treatment. As such, only the more severe levels of force are captured in a limited detail on Significant Event Messaging System database (SEMS) (Hine, Porter, Westera, & Alpert, 2018a). In New South Wales, wherever police use force they are then urged to complete mandatory use of force fields in the COPS database (Computerised Operational Policing System) (NSW Police, 2019). In Western Australia, following significant reform to their use of force policies and procedures in 2009, use of force data is collected and reported every time police use an instrument as a force option, or use handcuffs or empty hand tactics and cause an injury (Western Australia Police, 2010). Their system reporting appears very detailed and requires not only multiple information from drop down menus similar to what occurs in Victoria but also provision of comprehensive narrative explanations of the incident. It remains unclear what the level of compliance with the completion of these forms actually is and whether similar issues to those noted in Victoria arise elsewhere (Strong, 2009).

FATAL POLICE USE OF FORCE INCIDENTS

Dalton (1998) reported that between 1990 and 1997, of the 41 people who were fatally shot by the police in Australia, the vast majority were male, aged 33 on average, who were either threatening or attempting to assault or kill police during the incident. Between 1990 and 2004, there were 76 police shooting deaths across Australia, with the majority of these occurring in Victoria ($n = 29$), followed by the New South Wales ($n = 18$) (Brouwer, 2005). More recently, the Australian Institute of Criminology's National Deaths in Custody Program (NDICP) reported that there were 105 fatal police shootings between 1989 and

2011; and, of note, 1999–2000 saw 11 police fatal shootings nationwide (AIC, 2013).

Perhaps as a result of Victoria consistently having the highest number of police fatal shootings, the force has undergone significant changes in its policy and practice from the mid-1990s. Project Beacon, established in 1996, resulted in a number of significant changes to policy and practice, including the introduction of the *Safety First Philosophy* as a key element of all planned and unplanned police engagements, implementation of the situational tactical options model, and mandatory annual training (Brouwer, 2005). Consequent to these changes, there was a significant drop in the number of fatal shootings in Victoria; however, subsequently an increase in mental health issues among police fatalities emerged as a significant point of concern (Brouwer, 2005). Of note, there is a significant lack of research into fatal police force in Australia, notwithstanding official investigations, such as legally required coronial investigations. One notable study, conducted in Victoria by Kesic and colleagues, offered some insights into the situational characteristics of the 48 police fatalities that occurred between 1980 and 2007, namely, that the majority of these events occurred very rapidly and that most of the decedents were behaving aggressively, were resisting police, and were armed with a weapon (Kesic et al., 2012a).

NON-FATAL POLICE USE OF FORCE INCIDENTS

Examinations of non-fatal police use of force in Australia have been on the increase over the past decade, specifically; prior to then, there was a distinct lack of wider research and knowledge about what occurs locally. One of the first published analyses of non-fatal use of force incidents was conducted in Queensland and revealed that police used some form of physical force in 20% of arrests (Edwards, 2000).

An Office of Police Integrity review (Strong, 2009), using data from the Victorian Use of Force Register, reported that in 2008 Victoria Police resorted to using force every 2.5 hours, and that a critical incident occurred every 49 hours. Consistent with the extant research from the USA, Strong found that police use of force occurred rarely, with reported rates of use of force remaining steady at 0.14% of all reported police-public contacts between 2004 and 2008.

Using the same police database, Kesic and colleagues (Kesic, Thomas, & Ogloff, 2012b) examined a random sample of 4,627 cases recorded between 1995 and 2008. Although they focused mainly on the role of mental health issues in these events, overall they found that most common behavioural presentations were violent behaviour, abusive language, being alcohol affected, and being irrational/unstable. The strongest predictor of police threat or use of weapons was citizen's behaviour, in particular, their threat or use of weapons, followed by violent behaviour and use of verbal aggression. These findings are in line with other international research (Bolger, 2015).

There are a number of more recent studies conducted in Queensland. Some have examined police officers' attitudes to use of force, their intentions to use force and procedural justice measures (e.g. Bond, Murphy, & Porter, 2015; Fildes, Murphy, & Porter, 2017; Porter & Alpert, 2017). Others have used different methodologies to examine (1) police decision-making around use of force, and (2) official data on the characteristics of use of force events, providing some important insight into practices on a more national level.

Hine and colleagues (Hine, Porter, Westera, Alpert, & Allen, 2018b) used a Naturalistic Decision Making (NDM) paradigm to look at the police use of force decision-making in a sample of 91 recruits in Queensland. They found that although the most common was intuitive decision-making style, there was evidence that recruits also used analytical decision-making style. Davies (2017) examined 372 NSW police recruits in the final stages of their recruit training with respect to their decision-making during force simulation scenarios. The study found that: (1) threat to themselves and others, presence of weapons, and situational characteristics were most common factors that affected police decision-making, and (2) the factors that influenced use of force decisions in the field were: criticality of the incident, timing/pace of the incident, safety of all, teamwork, and ability to refer to the knowledge gained throughout the academy training.

More recently, McCarthy and colleagues (McCarthy, Porter, Townsley, & Alpert, 2019a) examined 8,357 use of force reports by QPS between 2013 and 2016. Similar to Kesic et al.'s 2012 findings in Victoria, most common citizen characteristics were being violent, using abusive language, and alcohol intoxication. They found that most common incident type involved younger male citizens, and that they occurred in areas with higher Indigenous populations, higher residential instability, and areas with higher proportions of residents who were in the lowest quartile for income. A follow-up examination of 18,322 serious use of force events across three years in Queensland found that areas with high crime rates, high density of alcohol-serving venues, higher levels of residential instability, high levels of residents on long-term unemployment benefits, and lower levels of migrants were associated with more frequent police use of force (McCarthy, Porter, Townsley, & Alpert, 2019b). Of note, however, their results also suggested that more severe levels of force are predicted by individual and situational factors rather than environmental considerations.

In a further examination of 202 cases from official QPS data on use of force, Hine and colleagues (2018a) found that in the majority of events, officers used similar levels of force to the levels of suspect resistance. However, when suspects showed high-risk behaviours such as physical violence or possession of weapons, officers were less likely to use higher relative force in response. The authors suggested this may mean that police: (1) underestimate the levels of force presented, risking self-injury, or (2) enter high-risk situations more prepared and are reluctant to use more force so as not to further escalate the incident. In a follow-up study using the same data, Hine and colleagues (2018c) examined officer injuries, reporting that in almost half of the events, officers sustained an injury. The strongest predictors of officer injuries were encounters with physically aggressive suspects and instances where the police reported using less force relative to the suspect's level of resistance.

In terms of other official data, the most prominent around Australia have been Ombudsmen investigations into police use of Tasers, with no published research studies on these. Tasers are now widely used by police forces around Australia: Some claim that their widespread use comes without solid evidence that Tasers decrease police injuries and reduce fatal use of force and in spite of significant concerns raised about their distinct potential for adverse health consequences. These concerns relate to their ability to cause serious injury and even death in some cases (Baker & Bacharach, 2017) and their potential overuse with people who appear or are known to be experiencing mental health issues (Dymond, 2018; Hallett et al., 2020; O'Brien & Thom, 2014). Tasers are considered to be *used* by police any time they are presented/drawn, aimed, or discharged, and police forces around Australia have specific and similar provisions detailing when they can be used. For instance, NSW Police Taser Manual (New South Wales Police Force, 2016) specifies that Tasers be used only to protect: (1) human life, (2) self/other where violent confrontation is occurring or is imminent, (3) another officer in danger of being overpowered or self/others from risk of actual bodily harm, and (4) from animals. In their policies around the use of Tasers, police forces generally specify situations when Taser use should be avoided, such as on children, pregnant women, and people known to have a mental health issue (e.g. Barbour, 2012; Shoyer, 2017).

One of the earliest Australian examinations of Tasers was the Queensland Police Force's review (2009). Among other things, the review found that Tasers were most likely to be used on Caucasian males between the ages of 20 and 29, where the majority were under the effects of substances but did not possess weapons. In Western Australia, a post-implementation review of Tasers between 2007 and 2009 revealed variable trends, including an overall increase in Taser use (CCC, 2010; WA Police, 2010). Consequently, the Corruption and Crime Commission (2010) cautioned about a possibility of Tasers "mission creep", and a particular concern about their (over)use with some vulnerable populations (CCC, 2010).

The NSW Ombudsman's report into the use of Tasers (Barbour, 2012) reviewed 556 incidents, finding that most of the citizens involved did not have weapons (74%) when the police used their Taser, findings similar to those in Queensland. There were only a small number of incidents where the Taser was used instead of a firearm, thereby discounting the often-cited argument that their introduction would prevent the use of firearms. Similarly, the NSW Ombudsman opined that although there was a reduction in police injuries, this trend began prior to the introduction of Tasers and therefore that this reduction could not be attributed to the introduction of Tasers to operational members.

Following reports of inappropriate use of Tasers in the Northern Territory, its Ombudsman criticised police policy for lacking in clarity and detailed information, and officers for not being informed about the dangers of Taser use (Shoyer, 2017). Significantly, there have been no publicly available outcomes reported in relation to any subsequent investigations of Taser use in Australia. Interestingly, a recent media investigation, using NSW police use of force data obtained covering the period between 2014 and 2018, reported very limited Taser use-related information (Gladstone, 24/9/2019).

AUSTRALIAN POLICE USE OF FORCE ON PEOPLE EXPERIENCING MENTAL HEALTH ISSUES

Different states around Australia have provisions about police interactions with people who appear to be experiencing a mental illness. For instance, in NSW it is section 22 of the *Mental Health Act 2007* (NSW) and in Victoria it is section 351 of the *Mental Health Act 2014* (VIC). Similar to the rest of the Western countries, these provisions give police the power to use the necessary force in order to apprehend a person who appears mentally ill and is at risk of self-harm or harm to others, for the purpose of conveying them to appropriate psychiatric assessment.

Despite the limited research, the available findings suggest that the presence of a citizen's mental health issues is an important consideration in fatal force incidents. Of the 105 police fatal shootings between 1989 and 2011, 42% were recorded as decedents who had a mental illness diagnosis, schizophrenia being most common (AIC, 2013). Historically, Victoria Police had the highest proportion of fatal shootings nationwide, and also saw a concerning trend – fatally shooting people with a known history of mental illness, which resulted in an Office of Police Integrity (now the Independent Broad-based Anti-Corruption Commission) investigation into those shootings (Brouwer, 2005).

In one of the rare published research studies on this issue in Victoria, Kesic and colleagues (2010) found very similar rates of diagnosed mental illness in a sample of 48 police fatalities between 1980 and 2007 as those reported by the AIC at the national level. Concerningly, the study by Kesic and colleagues (2012a) also showed that, in a third of these incidents, there was evidence for suicide-by-police, where diagnosed mental illness, a history of suicide attempts, and alcohol intoxication were significantly more likely to occur in a subset who met the suicide-by-police criteria. In a follow-up study, Kesic and Thomas (2017) utilised a random 20% of all police-attended incidents in one year, finding that Victoria Police members reported attending incidents that meet attempted suicide-by-police criteria up to three times weekly, and resolve them successfully. Significantly, officers perceived that communication and negotiation were the most effective operational tactics used.

Brouwer's investigation highlighted two factors as contributing to the increased number of police shootings of persons with mental health issues: (1) police lack of training in effective management of incidents that involve persons experiencing mental illness and distress, and (2) a lack of effective partnerships and protocols between Victoria Police and other government agencies responsible for the care of people experiencing mental illness. Consequently, Brouwer found that training, procedures, and policies governing critical incidents and incidents involving people experiencing mental illness were not adequate and made 55 recommendations to Victoria Police to improve these. A subsequent Office of Police Integrity Review urged Victoria Police to commit to implementing those recommendations (Strong, 2009). In 2010, all operational officers received a full-day training in managing incidents involving people experiencing mental health issues (Kesic et al., 2012b). This training was a mix of scenario-based exercises and didactic learning. It is unclear what has occurred since 2010 with respect to the provision of ongoing training on how to engage with people who experience mental distress, specifically related to using effective communication and negotiation strategies, as historically and anecdotally these skills had been overlooked in their training in favour of weapons skills training (e.g. Brouwer, 2005). Indeed, Stoughton (2015) argued that the "warrior mindset" that characterises most police organisations undervalues police use of verbal/non-force tactical options, resulting in greater emphasis on an authoritarian style of interactions and force-tactics (see Thomas, Chapter 15).

There are very limited studies examining the incidents of mental distress in non-fatal use of force incidents in Australia. The most notable study to date was Kesic and colleagues' examination of a random sample of 4,267 incidents (Kesic, Thomas, & Ogloff, 2013a). A minority (7.2%) of these cases involved people whom Victoria Police officers perceived to have a mental illness at the time; however, they were more likely to use/threaten to use weapons on police and have weapons used/threatened to be used against them than those who were not perceived to appear to have a mental illness (Kesic et al., 2013a). Very similar rates were found in a recent study by McCarthy and colleagues in Queensland (2019a). Conversely, more than a third of these 4,627 cases in Victoria had a history of formally diagnosed mental illness, with rates of severe mental illness being significantly overrepresented in this sample as compared to their prevalence in the Victorian population (Kesic et al., 2013b).

Mental distress has most commonly been examined in investigations of police use of Tasers in Australia. For instance, the NSW Ombudsman found that almost a third of people involved in Taser-related incidents were thought to be experiencing a mental illness at the time (Barbour, 2012), a finding similarly echoed in a media analysis of police Taser use between 2014 and 2018 in NSW (Gladstone, 24/9/2019). Even prior to such a widespread roll-out of Tasers across Australia, the Crime and Corruption Commission warned of inappropriate use of Tasers in incidents where mental distress was a factor, at times even in the absence of attempts to first use other tactical options (CCC, 2010). Significantly, and in line with Australian investigations, the most recent international meta review of 33 studies found that the overall prevalence of Taser use on people in mental health distress was 28% (Hallett et al., 2020). It was reported that Tasers were used by police in a range of settings, including in residential settings, and that police often had prior knowledge about the person's mental health condition. The authors maintained that these results were very concerning, cautioning that "there is an increasing need to monitor the use of Tasers on people experiencing mental distress" (p. 12) especially when considering the proliferation of Tasers around the world.

CONCLUSION

Overall, there are a number of critical issues with respect to police use of force in Australia; many have been noted throughout this chapter, and a few will be highlighted here. At present, there is no uniform mandatory national reporting on police use of force. A level of standardised use of force recording across the different states that is regularly collated and published would not only provide a consistent unit of analysis to work from to improve policy and practice but would also serve to improve public perceptions of police legitimacy by means of the increased transparency. Further, and pertaining to the issues of over-representation of use of force, including Tasers, on people experiencing mental health issues, there is a crucial need for police forces around the country to provide regular publicly available data on this issue. The lack of focused examinations, both academic and official, in this area over the last decade is very concerning, yet extant evidence tells us that this issue requires specific and ongoing attention (e.g. Hallett et al., 2020). Furthermore, there are significant recent policing changes (e.g. introduction of the Hostile Vehicle policy, and roll-out of semi-automatic long-arms to police in regional Victoria for managing high-risk incidents) that need to be carefully monitored against their impact on vulnerable populations. Lastly, a lack of published research examinations of police use of force in Australia in general, and particularly to do with the issues pertaining to police contact with people experiencing mental health issues, needs immediate attention. It is crucial that research, which accelerated in the last decade, continues to be built on and prioritised by policing organisations in partnership with academic institutions. Crucially, future research ought to heed the findings of recent meta-analyses and ongoing critiques of extant international research to ensure meaningful progression in the field. Therefore, as advocated by Klahm IV and colleagues (2014), instead of continuing to examine individual factors that may influence police use of force through inconsistent and weak methodologies, future research should focus on multilevel modelling of organisational, environmental, and situational factors so as to be able to provide a reliable and valid picture of the complexity of the actual relationships and to meaningfully contribute to improvements in policing policy and practice.

NOTE

1 Current preferred less stigmatising terminology: The broader term *mental health issues*, which may include a formal diagnosis of a mental illness, will be used throughout. Where required, formally diagnosed *mental disorder* is termed *mental illness*.

REFERENCES

ACT Police. (2016). *ACT policing annual report 2016/17*. Retrieved from https://police.act.gov.au/sites/default/files/PDF/ACTPAnnualReport2016-17.pdf

Australian, New Zealand Policing Advisory Agency (ANZPAA). (2014). *Australia New Zealand use of force principles*. Retrieved from www.anzpaa.org.au›police-use-of-force-principles.pdf.aspx

Australian Institute of Criminology (AIC). (2013). *Police shootings of people with a mental illness*. Research in Practice, No. 34, May. Retrieved from https://aic.gov.au/publications/rip/rip34

Australian, New Zealand Policing Advisory Agency (ANZPAA) (2014). *Australia New Zealand use of force principles*. Retrieved from www.anzpaa.org.au›police-use-of-force-principles.pdf.aspx

Baker, M. A., & Bacharach, V. R. (2017). Police officer-civilian confrontations caught on camera: The influence of contextual frames on judgements of excessive force. *American Journal of Criminal Justice, 42*(4), 683–697.

Barbour, B. (2012). *How are Taser weapons used by the NSW police force*, October. Retrieved from www.ombo.nsw.gov.au/__data/assets/pdf_file/0004/6970/How-are-Taser-weapons-used-by-NSW-Police-Force-Special-report-to-Parliament-October-2012-.pdf

Best, D., Quigley, A., & Bailey, A. (2004). Police shootings as a way of self-harming: A review of the evidence for 'suicide by cop' in England and Wales between 1998 and 2001. *International Journal of the Sociology of Law, 32*, 349–361.

Bolger, P. C. (2015). Just following orders: A meta-analysis of the correlates of American police officer use of force decisions. *American Journal of Criminal Justice, 40*(3), 466–492.

Bond, C. E. W., Murphy, K., & Porter, L. E. (2015). Procedural justice in policing: The first phase of an Australian longitudinal study of officer attitudes and intentions. *Crime, Law and Social Change, 64*(4), 229–245.

Brouwer, G. E. (2005). *Review of fatal shootings by Victoria Police*. Melbourne: Office of Police Integrity.

Carroll, M. (2005). Mental health system overburdening police. *Police Journal*, 18–22.

Corruption and Crime Commission (2010). *The use of Taser weapons by Western Australia police*. Retrieved from www.ccc.wa.gov.au/sites/default/files/Full%20 Report%20-%20Use%20of%20Taser%20Weapons%20by%20WAPOL.pdf

Dalton, V. (1998). Police shootings 1990–97. *Trends and Issues in Crime and Criminal Justice*, 89, 1–6. Retrieved from www.aic.gov.au/publications/tandi/tandi89.html

Davies, J. A. (2017). Shoot/do not shoot: What are the factors? The police recruit perspective. *Policing and Society*, 27(5), 494–507. doi:10.1080/10439463.2015.1 077835

Dymond, A. (2018). 'Taser, Taser'! Exploring factors associated with police use of Taser in England and Wales. *Policing and Society*. doi:10.1080/10439463.2018.1 551392

Edwards, A. (2000). Reported use of force by Queensland police: Findings from the 1999 Queensland defendants survey. *Queensland Criminal Justice Commission*, 6(2), 1–8. Retrieved from www.ccc.qld.gov.au/sites/default/files/Docs/ Publications/CJC/Issues%2Cseries-and-discussion-papers/Research-paper/ Research-Paper-Series-Vol6No2-Reported-use-of-force-by-qld-police-2000.pdf

Fildes, A., Murphy, K., & Porter, L. (2017). Police officer procedural justice self-assessments: Do they change across recruit training and operational experience? *Policing and Society*. doi:10.1080/10439463.2017.1290089

Fry, A. J., O'Riordan, D. P., & Geanellos, R. (2002). Social control agents or front-line carers for people with mental health problems: Police and mental health services in Sydney, Australia. *Health & Social Care in the Community*, 10(4), 277–286.

Gill, J. R., & Pasquale-Styles, M. (2009). Firearm deaths by law enforcement. *Journal of Forensic Sciences*, 54(1), 185–188.

Gladstone, N. (2019, September 24). *NSW police database unlocked: The where, when and why officers used force*, September 24. Retrieved from www.smh.com.au/ national/nsw/nsw-police-database-unlocked-the-where-when-and-why-officers-used-force-20190917-p52s1p.html

Hallett, M., Duxbury, J., McKee, T., Harrisson, N., Haines, A., Craig, E., & O'Brien, A. (2020). Taser use on individuals experiencing mental distress: An integrative literature review. *Journal Psychiatric Mental Health Nursing*, 1–16. doi:10.1111/ jpm.12594

Hickman, M. J., Piquero, A. R., & Garner, J. H. (2008). Toward a national estimate of police use of nonlethal force. *Criminology & Public Policy*, 7(4), 563–604.

Hine, K., Porter, L., Westera, N., & Alpert, G. (2018a). Too much or too little? Individual and situational predictors of police force relative to suspect resistance. *Policing and Society*, 28(50), 587–604. doi:10.1080/10439463.2016.1232257

Hine, K., Porter, L., Westera, N., & Alpert, G. (2018b). Exploring police use of force decision-making processes and impairments using a naturalistic decision-making approach. *Criminal Justice and Behavior*, 45(11), 1782–1801.

Hine, K., Porter, L., Westera, N., & Alpert, G. (2018c). The understated ugly side of police – citizen encounters: Situation, suspect, officer, decision- making, and force predictors of officer injuries. *Policing and Society*, 28(6), 665–683. doi:10. 1080/10439463.2016.1251430

Hollis, M. E., & Jennings, W. G. (2018). Racial disparities in police use of force: A state-of-the-art review. *Policing: An International Journal of Policing Strategies and Management*. 41(2), 178–193.

International Association of Chiefs of Police. (2001). *Police use of force in America 2001*. Alexandria, VA: International Association of Chiefs of Police.

Johnson, R. R. (2011). Suspect mental disorder and police use of force. *Criminal Justice and Behavior, 38*(2), 127–145.

Kaminski, R. J., DiGiovanni, C., & Downs, R. (2004). The use of force between the police and persons with impaired judgment. *Police Quarterly, 7*(3), 311–338.

Kesic, D., & Thomas, S. D. M. (2017). Attempted suspect-provoked shootings in Victoria: Prevalence and characteristics. *Policing: An International Journal of Police Strategies & Management, 40*(4), 704–718. doi:10.1108/PIJPSM-04-2016-0050

Kesic, D., Thomas, S. D. M., & Ogloff, J. R. P. (2010). Mental illness among police fatalities in Victoria 1982–2007: A case linkage study. *Australian and New Zealand Journal of Psychiatry, 44*, 463–468.

Kesic, D., Thomas, S. D. M., & Ogloff, J. R. P. (2012a). Time, space and suicide by police: Coronial reports analysis of fatal police shootings. *Criminal Justice and Behavior, 39*, 1107–1125. doi:10.1177/0093854812440084

Kesic, D., Thomas, S. D. M., & Ogloff, J. R. P. (2012b). Estimated rates of mental disorders in, and characteristics of, incidents of nonfatal use of force by police. *Social Psychiatry & Psychiatric Epidemiology*. doi:10.1007/s00127-012-0543-4

Kesic, D., Thomas, S. D. M., & Ogloff, J. R. P. (2013a). Use of nonfatal force on and by persons with apparent mental disorder in encounters with police. *Criminal Justice and Behavior, 40*, 321–337.

Kesic, D., Thomas, S. D. M., & Ogloff, J. R. P. (2013b). Do prior histories of violence and mental disorders impact on violent behaviour during encounters with police? *International Journal of Law and Psychiatry*. doi:10.1016?j.ijlp.2014.02.012

Klahm IV, C. F., & Tillyer, R. (2010). Understanding police use of force: A review of the literature. *Southwest Journal of Criminal Justice, 7*(2), 214–231.

Klahm IV, C. F., Frank, J., & Liederbach, J. (2014). Understanding police use of force: Rethinking the link between conceptualisation and measurement. *Policing: An International Journal of Policing Strategies and Management, 37*(3), 558–578.

Klein, G. C. (2010). Negotiating the fate of people with mental illness: The police and the hospital emergency room. *Journal of Police Crisis Negotiations, 10*(1), 205–219.

Knott, J. C., Pleban, A., Taylor, D., & Castle, D. (2007). Management of mental health patients attending Victorian emergency departments. *The Royal Australian and New Zealand College of Psychiatrists, 41*, 759–767.

Lawton, B. A. (2007). Levels of nonlethal force: An examination of individual, situational, and contextual factors. *Journal of Research in Crime and Delinquency, 44*(2), 163–184.

McCarthy, M., Porter, L., Townsley, M., & Alpert, G. (2019a). Influence of community characteristics on serious police use of force events in an Australian policing jurisdiction: A test of minority threat, social disorganisation, and ecological contamination theories. *Policing and Society, 29*(9), 1091–1108. doi:10.1080/10439463.2018.1493109

McCarthy, M., Porter, L., Townsley, M., & Alpert, G. (2019b). The typology of citizen presentations in use of force events: Are there ecological drivers. *Police Quarterly, 22*(3), 360–387.

McElvain, J. P., & Kposowa, A. J. (2008). Police officer characteristics and the likelihood of using deadly force. *Criminal Justice and Behavior*, *35*(4), 505–521.

McKenzie, I. K. (2006). Forcing the police to open fire: A cross-cultural/international examination of police-involved, victim-provoked shootings. *Journal of Police Crisis Negotiations*, *6*(1), 5–25.

Mohandie, K., Meloy, J., & Collins, P. I. (2009). Suicide by cop among officer-involved shooting cases. *Journal of Forensic Sciences*, *54*(2), 456–462.

Mumola, C. J. (2007). *Arrest-related deaths in the United States 2003–2005 (NCJ-219534)*. Washington, DC: United States Department of Justice.

New South Wales Police Force. (NSW) (2016). *Use of conducted electrical weapons (Taser)*. Retrieved from https://www.police.nsw.gov.au/__data/assets/pdf_file/0010/583705/taser-use-public-information.pdf

NSW Police. (2019). *NSW police handbook*. Retrieved from www.police.nsw.gov.au/__data/assets/pdf_file/0014/631004/nsw_police_force_handbook.pdf

O'Brien, A. J., & Thom, K. (2014). Police use of TASER devices in mental health emergencies: A review. *International Journal of Law and Psychiatry*, *37*(4), 420–426.

Porter, L., & Alpert, G. (2017). Understanding police recruits attitudes towards public interactions: An Australian example. *Police Quarterly*, *20*(4), 449–480.

Queensland Police Force. (2009). *Review of the Queensland Police Service Taser Trial*. Retrieved from https://www.cabinet.qld.gov.au/documents/2009/jun/qps%20taser%20trial/Attachments/Review%20of%20QPS%20Taser%20Trial.pdf

Senate Select Committee on Mental Health. (2006). *A national approach to mental health – from crisis to community: First report*. Canberra: Commonwealth of Australia.

Shoyer, P. (2017). *Taser use and management of NT police conduct issues*. Retrieved from www.ombudsman.nt.gov.au/sites/default/files/downloads/taser_use_and_management_of_nt_police_conduct_issues.pdf

Stoughton, S. (2015). Law enforcement's "warrior" problem. *Harward Law Review*, *128*, 225–234. Retrieved from https://harvardlawreview.org/2015/04/law-enforcements-warrior-problem/

Strong, M. (2009). *Review of the use of force by and against Victorian police*. Melbourne: Office of Police Integrity.

Terrill, W., & Mastrofski, S. D. (2002). Situational and officer-based determinants of police coercion. *Justice Quarterly*, *19*(2), 215–248.

Tuckey, M. (2004). *National guidelines for incident management, conflict resolution and use of force: 2004*. Payneham, SA: Australasian Centre for Policing Research.

Victoria Police. (2004). *Operational safety: 101-4 Use of force*. Melbourne: Victoria Police.

Western Australia Police. (2010). *Post Implementation Review of Tasers*. Retrieved from www.police.wa.gov.au

CHAPTER 12

Working with others
Future policing partnerships

Douglas E. Abrahamson and Jane Goodman-Delahunty

INTRODUCTION

Roles, responsibilities, policies, and practices of contemporary police officers and organisations evolve and adapt to changing needs of their communities, society, and the world around them. Continued police policy and practice review, adaptation, and evolution correspond to increasingly complex, dynamic, and persistent manifold public safety and security issues within Australia and beyond. Further, many public policy safety and security issues extend beyond conventional regional, state, or national boundaries, stretching the limits of traditionally conceived police knowledge and policy capacities. Critically, many police policy and practice adaptations and expansion of roles and responsibilities developed ad hoc as police leaders and organisations attempted to meet new threats without requisite human, financial, or technological resources, knowledge, skills, and/or partnerships. Increasingly, within Australia and elsewhere around the globe, complex criminal justice policy issues cannot be understood, ameliorated, or resolved without considering sustainable multisectoral analysis, collaborations, debate, reflection, and application of evidence-based responses (Deckert & Sarre, 2017). At the core of this process is the need for public policy collaboration and partnerships that can share policy responsibility, knowledge, effective practices, and overcome the inherent inflexibility of traditional organisational and sectoral boundaries.

Police personnel, whether at the front line, manager/supervisor, or executive management level, must effectively reconcile past policies, practices, and understanding of the world around them through the lens of new information, knowledge, social values, and critically important – a multitude of stakeholder perspectives. The complexity of the issues to be addressed requires police practitioners and support staff to incorporate a broad range of "knowledge, skills, contextual understandings and critical reflection into a sophisticated repertoire for professional practice" (O'Hara & Pockett, 2011, p. 339).

When we think about public policy issues such as cybercrime, gun violence, human trafficking, organised crime, and acts of terrorism, we find that the levels of stakeholder conflict, solution ambiguity, political debate, and stakeholder polarisation are often elevated due to the complexity and pluralistic nature of the issues. This necessitates the question as to how police leaders can demonstrate the requisite *professional* practice and community accountability if the very issue they are addressing lacks apparent solution through conventional contextual interpretation, knowledge, skills, policies, or practices. Further, how can police organisations present a professional persona when dealing with a policy problem set that highlights the organisation's lack of awareness and understanding of interconnected contexts and knowledge of effective, manageable, and sustainable solutions? To effectively deal with complex and sometimes intractable policy issues, from issue management to sustainable solution delivery, police leaders must constantly assess and monitor whether their organisations' policy and practice capacities, culture, knowledge, and skills are up to the task. Competent organisations require "stronger understandings of how policy problems evolve, how debates are shaped around issues and solutions, and how to identify a range of methods (e.g. analytical tools, managerial capacities, consultative processes) that might develop more effective policy responses" (Head, 2019, p. 181). One key method is understanding why collaboration is critical to public policy and policing today, what collaboration entails, how it has been used, and how to apply effective strategic partnership arrangements within your own organisation.

EFFECTIVE STRATEGIC PARTNERSHIPS

Complex socially constructed and politically constrained public policy issues cannot always be understood or addressed through myopic monodisciplinary approaches. Cross-disciplinary approaches provide different policy perspectives that facilitate better understanding of the issue context, increase policy legitimization, promote trust, and improve stakeholder alignment (Kivits, 2011; Lawrence, 2017). A cross-disciplinary or cross-sector approach is a way of working with other fields of practice or disciplines (e.g. academe, economics, health sciences, social sciences) that have knowledge, insights, and experience in addressing the same policy issue – from a different perspective. Cross-sector collaboration is:

> *the voluntary linking of organizations in two or more sectors in a common effort that involves a sharing of information, resources, activities, capabilities, risks and decision-making aimed to achieve an agreed to public outcome that would have been difficult or impossible to achieve by one organization acting alone* (Forrer et al., 2014, pp. 9–10).

Benefits of cross-sector collaborations include improved problem management and better solutions and public service delivery. For example, human trafficking cannot simply be addressed through police investigation and enforcement of federal laws. Other fields of practice, such as political science (re: political instability), economics (re: poverty, human migration), social sciences (re: gender inequality), and health sciences (re: mental and physical health, addiction) have obvious contributions to help understand human trafficking in a broader context. Professionals from these fields of expertise can assist police in developing more effective, holistic, and sustainable policies and practices, across disciplines and traditional problem solving and decision-making boundaries.

When considering public policy collaboration options, Australian police have a choice in entering into different levels of cross-disciplinary engagement. Expanding upon the concept of the "three Cs" (cooperation, coordination, collaboration), Keast (2016) suggested a "five Cs" continuum of inter-organisational relationships, from competition and cooperation at the low end, coordination in the mid-range, to collaboration and consolidation at the high end. Each option has corresponding characteristics in terms of: level of organisational autonomy, personnel involved, level of information sharing, decision-making processes, conflict management requirements, resource allocation, need for and level of trust, and the degree of *systems level* thinking (McNamara, 2012).

Each inter-organisational relationship option has its own unique needs and issues that must be balanced in terms of context-specific organisational goals, objectives, resources, risks, and likelihood of achieving desired outcomes. Notably, while cross-disciplinary and collaborative approaches are core to contemporary public policy governance (Craven et al., 2018), these partnerships are not simple, nor do they guarantee success. They require organisations to cross a broad range of *dynamic* cultural, knowledge, policy, professional, social, structural, and technical boundaries between people, organisations, and institutional entities. Thus, bridging organisational entities requires context-specific boundary-spanning processes that draw upon a combination of human agency (e.g. individual action, issue conceptualization, leadership, motivation, and professionalism) and structural factors (e.g. organisational capability and capacity, incentives, and resources).

GOOD PARTNERSHIP IN PRACTICE

Creating *shared value* is one hallmark of good public policy partnerships and has been the goal of organisations and democratic governments around the world for several years. Creating good collaborative cross-disciplinary practices requires a combination of committed leadership and support from governments, stakeholders, and organisational leaders. While many police-academic partnerships focus on solving specific crime-control issues (e.g. transnational crime) they also serve important functions outside the crime-control remit. For instance, shared value may be created through: mutual context and knowledge sense-making, research gap analysis, capability and capacity building, relationship building, workforce development, and strategic policy coordination. Within Australia, examples of good police partnerships in practice exist within the areas of research, problem solving, and training, which are discussed next.

Research partnerships

Over the last 20 years, mere anecdotal evidence of successful police policy and practice led to the demand for and application of evidence-based policies and practices based upon best available evidence (i.e. research *and* craft) of "what works" after careful and considered planning and systematic analysis of program or policy efficacy (Farrington, 2013; Sherman, 1998; Telep, 2017). A recent report, *Social Science Research and Intelligence in Australia* (Academy of the Social Sciences in Australia, 2019), highlights the desirability of and need for collaborative partnerships between social and behavioural science researchers and intelligence communities within Australia. This need for well-informed, educated, capable, and connected intelligence analysts and police officers in democratic countries cannot be understated, as evidenced by events such as the Christchurch, New Zealand, mosque attack (British Broadcasting Corporation, 2019) and hostage-taking in the Brighton community of Melbourne, Australia (British Broadcasting Corporation, 2017). Endorsing this police-research partnership agenda, the Director General of the UK MI5 stated:

> [W]e identified ways in which advances in that field enable us to sharpen our "radar" and increase insight. . . . Used in combination with knowledge from our behavioural science experts, this will give us an earlier and richer picture of our cases (Melanie, 2019, p. 1).

The inherent value of *co-created* contextual and behavioural knowledge, through data and knowledge analytics before, during, or after such events, should be readily apparent as police and researchers attempt to answer independent but often overlapping questions regarding contextual factors, processes that support or hinder the achievement of desired outcomes, and how to improve efficacy of policy and practice.

A noteworthy example of effective research partnerships to support policy and practice reforms comes from the area of child sexual abuse investigations, which have direct implications for police in terms of prevention, identification, response, and justice for victims. Then the Australian Royal Commission underscored the value of research and collaboration with multidisciplinary advisory groups, researchers, and experts in "obtaining background information, filling key evidence gaps, exploring what is known and what works, analyzing information we have collected" (Royal Commission Into Institutional Responses to Child Sexual Abuse, 2014, p. 69) and made research one of three pillars of the inquiry. Not only did this research inform the outcomes, policy, and practice recommendations, outlined in the final Criminal Justice Report (Royal Commission Into Institutional Responses to Child Sexual Abuse, 2017) but elements were incorporated into the larger practitioner literature (Westera et al., 2019). Now that this research and knowledge is more readily available, police organisations will be better equipped to problem-solve policy and practice issues at the local, regional, or national level.

Problem-solving partnerships

Problem solving within the field of policing has evolved from what Goldstein initially described as Problem-Oriented Policing (Goldstein, 1990) to extensive variations on the theme that have a singular goal – crime reduction. Within this framework, crime reduction involves identifying *problems* within the community (e.g. organised crime) and reducing associated crimes by "implementing tailored responses directly linked to the findings of comprehensive problem analyses" (Community Oriented Policing Services, 2011, p. 3). Key elements of police problems include: (1) concerns to the public and to police; (2) conduct or conditions within the broad responsibilities of the police; (3) multiple, recurring incidents or cases related in one or more ways; and (4) unlikely resolution without police intervention (Scott, 2015, p. 9).

Examples of crime reduction problem-solving models include SARA, SPATIAL and CAPRA, which incorporate a combination of environmental scanning, analysis, response, assessment, stakeholder engagement, and intervention techniques (McGarry, 2010; Sidebottom & Tilley, 2011). Those six core principles require collaboration and partnership between police, community, researchers, and other stakeholders. Critics of the narrowly focused *crime reduction* police problem-solving model recommend a more expansive and inclusive problem-solving model which means:

> *reconsidering the role of police officers and other crime reduction practitioners within a broader multidisciplinary frame and – in moving from the consensual goal of reducing crime to a wider arena of policy issues engaged by preventive interventions in the causes of crime and to the reconciliation of security with other policy requirements* (Borrion et al., 2020, p. 234).

The Australian Federal Police (AFP) has already acknowledged this issue, per its Futures Centre website:

> *The use of multidisciplinary and multi-agency teams, comprising detectives and specialist investigative capabilities, to resolve standard investigations will become the norm. This will require a recalibration of the AFP's existing workforce and greater public sector partnerships* (Australian Federal Police, 2020a).

As with all models of policing policy and practice, each evolves through changes in society; pressure from internal and external stakeholders; and advances in academic research and theory, technology, and our knowledge of what actually works versus conjecture, personal opinion, or past practice. Within this multidisciplinary frame, police officers must be made aware of relevant advances within and outside their field of practice and must understand that new information gathering, data analysis, critical thinking, and collaboration skills will be needed within a multisectoral policy environment.

An example of how academics and police can collaborate on important practical problems was developed by applying Robson's (1995) Model for Real World Enquiry to criminal investigations (Ryan & Kebbel, 2020). The model uses relationships with practitioners to identify a problem, analyse the context, formulate a potential solution based on existing evidence, develop a way of testing this "solution," and refine it based on the results of research and practitioner feedback (p. 19).

Training partnerships

Historically, police training has been self-insulated, with police training police in local, regional, or national training academies with little to no requirement for higher education or partnerships with tertiary education institutions. This self-contained and restricted training culture has long been criticized. Calls for professionalism of policing, policing reforms, and more evidence-based approaches abound (Neyroud, 2017; Rogers & Frevel, 2018). Though Green (2018) noted progress in Australian police recruit training and partnerships with tertiary education institutions, notably the 17-year partnership between Charles Sturt University and the New South Wales Police Force, recruit level training "remains entrenched in a practitioner-focused, skills-based, training environment" (p. 252).

Whilst the application of formalized police (recruit) training and tertiary education partnerships remain underpotentiated within Australia and abroad, examples of successful multisector police training partnerships and/or potential opportunities prevail. For instance, the AFP does not partner with tertiary education institutions for recruit training modules, but does partner with and share information, skills, and strategies with external government agencies, members of Commonwealth investigative agencies, and international police services through its Management of Serious Crime Program (Australian Federal Police, 2020b). Recognising future training needs, challenges, and opportunities, the AFP suggests that it:

> *should assume a greater leadership role in the delivery of national investigative standards and training curricula for its Commonwealth law enforcement partners. The establishment of an investigations training and accreditation centre of excellence could deliver national investigative standards and training curricula for all Commonwealth law enforcement agencies. Such a centre could establish capability benchmarks for the standard of investigations, and drive*

continuous improvement by sharing capabilities and experiences. It would help generate a common understanding of techniques and investigative tools, including technology, harmonise the interpretation of legislation, ensure better information-sharing and help strengthen the personal networks of law enforcement professionals (Australian Federal Police, 2020a).

Bearing in mind the need for partnerships, delivering curricula, and establishing (evidence-based) benchmarks for good practice, academic researchers within Australia and around the globe often suggest the need for and offer opportunities for police training on issues that are relevant, timely, and critical to police operations, policy, and practice – including evidence-based investigative techniques (Goodman-Delahunty et al., 2020, in press; 2021, in press). Such collaborations and partnerships would support the future needs, challenges, and opportunities of the AFP and state policing agencies.

GOOD PARTNERSHIP MECHANISMS, METHODOLOGIES, AND SKILLS

Mechanisms of good partnership

Changes in police policy and practice innovation and diffusion are driven by diverse motivations or mechanisms, including: the need to demonstrate legitimacy, dealing with network structure pressure, spreading best practices within and across governments and organisations, learning by example, participating in economic competition, and combating coercion from government (Jagers et al., 2019; Shipan & Volden, 2008).

Three significant and interrelated shifts within democratic societies occurred over the last 20 years, each of which directly affected demands for improved collaborative capability and capacity within policing:

1. Effective information and knowledge communication, management, and sharing, within and across police organizations and teams became a critical organizational resource and governance capability, since all contemporary policing models are knowledge-intensive (Abrahamson & Goodman-Delahunty, 2013);
2. Police organizations had to demonstrate greater accountability to stakeholders through proper governance practices and the application of *evidence-influenced* policies and practices requiring police to use the best available evidence (i.e. formal research, professional consensus and/or peer reviewed evidence) to inform and guide police problem solving, decision-making, policies, practices, and achievement of organizational outcomes (Mitchell & Huey, 2019); and
3. Due to the complex (cultural, economic, geographical, political, social, and/or technical) nature of contemporary public policy issues, the need increased for greater strategic collaboration, partnerships, and teamwork within and across organizations, institutions, and disciplines (Abrahamson, 2019; Brown et al., 2010).

Compounding the need to address complex public policy issues, police leaders must concomitantly demonstrate their ability to improve police policy and practice efficiency, effectiveness, and accountability through accepted *good governance* practices. By demonstrating and adhering to good governance practices and the achievement of organisational and societal goals and outcomes, police leaders garner and maintain public trust, legitimacy, and cooperation.

The concept of good governance within democratic societies and organisations includes principles related to the need for and adherence to the basic principles of: legitimacy (stakeholder engagement and consensus orientation); strategic vision; performance (responsiveness, effectiveness, and efficiency); accountability; transparency, and fairness (equity and rule of law) (Addink, 2019; Graham et al., 2003). Police openness to organisational change and to adopting evidence-based techniques is fostered by the presence of features of organisational justice such as a procedurally fair workplace climate (Brimbal et al., 2020).

Within these governance mechanisms, police leaders must also explore, understand, and improve their organisation's *policy capacity*. Policy capacity is the organisation's ability to address public problems and "the set of skills and resources – or competences and capabilities – necessary to perform policy functions . . . categorized into three types: analytical, operational and political" (Wu et al., 2015, p. 166). By assessing and understanding an organisation's policy capacities, police leaders will be better equipped to understand their organisations' stress points, strengths, and weaknesses in relation to the context in which the organisation operates and its ability to enter into collaborative partnerships. This assessment process supports organisational decision-making and problem solving, and demonstrates good governance practices to stakeholders. It is imperative that police update their knowledge and their decision-making and problem-solving capacities through ongoing reflection and reflexivity.

Self-reflection involves self-awareness and critical examination of our personal assumptions, experiences, emotional responses, and practices. Reflexivity builds on reflection by asking police practitioners to critically examine things that influence their professional "thoughts, behaviours and actions" (Bassot, 2016, p. 130), including practice context, politics, and social relationships. This extends to assessing the need for and value of entering into specific collaborative partnerships. Norris-Tirrell (2010) identified five *collaboration preconditions:* (1) a legitimate and pressing need to collaborate; (2) critical mass and sufficient representativeness; (3) skilled and committed leadership; (4) competence for collaboration; and (5) reasonable likelihood of consequential change.

Effective collaboration entails "nurturing new and building on existing relationships, establishing trusting relationships, forging agreements on what to work on together and how to work together, building new leadership capacities and identifying and managing conflicts" (Keast, 2016). This process is depicted in Figure 12.1, which shows the continuum of interaction between police agencies and community (cross-sector participants).

CHAPTER 12: WORKING WITH OTHERS 207

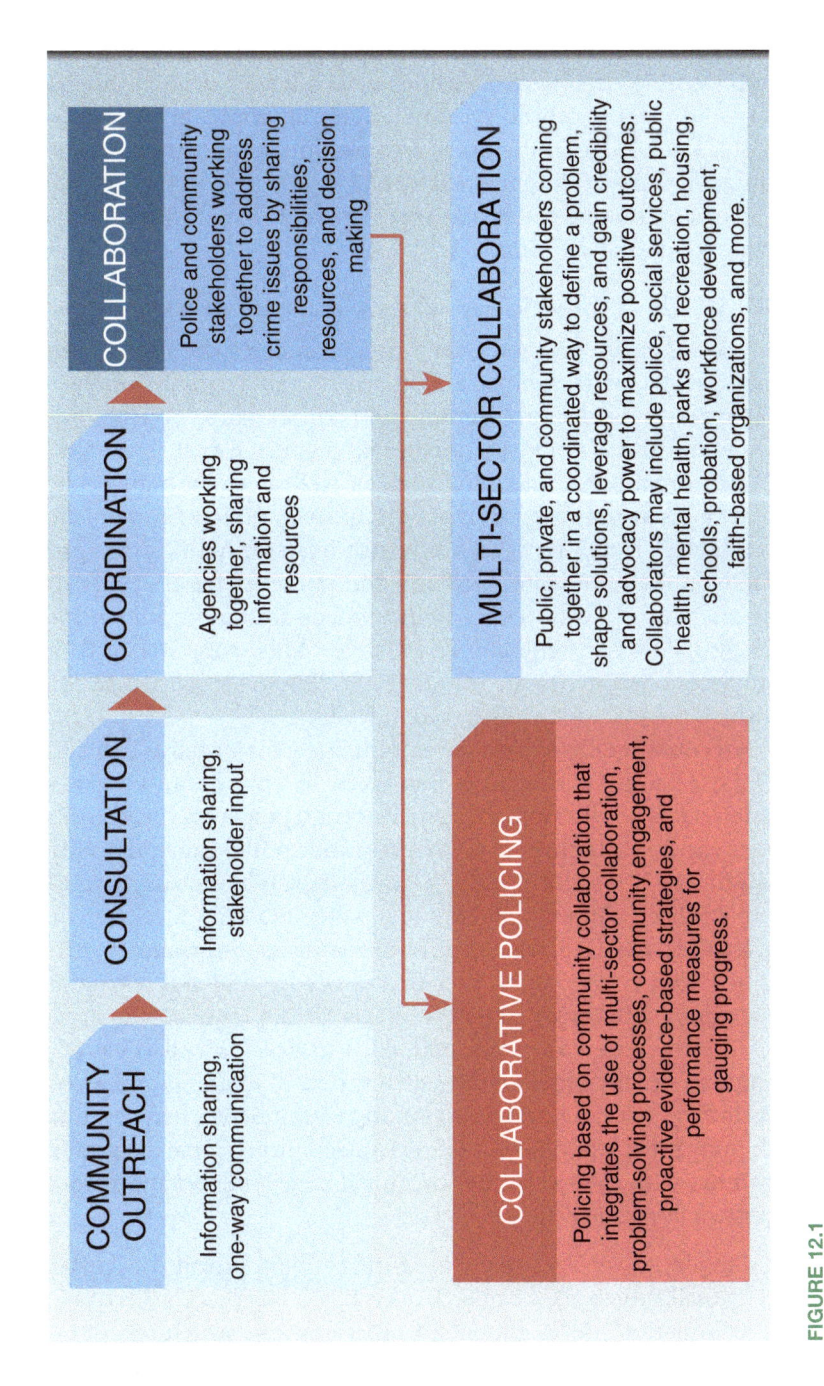

COMMUNITY OUTREACH
Information sharing, one-way communication

CONSULTATION
Information sharing, stakeholder input

COORDINATION
Agencies working together, sharing information and resources

COLLABORATION
Police and community stakeholders working together to address crime issues by sharing responsibilities, resources, and decision making

MULTI-SECTOR COLLABORATION
Public, private, and community stakeholders coming together in a coordinated way to define a problem, shape solutions, leverage resources, and gain credibility and advocacy power to maximize positive outcomes. Collaborators may include police, social services, public health, mental health, parks and recreation, housing, schools, probation, workforce development, faith-based organizations, and more.

COLLABORATIVE POLICING
Policing based on community collaboration that integrates the use of multi-sector collaboration, problem-solving processes, community engagement, proactive evidence-based strategies, and performance measures for gauging progress.

FIGURE 12.1
Police-community Continuum of Interaction

Source: Reprinted from CNA Analysis and Solutions (2017, p. 2).

In terms of operational mechanisms for collaborative partnerships at the state and/or federal levels, options include multi-jurisdictional memoranda of understanding, harmonised legal (criminal law and procedure) frameworks, and compensatory strategies (e.g. education and training) that work to mitigate "challenges of their internal diversity and created central systems of coordination, or mechanisms that foster knowledge of the laws, organisational structures and cultures of other agencies" (Hufnagel, 2016, p. 11).

Next we discuss collaborative processes and methods to support strategic collaborative initiatives.

Methods to develop strategic partnerships

In considering processes and methodologies for the development of strategic partnerships, a framework can facilitate understanding. Figure 12.2 displays an example of a collaborative policing framework showing interactions of individual, organisational, and system-level policy capabilities and capacities as well as collaborative knowledge and skill sets that support cross-disciplinary policies and practices. This framework is neither prescriptive nor necessarily linear in application. The foundation is the need for and value of baseline collaboration and teamwork knowledge, skills, and understanding how the lack of or availability of requisite knowledge, skills, supports, and decisions impedes or supports the building of *collaborative policy capacity* at individual, organisational, and system levels.

In conceptualizing and developing the Collaborative Policing Framework, careful consideration was given to commonly understood and interrelated good governance processes and practices (Gleeson et al., 2011; Rotberg, 2014; Termeer et al., 2015), public policy capabilities (Andriof & Waddock, 2017; Head, 2019; Tiernan, 2011), levels and types of policy capabilities (Wu et al., 2015), and policy maturity measurement scales (New Zealand Department of Prime Minister and Cabinet, 2017) combined with collaboration-specific knowledge and skill elements (Abrahamson, 2019; Choo, 2001; Mathieu et al., 2017; McDonald et al., 2009).

The requisite knowledge and skills to develop collaborative partnerships are readily acquired through a variety of methods and mechanisms, including, but not limited to, working with independent consultants and training providers, online training courses, professional associations, and/or tertiary education institutions. This strategic collaboration process comprises a five-stage life cycle:

1. Exploration: informal or formal exploration of collaborative possibilities;
2. Formation: development of processes and structures;
3. Growth: growth through goals and consensus building;
4. Maturity: stakeholder engagement and collaboration, processes, resources, and structures are in place and functioning; and
5. Ending: collaboration may end or transform (Norris-Tirrell, 2010, p. 30).

COLLABORATIVE POLICING FRAMEWORK

5. Unit Level Capabilities
- System Level
- Organisation Level
- Individual Level

(ANALYTICAL, OPERATIONAL & POLITICAL CAPABILITIES)

4. Implementation Level
- Embedded Systems & Culture
- Practiced
- Enabled
- Ad Hoc Policies & Practices

3. Policy Capacity

COLLABORATION POLICY CAPACITY (+-)

2. Impediments

IMPEDIMENTS
(LACK OF KNOWLEDGE, SKILLS & SUPPORT SYSTEMS)

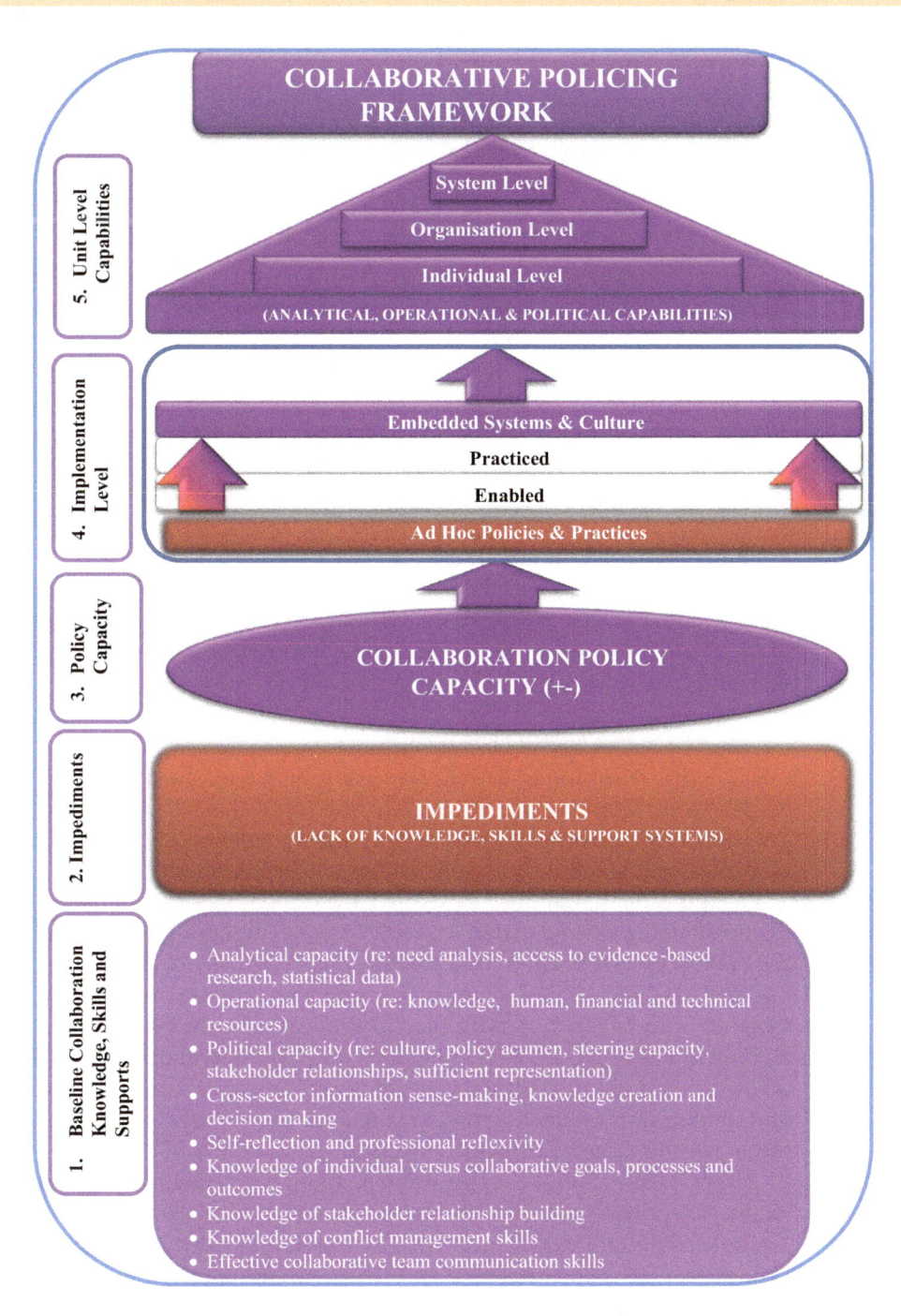

1. Baseline Collaboration Knowledge, Skills and Supports
- Analytical capacity (re: need analysis, access to evidence-based research, statistical data)
- Operational capacity (re: knowledge, human, financial and technical resources)
- Political capacity (re: culture, policy acumen, steering capacity, stakeholder relationships, sufficient representation)
- Cross-sector information sense-making, knowledge creation and decision making
- Self-reflection and professional reflexivity
- Knowledge of individual versus collaborative goals, processes and outcomes
- Knowledge of stakeholder relationship building
- Knowledge of conflict management skills
- Effective collaborative team communication skills

FIGURE 12.2
Collaborative Policing Framework

A series of institutional barriers may impede acquisition of relevant information, knowledge, and skill sets. Three common institutional barriers are: (1) cultures of secrecy, (2) difficulties sharing information within and across agencies and institutions, and (3) inadequate funding.

Institutional barriers to effective partnership

Many police leaders, managers, and personnel espouse the value of and are committed to collaborative partnerships within, across, and outside of their organisation(s), but these processes may go awry in practice (Abrahamson & Goodman-Delahunty, 2014). This disconnect between stated organisational values, espoused theories, rational decision-making, and what is achieved in practice, has long been examined (Argyris & Schön, 1978; March, 1994: Simon, 1997). Faulty logic, outdated assumptions, personal biases (conscious or unconscious), outdated or limited knowledge and skills, along with personal beliefs, dysfunctional organisational cultures, and lack of decision-support systems can all affect the ability of a police officer or an organisation to make sound, fair, and informed decisions. Next, we discuss (1) cultures of secrecy, (2) barriers to information and knowledge acquisition and sharing, and (3) inadequate funding.

Cultures of secrecy in policing

Cultures of "police and policing" have been studied for decades, uncovering broad cynicism, solidarity, secrecy, and conservatism (Chan, 1996; Prenzler, 1997). However, these stereotypical personae are, in reality, neither monolithic nor static and can be subject to change.

Organisational "culture" is shaped by values, place, and history demonstrated through *shared* artifacts (e.g. documents, norms, policies, practices, symbols, or technologies) espoused beliefs, meanings, orientations, underlying assumptions, and the actions of its people. Organisations often have multiple cultures, or subcultures, since not all individuals or groups of people necessarily agree with the espoused organisational identity. Others may "orient themselves to other social units and sources of identity than the organisation as a whole, for example, a division or a department" (Alvesson, 2013, p. 40).

Recent debates about the culture of Australian policing focus on the issue of silence and secrecy within policing and government (Denereaz, 2019; Ransley & Mazerolle, 2009). Compounding this issue is the Crimes Act 1914 which makes it an offence for an officer to publish or communicate "any fact or document which comes to his or her knowledge, or into his or her possession, by virtue of being a Commonwealth officer, and which it is his or her duty not to disclose" (Cave, 2019, Section 70).

Obviously, a prevailing culture that demands strict adherence to non-disclosure of information between individuals or agencies, without explicit authority from supervisors, upon penalty of conviction, inhibits personnel from entering into collaborative arrangements with outside agencies or entities. Without debating the relative merits or demerits of a culture of secrecy within a liberal democracy or our current globalized policing environment, we simply highlight how solidarity and secrecy within policing can impede effective collaborative partnership arrangements. Kinshott et al. (2004, p. 197) suggest: "police officers are members of a unique occupational culture that imbues officers with both a unique world-view, and a working personality." A culture of secrecy can breed world views and working personalities framed by mistrust, cynicism, information and knowledge hoarding, an "us against them" mentality, antithetical to ethical, productive, and (collaborative) democratic policies and practices. In stark contrast, a collaborative organisational culture is open and transparent in its actions and sharing of information; cross-sector relationships are built on mutual trust and respect; and organisational policies, practices, and assumptions are openly challenged in a mutually respectful manner.

Tensions between the need for secrecy and the need for openness will always be a part of policing policy and practice. However, effective sharing of information, building of inter-organisational and cross-sector relationships, and mutual trust form the cornerstones of collaborative partnerships and must be reconciled within the current organisational milieu and against potential barriers to desired policy and practice.

Barriers to information/knowledge acquisition and sharing in policing

Considering that contemporary policing models are information and knowledge intensive, effective information and knowledge sharing, within and across units, agencies and outside institutions, is of primary value, and is the focus of all police personnel, units, and organisations (Abrahamson & Goodman-Delahunty, 2014). Unfortunately, despite the rhetoric and core principles of contemporary policing models, information and knowledge are not always acquired or shared, effectively or otherwise. Barriers to information and knowledge acquisition and sharing within policing are numerous.

Due to the complexity and impact of modern public policy issues, the importance of having the right information and knowledge at the right time and providing them to the right people cannot be understated. Building policy capacity in support of sustained policy implementation requires individuals, organisations, and systems to have the right knowledge, skills, and supports in place at any given point in time. The absence of requisite training for collaboration and partnership arrangements creates a foundational barrier. The New Zealand Department of the Prime Minister and Cabinet (2017) identified several barriers to policy capacity information and knowledge training, displayed in Figure 12.3, supporting the premise that the requisite information, knowledge, training, and supports is critical to building policy capacity, collaborative or otherwise.

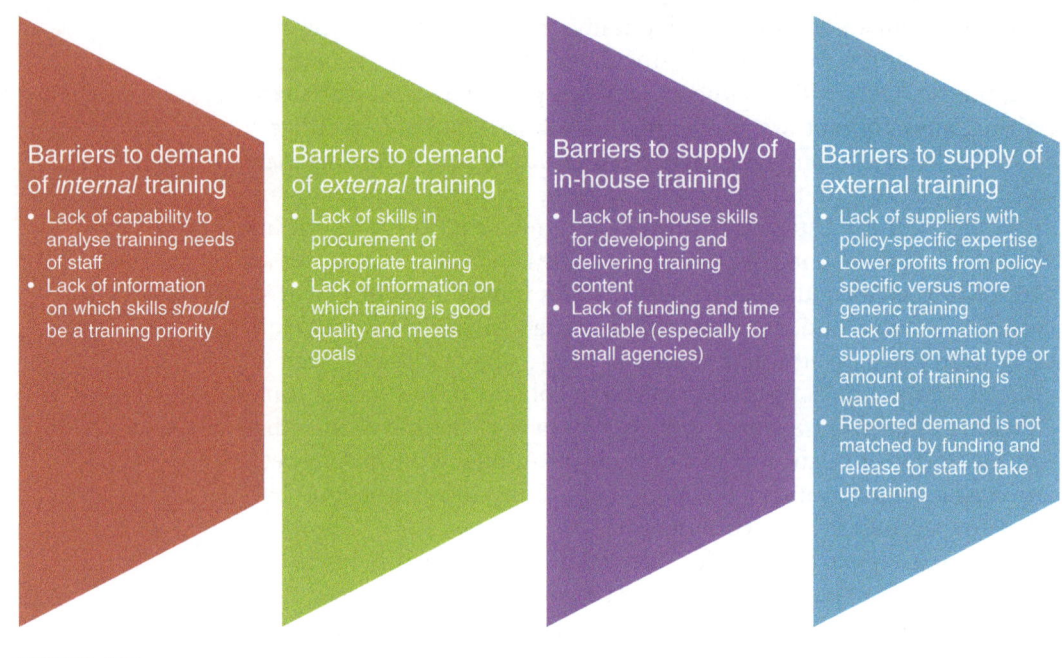

Barriers to demand of *internal* training
- Lack of capability to analyse training needs of staff
- Lack of information on which skills *should* be a training priority

Barriers to demand of *external* training
- Lack of skills in procurement of appropriate training
- Lack of information on which training is good quality and meets goals

Barriers to supply of in-house training
- Lack of in-house skills for developing and delivering training content
- Lack of funding and time available (especially for small agencies)

Barriers to supply of external training
- Lack of suppliers with policy-specific expertise
- Lower profits from policy-specific versus more generic training
- Lack of information for suppliers on what type or amount of training is wanted
- Reported demand is not matched by funding and release for staff to take up training

FIGURE 12.3
Policy Capability Knowledge Barriers

Source: Reprinted from The Policy Project, New Zealand, New Zealand Department of the Prime Minister and Cabinet (2017, p. 4).

An examination of other potential barriers to information and knowledge capabilities within three Canadian police organisations identified seven mutually exclusive impediments to information and knowledge sharing across organisations, namely: processes/technology, individual unwillingness, organisational unwillingness, workload/overload, location/structure, leadership, and risk management (Abrahamson & Goodman-Delahunty, 2014). Figure 12.4 illustrates these barriers by relative perceived importance to police officers.

Notably, the "three most significant discrete impediments to information and knowledge sharing within all three police organisations were processes and technology, individual unwillingness, and organisational unwillingness" (p. 12). Thus, the confluence of lack of effective organisational supports, individual awareness, and organisational culture create effective barriers to information and knowledge acquisition, sharing, and policy capability development. A related barrier, inadequate funding, is discussed next.

Inadequate funding for collaborative policing policy

Inadequate funding as a barrier to developing police policy capability is a perennial issue for most police agencies worldwide. Government funding for programs is constantly balanced against the real or perceived needs of competing agencies and programs along with the economics and politics of the day. Despite limited traditional policy

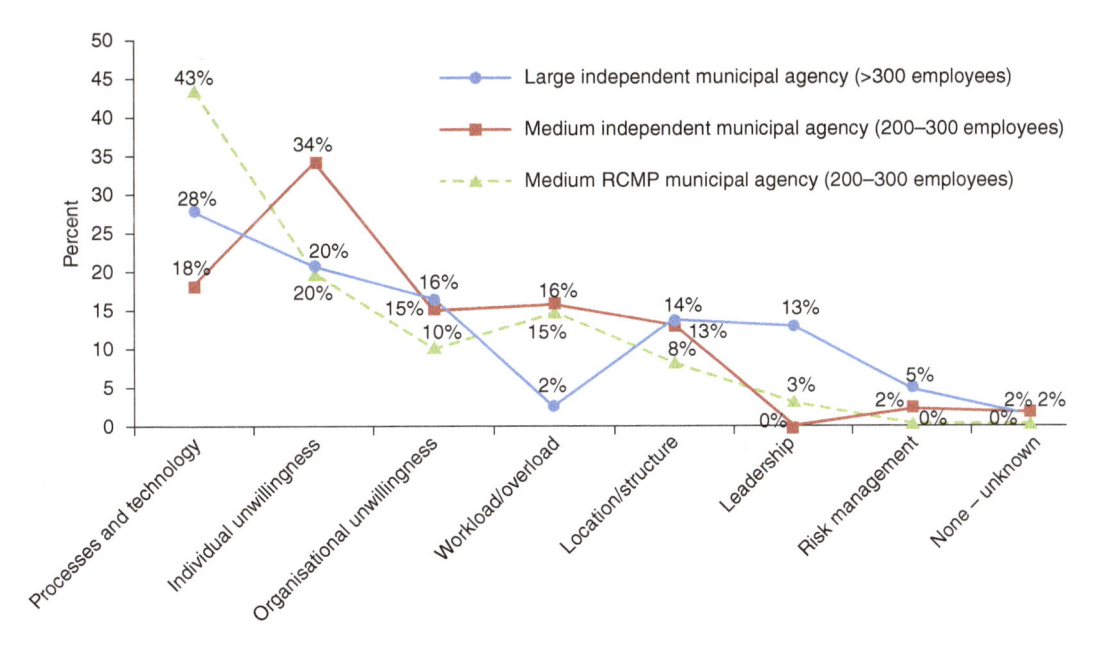

FIGURE 12.4
Perceived Impediments to Information and Knowledge Sharing by Police Agency

Source: Reprinted from Abrahamson and Goodman-Delahunty (2014, p. 9).

funding, the Australian government recognises the need to fund collaborative policing policy efforts that are "integrated, united, capable and evolving", as illustrated by the national strategy to fight transnational, serious, and organised crime (Australian Department of Home Affairs, 2019).

The availability of stable funding within AFP was acknowledged (Hufnagel, 2016) as a core strength in the AFP ability to leverage information sharing, databases, human resources, and analytical capacity within a joint investigative team partnership. This stable funding, however, is a double-edged sword since it may become a significant point of contention and create jealousy within other less-recognised or lesser-funded police agencies or institutions. Such instances might negatively impact the willingness of lesser-funded agencies to cooperate and collaborate, take advantage of available training and networking, and reduce trust and the ability of partners to harmonise resources (Hufnagel, 2016). Stable funding enables police organisations to make full use of available collaborative partnership arrangements regionally, nationally, internationally, and across disciplines.

Transdisciplinary partnerships

Transdisciplinary practices are integrative joint processes to develop new conceptual frameworks and combine knowledge and efforts to create new approaches addressing joint policy and practice issues. As illustrated by the Australian *National Strategy to Fight Transnational, Serious and Organized Crime Model*, creation of transdisciplinary partnerships entailed development of a four-pronged integrated, united, capable, and evolving approach that ultimately supported national policy capability (Commonwealth Transnational Serious and Organised Crime Centre, 2018, p. 9):

1. Deploy multiple available tools (legislation, education, research and innovation, operations, policy, technology and intelligence) to disrupt transnational and serious organized crime;
2. Develop and maintain trust in partnership engagement with:
   - International partners to assist in the detection, disruption and dismantling of transnational, serious and organized crime;
   - Commonwealth, state and territorial intelligence, law enforcement, border control, legal and social policy partners, who assist through good governance practices;
   - Private sector, civil society and academic partners, who help to develop effective policies, practices, regulations and operational responses; and
   - Community engagement partners, whose local knowledge, expertise and experience helps to build local and institutional resilience;
3. Support the national policy capability model by ensuring that people (with appropriate knowledge and skills), systems and processes, technology and infrastructure, intelligence and data work together to create key assets, inform approaches and improve outcomes; and
4. Continuous improvement through research, innovation, measurement of capabilities, understanding outcomes and recognizing success.

IMPLICATIONS FOR PRACTICE AND POLICY

Transitioning from traditionally insular, self-reliant, pragmatic, and sometimes secretive organisational cultures, policies and practices to the exploration, formation, and growth of evidence-based collaborative partnerships will stretch some police leaders, personnel, and organisations. Prudent police leaders will satisfy the five preconditions for collaborative policy transformation listed earlier (Norris-Tirrell, 2010), each of which has policy and practice implications.

Many current police policy issues are complex, demanding complex analysis and multisectoral approaches. Police require the assistance of cross-sector knowledge, expertise, perspective, and support. Police must first identify appropriate partners, engage those parties, and build trusted, sustainable relationships. Through informal and formal engagement, police will identify appropriate partnership targets, identify when sufficient representativeness is achieved, and be able to professionally communicate, negotiate, and deal with conflicts in an effective and respectful manner. Thus, police organisations must ensure that policy, practice, and supporting systems equip police leaders to fulfill this role. Policies and practices have to be devised regarding who, what, when, where, and how these potential partners are to be engaged, the levels of partnerships allowed, and who within the agency is responsible for these partnerships.

Whoever is selected to lead collaborative change processes must ensure that the organisation is fully aligned in terms of vision, need for change, strategic initiatives, communications, cultural readiness (i.e. values, ability to learn, share information, and make decisions), employee empowerment, and resource commitment (i.e. human, technical, structural, financial). Depending on the scale of implementation, these leaders need to guide and deal with individuals who resist collaborative change initiatives, since this change requires affected officers to transition from primarily individual (me) roles to primarily team (we) roles. Requiring "individual" officers to change values, beliefs, and assumptions about how policing works and their relationships with "outside" organisations and people is challenging. Employing a qualified team *business coach* to facilitate the team process on behalf of the organisation and/or police leader may be advisable.

Whether the organisation has the requisite knowledge, skills, and support systems for collaborative policies and practices is critical. Without the requisite collaboration and partnership development knowledge, skills, and supports, true collaborative efforts may diminish. Questions to ask are (1) whether your organisation has an issue with academe, collaboration, partnerships, teamwork, information, or knowledge sharing; and (2) whether you or your colleagues have received training on the value, interpretation, and application of evidence-based research in practice? Collaborative partnerships are about teamwork. Police officers generally lack knowledge or training in "team" theories, concepts, processes, or capabilities. Thus, a combination of reflexivity, analysis, and training is required in policy and practice.

Last, the likelihood of achieving consequential change in alignment with overall goals and strategic direction requires a combination of analytical, operational, and political policy and practice capabilities. In this collaborative partnership landscape, police leaders must constantly analyze and assess the value of partnerships, resources required, and the degree of partnership commitment, in part or in whole. Additionally, the question as to whether *shared value* is created requires partnership group and organisational reflection, discussion and debate.

CONCLUSION

Policy and practice implications center on aligning good governance capabilities with collaborative partnership specific knowledge, skills, and support systems. Collaborative partnerships, sometimes difficult to implement, are integral to current government policies and practices. They provide the opportunity to better understand police issues from multiple perspectives, using of a variety of policy tools and instruments, building national and state policy capability, increasing policy legitimization, promoting trust, and improving stakeholder alignment. Australian examples highlighted the feasibility of strategic cross-sector collaboration partnerships and sharing value across partnering organisations. This journey begins with the first steps: exploring potential informal and formal collaboration partnerships, the formation and development of supportive processes and structures (through committed leadership), the growth of partnerships through shared goals and consensus building, and the final integration of stakeholder engagement, processes, resources, and structures. The path is yours to build.

REFERENCES

Abrahamson, D. E. (2019). Shifting policing paradigms: The roles of collaboration and team coaching in evidence-based policing implementation. In D. Clutterbuck, J. Gannon, S. Hayes, J. Iordanou, K. Lowe, & D. MacKie (Eds.), *The practitioner's handbook of team coaching* (1st ed., pp. 497–505). London: Routledge.

Abrahamson, D. E., & Goodman-Delahunty, J. (2013). The impact of organizational information culture on information use outcomes in policing: An exploratory study. *Information Research*, *18*(4). Retrieved from: http://informationr.net/ir/18-4/paper598.html

Abrahamson, D. E., & Goodman-Delahunty, J. (2014). Impediments to information and knowledge sharing within policing: A study of three Canadian policing organizations. *Sage Open*, *4*(1). https://doi.org/10.1177/2158244013519363

Academy of the Social Sciences in Australia. (2019). *Social science research and intelligence in Australia*. Author. Retrieved from: https://socialsciences.org.au/publications/social-science-research-intelligence-in-australia/

Addink, H. (2019). *Good governance: Concept and context*. Oxford: Oxford University Press. https://doi.org/10.1093/oso/9780198841159.001.0001

Alvesson, M. (2013). *Understanding organizational culture* (2nd ed.). London: Sage Publications.

Andriof, J., & Waddock, S. (2017). Unfolding stakeholder engagement. In J. Andriof, S. Waddock, B. Husted, & S. Sutherland-Rahman (Eds.), *Unfolding stakeholder thinking: Theory, responsibility and engagement* (pp. 19–42). London: Routledge. https://doi.org/10.4324/9781351281881-2

Argyris, C., & Schön, D. A. (1978). *Organizational learning: A theory of action perspective*. Boston: Addison-Wesley.

Australian Department of Home Affairs. (2019). Transnational, serious and organised crime. *National Security*. Retrieved from: www.homeaffairs.gov.au/about-us/our-portfolios/national-security/tsoc

Australian Federal Police. (2020a). *AFP futures centre: Complex challenges- implications for the AFP*. Australian Federal Police. Retrieved from: www.afp.gov.au/futures/implications

Australian Federal Police. (2020b). Management of serious crime program. *Training for Agencies*. Australian Federal Police. Retrieved from: www.afp.gov.au/what-we-do/services/training-agencies/management-serious-crime-program

Bassot, B. (2016). *The reflective journal*. London: Macmillan International Higher Education.

Borrion, H., Ekblom, P., Alrajeh, D., Borrion, A. L., Keane, A., Koch, D., Mitchener-Nissen, T., & Toubaline, S. (2020). The problem with crime problem-solving: Towards a second generation POP? *The British Journal of Criminology, 60*(1), 219–240. doi:10.1093/bjc/azz

Brimbal, L., Bradford, B., Jackson, J., Hartwig, M., & Joseph, E. (2020). Acceptance and implementation of evidence-based policing: On the importance of a procedurally fair organizational climate to openness to change among law enforcement investigators. *PsyArXiv*. Retrieved from: https://psyarxiv.com/vk5qe/029

British Broadcasting Corporation. (2017, June 6). Melbourne siege a 'terrorist incident'. *BBC*. Retrieved from: www.bbc.com/news/world-australia-40168085

British Broadcasting Corporation. (2019, March 15). Christchurch shootings: 49 dead in New Zealand mosque attacks. *BBC*. Retrieved from: www.bbc.com/news/world-asia-47578798

Brown, V. A., Harris, J. A., & Russell, J. Y. (Eds.). (2010). *Tackling wicked problems through the transdisciplinary imagination* (1st ed.). London: Earthscan. https://doi.org/10.4324/9781849776530

Cave, D. (2019, June 5). Australia may be the world's most secretive democracy. *The New York Times*. Retrieved from: www.nytimes.com/2019/06/05/world/australia/journalist-raids.html

Chan, J. (1996). Changing police culture. *British Journal of Criminology, 36*(1), 109–134. https://doi.org/10.1093/oxfordjournals.bjc.a014061

Choo, C. W. (2001). The knowing organization as learning organization. *Education & Training, 43*(4–5), 197–205. https://doi.org/10.1108/EUM0000000005482

CNA Analysis Solutions. (2017). *Smart policing collaboration principles*. Bureau of Justice Assistance. Retrieved from: www.lisc.org/media/filer_public/9d/c4/9dc46966-b5f1-4549-b295-2676c99ba6f3/spi-collaboration_principles.pdf

Commonwealth Transnational Serious and Organised Crime Centre. (2018). *National strategy to fight transnational, serious and organized crime*. Department of Home Affairs. Retrieved from: www.homeaffairs.gov.au/nat-security/files/strategy-transnational-serious-organised-crime.pdf

Community Oriented Policing Services. (2011). *Problem-solving tips: A guide to reducing crime and disorder through problem-solving partnerships*. U.S. Department of Justice. Retrieved from: https://cops.usdoj.gov/RIC/Publications/cops-p019-pub.pdf

Craven, L., Dickinson, H., & Carey, G. (Eds.). (2018). *Crossing boundaries in public policy and management: Tackling the critical challenges*. London: Routledge. https://doi.org/10.4324/9781315206271

Deckert, A., & Sarre, R. (Eds.). (2017). *The Palgrave handbook of Australian and New Zealand criminology, crime and justice*. Melbourne: Palgrave Macmillan.

Denereaz, S. (2019, August 22). Warning signs remain: AFP culture change is needed. *Independent Australia*. Retrieved from: https://independentaustralia.net/politics/politics-display/warning-signs-remain-afp-culture-change-is-needed-13025

Farrington, D. P. (2013). Encouraging policy makers and practitioners to make rational choices about programs based on scientific evidence on developmental crime prevention. *Criminology & Public Policy, 12*(2), 295–301. https://doi.org/doi:10.1111/1745-9133.12043

Forrer, J. J., Kee, J. E., & Boyer, E. (2014). *Governing cross-sector collaboration.* San Francisco: Jossey Bass.

Gleeson, D., Legge, D., O'Neill, D., & Pfeffer, M. (2011). Negotiating tensions in developing organizational policy capacity: Comparative lessons to be drawn. *Journal of Comparative Policy Analysis: Research and Practice, 13*(3), 237–263. https://doi.org/10.1080/13876988.2011.565912

Goldstein, H. (1990). *Problem solving policing.* New York: McGraw-Hill.

Goodman-Delahunty, J., Martschuk, N., Hale, S. B., & Brandon, S. E. (2020, in press). Interpreted police interviews: A review of contemporary research. In M. Miller & B. H. Bornstein (Eds.), *Advances in psychology and law.* New York: Springer.

Goodman-Delahunty, J., Corbo Crehan, A., & Brandon, S. E. (2021, in press). The ethical practice of police psychology. In P.B. Marques & N. Paulino (Eds.), *Police psychology: New trends in forensic psychological science.* Amsterdam: Elsevier Science Publishing Co.

Graham, J., Plumptre, T. W., & Amos, B. (2003). *Principles for good governance in the 21st century* [Policy Brief]. Institute on Governance. Retrieved from: https://iog.ca/docs/2003_August_policybrief15.pdf

Green, T. (2018). Down under: Police education at the Charles Sturt University, Australia. In C. Rogers & B. Frevel (Eds.), *Higher education and police: An international view* (pp. 247–269). London: Palgrave Macmillan.

Head, B. W. (2019). Forty years of wicked problems literature: Forging closer links to policy studies. *Policy and Society, 38*(2), 180–197. https://doi.org/10.1080/14494035.2018.1488797

Hufnagel, S. (2016). *Policing cooperation across borders: Comparative perspectives on law enforcement within the EU and Australia.* London: Routledge.

Jagers, S. C., Matti, S., & Nordblom, K. (2019). The evolution of public policy attitudes: Comparing the mechanisms of policy support across the stages of a policy cycle. *Journal of Public Policy*, 1–21. https://doi.org/10.1017/S0143814X19000023

Keast, R. (2016). Shining a light on the black box of collaboration: Mapping the prerequisites for cross-sector working. In J. R. Butcher & D. J. Gilchrist (Eds.), *The three sector solution: Delivering public policy in collaboration with not-for-profits and business* (pp. 157–178). Canberra: ANU Press.

Kingshott, B. F., Bailey, K., & Wolfe, S. E. (2004). Police culture, ethics and entitlement theory. *Criminal Justice Studies, 17*(2),187–202. https://doi.org/10.1080/0888431042000235020

Kivits, R. (2011). Three component stakeholder analysis. *International Journal of Multiple Research Approaches, 5*(3), 318–333. https://doi.org/10.5172/mra.2011.5.3.318

Lawrence, A. T. (2017). *Business and society: Stakeholders, ethics, public policy* (13th ed.). New York: McGraw-Hill, Irwin.

March, J. G. (1994). *Primer on decision making: How decisions happen.* New York: Simon and Schuster.

Mathieu, J. E., Hollenbeck, J. R., van Knippenberg, D., & Ilgen, D. R. (2017). A century of work teams in the journal of applied psychology. *Journal of Applied Psychology, 102*(3), 452–467. https://doi.org/10.1037/apl0000128

McDonald, D., Bammer, G., & Deane, P. (2009). *Research integration using dialogue methods*. Canberra: ANU Press. https://doi.org/10.26530/OAPEN_459494

McGarry, M. (2010). Police and problem solving: Beyond SARA. *Australasian Policing, 2*(2), 42–45.

McNamara, M. (2012). Starting to untangle the web of cooperation, coordination, and collaboration: A framework for public managers. *International Journal of Public Administration, 35*(6), 389–401. https://doi.org/10.1080/01900692.2012.655527

Melanie, P. (2019, March 29). MI5 and the Met sharpen fight on terror: Two organisations on the front line of violent extremism have new ways to tackle the problem. *Times Newspapers*. Retrieved from: www.thetimes.co.uk/article/mi5-and-the-met-sharpen-fight-on-terror-lpmrffmb0

Mitchell, R., & Huey, L. (Eds.). (2019). *Evidence based policing: An introduction*. Bristol: Policy Press.

New Zealand Department of the Prime Minister and Cabinet. (2017). *Policy capability framework: Measuring capability*. Policy Project. Retrieved from: https://dpmc.govt.nz/sites/default/files/2017-03/policy-capability-framework-development-insights-and-applications-v3.pdf

Neyroud, P. (2017). Policing with science: A new evidence-based professionalism for policing? *European Law Enforcement Research Bulletin, 2*, 39–44. Retrieved from: https://bulletin.cepol.europa.eu/index.php/bulletin/article/view/201

Norris-Tirrell, D. (2010). *Strategic collaboration in public and nonprofit administration a practice-based approach to solving shared problems*. Boca Raton, FL: CRC Press.

O'Hara, A., & Pockett, R. (2011). *Skills for human service practice: Working with individuals, groups and communities*. Oxford: Oxford University Press.

Prenzler, T. (1997). Is there a police culture? *Australian Journal of Public Administration, 56*(4), 47–56. https://doi.org/10.1111/j.1467-8500.1997.tb02488.x

Ransley, J., & Mazerolle, L. (2009). Policing in an era of uncertainty. *Police Practice and Research: An International Journal, 10*(4), 365–381. https://doi.org/10.1080/15614260802586335

Robson, C. (1995). *Real world research: A resource for social scientists and practitioner-researchers*. Oxford: Wiley-Blackwell.

Rogers, C., & Frevel, B. (Eds.). (2018). *Higher education and police: An international view*. London: Palgrave Macmillan.

Rotberg, R. I. (2014). Good governance means performance and results. *Governance, 27*(3), 511–518. https://doi.org/10.1111/gove.12084

Royal Commission Into Institutional Responses to Child Sexual Abuse. (2017). *Royal Commission Into Institutional Responses to Child Sexual Abuse - Criminal justice report: Executive summary and parts I and II*. Commonwealth of Australia. Retrieved from https://www.childabuseroyalcommission.gov.au/sites/default/files/file-list/final_report_-_criminal_justice_report_-_executive_summary_and_parts_i_to_ii.pdf

Royal Commission Into Institutional Responses to Child Sexual Abuse. (2014). *Royal Commission Into Institutional Responses to Child Sexual Abuse: Interim report, Vol. 1*. Commonwealth of Australia. Retrieved from https://www.childabuseroyalcommission.gov.au/sites/default/files/file-list/interim_report_volume-1.pdf

Ryan, N., & Kebbell, M.R. (2020). Developing a psychological research base for criminal investigations: Academics and practitioners working together. In P. Marques & N. Paulino (Eds.), *Police psychology: New trends in forensic psychological science*. Amsterdam: Elsevier Science Publishing Co.

Scott, M. S. (2015). *Identifying and defining policing problems*. U.S. Department of Justice. Retrieved from: https://popcenter.asu.edu/content/identifying-and-defining-policing-problems

Sherman, L. W. (1998). *Evidence-based policing*. Arlington: Police Foundation.

Shipan, C. R., & Volden, C. (2008). The mechanisms of policy diffusion. *American Journal of Political Science, 52*(4), 840–857.

Sidebottom, A., & Tilley, N. (2011). Improving problem-oriented policing: The need for a new model? *Crime Prevention and Community Safety, 13*(2), 79–101. https://doi.org/10.1057/cpcs.2010.21

Simon, H. A. (1997). *Models of bounded rationality: Empirically grounded economic reason* (Vol. 3). Boston: MIT Press.

Telep, C. W. (2017). Police officer receptivity to research and evidence-based policing: Examining variability within and across agencies. *Crime & Delinquency, 63*(8), 976–999. https://doi.org/10.1177/0011128716642253

Termeer, C. J., Dewulf, A., Breeman, G., & Stiller, S. J. (2015). Governance capabilities for dealing wisely with wicked problems. *Administration & Society, 47*(6), 680–710. https://doi.org/10.1177/0095399712469195

Tiernan, A. (2011). Advising Australian federal governments: Assessing the evolving capacity and role of the Australian public service. *Australian Journal of Public Administration, 70*(4), 335–346. https://doi.org/10.1111/j.1467-8500.2011.00742.x

Westera, N. J., Powell, M. B., Milne, B., & Goodman-Delahunty, J. (2019). Police interviewing of sexual assault victims: Current organisational responses and recommendations for improvement. In R. Bull & I. Blandon-Gitlin (Eds.), *The Routledge international handbook of legal and investigative psychology* (pp. 182–196). London: Routledge.

Wu, X., Ramesh, M., & Howlett, M. (2015). Policy capacity: A conceptual framework for understanding policy competences and capabilities. *Policy and Society, 34*(3–4), 165–171. https://doi.org/10.1016/j.polsoc.2015.09.001

CHAPTER 13

Policing and security
Critiquing the privatisation story in Australia

Rick Sarre and Tim Prenzler

INTRODUCTION

The provision of security in Australia (and indeed across the entire world) has undergone a major transformation in recent decades. No longer are the police the predominant players in the security market, if they ever were. Today, security roles are dominated by nationally and internationally owned and operated private security firms. Australians now have access to a vast array of such businesses. They provide a wide variety of services to both public and private instrumentalities acting under regulatory structures that typically require formal training regimes and pre-entry standards. Together they join with public police to form what has been referred to as "pluralised policing" or a security "quilt" (Sarre & Prenzler 2018). This chapter identifies the privatisation trends in the provision of security services generally and reviews the regulatory requirements and legal frameworks that are intended to allow governments and the public alike to have confidence in the way in which private operators regularly join with public police operations to tackle crime, corruption, and disorder.

DIVERSIFIED POLICING

The modern diversification in policing, by virtue of an expansion of non-governmental participants and agencies, takes many forms. It is not uncommon to find "non-police" engaging in investigations, taking witness statements, inspecting bags, detaining suspected shoplifters, patrolling shopping centres, and participating in crowd control operations around sporting and other community events. Certainly, a citizen, when moving around the community in daily life, is far more likely to be directed, questioned, challenged, or searched by private security personnel than by a police officer.

The private policing field is thus characterised the world over by a heterogeneous composition of companies that offer capital-intensive and labour-intensive services (Stenning & Shearing 2012; BIGS 2014,

25; Sarre & Prenzler 2017; Button 2019). This has had major consequences for the way in which society perceives the "policing" task. As Philip Stenning identified a decade ago:

> *"The police", as commonly thought of, are now but one member – albeit still a very significant and influential one – of an ever extended "policing family"* (Stenning 2009, 23).

His words echo those of Lucia Zedner, who offers the view that the publicly employed officers of state police:

> *may come to be seen as an historical blip in a more enduring schema of policing as an array of activities undertaken by multiple private and public agencies, and individual and communal endeavours* (Zedner 2006, 81).

HOW DO WE BEST DEFINE AND CHARACTERISE "PRIVATE" POLICING?

A definition that we have usefully employed for the purpose of defining private security is as follows:

> *Those persons who are employed or sponsored by a commercial firm on a contract or "in-house" basis, using public or private funds, to engage in tasks (other than vigilante action) where the principal component is a security or regulatory function* (Sarre & Prenzler 2009, 4).

This definition covers private security guards and all manifestations of security operatives who are privately financed and managed. It also acknowledges the importance of those non-state personnel who are sponsored and managed by governments and local (public) instrumentalities to engage in policing roles that are private in nature, for example, private investigators who do anti-fraud work for a government welfare department, or private security personnel working for a contract firm in a public instrumentality such as a hospital or university. The finance industry sector, too, buys a large range of security services in order to enable their managers to ensure the safety and security of their premises and their staff. Specialist cash handling services, property and business services, community services, and cultural and recreational services all regularly call upon private security firms to provide appropriate levels of safety for participants. Additionally, there would not be a major shopping centre or sports complex in Australia today that would not, on a regular basis, hire and instruct a considerable number of security guards – often working on a casual, part-time basis – for the purposes of patrolling and maintaining order in these pseudo-public spaces.

There are a number of key factors and business drivers that have given considerable impetus to this growth. These include greater demand from consumers for effective local security in their neighbourhoods, an increasing cost differential between private security options and police (with the former becoming more cost-effective as competition in the market-place grows), and vast improvements in the ability of security services to provide inexpensive technological solutions (especially in the provision of hardware and software) to security problems (Prenzler & Sarre 2017).

Governments, too, are keen to access these private services and to link with private providers. The state, through its purchasing power to supplement its police services, is a key driver of this mixed economy of policing (Sarre & Prenzler 2011). It is not uncommon to find state governments hiring and deploying transit officers, and local government councils hiring private personnel to maintain a security presence in parks and at beachfronts. CCTV installations, monitored chiefly by private personnel, are now ubiquitous in public spaces under the auspices of local and state governments. At the national level, too, the counter-terrorism agenda has allowed private security operators to exhibit their skills and deploy their hardware in an antiterrorism environment (Sarre 2012). Indeed, the Australian Strategy for Protecting Crowded Places from Terrorism cites a key role for the private sector in prophylactic measures (Australian Government 2017).

It is clear, therefore, that both locally, nationally, and internationally there has been a burgeoning of privately financed security services in both their demand and provision, and a commensurate and vast improvement in the ability of such services to provide solutions to key security and crime-prevention problems (Prenzler & Sarre 2017).

THE SIZE OF THE INDUSTRY

Measuring the size of the private security sector has been notoriously difficult, and there have been widely varying accounts. In Australia, the category "Guards and Security Officers" – both public and private – was first included in the national census in 1986, with 22,975 persons recorded (Prenzler 2014, 136). This compared to 33,881 police officers at that time. Since then, security has been categorised in different ways. In the most recent census, the core occupations most closely related to the original security category numbered 41,913 (ABS 2016). This represented an 82% increase over 30 years. At the same time, the number of police increased by 53% to 51,913, while the Australian population increased by 50%. However, it should be noted that the census only covers the main occupation of respondents. Research has indicated that there could be twice as many people in the industry who hold a security license, many of whom work part-time or casually. A study by the Australian Security Industry Association Limited identified a total of 147,729 individual license holders in Australia in 2019, and 11,170 security firm license holders (ASIAL 2020, 15). At the same time, the most recent data, in 2018, on employment in Australia recorded 54,800 persons working (principally) as "Security Officers and Guards" (Department of Jobs and Small Business 2019, 22). True, there were slightly more police (at 63,500) concurrently, but the numbers of private operators remain considerable. It should also be noted that approximately half of this security market is serviced by a large number of small businesses, and the other half is concentrated in five big companies (Prenzler 2014).

Despite the difficulties in counting and weighting, it is reasonable to conclude that there are as many people operating part-time in a security role in Australia as there are full time employees in that role. With that assumption in mind, there are at least twice as many people carrying out a security function in a private capacity in Australia today than sworn police officers.

THE RELATIONSHIPS BETWEEN PRIVATE AND PUBLIC POLICING SERVICES

In recent years there has been a marked development of ties between police and private security, and a considerable improvement in their relationships. The private security sector itself has been keen to expand its markets and establish its credibility with public agencies. But, as indicated earlier, calls for cooperation have come from governments, too, seeking cost savings, especially in relation to the sorts of tasks that do not necessarily need specialist policing services, such as guarding, monitoring CCTV (see Prenzler & Wilson 2019), issuing fines, and checking bags. Governments would also have in mind the record of ongoing failures related to crime reduction through conventional policing (UNODC 2011).

The most common form of engagement of the private sector by Australian governments in policing has been through the development of public-private partnerships (Prenzler & Sarre 2016; Sarre & Prenzler 2000). These engagements include private agents working with state and regulatory authorities, with community groups (government funded and privately funded), and with non-public third parties in a variety of crime-control roles, referred to as "third-party" policing (Mazerolle & Ransley 2006; Webster 2015).

There are a number of examples of successful partnerships in the field of crime reduction in Australia. One of the better examples remains the National Motor Vehicle Theft Reduction Council (NMVTRC), which brings together federal and state governments, police, insurers, and transport and motoring bodies. The NMVTRC, which was created in 1991, has been described as "arguably Australia's most enduring and successful business and government partnership in crime prevention" (Australian Crime Prevention Council 2012, 1). Its members include police, representatives of Australia's insurance industry, motoring groups, and transport bodies. This cooperative endeavour has contributed to significant reductions in motor vehicle thefts through a range of strategies, including the promotion of immobiliser technology and programs for young offenders (NMVTRC, n.d).

Another example is the award-winning Strike Force Piccadilly, initiated to stop an outbreak of automatic teller machine (ATM) ram raids (and later, explosive gas attacks on ATMs) that began in the mid-2000s. The partnership strategy involved police, banks, ATM operators, and retail security teams. The countermeasures implemented, including a specialised alarm-response system, ATM relocations, and anti-ramming and anti-explosive equipment, resulted in the virtual elimination of the crime problem (Prenzler 2011; also Chapter 17 of the present volume).

There are other notable examples of public/private cooperative endeavors. In 1999, Centrelink formally adopted covert surveillance as a tool in its armory against welfare fraud. Formerly, cases of suspected benefit malfeasance were handed over to the police. Cases amenable to this type of examination were outsourced to a panel of private investigation firms across Australia. By 2010, Centrelink had 11 contracted surveillance providers on its panel. In the first year of operation, 1,063 cases were finalized, leading to almost AU$4 million in payments targeted for recovery (Sarre & Prenzler 2011, 97). Savings were estimated at AU$26,126 per investigation.

Eyes on the Street was an initiative involving a partnership between Western Australia Police, local government, local businesses, and the private security industry, managed by the government Crime Prevention and Community Liaison Unit. The partners received training in recording and reporting suspicious persons or events. The program involved these players gathering and reporting information to police. This allowed police to make further inquiries. According to an evaluation of the program, security personnel and the business owners, generally speaking, developed a good relationship with police, understood well the protocols and practices of reporting incidents, and thus provided a valuable service (CRC 2008). The program has since merged with Crime Stoppers WA.

Not all partnerships need be formal. Some relationships between public and private policing personnel are typically informal. One example is the modern battle against cybercrime. The borderless nature of the internet means that governments, businesses, and individuals can be targeted by criminals from anywhere in the world. Moreover, today's criminals can engage in cybercrime without the need for high-level technical skills (McGuire & Dowling 2013). Ironically, "do-it-yourself" malware kits, for example, are available from online forums. The 2018 PwC Global Economic Crime and Fraud Survey revealed that 43% of their business respondents said that they had suffered a cyberattack (PwC 2018, 7). CEOs overwhelmingly reported to PwC that cybercrime is the number-one threat to their organisation's growth prospects.

It can be a challenge to ensure effective crime prevention. Surveillance by government agencies can be an effective crime deterrent at some level. To that extent, state police activity is essential but not sufficient. In the short term, such responses are usually a case of "too little, too late", assuming that police can detect the behaviour at all. It is rarely the case that they can thwart it ahead of time (Broadhurst & Chang 2013). In the longer term, the best responses to cybercrime are the education of those who are most vulnerable and the deployment of electronic crime detection and prevention tools. It is in relation to the latter of these that the private sector adds significant value, for one is more likely to find private instrumentalities involved in the development and production of advanced cyber technologies than cash-strapped police agencies.

Thus, as Chang, Zhong and Grabosky (2018) point out, there is now a diverse constellation of individuals and non-state organisations that exist to safeguard cyberspace, ranging from those that are purely commercial, providing services for a fee, to those that operate on a pro bono basis. They conclude that, while some private actors may become overzealous in the protection of their own interests, "where state capacity to control cybercrime is limited, the socially and economically marginalized may suffer, directly or indirectly, no less than the privileged among us. A degree of citizen involvement in securing cyberspace can, thus, be useful" (Chang, Zhong & Grabosky 2018, 111).

A report commissioned by the Australian Security Industry Association Limited (ASIAL) examined developments internationally regarding private security and crime prevention efforts (Prenzler 2013). The author's conclusions concurred with those of Farrell et al. (Farrell, Tseloni, Mailley & Tilley 2011; also Farrell 2013), who state that the historical downward trajectory of crime internationally since the mid-1990s was largely attributable to the widespread uptake of private security services across a vast range of institutional, business, and domestic settings. The report concluded that there remain enormous opportunities for governments, police, and private security firms to operate in a synergetic fashion to reduce crime. This can be done, it reported, in ways that meet public interest criteria while at the same time satisfying principles of democratic accountability and transparency.

The examples just presented suggest strongly that private and public-sector security managers can work synergistically with a range of partners to produce successful outcomes in policing, crime prevention, and crime reduction (Prenzler & Sarre 2014a).

Partnerships are not, however, unproblematic. There may be risks to civil liberties by virtue of, for example, non-police "eyes" having access to confidential data, and where different rules, protocols, and procedures (if not ideologies) apply to relevant agents, depending upon who their paymasters are (Chang, Zhong & Grabosky 2018, 108–110). Moreover, if there are inadequate licensing systems, and poor training and supervision of private operatives(such as occurred in the 2020 Melbourne COVID-19 quarantine hotel supervision lapses), then these partnerships quickly break down. On the other side of the coin, there is also a danger, at least in perception, that government resources sometimes privilege particular security firms, although these perceptions can be reduced or eliminated through proper tendering processes.

The crucial message here is that the partnerships that are now commonplace are to be welcomed, if not applauded, but they need to be carefully managed, with a requirement of a clear public interest benefit at the forefront of any planning and practice.

THE SAFETY OF SECURITY OFFICERS

With security work comes a range of physical risks for those involved and for those with whom security personnel come into contact. Security officers work in a high-risk environment. The data are indicative of the considerable "first responder" role played by security officers, mainly crowd controllers, in dealing with risky offenders outside of, or preceding, a police response. The scale of the problem, and the financial and personal costs involved, show the need for a sophisticated approach to protecting security officers and members of the public (Ferguson, Prenzler, Sarre & de Caires 2011).

Research data provide for a comparison of police and security officer experiences of workplace violence and injury. At the time of a survey undertaken a decade ago, security and police were in the top three highest claiming occupations for work-related injuries and deaths from occupational violence, with security officers at number one in both instances (Sarre & Prenzler 2011). Between 2000–2001 and 2007–2008, security officers and police in Australia made compensation claims for 17,231 work-related injuries. While the rate of police officers' work-related injuries overall occurred at twice the rate for security officers, the rates of occupational violence were about equal, and followed the same trend over time, rising during the mid-2000s and then declining steadily. Despite the similarity in rates of occupational violence, however, the nature of the injuries suffered by police and security officers differed. Australian security officers appeared more likely to sustain serious non-fatal injuries than police, as evidenced by the high rates of head injuries and substantial differences in the amount of time lost as a result of an incident (Sarre & Prenzler 2011, 122–123).

The research revealed that security officers suffered unacceptably high rates of workplace injuries, violence, and fatalities. Situational analyses of police deaths suggest that the majority of these are preventable, and it is likely that this also applies to security officer risks (Allard & Prenzler 2009).

The higher compensation claim rates for males over females for both police and security work suggested a culture of male risk-taking behaviour that might be amenable to modification. Encouraging more women into security work, too, is another option available to address this problem. In 2018, women were recorded as just 18% of security officers and guards in Australian employment data (Department of Jobs and Small Business 2019, 48). The risk here – as in any occupations that involve working with offenders – is that women are employed because of stereotypically female traits of pacification (Prenzler & Sinclair 2013). However, this approach does give an employment equity outcome for women, so long as they are deployed on an egalitarian basis. Intensive training in de-escalation techniques and low impact physical control techniques is another important strategy in this regard.

REGULATION AND TRAINING

There is no shortage, sadly, of examples of inappropriate conduct and scandals that have alerted us to the need for appropriate regulation of the security industry worldwide (Button 2012). Australia has not remained aloof from these trends. We have seen an infiltration of nightclub security by organised crime figures trading in illicit drugs (ACC 2008, 56, 2011). Enquiries by the Fair Work Ombudsman and the New South Wales Independent Commission Against Corruption (ICAC) found extensive and entrenched forms of misconduct in key parts of the industry, including extortion, fraud, and under-award employment conditions (Prenzler & Milroy 2012). There have been widespread and ongoing problems, too, with serious assaults by crowd controllers (Prenzler, Sarre & Kim 2017). A number of people (typically patrons at licensed premises) have lost their lives or have been seriously injured at the hands of security staff (Sarre & Prenzler 2009, 127–129). There have also been incidents of information corruption, fraud, assaults, insider crime, incompetence, and inattention to the required standards (Prenzler & Sarre 2008a).

As a result of the negative perceptions arising from this state of affairs, major reforms have been introduced in Australia to strengthen private security licensing regimes and to increase training requirements. In terms of coverage of the industry, government licensing, which requires all persons undertaking a security task to have the appropriate license, was ultimately extended a decade ago to all areas of security work, including locksmiths, consultants, in-house security personnel, trainers, and electronic system installers and monitors (Sarre & Prenzler 2011). The number of disqualifying offences has also been enlarged to cover firearms offences and drug offences. Regulators have been given greater powers to deny or suspend licenses on discretionary grounds, including evidence of poor character or associating with undesirables. In two jurisdictions, New South Wales and South Australia, regulators can use confidential intelligence to reject an application for a license; that is, there is no need to provide access to the applicant to that intelligence, nor to give any reason for the rejection of the application. Most jurisdictions also suspend licenses if a license-holder has been charged with a criminal offence. Indeed, license-holders are required to inform the regulator if they have been charged. Mandatory fingerprinting or palm-printing has been introduced in all jurisdictions in order to allow regulators to undertake more reliable criminal history checks ahead of a license being granted.

There have been efforts, too, by professional security associations to address conduct issues through membership standards. However, associations usually have limited investigative capacity and a limited reach, since membership is usually voluntary. Accountability has also occurred less directly (but arguably no less effectively) through the criminal and civil law, employment law, privacy legislation, and weapons legislation, in addition to the security market itself (Sarre & Prenzler 2009, 232) and fair-trading requirements (Office of Fair Trading 2012). However, each of these mechanisms is limited in its capacity to bring poor operators and criminally minded security personnel to justice or to deter misconduct more generally.

Pleasingly, the Council of Australian Governments (COAG) has repeatedly sought a national approach to regulation (Prenzler & Sarre 2014b, 187–188), based in part on "the important contribution the private security industry makes in supporting Australia's counter-terrorism arrangements" (COAG 2005, 5). A report to the Federal Attorney-General's Department published in 2007 recommended regulatory "harmonisation" (Centre for International Economics 2007), although the process of pursuing that outcome has stalled in all but the guarding sector (COAG 2008). That being the case, there is a great urgency for state governments and industry associations to continue to explore and experiment with regulatory options (Prenzler & Sarre 2008b).

Hand in hand with regulation goes the requirement of training. COAG has been concerned with boosting pre-employment competencies through a prescribed training curriculum and associated qualifications framework (consistent with established competency development principles) and ensuring training standards for guards are nationally consistent (COAG 2008). But there are grounds for ongoing concern. Training requirements are intended to guarantee adequate competencies and operate in tandem with probity tests, complaints investigation and adjudication, and inspections and audits. At present, there is no legislative requirement for public disclosures of training methods and quality control in Australia. In that regard, a key regulatory task of reassuring consumers about the competency of security providers has not been realised (Prenzler, Sarre & Kim 2017). The national certificate requirements represent a major step forward, but these are limited to operatives, with no requirements for the holder of a company license or government security managers to have training. This aspect of regulation needs serious attention.

POWERS AND IMMUNITIES

Given the rapid expansion of the tasks now being carried out by private security personnel in policing partnerships, one might assume that careful attention would have been paid to the legal framework within which these cooperative activities take place. Regrettably, this has not been the case (Sarre 2014). One can sympathise with lawmakers. It would be a very difficult task for parliaments to specify private security powers across the board, given the many forms and varieties of private operatives and the multitude of activities in which they may be engaged. In addition, many private security firms are national, indeed global, corporations, and any general attempt to set legislative rules which transcend national and international boundaries would be difficult to do, let alone to implement and enforce. That being the case, those wishing to add a legal "touch" to private policing in Australia have tended to focus more on how to ensure security provider conduct is lawful rather than curtailing and shaping the legal powers that should apply (Stenning 2000).

The consequence of this legislative reluctance to do anything more than tinker around the edges is that the legal authority, powers, and immunities of private security providers are found mainly, and obscurely, in bits and pieces of the criminal law, the law of property, the law of contract, and employment law (Sarre 2014, 151). It is unlikely that these common law powers, however, would ever be limited by legislation, for to do so would be to limit the rights of all property owners to protect their families and properties.

As mentioned earlier, while there has been regulatory legislation passed in all Australian jurisdictions concerning the registration, licensing, and training of private security personnel, the main aim of this legislation is to oversee those who operate within the industry and to check those who wish to enter it against certain criteria. This legislation, however, does not deal with powers and immunities at all. There is no legislation in Australia that permits security guards generally to wield specific powers. This lack of legislative direction is potentially confusing for security personnel and the public alike. Moreover, there are few legal precedents emerging from the courts, essentially because only a very small number of claims (typically seeking compensation for negligence) wind up in court, and the results of these cases are rarely reported. The vast majority are either abandoned or settled by negotiation out of court. Criminal prosecutions are confined to the more blatant assaults by crowd controllers, and these are typically unreported matters heard in magistrates' courts. Rarely do they go on appeal where they are more likely to be reported. Hence it is difficult to find a comprehensive body of law on the subject of private security powers. For the tens of thousands of private security personnel who don a uniform each day, then, the law remains inaccessible and thus uncertain.

That having been said, there are certain powers that do exist, and these are regularly resorted to. Private citizens (which include private security officers) have the right to make a citizen's arrest. However, it is highly unlikely that a citizen (or a trained security guard, for that matter) will know precisely which rules concerning such arrests and which definitions apply in any given jurisdiction, and, if they do apply, what the consequences might be.

Other possibilities for confusion emerge from the common law rights of persons to sue others for breach of their rights of liberty. For example, retail managers who detain shoplifters upon reasonable suspicion of theft have had damages awarded against them (paid to wrongly accused suspects) in some cases, but not in others. The outcome, it seems, depends upon the level of restraint, the length of time involved, and the extent to which the accused person was given an opportunity to allay suspicion (Sarre & Prenzler 2009, 108). The confusion stems from the fact that the laws that apply to private personnel have developed over the years to apply not to those doing police-type work but to journalists, landowners, and employers. They may translate into something potentially quite different in the hands of the agents of these individuals.

Should we embark upon a new legislative crusade, one that settles powers and immunities once and for all? There is a view that says that leaving the law ambiguous encourages fewer lawsuits against private security, forcing those aggrieved to negotiate more and litigate less. What this means for the general law, however, is that there is little guidance concerning when security personnel can safely rely upon legal immunity from a lawsuit. There is an alternative view that parliaments could and should legislate to grant certain powers and to protect security personnel by immunities in certain circumstances. The idea of a person being protected from legal suit when exercising good faith is not novel (Sarre 2011). A "reasonable suspicion and good faith immunity" could be installed into legislation, applying to all people who engage in security functions, especially those who have satisfied a specified level of training. This is likely to be controversial, given that it would allow private security personnel a level of immunity that the common law does not permit them currently. If this position were to be adopted by lawmakers (although there are no signs of that occurring in the immediate future) one would expect the common law to develop standards related to conduct that are appropriate in balancing the desire to reduce public disorder with the necessity of keeping the potential of public harm to a minimum. Any move towards enhanced enforcement powers for security officers would need to include a training program in the law. This would be a very helpful initiative. It is time that legislators moved in this direction.

CONCLUSION

There has been an undeniable shift in confidence in Australia regarding privatised forms of policing. In the past, it was nearly impossible to conceive of private security personnel operating entirely in the public interest (Loader & White 2015). That notion has been consistently challenged in the last three decades, as public expectations of security have shifted and as policy-makers and the public alike have witnessed successful policing partnerships (Stiernstedt, Button, Prenzler & Sarre 2019). Private security industries in Australia have seen significant growth and are now an established part of the policing and crime-prevention environment. There has been evidence of increasing confidence in government about the policing abilities of the non-government sector. Complementary public and private arrangements have been put in place to control violence and disorder in and around local communities, businesses, and major events.

Provision of security services sometimes comes at a high cost, however, as evidenced in the health and welfare studies, and it is important for policy-makers not to lose sight of the importance of protecting the welfare of security personnel. It is also important to ensure that the public feels safe at the hands of those who are deployed to carry out policing and security tasks.

In response to scandals regarding the private sector delivery of security services, reforms have been introduced in Australia to lift the standards of regulation. The accountability measures, however, require further development. Powers and immunities need to be better defined, too.

What can we anticipate for the future? The trend towards greater reliance on private security for protection from crime and violence in our society is strong and enduring. That being the case, Australians will continue to witness a privatised and consequently pluralised policing landscape well into the foreseeable future. The safety and security of all Australians depends upon continuing the research, testing the assumptions and, ultimately, getting an appropriate balance between the powers, functions, and abilities of public and private actors.

REFERENCES

ABS (2016). *Census of Population and Housing, Customised Data Report, Table 1: Count of Employed Persons by Selected Occupations*. Canberra: Australian Bureau of Statistics.

ACC (2008). *Annual Report 2007–08*. Canberra: Australian Crime Commission.

ACC (2011). *Private Security Industry Criminal Infiltration*. Canberra: Australian Crime Commission.

Allard, T. & Prenzler, T. (2009). A Summary Analysis of Police Deaths in Australia: Implications for Prevention. *International Journal of Comparative and Applied Criminal Justice*, 33(1), 61–81.

ASIAL (2020). ASIAL Security Industry Licensing Report 2020. *Security Insider*, 26(1), 14–17.

Australian Crime Prevention Council (2012). A Case Study in Valuing Crime Prevention Outcomes: The National Motor Vehicle Theft Reduction Council. *Newsletter*, June, 1–4.

Australian Government (2017). *Australia's Strategy for Protecting Crowded Places from Terrorism, Australia-New Zealand Counter-Terrorism Committee (ANZCTC)*. Canberra: Commonwealth of Australia.

BIGS (2014). *Civil Security and the Private Security Industry in Germany, Brandenburg Institute for Society and Security*. Paper no. 4, August. Canberra: BIGS.

Broadhurst, R. & Chang, L. (2013). Cybercrime in Asia: Trends and Challenges. In: Liu, J., Hebenton, B. & Jou, S. (eds) *Handbook of Asian Criminology*. New York: Springer, 49–63.

Button, M. (2012). Optimizing Security Through Effective Regulation: Lessons from Around the Globe. In: Prenzler, T. (ed) *Policing and Security in Practice*. Houndmills: Palgrave Macmillan, 204–220.

Button, M. (2019). *Private Policing* (2nd ed). Abingdon: Routledge.

Centre for International Economics (2007). *Harmonisation of Private Security Industry Regulation*. Report to the Federal Attorney-General's Department. Canberra: CIE.

Chang, L., Zhong, L. & Grabosky, P. (2018). Citizen Co-Production of Cyber Security: Self-Help, Vigilantes, and Cybercrime. *Regulation & Governance*, 12(1), 101–114.

COAG (2005). *Special Meeting on Counter-Terrorism*, 27 September. Canberra: Council of Australian Governments.

COAG (2008). *Regulation of the Private Security Industry: Manpower (Guarding) Sector*. Canberra: Council of Australian Governments.

CRC (2008). *Evaluation of the Eyes on the Street Program*. Canberra: Crime Research Centre, University of Western Australia.

Department of Jobs and Small Business (2019). *Australian Jobs 2019*. Canberra: Department of Jobs and Small Business.

Farrell, G. (2013). Five Tests for a Theory of the Crime Drop. *Crime Science*. 2(5), 1–8, Open Access.

Farrell, G., Tseloni, A., Mailley, J. & Tilley, N. (2011). The Crime Drop and the Security Hypothesis. *Journal of Research in Crime and Delinquency*, 48(2), 147–175.

Ferguson, P., Prenzler, T., Sarre, R. & de Caires, B. (2011). Police and Security Officer Experiences of Occupational Violence and Injury in Australia. *International Journal of Police Science and Management*, 13(3), 223–233.

Loader, I. & White, A. (2015). How Can We Better Align Private Security with the Public Interest? Towards a Civilising Model of Regulation. *Regulation and Governance*, 11(2), 166–184.

Mazerolle, L. & Ransley, J. (2006). *Third Party Policing*. Cambridge: Cambridge University Press.

McGuire, M. & Dowling, S. (2013). *Cybercrime: A Review of the Evidence: Summary of Key Findings and Implications*. Home Office Research Report 75, October. London: Home Office.

National Motor Vehicle Theft Reduction Council (NMVTRC) (n.d.). Available from: www.carsafe.com.au [Accessed 2 March 2020].

Office of Fair Trading (2012). *Security Adviser*. Available from: www.fairtrading.qld.gov.au/security-adviser.htm [Accessed 2 March 2020].

Prenzler, T. (2011). Strike Force Piccadilly and ATM Security: A Follow Up Study. *Policing: A Journal of Policy and Practice*, 5(3), 236–247.

Prenzler, T. (2013). *Outsourcing of Policing Tasks: Scope and Prospects*. Report to the Australian Security Industry Association Limited (ASIAL), ARC Centre for Excellence in Policing and Security. Available from: www.asial.com.au/documents/item/13 [Accessed 2 March 2020].

Prenzler, T. (2014). The Security Industry: Dimensions and Issues. In: Prenzler, T. (ed) *Professional Practice in Crime Prevention and Security Management*. Brisbane: Australian Academic Press, 129–147.

Prenzler, T. & Milroy, A. (2012). Recent Inquiries into the Private Security Industry in Australia: Implications for Regulation. *Security Journal*, 25(4), 342–355.

Prenzler, T. & Sarre, R. (2008a). Developing a Risk Profile and Model Regulatory System for the Security Industry. *Security Journal*, 21, 264–277.

Prenzler, T. & Sarre, R. (2008b). Protective Security in Australia: Scandal, Media Images and Reform. *Journal of Policing, Intelligence and Counter Terrorism*, 3(2), 23–37.

Prenzler, T. & Sarre, R. (2014a). The Role of Partnerships in Security Management. In: Gill, M. (ed) *Handbook of Security* (2nd ed). Basingstoke: Palgrave Macmillan, 769–790.

Prenzler, T. & Sarre, R. (2014b). Smart Regulation for the Security Industry. In: Prenzler, T. (ed) *Professional Practice in Crime Prevention and Security Management*. Samford Valley: Australian Academic Press, 175–191.

Prenzler, T. & Sarre, R. (2016). Public-Private Crime Prevention Partnerships. In: Prenzler, T. (ed) *Policing and Security in Practice: Challenges and Achievements* (2nd ed). Houndmills: Palgrave Macmillan, 149–167.

Prenzler, T. & Sarre, R. (2017). The Security Industry and Crime Prevention. In: Prenzler, T. (ed) *Understanding Crime Prevention: The Case Study Approach*. Brisbane: Australian Academic Press, 167–183.

Prenzler, T., Sarre, R. & Kim, D. W. (2017). Reform of Security Industry Training Standards: An Australian Case Study. *International Journal of Comparative and Applied Criminal Justice*, 41(4), 323–334.

Prenzler, T. & Sinclair, G. (2013). The Status of Women Police Officers: An International Review. *International Journal of Law, Crime and Justice*, 41(2), 115–131.

Prenzler, T. & Wilson, E. (2019). The Ipswich (Queensland) Safe City Program: An Evaluation. *Security Journal*, 32(2), 137–152.

PwC (2018). Global Economic Crime and Fraud Survey: Australian Report. *The New Face of Economic Crime*. Available from: www.pwc.com.au/consulting/assets/gecs-report18.pdf

Sarre, R. (2011). Private Security Powers and Immunities: Is It Time for Legislative Action? *Australian Security*, December, 37–38.

Sarre, R. (2012). Public-Private Cooperation in Policing Crime and Terrorism in Australia. In: Taylor, S. C., Torpy, D. J. & Das, D. (eds) *Policing Global Movement: Tourism, Migration, Human Trafficking and Terrorism*. New York: CRC Press, Taylor and Francis, 75–90.

Sarre, R. (2014). Legal Powers, Obligations and Immunities. In: Prenzler, T. (ed) *Professional Practice in Crime Prevention and Security Management*. Samford Valley: Australian Academic Press, 149–161.

Sarre, R. & Prenzler, T. (2000). The Relationship Between Police and Private Security: Models and Future Directions. *International Journal of Comparative and Applied Criminal Justice*, 24(1), 91–113.

Sarre, R. & Prenzler, T. (2009). *The Law of Private Security in Australia* (2nd ed). Pyrmont, New South Wales: Thomson LBC.

Sarre, R. & Prenzler, T. (2011). *Private Security and Public Interest: Exploring Private Security Trends and Directions for Reform in the New Era of Plural Policing*. Sydney:

Report prepared for the Australian Research Council and the Australian Security Industry Association Ltd (ASIAL).

Sarre, R. & Prenzler, T. (2017). Privatisation in the Criminal Justice System. In: Palmer, D., de Lint, W. & Dalton, D. (eds) *Crime and Justice: A Guide to Criminology* (5th ed), Pyrmont, New South Wales: Thomson Reuters, 427–444.

Sarre, R. & Prenzler, T. (2018). Privatisation of Police: Themes from Australia. In: Hucklesby, A. & Lister, S. (eds) *The Private Sector and Criminal Justice*. London: Palgrave Macmillan, 97–134.

Stenning, P. (2000). Powers and Accountability of Private Police. *European Journal on Criminal Policy and Research*, 8, 325–352.

Stenning, P. (2009). Governance and Accountability in a Plural Policing Environment: The Story so Far. *Policing: A Journal of Policy and Practice*, 3(1), 22–33.

Stenning, P. & Shearing, C. (2012). The Shifting Boundaries of Policing: Globalisation and Its Possibilities. In: Newburn, T. & Peay, J. (eds) *Policing: Politics, Culture and Control – Essays in Honour of Robert Reiner*. London: Hart Publishing, 265–284.

Stiernstedt, P., Button, M., Prenzler, T. & Sarre, R. (2019) The 'Three-Pillars' Model of Regulation: A Fusion of Governance Models for Private Security. *Security Journal*. DOI:10.1057/s41284-019-00224-3.

UNODC (2011). *Civilian Private Security Services: Their Role, Oversight and Contribution to Crime Prevention and Community Safety*. Vienna: United Nations Office on Drugs and Crime.

Webster, J. (2015). Effective Third-Party Policing Partnerships or Missed Opportunities? *Policing and Society*, 25(1), 97–114.

Zedner, L. (2006). Liquid Security: Managing the Market for Crime Control. *Criminology and Criminal Justice*, 6(3), 267–288.

SECTION 3

Operational practices and procedures

CHAPTER 14

Police, media, and the digital age in Australia

John Gaffey

INTRODUCTION

This chapter examines contemporary aspects of the relationship between the police and the media. This relationship has undergone substantial change recently, particularly to the way journalists produce crime news and images of policing for public consumption. The advent of a fast-paced, 24-hour news cycle and the explosion of digital news outlets have led to significant changes in the work of journalists (McGovern & Lee, 2010). Further impact on traditional journalism comes from the introduction of social media into the news environment, which has left a situation where "the mainstream media often sources its news from social media and social media sites are populated with news reports from the mainstream media, and as such it is not easy at times to differentiate between the two mediums" (Allan, Kelly, & Stephenson, 2016).

In the changing contemporary news environment, policing organisations have been found to be successfully developing greater control over the framing of crime news and its reporting by the traditional media. This has improved the ability of increasingly professionalized police public relations practices to leverage the reporting of crime news for public relations goals or "image work" (Lee & McGovern, 2014; McGovern & Lee, 2010). Accordingly, this chapter explores recent developments in the relationship between police organisations, journalism, and the production of crime news. Also considered here is the ongoing shift of police public relations activities into the online and social media space. This change offers a range of opportunities and challenges to policing organisations and serves as one of the more significant challenges to the relationship between policing organisations and the media (Ellis & McGovern, 2016).

Finally, this chapter discusses recent media-related technological developments that have impacted on the public's perception of policing organisations and their legitimacy. Citizen journalism, where the public become producers and mediators of policing images, has become a fixed element of the contemporary media environment (Farmer, 2016; Greer & McLaughlin, 2010; Mythen, 2010). Citizen journalism deserves some consideration, as it contests the ability for current policing organisations to maintain authority over the distribution of policing images available to the public and thus represents a major challenge to their perceived legitimacy (Brucato, 2015a).

POLICE AND THE PRODUCTION OF CRIME NEWS

The production of crime news has been examined in a variety of ways. An often-adopted approach to explaining the production of crime news is to consider the systemic journalistic practices that influence both the amount of crime coverage and the nature of that coverage. Jewkes (2015) argues that news, like any media image or representation, is heavily influenced by the "production processes of news organisations and the structural determinants of news making" (Jewkes, 2015, p. 45). These processes may include elements such as a tendency towards the over-reporting of crimes as solved; a consideration of how reporters are deployed, including the scheduling demands of news production; a focus on details of crime with little account for causes; and an over-reliance on official sources of information, such as the police (Jewkes, 2015).

A second set of influences are the assumptions journalists make about their audience. Jewkes (2015) further argues that media professionals actively select news stories, prioritising some over others; choose words and images; and adopt a particular tone. Together, these influences serve to, first, routinely prioritise some types of crime stories at the expense of others which has an agenda-setting effect and second frame crime news in particular ways (Jewkes, 2015).

News stories are not selected randomly, nor with the aim of presenting a broad snapshot of all crimes or events. Instead, an expanded range of professional criteria are employed to determine a story's newsworthiness. The concept of newsworthiness has been understood in terms of "news values". News values are a range of socially, culturally, and historically contingent criteria that inform the newsworthiness of crime events (Jewkes, 2015). The most well-known formulations of news values come from Chibnall (1977), who examined crime news in the UK in the 1970s, and Jewkes (2015), who reformulated news values in light of contemporary news production. While it is beyond the scope of this chapter to examine news values in detail, they can be understood as elements of an event that create newsworthiness. Some common and recognisable news values are predictability, proximity, sex, and violence and graphic imagery (Jewkes, 2015). While these news values may undergo some revision due to changes in journalistic practices as well as social and historical contingencies, they tend to remain relatively constant (Clifford & White, 2017). However, what has undergone some significant changes are the sources journalists rely on for information about crime.

Sources of crime news

The types of sources journalists turn to for information about crime is influenced by a range of competing demands. Journalists need sources that are both accessible and credible (Clifford & White, 2017). Historically, agencies within the criminal justice system have been a key source of information to journalists, and the police are often the principal source journalists rely on (Lee & McGovern, 2014; Mawby, 2010a; McGovern & Lee, 2010).

News is also currently produced in a rapidly changing media environment. Many media outlets have downsized the number of journalists they employ, while demand for crime stories and content rise. Demand is driven by changes to the news cycle brought about by the demands of online news delivery and the immediacy of social media formats (Lee & McGovern, 2014; McGovern & Lee, 2010). Linked to this are significant shifts in news formats and distribution mediums, with the rapid growth of online news and the distribution of news through social media (Watkins et al., 2015). Social media is cited as a common source of news in addition to traditional news sources with an online presence. Social media is a rising source of news, especially for consumers in younger age groups. According to Watkins et al. (2015), 48.0% of Australian news consumers indicated they had used Facebook for news in the prior week, 15.4% had used YouTube and 7.5% had used Twitter. This represents a significant change.

The contemporary role of Australian police organisations in the construction of crime news has been examined at length recently. This research has shown that, in New South Wales, the police actively provide crime news to the media through highly organised and increasingly professionalized media units (McGovern & Lee, 2010).

McGovern and Lee (2010) argue that previously the relationship between journalists and the police was one where police-produced information served as a starting point for the generation of crime news. More recent practices involve increasingly professionalized police media units with a public relations focus, such as the New South Wales Police Media Unit (PMU). The material produced by the police has been found to be much more central to the final crime news product. In short, according to McGovern and Lee, "In many cases the PMU story *is* the news story" (McGovern & Lee, 2010, p. 456).

While demonstrating the power of the PMU, McGovern and Lee (2010) caution against a view that this is a one-way relationship. There are still power struggles found between police and journalists, and contests over the reporting of crime. Further, McGovern and Lee's (2010) examination of the New South Wales Police Media Unit shows that the close relationship between the PMU and crime news provides potential for policing organisations to maintain a level of control over the view of crime the public may develop when exposed to crime news in the media. They position this contemporary relationship as one where the PMU have influence over not only crime news but over news concerning the New South Wales police more generally. This includes the public relations goal of managing images or representation of police activity and, accordingly, the legitimacy of policing practices.

Police involvement in communicating with the public via the media sometimes highlights the tension between the goals of the media and the police. In one recent example, the police narrative directly undermined a media narrative driven by law-and-order concerns. This occurred in Victoria, Australia, during extended media coverage of what elements of the media labelled "African gang crime". While much of the media coverage used the term "gang" along with the specific "African" identifier, the Victorian police made several public statements that contradicted the media narrative, stating via press conference and media releases that there was no "gang" crime problem. Some sections of the media said this response by the police was a further failure of the police organisation, arguing that gangs *were* involved and that the police were only countering media claims because they were crippled by the demands of political correctness (Gaffey, 2019). This conflict suggests that despite the close relationship between crime news and police media engagement, tensions between their goals remain.

What has changed over time are the processes that decide what type of crime news is ultimately reported in the media and, accordingly, is communicated to audiences. An examination of the relationship between contemporary aspects of policing practice, such as the rise of police media units and crime news, shows a concerted effort on the part of policing organisations to maintain both a positive policing image and a related agenda-setting role. The agenda-setting role provided by this relationship between the police and crime news production is one where police organisations that employ professionalized media units increase the potential for that organisation to exercise some influence over the way crime is reported.

POLICE MEDIA UNITS AND "IMAGE WORK"

As just described, the relationship between policing organisations and the production of media content such as crime news is not characterised by a passivity on behalf of the police coupled with proactive journalists and media institutions. This has been a popular image of the police/media relationship in the past, but there have been significant changes to this relationship (Clifford & White, 2017).

The media and the police fill public roles that will bring them into contact with each other, but they often have different agendas (Mawby, 2002). Journalists are attempting to both maximise revenue while operating as a fourth estate, challenging the state on behalf of the public.

Police maintain a primary goal of responding to crime and maintaining social order. Yet beyond this goal, the police have a related interest: "to promote favourable images, to control the flow of content of information through the media to the public, but also to inform and to demonstrate public accountability" (Mawby, 2002, p. 305).

Policing organisations have long recognised the benefits of media engagement when promoting a positive image (Chermak & Weiss, 2005; Lee & McGovern, 2014; Mawby, 2002). The benefit flows partly from the public's expectations of both the police and the media, where "[t]he public is more likely to know its police organizations, and what they are doing to respond to crime and enhance public safety in society, by viewing mass media images" (Chermak & Weiss, 2005, p. 503).

However, the media engagement goals of policing organisations have moved beyond just assuring the public that they are addressing crime or maintaining order. A recognised core goal of contemporary, and increasingly professionalized, police media work is also understood as an attempt to manage the police "image" (Lee & McGovern, 2013, 2014, 2016; Mawby, 2002, 2010b; McGovern, 2008). "Image work" is coupled with other interrelated "logics" of media engagement, such as risk management and public responsibilisation as well as the promotion of trust and legitimacy (Lee & McGovern, 2014). The public relations practices of the police, including the promotion of a positive image, are concerned with both the public's and the organisation's perception of police legitimacy and the creation of trust (Lee & McGovern, 2013).

Accordingly, the public relations goals of policing organisations and their engagement with the media have shifted as policing organisations have reformed and professionalized. In New South Wales, for example, there was an evolution of the police approach to media engagement culminating in the NSW Police Media Unit mentioned earlier (Lee & McGovern, 2014). The advent of professional police media units such as this represents a transformation of the relationship between the media and police organisations, and accordingly, police organisations and the public (Lee & McGovern, 2013).

POLICE-MEDIA ENGAGEMENT ONLINE

Online and social media are thought to provide policing institutions with innovative image-management and public relations opportunities and prospects for police and community engagement. Social and online media sites such as Facebook and Twitter are increasingly leveraged by police services for a variety of goals, with social media assuming a key role in investigations, risk management, and public relations (Lee & McGovern, 2012)

There is a significant recognition by policing organisations that social media present a new range of opportunities to engage with the public in ways that still promote police goals. As Lee and McGovern (2014, p. 117) point out: "With pressure on the police to increase public confidence and reduce community concerns over crime, social media has emerged as a valuable tool for proactive police communication strategies". As with many professional and corporate entities, the police may see social media as a useful way of increasing dialogue with the public with the goal of improving public relations and promoting a positive public image and increased legitimacy.

There are a variety of ways policing organisations employ social media. These fall broadly into the categories of (1) information sharing or gathering, and (2) community engagement (Ruddell & Jones, 2013). Information sharing may be, for example, distribution of information concerning "wanted" offenders where the public is asked to provide information that may lead to the offender's arrest. The use of social media as part of a tactical response can also refer to the utilisation of social media to disseminate information about exigent or ongoing risks to the public with ease and immediacy, factors that police view as advantageous (Lee & McGovern, 2014).

When considering the "image work" discussed earlier, community engagement via social media also provides police organisations with novel ways of engaging with the public while promoting a positive image. The type of activity considered may be direct, covering specific aspects of policing, or may be less direct, such as the sharing of police-related memes or other humorous content (Wood, 2020). Activities that fall into this category would often be generated by some element of the policing organisation's public relations team. This has been seen with the use of memes, with the police making humorous posts about sporting rivalries or similar public interests that fall outside of traditional police activity (Wood, 2020).

Considering the image management goals of policing organisations, one of the core advantages of social and online media use is the ability for police organisations to interact with the public minus a reliance on traditional media organisations (Colbran, 2020; Ellis & McGovern, 2016; Lee & McGovern, 2013, 2014; McGovern, 2010). Doing so grants the policing organisation a greater ability to choose how they and their work is presented. One of the significant challenges faced by the police when using social media is an inherent lack of control over access and distribution (Bullock, 2018). Lee and McGovern (2012) acknowledge that the rapid growth of social media presents challenges for policing organisations partly due to inherent unpredictability but point out that in the case of the New South Wales Police Facebook page, negative reactions to posts are often policed by users rather than the police themselves. The New South Wales Police Facebook page is an online space where "policing is simulated and played out in an online web culture where interested members of the public engage in crime talk and policing discourse – a kind of online virtual or simulated community policing" (Lee & McGovern, 2012, p. 126).

Ultimately, the expanded use of social media, especially for police "image work" has provided policing organisations with a range of new public engagement opportunities while simultaneously diminishing their reliance on journalists and the media to achieve these goals. Journalists have attempted to address this shift in power, often also utilising social media to achieve their own goals, which are sometimes at odds with those of the police (Colbran, 2020). However, there is more police-generated information available to the public, and the police are increasingly able to maintain greater control over it (Ellis & McGovern, 2016).

NEW FORMS OF TECHNOLOGICAL ACCOUNTABILITY

If, as discussed here, online and social media have provided a range of new opportunities for the police to engage with the public, other forms of new technology have provided a number of challenges. Recent technological advances mean that policing organisations sometimes have reduced control over images of policing, including negative ones, and these can spread quickly in the online space.

Citizen journalism

The increasing number of cameras carried by citizens through the widespread use of smartphones over the last decade or so has meant that most people have a camera with them at all times. A related technological change is the always-connected nature of contemporary technology. The introduction of live-streaming means that interactions between the public and the police can be distributed online in real time.

The advent of such technology reduces the ability for the police to control how their "performances" are received by the public.

> *The police are no longer the only actors, nor do they control all elements of stage production. There is simultaneously more participation in the staging through the production of unofficial recordings (readings/accounts) of policing events, as well as a larger and more heterogeneous audience for those stagings* (Goldsmith, 2010).

This set of connected practices, sometimes defined as citizen journalism, represents perhaps the most significant threat to police image management. Citizen journalism has the power to undermine the image-management practices of the police. This includes the media-related practices of institutional public relations bodies within police organisations.

Broadly, citizen journalism refers to the mass distribution of user-generated content. In its most contemporary form, citizen journalism is "participation brought about by mass ownership of mobile phones with built-in cameras, image sharing networking sites including YouTube and Twitter, and the popularity of blogs" (Jewkes, 2015, p. 294).

Citizen journalism, especially during its formative stages, was helped by technological convergence, smartphones with video, now with always-connected internet, and the growth of an interactive media environment (Mythen, 2010). This media environment includes user-driven content filtering and distribution through social media platforms such as Facebook and Twitter. It is in this environment that, according to Mythen (2010), bystanders and everyday citizens who capture images are not simply suppliers and/or audiences, they are also creators of news.

Citizen journalism represents what could be considered as a "democratising" and participatory form of journalism. However, Mythen (2010) points out that there are limits to citizen journalism. One of these is the issue of unequal access where there is an economically driven inequality potentially driving the access to technology and to the ability to distribute any material produced.

An issue impacted by citizen journalism is police accountability and critical examination of the criminal justice system. One example of this is the increasing use of emerging media technologies by political activists and similar groups. Some of the most widely distributed examples of citizen journalism affecting the police image are those where information, usually video that is captured and distributed by the public, demonstrates contested police practices such as the use of force. In the widely documented case of the London G20 protests in 2009–2010, bystander footage captured the moment a police officer struck a member of the public as he made his way home attempting to avoid police and protesters. Greer and McLaughlin (2010) examined the impact of citizen journalism on this case and how it was able to "disrupt the traditional flows of communication power" (p. 1). The authors argue that in this case, the death of Ian Tomlinson, citizen journalism was able to intervene in the context of a miscarriage of justice after the police promoted an anti-protester narrative and "prioritized the police perspective" (Greer & McLaughlin, 2010, p. 1049).

As further noted by Greer and McLaughlin (2010), the images provided by citizen journalists disrupted the police image work, exposing the police media releases concerning the incident as partial fabrications. This was in line with a series of police media releases which sought to establish a discourse that legitimised public-order policing practices prior to the protests taking place. These media releases defined protesters as, for example, violent. This same discourse was then drawn on in public police statements concerning the death and were undermined once footage produced by a citizen journalist went viral.

In Australia, Ellis (2019) examined the use of amateur video in a well-publicised incident during the 2013 Sydney Gay and Lesbian Mardi Gras. This was an incident of police excessive force captured on video and distributed online. In this case, it was the police use of force against Jamie Jackson. Jackson's arrest was captured on video by multiple bystanders, several of whom can be heard arguing with the police and questioning police behaviour. With the emergence of this footage, which was quickly distributed via social media and then the mainstream media, claims of excessive force were levelled at the NSW police members involved.

In a similar progression of events as those seen in the London G20 protest coverage discussed previously, in the case of the 2013 Sydney Gay and Lesbian Mardi Gras, the police narrative prior to the release of the arrest video was one that differed from the images captured by bystanders. Shortly after the release of the video, New South Wales Police addressed the media and played down the incident (Ellis, 2019). Ellis (2019, p. 421) argues that this response fell short of public expectation and "fell short of the 'dynamic' legitimacy demanded of online audiences who expected real-time, meaningful responses to their queries through the NSW Police Force LGBTI Corporate Sponsor Facebook page". While it was found that not all responses to the footage were opposed to the behaviour of the police, the reaction to the footage highlights the impact citizen journalism can have on perceived police legitimacy. Further, these cases highlight how significant an impact the subsequent behaviour of police can have on perceived legitimacy, especially if the police are found to be misrepresenting events. This suggests that for the public, demonstrating transparency on behalf of the police is central to perceived legitimacy.

The impact of citizen journalism on police legitimacy amplifies in the online, and particularly the social media, space. It is in this social network-driven space where much citizen produced content gains wide circulation. One of the key differences here is that social media sharing is characterised by user editorials. The sharing through these networks is premised on the idea that users will not only share citizen journalism artefacts but will often editorialise in a way that signifies their views on the artefact.

The concept of visibility has been a pillar of police operations where visibility through uniforms or marked vehicles has added operational effectiveness and asserted authority to the public (Goldsmith, 2010). This same analysis could be applied to attempts by policing organisations to promote a positive image where visibility is a central requirement and control of that visibility is a must. However, just as visibility can produce good effects for policing organisations, a lack of control over visibility can trigger arrangements of accountability where "[p]ublic exposure of misdeeds or neglect therefore has the potential to reflect badly upon the police as an organization and lead them to being held to account collectively as well as individually for the actions revealed" (Goldsmith, 2010, p. 915).

Visibility of particular policing practices also matters for accountability and perceived legitimacy. Operational practices such as the use of discretion have tended to be low-visibility and therefore difficult targets for oversight or accountability (Goldsmith, 2010, 2015). The new possibilities for citizen journalism due to technological change have shifted the balance, and previously relatively invisible aspects of policing such as the use of discretion and the use of force are often the subject of public produced policing images (Brucato, 2015a, 2015b; Goldsmith, 2010; Parry, Moule, & Dario, 2019). Goldsmith (2010) argues that the advent of media technology in the hands of the public creates a "new visibility" of policing. In an era of new visibility, new forms of accountability also emerge, such as problematic behaviour of individual off-duty police officers in online or social media spaces. Such behaviour is seen to reflect on the police organisation and impact on public confidence (Goldsmith, 2015).

When considering the concept of transparency in the context of police legitimacy, Brucato (2015a) argues that transparency, and therefore elements of police accountability, rely on visibility. Historically, visibility of the police has only been a product of types of surveillance. Brucato (2015a, p. 48) argues that with increased access to technology such as smartphones, there has been a shift towards citizen empowerment "where the ability for civilians to produce policing's visibility empowers them in ways previously never imagined. These powers emerge from the mechanically objective qualities of cameras and the self-evident – even scientific – qualities of the media they produce".

Considerations of citizen journalism need not be limited to images of the police in action. Police legitimacy may be questioned by citizen journalism in ways found in the traditional media. Rather than images that show particular police action such as the use of force, there may be images that demonstrate a lack of policing where the police are present but operating in a way that suggests a type of under-policing. Similarly, there may be a reaction to citizen-generated footage where the police are absent, despite a perceived need. This would be similar to coverage that may be found in other media formats such as television news and current affairs where police as primary definers and responders are also held to account for a lack of intervention deemed suitable by the media producers (Gaffey, 2019).

Sousveillance

Sousveillance, an increasingly popular term in regard to citizen journalism, refers to the concept of watching "from below" where surveillance could be relatively defined as the act of watching from above (Mann, 2004; Mann, Nolan, & Wellman, 2003). Importantly, both of these are types of "watching", and not just simply "seeing". Sousveillance is a form of "reflectionism" where "[r]eflectionism holds up the mirror and asks the question: 'Do you like what you see?'" (Mann et al., 2003, p. 333). Sousveillance also involves a level of transparency generally not present in surveillance. Surveillance benefits from being secretive or undetected, while sousveillance, in the context of contemporary citizen journalism, tends to decentralise observation (Goldsmith, 2010; Mann, 2016).

Certainly, several of the examples of citizen journalism included earlier may qualify as forms of sousveillance. That is, police may have been captured on film by a citizen who was "watching" the police. The accountability that emerges from this comes after the act and this new form of accountability has been put into action by a variety of groups who aim to use sousveillance in an organised way. Perhaps the best known example of this is "Copwatch", a movement which began in the United States (Brucato, 2016). "Copwatch" is an activist group that aims to not only promote citizen journalism but to promote citizen journalism as a legitimate response to previously unrecognised police violence and misconduct (Brucato, 2016). The "copwatch" movement has also used elements of citizen journalism, coupled with strong social media utilisation in an attempt to promote civil rights (Miller, 2016). In this sense, sousveillance moves beyond simply watching or recording. Rather, it becomes an attempt to in part shift the balance of power between citizens and the police in terms of image. As Mann et al. (2003, p. 332) put it: "One way to challenge and problematize both surveillance and acquiescence to it is to resituate these technologies of control on individuals, offering panoptic technologies to help them observe those in authority".

An important recent development in light of observing those in authority is the investment by the police in body-worn cameras (BWC). It is beyond the scope of this chapter to discuss police BWC fully, but in short, they and the footage they produce are seen as having the potential to "enhance public trust in police, provide transparency in policing activity, increase police accountability, reduce conflict between police and public, and provide a police perspective of incidents and events" (Lee, Taylor, & Willis, 2019, p. 174). This is a list of potential benefits that closely echo those of citizen journalism.

Citizen-produced images and BWC footage captured by the police may be very similar. They are often captured at the moment of police use of discretion and application of police powers. BWC footage captured by on-body cameras, much like public-produced images, have led to police being held to account for misconduct, including the misuse of force (Taylor, 2016b). Conversely, it has been determined that the police tend to hold control over what type of BWC images are produced and when (Lee et al., 2019; Palmer, 2016; Taylor, 2016a, 2016b). Police agencies view the utility of BWC as a way of protecting officers from false claims and public misconduct (Brucato, 2015a). Further, the compelling "bottom-up" nature of BWC footage may lead to less focus on those police actions and behaviours not captured (Taylor, 2016b).

The similarity between citizen-produced images and BWC footage creates potential for the police to utilise such footage for public relations purposes. In an age of citizen journalism, police may rely on BWC footage as a type of authority due to its format and its privileged source. The persuasive characteristics of public-produced sousveillance, such as presumed objectivity and the negation of institutional power, may be co-opted by police with the distribution of BWC images. On the relationship between citizen journalism and the use of BWC, Brucato argues that BWC do not simply increase the likelihood of prosecution or protect citizens from police misconduct. Instead:

> *These cameras function to nullify third-party videos, and especially civilian sousveillance. The video shot from the position of the officer is legally and culturally privileged. As such, rather than being just a new surveillance technology, on-officer wearable cameras work as counter-sousveillance technology* (Brucato, 2015b, p. 470).

CONCLUSION

This chapter has examined the relationship between policing institutions and contemporary media and has examined some of the significant changes this relationship has undergone as we progress further into the digital age. The changes to the instruments policing institutions use to leverage positive public relations goals via the media represent a longer set of established media engagement practices that are now translating to new formats due to new technologies such as online and social media (Lee & McGovern, 2014). The key challenges faced by policing organisations in navigating this transition are yet to be resolved, but the ability of police organisations to employ new media formats to engage with the public holds potential benefits for both the police and the public (Goldsmith, 2010; Lee & McGovern, 2013, 2014; Lee et al., 2019; Mawby, 2002).

As the digital age progresses, public demands for police legitimacy and accountability are closely related to the relationship both the public and policing organisations share with a growing number of media sources. Even though contemporary technology provides a range of avenues to promote policing goals, public-produced media, or citizen journalism, is increasingly fulfilling a particularly contemporary yet contested role by confronting existing police practices that have formerly enjoyed a lack of public scrutiny.

REFERENCES

Allan, D. M. C., Kelly, A., & Stephenson, A. (2016). The impact of a changing media landscape on police practice and legitimacy. *Global Media Journal: Australian Edition*, *10*(2), 1–14. Retrieved from: www.hca.westernsydney.edu.au/gmjau/?p=2927

Brucato, B. (2015a). The new transparency: Police violence in the context of ubiquitous surveillance. *Media and Communication*, *3*(3), 39–55.

Brucato, B. (2015b). Policing made visible: Mobile technologies and the importance of point of view. *Surveillance & Society*, *13*(3–4), 455–473.

Brucato, B. (2016). Standing by police violence: On the constitution of the ideal citizen as Sousveiller. *American Studies Journal*, *61*, 1–16.

Bullock, K. (2018). (Re)presenting 'order' online: The construction of police presentational strategies on social media. *Policing and Society, 28*(3), 345–359.

Chermak, S., & Weiss, A. (2005). Maintaining legitimacy using external communication strategies: An analysis of police-media relations. *Journal of Criminal Justice, 33*(5), 501–512.

Chibnall, S. (1977). *Law-and-order news: An analysis of crime reporting in the British press.* London: Tavistock Publications.

Clifford, K., & White, R. (2017). *Media and crime: Content, contexts and consequence.* Oxford: Oxford University Press.

Colbran, M. P. (2020). Policing, social media and the new media landscape: Can the police and the traditional media ever successfully bypass each other? *Policing and Society*, 1–15.

Ellis, J. (2019). Renegotiating police legitimacy through amateur video and social media: Lessons from the police excessive force at the 2013 Sydney gay and lesbian Mardi Gras parade. *Current Issues in Criminal Justice, 31*(3), 399–419.

Ellis, J., & McGovern, A. (2016). The end of symbiosis? Australia police – media relations in the digital age. *Policing and Society, 26*(8), 944–962.

Farmer, A. (2016). *Copwatchers: Citizen journalism and the changing police-community dynamic.* Delaware: University of Delaware Press.

Gaffey, J. (2019). Melbourne's African gangs' and media narratives. *Salus Journal, 7*(2), 68–84.

Goldsmith, A. J. (2010). Policing's new visibility. *The British Journal of Criminology, 50*(5), 914–934.

Goldsmith, A. J. (2015). Disgracebook policing: Social media and the rise of police indiscretion. *Policing and Society, 25*(3), 249–267.

Greer, C., & McLaughlin, E. (2010). We predict a riot?: Public order policing, new media environments and the rise of the citizen journalist. *The British Journal of Criminology, 50*(6), 1041–1059.

Jewkes, Y. (2015). *Media and crime.* London: Sage Publications.

Lee, M., & McGovern, A. (2012). Image work(s): The new police (popularity) culture. In K. Carrington, M. Ball, E. O'Brien, & J. Tauri (Eds.), *Crime, justice and social democracy.* London: Palgrave Macmillan.

Lee, M., & McGovern, A. (2013). Force to sell: Policing the image and manufacturing public confidence. *Policing and Society, 23*(2), 103–124.

Lee, M., & McGovern, A. (2014). *Policing and media: Public relations, simulations and communications.* New York: Routledge.

Lee, M., & McGovern, A. (2016). Logics of risk: Police communications in an age of uncertainty. *Journal of Risk Research*, 1–12.

Lee, M., Taylor, E., & Willis, M. (2019). Being held to account: Detainees' perceptions of police body-worn cameras. *Australian & New Zealand Journal of Criminology, 52*(2), 174–192.

Mann, S. (2004). "Sousveillance": Inverse surveillance in multimedia imaging. Paper presented at the Proceedings of the 12th annual ACM international conference on Multimedia, New York. https://doi.org/10.1145/1027527.1027673

Mann, S. (2016). Surveillance (oversight), sousveillance (undersight), and metaveillance (seeing sight itself). 2016 IEEE Conference on Computer Vision and Pattern Recognition Workshops (CVPRW), Las Vegas, NV, pp. 1408–1417.

Mann, S., Nolan, J., & Wellman, B. (2003). Sousveillance: Inventing and using wearable computing devices for data collection in surveillance environments. *Surveillance & Society*, *1*(3), 331–355.

Mawby, R. C. (2002). Continuity and change, convergence and divergence: The policy and practice of police – media relations. *Criminal Justice*, *2*(3), 303–324.

Mawby, R. C. (2010a). Chibnall revisited: Crime reporters, the police and 'law-and-order news'. *The British Journal of Criminology*, *50*(6), 1060–1076.

Mawby, R. C. (2010b). Police corporate communications, crime reporting and the shaping of policing news. *Policing and Society*, *20*(1), 124–139.

McGovern, A. (2008). *Policing media: Controlling representations of the New South Wales police force.* (Doctoral dissertation, University of Western Sydney, Sydney). Retrieved from: https://researchdirect.westernsydney.edu.au/islandora/object/uws:7081

McGovern, A. (2010). *Tweeting the news: Criminal justice agencies and their use of social networking sites.* Paper presented at the Australian and New Zealand Critical Criminology Conference 2010, Sydney Law School, University of Sydney, Sydney.

McGovern, A., & Lee, M. (2010). 'Cop[ying] it sweet': Police media units and the making of news. *Australian & New Zealand Journal of Criminology*, *43*(3), 444–464.

Miller, K. (2016). Watching the watchers: Theorizing cops, cameras, and police legitimacy in the 21st century. In *The politics of policing: Between force and legitimacy* (Vol. 21, pp. 257–276). Bingley: Emerald Group Publishing Limited.

Mythen, G. (2010). Reframing risk? Citizen journalism and the transformation of news. *Journal of Risk Research*, *13*(1), 45–58.

Palmer, D. (2016). The mythical properties of police body-worn cameras: A solution in the search of a problem. *Surveillance & Society*, *14*(1), 138–144.

Parry, M. M., Moule, R. K., & Dario, L. M. (2019). Technology-mediated exposure to police – citizen encounters: A quasi-experimental assessment of consequences for citizen perceptions. *Justice Quarterly*, *36*(3), 412–436.

Ruddell, R., & Jones, N. (2013). Social media and policing: Matching the message to the audience. *Safer Communities*, *12*(2), 64–70.

Taylor, E. (2016a). Debate lights, camera, redaction . . . police body-worn. *Surveillance & Society*, *14*(1), 129.

Taylor, E. (2016b). Lights, camera, redaction . . . police body-worn cameras; autonomy, discretion and accountability. *Surveillance & Society*, *14*(1), 128–132.

Watkins, J., Park, S., Blood, R. W., Breen, M. D., Fuller, G., Papandrea, F., & Ricketson, M. (2015). *Digital news report: Australia 2015.* Retrieved from: http://apo.org.au/resource/digital-news-report-australia-2015

Wood, M. A. (2020). Policing's 'meme strategy': Understanding the rise of police social media engagement work. *Current Issues in Criminal Justice*, 1–19.

CHAPTER 15

Public health and its interface with police practice in the 21st century

Stuart D.M. Thomas

INTRODUCTION

Researchers, practitioners, and policy-makers have increasingly spoken about the inextricable links and similarities between the people who come into frequent contact with health services and criminal justice services. Fundamentally, Crofts and Thomas (2017) argue that these are in fact, on the whole, the same people; or, what van Dijk et al. (2019) refer to as a "common clientele" so, in many ways, this should not come as much of a surprise.

Much has been written about the social determinants of health. Perhaps most prominently, Michael Marmot (e.g. Marmot & Wilkinson, 2005) has argued extensively that the major determinants of health are social, and therefore in order to address health inequalities we must necessarily have a social focus. Braveman, Kumanyika, Fielding, LaVeist, Borrell, Manderscheid, and Troutman (2011) also referred to the need to strive for a more just society; equitable access to support and services being the cornerstone of preventing and ameliorating health inequalities that are present in our societies (Whitehead, 1991). It is these arguments that have led researchers, practitioners, and more recently, policing leaders, to talk about public health and policing much more interchangeably and sometimes even in the same sentence.

Public health, broadly defined, has a central remit to provide citizens with the array of living situations that are associated with physical, mental, and social wellbeing. The World Health Organisation defines public health's aim as being to prevent disease, promote health, and prolong life (WHO, 2004). While, at least initially, this may not resonate with what we may (at least traditionally) think of as policing, or core policing functions, a more detailed consideration reveals a number of distinct overlaps and potential synergies. van Dijk and Crofts (2017) make an interesting point here that law enforcement does not tend to function with a specific public health remit, except in times of a major health crisis which has an associated public order component, such as an epidemic or other emergency. Despite this, they add that to the argument that public health and policing share a common purpose. They base their argument on the position that both public health and law enforcement seek to protect people from their fear of ill-health, injury, and the possibility of death, clarifying that much of what policing seeks to do is to preserve the health states of its community members. Interestingly, though, these actions may be hidden under the guise of what might be considered more standard police practices of maintaining public safety or responding to other matters of security. van Dijk and colleagues (2019) argue that, for this reason, the police's role in protecting, supporting, and promoting public health is rarely recognised and, as a consequence, goes largely unacknowledged.

van Dijk and Crofts (2017) describe the gradual aligning of what they refer to as "distinctly separate systems" towards an emerging field of law enforcement and public health. The authors attribute this to a process of "disruptive thinking" (Crofts & Thomas, 2017) and the adoption of a more socially engaged policing ethos associated with the recognition of, and willingness to try, multi-agency collaborations and initiatives. Such arrangements were highlighted as a means of addressing what were increasingly seen to be complex social problems and increased recognition that the traditional siloed approach to responding to what amounts to intergenerational social and economic disadvantage is simply not going to work. van Dijk and colleagues (2019) further this argument, asserting that law enforcement and public health both make use of concrete interventions that seek to change what is considered to be unhealthy or criminal behaviour. The authors argue that policing has needed to reform its practices and place the need of its community and citizens at the forefront of its policies and practices.

A significant development towards realising the common ground between public health and policing has been the increasing focus on the development and application of evidence-based policy (van Dijk et al., 2019). While it is clear that there are broad-reaching benefits of adopting evidence-informed policing services to help improve the health and wellbeing of citizens, to be effective, this needs to occur at both the strategic and front-line levels. Christmas and Srivastava (2019) refer to such changes in terms of moving away from the more traditionalist approach of "response policing" which focuses on individuals and enforcement to one of "neighbourhood policing" and "problem solving". The authors align this shift in orientation and practice to the evolution of public health approaches to policing coupled with changes in language and attitudes towards evidence-based practice, problem solving through partnerships, responding to vulnerability, and whole of system approaches.

Internationally, we have seen policing services becoming more professionalized and making use of what Skogan and Frydl (2004) describe as more sophisticated practices. Four examples are drawn upon here that demonstrate the practical application of these kinds of more "sophisticated practices" and show the utility of a public health-informed policing strategy focusing on the Australian context. The four areas highlighted are: reducing violence, road safety, illicit drug use, and pandemics.

REDUCING VIOLENCE

Broad consideration of violence as a public health issue is relatively new phenomenon (Dahlberg & Mercy, 2009), with violence being termed a leading worldwide public health problem in 1996 through the World Health Assembly WHA49.25 (cited in van Dijk et al., 2019). The economic argument grounding this is clear, with a United Kingdom-based report by Bellis, Hughes, Perkins, and Bennett (2012) noting the significant costs to the health systems associated with violence, its "contagious" character, and what they described as a strong inequality gradient.

One particular area of growth for law enforcement calls for service relates to family and intimate partner violence. The World Health Organisation (WHO) only more recently identified family and intimate partner violence as a major public health concern (WHO, 2013). The extent, and impacts of, of this type of offending cannot be overstated. For example, Victorian data published by the Crime Statistics Agency (CSA; Millsteed, 2016) reported that, over the ten-year period from January 2006 to December 2015, Victoria Police recorded a total of 470,645 family violence incidents that corresponded to 217,995 individual perpetrators. These figures alone suggest that a substantial proportion of the perpetrators are offending more than once; in fact, over a third (38.4%, n=83,705) of the perpetrators had more than one family violence incident recorded on Victoria Police files, around 7% had five or more incidents recorded, and some (0.2%) had more than 20 incidents that had been recorded. Further, related CSA data show that the number of family violence incidents reported to Victoria Police increased from 43,846 incidents in 2011 to 74,385 incidents in 2015 (Millsteed & Coghlan, 2016), while the proportion of perpetrators with more than one recorded incident of family violence in a year also increased from 18.4% in 2006 to 27% in 2015. Reasons for these increased rates are likely due to several factors associated with an increased focus on family violence by policing services, increased reporting by victims, and an increase in the number of incidents occurring in the community. The lack of a clear health-based solution (Gover, 2011) has led to the need to bring together and consider a range of other "non-health focused" solutions.

The role of front-line police, as with other first responders, in relation to family and intimate partner violence has been articulated as detecting which cases are most likely to lead to significant ongoing harm (Messing & Campbell, 2016), as this means that these cases can be directed to appropriate community supports, thus ameliorating possible harm in the longer term. Early identification and intervention are necessary to help reduce harms, as it has been established that the psychological and other personal costs to the victims involved are significant and enduring, leading to long-term health impacts. As such, it becomes necessary for front-line officers and other first responders to be able to accurately assess risk. An interesting example of a joint initiative to tackle family and intimate family violence involving a police service, health provider, and academics is described by McEwan, Bateson and Strand (2017). The key elements of this police-health-research partnership are outlined briefly here, as they demonstrate some key learnings regarding the policing-public health interface.

The partnership came about as a result of two significant family and intimate partner violence homicides in Melbourne in February 2014 – Kelly Ann Thompson and Luke Batty. These tragedies led to significant media and community attention and, more specifically, questioning whether the police could have done anything to prevent these deaths. Coronial Inquests into the two deaths concluded that the current police risk assessment processes were vastly inadequate. This led Victoria Police to review their family violence risk assessment processes. This started with the creation of a Family Violence Command, which was touted as a first across Australia. A subsequent change in police command with this portfolio led to a request for collaboration between Victoria Police, Swinburne University of Technology, and the Victorian Institute of Forensic Mental Health to develop an evidence-based approach to their risk assessment practices.

McEwan and colleagues (2017) describe the development of the Victoria Police Screening Assessment for Family Violence Risk (VP-SAFvR). Its development incorporated results from the analysis of 12 months of reported family violence incidents and used the legislative definition of family violence in Victoria as a guide for its scope. Victoria Police Family Violence Team members were also trained in the application of the VP-SAFvR, and supported by senior psychologists, to aid implementation. Early findings have been interesting, with officers having mixed views about adopting a different risk assessment tool in practice, despite the compelling evidence that existing practices were not adequate to protect public safety. Only just over half of those canvassed indicated they preferred the VP-SAFvR over the pre-existing Victoria Police assessment. Most commonly it was commented that the evidence-based approach was considered too time-consuming to complete due to the comprehensiveness of the assessment and the need to collate additional detailed information; therefore, feasibility and utility were both compromised. A follow-up study published in 2019 demonstrated some statistical utility of this evidence-based assessment of family violence (McEwan, O'Shea & Ogloff, 2019). However, this study also demonstrated the ongoing schisms associated with translating traditional research evidence and tools into routine practice. The authors noted that the tool did not work equally as well across different family violence perpetrator groupings and that it was likely that VP-SAFvR item wording would need to be developed to aid its application by police in the field. Both of these factors likely contribute to the acceptability and uptake of evidence-based practice by officers. Further field trials will ultimately determine its utility in the field and the degree to which it is adopted more routinely across the State.

It is important to note here that even for these changes to happen, a number of factors were in play at or around the same time: (1) there was a significant event (or events in this case) that led to significant scrutiny of current policing practices; (2) current policing practices were identified by independent Coronial inquiry to be highly compromised and insufficient; (3) there was a commitment to change at a strategic level and change in leadership of the portfolio covering family violence at Victoria Police; and (4) there was identifiable clinical and academic expertise available locally to guide the development of evidence-based practices. Arguably, if one or more of these had not been in place, this partnership may not have happened at all, and policing practice may not have changed to the extent that it has. The benefits of this particular evidence-based practice to address family and intimate partner violence remain to be seen, but the centrally important front-line role of the police in tackling what is a significant public health concern is clear.

ROAD SAFETY

A different example of how policing services have proactively engaged with academics and other agencies is evident in their approaches to tackling road safety. While framed under a focus on procedural justice, the Queensland Community Engagement Trial (QCET) (e.g. Mazerolle, Bennett, Antrobus & Eggins, 2012) provides a strong argument in support of public health-informed and indeed public health-driven policing strategy. The QCET study is briefly outlined here.

QCET was set up as a result of ongoing recognition of the low levels of confidence and trust in the police by its community members. The focus of the trial intervention, conducted by academics from the University of Queensland in partnership with Queensland Police, was on developing a brief script that front-line police officers could use during a short, routine traffic stop for random breath testing. Of note, random breath testing serves a couple of overlapping purposes relevant here: it seeks to catch drunk drivers and serves as a general visual deterrent to drink or drug driving through seeing the random breath (or indeed drug) test roadblocks or by having been stopped and tested.

The public health importance of such an initiative is pretty clear, even if not being the primary rationale for the partnership between the academics and Queensland Police. A recent Australian Institute of Criminology paper notes that while drink driving has been on the decline since the 1980s, it still represents the leading cause of road fatalities and injuries, with recidivist drunk drivers disproportionately contributing to road trauma (Terer & Brown, 2014). As an indicator of the frequency of random breath testing, Watson and Freeman (2007) reported that there were 2.6 million tests across two financial years (2001–2002 and 2002–2003). A more contemporary estimate reported in a 2019 news article in *The Guardian* newspaper demonstrates the significant increases in its use, noting that Victoria Police completed 17.5 million random breath tests in the previous five years, with a target set in 2017 of conducting 4.5 million random breath tests annually (Martin, 2019). The implementation of random breath tests has consistently shown to have a positive effect, reducing rates of drink driving, serious road injuries, and road fatalities (Terer & Brown, 2014).

The QCET script provided to police officers involved in the trial covered several different aspects: attitudes towards drink driving, perceptions of compliance with the law, and people's satisfaction with the police (it should also be noted here that there was a "business as normal", aka treatment as usual, arm to the trial to compare results against). The aim of the intervention was to help build trust and confidence in the police. The role of procedural justice is important here, as prior research has reported a strong association between people's perceptions of procedurally just interactions with law-enforcement agencies and their subsequent law-abiding behaviour, including their likelihood of criminal recidivism (Strang & Sherman, 2003). Mazerolle and colleagues (2012) noted that a central part of the intervention was to change the way that police interacted with community members. The random breath test was seen as an excellent opportunity to intervene, as it fundamentally changed what the authors described as a "very quick, abrupt and often devoid of anything . . . compulsory communication" to something, still brief but more socially informed and engaged.

Findings from the QCET study neatly demonstrate how a socially orientated police intervention can change community members' attitudes and behaviour and therefore lead to a public health impact; as Mazerolle and colleagues note, "[S]hort, but quality, encounters can and do leave an impression on citizens".

ILLICIT DRUG USE

A 2010 report by the Australian Institute of Criminology clearly demonstrates the impact of illicit drug use on society, reporting that harm caused by illicit drug use was estimated to cost $8.2 billion per year (Gaffney, Jones, Sweeney & Payne, 2010). Since 1985, Australia has had a National Drug Strategy. Its aims, articulated in its most recent publication (Department of Health, 2017) represent the three pillars of harm reduction: to improve health, social, and economic outcomes by reducing demand, supply, and therefore harm. The police have a central role in the realisation of this multipronged strategy.

Police efforts to intervene to limit the supply and use of illicit drugs have had a long and somewhat chequered history. Early street-level policing efforts that targeted specific populations were heavily criticised for contributing to a range of other harmful health and social impacts. Policing crackdowns led to individuals engaging in alternative high-risk behaviours such as unsafe injecting practices and to the displacement of criminal activity to other locations, thereby affecting adjacent suburbs and broader communities (e.g. Maher & Dixon, 1999). More recent policing efforts have shifted to operate much more within a harm minimisation framework; these have sought to minimise harm to direct users and the general community. As such, the following police initiatives have been witnessed in Australia and overseas: (1) involving greater use of problem solving; (2) increased use of discretionary powers, through providing alternatives to arrest through diversion programs (e.g. to healthcare, housing and related services); and (3) decriminalisation of certain drug possession offences.

There has been a lot of variability reported with respect to the successes (or otherwise) of harm reduction initiatives involving the police. Blaustein, McLay and McCulloch (2017) comment that this is likely due to ongoing challenges associated with the "institutionally entrenched understandings of police work". They suggest that harm minimisation approaches have had the most impact on policing in relation to domestic drug enforcement activities.

On a practical level (both in Australia and overseas), the most beneficial outcomes (i.e., reduced drug use/trade and reductions in other criminal activity) have been found in instances where policing services have worked in proactive partnerships with other agencies and community services (Mazerolle, Soole & Rombouts, 2007). A study by Midford, Acres, Lenton, Loxley and Boots (2002) additionally demonstrates the importance of harm minimisation interventions being set up with a long-term agenda and how vitally important early community and service consultations are, coupled with ongoing engaged communication. The authors noted that interventions that were rushed and not tailored to the local context proved challenging to implement and sustain. A constant criticism here relates to the poor quality of the evaluations that have been undertaken; this continues to compromise meaningful opportunities for dialogue around evidence-based, public health-informed policing practices to tackle illicit drug use.

PANDEMICS

As highlighted earlier in this chapter, police do have a much better defined and well-established role to play in response to pandemics. At the time of writing this chapter, we were facing a global epidemic surrounding COVID-19 which was an infectious disease caused by a new coronavirus. The rate of infection, its exponential spread, and our lack of understanding of the specifics of the disease led to significant restrictions being placed on the daily lives and activities of community members across the world. It was declared a global pandemic by the World Health Organisation (WHO) on March 11, 2020.

An unequivocal directive for social (or physical) distancing and widespread panic across many communities has led to the establishment of new specific powers for the police, both overseas and here in Australia. Their primary function has been to check up on community members' adherence to imposed quarantine measures and to police supermarkets and other "essential services" to help restore and maintain public order. The measures put in place at federal and state levels are unprecedented.

Police powers regarding responding to pandemics were already present and detailed under state and territory-based Public Health Act legislation (including the Western Australia Public Health Act 2016; the South Australian Public Health Act 2011; the New South Wales Public Health Act 2010; the Queensland Public Health Act 2005; and the Public Health and Wellbeing Act 2008 in Victoria). The primary function of this legislation is to promote and protect public health through controlling the risks, and preventing the spread, of infectious diseases. New police powers were enacted to enforce compliance with these self-isolation rules at individual and group levels; these operated at both operational and strategic levels.

At an individual level, it was required that people who tested positive for COVID-19, or who had returned to Australia from overseas after midnight on March 29, 2020, had to self-isolate for 14 days. This was also extended to include people with symptoms of the virus, who were also told to self-isolate. At a group level, businesses determined to be "non-essential" were required to close with pretty much immediate effect. A system of fines (and in some cases the added risk of imprisonment) were put in place as a strong general deterrence strategy, with operational police monitoring their communities for compliance and asking neighbours and general community members to report incidents of non-compliance.

It has been acknowledged that this system of fines is difficult to police in practice, primarily because their powers are very much based on an honour system, but early anecdotal reports of their enactment in response to COVID-19 found that police in some Australian jurisdictions have issued fines to individuals who were found to be not self-quarantining. A further example exists of a person being charged for breaching self-isolation orders and then being refused bail (Cornwell, 2020). Interestingly, there have also been examples reported of police using mobile phone video technologies to speak with those with quarantine periods imposed to check up on their self-isolation status; suggestions have also been reported in the print media that the police may make use of mobile phone tracking via metadata to further track people's movements (e.g. Taylor, 2020) in order to help contain the risks of additional contamination. It was also noted in news media on April 2, 2020, that these new police powers would be limited to just 90 days (Godfrey, 2020); despite assurances made that police would not be seeking to extend these powers, only time will tell if this transpires or not.

OPPORTUNITIES CHALLENGING THE RHETORIC AND REDEFINING POLICING IN THE 21ST CENTURY

One of the central challenges for front-line police in responding to any call for service, whether it be public health-related or not, is that police tend to prefer to respond to situations using tactics that have worked for them in the past (Cherney, Antrobus, Bennett, Murphy, & Newman, 2019). This relates to what we know is their preferred on-the-job learning style and focus on experiential learning (Thomas & Watson, 2017). Incorporating and implementing new approaches to help manage and mitigate risks in the community may therefore be significantly challenging for frontline police, especially if it involves incorporating other forms of knowledge and ways of working. This circumstance leads to additional challenges when it comes to envisioning more fully immersed public health-informed policing.

Many authors have written about the need to be cognisant of the need to overcome what could be significant cultural barriers and overt resistance amongst police officers to changes to their practice. This attitude has been found to manifest as antipathy towards outsiders and includes the labelling of such activities as "shit work", which is thought to be taking police away from their other core business (Punch & James, 2017). Recognising this widespread variability in police officers' perceptions of the scope of their role, how they should act with community members, and more generally, how their role should be performed are all important considerations in understanding what it is that a "good police officer should be doing" (Ingram, Paoline & Terrill, 2013).

Adopting a more structural approach involving partnerships with public health agencies may lead the way towards innovative practices and potentially contribute to better public safety and public health outcomes. Indeed, Christmas and Srivastava (2019) describe these partnerships as essential to the implementation of effective public health approaches in policing. There are real problems here with respect to data sharing and issues around privacy that, despite significant debate and consideration, have not been clearly resolved beyond a local level. Again, disruptive thinking will be required to find joined-up solutions for this state of affairs and what will inevitably be many other common problems.

Policing and public health are interdependent, but true partnerships may actually require a more fundamental deconstruction of traditional disciplinary boundaries. As noted by Bartkowiak-Theron and Asquith (2017), we have long acknowledged that police work is not just about solving crime, and that it involves a significant social role and function (e.g. Punch, 1979). So as we learn more and gain a more detailed understanding about the breadth of contemporary policing practice through better transparency and measurement of police activity, the role of police in the 21st century needs to be re-examined and rearticulated around population level health, safety, and wellbeing.

Wood and Watson (2017) posit that police should reimagine themselves as "guardians" instead of "warriors"; this kind of sentiment resonates well here but has been questioned by others, especially as it relates to dominant policing cultures and professional pride in referring to police as warriors (Stoughton, 2015). Stoughton (2016) goes on to argue that this reimagining of modern-day policing is necessary due to the low levels of confidence and trust in policing services and talks about the notion of tactical restraint as it relates to police officer and citizen safety (for more details on use of force, refer to Chapter 11 by Kesic and Thomas). Others have also outlined a number of key benefits to this kind of reframing exercise. McLean, Wolfe, Rojek, Alpert and Smith (2019) agree that the "police as guardians" orientation is superior to the warrior-style orientations in contemporary society. Their study found that guardians and warriors were distinct but related constructs; the authors concluded that police operating through a guardianship lens was likely to lead to more positive community relations and concomitantly greater trust and legitimacy.

The examples provided earlier on violence prevention, road safety, illicit drug use, and responding to pandemics do not necessarily represent new challenges for the police, but they demonstrate how contemporary police services have needed to adapt to a constantly changing landscape. With all four case examples, the police can be seen to be operating under a public health-informed strategy by proactively targeting high-risk groups and by making use of evidence-based strategies in order to have a broader community-level impact through intervening with those who present with the greatest risks and needs. Marmot (2010) refers to this as proportional universalism and talked of how this type of targeted approach can help to narrow the gap in existing social and health inequalities.

What has perhaps been most interesting with these developments is that internationally we still generally see policing services refraining from referring to themselves as "public health actors" and a continued lack of an internationally accepted definition of public health policing (Christmas & Srivastava, 2019). While the label perhaps doesn't sit neatly with policing services, this chapter demonstrates that police can clearly be seen to be acting as public health interventionists through the broad range of activities and initiatives that they have both initiated and or contributed to, with examples of such partnerships becoming evident domestically and internationally.

What is also interesting is that the police just don't refer to what they are doing as public health; instead they describe their interventions in relation to other "core" police roles and duties relating to community order and safety. Perhaps this kind of comfort zone relates to what Kerr,

Small and Wood (2005) report in relation to police fulfilling their core law-enforcement role whilst having simultaneous (but not necessarily intended) public health benefits for individuals and communities. Whether these issues reflect a nuance of language, or lack of a common language, it is clear is that policing and public health can and do go hand in hand. What is needed moving forward is a greater emphasis on public health-informed policing and a commitment to what van Dijk et al. (2019) refer to as a "joined-up approach" with multi-agency commitments to proactive preventative activities and to working together (Christmas & Srivastava, 2019). These kinds of partnerships are costly in all senses of the word; they take time, effort, resources, and a sustained commitment from all parties to develop, sustain, and thrive. That doesn't mean that public health-informed policing shouldn't be supported or continue to happen.

It is reasonable to predict that what we will see moving forward are increasing examples, and increasing visibility, of police-health-academic partnerships and the forging of a common ground and strong foundation from which the health and social inequalities present in our communities can be tackled using multifaceted, evidence-based approaches. Creating platforms to share these initiatives, and the challenges and opportunities afforded by such partnerships, will be vital as we move forward. Such platforms would serve to provide additional evidence-based interventions for police beyond the site-specific reach most initiatives have had to date. There is a changing face to policing practice in the 21st century. It will be exciting to see how policing services and public health services continue to navigate and engage in this space. A range of tried-and-tested as well as much more novel approaches will be required if we are to maximise opportunities that serve to reduce social and health inequalities and improve health and justice-related outcomes for individuals and communities.

REFERENCES

Bartkowiak-Theron, I., & Asquith, N.L. (2017). Conceptual divides and practice synergies in law enforcement and public health: Some lessons from policing vulnerability in Australia. *Policing and Society*, 27, 276–288. https://doi.org/10.1080/10439463.2016.1216553

Bellis, M.A., Hughes, K., Perkins, C., & Bennett, A.M. (2012). *Protecting people, promoting health: A public health approach to violence prevention for England*. London: United Kingdom Department of Health. Retrieved from: https://assets.publishing.service.gov.uk/government/uploads/system/uploads/attachment_data/file/216977/Violence-prevention.pdf

Blaustein, J., McLay, M., & McCulloch, J. (2017). Secondary harm mitigation: A more humanitarian framework for international drug law. *International Journal of Drug Policy*, 46, 66–73. https://doi.org/10.1016/j.drugpo.2017.05.038

Braveman, P.A., Kumanyika, S., Fielding, J., LaVeist, T., Borrell, L.N., Manderscheid, R., & Troutman, A. (2011). Health disparities and health equity: The issue is justice. *American Journal of Public Health, 101*(Suppl 1), S149–S155. https://doi.org/10.2105/AJPH.2010.300062

Cherney, A., Antrobus, E., Bennett, S., Murphy, B., & Newman, M. (2019). *Evidence-based policing: A survey of police attitudes*. Trends & Issues in Crime and Criminal Justice no. 579. Canberra: Australian Institute of Criminology.

Christmas, H., & Srivastava, J. (2019). *Public health approaches in policing: A discussion paper*. London: United Kingdom College of Policing.

Cornwell, D. (2020). Coronavirus: Sydney man breached self-isolation order 3 times in 24 hours. *The Australian*, 30 March. Retrieved from: www.theaustralian.com.au

Crofts, N., & Thomas, S. (2017). Law enforcement and public mental health: Finding common ground and global solutions to disparities in health and access the criminal justice. *Journal of Community Safety & Wellbeing, 2*(3).

Dahlberg, L.L., & Mercy, J.A. (2009). History of violence as a public health problem. *American Medical Association Journal of Ethics, 11*, 167–172.

Department of Health (2017). *National drug strategy 2017–2026*. Publication no. 11814. Canberra: Department of Health.

Gaffney, A., Jones, W., Sweeney, J., & Payne, J. (2010). *Drug use monitoring in Australia: 2008 annual report on drug use among police detainees*. Monitoring Reports 9. Canberra: Australian Institute of Criminology.

Godfrey, A. (2020). *NSW coronavirus social distancing rules to last 90 days*. Retrieved from: https://7news.com.au/lifestyle/health-wellbeing/nsw-coronavirus-social-distancing-rules-to-last-90-days-c-948010

Gover, A.R. (2011). New directions for domestic violence offender treatment standards: Colorado's innovative approach to differentiated treatment. *Partner Abuse, 2*, 95–120. https://doi.org/10.1891/1946-6560.2.1.95

Ingram, J.R., Paoline, E.A., & Terrill, W. (2013). A multilevel framework for understanding police culture: The role of the workgroup. *Criminology, 51*, 365–397. https://doi.org/10.1111/1745-9125.12009

Kerr, T., Small, W., & Wood, E. (2005). The public health and social impacts of drug market enforcement: A review of the evidence. *International Journal of Drug Policy, 16*, 210–220. https://doi.org/10.1016/j.drugpo.2005.04.005

Maher, L., & Dixon, D. (1999). Policing and public health: Law enforcement and harm minimisation in a street-level drug market. *The British Journal of Criminology, 39*, 488–512. https://doi.org/10.1093/bjc/39.4.488

Marmot, M. (2010). *Fair society, healthy lives: Strategic review of the health inequalities in England post 2010*. London: The Marmot Review.

Marmot, M., & Wilkinson, R. (2005). *Social determinants of health*. 2nd Edition. London: Oxford University Press.

Martin, L. (2019). Victoria Police falsified breath tests to meet 'unachieveable' targets, inquiry finds. *The Guardian*, 16 January. Retrieved from: www.theguardian.com/australia-news/2019/jan/16/victoria-police-falsified-breath-tests-to-meet-unachievable-targets-inquiry-finds

Mazerolle, L., Bennett, S., Antrobus, E., & Eggins, E. (2012). Procedural justice, routine encounters and citizen perceptions of police: Main findings from the Queensland community engagement trial (QCET). *Journal of Experimental Criminology, 8*, 343–367. Doi:10.1007/s11292-012-9160-1

Mazerolle, L., Soole, D., & Rombouts, S. (2007). Drug law enforcement: A review of the evaluation literature. *Police Quarterly, 10,* 115–153. https://doi.org/10.1177/1098611106287776

McEwan, T., Bateson, S., & Strand, S. (2017). Improving police risk assessment and management of family violence through a collaboration between law enforcement, forensic mental health and academia. *Journal of Criminological Research, Policy and Practice, 3,* 119–131.

McEwan, T., O'Shea, D.E., & Ogloff, J.R.P. (2019). An actuarial instrument for police triage of Australian family violence reports. *Criminal Justice and Behavior, 46,* 590–607. Doi:10.1177/0093854818806031

McLean, K., Wolfe, S.E., Rojek, J., Alpert, G., & Smith, M.R. (2019). Police officers as warriors or guardians: Empirical reality or intriguing rhetoric? *Justice Quarterly.* doi.org/10.1080/07418825.2018.1533031

Messing, J.T., & Campbell, J.C. (2016). Informing collaborative interventions: Intimate partner violence risk assessment for front line police officers. *Policing: A Journal of Policy and Practice, 10,* 328–340. DOI:10.1093/police/paw013

Midford, R., Acres, J., Lenton, S., Loxley, W., & Boots, K. (2002) Cops, drugs and the community: Establishing consultative harm reduction structures in two West Australian locations. *International Journal of Drug Policy, 3,* 181–188.

Millsteed, M. (2016). *How many repeat family violence perpetrators were there in Victoria over the last ten years?* Fact Sheet no. 2. Melbourne: Crime Statistics Agency. Retrieved from: www.crimestatistics.vic.gov.au/sites/default/files/embridge_cache/emshare/original/public/2016/05/4b/e9463044e/20160420_in%2Bfact_fv%2Brecidivism.pdf

Millsteed, M., & Coghlan, S. (2016). *Predictors of recidivism amongst police recorded family violence perpetrators.* Fact Sheet no. 4, May. Melbourne: Crime Statistics Agency. Retrieved from: www.crimestatistics.vic.gov.au/sites/default/files/embridge_cache/emshare/original/public/2016/06/96/97f49b66e/20160530_final_in_brief4.pdf

Punch, M. (1979). *Policing the inner city. A study of Amsterdam's Warmoesstraat.* London: Palgrave Macmillan.

Punch, M., & James, S. (2017). Researching law enforcement and public health. *Policing and Society. An International Journal of Research and Policy, 27,* 251–260. https://doi.org/10.1080/10439463.2016.1205066

Skogan, W., & Frydl, K. (2004). *Fairness and effectiveness in policing.* Washington, DC: National Academy Press.

Stoughton, S.W. (2015). Law enforcement's "warrior" problem. *Harvard Law Review Forum, 128,* 125.

Stoughton, S.W. (2016). Principled policing: Warrior cops and guardian officers. *Wake Forest Law Review, 51,* 611–676.

Strang, H., & Sherman, L. (2003). Repairing the harm: Victims and restorative justice. *Utah Law Review, 15,* 17–23.

Taylor, J. (2020). Australia's civil liberties under coronavirus: Advocates warn laws must be temporary. *The Guardian,* 26 March. Retrieved from: www.theguardian.com/world/2020/mar/26/australias-civil-liberties-under-coronavirus-advocates-warn-laws-must-be-temporary

Terer, K., & Brown, R. (2014). *Effective drink driving prevention and enforcement strategies: Approaches to improving practice.* Trends & Issues in Crime and Criminal Justice no. 472. Canberra: Australian Institute of Criminology.

Thomas, S., & Watson, A. (2017). A focus for mental health training for police. *Journal of Criminological Research, Policy and Practice, 3,* 92–104.

van Dijk, A., & Crofts, N. (2017). Law enforcement and public health as an emerging field. *Policing and Society: An International Journal of Research and Policy, 27,* 261–275.

van Dijk, A., Herrington, V., Crofts, N., Breunig, R., Burris, S., Sullivan, H., Middleton, J., Sherman, S., & Thomson, N. (2019). Law enforcement and public health: Recognition and enhancement of joined-up solutions. *The Lancet, 393,* 287–294. https://doi.org/10.1016/S0140-6736(18)32839-3

Watson, B., & Freeman, J. (2007). Perceptions and experiences of random breath testing in Queensland and the self-reported deterrent impact on drunk driving. *Traffic Injury Prevention, 8,* 11–19. https://doi.org/10.1080/15389580601027360

Whitehead, M. (1991). The concepts and principles of equity and health. *Health Promotion International, 6,* 217–228.

Wood, J.D., & Watson, A.C. (2017). Improving police interventions during mental health-related encounters: Past, present and future. *Policing and Society. An International Journal of Research and Policy, 27,* 289–299. DOI:10.1080/10439463.2016.1219734

World Health Organisation. (2004). *Promoting mental health: Concepts, emerging evidence, practice.* Retrieved from: https://www.who.int/mental_health/evidence/en/promoting_mhh.pdf

World Health Organisation. (2013). *Violence against women: 'A global health problem of epidemic proportions'.* Retrieved from: https://www.who.int/mediacentre/news/releases/2013/violence_against_women_20130620/en/

CHAPTER 16

Emergency management and the role of state police

Ian Manock and Simon Robinson

INTRODUCTION

Police have always had a role to play in one form or another when disasters strike. These roles have included emergency response, rescue, and identification of victims; securing and cordoning of impacted areas; and in recent times, the actual management and coordination of multi-agency response. Throughout history, our police agencies have been asked to look after the day-to-day community needs with respect to policing and law enforcement, and in recent times, public expectations during disaster situations have forced additional roles onto them relating to disaster/emergency-management-related prevention/mitigation, preparedness, response, and recovery. Police today are expected to not only be the upholders and enforcers of our laws but to take an active, and in some cases a leading, role in the preparation for and response to disasters and emergencies.

HISTORY

The very first Police Force in Australia was formed in New South Wales by Governor Arthur Philip in 1788, just after the arrival of the First Fleet. The Royal Marines were initially tasked with maintaining the laws set by Governor Philip, but he decided the colony needed its own police force and thus created the Night Watch, comprised of 12 of the best-behaved convicts (Crofts, 2016). The Night Watch teams were combined in 1862 to form the NSW Police Force (NSW Police, 2019). As with NSW, similar initial law-enforcement groups were formed in the other colonies as they were established. Formal police forces were eventually established in South Australia in 1838, Victoria and Western Australia in 1853, Queensland in 1864, and Tasmania in 1899. On January 1, 1901, the Commonwealth of Australia came into being and the six colonies became the six states of Australia, forming the first state police agencies in Australia. Following on from Federation, the Northern Territory Police was formed in 1911 and finally the Australian Federal Police, who also police the Australian Capital Territory, in 1979.

There is very little written relating to actual police involvement in major emergencies and disasters during the late 1800s and early 1900s, but it can be assumed that the police agencies around Australia would have undertaken life- and property-saving activities during natural disasters as they do today.

Civil defence to emergency management

Following World War II (WWII), response to disasters in Australia was carried out in the main by the emergency services and the various civil defence units/organisations that had been formed during WWII and maintained afterwards, as the impact of the cold war era (1950s–1960s) caused concern and worry in Australia. These units provided civil defence and protection services to Australian communities throughout the post-WWII period. A number of major disaster events in the 1950s and 1960s (including the 1967 Tasmanian Bushfires), saw these civil defence units provide major response to communities impacted by bushfires, floods, and tropical cyclones. These civil defence units continued to operate within the various states and territories into the 1970s. In 1956, the Commonwealth Government established the Civil Defence School at Mt Macedon, Victoria, in order to provide training to civil defence units throughout Australia. The training sought to train police in "offering maximum protection from the effects of hostilities on Australian soil to all Australians" (Pearce, 2006, p. 2).

When Cyclone Tracy hit Darwin in December 1974, the devastating impact it had resulted in a nationwide response to the event. Response and support resources from the States and Territories, together with the military, converged on Darwin to provide support to the Territory's administration and emergency services in their response to the event. Numerous police agencies from around Australia dispatched police officers to assist the stricken Darwin community and support the NT Police in restoring and maintaining law and order (NSW Police, 2019), (Queensland Police, 2020). The impact of Cyclone Tracy on Darwin in 1974 was a major catalyst in reforming Australia's civil defence organisations into the counter-disaster and emergency-management agencies of today.

Following on from a series of major disasters in the late 1960s and early 1970s, the Commonwealth Government in 1974 formed Australia's first counter-disaster agency, the Natural Disasters Organisation (NDO). The NDO was formed to "coordinate Commonwealth physical assistance to states and territories in the event of a natural disaster" (Dwyer, 2006, p. 42). The NDO also provided support to the states and territories in the transitioning from civil defence to the development of a counter-disaster capability, later to become emergency management. The impact and devastation caused by Cyclone Tracy in December 1974 demonstrated the need for an ongoing role for the Commonwealth Government in support of the states and territories during natural disasters. The NDO upgraded the Civil Defence School at Mt Macedon, renaming it the Australian Counter Disaster College (ACDC), where a range of short residential courses continued to be delivered to representatives from each state and territory, but with more emphasis on counter-disaster training rather than cold war civil defence. Over the years following, as the NDO became Emergency Management Australia (EMA), the ACDC became the Australian Emergency Management Institute (AEMI) and delivered residential emergency-management courses until its closure in 2014.

Legislation

Within Australia, "state and territory governments have primary responsibility for protecting life, property and environment within their borders" (Australian Institute for Disaster Resilience [AIDR], 2019, p. 7). The Australian Constitution provides that "State Parliaments can pass laws on a wider range of subjects than the Commonwealth Parliament, and for this reason important areas such as education, criminal law, and roads are regulated primarily by laws of the States rather than by laws of the Commonwealth Parliament" (Commonwealth of Australia, 2010, p. vi). Emergency Management Australia [EMA], (2000) state that "Australia's emergency management and counter-disaster arrangements are founded on the premise that, when the Australian Constitution was prepared, State and Territory Governments retained responsibility for those matters not addressed. This includes protection and preservation of the lives and property of their citizens" (p. 2). Therefore, in accordance with the Australian Constitution, the establishment of emergency-management and police-specific legislation as well as the development of emergency/disaster management arrangements, plans, and strategies are the responsibility of the state and territory governments.

Following the impact of Cyclone Tracy in 1974, states began the process of developing specific disaster management/emergency-management legislation to establish roles, responsibilities, arrangements, and powers associated with disaster management. Today, all states and territories in Australia have specific emergency/disaster management legislation in place. These pieces of legislation generally provide requirements for the establishment and membership of state, regional, and local emergency/disaster management committees, emergency-management roles and responsibilities, emergency- management planning, recovery management and declarations of states of emergency/disaster, and the powers that go along with those declarations (*Disaster Management Act, 2003* (Qld), *Emergencies Act, 2004* (ACT), *Emergency Management Act, 2004* (SA), *Emergency Management Act, 2005* (WA), *Emergency Management Act, 2006* (Tas), *Emergency Management Act, 2013* (NT), *Emergency Management Act, 2013* (Vic), *State Emergency and Rescue Management Act, 1989* (NSW)). The linkage between legislation and the roles of police in emergency management will be discussed further in the "Roles and responsibilities" section later in this chapter.

Education and training

With the establishment of the Civil Defence School in 1956, and then its transition to the ACDC and then AEMI, opportunities for police officers to receive counter-disaster and emergency-management-related training expanded. Courses were initially delivered at Mt Macedon as national courses, with limited representatives from each state and territory participating. In the 1990s state- or territory-focused courses began to be conducted in each state and territory by the AEMI but funded by the Commonwealth Government. Police officers were regular attendees at courses such as "Introduction to Disaster/Emergency Management, Emergency Planning and Exercise Management". In fact, the national exercise-management course at Mt Macedon was developed, coordinated, and delivered by police officers from the South Australia Police, demonstrating that state police agencies had a role to play in emergency-management education and training.

State police emergency-management units

From the 1990s onwards, several state and territory police agencies around Australia began developing their own emergency-management capabilities with the establishment of specialised emergency-management units. These units are responsible not only for assisting operational police develop and prepare emergency-management plans and strategies for major events but also for providing training for operational police officers in areas of emergency management, such as risk assessments, community emergency-management planning, and mass gathering/major event planning. For example, the ACT Policing Emergency Management and Planning Team was established in 2009 and has as its role "increasing the preparedness and response capabilities of ACT Policing to major events, Guest of Government visits and major incidents including, but not limited to; terrorism related occurrences, natural disasters, health pandemics, the coordination of recovery operations and crowded places" (Australian Federal Police, 2020).

In South Australia, the South Australian Police (SAPol) established their Emergency and Major Events Section in 1998. The unit was initially responsible for the three key areas of major event planning, terrorism exercising, and traffic management and emergency management across all portfolios. The emergency-management role expanded in the years following formation of the section, with the Emergency Management Coordinator position established. The emergency-management function now addresses national capability development, exercising, state emergency-management policy and development, and the day-to-day policy and operational support to the SAPol Commissioner, who is the South Australian State Emergency Coordinator (Dippy, personal communication April 20, 2020).

9/11 and beyond

The September 11, 2001, (9/11) terrorist attacks on targets in the United States, including the World Trade Centre, the Pentagon, and four commercial flights, killed nearly 3,000 people. The attacks on 9/11 triggered major initiatives around the world to combat terrorism (Hoffman, 2002). For the first time in history, terrorism became a recognised major disaster threat to communities. According to Mehta (2018), between 2002 and 2017, the US alone spent US$2.8 trillion on counterterrorism funding. That was an average of US$186.6 billion per year over that 15-year period.

In the years since 9/11, the roles and responsibilities of Australian police relating to public order, public security, and counterterrorism have changed quite dramatically. In 2002, we saw the establishment of the Australian National Counter Terrorism Committee as well as the establishment in each state and territory of joint Australian Federal Police (AFP) – State/Territory police counterterrorism teams. The responsibility for responding to domestic terrorist attacks lies with each state and territory, led by the state and territory police (Council of Australian Governments [COAG], 2015). Post-9/11 there was also an increase of funding provided by federal and state governments for the expansion and enhancement of the counterterrorist capability of all intelligence and response agencies. As 9/11 demonstrated, the impact of a terrorism event not only affected the immediate victims of the event but also the emergency services responding to the event and the wider community with connections to the event, be they geographical location, relationships with victims and responders, or social connections.

POLICE ROLES AND RESPONSIBILITIES IN EMERGENCY MANAGEMENT

In order to better understand the roles of the state police agencies in emergency management, it is beneficial to understand the relationship of state police agencies within the national emergency-management context and also the role that emergency-management legislation plays.

National emergency-management relationships

In Australia, national emergency management is overseen by the Council of Australian Governments (COAG), established in 1992. Members of COAG are the Prime Minister, state and territory first Ministers, and the President of the Australian Local Government Association. Reporting to COAG specifically on police and emergency-management issues is the Ministerial Council for Police and Emergency Management (MCPEM). The Australian Department of Home Affairs [DHA] (2020) states that the MCPEM was established in 2017 and consists of Ministers for Police and Emergency Management from the Commonwealth, each state and territory, New Zealand, and the President of the Australian Local

Government Association. The MCPEM is responsible for broad areas of law-enforcement reform and emergency management, and increased collaboration across these areas. Reporting to the MCPEM specifically on emergency-management issues is the peak Government committee responsible for emergency management, the Australia-New Zealand Emergency Management Committee (ANZEMC), consisting of senior officials from each state and territory, plus a member from New Zealand and the Australian Local Government Association (DHA, 2020).

State-level roles and responsibilities

Currently, in most states and territories, the Commissioner of Police or a nominated senior executive member of the police force is designated as the state or territory emergency/disaster controller or coordinator, or a similar title. These roles, and the functions and responsibilities associated with the roles, are established by the relevant emergency/disaster management legislation. For example, the *State Emergency and Rescue Management Act 1989* (NSW) states that there shall be a State Emergency Operations Controller and a Deputy State Operations Controller, and that the State Emergency Operations Controller is to be the Commissioner of Police. However, there is also an alternative identified, in that the Governor of NSW, on the recommendation of the Minister, "may designate a position in the NSW Police Force Senior Executive Service as the position of State Emergency Operations Controller". The Deputy State Emergency Operations Controller is to be a person holding a position in the NSW Police Force Senior Executive Service. In 2020, that position was held by a Deputy Commissioner of Police.

In the Australian Capital Territory, arrangements are slightly different. The *Emergencies Act 2004* (ACT), provides for the appointment of an Emergency Controller by the Territory Chief Minister under two differing circumstances, when there is no declared state of emergency and when there is. Appointments where there is no declared state of emergency only last a maximum of seven days and the Chief Minister is required to review the appointment after 48 hours. When a state of emergency is declared, the Chief Minister will again appoint an Emergency Controller, but the length of appointment continues until the declaration of emergency is rescinded or the Chief Minister directs otherwise. Due to the size of the ACT, there is no provision for regional or local/municipal emergency controllers. The Territory Emergency Controller takes on these responsibilities.

In South Australia, the *Emergency Management Act 2005* (SA) stipulates that the Commissioner of Police shall be the State Emergency Coordinator (SEC), but the presiding member of the State Emergency Management Committee (SEMC) is to be the Chief Executive Officer of the administrative unit administering the Act. The SEC is listed as an ex-officio office holder in the SEMC but not its Chairperson. In addition, the South Australian legislation makes no reference to district or local emergency-management control or coordination, delegating all decisions and control to the SEC.

In Queensland, the role of State Disaster Controller is determined by the Chairperson of the State Disaster Committee (SDC) (the State Premier), Under the *Disaster Management Act 2003* (Qld). The Queensland legislation requires that the Chairperson of the SDC must appoint either a Deputy Commissioner of Police as the State Disaster Controller or another person who the chairperson chooses after consultation with the Commissioner of Police should be appointed to coordinate operations.

The *Emergency Management Act 2006* (Tas) provides for the Minister to appoint a person to be the Tasmanian State Emergency Management Controller (SEMC), but if no appointment is made, the Commissioner of Police, by default, becomes the SEMC. Similarly, the Deputy SEMC can be appointed by the Minister, or if no appointment is made, the Deputy Commissioner of Police becomes the Deputy SEMC. Under the *Tasmanian Act*, the SEMC also chairs the State Emergency Management Committee.

Next are two other examples, this time from Western Australia and the Northern Territory, where under the *Emergency Management Act 2005* (WA) the Commissioner of Police is designated as the State Emergency Controller and in the NT, under the *Emergency Management Act 2013* (NT), the Commissioner of Police is designated as the Territory Emergency Controller. In WA, the State Emergency Controller also chairs the State Emergency Management Committee, whereas in the NT, the Territory Emergency Controller and the Territory Recovery Controller (Chief Executive Officer of the Department of the Chief Minister) co-chair the Territory Emergency Management Council.

Finally, in Victoria, state emergency-management arrangements are a little different and have gone through some major changes in the years following the Black Saturday Bushfires of 2009 (Emergency Management Victoria, 2015). Numerous recommendations were made by the Victorian Bushfires Royal Commission (Teague, McLeod & Pascoe, 2010), some of which resulted in further developments within Victoria's emergency-management arrangements. These recommendations led to the revision of existing legislation and enactment of the *Emergency Management Act 2013* (Vic). Under this legislation, the position of Emergency Management Commissioner was established. In essence, this position equates to the State Disaster/Emergency Operations Controller roles established in other states and territories. This person is either the successor in law to the State's Fire Services Commissioner, as established under the *Fire Services Commissioner Act 2010* (Vic), which was repealed in 2013 with the enactment of the *Emergency Management Act 2013* (Vic). Under this legislation, the Governor in Council may appoint a person to the role as Emergency Management Commissioner. The Governor in Council must be satisfied that the person has appropriate management, professional, technical, and operational expertise in emergency management. Therefore, in Victoria's case, the police do not have a multi-agency state-level control or coordination role for emergency management as they do in most other states and territories. Some argue that the Victorian model is the wave of the future, as strategic coordination is a function that can be carried out by skilled and qualified persons who are not necessarily police officers.

As can be seen here, apart from Victoria, the roles are generally similar in that the Commissioner of Police or his/her deputy has a major role to play in the control and coordination of emergency-management operations. However, this role does not necessarily also encompass the role of chairperson of the state/territory emergency-management committee.

Regional/district roles and responsibilities

The establishment of emergency-management roles and responsibilities at the regional or district levels is also determined by the relevant state and territory emergency/disaster management legislation. Again, in most states and territories, the primary roles are generally undertaken by senior regional/district police officers.

In Tasmania, for example, the *Emergency Management Act 2006* (Tas) states that the Chairperson of a Regional Emergency Management Committee (REMC) is to be the appointed Regional Emergency Management Controller. The Regional Emergency Management Controller is a person appointed by the Minister, but if no such person is appointed, then the Commissioner of Police will determine which Commander within Tasmania Police will be the respective Regional Emergency Management Controller. This, in effect, means that the Regional Police Commander is both the Chair of the REMC and the Regional Controller. This provides senior police in each region with a major role in the development and coordination of emergency-management arrangements, plans, and strategies.

In Queensland, under the *Disaster Management Act 2003* (Qld), the Commissioner of Police appoints the District Disaster Controller (DDC). This is not stipulated as having to be a police officer, but it is highly likely that this position is undertaken by the senior district police officer. The DDC is also appointed as the chairperson of the District Disaster Management Group.

In Victoria, arrangements are slightly different. Under the *Emergency Management Act 2013* (Vic), the Emergency Management Commissioner may undertake the role of regional or municipal emergency response coordinator in emergency situations that cross multiple regional boundaries. In these cases, the Chief Commissioner of Police appoints a Senior Police Liaison Officer to advise the Emergency Management Commissioner. Where an emergency impacts just one regional area, the Chief Commissioner of Police, on the request of the Emergency Management Commissioner, appoints a police officer to be the Emergency Response Co-ordinator for each region and municipal district.

Therefore, whereas the police do not have the state-level, multi-agency coordination role for emergency management, they still retain a fairly major emergency-management role at regional and municipal district levels.

As can be seen from the examples here, the role of the state/territory police at the regional/district level can differ between states and territories. In some states, the senior police officer in the region or district has the regional emergency-management controller/coordinator role, whereas in other states, there is opportunity for other persons to be appointed. Also, the regional/district controller does not necessarily chair the regional/district emergency management committee.

Local/municipal roles and responsibilities

Local/municipal roles and responsibilities are generally also established by the relevant emergency/disaster management legislation. However, in most cases, because local government is given the responsibility and accountability for developing local/municipal emergency-management arrangements, the police role is often reduced to a more operational role, with the coordination and control role at the local/municipal level being undertaken by a member of the local government authority.

In WA, the State Emergency Coordinator (SEC) appoints the local emergency coordinator for each local government area. It is not stipulated that this person should be a police officer. The stipulation is that the SEC consult with the relevant local government and to take into account any submissions that they may make (*Emergency Management Act 2005* (WA)). It is quite likely that this role may be undertaken by the local senior police officer, but there is latitude for this role to be undertaken by another person, possibly a member of the local government staff.

In Tasmania, the Emergency Management Act 2006 (Tas) provides for the Minister to appoint a Municipal Emergency Management Coordinator and deputy. There is no stipulation as to who this person might be, other than, "A council may only nominate a person for the position of Municipal Emergency Management Coordinator or Deputy Municipal Emergency Management Coordinator if the person, once appointed to the position, would have the authority and ability to make decisions relating to the coordination of emergency management in the municipal area during an emergency without first seeking the approval of the council" (S.23(8)).

In Queensland, the *Disaster Management Act 2003* (Qld), requires local governments to establish a Local Disaster Management Group (LDMG) for their individual areas. The Chairperson of the LDMG appoints either the Chief Executive Officer of the local government area or an employee of the local government to be the Local Disaster Coordinator.

Emergency/disaster response

State and territory police undertake numerous roles when it comes to disaster/emergency response above and beyond those that relate specifically to their bread-and-butter roles in law enforcement. Some emergency-management legislation actually stipulates which agencies should coordinate or control certain hazard-related events.

In South Australia, the police have been directed to be the *coordinating agency* for all emergencies, apart from where the State Emergency Management Plan identifies a different body or organisation (e.g. bushfires are coordinated by the Country Fire Authority) (*Emergency Management Act, 2004* (SA)).This coordination role is present in other states and territories as well (NT, QLD, NSW, Victoria, Tasmania, for example). This coordination role is separate from the control role that is also stipulated in the Act. It is probably best at this stage to determine what the differences are between coordination and control. Emergency Management Australia (1998) defines *control* as:

> *The overall direction of* **emergency management** *activities in an emergency situation. Authority for control is established in legislation or in an* **emergency plan** *and carries with it the responsibility for tasking and coordinating other organisations in accordance with the needs of the situation. Control relates to situations and operates horizontally across organisations* (p. 34; emphasis added).

The Glossary defines *coordination* as:

> *[T]he bringing together of organisations and elements to ensure an effective response, primarily concerned with the systematic acquisition and application of resources (organisation, manpower and equipment) in accordance with the requirements imposed by the threat or impact of an emergency. Coordination relates primarily to resources, and operates, vertically, within an organisation, as a function of the authority to command, and horizontally, across organisations, as a function of the authority to control* (p. 35).

Therefore, we can see that in South Australia, the *Emergency Management Act 2004* (SA) specifically differentiates between the control role (direction of activities and organisations) and the coordination role (resource management).

Over the past 40 years, we have seen police regularly carry out a variety of non-law-enforcement operational-related roles during major emergency/disaster events. In 1977, NSW Police worked alongside the NSW Fire Brigades in the rescue of trapped victims in the Granville Rail Disaster and again in 1989 assisted in the rescue and retrieval of victims from the Kempsey Bus Crash. In Tasmania in 1996, responding to the Port Arthur Massacre, we saw police not only deploying special operations officers to respond to the shooter but carrying out alerting and warning of the community in the Port Arthur vicinity, enforcing a major cordon of the area, and in the aftermath, working with the local community in their recovery. During the Newcastle Earthquake of 1989 and the Thredbo Landslide of 1997, we saw police search-and-rescue units, assisted by fire and other emergency service personnel, conduct search, rescue, and retrieval operations of victims trapped under collapsed buildings. During the Beaconsfield Mine Collapse in 2006, Tasmania Police worked in conjunction with the mine owners and mines rescue staff to rescue two trapped miners. These are just a few examples of the many times that state and territory police have been involved over the years in the response to emergency/disaster events.

More recently, in December 2019 to February 2020, we saw police agencies across every state and territory in Australia engaged in evacuation of vulnerable persons and communities from bushfire-threatened areas as part of the Black Summer bushfire crisis response. In March 2020, as part of the response to the COVID-19 health crisis, police agencies across Australia have been given powers to enforce social distancing, isolation, and lockdown requirements for parts of the population and issue fines to those who violate the new legislation. During the COVID-19 pandemic crisis, we also saw New South Wales's strategic coordination of overall response transferred from the Department of Health to the Commissioner of the NSW Police Force, in his role as State Emergency Operations Controller. This was implemented to enable the multi-agency strategic response to be coordinated by the State Emergency Operations Controller, as designated in the *State Emergency Rescue Management Act, 1989* (NSW), leaving the NSW Department of Health to coordinate the actual health response to the incident as the lead management agency for health-related emergencies. These two examples highlight the extremes of involvement and roles that police have during times of civil emergency. In these two cases, from a supportive role to the community in times of natural disaster to a law-enforcement role during a biological and economic disaster.

Community recovery and beyond

In the past 15 years, we have seen an increase in the development of planning and strategies relating to the recovery of communities following a major emergency/disaster. Following most major emergency/disaster events, we now see the appointment of a Recovery Coordinator whose role is to coordinate the long-term recovery of the affected communities. These roles are often given to retired senior military officers or civil servants with track records in effective and efficient management, particularly with regard to multi-agency activities. For example, the recovery efforts following Tropical Cyclone Larry in 2006 were led by the former head of the Australian Defence Force, General Peter Cosgrove AK, CVO, MC, who later went on to become Australia's 26th Governor General. In January 2020, Dick Adams, a retired Assistant Commissioner of the NSW Police Force, was appointed Recovery Coordinator for southern NSW by the NSW Premier in response to the Black Summer bushfire crisis. Similarly, in Queensland, the retired Commissioner of Police, Ian Stewart, was appointed by the Premier to head the Queensland bushfire recovery. Stewart, in his previous position as Commissioner of Police had been the State Disaster Coordinator during Cyclone Yasi in 2011 and the devastating floods that impacted Toowoomba, Grantham, and Brisbane also in 2011. This recovery coordination role has generally not been given to serving police because of the protracted nature and specialised needs and requirements of recovery management activities, but as can be seen by the examples given, retired senior police officers are also being asked to undertake these roles, given their often-extensive emergency-management knowledge and experience.

In the past 20 years, we have also seen an increase in the number of commissions and enquiries that have been conducted following major emergency/disaster events. These commissions and enquiries are required to investigate, analyse, and report findings back to Government on all aspects of the emergency/disaster event and are led by retired judges, retired Police Commissioners, and the like. For example, the Royal Commission into the 2019–2020 Black Summer Bushfires was headed up by the retired Chief of Air Force and Chief of the Defence Force, Air Chief Marshall Mark Binskin, AC. In Western Australia, following the Perth Hills bushfires of 2014, retired Australian Federal Police Commissioner Mick Keelty was appointed to head up the inquiry, examining bushfire risk management. Following the 2009 Victorian Black Saturday Bushfires, retired Victorian Supreme Court Judge, the Hon Bernard Teague, AO headed the Victorian Bushfires Royal Commission.

Again, as police are a major organisation involved in emergency/disaster management, it would be inappropriate to have these commissions and enquiries led by serving senior police officers, or for that matter, senior officers/staff from any other agency that was involved in the emergency response. However, the extensive amount of emergency-management knowledge and experience often held by retired heads of agencies would definitely be of value in the conduct of post-event enquiries.

THE FUTURE

A working crystal ball would always be a handy thing to have, but the reality is that we can't see into the future. But we *can* use what has happened in the past to better prepare us for the future and possibly anticipate issues that might arise down the track.

So what is the future for police in emergency management? Is the Victorian emergency-management model the way of the future, where an Emergency Management Commissioner or similar title is appointed by the state government or Governor and that person has appropriate management, professional, technical, and operational expertise in emergency management? Will police continue to coordinate and control state/territory and regional/district emergency-management operations, or will lead agencies take on these roles? As roles and responsibilities for police changed after 9/11, will the roles and responsibilities of police also change after the Coronavirus pandemic crisis of 2020? Will legislative changes that occurred in the Coronavirus pandemic be a thing of the future for other major events? Is the size of Australia and its small population, which is spread predominantly around the eastern coastline, a hindrance to effective and efficient emergency management, particularly in large cross-border emergencies, over very large areas, with sparsely populated communities?

CONCLUSION

In this chapter we have examined the role that our state police agencies play in emergency management. We have examined the roles that police have at state/territory level, district/regional levels, and at the local/municipal level. We have also looked at how legislation influences those roles.

Police continue to provide a valuable operational response role in disaster/emergency situations, carrying out a wide range of duties, many of them not associated with their daily law-enforcement role. However, we have recently seen the expansion of the law-enforcement role into emergency management with the Coronavirus pandemic and the new pieces of legislation that have been enacted throughout Australia to combat this emergency. The emergency-management landscape is ever changing, and the role of police in that landscape is constantly being revised and fine-tuned, as we have seen in Victoria. What we do know for a fact is that emergencies and disasters will continue to occur, and the more we learn from these events, the better prepared we can be for the future. The police, because of their position and standing within our society and communities, will always have a role to play in emergency/disaster management.

Final word

Our response to the virus has changed a little from both an emergency management and a police perspective. The enormity of the situation and the consequences it was spinning up were beyond the "Health response" as the combat Agency for this Pandemic. As such, the SEOCON was handed the overall control and co-ordination of the response. NSW Health moved back into a lead agency response. Commissioner Fuller then assumed his role as the SEOCON and I moved back to his Deputy SEOCON role. We are still working from the RFS control centre at Homebush and the police footprint here has been expanded.

> *Mr Fuller and I sit here alongside NSW Health and a full range of other combat agencies and functional areas that make up the SEMC (State Emergency Management Committee). We have been in this new posture for a week now and it's working remarkably well.*
>
> *I also want to acknowledge our response as regional, rural and remote officers and all our good people in our Capability Performance and Youth Command to what has been extraordinary times (notice I didn't use unprecedented). Not just as police officers and employees but managing our families and friends who always look to those in policing for strength, safety and comfort. I continue to learn a lot about the virus, ICU beds, disease management and so on. However, what I have noticed most when we are challenged like we are right now is that police and the NSWPF stand tall. You folks just get on with your tasks and show the community who they can trust and who will never let them down* (Worboys,[1] 2020).

NOTE

1 At the time of the COVID-19 pandemic crisis of 2020, Deputy Commissioner Gary Worboys was the NSW Police Deputy Commissioner Regional NSW Field Operations and also the NSW Deputy State Emergency Operations Controller.

REFERENCES

Australian Federal Police. (2020). *ACT policing: Emergency management*. Retrieved from: https://police.act.gov.au/safety-and-security/emergency-management.

Australian Institute for Disaster Resilience. (2019). *Australian emergency management arrangements*. Canberra: Commonwealth of Australia.

Commonwealth of Australia. (2010). *Australia's constitution: With overview and notes by the Australian Government Solicitor*. Canberra: Parliamentary Education Office.

Council of Australian Governments. (2015). *Australia's counter-terrorism strategy: Strengthening our resilience*. Canberra: Commonwealth of Australia.

Crofts, C. (2016). Australia's first cops were all criminals. *National Geographic*. Retrieved from: www.nationalgeographic.com.au/history/australias-first-cops-were-all-criminals.aspx.

Department of Home Affairs. (2020). *Committees and fora*. Retrieved from: www.homeaffairs.gov.au/help-and-support/how-to-engage-us/committees-and-fora.

Disaster Management Act 2003 (Qld). Retrieved from: www.legislation.qld.gov.au/view/pdf/inforce/current/act-2003-091.

Dwyer, A. (2006). Cyclone Tracy and Whitlam's 'new' federalism: Implications for the management of natural disasters in Australia. *Australian Journal of Emergency Management*, 21(3), 41–46.

Emergencies Act 2004 (ACT). Retrieved from: www.legislation.act.gov.au/a/2004-28.

Emergency Management Australia. (1998) *Australian emergency management glossary*. Canberra: Commonwealth of Australia.

Emergency Management Act 2004 (SA). Retrieved from: www.legislation.sa.gov.au/LZ/C/A/EMERGENCY%20MANAGEMENT%20ACT%202004.aspx.

Emergency Management Act 2005 (WA). Retrieved from: www.legislation.wa.gov.au/legislation/statutes.nsf/main_mrtitle_294_homepage.html.

Emergency Management Act 2006 (Tas). Retrieved from: www.legislation.tas.gov.au/view/html/inforce/current/act-2006-012.

Emergency Management Act 2013 (NT). Retrieved from: https://legislation.nt.gov.au/en/Legislation/EMERGENCY-MANAGEMENT-ACT-2013.

Emergency Management Act 2013 (Vic). Retrieved from: https://content.legislation.vic.gov.au/sites/default/files/2020-04/13-73aa016%20authorised.pdf.

Emergency Management Australia. (2000). *Manual 2: Australian emergency management arrangements.* Canberra: Commonwealth of Australia.

Emergency Management Victoria. (2015). *Foundations of emergency management: Class 1 emergencies.* Emergency Management Victoria. Retrieved from: https://files-em.em.vic.gov.au/public/Doctrine/Found/Foundations-EMC1.pdf.

Hoffman, B. (2002). Rethinking terrorism and counterterrorism since 9/11. *Studies in Conflict and Terrorism*, 25(5), 303–316. https://doi.org/10.1080/105761002901223.

Mehta, A. (2018, May). Here's how much the US have spent fighting terrorism since 9/11. *Defence News.* Retrieved from: www.defensenews.com/pentagon/2018/05/16/heres-how-much-the-us-has-spent-fighting-terrorism-since-911/.

NSW Police. (2019). *History.* Retrieved from: www.police.nsw.gov.au/about_us/history.

Pearce, T. (2006). Foreword: Mt Macedon 50th anniversary. *The Australian Journal of Emergency Management*, 21(3), 2.

Queensland Police. (2020). *myPolice Museum.* Retrieved from: https://mypolice.qld.gov.au/museum/2013/08/20/from-the-vault-help-at-hand-cyclone-tracy-the-queensland-police-contingent/.

State Emergency and Rescue Management Act 1989 (NSW). Retrieved from: www.legislation.nsw.gov.au/#/view/act/1989/165.

Teague, B., McLeod, R., & Pascoe, S. (2010). *2009 Victorian bushfires royal commission: The final report.* Melbourne: Government of Victoria.

Worboys, G. (2020). *Personal communications.*

CHAPTER 17

Community safety, crime prevention, and 21st century policing

Tim Prenzler and Rick Sarre

INTRODUCTION

This chapter explores the evolution of crime policy in Australian policing, focusing on philosophical shifts, primarily from the 1980s, away from a crime containment model towards sustainable crime reduction, primarily through the adoption of imported models of Community Policing, Problem-Oriented Policing, and Intelligence-Led Policing. The chapter explores diverse case studies of effective practice, including partnership-based approaches. However, it will be argued that the reform agenda was largely unsuccessful, and 21st century policing remains locked into a reactive mode of practice with limited outcomes. This proposition is developed with reference to the extensive harms associated with two very different crime problems: fraud and vehicle crashes. The chapter concludes with a set of recommendations for improving community safety and security by integrating principles from established policing frameworks centred on a data-driven problem-solving process.

THE CRISIS IN POLICING AND AN AGENDA FOR CHANGE

For much of its history, and up to the 1970s, policing in Australia operated within a broad consensus of public and political support based on a "crime containment" model (Drew & Prenzler, 2015). Granted many exceptions and, from time to time, detractors, police in general kept crime to acceptable levels by a combination of mobile patrolling and rapid response, investigation, prosecution, and various other peacekeeping and emergency service activities. The main areas of innovation were technical – in improved communications, rapid response, and forensic science. However, the explosion of crime in the 1970s put an end to the idea of a natural police monopoly in crime control. The crisis came to a head in Australia in the late-1970s/early-1980s, involving "multi-layered" problems and issues (Bradley, 1992). Apart from burgeoning crime, these including entrenched police corruption, routine excessive force, sexual and racial discrimination, neglect of victims of crime, and repeated miscarriages of justice.

The crisis in Australian policing provided some receptivity to philosophical and practical developments occurring overseas which had arisen out of similar circumstances. The first challenge came from the Community Policing movement of the 1980s (Trojanowicz, 1982). The idea that police could not reduce crime on their own, and that they needed to work closely with their local communities in a genuine power-sharing arrangement, was revolutionary at the time (Sarre, 1996). Community Policing initiatives included consultative committees, and public opinion and experience surveys. It incorporated the Neighbourhood Watch movement, and encouraged police shopfronts, foot patrols, crime-awareness programs, and security-advice services. More recently, it readily embraced social media platforms to communicate messages (Fleming, 2005; Putt, 2010).

Problem-Oriented Policing provided another challenge, focusing on an innovative and systematic approach to reducing or eliminating crime by analysing and addressing causal factors (Goldstein, 1979). Variants of Problem-Oriented Policing arrived in Australia in the 1990s, including Intelligence-Led Policing (HMIC, 1997; Ratcliffe, 2003) and Third-Party Policing (Mazerolle & Ransley, 2006). These frameworks included ideas for concentrating crime prevention efforts on repeat offenders, repeat victims, "linked" crimes, and geographic "hotspots". Police personnel were encouraged to engage stakeholders such as landlords, business owners, and local government regulators to enforce laws more effectively within their spheres of influence and authority. Subsequent variants have included Harm-Focused Policing (Prenzler, 2014; Ratcliffe, 2015) and Reassurance Policing (Fleming, 2005; Innes & Fielding, 2002).

These concepts are now de rigueur in police policy documents and annual reports, with a wide range of associated performance indicators. The New South Wales Police *Annual Report* for 2018/19, for example, states that "we focus on reducing rates of crime, particularly violent crime", and that "targeting of crime hotspots and repeat offenders has contributed to crime levels across all major key indicators falling or remaining stable" (2019, p. 11). For a period, the Queensland Police Service adopted a Problem-Oriented and Partnership Policing policy – POPP (Thorne, 2003, pp. 248–249). The *Victoria Police Blue Paper: A Vision for Victoria Police in 2025* integrates "Evidence-based policing", "Intelligence-led and predictive policing", "Community policing", and "Problem-oriented policing", including "a focus on prevention, victim support and targeting the greatest harms"; with a commitment to "genuine partnerships" with "citizens, businesses, other government agencies and not-for-profit agencies in Victoria, plus other Australian and international law enforcement agencies" (Victoria Police, 2014, p. 52).

SUCCESSFUL CASE STUDIES

The international crime prevention literature contains very few Australian exemplars, and even fewer police-led case studies (Prenzler, 2017b). Nonetheless, there are examples on the record where police appear to have taken a leading role in applying science to solve crime problems in Australia, achieving substantial success, and demonstrating the potential for further gains from proactive measures. Four examples are summarised below.

Random breath testing

In their meta-analysis of the impacts of driver alcohol testing, Erke, Goldenbeld and Vaa (2009) reported that Australia was the most successful country in the world in reducing crashes through Random Breath Testing (RBT). Success was attributed to the "high intensity" of the best Australian programs, including high visibility, widespread publicity, the large numbers of tests, and testing of all stopped drivers (p. 921). New South Wales, where RBT was introduced in 1982, has been considered the most successful location (Erke, Goldenbeld & Vaa, 2009). It has been estimated that over a ten-year period, starting from December 1982, RBT in New South Wales prevented 6,742 "serious accidents" and 1,487 fatal accidents (Henstridge, Homel & Mackay, 1997, p. 104).

Member of Parliament George Paciullo and criminologist Ross Homel are credited with leveraging RBT into practice in New South Wales, but police support was crucial to its success (Homel, 1993). One of the most important lessons for effective RBT is that police need to test all drivers at a checkpoint, and then prosecute all drivers who are in breach of the blood alcohol limit in order to maximise the deterrent effect. Drivers should only be permitted to dispute the charge in the courts. In Homel's formula, RBT has to be "highly visible . . . unpredictable, unavoidable and ubiquitous" (1993, p. 28S). This approach entailed a seismic shift away from the tradition of officers questioning drivers about their condition and making discretionary decisions about whether to charge, warn, and/or release drivers. It meant a major abrogation of power by front-line officers. In other words, RBT made for a whole new way of doing policing.

The Geelong Venues against Violence Accord

The Geelong Venues against Violence Accord operationalised an agreement between local police, liquor licensees, and the state Liquor Licensing Commission, beginning in the late-1980s (Felson, Berends, Richardson & Veno, 1997). The Accord was developed in response to alcohol-fuelled disorder in the Geelong city centre – which included public intoxication, under-age and outdoor liquor consumption, assaults, public urination, property damage, noise, intimidation, and drunk driving. Intense competition between pubs and clubs encouraged heavy alcohol consumption through free entry to venues and drinks discounting.

The Felson, Berends, Richardson and Veno (1997) report is unclear about who initiated the stakeholder meetings that led to the Accord. However, at one point the report states that "[p]olice organised and led the [Accord] process" (p. 126). It also notes that police "present[ed] the policy to publicans in a non-authoritarian manner", while the police and the Licensing Commission also "maintained a "hidden stick" – the ability to investigate and ultimately close down businesses" (p. 126). The Accord was managed through bi-monthly meetings of a Best Practices Committee, consisting of police, the Licensing Commission, venue representatives and the City Council. The consultation process led to managers of the 14 main hotels and nightclubs in the area signing up to a voluntary code of practice. The code included a cover charge after 11:00 p.m., no free re-entry, no rule exemptions for females, no extended "happy hour", no drinks promotions, no free drinks, common minimum pricing, non-alcohol-related entertainment, greater availability of taxis, and alcohol-free "blue-light" discos for under-age teenagers. There was a focus on enforcement of laws around public drinking, under-age drinking, and false identification cards. A key strategy was to use warnings and seizure of false IDs before resorting to arrest.

The main quantified impact measure was limited to the "serious assault" rate for the larger Geelong police region. Data were collected from the year before the Accord to three years following, showing an immediate fall from 117 serious assaults per 100,000 in 1988/89 to 73 in 1989/90 – the year the Accord was introduced. Overall, the rate fell by 45% to 64 in 1992/93 (p. 128). Comparative data were combined for six other cities in Victoria. In the same period, serious assaults per 100,000 rose 31% from an average of 77 to 101. Despite fears that nightclub revenue would fall, police reported a "100% increase in door takings at nightclubs" following the introduction of the Accord, "and a 160% increase in overall revenue" in the first 12 months (p. 126). Evidence regarding the positive effect of the Accord was also supported by qualitative data. According to Felson, Berends, Richardson & Veno (1997, p. 127):

> *The police reported that young people were going home earlier and problems were far fewer. The crowds of intoxicated youths moving about the CBD were no longer evident in such numbers. . . . The soft data indicate that young people were still attracted to Geelong but apparently did not get in as much trouble while there.*

The Accord evaluation team noted that the program was a classic example of Problem-Oriented Policing, particularly through the "analytic, problem-solving approach" (p. 129). Aspects of Third Party Policing were also evident. The researchers noted that the process required a major shift in police attitudes and strategies: "[P]olice, while not abandoning law enforcement, defined that traditional role as secondary and focused instead upon crime prevention" (p. 129).

Bsafe

"Bsafe" is a personal security program for victims of domestic violence established in 2007 by Women's Health Goulburn North East in Victoria and now operated by VincentCare (2020), Shepparton. The project received a 2010 Australian Crime and Violence Prevention Award, and five years later, the 2015 Victorian Automobile Chamber of Commerce (VACC) Regional Safety Award. The genesis of Bsafe was a 2003 Rotary study tour to Sweden by Victorian Police Sergeant Peter Milligan. He observed a domestic violence prevention program that provided alarm-based "safety kits" to victims (MacKay, 2011, p. 5). On his return to Australia, Milligan conducted a partial replication experiment, with feedback indicating considerable improvements in participants' safety. The Women's Health Goulburn North East and the Victoria Police obtained start-up funds under the National Community Crime Prevention Program for the Bsafe pilot.

BSafe is centred on the development of safety plans and supplying personal duress alarms to participants. Alarms can be activated when breaches of protection orders occur or are imminent, or when there is any sense of threat. In its initial format, the alarms consisted of waterproof pendants, linked by radio transmission to the landline phone system, which could be activated in the participant's residence; and a mobile device, similar to a mobile phone, linked to the mobile phone network in the Hume region (MacKay, 2011). The alarms were managed by a company specialising in medical alert services, which checked and then relayed calls to police. The system was predicated on a police commitment to prioritise their response in order to optimise the deterrent and incapacitative effects of the system. The Bsafe project was managed by a support network consisting of a Project Coordinator, local police, the alarm response company, and specialist staff from Women's Health.

The only available systematic evaluation of Bsafe was conducted for the extended pilot project (MacKay, 2011). This covered five years and included 72 women and 143 children. All the women had been assessed as being at high risk of violence, and the large majority had experienced repeated severe violence. Eighty-three percent of offenders had threatened, or attempted, to kill their partners, and many were known to have access to firearms. There was an extremely high risk of child abductions and assaults on children. The evaluation report involved a within-group study format and focused on self-reported levels of abuse before, during, and after the Bsafe experience.

The evaluation was hampered by an attrition problem with survey respondents. Nonetheless, the available data were extremely positive (MacKay, 2011). The pre-Bsafe survey showed that 92% of 36 respondents had experienced one or more breaches of their protection order. The average number of breaches was 2.5. The second survey, of 22 participants who had been on the program for three months, found that 64% had experienced at least one breach, with an average of two. This group reported substantial reductions in physical violence and threats of murder, with breaches mainly in the area of stalking and harassment. The third survey, of 19 participants on the program for six months, found that 21% had experienced a breach in the preceding three months, with an average of two, mainly lower-level, breaches. The final survey of 10 participants, who had completed the program, found that none had experienced a breach in the preceding three months. The final responses from all 36 respondents also showed that 83% had improved feelings of safety, with 58% stating they felt safe. In addition, 95% reported that Bsafe had helped them stay in their home (68%) or obtain another form of agreeable accommodation.

Overall, the respondents saw their ability to manage the alarm response system, and have confidence in the police response, as crucial to achieving safety and wellbeing for themselves and their children. The survey results indicated that offenders went through a learning process of trial and error regarding the timeliness and certainty of police interventions and the willingness of Bsafe participants to use the alarm system (MacKay, 2011). This demonstrated the utility of a traditional police rapid response strategy; one optimised through enhanced technology and partnerships. These findings were confirmed by feedback from the police and other professionals – although, inexplicably, no police data on breaches and arrests were included in the evaluation.

Strike Force Piccadilly

Strike Force Piccadilly is arguably the most successful police problem-solving initiative on record in Australia (Prenzler, 2017b). The Piccadilly team won two Australian Crime and Violence Prevention Awards and the international Herman Goldstein Award for Excellence in Problem-Oriented Policing. The Task Force was established in 2005 by the New South Wales Police Property Crime Squad after traditional policing methods failed to halt an outbreak of ATM ram raids in the greater Sydney area. In the peak period in 2006, there were 12 attacks in May, 14 in July and 12 in August, causing enormous destruction and financial losses.

The turning point occurred when the Piccadilly team convened a stakeholder forum, which led to the establishment of an ongoing partnership between police and security managers from the ATM Industry Association, cash-in-transit firms, the Australian Bankers' Association, and the Shopping Centre Council of Australia. Situational analyses and information-sharing identified diverse opportunity factors for ram raids, including easy vehicle access to machines, an operating window for the thieves in the period between alarm activations and the police response, and frequent false alarm activations that deterred police.

The analysis and stakeholder consultation process led to the adoption of a set of countermeasures that included a priority response system based on multiple alarm activations, relocations of ATMs away from vehicle access, the installation of high-quality bollards and anti-ramming devices (such as flexible base plates), and a police ATM installation advisory service based on Crime Prevention Through Environmental Crime Design (CPTED) principles.

The countermeasures were highly effective in deterring and disrupting ram raiders and incapacitating approximately one hundred offenders through arrests and imprisonment. However, this was followed by a shift in offender tactics to "bam raids", the name given to ram raids that involved explosive gas attacks. There were 19 attacks at a peak in November 2008. In response, the Strike Force Piccadilly Team was enlarged, with intensified interventions, including enhanced use of shared intelligence and the installation of gas detection and disabling equipment by ATM operators. Across the two crime categories, a long-term follow up study showed there was a 100% reduction in successful ram raids over a seven-year period and an 84% reduction in attempted ram raids. Moreover, there was a 100% reduction in successful bam raids over a four-year period and attempted bam raids were reduced by 95% (Prenzler, 2017b, pp. 112–113). Available evidence indicated that there was no displacement to other crimes.

Case study limits

Case studies such as those outlined above usually carry limitations in terms of project evaluation protocols. They often lack adequate comparison groups and triangulated impact measures, and they often leave questions unanswered about the longevity of programs and their effects. Nonetheless, the studies show the great potential for police to make large and sustained reductions in crime through a variety of innovations, usually involving working with community partners.

THE FAILURE OF REFORM

Despite examples of successful problem-solving by Australian police, and despite large reductions in crime in the last 25 years, particularly in property crime (Sarre, 2017), evidence of highly effective crime reduction programs led by police are difficult to find. In fact, the failure of the dominant model to deliver on community safety is more the case. A variety of reviews have made this point over the years (e.g. Sarre, 1996; Putt, 2010). The following examples illustrate the problem, using the findings of one government review; one case study evaluation report; and examples of poorly managed attempts to curb major crime problems, namely online fraud and road trauma.

Community policing in post-Fitzgerald Queensland

The 1987/89 "Fitzgerald Inquiry" in Queensland exposed entrenched corruption and mismanagement in the Queensland Police Force. The

Report recommended major changes to the control of police conduct and a complete reorientation of policing strategies. The Report declared that traditional "reactive" crime fighting methods had failed to protect the community – citing rising crime rates, especially increasing violent crime – and recommended that "Community policing be adopted as the primary policing strategy" (p. 381). Specifically:

a) preventive policing strategies are to be an integral part of the normal activities of every police officer; and
b) the community is to be involved with the police in preventing crime through establishment of community crime committees and community crime prevention programmes based on the needs of individual communities.

A series of reports in the 1990s found that Queensland Police had made some genuine efforts to innovate in the Community Policing space in areas such Community Consultative Committees and a Women's Safety Project. Nonetheless, more advanced and experimental projects – such as local beat policing – were initiated from outside the department, and the approach overall was tokenistic (Criminal Justice Commission, 1994; Queensland Police Service, 1996; see also Macintyre & Prenzler, 1997; Thorne, 2003).

The Fitzgerald vision for Community Policing as the principal operating philosophy of the Queensland Police was never realised, and the experience mirrored that of other Australian jurisdictions. Three decades later, organised community involvement remains very much at the margins of police operations in Australia, with a yawning gap between rhetoric and reality, particularly in terms of evidence of a preventive effect from diverse projects labelled "Community Policing" (Putt, 2010; see also Prenzler, 2009; Queensland Police Service, 2019, pp. 17–18).

Operation Anchorage

"Operation Anchorage" exemplifies the problem of sustaining police-led crime prevention initiatives. The four-month anti-burglary project in the Australian Capital Territory was based on Intelligence-Led Policing principles, using profiling techniques to identify prolific offenders and then to incapacitate them in prison by opposing bail and non-custodial penalties (Makkai, Ratcliffe, Veraar & Collins, 2004). Anchorage was "a dedicated burglary reduction initiative with four teams of about 10 to 12 investigators supported closely by six intelligence analysts, surveillance teams and, where necessary and available, other operational support" (Ratcliffe, 2001, p. 4.). As the project unfolded, police efforts to incarcerate offenders were partly undermined by judicial decisions to release charged persons. Moreover, a significant proportion of charges were dismissed. Nonetheless, the Operation was deemed a success in that there were large increases in the remand and imprisonment rates for the target group, reoffending by the group was substantially reduced, and burglary rates decreased. Post-Anchorage, burglaries dropped by approximately one-third for 11 months over pre-Anchorage rates, with an estimated 2,445 offences prevented (Makkai, Ratcliffe, Veraar & Collins, 2004, p. 12). A total of 2,969 offences were estimated to have been prevented and $7,125,600 in losses prevented during and after the Operation. This compared well against the "incapacitation costs" from the project, which were put at $3,465,822 (p. 12).

Despite these achievements, Operation Anchorage showed an eventual "decay" effect, with burglary rates returning to levels approximating those pre-Anchorage (Makkai, Ratcliffe, Veraar & Collins, 2004). A longer-term analysis showed that there had been two preceding efforts to crack down on burglary offenders – Operation Chronicle and Operation Dilute – both of which had also shown initial success followed by reversion to the norm once the operations were terminated. At the end of a three-year period, following three crackdowns, burglaries were occurring in the same numbers as they had been at the start.

Fraud

Fraud appears as the fastest growing area of crime in Australia and occurs over a wide range of locations (Prenzler, 2017a). Much of the growth is driven by the increasing adoption of internet-based communications and transactions. The increased opportunities provided by the internet for myriad types of crimes, starting in the early 1990s – including child exploitation, stalking, and money laundering – essentially caught police unawares, and authorities have been playing a game of catch-up ever since, often with little success.

The best national data that we have for fraud in Australia are from the Australian Bureau of Statistics (ABS) Crime Victimisation Survey, which includes offences not officially reported or recorded – although the category is limited to "personal fraud" and excludes some business fraud and fraud against governments. The most recent survey, from 2014/15, showed that 8.5% of the sample of persons aged 15 or over – or 1.6 million persons – said they had been victimised (ABS, 2016). This represented an increase from 6.7% in the 2010/11 survey and 5.0% in the first survey – conducted in 2007. Of those victimised in 2014/15, 1.2 million incurred a loss, with a total estimated loss of $3 billion. "Card fraud" was the most common category of victimisation.

One of the most revealing aspects of Australian research on fraud is the finding that victims are largely on their own, with police refusing to investigate most frauds and other agencies simply recording complaints (Prenzler, 2017a; Lacey, Goode, Pawada & Gibson, 2020). The wider field of fraud enforcement and prevention – involving federal agencies such as the Australian Competition and Consumer Commission (ACCC) and the Australian Securities and Investments Commission (ASIC) – as well as many other federal and state regulators – is also characterised by massive under-enforcement, with very few investigations and convictions, and very little available by way of restitution (Prenzler, 2017a).

Government negligence is also evident in responses to new financial technology, particularly the advent of "tap-and-go" ("contactless" or "pay wave") card payment systems. "Chip and PIN" technology, introduced in the early 2000s, was associated with large reductions in card fraud (Levi, 2008). However, many tap-and-go card providers in Australia set the Personal Identification Number requirement to $100, in a case of convenience over security. Although no precise figures are available, police in Australia have stated that tap-and-go has made a major contribution to rising rates of card fraud. "Thieves are breaking into homes and stealing credit cards from people and are able to very quickly fraudulently obtain property by simply going under $100 in every purchase" (Weber, 2018, p. 1).

The problem of maintenance of crime prevention programs (see earlier discussion) has also been evident in relation to fraud in Australia with the abandonment of the highly innovative and successful Project Sunbird, which ran from 2013 to early 2017 in Western Australia. The Project, reportedly an initiative of a police detective, was a joint venture of the Police Major Fraud Squad and the Department of Commerce Consumer Protection Division (Emerson, 2017). Project Sunbird was focused on preventing repeat online fraud, particularly from scams originating in West Africa. Bank account holders with suspicious payments – flagged by a "financial intelligence" system – received warning letters and offers of assistance. While reported outcomes have not been precisely measured, official accounts claim that approximately 50 new victims were identified each month and approximately three-quarters of victims stopped sending money, saving tens of millions of dollars over the life of the Project (Cross, 2016; Department of Commerce, 2017, p. 29; Mischin, 2017). Despite this success, the Project was shut down. The Western Australia Police cited "resource priorities" for putting a halt to their analysis of the data, noting that "there had been public warnings for many years about online scams" (Department of Commerce, 2017, p. 29; Emerson, 2017, p. 4). The ACCC shut down a similar "National Scams Disruption Project" in 2017 (see Cross, 2016; Australian Competition and Consumer Commission, 2019).

Road trauma

Road safety initiatives operationalised by police, such as Random Breath Testing (outlined briefly earlier), provide some of the better, more successful examples of Problem-Oriented Policing in Australia. Nonetheless, the evidence seems to be that police have often applied these strategies reluctantly in response to intense pressure associated with increasing carnage on the roads. For example, red light and speed cameras have also been associated with large reductions in crashes, injuries, and fatalities, leading to enormous financial savings from reduced hospitalisations, insurance payouts, repairs, and lost productivity, but these initiatives appear to have come from transport departments, not police (e.g. Bourne & Cooke, 1993).

What is now alarming is that many of the gains in road safety of the last 40 years are being undone by a failure by authorities to push the lessons further and to pre-empt new threats such as mobile phone use while driving. Road fatalities in Australia peaked at 3,798 in 1970, then trended downward to a low of 1,155 in 2013/14 (ABC, 2019; Steering Committee for the Review of Government Service Provision, 2020, Table 6A.17). This occurred on the back of a range of innovations including increased enforcement, improved vehicle and road design, and improved driver training. However, the last eight years have seen a concerning reduction in the rate of decline in fatalities, with more of an undulating rate in evidence (BITRE, 2019, p. 150). At the same time, serious injuries resulting in hospitalisations have been trending upwards over three decades, from a low of 21,512 in 1992 to 38,452 in 2016/17 and 37,893 in 2017/18 (BITRE, 2019, p. 154; Steering Committee for the Review of Government Service Provision, 2020, Table 6A.18). According to the Australian Automobile Association (2019), Australia is in the midst of a "road trauma crisis" (p. 8). Research commissioned by the Association put the total cost of vehicle crashes in 2015 at $22.2 billion, and also put the figure of permanent disability at 4,436 cases in the same year (Economic Connections, 2017, pp. iv, 19). Also of note is the fact that two-thirds of Australians consistently view "speeding cars" and "dangerous or noisy driving" as "problems in their neighbourhood" (Steering Committee for the Review of Government Service Provision, 2020, Table, 6A.5).

Australian research shows that intensified law enforcement on the roads would save lives and reduce injuries and disabilities. For example, using the example of Western Australia, an analysis of the relationship between RBT and traffic crashes showed that an increase in testing to achieve a likelihood target of one test per driver per year would reduce crashes by 15 per month (Ferris, Mazerolle, King, Bates, Bennett & Devaney, 2013). The apparent problem of police indifference to the science is not the only problem. A case study involving a policy process analysis by Bates, Watson and King (2010) showed how politicians and policy-makers often prioritise individual freedom and convenience over public safety in opposing restrictions on drivers. The courts are another element of this system-wide imbroglio. Drivers with a "deplorable traffic history" are frequently released and go on to maim and kill (e.g. Buckley, 2019, p. 6; see also Ransley & Prenzler, 2020, p. 26). The extent of the human toll from dangerous driving is appalling, and what is clear is that official interventions are well below the levels needed to protect the community.

THE WAY FORWARD

"Crime containment" is an essential task for police. The work is both unpredictable and routine, occurring in response to calls for assistance and other sources of information about crime and disorder problems.

Police actions in these cases solve problems, diffuse conflict, prevent the escalation of violence, and restore social equilibrium – but frequently on an incidental basis – without pushing down the overall crime rate. Consequently, the primary challenge for police management is to deliver on this essential task while also directing resources to large-scale programmatic crime reduction; that is, deliberate, planned, organised, and sustained crime prevention.

There is one primary means by which agencies such as police can optimise their capabilities in reducing crime: through the rigorous application of a classic problem-solving methodology. There is certainly no shortage of guides for police managers to follow. Goldstein's original article (1979) and book (1990) on problem-oriented policing (POP) remain essential sources, with the principal steps to successful POP codified by Eck and Spelman (1987) in the acronym SARA: "Scan, Analyse, Respond, Assess". Ekblom"s (2011) "5Is Framework" also provides a useful set of similar steps and requirements, entailing "Intelligence, Intervention, Implementation, Involvement and Impact – and Process Evaluation". Guidance is also available from the 25 techniques of Situational Crime Prevention (Cornish & Clarke, 2003); Clarke's (1997) version of five steps to stop crime, based on an Action Research model (p. 15); and the manual *Become a Problem-Solving Crime Analyst in 55 Small Steps* (Clarke & Eck, 2003). There are also guides that include standards around community consultation, social inclusiveness, observance of human rights, and democratic accountability (Mazerolle & Prenzler, 2004; Trojanowicz & Bucqueroux, 1990; United Nations Office on Drugs and Crime, 2010; White, Murray & Robbins, 1996).

Various guides also emphasise the large scope for governments to facilitate programs led by police, or involving police, and to ensure sustainability. Governments can provide start-up funds for pilot projects and demonstration projects, subsidies for private sector and community-sector participants, administrative support for management committees, and support for evaluation and sharing of results (International Centre for the Prevention of Crime, the World Bank and the Bogotá Chamber of Commerce, 2011; Marks, Meyer & Linssen, 2005; Prenzler & Sarre, 2014; Schmerler, Perkins, Phillips, Rinehart & Townsend, 2006). Federal, state, and local governments also need to employ specialist crime prevention officers who can work with police; and crime specialists within police departments – in areas such as financial crime or cybercrime – and can facilitate productive partnerships with outside agencies (Gill, 2013). The review of the Queensland Police Service (1996) usefully recommended the employment of crime analysts who would focus interventions in the areas of likely success, such as with repeat offenders and repeat victims and "systemic problems and high-density crime locations" (p. 208). It could be argued that police also need to take on more of an advocacy role with government, in bringing crime science to policy-makers while countering ideologically-based views about individual freedom that can undermine potentially effective initiatives.

CONCLUSION

The evidence presented in this chapter shows that police can make large and sustained reductions in crime and improve community safety by adopting a range of programmatic crime reduction strategies. But to do this most effectively, they need to move beyond a traditional crime containment model of policing (based on simple strategies of rapid response with follow-up investigations and prosecutions) and towards models based upon research findings regarding strategic effectiveness published over the last 30 years. Despite the adoption of many advanced models from the 1980s, 21st-century Australian policing struggles to demonstrate large gains against crime that are attributable to police initiatives. To turn this situation around, a new management culture is needed, one that fully embraces scientific methods and community partnerships.

REFERENCES

ABC. (2019). *Road fatalities, 1925–2017*. Retrieved from www.abc.net.au/news/2018-01-25/deaths-since-1925/9358692.

ABS. (2016). *4528.0 – Personal Fraud, 2014–15*. Retrieved from www.abs.gov.au/AUSSTATS percent5Cabs@.nsf/0/1FF970676E24FDFECA2574740015CA71?Opendocument.

Australian Automobile Association. (2019). *Reviving road safety*. Canberra: Author.

Australian Competition and Consumer Commission. (2019). *Scam disruption project*. Retrieved from www.accc.gov.au/consumers/consumer-protection/protecting-yourself-from-scams/scam-disruption-project.

Bates, L., Watson, B., & King, M. (2010). Mobility and safety are conflicting goals for transport policy makers when making decisions about graduated driver licensing. *International Journal of Health Promotion and Education, 48*(2), 46–51.

BITRE. (2019). *Yearbook 2019: Australian infrastructure statistics*. Canberra: Bureau of Infrastructure, Transport and Regional Economics.

Bourne, M., & Cooke, R. (1993). Victoria's speed camera program. *Crime Prevention Studies, 1*, 177–192.

Bradley, D. (1992). Escaping Plato's cave. In P. Moir & J. Eijkman (Eds.), *Policing Australia: Old issues new perspectives* (pp. 132–159). Melbourne: Palgrave Macmillan.

Buckley, D. (2019, November 13). Husband says decision not respectful of life: Appeal dismissal guts family. *Sunshine Coast Daily*, p. 6.

Clarke, R. (Ed.). (1997). *Situational crime prevention: Successful case studies*. Guilderland, NY: Harrow and Heston.

Clarke, R., & Eck, J. (2003). *Become a problem-solving crime analyst in 55 small steps*. London: Jill Dando Institute of Crime Science, University College London.

Cornish, D., & Clarke, R. (2003). Opportunities, precipitators and criminal decisions: A reply to Wortley's critique of situational crime prevention. *Crime Prevention Studies, 16*, 41–96.

Criminal Justice Commission. (1994). *Implementation of reform within the Queensland police service*. Brisbane: Author.

Cross, C. (2016). Using financial intelligence to target online fraud victimisation. *Criminal Justice Studies*, 29(2), 125–142.

Department of Commerce. (2017). *Final report 2016–2017*. Perth: Government of Western Australia.

Drew, J., & Prenzler, T. (2015). *Contemporary police practice*. Melbourne: Oxford University Press.

Eck, J., & Spelman, W. (1987). *Problem-solving: Problem-oriented policing in Newport News*. Washington, DC: National Institute of Justice.

Economic Connections. (2017). *Cost of road trauma in Australia 2015*. Canberra: Australian Automobile Association.

Ekblom, P. (2011). *Crime prevention, security and community safety using the 5Is Framework*. Basingstoke: Palgrave Macmillan.

Emerson, D. (2017, October 16). LOVE SCAM PLEA: Romance scam squad disbanded. *The West Australian*, p. 4.

Erke, A., Goldenbeld, C., & Vaa, T. (2009). The effects of drink-driving checkpoints on crashes–A meta-analysis. *Accident Analysis and Prevention*, 41(5), 914–923.

Felson, M., Berends, R., Richardson, B., & Veno, A. (1997). Reducing pub hopping and related crime. *Crime Prevention Studies*, 7, 115–132.

Ferris, J., Mazerolle, L., King, M., Bates, L., Bennett, S., & Devaney, M. (2013, November). Random breath testing in Queensland and Western Australia. *Accident Analysis and Prevention*, 60, 181–188.

Fleming, J. (2005). 'Working together': Neighbourhood Watch, reassurance policing and the potential of partnerships. *Trends & Issues in Crime and Criminal Justice*, 303, 1–6.

Gill, M. (2013). Engaging the corporate sector in policing. *Policing: A Journal of Policy and Practice*, 7(3), 273–279.

Goldstein, H. (1979). Improving policing: A problem-oriented approach. *Crime and Delinquency*, 25(2), 236–258.

Goldstein, H. (1990). *Problem-oriented policing*. New York: McGraw-Hill.

Henstridge, J., Homel, R., & Mackay, P. (1997). *The long-term effects of random breath testing in four Australian states*. Canberra: Department of Transport and Regional Development.

HMIC. (1997). *Policing with intelligence*. London: Her Majesty's Inspectorate of Constabulary.

Homel, R. (1993). Random breath testing in Australia: Getting it to work according to specifications. *Addiction*, 88(Supplement), 27S–33S.

Innes, M., & Fielding, N. (2002). From community to communicative policing: 'Signal crimes' and the problem of public reassurance. *Sociological Research Online*, 7(2), 1–22.

International Centre for the Prevention of Crime (ICPC), the World Bank and the Bogotá Chamber of Commerce. (2011). *Public-private partnerships and community safety: Guide to action*. Montreal: ICPC.

Lacey, D., Goode, S., Pawada, J., & Gibson, D. (2020). The application of scam compliance models to investment fraud offending. *Journal of Criminological Research Policy and Practice*, 6(1), 65–81.

Levi, M. (2008). Combating identity and other forms of payment fraud in the UK. *Crime Prevention Studies, 23,* 111–131.

Macintyre, S., & Prenzler, T. (1997). Officer perspectives on community policing. *Current Issues in Criminal Justice, 9*(1), 34–55.

MacKay, R. (2011). *Bsafe pilot project 2007–2010 final report.* Wangaratta: Women's Health Goulburn North East.

Makkai, T., Ratcliffe, J., Veraar, K., & Collins, L. (2004). *ACT recidivist offenders.* Canberra: Australian Institute of Criminology.

Marks, E., Meyer, A., & Linssen, R. (2005). *Beccaria-standards for ensuring quality in crime prevention projects.* Hannover: Council for Crime Prevention of Lower Saxony.

Mazerolle, L., & Prenzler, T. (2004). Third party policing: Considering the ethical challenges. In M. Hickman, A. Piquero, & J. Greene (Eds.), *Police integrity and ethics* (pp. 163–187). Belmont, CA: Wadsworth.

Mazerolle, L., & Ransley, J. (2006). *Third party policing.* Cambridge: Cambridge University Press.

Mischin, M. (2017, January 18). *WA victims lose $10 million to scams in 2016.* Retrieved from www.mediastatements.wa.gov.au/Pages/Barnett/2017/01/WA-victims-lose-10-million-to-scams-in-2016.aspx.

New South Wales Police Force. (2019). *Annual report 2018–2019.* Sydney: Author.

Prenzler, T. (2009). An assessment of reform in politics, criminal justice and the police in post-Fitzgerald Queensland. *Griffith Law Review, 18*(3), 576–595.

Prenzler, T. (2014). Re-thinking counter-terrorism and crime prevention strategies from a harm perspective. *Australasian Policing, 6*(2), 22–23.

Prenzler, T. (2017a). Fraud victimisation and prevention. In A. Deckert & R. Sarre (Eds.), *The Australian and New Zealand handbook of criminology, crime and justice* (pp. 269–283). London: Routledge.

Prenzler, T. (Ed.) (2017b). *Understanding crime prevention: The case study approach.* Brisbane: Australian Academic Press.

Prenzler, T., & Sarre, R. (2014). The Role of partnerships in security management. In M. Gill (Ed.), *Handbook of security* (pp. 769–790). Houndmills: Palgrave Macmillan.

Putt, J. (Ed.) (2010). *Community policing in Australia.* Canberra: Australian Institute of Criminology.

Queensland Police Service. (1996). *Report on the Review of the Queensland Police Service.* Brisbane: Minister for Police.

Queensland Police Service. (2019). *2018–2019 annual report.* Brisbane: Author.

Ransley, J., & Prenzler, T. (2020). Defining crime. In H. Hayes & T. Prenzler (Eds.), *An Introduction to crime and criminology* (pp. 17–34). Sydney: Pearson.

Ratcliffe, J. (2001). Policing urban burglary. *Trends and Issues in Crime and Criminal Justice, 213,* 1–6.

Ratcliffe, J. (2003). Intelligence-led policing. *Trends and Issues in Crime and Criminal Justice, 248,* 1–6.

Ratcliffe, J. (2015). Towards an index for harm-focused policing. *Policing: A Journal of Policy and Practice, 9*(2), 164–182.

Sarre, R. (1996). The state of community-based policing in Australia: Some emerging themes. In D. Chappell & P. Wilson (Eds.), *Australian policing: Contemporary issues* (pp. 26–41). Sydney: Butterworths.

Sarre, R. (2017). How I would spend $100 million to reduce crime. *Current Issues in Criminal Justice, 28*(3), 339–353.

Schmerler, K., Perkins, M., Phillips, S., Rinehart, T., & Townsend, M. (2006). *A guide to reducing crime and disorder through problem-solving partnerships*. Washington, DC: Office of Community Oriented Policing Services, US Department of Justice.

Steering Committee for the Review of Government Service Provision. (2020). *Report on government services 2020 – Police*. Canberra: Productivity Commission.

Thorne, C. (2003). *Implementation of community policing within the Brisbane Metropolitan North Police Region: Issues and problems* (Unpublished doctoral dissertation). Queensland University of Technology, Brisbane, Australia.

Trojanowicz, R. (1982). *An evaluation of the neighborhood foot patrol program in Flint, Michigan*. East Lansing: Michigan State University.

Trojanowicz, R., & Bucqueroux, B. (1990). *Community policing: A contemporary perspective*. Cincinnati: Anderson.

United Nations Office on Drugs and Crime. (2010). *Handbook on the United Nations crime prevention guidelines*. Vienna: Author.

Victorian Government. (2014). *Victoria police blue paper: A vision for Victoria police in 2025*. Melbourne: Author.

VincentCare. (2020). *Our services*. Retrieved from www.vincentcare.org.au/our-services/marian-community/.

Weber, D. (2018, July 26). *Tap-and-go credit card fraud on the rise, prompting warning from senior police*. Retrieved from www.abc.net.au/news/2018-07-26/tap-and-go-fraud-on-the-rise/10040890.

White, R., Murray, G., & Robbins, N. (1996). *Negotiating youth-specific public space: A guide for youth and community workers, town planners and local councils*. Sydney: Youth Programs Unit, New South Wales Department of Training and Education Co-ordination.

CHAPTER 18

Terrorism and the role of state police

Nick Kaldas

INTRODUCTION

There is no escaping the ubiquitous incidence of terrorism in the world today. It seems there is an endless flood of individuals, groups, and causes wishing to mount attacks across the globe. Their impact is significant, and hence, the duty to be aware of and effectively deal with these threats rests to a large extent on domestic law enforcement. Consider the following:

> *Since 2003, in the U.S., 663 people have died in mass shootings, defined as indiscriminate attacks in public with at least three fatalities (each), excluding the shooter. More than 1 in 4 victims were killed by an attacker who adhered to an extreme ideology* (Bergengruen and Hennigan, 2019, p. 20).

> *In 2018, terrorism continued to constitute a major threat to security in EU Member States* (Europol, 2019, p. 4).

Or as ASIO has stated:

> *The threats of terrorism, espionage and foreign interference recognise no borders. They are persistent, and their enduring nature means we cannot afford to rest on our successes* (ASIO, 2019, pp. 3–4).

As discussed in this chapter, terrorism is not new, and is not likely to fade or disappear anytime soon. It is a phenomenon which will be with us, our children, and most probably our grandchildren. The threat of terrorism we face in the Western world, and in Australia, sadly, is brought into stark relief for us on an almost weekly basis with news of yet another attack. For police, being the guardians of the population, it is important that their leadership and the rank and file understand the true nature of the threat and develop measures covering the four pillars of dealing with these risks: prevention, preparedness, response, and recovery.

The following has been stated by our national security agency in Australia, the Australian Security Intelligence Organisation (ASIO): "The world in which we live is becoming ever more complex, more uncertain and, as a result of globalisation, more 'connected' than at any other time in history" (ASIO, 2019, p. 3). It is necessary when developing responses to have a basic understanding of the history of the threats we face, their evolving nature, and how we got here. While the present-day threat has trans-morphed constantly, there are some almost predictable outcomes that can be guarded against if one studies the past and learns from it. John Timoney, who was a renowned and innovative police leader in the US and somewhat of a philosopher, served as the Deputy Commissioner in the New York Police Department and went on to be Chief of Police in Philadelphia and in Miami. He often said: "Those who don't study history are doomed to repeat it, and police don't study history". But that need not be so; the senior ranks of policing in Australia are filled with educated, forward thinking, exceptional leaders who are more than capable of a deep understanding of terrorism and mitigating steps that can and must be taken in a liberal democratic society such as Australia. This chapter is a small step in continuing the narrative or dialogue on this topic.

BACKGROUND

In attempting to understand the nature of the threat of terrorism, it is helpful for police leadership to consider the theory and history, the fact that the threat is evolving, and that some patterns can be anticipated.

Professor David Rapoport (2004) a highly influential thinker and prolific writer on terrorism, developed a seminal theory of the "four modern waves of terrorism". Firstly, he posited that terrorism is not new; secondly, that until the end of the 19th century, the causes of terrorism were primarily religious; thirdly, that there are four modern waves of terrorism that are discernible. These four waves are: Anarchist, (1878–1919); the Anti Colonial, (1920s – early 1960s), for example the anti-colonial struggles in Cyprus and Algeria in the 1950s; followed by the Communist or new-left wave, (mid 1960s – 1990s), for example the Baader-Meinhoff gang in Germany, the Red Brigades in Italy, the Red Army Faction in Japan; and the current wave we face, the extreme Islamic fundamentalist terror – and so it is back to religion again (1979–) (Kaplan, 2016). Rapoport alluded to each wave being approximately a 40-year cycle. There is much debate regarding what threat may next emerge after the current wave, if and when it abates, but no consensus. However, the modern extreme Islamic fundamentalist phase has to be seen as more sustained, virulent, and having a far more devastating effect than earlier waves. For example: "While terrorists in the 1970s and 1980s killed in tens, in the 1990s killed in hundreds, today's terrorists want to kill in thousands" (Gunaratna, 2005, p. xxii), increasing the pressure on authorities to act effectively.

A brief recap of more recent history may illustrate how we arrived at this point. Following the 9/11 attacks, the Western and USA-led international coalition went after Al Qaeda in Afghanistan. In a sense, matters were easier pre-9/11 in that the main enemy, Al Qaeda, was geographically headquartered in Sudan and then Afghanistan, and the whereabouts of our target were known. The Western-led campaign on "Al Qaeda central" in Afghanistan was largely successful and greatly degraded the capability of Al Qaeda to operate freely. What happened next was unintended and perhaps unforeseen. "In disbanding the centralized group, the Coalition, unintentionally, created an enemy which is now harder to pin down, in that there is no longer a geographic location where the enemy resides, and where strikes could be directed" (Kaldas, 2007, p. 61). However, while Al Qaeda is diminished, with its leadership largely decapitated, it is still an organisation which is more than capable of commissioning, directing, and inspiring attacks globally. We now have a plethora of self-radicalised individuals who do not need specific guidance but are inspired by their jihadi ideals, acting in "lone wolf" mode. This has been aptly described as "Leaderless Jihad" (Sageman, 2008).

THE RISE AND PARTIAL FALL OF ISIS AND THE GLOBAL IMPACT: A GAME CHANGER

ISIS, or Islamic State in Iraq and the Sham (the Levant in Arabic), burst onto the scene as a jihadist group in Syria and Iraq, with what seemed to be unprecedented violence and savagery "so brutal and out of control that it was officially disavowed by Al Qaeda" (Stern and Berger, 2016, p. 3).

The group was made up of remnants of other groups and attracted a huge following from across the globe, flocking to join their fight. ISIS was estimated at one point to have a fighting force of around 25,000 men Stern and Berger (2016, p. 51). Some of those fighters were Australian citizens. But in many ways this group was unlike any other. Its ambition was to rule the world in an extreme fundamentalist Islamic empire, crushing all before it. On June 29, 2014, ISIS declared "that it was reconstituting the caliphate, a historic Islamic empire with resonance for Muslims around the world, but especially for Salafi jihadists" (Stern and Berger, 2016, p. 46). However, one of the distinguishing features of the group from its early days was its ability to self-promote with the use of social media. "ISIS has made its name on the marketing of savagery, evolving its message to sell a strange but potent new blend of utopianism and appalling carnage to a worldwide audience" (Stern and Berger, 2016, p. 125). ISIS mastered social media as never before.

In a strange twist, nevertheless, which illustrated how innovative this group was, it was discovered that ISIS recruiting videos were built on a

12-step Hollywood formula, used in such films as *Titanic*, *The Wizard of Oz*, and *Star Wars* (Goudie and Markoff, 2016). ISIS invaded and held vast areas of both Syria and Iraq, and held onto those spaces for some years, inflicting a harsh, extreme fundamentalist regime on inhabitants of those areas who could not flee. They instituted slave markets and practiced beheadings and other savage acts forgotten by mankind from previous, ancient eras (Stern and Berger, 2016).

Eventually, the overwhelming array of forces fighting against ISIS included a US-led coalition, the Russian military presence supporting the Syrian regime (both with significant air power), together with Lebanese Hezbollah fighters and Iranian Revolutionary Guard Corps, as well as other insurgent groups in Syria. Strange bedfellows indeed. In Iraq, ISIS faced the regular Iraqi security forces, as well as numerous militias which sprang up with the aim of defeating ISIS, backed by Iran. In both Iraq and Syria, Kurdish fighting forces also joined the fight against ISIS. (Stern and Berger, 2016)

Finally in December 2018, President Trump claimed the total defeat of ISIS, and around March 2019, the international community felt it could announce that ISIS had in fact been defeated and had lost control of the last shards of the cities it once controlled (Chulov, 2018).

THE CURRENT STATE

While ISIS may have been militarily defeated, the threat it poses, like Al Qaeda, remains, albeit in a different form. It has been described thus:

> *The reduction of the physical caliphate is a monumental military accomplishment. But the fight against ISIS and violent extremism is far from over . . . what we are seeing now is not the surrender of ISIS as an organization, but a calculated decision . . . waiting for the right time to resurge. [T]he ISIS population being evacuated from the remaining vestiges of the caliphate largely remain unrepentant, unbroken and radicalized* (Votel, 2019).

Those advocating violent jihad have refined their exhortations to the faithful continuously and co-opted events to support their arguments. There is no doubt that the invasions, followed by protracted wars against insurgencies in both Afghanistan and Iraq, have had a "profound impact on radicalised and politicised Muslims. By exploiting the anger and the suffering of Muslims, . . . existing terrorist and extremist groups are growing, and new groups are emerging" (Gunaratna, 2005, p. xxvi). This impact is also true for communities in Australia. So we see a pattern of extremist groups using the presence of Western, primarily US, forces in the Middle East and elsewhere, specifically in Muslim majority nations, as a rallying cry, denouncing occupation and imperialism, feeding anger and radicalisation (Nelson and Sanderson, 2011, p. 20).

Following comprehensive research and the establishment of a database cataloguing the motivation for terrorism, Robert Pape argues that perhaps the most significant motivation for suicide attacks is in fact a reaction to and attack on "alien" occupations of a country (Pape, 2006). But in this environment, lest anyone think that those who wish us harm may demur if faced with our obstacles, one should consider this. Enormous efforts have gone into protecting air travel. Terrorists have not backed away or given up, despite numerous failures. On the contrary, that sector has remained a primary target, they are not deterred. Instead, there has been assessment and new techniques shown by them. So, too, must we reflect on outcomes, and adjust our thinking.

One other significant factor remains largely unappreciated by the policing population. Muslims, like other vulnerable communities, are not homogenous. Specifically, the Sunni-Shia divide within the Muslim faith must be understood by police leaders before delving into the community. While one could spend hours explaining the history and current status of that conflict; it is sufficient to say it is a deep, irreparable split, and must be factored into any engagement program. It is the author's view that, apart from the Palestine-Israel issue, most other conflicts in the Middle East today are centred on this historic quarrel.

THE ROLE OF STATE AND TERRITORY POLICE IN COUNTERING TERRORISM

Australia has a mature framework governing policy and programs around countering terrorism, with the peak policy body being the Australia and New Zealand Counter Terrorism Committee.

A brief examination of the national counterterrorism framework in Australia illustrates the different levels, roles, and responsibilities allocated to the state and federal authorities (Australian Government website, 2020). While all Australian jurisdictions and police forces are members of the Australia and New Zealand Counter-Terrorism Committee, New Zealand was added as a full member in 2012, marking the tenth anniversary of the establishment of the committee following the September 11 attacks.

There are three key indicators for state and territory police being pivotal in the fight against extremism, radicalisation, and the response to terrorist attacks. Accordingly, it behoves leaders of policing in Australia to be aware of this operating environment; to remain abreast of trends, developments and issues; and to inform their operational and planning decision-making. Firstly, the Australian government framework for dealing with terrorism allocates significant responsibility to states and territories:

- States and territories have primary operational responsibility for responding to a terrorist situation in their jurisdiction; and

- They determine prevention strategies and operational responses to threats, including seeking assistance from other jurisdictions (Australian Government Website, 2020).

Secondly, consider the range of activities local police attend to, in and amongst the communities on a daily basis: parking and traffic, domestic violence and other issues, volume crime and higher-level organised crime, youth and gang crime and issues, and simple matters such as noise and domestic violence complaints. Thus, the role of police at the state level is central. They are one of the few 24/7/365 agencies, out where "the rubber meets the road" to use the colloquial saying, and are thus ideally placed to communicate with and take the pulse of the communities in order to understand their concerns, fears, needs, and aspirations.

Thirdly, state and territory police will always be the first responders, the front line, not only interfacing with communities in a crisis but possessing on-the-ground capability such as forensic services, investigators, and requisite assets. Thus, they have the knowledge, relationships, and hopefully rapport and trust with the communities, as well as the operational capability. It is logical that police forces must then be the conduit to efforts in countering radicalisation and responding to incidents, working hand-in-glove with federal colleagues.

A SHIFT IN PARADIGM

The traditional policing model in Australia and most of the Western world has been based on responding to events or incidents. Crimes such as robbery, murder, or fraud usually occurred before police were informed; they then responded to solve the crime and bring offenders to justice. In facing terrorism and extremism, the state cannot afford to wait until an offence occurs – lives are at stake. Thus, police have had to adjust their whole operational framework so as not to respond, but to prevent, and be prepared to deal with incidents they fail to prevent.

Similarly, in terms of legislation, our justice system is geared to deal with offences that have already occurred. New measures and a raft of state and Commonwealth legislation had to be introduced to create offences such as belonging to a proscribed group, plotting attacks (that have not occurred), assisting others materially to plan or mount attacks, and most problematically, to deal with those citizens who committed these acts offshore, outside the jurisdiction (see the discussion later in the subsection "Returning fighters").

Our whole system, when first facing terrorism, had historically been responsive, and this mindset had to be challenged, firstly, in terms of the necessity for preventative and protective measures, including legislation; secondly, in focusing on the significance of engagement with vulnerable communities and counter radicalisation methods; and thirdly, in terms of disruption and pre-emptive strikes, arrests, and operations before an attack occurs. In those spheres, the local police are an integral part of the equation.

THE CHALLENGES

Accountability and scrutiny

There is no escaping the fact that whether police perform brilliantly or fail miserably in dealing with incidents of terrorism in a Western democracy, there will inevitably be commissions of inquiry, Coronial inquests, or parliamentary inquiries after the event, or all of these. All aspects of their performance will be scrutinised. For example, following the Munich Olympic attack in 1972 where all nine hostages and a police officer were killed, much criticism was levelled at the authorities (Hoffman, 2017, pp. 69–71).

Similarly, in recent times, following the Lindt café siege in Sydney in 2014, where two victims and the gunman were killed, one of the victims' families summed up the incident and the police handling of it in these terms: "[T]he entire management of the siege was a disaster. It cannot happen again that way, ever" (Snow, 2018, p. 293). There were also many criticisms of state agencies not calling on federal capabilities, including the military (see the subsection "Interoperability" later in the chapter).

Compounding this pressure on police leaders, these operations are almost always carried out under the intense glare of media and public attention. Senior police should not need motivation to prepare for terrorist incidents. However, fairly or unfairly, the point here is that while police take their sacred duty to protect seriously, there are always consequences for those who do not prepare adequately in advance and measure up in the crisis.

Returning fighters

> *Australia should be doing more to bring back all its citizens and placing those of them involved in the commission of international crimes on Trial* (Araf, 2019, p. 25).

Conversely it has been argued:

> *These ideologically indoctrinated, hardened fighters can pose a serious threat to their country of origin and elsewhere in the event that they would return. They have witnessed or perpetrated large-scale violence, are capable of handling weapons and explosives, and frequently hold a grudge against the West* (Acheson and Paul, 2019, p. 111).

These are two views about what authorities in Australia should or should not be doing in relation to those who left the country to join

ISIS or similar groups, lived and probably fought in conflict zones, and then sought return to Australia.

This is a complex issue that has stirred deep emotions for and against the notion that citizens who left Australia and fought overseas should be allowed to return and possibly face charges for their actions in joining ISIS or other similar groups. There are some who call for that to occur and for the Australian government to do all in its power to bring them back. On the other hand, there are many who feel that these individuals have forfeited their rights to be an Australian citizen and be protected by their government, and it has been argued that on the occasions when they have faced trials, the punishment has usually been inadequate, or too lenient (Acheson and Paul, 2019). The issue is complicated further by the presence of many women and children, families of the fighters, whose complicity is uncertain and may vary greatly.

Moreover, it is very difficult if not impossible in most cases to prove exactly who did what in that environment to a level that would satisfy an Australian court beyond a reasonable doubt. The gathering of battlefield evidence is always difficult, complicated further in a live war zone, as has been shown in these cases and similar investigations such as the investigations into the use of chemical weapons in Syria, which the author led. Worse, it has been argued that there are inadequate mechanisms to rehabilitate these individuals on return (Fabri and Paul, 2018, p. 70).

The debate rages as we write, and to some extent it has become politicised with the left and right of the political landscape divided along ideological lines. But what is certain is that police in Australia have had to and will have to grapple with at least some of these individuals on their return. This will be a risk management exercise with serious implications if police misstep.

Yet another aspect to this problem is the presence of a sizable number of people within Australia who were identified as wanting to join jihadist groups offshore but then had their passports cancelled and their ability to travel removed. They are then stuck in Australia, often with anger and evil intent towards Australia and its government. The government has sought to contain these individuals with the introduction of Control Orders, to detain individuals and dictate their movements. Police are often the ones left to deal with these individuals and manage that risk.

Clearly there has already been a great deal of discussion and collaboration between police, education, health, immigration, and judicial officers in the major capital cities in Australia where the largest numbers were drawn from. It is essential that this dialogue and collaboration continue, and it must be understood that no one organisation can deal with this vexed issue by themselves, an all-hands-on-deck approach is essential. These are, of course, problems faced by most Western countries, and there are no easy answers, nor is there consistency or consensus as to how to deal with them.

The re-emergence of right-wing extremism

Right wing terrorism is a global problem, resulting in devastating attacks from New Zealand to Norway (Bergengruen and Hennigan, 2019, p. 21).

White supremacy is a greater threat than international terrorism right now (former USA Attorney, quoted in Bergengruen and Hennigan, 2019).

Likewise, the United Nations has estimated a 320% rise in attacks from those affiliated with right-wing extremists in the past five years (UN. CTED, 2020, p. 3). Right-wing or alt-right extremism, like other forms of terrorism, is not new. One only needs to consider the Ku Klux Klan as one example, dating back over 100 years. However, in recent times there has been a clear escalation and re-energising of those who adhere to these beliefs, facilitated by the internet. Internet chatrooms and other social media give them anonymity and a global reach. To put things in some context, in Texas on August 3, 2019, a right-wing extremist launched an attack after posting a message on 8chan, a right-wing forum. "More people were killed that day in El Paso than all 14 service members killed this year on the battlefields in Afghanistan, Iraq, and Syria" (Bergengruen and Hennigan, 2019, p. 21). Thus, the problem is significant and often underestimated by law enforcement. Targets can include significant segments of society: Jewish, Arabic, African American, LGBTQ, Hispanic communities, and left-wing organisations (Bergengruen and Hennigan, 2019; Hassan, 2019).

While the magnitude of this problem is not as great as the extreme Islamic fundamentalist threat and must be kept in context, it is still sizable, and there are very clear indications it is on the rise (Hassan, 2019; FBI, 2018).

The problem is compounded in Australia by the lack or inadequacy of accurate statistics being kept by law enforcement nationally that identifies specific hate crimes committed in this way The US has in excess of 15,000 police agencies, yet the FBI manages to gather and analyse data, publishing an annual report on the status of hate crimes and alt-right crime. The eight forces in Australia should consider moving towards a consistent focus on this issue and a more coordinated approach to identifying, gathering, and analysing this data. The old adage, if you cannot measure a problem, you cannot deal with it, comes to mind.

Mindset: but we've always done it that way

For some decades, the national counterterrorism exercises, testing various jurisdictions' capabilities, focused on a siege scenario, with hostages and a stronghold. Then the advent of a moving, armed assailant emerged, highlighted in the attacks in Mumbai, India, in 2008 and repeated many times since then. This was a significant shift, with huge implications for what were then called "places of mass gatherings", e.g. shopping centres, sporting stadiums, etc.

Yet it took some years at the national and state level for a consensus to be reached that different things needed to be done to prepare police for that type of attack. In essence, police had been trained in the mantra of "contain and negotiate", a policy which had served us well for some years, and statistics showed that the longer a siege situation went, the more likely it would be resolved peacefully. The active shooter scenario turned that logic on its head. In that situation, the longer police delayed entry and confrontation, the more people would almost certainly be killed. So the approach had to shift dramatically to deal with this new threat.

Likewise, the type of weapon and training used by most front-line police suddenly appeared under-powered, and another debate commenced regarding issuing long arms to front-line officers. Some leaders felt the risk of issuing long arms was too much to bear. The point here is that the ground had shifted. There had to be a fundamental change in planning, training, and equipping police going forward in order to save lives, one brought on by a completely different terrorist methodology that came in the form of a mobile shooter,.

That discussion and the whole process of change took some years, was somewhat torturous, and was opposed on a number of levels as too risky, but approval at the national level was ultimately given. This issue clearly highlighted the fact that law enforcement, policy-makers, and legislators had to be more agile and keep their operational tempo abreast, or preferably ahead, of such emerging issues in terrorism.

OPPORTUNITIES

Community engagement, countering radicalisation

In the process of radicalisation, communities are often the ones to notice the signs. Yet often they do not know where to turn. Informing police may cause their loved one to be arrested and charged. They may not have enough information or lack faith in authorities to do something without ruining their loved one's life. Dedicated community contact or engagement officers can break through that barrier using pre-established rapport and harness that trust and even friendship with key individuals in the community, who would then have the faith to entrust police with information. The community members can then be directed towards counter radicalisation programs.

Thus, the role of dedicated community engagement teams is important, while recognising that all front-line police as well the senior executive have a role to play. There are several benefits to having a specialised, focused community contact team, quarantined from the daily operational imperatives, so that engagement does not simply get pushed to the back of the line when busy. The broad aim should be to foster communication and rapport with the communities that are at risk of radicalisation. It is a force multiplier. Aims to be pursued include:

1. Enhance community understanding of police actions and their use of specific counterterrorism legislative powers, thus addressing concerns. This would reduce community anxieties regarding counter-terrorism efforts generally and the use of specific powers.
2. Conversely, keeping up communication would inform police of concerns held by communities so that they may be addressed. Better informed decisions can be made and then conveyed to communities to continue the cycle. For example, one constant issue raised by communities is the issue of hate crime and the perception that police generally do not treat these offences seriously enough. The NSW experience is that once a unit was set up and focused on this issue, it meant a great deal in the relationship with the community.
3. Working with community leaders to build resilience against the spirit of extremism within and from the community.
4. Assist, and complement the relationships that communities have with their local police, but without replacing that relationship. Community contact officers should tap into and utilise existing relationships at a local level with communities.
5. Hate crime unit duties should include monitoring actual offences, identifying, analysing, and advising on trends and then looking at corporate systems, policies, and procedures and recommending any required changes.
6. Dedicated community engagement teams should also play a role in education and training of the general policing population, the community and the media.

Engagement with international partners

In countering terrorism and dealing with the complex issues of returning fighters, holding those who fought with ISIS, and radicalisation, it is often overlooked that there is a plethora of international bodies that hold significant information and evidence relating to Australian citizens.

It has traditionally been left to the AFP to deal with these bodies, but in the current environment it is almost unfair to expect the AFP to solely shoulder the responsibility. There would be benefit in allowing state jurisdictions to engage, with full transparency, with bodies that can assist their investigations in the UN or elsewhere. Furthermore, when state police have been given opportunities to work briefly or study overseas, either through the AFP in peacekeeping or otherwise, the benefits have been significant, not just for their organisation and personal development but also for the greater good. They returned with many initiatives, experiences, and networks that assist greatly, enhancing the overall capability of the nation.

SOME ISSUES FOR POLICE LEADERS TO CONSIDER MOVING FORWARD

Engagement

As outlined earlier, dedicating resources to these efforts of engagement and paying attention to the issues that are of concern to vulnerable communities are an investment in goodwill, which stand policing organisations in good stead in a time of crisis.

We have discussed the nature of policing having traditionally been responsive rather than proactive. So it is with engagement activities. It is essential the police build these bridges in a time of peace, when there is no emergency, as it is much more difficult to make friends, and establish, rely on, and call on trust if one has not made the effort prior to the crisis. In this battle for hearts and minds, communication with communities is not only crucial but "there is an urgent need to develop effective counter-narratives to extremist ideologies" (Fabri and Paul, 2018, p. 71).

Interoperability

Counterterrorism is a labour-intensive operational space. There are a number of areas and situations where no one police force can adequately deal with a problem in that space. For example, in the process of analysing electronic data seized from accused groups of extremists, a growing problem, there have been cases like Operation Pendennis, a joint operation between NSW Police, Victoria Police, and the Australian Federal Police in 2005/6.

This operation ultimately resulted in the arrest of some 20 individuals and the seizure of thousands of electronic files and materials from laptops, phones, USB memory sticks, and discs. Police struggled to analyse this huge amount of data in time for court, some of which was in Arabic, requiring translation. It is fair to say that even with three of the largest police forces involved, there was still a struggle. Despite some interoperability at the time, we have not seen the establishment of a framework which allows jurisdictions across the nation to call on each other in a seamless fashion to assist in a time of need. Striving for interoperability thus continues. The network of Joint Counterterrorism Teams, bringing together federal and state agencies, which began in Sydney, provides an excellent example of the benefits of integrated, aligned teamwork.

Furthermore, in the tactical operations space (SWAT, essentially) and with respect to hostage negotiators and other highly specialised operators, the framework exists for interoperability between the states, territories, and the AFP. Officers in state/territory police and federal police (AFP) train together to the same level, have agreed-upon common standard operating procedures, and equipment, and often know each other well, making it easy to deploy on joint operations, seamlessly. These arrangements were activated very successfully during a number of major events such as the APEC conference in Sydney in 2007, the Sydney Olympics in 2000, CHOGM conferences, and World Youth Day in 2008. The military were also included in some of those efforts with great benefit, and they should be considered for inclusion in some areas. There was some severe criticism of police in the Lindt café siege for precisely that point, not considering adequately the support available from the ADF.

Thus, broadening that cooperative approach to other policing disciplines and the military would yield many benefits, building much larger capacities for each police force; effectively creating stronger, better resourced regional and national capability; enhancing resilience; and standardising command and control doctrine across the nation.

Engagement with business sector and private security

There has been much discussion regarding police engaging more closely with the private sector, and particularly with the private security industry. There have always been obstacles. Among other things, there have been allegations that some of the private security business organisations have been infiltrated by organised crime figures. A lack of trust had caused that dialogue to stall.

However, it has been convincingly argued in two groundbreaking papers published recently that the private security industry and the private sector generally can and must play a vital role in national security, and that what problems exist are not insurmountable. These problems, should be resolved, and the industry and the private sector should be at the table for national security issues, after appropriate vetting (Bergin, Williams, and Dixon, 2018, p. 6). In short:

> *Our approach to national security planning should now include key companies and their supply chains: it's time to rethink our national security approach in a more complex, dynamic and interconnected world. Our corporate sector is now a key component of our deterrent posture against a range of threats* (Bergin, Williams, and De Wild, 2019).

Certainly, the issue of securing our nation's supply chains for essential commodities ranging from petrol and face masks to toilet paper has been exposed as vulnerable during the COVID-19 virus crisis.

There are examples of this cooperation occurring successfully in other countries, such as Operation Griffin in the UK and Operation Shield in New York. In the current threat environment, this is an idea whose time has now come in Australia – "all hands on deck".

Leadership

Finally, it is impossible to overstate the importance of leadership in policing on these issues. The tone starts at the top. Leaders must be "aware" and "involved". For example, decades of experience have shown that where police commanders are committed to serious engagement programs, the troops follow; where police commanders are not committed to such programs, or worse, if they are antagonistic to that effort, programs and the whole effort fails.

If we accept that "to end terrorism it is essential to address the root causes" (Gunaratna, 2005, p. xxiii), then one must first understand the problem. Leadership is required to actually drive that effort to reflect on events and incidents, learn lessons, and apply those learnings. Following September 11, much was written about "the failure of imagination". We cannot afford to let that happen again. To quote an old police saying, "there is a difference between being in charge and taking charge". Police leaders in countering terrorism must "take" charge.

CONCLUSION

As has often been said of attacks, we will continue to stop most of them, but we cannot stop all of them. Police leadership in Australia is among the best in the world. However, there are a number of issues highlighted here worthy of consideration:

- Raising awareness of the terrorism environment;
- Systemic reflection on and analysis of experiences, positive and negative;
- Enhancing and strongly focusing on community engagement;
- Enhancing interoperability;
- More meaningful engagement with the private security industry and the business community; and
- Focusing on leadership in the terrorism space.

We should all remember this: "Equality and freedom can only thrive where citizens can trust that they can exercise their rights and participate in public life without intimidation or fear of violence" (Europol, 2019, p. 4).

REFERENCES

Acheson, I., & Paul, A. (Eds.). (2019). *Guns and Glory: Criminality, Imprisonment and Jihadist Extremism in Europe*. Belgium: European Policy Centre, Counter Extremism Project.

Araf, R. (2019). Bring Australian Families to Home, to Justice. *The Sydney Morning Herald*, 11 October, p. 25.

Australian Government Website. (2020). *The Australia and New Zealand Counter Terrorist Committee*. Retrieved from: www.nationalsecurity.gov.au/whataustraliaisdoing/pages/australia-new-zealand-counter-terrorism-committee.aspx.

Australian Security Intelligence Organisation (ASIO). (2019). *Annual Report, 2018–2019*. Canberra: ASIO.

Bergengruen, V., & Hennigan, W. J. (2019). The Terror Within, Special Report. *Time Magazine*, 19 August, pp. 18–32.

Bergin, A., Williams, D., & De Wild, R. (2019). *From Board Room to Situation Room: Why Corporate Security Is National Security*. Canberra: Australian Strategic Policy Institute.

Bergin, A., Williams, D., & Dixon, C. (2018). *Safety in Numbers: Australia's Private Security Guard Force and Counter Terrorism.* Canberra: Australian Strategic Policy Institute.

Chulov, M. (2018). Has ISIS Been Defeated in Syria as Trump Claims? *The Guardian Newspaper.* 20 December. Retrieved from: www.theguardian.com/world/2018/dec/19/has-isis-been-defeated-in-syria-as-trump-claims).

Europol. (2019). *European Union Terrorism Situation and Trend Report 2019.* The Hague: Europol.

Fabri, F., & Paul, A. (Eds.). (2018). *Fighting Terrorism and Radicalisation in Europe's Neighbourhood: How to Scale Up E.U. Efforts.* Belgium: European Policy Centre, Counter Extremism Project.

Federal Bureau of Investigation (FBI). (2018). *Hate Crime Statistics Report.* Retrieved from: https://ucr.fbi.gov/hate-crime/2018/hate-crime.

Goudie, C., & Markoff, B. (2016). *How ISIS Recruiting Videos Mirror Hollywood Scripts.* Chicago: ABC7 I-Team Investigation.

Gunaratna, R. (2005). *Inside Al Qaeda: Global Network of Terror.* Carlton South, Victoria: Scribe Publishing.

Hassan, A. (2019). Hate Crime Violence Hits 16 Year High. *New York Times*, 12 November, p. 19.

Hoffman, B. (2017). *Inside Terrorism,* 3rd edition. New York: Columbia University Press.

Kaldas, N. (2007). Australia and the Changing Terrorist Threat. *Policing: A Journal of Policy and Practice,* 1(1), 61–62.

Kaplan, J. (2016). Waves of Political Terrorism. Retrieved from: https://pdfs.semanticscholar.org/0fd2/cb18d42a2387b03a231b26520df913dfa70a.pdf.

Nelson, R., & Sanderson, T. (2011). *A threat Transformed: Al Qaeda and Associated Movements in 2011.* Washington, DC: Centre for Strategic and International Studies.

Pape, R. (2006). *Dying to Win: The Strategic Logic of Suicide Terrorism.* New York: Random House.

Rapoport, D. (2004). The Four Waves of Modern Terrorism. In A. K. Cronin & J. M. Ludes (Eds.), *Attacking Terrorism: Elements of a Grand Strategy* (pp. 46–73). Washington, DC: Georgetown University Press.

Sageman, M. (2008). *Leaderless Jihad: Terror Networks in the Twenty First Century.* Philadelphia: University of Pennsylvania Press.

Snow, D. (2018). *Siege: Inside the Lindt Café.* Sydney: Allen and Unwin.

Stern, J., & Berger, J. M. (2016). *ISIS: The State of Terror.* London: William Collins Books.

United Nations Security Council Counter-Terrorism Executive Directorate (UN, CTED). (2020). *Member States Concerned by the Growing and Increasingly Transnational Threat of Extreme Right-Wing Terrorism.* New York: United Nations.

Votel, J. (2019). *Evidence Before House Armed Services Committee Hearing on U.S. Central Command.* Washington, DC: US Government, 3 April.

CHAPTER 19

Organised and transnational crime
The impact on Australian police

Anthony Morgan, Rick Brown, Isabella Voce, and Timothy Cubitt

INTRODUCTION

The threats posed by organised and transnational crime have become important considerations for all policing and law-enforcement agencies operating in Australia. The very fact that we are more globally connected, and simultaneously more anonymous than ever before, creates an environment in which organised crime can flourish – allowing it to operate internationally in real time, just as any multinational corporation might.

Before proceeding, the chapter begins by defining "organised" and "transnational" crime. There are many definitions of organised crime. For example, at last count, von Lampe (2020) had amassed over 180 different definitions. Here, we will use a working definition from section 4 of the *Australian Crime Commission Act 2002*, which contains many of the key elements found in others internationally. This Act defines "serious and organised crime" as an offence that involves two or more offenders and substantial planning and organisation; typically involves the use of sophisticated methods and techniques; and is typically committed in conjunction with other similar offences. The 2002 Act goes on to specify 20 crime types that define a serious offence, but for our purposes, the preceding elements are largely sufficient to characterise what is implied by organised crime – multiple offenders planning criminal acts that employ sophisticated methods. However, we could also add the element of financial/material benefit that is found in many definitions, including the United Nations Convention against Transnational Organised Crime (United Nations, 2000).

Transnational crime includes crimes that occur in more than one state in the country, as well as those that are planned and directed from one state but which take place or impact people in another state (United Nations Office on Drugs and Crime [UNODC], n.d.). This definition of transnational crime includes offending by both organised crime groups (assumed to be non-state actors) and state actors, although for the purposes of this chapter it will be assume they involve organised crime groups.

While crimes will often be both organised *and* transnational, they can also be transnational *or* organised. For example, Mexican drug cartels that ship methamphetamine into Australia are clearly both organised and transnational, but a clandestine methamphetamine laboratory in rural New South Wales that supplies a local demand will be organised but not transnational. In contrast, a teenager in Belarus who orchestrates a distributed denial of service attack on an Australian company would meet the definition of transnational but would probably not be termed "organised". This chapter is concerned with those crimes that are both organised *and* transnational. It should be noted that organised and transnational crime in Australia is largely concerned with trade in physical (rather than virtual) commodities, particularly illicit drugs (such as methamphetamine, cocaine, and MDMA). Smith (2018) estimated that the cost to Australia from serious and organised crime in 2016–2017 was up to $47.4 billion. Of this, illicit drug activity accounted for $9.6 billion, with a further $4.1 billion associated with trade in other illicit commodities (such as intellectual property, native flora and fauna, and illicit tobacco). While many other types of organised and transnational crime impact upon Australia and are addressed by law-enforcement agencies, the primary focus remains the trade in these illicit commodities – especially drugs.

IMPACT OF TRANSNATIONAL AND ORGANISED CRIME ON THE AUSTRALIAN COMMUNITY

Methamphetamine is the illicit drug currently having the greatest impact on the Australian community, with the growth over the last decade being described as an "ice epidemic" (Law Reform, Drugs and Crime Prevention Committee, 2014). According to the Australian Institute of Criminology's Drug Use Monitoring in Australia program, there has been a more than threefold increase in the proportion of detainees who tested positive for methamphetamine over a ten-year period, with more than half testing positive in 2018 (Voce & Sullivan, 2018). The most recent report of the National Wastewater Drug Monitoring Program found the national average consumption of methamphetamine to be the highest since that collection began in August 2016 (Australian Criminal Intelligence Commission [ACIC], 2020). It has the highest usage rates of all illicit substances tested with available dose data. In fact, among the 25 countries with comparable wastewater data, Australia ranks second for methamphetamine use. The harms associated with methamphetamine use and dependence are significant. This includes the impact on crime – methamphetamine use is associated with increased involvement in violence (McKetin et al., 2014), domestic violence (Dowling & Morgan, 2018), and property crime (Bradford & Payne, 2012) – and incurs significant criminal justice costs (Whetton et al., 2016). There are also substantial mortality costs, healthcare costs, and costs from child maltreatment, among other harms (Whetton et al., 2016).

These harms can be attributed, albeit indirectly, to the transnational (and domestic) serious and organised crime groups that profit from the production, distribution, and sale of methamphetamine. While a significant proportion of Australia's methamphetamine is produced domestically in clandestine laboratories, amphetamine-type stimulants (ATS; excluding MDMA) account for the highest proportion of border detections in terms of weight seized, indicating a sizeable quantity of methamphetamine is imported from overseas (ACIC, 2019). This reflects the high level of involvement by transnational syndicates operating across borders. While North America remains the primary embarkation point for ATS seizures (ACIC, 2019), South East Asia is a growing source of methamphetamine and precursor products, involving a growing number of transnational criminal networks which previously operated outside the region (UNODC, 2019). South East Asia is also a major source of other illicit commodities shipped to Australia, including heroin and illicit tobacco (UNODC, 2019).

Outlaw motorcycle gangs (OMCG) are widely regarded as one of the most visible manifestations of organised crime in Australia, and are heavily involved in methamphetamine distribution and other illicit activities. Although the number of members has reportedly decreased in some jurisdictions in response to law-enforcement disruption (Caldwell, 2019), there remains nearly 6,000 members nationally in 39 active gangs. Recent research highlights the high prevalence of organised crime-type offending among OMCG members, including among members in executive roles, and revealed that many gangs show signs of operating as criminal organisations (Morgan et al., 2020). Most of this organised crime offending is related to commercial drug supply and enabling activities, particularly violent crime. Of course, not all of this criminal activity, organised or otherwise, is transnational in nature; however, there is evidence that Australian OMCGs have established chapters in South East Asia, where they are involved in drug trafficking (United Nations Office of Drugs and Crime, 2019). OMCGs have been a major focus for law enforcement and legislators, with a proliferation of new legislation and expanded powers introduced in the past decade following high profile incidents, most notably the brawl at Sydney Airport in 2009 involving members of the Hells Angels and Comancheros (Ayling & Broadhurst, 2014).

Drug traffickers, be they OMCGs or other criminal groups, rely on money laundering to both move and legitimise their illicit income (ACIC, 2017; Crime and Misconduct Commission (CMC), 2009). Money laundering is both an enabler of organised crime and a profitable enterprise in and of itself. The scale of money laundering, and associated harms (particularly where money laundering is secondary to other illicit activity), has proven difficult to measure (Levi, 2014; Smith,

2018). The mechanisms through which organised crime groups launder the proceeds of their illicit activities are numerous and wide ranging. Increasingly, these funds are being transferred offshore, sometimes with the assistance of transnational money laundering organisations and professional money launderers (ACIC, 2017). There is evidence that organised crime groups have responded to the introduction of civil penalties such as unexplained wealth laws and proceeds of crime, alongside criminal sanctions, with new and more sophisticated methods to hide their income (CMC, 2009). Despite extensive regulation of the financial system to reduce the risk of money laundering, several recent high-profile cases involving large banks have highlighted the risk that persists (AUSTRAC, 2018).

Money laundering is also an important enabler of organised financial crime. Organised tax fraud is the focus of growing attention by law enforcement because of the large-scale financial loss to government (Smith, 2018). For example, a sophisticated tax-fraud case involving two Australian co-conspirators using a complex structure of domestic and international trusts to evade their tax obligations resulted in $135m in losses to the Commonwealth, while the offenders obtained more than $60 million (Australian Tax Office (ATO), 2019). They were both sentenced to more than ten years in prison. Collectively, organised fraud cost close to $9 billion in 2017–2018, including the costs associated with superannuation fraud, illegal phoenixing, and payment-card fraud (Smith, 2018).

The rapid development of online technology has quickly seen cybercrime become a major threat to the safety and security of countries around the world. While more traditional organised crime groups have demonstrated a growing willingness to employ the services of professional facilitators with information and communication technology (ICT) knowledge and skills, the greater cybercrime threat likely comes from transnational networks of individuals who are connected online (ACIC, 2017; Choo & Grabosky, 2014). Many of these criminal networks do not meet more conventional definitions of organised crime (Leukfeldt et al., 2017). However, they are increasingly recognised by criminal intelligence organisations as a feature of the organised crime landscape. And, because of the overlap, a consideration of the response to organised crime necessarily requires thinking about how police respond to a growing cybercrime threat.

While the harms briefly described here are expansive, it is sometimes difficult to distinguish between the harms from organised criminal activity that is transnational in nature, and that which is domestic. The ACIC (2017) reports that as much as 70% of serious and organised crime impacting Australia is either based offshore or has strong offshore links. As observed elsewhere, there has been a shift away from hierarchical crime groups (with the exception of OMCGs) towards smaller, more flexible entrepreneurial groups that operate across borders in multiple markets (Ayling & Broadhurst, 2014).

POLICING ORGANISED AND TRANSNATIONAL CRIME AT THE COMMONWEALTH LEVEL

These transnational and organised crime threats faced by the Australian community pose a significant challenge to law enforcement, which typically evolves slowly and is, of course, bound by the laws of the land. The Australian Constitution helps to define what has become a demarcation of responsibility for policing organised and transnational crime, with the Commonwealth responsible for a narrowly defined set of issues, including those associated with trade and commerce, taxation, defence, and external affairs (Australian Bureau of Statistics, 1997). All else is the responsibility of the states and territories, each of which have their own legal systems. From a policing perspective, the Commonwealth typically focuses on crimes associated with trafficking across borders and with communications (use of the postal system and telecommunications), as well as with various other matters, including fraud against the Commonwealth and corruption involving Commonwealth officials/politicians.

The Australian Federal Police (AFP) is the primary law-enforcement agency at the Commonwealth level and is responsible for providing police services in relation to Commonwealth law and Commonwealth property and for safeguarding Commonwealth interests. It also provides other functions, including protective and custodial services; assistance and cooperation with Australian and foreign law-enforcement agencies, intelligence/security agencies, and government regulatory agencies; police services to support peace, security and stability in foreign countries, and community policing services to a number of Australian territories (AFP, 2019). In practice, this has led to significant law-enforcement activity focused on organised and transnational crime. For example, in 2018–2019, almost 15 tonnes of illicit drugs and their precursors were seized at the border/domestically, plus a further 40 tonnes were seized by overseas police, supported by the AFP; $53m in assets from the proceeds of crime was seized; 502 arrests for Commonwealth offences were made, and 112 overseas children were rescued from child sexual abuse (AFP, 2019).

The AFP is part of the Department of Home Affairs portfolio and works closely with other parts of the portfolio on a day-to-day basis. For example, it works closely with the Australian Border Force (ABF), a hybrid agency within the Department itself. The ABF has responsibility for facilitating travel and trade and for securing Australia's borders. From an organised crime/transnational crime perspective, the ABF is responsible for seizing illicit goods (particularly drugs) at the border through its customs function at ports and airports (including over 35,000 drugs and precursor detections in 2018–2019); preventing the smuggling of tobacco (over 285,000 detections in 2018–2019); preventing and interdicting people smuggling and human trafficking; preventing the criminal exploitation of migrant labour; and removing those whose visa has been cancelled for engaging in organised crime (Department of Home Affairs, 2019).

Beyond these large organisations, there are numerous smaller agencies in the Commonwealth that play a law-enforcement role in tackling transnational and organised crime. These include the ACIC (responsible for generating intelligence on serious and organised crime and for managing national police information systems); AUSTRAC (responsible for generating financial intelligence that can identify money laundering by organised crime groups); the Australian Securities and Investments Commission (responsible for preventing financial/white collar crime); Australian Signals Directorate (responsible for responding to serious cyberattacks and targeting cyber-criminals); and the Australian Commonwealth Law Enforcement Integrity Commission (which provides a police oversight function that addresses misconduct and corruption). That is in addition to other specialist agencies, such as the newly formed Sports Integrity Australia, which aims to address organised crime in sport (Holmes, 2020). This complex network of Commonwealth agencies, with specific powers and functions, provides a distributed array of competencies for addressing transnational and organised crime.

In addition, specialist multi-agency police units/squads/task-forces are often formed to address specific organised crime threats, and these can draw on a range of skills provided by agencies working at the Commonwealth and state/territory level, each of which can draw on intelligence from their own organisation and use their agency's specific powers and capabilities to address known organised crime problems. For example, the National Anti-Gangs Squad is led by the AFP but also includes personnel from the ABF, ACIC, ATO, and state/territory level police members. Similarly, the Joint Agency Ice Strike Team draws together resources from the AFP, ATO, and local state/territory police to provide a coordinate response to methamphetamine supply. These task forces are not limited to gang and drug-related crime; the Serious Financial Crime Taskforce is an ATO-led joint-agency task force established in 2015, and includes the AFP, ACIC, Attorney General's Department, AUSTRAC, Australian Securities and Investments Commission, Commonwealth Director of Public Prosecutions, and ABF.

POLICING ORGANISED AND TRANSNATIONAL CRIME AT THE STATE AND TERRITORY LEVEL

At the state and territory level, each police service also has a responsibility for tackling transnational and organised crime as defined by local legislation. This will typically include targeting organised crime groups and OMCGs operating within their jurisdictions. Their enforcement activity will also involve dealing with the impacts of transnational/organised crime – particularly street-level illicit drug supply and possession but also including the full range of organised crime activity at the local level.

A number of states and territories have law-enforcement agencies specifically established to address organised crime and (particularly) corruption that work closely with their police counterparts. For example, in Queensland, the Crime and Corruption Commission is a statutory body established to address major crime (such as drug trafficking, money laundering, and fraud) and tackle corruption in the public sector, as well as running the state's proceeds-of-crime regime and witness protection program. Other similar organisations (although with somewhat varying remit) include the New South Wales Crime Commission, Victoria's Independent Broad-Based Anti-Corruption Commission, Tasmania's Integrity Commission, South Australia's Independent Commissioner Against Corruption, Western Australia's Corruption and Crime Commission, and Northern Territory's Office of the Independent Commission Against Corruption.

AUSTRALIA'S RELATIONSHIPS WITH INTERNATIONAL PARTNERS

Transnational, organised crime has driven a surge in global law-enforcement cooperation, highlighting the need for countries to work together in information collection and proactive policing. In addition to law-enforcement agencies working together within and across states/territories and at the national level with Commonwealth law-enforcement agencies, they also work with international law-enforcement partners. Australian law-enforcement agencies work closely with counterpart organisations in neighbouring and distant regions in many different contexts (Fijnaut, 2012). This occurs in three main forms: formal requests for mutual legal assistance (MLA) from overseas agencies with an investigation/prosecution, made through the Commonwealth Attorney General's Department; officers going overseas to carry out specific investigative tasks; and the high-level coordination of multiple police jurisdictions or task forces, such as the Pacific Transnational Crime Network and INTERPOL.

The nature of international cooperation depends largely on the seriousness of the transnational crime problem, whether countries view this in the same way, and whether they have common political and economic interests (Fijnaut, 2012). While Australian law-enforcement agencies work collaboratively with a wide range of international law-enforcement agencies (particularly those in the Asia-Pacific Region), there is a special relationship with the Five Eyes nations (Australia, New Zealand, Canada, United States, and United Kingdom). This involves the sharing of intelligence products, investigative tools, and resources to a degree that is typically unmatched with law-enforcement agencies outside of the Five Eyes.

Australian police regularly request that overseas authorities provide information or operational assistance in organised crime investigations. MLA is the formal process by which different jurisdictions and countries provide and receive assistance in gathering information, intelligence, and evidence for investigations (Brun et al., 2011). Australia had ongoing MLA treaties with 30 countries in 2019 (AGD, 2019), with MLAs increasingly being used to assist the process of criminal investigations and prosecutions of international organised crime (Broadhurst & Ganapathy, 2008).

Many organised crime investigations involve law-enforcement officers working in another country, usually in a specific capacity for a certain investigation (such as undercover operations) or in long-term roles (such as joint teams, parallel investigations and liaison officers). In 2018–2019, the AFP had an extensive network of 225 staff across more than 30 countries (AFP, 2019). Similarly, the ACIC deployed 30 officers to 15 international locations to undertake joint agency investigations and intelligence gathering operations in 2017–2018 (ACIC, 2018).

While these arrangements exist, challenges remain. Foreign law-enforcement agencies may not have the willingness, regulations, or resources to assist or host Australian officers during investigations. The MLA process can be resource-intensive and time-consuming. In some cases, there is a lack of accountability, willingness to cooperate, or a sufficient legal framework for a foreign jurisdiction to provide the required information in a timely manner (Brown & Gillespie, 2015). Cultural and legal differences may also adversely affect the information provided, and significant differences in resourcing between jurisdictions influence the ability to provide information in a timely manner (Brown & Gillespie, 2015). That said, there have been significant advancements in terms of international cooperation, and numerous examples of transnational crime groups targeting Australia being disrupted due to the combined efforts of local and overseas law enforcement.

This brief survey of the Australian law-enforcement landscape demonstrates a high degree of specialisation in roles and collaboration (intrastate, interstate, internationally, and interdisciplinary), which is necessary to tackle contemporary, sophisticated, organised, and transnational crime groups. Despite this significant law-enforcement response, which costs the Australian taxpayer more than $8 billion per year (Smith, 2018), there remain significant challenges resulting from both internal and external pressures.

A CHANGING WORKFORCE, BUT THE RISK OF CORRUPTION REMAINS

Corruption of public officials, including police, is an important enabler of transnational organised crime (Smith et al., 2018). However, the risk of corruption from organised criminal groups is not a new problem. Police were widely criticised for entrenched corruption that existed throughout the last half of the 20th century as part of Royal Commissions in Queensland (Fitzgerald, 1987), New South Wales (Wood, 1997), and Western Australia (Kennedy, 2004), as well as special inquiries in Victoria (Office of Police Integrity, 2007). The scope of this misconduct and corruption extended well beyond organised criminal activity; however, there was widespread evidence of police turning a blind eye to prostitution and drug rings, with well-known organised crime links as well as direct involvement in the supply of illicit drugs.

Despite the events of the past, and the way in which corruption erodes trust, police still compare favourably in terms of public perceptions of government entities most at risk of corruption (Graycar, 2015). This might be due to the significant organisational reform that has followed findings of these reviews. These include internal complaints investigation and disciplinary systems, increasingly robust security assessment procedures, surveillance measures and the establishment of oversight bodies, some of which were described earlier. This is combined with more widespread cultural change within law-enforcement agencies, with the goal of increasing diversity and better representing the communities they serve.

While there is little evidence of the highly organised, corrupt networks that existed during the 1960s, 1970s and 1980s, the extent to which corruption exists within modern policing is difficult to assess. There are certainly recent examples upon which to draw. Perhaps the most obvious is the involvement of former Assistant Director of Investigations at the NSW Crime Commission, Mark Standen, who received a lengthy jail sentence for his involvement in a drug trafficking organisation and attempt to import methamphetamine precursors from a Dutch organised crime syndicate (Rowe et al., 2013). Of course, corruption risk does not merely entail organised crime groups infiltrating law enforcement – there are different levels of corruption that can take place (Smith et al., 2018). The current Royal Commission into the Management of Informants in Victoria, which examines the use of a high-profile barrister as an informant during Melbourne's gangland wars during the 1990s and 2000s (McCurdo, 2019), is a reminder of the risks associated with alleged noble-cause corruption, where the corrupt conduct takes place because there is a perception that the ends justify the means.

While few roles demand the level of integrity required of police, the sheer size of the law-enforcement workforce and the highly lucrative illicit activities to which police are exposed mean that corruption remains a risk, irrespective of the reforms and measures that have been introduced. Identifying those officers and roles most at risk, and putting in place safeguards to minimise opportunity for corruption, remains the best defence against infiltration by organised crime groups.

RAPID DEVELOPMENT OF INFORMATION AND COMMUNICATIONS TECHNOLOGIES

The rapid development and expansion of modern ICT presents new investigative challenges for law enforcement. The last decade has seen the introduction of encryption, the darknet, cloud data storage platforms, cryptocurrency, social media, and messaging apps. These ICTs can be used by criminals to hide their identity, operate undetected, and commit crime across borders and, according to criminal intelligence organisations, are exploited by terrorists, child sex offenders, cybercriminals, and organised crime syndicates (Parliamentary Joint Committee on Law Enforcement (PJCLE), 2019).

Encryption is a process that encodes a message or file so that it can only be read by certain people. The process uses an algorithm to scramble data as it is being sent and then uses a key for the receiving party to unscramble the information. This provides secure access to online content while separating a person's identity from their online activity. End-to-end encryption on instant messaging apps and devices can only be accessed from the receiving end-point device such as a mobile phone, and the service provider is not able to access the content that passes through the app. Law enforcement have identified encryption as a significant barrier to investigations – in Australia, the ACIC has reported that 90% of investigations involve some type of encryption (Phelan, 2019), while in the United Kingdom, it has been encountered in 100% of investigations (National Crime Agency, 2020). The introduction of end-to-end encryption has resulted in difficulties in accessing and obtaining data and digital evidence for law-enforcement purposes, with alleged criminal and terrorist targets using increasingly sophisticated encryption services (PJCLE, 2019).

Cryptocurrencies are a form of decentralized digital currency where encryption processes are used for currency regulation and transfer verification. Transactions are sent between peers, generally outside a regulated financial system, such as banking institutions. Since the first decentralized cryptocurrency called Bitcoin was created in 2009, over 6,000 variants of cryptocurrencies have been created. Several features of cryptocurrencies make them attractive to organised criminal groups, including a cheaper, more efficient, and faster method of payment. More importantly, they also offer significantly greater anonymity compared with traditional non-cash payment methods, with systems that are often located in many countries and subject to varying degrees of oversight (PJCLE, 2019).

Darknet markets (also referred to as cryptomarkets) are commercial websites that operate on the darknet and predominately use cryptocurrency. The darknet is a part of the internet that is not readily accessible through typical search engines such as Google and can only be accessed with specific software and configurations. Darknets overlay an internet connection with an anonymous network layer that conceals a user's location and usage from anyone conducting network surveillance or traffic analysis. Common darknets include The Onion Router (TOR), the Invisible Internet Project (I2P), and Freenet.

Darknet markets function as black markets, with users selling or dealing in drugs, weapons, counterfeit currency, stolen credit card details, forged documents, unlicensed pharmaceuticals, and other illicit goods as well as the sale of legal products. Darknet markets provide increased anonymity, access, and convenience for both sellers and buyers (Foley et al., 2019), are expanding quickly, and are attracting a greater share of organised crime (Lavorgna, 2015). Darknet market sales in Australia are predominately domestic, which may reflect consumer unwillingness to buy offshore products that may be detected by border security (Cunliffe et al., 2017). The constant closing and reopening of different darknet markets, limited visibility of transactions, and the use of virtual currencies is making it increasingly difficult for law-enforcement agencies to undertake criminal investigations (PJCLE, 2019).

Collectively, these advances mean that law enforcement is increasingly reliant on international collaboration, national information and intelligence sharing initiatives, a responsive legislative framework, and collaboration between the public and private sectors (PJCLE, 2019). Australia is party to several inter-jurisdictional treaties and alliances that facilitate international cooperation in relation to ICT-enabled criminal activity. These include the Budapest Convention (Council of Europe Convention on Cybercrime), which was adopted by the Australian government in 2010 and sets out ICT-enabled offences, harmonises legal cybercrime frameworks, provides for domestic powers to investigate and prosecute cybercrime, and establishes a system of international legal cooperation. Law enforcement can also engage in MLA processes to access stored communications and telecommunications data held offshore.

At a national level, a number of initiatives have been established in Australia to improve information and intelligence-sharing across jurisdictions; however, these have not overcome some of the workforce challenges that are posed by technologically sophisticated criminal networks. The Australian Cybercrime Online Reporting Network (ACORN), modelled on systems operating in the United States and the United Kingdom, was a national online system that allowed the public to securely report instances of cybercrime and assist law enforcement to identify offenders who were in a different jurisdiction than their victims (Morgan et al., 2016). However, an evaluation of the system identified a range of problems, many of which resulted from the sheer volume of reports received – many of which were for relatively minor scams – and the capacity of law-enforcement agencies to respond (Morgan et al., 2016). More recently, the National Criminal Intelligence System was developed to enable the sharing of criminal intelligence and information across all Australian jurisdictions in real time. While these systems often have grand aims, the reality is that they do not always deliver tangible benefits to law enforcement, for a whole range of reasons. In the case of NCIS, early pilot results were promising, and the ACIC reported it helped lead to the apprehension of a UK-based cybercriminal who had defrauded Australian bank accounts (ACIC, 2018).

Australia's legislative framework must also keep pace with the rapidly changing ICT environment. In 2015, the Australian government introduced the Data Retention regime through amendments to the *Telecommunications (Interception and Access) Act 1979*, which required that telecommunications metadata be retained by service provider companies for law-enforcement purposes. In April 2018, new legislation providing for digital currency exchange providers operating in Australia was implemented. The legislation which covered regulation of cryptocurrency service providers, including Bitcoin. In December 2018, the Australian Parliament passed the *Telecommunications and Other Legislation Amendment (Assistance and Access) Act 2018*, introducing a new framework for industry assistance, including new powers to secure assistance from key companies in the communications supply chain both within and outside Australia. Under this legislation, law-enforcement agencies may request or compel communication providers to provide access to encrypted communications. This legislation is not without its critics; in fact, few pieces of legislation have been as hotly debated as the metadata retention laws, with concerns raised about privacy, mission creep, compliance, and access to data (Sarre, 2017). It highlights the delicate tension that exists between ensuring law-enforcement have the tools necessary to tackle the growing threat of sophisticated, technology-enabled transnational organised crime, and not encroaching on the rights of those sections of the community (e.g. journalists) that rely on protecting access to sensitive information but do not use it for nefarious purposes.

Law enforcement must also partner with the private sector to facilitate (1) the exchange of information and communications technology expertise, and (2) the development of novel approaches to tackling cybercrime. AUSTRAC has built public-private collaborative partnerships for financial intelligence, including with digital currency exchange providers to gain greater insight into the operation of the sector and to assist them in implementing the regulatory reforms (PJCLE, 2019).

EMERGING TRENDS IN TRANSNATIONAL AND ORGANISED CRIME

This chapter has already highlighted several emerging challenges for law enforcement. These relate primarily to the *how* of transnational organised crime, rather than the *what*. While entities continue to look to exploit new methods to profit from illicit activities, so too are they constantly exploring new opportunities and markets, driven by a combination of demand for illicit commodities, changing social and economic conditions, and weak regulatory systems. In this way, law enforcement and offenders are engaged in a co-evolutionary arms race, whereby offenders are constantly innovating to try to bypass the measures introduced to try to stop them (Brown, 2017).

Many of the illicit activities described here – drug trafficking, money laundering, organised tax fraud, and cybercrime – will continue to impact on Australia in the future. Transnational syndicates will undoubtedly find ways to circumvent current legislative, policy and law-enforcement responses and to modify the way in which they commit these crimes. But the threat of diversification also exists. An example is what has happened in North America with respect to the opioid crisis that first saw a shift from prescribed oxycodone to heroin, and then from heroin to synthetic opioids, most notably fentanyl and its analogues (often mixed with the heroin; see Brown & Morgan, 2019). Almost the entire fentanyl supply is sourced from Mexico and China, courtesy of more traditional drug trafficking networks and online purchases (Pardo et al., 2019). While the same demand does not exist in Australia, harms from prescription opioids have increased in recent years, and there has been evidence of fentanyl-contaminated methamphetamine (Voce & Sullivan, 2020).

In 2020 it is difficult to ignore the potential of COVID-19 to transform the transnational and organised crime landscape, and to understand how this might impact on law enforcement in Australia and overseas. It is too early to say with any certainty what will change as a result of the pandemic, but reports have already emerged of impacts on drug supply and emerging threats related to organised fraud and cyber-enabled crimes (Europol, 2020; Global Initiative Against Transnational Organized Crime, 2020). There is already evidence of profit-motivated offenders adapting to the opportunity to sell medical products – be they legitimate or scam products – on the Tor darknet markets (Broadhurst et al., 2020). Other trends will likely emerge, especially because the pandemic has had global repercussions.

CONCLUSION

The challenges faced by law-enforcement agencies in Australia in their attempts to tackle organised and transnational crime should not be underestimated. From an external perspective, there are multiple factors that place significant pressures on policing agencies. These include a seemingly insatiable desire for illicit drugs – especially methamphetamine – that drives commodity-focused organised-crime groups to import illicit drugs and their precursors into the country; a financial infrastructure that allows illicit funds to be laundered into the mainstream system; and ICT developments that provide offenders with both anonymity and security. At the same time, policing agencies in Australia have developed complex networks of partner agencies (both domestically and internationally) that provide access to knowledge, skills, legislative mandates, and resources to tackle organised and transnational crime. Yet the fact remains that this is (and probably always will be) a constantly changing game of cat and mouse – a game in which the mouse often gets to read (and sometimes write) the rule book before the cat gets to see it. This means that law-enforcement agencies in Australia, and the legislative framework in which they operate, must continually evolve to counter the constantly changing threat of organised and transnational crime.

REFERENCES

Attorney General's Department. (2019). *Australia's Bilateral Mutual Assistance Relationships*. Retrieved from: www.ag.gov.au/Internationalrelations/International crimecooperationarrangements/Documents/bilateral-treaties-on-mutual-assistance-in-criminal-matters.pdf.

Australian Bureau of Statistics. (1997). *Crime and Justice: The Criminal Justice System*. Retrieved from: www.abs.gov.au/AUSSTATS/abs@.nsf/2f762f95845417aeca257 06c00834efa/a4d719473be50fdfca2570ec001b2c95!OpenDocument.

Australian Criminal Intelligence Commission (ACIC). (2017). *Organised Crime in Australia 2017*. Retrieved from: www.acic.gov.au/publications/intelligence-products/organised-crime-australia.

Australian Criminal Intelligence Commission (ACIC). (2018). *2017–18 Annual Report*. Retrieved from: https://acic.govcms.gov.au/sites/g/files/net3726/f/acic_2017-18_ar_digital.pdf?v=1539748074.

Australian Criminal Intelligence Commission (ACIC). (2018, December 6). *National Criminal Intelligence System* [Text]. Retrieved from: www.acic.gov.au/ncis.

Australian Criminal Intelligence Commission (ACIC). (2019). *Illicit Drug Data Report 2017–18*. Retrieved from: www.acic.gov.au/publications/reports/illicit-drug-data-report.

Australian Criminal Intelligence Commission (ACIC). (2020). *National Wastewater Drug Monitoring Program: Report 9*. Retrieved from: www.acic.gov.au/sites/default/files/2020/03/nwdmp-r9-060220_ec_v8_small.pdf?v=1583758864.

Australian Federal Police. (2019). *Annual Report 2018–19*. Retrieved from: www.afp.gov.au/sites/default/files/PDF/Reports/AnnualReport2018-19.pdf.

Australian Tax Office. (2019, March 28). *Serious Financial Crime Case Studies*. Retrieved from: www.ato.gov.au/General/The-fight-against-tax-crime/News-and-results/Case-studies/Serious-financial-crime-case-studies/?default.

Australian Transaction Reports and Analysis Centre (AUSTRAC). (2018, June 4). *AUSTRAC and CBA Agree $700m Penalty*. Retrieved from: www.austrac.gov.au/austrac-and-cba-agree-700m-penalty.

Ayling, J., & Broadhurst, R. (2014). Organized Crime Control in Australia and New Zealand. In L. Paoli (Ed.), *The Oxford Handbook of Organized Crime* (pp. 612–633). Oxford: Oxford University Press.

Bradford, D., & Payne, J. (2012). Illicit Drug Use and Property Offending Among Police Detainees. *Crime and Justice Bulletin*, 157, 1–12.

Broadhurst, R., Ball, M., & Jiang, C. J. (2020). Availability of COVID-19 Related Products on Tor Darknet Markets. *Statistical Bulletin*, 24, 1–12.

Broadhurst, R., & Ganapathy, N. (2008). Organised Crime in Asia: A Review of Problems. *Asian Criminology*, 3(1), 1–12.

Brown, R. (2017). Vehicle Crime Prevention and the Co-Evolutionary Arms Race: Recent Offender Countermoves Using Immobiliser Bypass Technology. *Security Journal*, 30(1), 60–73.

Brown, R., & Gillespie, S. (2015). Overseas Financial Investigation of Organised Crime: Examining the Barriers to Effective Implementation. *Journal of Money Laundering Control*, 18(3), 371–381.

Brown, R., & Morgan, A. (2019). The Opioid Epidemic in North America: Implications for Australia. *Trends and Issues in Crime & Criminal Justice*, 578, 1–15.

Brun, J. P., Gray, L., Scott, C., & Stephenson, K. M. (2011). *Asset Recovery Handbook: A Guide for Practitioners (English)*. World Bank Group. Retrieved from: https://star.worldbank.org/sites/star/files/asset_recovery_handbook_0.pdf.

Caldwell, F. (2019, June 18). Push to Force Out Bikies Leads to 139 Fewer Patched Members in Four Years. *Brisbane Times*. Retrieved from: www.brisbanetimes.com.au/politics/queensland/push-to-force-out-bikies-leads-to-139-fewer-patched-members-in-four-years-20190618-p51yqt.html.

Choo, K.-K. R., & Grabosky, P. (2014). Cybercrime. In L. Paoli (Ed.), *The Oxford Handbook of Organized Crime* (pp. 482–499). Oxford: Oxford University Press.

Crime and Misconduct Commission. (2009). *Money Laundering and Organised Crime in Queensland: A Strategic Assessment* (No. 11; Crime Bulletin Series). Crime and Misconduct Commission.

Cunliffe, J., Martin, J., Décary-Hétu, D., & Aldridge, J. (2017). An Island Apart? Risks and Prices in the Australian Cryptomarket Drug Trade. *International Journal of Drug Policy*, 50, 64–73.

Department of Home Affairs. (2019). *Department of Home Affairs Annual Report*. Retrieved from: www.homeaffairs.gov.au/reports-and-pubs/Annualreports/home-affairs-annual-report-2018-19.pdf.

Dowling, C., & Morgan, A. (2018). Is Methamphetamine Use Associated with Domestic Violence? *Trends & Issues in Crime and Criminal Justice*, 563, 1–15.

Europol. (2020). *Catching the Virus Cybercrime, Disinformation and the COVID-19 Pandemic*. European Union Agency for Law Enforcement Cooperation. Retrieved from: www.europol.europa.eu/publications-documents/catching-virus-cybercrime-disinformation-and-covid-19-pandemic.

Fijnaut, C. (2012). The Globalisation of Police and Judicial Cooperation: Drivers, Substance and Organisational Arrangements, Political Complications. In S. Hufnagel, C. Harfield, & S. Bronitt (Eds.), *Cross-Border Law Enforcement: Regional Law Enforcement Cooperation – European, Australian and Asia-Pacific Perspectives*. London: Routledge.

Fitzgerald, G. E. (1987). *The Fitzgerald Inquiry: Commission of Inquiry into Possible Illegal Activities and Associated Police Misconduct*. Queensland Parliament. Retrieved from: www.ccc.qld.gov.au/publications/fitzgerald-inquiry-report

Foley, S., Karlsen, J. R., & Putniņs, T. J. (2019). Sex, Drugs, and Bitcoin: How Much Illegal Activity Is Financed Through Cryptocurrencies? *The Review of Financial Studies*, 32(5), 1798–1853.

Global Initiative Against Transnational Organized Crime. (2020). *Crime and Contagion: The Impact of a Pandemic on Organized crime*. Global Initiative Against Transnational Organized Crime. Retrieved from: https://globalinitiative.net/crime-contagion-impact-covid-crime/.

Graycar, A. (2015). Corruption: Classification and Analysis. *Policy and Society*, 34(2), 87–96.

Holmes, T. (2020). Anti-Doping Boss David Sharpe Handed More Power, Promoted to Head Up New Sport Integrity Agency. *ABC News*, 3 May. Retrieved from: www.abc.net.au/news/2020-05-03/anti-doping-boss-heads-new-sporting-integrity-agency/12209624.

Kennedy, G. A. (2004). *Royal Commission into Whether There Has Been Corrupt or Criminal Conduct by Any Western Australian Police Officers: Final Report (Volume 1)*. Parliament of Western Australia. Retrieved from: www.parliament.wa.gov.au/

intranet/libpages.nsf/WebFiles/Royal+Commission+into+whether+there+has+been+any+corrupt+or+criminal+Conduct+by+Western+Australian+Police+officer+final+report+Volume+1+part+1/$FILE/WA+police+vol+1+part+1.pdf.

Lavorgna, A. (2015). Organised Crime Goes Online: Realities and Challenges. *Journal of Money Laundering Control*, *18*(2), 153–168.

Law Reform, Drugs and Crime Prevention Committee. (2014). *Inquiry into the Supply and Use of Methamphetamines, Particularly 'Ice', in Victoria: Final Report* (p. 428). Parliament of Victoria. Retrieved from: www.parliament.vic.gov.au/57th-parliament/lrdcpc/article/2135.

Leukfeldt, E. R., Lavorgna, A., & Kleemans, E. R. (2017). Organised Cybercrime or Cybercrime That Is Organised? An Assessment of the Conceptualisation of Financial Cybercrime as Organised Crime. *European Journal on Criminal Policy and Research*, *23*(3), 287–300.

Levi, M. (2014). Money Laundering. In L. Paoli (Ed.), *The Oxford Handbook of Organized Crime* (pp. 419–443). Oxford: Oxford University Press.

McCurdo, M. (2019). *Royal Commission into the Management of Police Informants: Progress Report*. State of Victoria. Retrieved from: www.rcmpi.vic.gov.au/.

McKetin, R., Lubman, D. I., Najman, J. M., Dawe, S., Butterworth, P., & Baker, A. L. (2014). Does Methamphetamine Use Increase Violent Behaviour? Evidence from a Prospective Longitudinal Study: Methamphetamine Use and Violence. *Addiction*, *109*(5), 798–806.

Morgan, A., Dowling, C., Brown, R., Mann, M., Voce, I., & Smith, M. (2016). *Evaluation of the Australian Cybercrime Online Reporting Network*. Australian Institute of Criminology. Retrieved from: https://aic.gov.au/sites/default/files/2018/08/acorn_evaluation_report_.pdf.

Morgan, A., Dowling, C., & Voce, I. (2020). Australian Outlaw Motorcycle Gang Involvement in Violent and Organised Crime. *Trends & Issues in Crime and Criminal Justice*, *586*, 1–18.

National Crime Agency. (2020). *National Strategic Assessment of Serious and Organised Crime 2020*. Retrieved from: www.nationalcrimeagency.gov.uk/who-we-are/publications/437-national-strategic-assessment-of-serious-and-organised-crime-2020/file.

Office of Police Integrity. (2007). *Past Patters – Future Directions: Victoria Police and the Problem of Corruption and Serious Misconduct:* Office of Police Integrity. Retrieved from: www.ibac.vic.gov.au/docs/default-source/reports/opi-report/past-patterns-future-directions – feb-2007.pdf?sfvrsn=dc586175_8.

Pardo, B., Taylor, J., Caulkins, J., Kilmer, B., Reuter, P., & Stein, B. (2019). *The Future of Fentanyl and Other Synthetic Opioids*. RAND Corporation.

Parliamentary Joint Committee on Law Enforcement. (2019). *Impact of New and Emerging Information and Communications Technology*. Retrieved from: www.aph.gov.au/Parliamentary_Business/Committees/Joint/Law_Enforcement/NewandemergingICT/~/media/Committees/le_ctte/NewandemergingICT/report.pdf.

Phelan, M. (2019, February 19). *ACIC CEO Press Club address: Child exploitation*. Retrieved from: www.acic.gov.au/media-centre/media-releases-and-statements/acic-ceo-press-club-address-child-exploitation.

Rowe, E., Akman, T., Smith, R. G., & Tomison, A. M. (2013). Organised Crime and Public Sector Corruption: A Crime Scripts Analysis of Tactical Displacement Risks. *Trends & Issues in Crime and Criminal Justice*, *444*, 1–7.

Sarre, R. (2017). Metadata Retention as a Means of Combatting Terrorism and Organised Crime: A Perspective from Australia. *Asian Journal of Criminology*, *12*(3), 167–179.

Smith, R. G. (2018). *Estimating the Costs of Serious and Organised Crime in Australia 2016–17* (No. 9; Statistical Report). Canberra: Australian Institute of Criminology.

Smith, R. G., Oberman, T., & Fuller, G. (2018). Understanding and Responding to Serious and Organised Crime Involvement in Public Sector Corruption. *Trends & Issues in Crime and Criminal Justice*, *534*, 1–16.

United Nations. (2000). *United Nations Convention against Transnational Organised Crime*. General Assembly Resolution 55/25. Retrieved from: www.unodc.org/documents/treaties/UNTOC/Publications/TOC%20Convention/TOCebook-e.pdf.

United Nations Office of Drugs and Crime. (2019). *Transnational Organised Crime in Southeast Asia: Evolution, Growth and Impact*. Retrieved from: www.unodc.org/unodc/en/frontpage/2019/July/organised-crime-syndicates-are-targeting-south east-asia-to-expand-operations_-unodc.html.

United Nations Office on Drugs and Crime. (n.d.) *Transnational Organised Crime*. Retrieved from: www.unodc.org/ropan/en/organized-crime.html.

Voce, A., & Sullivan, T. (2018). *Drug Use Monitoring in Australia: Drug Use Among Police Detainees, 2018* (No. 18; Statistical Report). Australian Institute of Criminology.

Voce, A., & Sullivan, T. (2020). Is There Fentanyl Contamination in the Australian Illicit Drug Market? *Statistical Bulletin*, *21*, 1–7.

von Lampe, K. (2020). *Definitions of Organised Crime*. Retrieved from: www.ceic.gouv.qc.ca/fileadmin/Fichiers_client/centre_documentaire/CEIC-R-3538.pdf.

Whetton, S., Shanahan, M., Cartwright, K., Duraisingam, V., Ferrante, A., Gray, D., Kaye, S., Kostadinov, V., Mcketin, R., Pidd, K., Roche, A. M., Tait, R. J., & Allsop, S. (2016). *The Social Costs of Methamphetamine in Australia 2013/14*. National Drug Research Institute. Retrieved from: http://ndri.curtin.edu.au/ndri/media/documents/publications/T246updated.pdf.

Wood, J. R. (1997). *Royal Commission into the New South Wales Police Service*. NSW Parliament. Retrieved from: https://data.gov.au/dataset/ds-nsw-189a1a08-cdf6-4901-9e33-dedc8e82d87e/details?q=royal%20commission.

CHAPTER 20

Policing cybercrime
An inside look at private and public cybercrime investigations

Alana Maurushat and Hadeel Al-Alosi

INTRODUCTION

As a general rule, cybercrime presents a plethora of policing challenges that are not as prevalent in traditional crimes. It is often a false belief amongst lawmakers that if the right legislation is enacted and if enough resources are allocated to the task, that both the law and its enforcement can rise up to the challenge and overcome a myriad of obstacles to combat cybersecurity and cybercrime. Cybercrime investigations, whether it be for online sale of drugs, online fraud, or hacking (unauthorised access, modification or impairment/interference with data or data systems), involve unique challenges. The challenges involve difficulties with harmonisation of laws, jurisdictional issues, policing resource implications, lack of training, ambiguity in terms of how a criminal provision will be interpreted alongside human rights protections, and, above all, a host of technical hurdles making tracing back to the "offender" difficult (Huey, 2002). Depending on the type of cybercrime, the ideal remedy sought by the victim is not a prison sentence for the offender – for example, in online fraud, it is asset recovery; in cyber-intrusion, it is mitigating damages and asset recovery; and in child sexual abuse, it is saving and removing the child from a dangerous situation. In spite of advances in machine learning, big data techniques, and artificial intelligence, attribution remains a formidable challenge (Maurushat, 2016).

This chapter excludes the policing of a number of other cybercrimes such as cyber-intrusion (hacking), sextortion, identity crime, online counterfeit goods sales, ransomware, and online copyright infringement; however, focus on three subsets which provide a good contrast in private versus public policing are presented. Each section is further broken down to address terminology and overview, case studies, and an analysis of key issues and challenges for policing. Where possible, the chapter refers to case studies in which Australia had either a victim link or where an Australian private or law enforcement was involved in the investigation. Accordingly, any reference to law is to Australian law.

ORGANISED ONLINE INVESTMENT FRAUD

Organised online fraud is a billion-dollar industry performed by both solo perpetrators and syndicates with organisations as complex as any legitimate medium-size company. There are hundreds of different types of online fraud, including, but not limited to, sextortion, investment fraud, business email compromise, ransomware, Nigerian Prince scams, lotto scams, love scams, cryptocurrency trading, binary option scams, sports trading scams, predatory pricing scams, ticket scams, investment fraud, boiler room scams, and others (PWC, 2018). This section will focus on two organised online fraud investigations: cryptocurrency fraud and boiler room fraud. The names, organisations, and any detailed personal information have been changed for security and privacy reasons. Pseudonymised interviews were conducted with the lead private investigators for each of these instances. For further discussion of these types of crimes, see the *60 Minutes* TV program report, "Scammers" (60 Minutes, 2019).

Terminology and overview

Cryptocurrency: The successes of Bitcoin and other online cryptocurrencies have provided a windfall for scammers. Using the same public funding model as many legitimate businesses, criminals posing as tech start-ups make an Initial Coin Offering (ICO) to investors, with the guarantee that their cryptocurrency will be valuable in the future. The fraudsters then disappear.

Boiler room fraud: A boiler room investment scam uses high-pressure cold calling and dishonest sales tactics to sell a range of investments over the phone. Criminals promote purported stocks they have shares in, which drives up their value, so they can profit without returning anything to the investor. Boiler room scams are usually a cross-border crime, with call centres in the Philippines and other countries that use virtual offices to create the illusion of a large international financial advisory firm.

Key issues and challenges

Ironically, the main reason why using a private investigator is more effective than the use of law enforcement is the highly practical issue of remedy. If you lose $2 million dollars, it is likely that recovering the money would be your first priority. A successful arrest and prosecution resulting in prison time would be a secondary benefit. The laws in many jurisdictions, however, are designed such that a successful police operation may result in arrest, prosecution, and jail time, but no money is recovered. Often the money has been laundered in safe-haven

CASE STUDIES

Case A: Cryptocurrency Fraud of John Smith for SoMEMoney Cryptocurrency

SoMEMoney set up a website and advertised heavily on social media about investment opportunities in a new cryptocurrency. This is known as an initial coin offering (ICO). Investors are offered the opportunity to receive coin tokens in the cryptocurrency in exchange for money. While legitimate initial coin offerings exist, many are fraudulent. SoMEMoney was an ICO that was marketed as the next Bitcoin. The company did not have any real technology or business plan to back it, and in this instance, likely no industry or computer science experience. The only notable experience was in marketing. There were links on social media sites Facebook and Linked-In for the opportunity.

John Smith clicked on the link, was directed to a website that looked very professional and legitimate. There was a number to call for more information or you could leave your information and have a broker return the call. An unregistered broker called John Smith and walked him through the investment. He then transferred an investment of $10,000 to a bank in Hong Kong. The website was linked to what appeared to be an Online Trading Platform. When John logged onto the platform it appeared as though the SoMeMoney was being heavily invested in, and he would receive great return on an investment, so he invested $100,000. John spoke about his investment with friends, and one of them notified him that this looked similar to some of the scams found on the Australian Competition and Consumer Commission's (ACCC) website. The ACCC is the Australian regulator for competition and national consumer law with jurisdiction over scams.

John contacted his local police and lodged the crime with the Australian Cybercrime Online Reporting Network (ACORN) and the ACCC. They all told him that, unfortunately, there was nothing they could do to recover his funds, or to investigate the fraudsters. John contacted a private firm that informed him that they had five other clients in the same situation. The private firm was able to trace the call centre to a South East Asian country. The mastermind behind the scam is a known fraudster from Canada. The investigation is ongoing, and measures to recover assets are also ongoing. The private firm is working with local police authorities in the South East Asian country to prosecute and recover assets of the victims.[1]

Case B: AI-enabled predictive analytics software for sports trading fraud – organised criminal syndicate

A private firm was retained by media to do surveillance work on a fraudster operating in the Gold Coast of Australia. The private firm discovered that the known fraudster was working with very well-known fraudster who had served multiple short jail sentences for previous fraud scams. The private firm as a matter of coincidence received a phone call from a new client detailing how they invested $50,000 in a sports trading AI-enabled predictive analytics software. The product was said to be able to predict the outcome of sporting events and thereby enable the user to place winning gambling bets on various upcoming sports matches. This online scam promised lucrative returns to investors who paid for exclusive access. When users complained that they weren't making money, the company responded by saying that they must not have configured it properly, and for extra money the company would assist them with this configuration. The firm was quickly able to find several more people who had experienced similar frauds by the same scam.

After a six-month investigation, the private firm was able to map out the organised syndicate's structure, members, and money-laundering structure. The firm was able to track bank accounts in Vanuatu, the Cayman Islands, and Hong Kong, and were able to freeze some accounts owned by the fraudsters (Murphy, 2010). However, the surrendering of $100,000 AUD in Hong Kong to freeze the assets, which is only given back after a successful criminal or civil litigation, is required.[2] After a lengthy class action lawsuit in Australia, the stolen assets were recovered. Unfortunately, the fraudster was able to drag out the proceedings for a significant time. A litigation funder was sought to ensure that the case could continue. Even though nearly $2 million dollars was recovered, most of this money had to be returned to the litigation funder, lawyers, and to pay for the investigation. This is because Australia has a bifurcated system for fraud whereby law enforcement prosecutes the offender but does not provide any assistance in asset recovery. Victims must seek the help of a law firm or investigation firm to help them recover stolen money. In other jurisdictions such as the United States and even in South East Asia countries, these two processes are merged, and law enforcement assists in both matters. The fraudster spent a few years in jail. He is now out and within a week of release, has set up new online scams with websites registered in Cambodia.[3]

Similar to the cryptocurrency fraud, when the victims contacted state and federal agencies, as well as Interpol, they were told that there was nothing that could be done or were merely given a case file number with no follow up.

jurisdictions, or increasingly is stored as a cryptocurrency – both of which are tremendously difficult to recover funds from. Or if money was miraculously recovered, the enabling legislation for proceeds of crime is inherently complex, expensive, and challenging, as the victim must bring a case before the court. Even when there has been a successful civil claim to recover funds, it is often the case that the defendant will claim bankruptcy. The portion of assets recovered generally is merely the tip of the iceberg. The remainder of money obtained through fraudulent means (anywhere from a few million to hundreds of millions) is nearly always located in tax and money-laundering havens or in untouchable cryptocurrencies.

The cryptocurrency case involved people, technology, workplaces, and banks in 32 jurisdictions. In jurisdictions such as Australia, fraud is handled by state law enforcement. This typically means that most successful fraud cases are ones where the criminal and victim are located in the same state. Online fraud is rarely based in one jurisdiction, and organised online fraud even less so. The author has seen cases involving more than 52 jurisdictions, and based on the interview with Investigator 1, he has worked on over 3,000 fraud cases with only two being based solely within the State of NSW, Australia. Organised online crime is sophisticated. Tackling this successfully requires both national and international coordination. In Australia at least, the Australian Federal Police (AFP) needs to take the lead on fraud cases instead of the state. For example, asking for help from overseas law enforcement must go through the designed authority under the Convention on Cybercrime. If a police officer in the State of Queensland had a lead on someone in England, a request to assist would have to go through the AFP.

In a 2019 Parliamentary Business Committee Report the Australian Securities and Investment Commission (ASIC) discussed key challenges for the investigation of scams where the darknet is involved, stating that there was a "lack of technological software and tools that have a specific focus on financial crimes, as typically the focus is on narcotics and terrorism" (ASIC Submission, 2019).

Statistics are frightfully poor for organised fraud. Often a victim will contact law enforcement and then be told that there is nothing that they can do about it given the complexity and jurisdictional issues. If an organisation lost $20,000 due to online fraud, this simply wouldn't be sufficient to warrant an investigation. But the real crime is that the details of the fraud are not necessarily captured into databases allowing fraud cases to be linked within the state, nation, and around the world.

This is very problematic. On paper a victim may only have lost $20,000, but collectively, if the data were analysed, the same fraud may have affected hundreds of victims around the world with totals lost closer to the $200,000,0000 AUD mark. This is simply not captured in the way law enforcement collects data or chooses not to record data accurately. Indeed, there are many barriers to law enforcement sharing raw data, as well as data analytics both between states within Australia, with regulators such as the ACCC, and especially with overseas law enforcement.

Hiring a private investigation firm specialising in asset recovery is a more effective way of recording funds lost, but this is simply not an option for most victims. A typical investigation will cost between $250,000 to $500,000 AUD. A victim would have to put this money up front to run the investigation without the guarantee of asset recovery. Often multiple victims will pool their money to run the investigations, but more times than not, a private investigation is out of reach for the victim.

Some victims, no matter how much assistance or education gained, continue to be victimized on countless occasions. Dealing with protective strategies for vulnerable people remains a difficult task (Drew, 2020).

One concept that has yet to be fully explored in the online fraud space is to offer a bounty for information leading to the arrest behind organised cybercrime fraud. A firm would invest their own money to investigate online fraud syndicates and then receive a large portion of the funds recovered. The incentive would have to be substantial, but it could prove to be an effective method in the future. How such a program would look in practice would clearly present with many significant challenges. As online fraud becomes more advanced incorporating AI enabled malware, traceback to the individuals and organisations involved in fraud will become more difficult. New methods such as bounties may be required as the technologies progress.

ONLINE DISTRIBUTION AND SALE OF DRUGS IN DARKNET FORUMS

Technology has disrupted the way in which drugs have been traditionally sold. Both the wholesale market (where drugs are trafficked in large quantities), and the retail market (where drugs are sold in smaller quantities directly to users) have undergone change. Instead of transacting on the street where law enforcement may be watching, or by phone that is subject to phone tapping, or on the net which is increasingly subject to surveillance by the state, buyers and sellers are able to transact online, using what is known as a "darkweb" (also known as the "darknet"). In addition, instead of paying in cash, bank transfer, or more traditional means, payments can now be made using "cryptocurrencies" (Aldrige & Decary-Hétu, 2016). Both the darkweb and cryptocurrencies use online encrypted communications, which add a layer of complexity to the communications, making surveillance by law enforcement more difficult.

Terminology and overview

Transacting on the darkweb requires the use of anonymising technologies. The darkweb is a free non-indexed network. However, instead of using a mainstream browser (Firefox or Chrome) darknet users download a different browser, known as a TOR browser. The TOR browser still communicates via a commercial internet service provider, which then sends all communication directly to the TOR network (TOR Project). Communications between the TOR browser and TOR network are encrypted, often via a VPN (virtual private network). Sellers and distributors of illegal goods on the darkweb often additionally use TAILS. TAILS is a live operating system that you can start on almost any computer from a USB or DVD. It ensures that the user cannot accidently forget to log into a darknet forum without the use of TOR. The only evidence TAILS leaves on a laptop is a temporary file (e.g. tails-i8584–5.8.1) in the desktop admin. This only indicates that someone searched for TAILS and may have used it. It does not indicate if the device was used to connect to the darknet, or anything further, other than TAILS may have been used for something.

In addition, instead of paying in cash, bank transfer or more traditional means, payments use cryptocurrencies such as Bitcoin and Monero (Sharma, 2018). Both the darkweb and cryptocurrencies use online encrypted communications, which add a layer of complexity to the communications, making surveillance by law enforcement more difficult (Bartlett, 2015).

Drugs purchased for personal use on the darknet are often sent via public postal services and private couriers, often disguised in DVD cases or letters, either to a home address, or to a rented post box. Australian Border Enforcement and Postal Services seize hundreds of packages containing narcotics on a daily basis (ABC 730, 2017).

International law enforcement cooperates on a range of investigations and prosecutions of online sale of illicit drugs. Recent examples include the takedown of two darknet markets, Hansa and AlphaBay (Greenberg, 2017). The FBI and US Drug Enforcement Agency organised and collaborated with law enforcement from around the world to shut down AlphaBay, which was in 2017 the world's largest darknet. AlphaBay boasted over 40,000 vendors and nearly a quarter of a million users/customers. Authorities arrested the mastermind and administrator of the site, Canadian Alexandre Cazes, in Thailand. Additionally, hundreds of arrests were made in countries around the world of various narcotic and weapons vendors selling on AlphaBay. In June 2017 Dutch police and Europol had secretly taken over the darknet market Hansa. At that time, when AlphaBay disappeared, many users and vendors flocked to competitor Hansa (Greenberg, 2017). Later in July 2017, it was publicly announced that Dutch police had been running Hansa for a month, gathering intelligence and evidence (MIX, 2017). That site was also then shut down (Aldrige & Decary-Hétu, 2016). Hundreds of arrests of vendors were made following the takedowns. Following the closure of the two largest and most popular darknet marketplaces, the ABC did a story on the amount of drugs arriving through the post and how these takedowns have given the Australian Federal Police "a trove of information about some of the darknet's anonymous users" (ABC 7:30 July 25, 2017). Thousands of people have died globally due to fentanyl overdoses; we saw much international cooperation in tackling online drug sales presumably motivated by the death toll now numbering well over 100,000 globally (National Vital Statistics Report, 2019).

> **CASE STUDY**
>
> **Strike Force Colette**
>
> Following the FBI's takedown of AlphaBay, several arrests were made around the world of those online dealers using the site to sell illicit products, and drugs in particular. Strike Force Colette was a joint investigation by NSW Police Force and the Australian Federal Police investigating illicit sale of drugs on the darknet AlphaBay (AFP Media Release 2017).
>
> Shortly following the FBI's take down of AlphaBay, a 43-year-old man was arrested in Sydney and charged with eight counts of drug supply, dealing with property proceeds of crime, and supplying prohibited drugs on an ongoing basis – all trading done over AlphaBay. The only further publicly available information about the arrest is video footage on Channel 9 News (9 Nws Dark Web Arrest: Sydney Man Charged Over Secret Drug Network). Whether he was convicted of these counts in not publicly available information. It was reported that "sophisticated hardware and software encryption" was used, while MDMA, magic mushrooms, and $12,000 cash was found; fentanyl was not found.

Key issues and challenges

Sites that have been taken down by law enforcement provide a rich source of data to analyse to study the functioning of online drug markets, such as the number and location of the vendors and purchasers, the quantities of drugs sold, the types of drugs sold, and the revenue generated. One such analysis of the activity on Silk Road 1 revealed that wholesale activity (sales for listings over USD $1,000) accounted for approximately one quarter of the overall revenue, with specific countries (China, the Netherlands, Canada, and Belgium) and some drugs (Ecstasy & MDMA and prescription drugs) being associated with wholesale revenue generation (Mullin, 2015). However, most crypto markets transactions are consistent with purchase for personal use or social supply (Bartlett, 2015).

There are a number of advantages for the various stakeholders that continue to drive the reincarnation of drug crypto markets. For buyers, there is a wide variety of drugs available via a convenient delivery system. Buyers have the opportunity to select from a global market of distributors, allowing purchasers to restrict their purchases to suppliers in specific countries. Purchasers are able to transact anonymously from their home, without the need to meet a seller in an unsafe location. However, if the drugs are posted via the mail, the purchaser ultimately needs to provide a physical address.

An extensive report by the European Monitoring Centre for Drugs and Drug Addiction investigated the world of online drug markets and found that drugs purchased via the darknet tend to be of higher purity than drugs purchased off the streets (Mountenay, 2016). In other words, the quality of the drugs supplied tends to match the quality marketed, and so buyers tend to get what they pay for. However, lower-cost prescription medicine is also sold and traded on these markets (Zabyelina, 2017).

Some sites incorporate harm reduction forums into their sites, enabling users to seek advice and support in order to use the drugs purchased in as safe a way as possible, creating a supportive community. Many of the middlemen in the transaction are cut out of the conventional supply chain, such as bikie gangs; international traffickers; and organised crime syndicates, who traditionally use violence, intimidation, and corruption of law enforcement to dominate and control. Online sales encourage non-violent markets for illicit drug trading.

Sellers no longer require personal introductions to buyers. Therefore, sellers are not limited by physical boundaries and distance and have the ability to trade globally, which greatly increases their reach to new markets. They no longer need to resort to traditional forms of intimidation and violence to promote sales and eliminate competition – taking out competition is done through reputation, just like legitimate competition between two companies in the real world. Ratings and customer feedback are similar to those used by EBay and Airbnb, which provide a powerful incentive for sellers to provide quality service and product. They even provide free samples for new clients.

The darknet continues to be attractive to those wishing to buy and sell drugs, due to the illicit nature of the enterprise, with new technologies and strategies constantly being developed to reduce the risk of detection. As a result of a combination of factors, including sustained international demand for drugs, a growing population of tech-savvy users, expanding access to the internet, and ever-developing technology to stay one step ahead of law enforcement, the darknet will continue to be attractive to the online sale and purchase of illicit drugs. While the use of new forensic tools such as Cellebrite is greatly assisting law enforcement by allowing them to perform forensics on heavily encrypted devices such as iPhones, the criminals will look to new technologies to assist them, or they will merely move back to traditional sale on the streets. Criminals are now using new unsuspecting avenues such as the video game platform Discord (Brewster, 2019). The FBI is actively investigating cybercriminal activity on the platform, including child grooming, stolen data, criminalised hate speech, and the sale of drugs (FBI, 2018).

ONLINE CHILD SEXUAL ABUSE MATERIAL

The market for child abuse material (CAM) has proliferated with the rapid expansion of the internet since the 1990s, creating unique challenges for law-enforcement agencies. The market for child abuse material (CAM) has proliferated with the rapid expansion of the internet since the 1990s, creating unique challenges for law-enforcement agencies (see Al-Alosi, 2018 for an extensive discussion about this issue). This situation exists largely because of the relative anonymity the internet provides for offenders to instantly access CAM online. The focus of this part of the chapter is on what CAM is, its prevalence, nature, law-enforcement responses to tackle such material, and some of the pressing challenges and issues associated with policing online CAM.

Terminology and overview

In Australia, which has a federal system style of government, the Commonwealth and each state and territory have their own police forces and legislation dealing with CAM. In Australia, which has a federal system style of government, the Commonwealth and each state and territory have their own police forces and legislation dealing with CAM (see Al-Alosi, 2018). The police are primarily responsible for conducting criminal investigations and then refering suspects to prosecutors who have the discretion to start criminal proceedings for breach of the law.

Many jurisdictions have now formed specialist units dedicated specifically to combating CAM. For example, in New South Wales, the Child Exploitation Internet Unit, which is part of the Child Abuse Sex Crime Squad, was established to target the production, dissemination, and possession of CAM facilitated by the internet and telecommunication systems. Other Australian jurisdictions have also formed specialist forces, such as the Queensland Task Force Argos.

Law-enforcement agencies use a range of strategies to identify and locate offenders. This includes covert policing and sting operations, which involve deceiving suspects and may involve police engaging in activity that is criminal to obtain evidence. Covert policing may also entail undercover officers encouraging suspects to commit a crime, which raises "the serious issue of crime amplification: the possibility that the very undercover investigation meant to catch criminals in the act may actually produce more crime" (Joh, 2009).

Given the global spread of CAM and borderless nature of the internet, police forces in Australia and other parts of the world have recognised the need to coordinate sting operations. For example, in 2003, the United Kingdom National Crime Squad worked with forces from countries such Australia, Canada, and the United States to introduce "Operation PIN". The purpose of the operation was to catch internet users seeking CAM. They worked with search engine operators to create fake websites purporting to offer illegal images (Ward, 2003). Another controversial example is Operation Ore, which was launched in the

> **CASE STUDY**
>
> Queensland Taskforce Argos is a specialist unit within the Queensland Police Service, formed in 1997 to investigate online child exploitation and abuse. It is recognised as a global leader in the policing of online child sexual abuse and has established relationships with international counterparts to tackle this global problem (Queensland Organised Crime Commission of Inquiry, 2015).
>
> Taskforce Argos have engaged in several noteworthy operations that have effectively led to the identification and prosecution of offenders and have saved victims. This includes involvement in the multinational Operation Auxin in 2004, which detected 720 suspects, resulting in the arrest of over 200 people and the seizure of more than 10 million CAM images (Queensland Sentencing Advisory Council, 2017). In 2017, Taskforce Argos took over the website Child's Play – claimed to be "the world's largest" CAM forum on the darkweb with approximately a million members (McInnes, 2017; Fairless, 2019). After the creators of the website in the United States were arrested, the task force was able to obtain the passwords from the creators and then posed as the administrators of the forum. During the 11-month operation, the task force regularly posted pre-existing CAM to prevent raising suspicion among members, which has led to criticism of the methods used by the officers (Hoydal et al., 2017). However, the officers involved have justified their actions as necessary to achieve the goals of the investigation and ultimately shut down the website (Hoydal et al., 2017). At the conclusion of the operation, Taskforce Argos had identified up to 90% of users and made 1,000 arrests (Iaccino, 2017). In many jurisdictions, the police officer's actions would have been illegal, but the task force was protected under the provisions of the Queensland Police Powers and Responsibilities Act 2000, which gives the police broad powers to conduct controlled operations.

United Kingdom in 2002 (Gillespie, 2011). Police in Australia, such as police from the NSW Child Abuse and Sex Crimes Squad's Child Exploitation Internet Unit, have also adopted fictitious personas online to catch predators (Noyes, 2019).

Key issues and challenges

The internet has made it possible for individuals to create and disseminate CAM anywhere around the globe, and CAM offences tend to involve multiple jurisdictions. The transnational nature of CAM offences creates challenges for law enforcement in tracing the origin of the images as well as detecting offenders and identifying victims. Accordingly, cooperation and mutual assistance to extradite offenders is vital. The global reach of the internet may also require extending law-enforcement powers beyond their respective national borders.

Inconsistent legislation in different jurisdictions may further hinder law enforcement, as many states require the laws to be equivalent as a condition of providing mutual legal assistance (Broadhurst, 2019). For example, in some jurisdictions, viewing CAM online (but not storing or downloading it) may not be considered possession, making it difficult to prosecute viewers of such material. The lack of a unified definition of the term "child" and consensus regarding what content is explicit enough to constitute CAM among some states also raises issues for law enforcement. For instance, in some jurisdictions, a child is defined as a person less than 18, while in others a child is a defined as less than 16 (Wells et al., 2007). Consequently, what may be considered CAM in one jurisdiction may be legal in another.

Another challenge for law enforcement is the rise of youth-produced sexual images (also known as "sexting"). Sexually explicit images of youths may meet the definition of CAM in some jurisdictions if the person depicted appears to be a child in a sexual context. Since it is not always easy to determine the age of older juveniles, law enforcement may experience difficulty, and incur considerable costs, trying to ascertain the age of the person depicted. Another challenge is establishing whether the material was produced "as part of coercive activity by adults or peers, or represent behaviour that is consistent with adolescent development and risk-taking" (ECPAT, 2018).

Of course, keeping up to date with technology carries further significant cost implications. This includes costs associated with training staff and being able to fund the required technology. Coordinated efforts may partly alleviate the issue of scarce resources by allowing law-enforcement agencies to pool their resources and expertise as well as avoid duplication efforts. Notably, in 2018, the Australian Government announced it will provide the Australian Federal Police $68.6 million over the next four years to foster a collaborative response to tackle online CAM (AFP, 2019).

Law enforcement engaging in sting operations to catch offenders raises serious ethical concerns. Little is known about the nature and frequency of these operations, which restricts public scrutiny and creates a greater risk of police abusing their powers (Joh, 2009). Of course, transparency in policing is vital, but publicity of police tactics may also reduce their effectiveness, thereby creating another dilemma of whether to publicise their efforts or not.

Nevertheless, it is important for police investigators not to breach their ethical obligations when conducting investigations, but this may limit their ability to combat CAM (Al-Alosi, 2017). Does the end (protecting children) justify the means (using CAM to entrap suspects)? It remains contentious whether law enforcement should be allowed to use fake identifies to simulate the sale or purchase of CAM to trap suspects. If, for example, the police do not share CAM as part of covert operations, as occurred with Taskforce Argos, they may arouse suspicion among offenders. Another issue is that trading images is sometimes a condition of membership. Given the seriousness of harm to children, police deception and sting operations may in this context be seen as a "necessary though unpleasant evil" (Joh, 2009). The challenge for police is avoiding re-victimising victims in the process and ensuring they do not incite suspects to commit an offence that person would have not otherwise committed.

Often, investigators will need to examine the material seized to assess its nature, classify it, prosecute offenders, and to identify victims (Gillespie, 2011). The task of analysing the material, as well as engaging in CAM sting operations, can have significant impact on the physical and mental health of investigators, and this can impede their productivity in tackling CAM (Wortley et al., 2014; Powell et al., 2014). The harmful impact on investigators takes its emotional toll (Hoydal et al., 2017).

Thankfully, technology has provided a partial solution to the problem of having to analyse a large collection of material by the introduction of programs that scan images and identify duplicates (Gillespie, 2011). However, a need remains for more research and innovative ways to reduce investigators' exposure to CAM, as well as measures to protect investigators from the effects of dealing with CAM. While there are still many uncertainties about CAM – such as its prevalence, its impact on viewers, and the ethicality of sting operations – there is certainly a need for law-enforcement agencies worldwide to continue their collaborated efforts.

CONCLUDING REMARKS

Law enforcement has limited capability in dealing with many types of cybercrime, such as online organised fraud due to issues of jurisdiction, culture, attribution, resources, and the ability to follow leads in a timely fashion. Hiring a private cybercrime investigation firm can be effective in dealing with frauds involving multiple jurisdictions. However, the money involved makes the option simply out of reach for many individuals and organisations.

Moving forward, the emerging field of blockchain used for logistics in supply chains is promising, as is the progression towards quantum encryption and quantum decryption. Both of these methods, however, will only help prevent some forms of fraud. Their biggest contribution will be the ability to quickly de-identify devices and possibly people who are using obfuscation methods such as TAILS and TOR. Criminals are smart. They evolve to ensure a continued livelihood. Even if detection, prevention, and mitigation techniques are significantly improved, targeting the weaknesses of human beings to be socially engineered will never completely disappear. Eventually quantum-enabled equipment will be affordable and available for criminals in the future as well.

The development of specialist cybercrime units in a private/public cooperative arrangement may be one way to better assist victims of fraud (Harkin et al., 2018). The reality is that many law-enforcement units simply do not possess the requisite training and ability to tackle most emerging forms of cybercrime, and many police officers have a very specific (and sometimes narrow) view of policing cybercrime (Hadlington et al., 2018). Fortunately, organisations with capability and political will to prosecute, such as the FBI, are very proactive and collaborative in assisting with cybercrime investigations anywhere in the world.

The ability to intercept telecommunications is severely challenged at present as the existing technologies used for law-enforcement work for 3G, work somewhat for 4G, and not at all with 5G (Parliamentary Business Committee Report, 2019). This will remain a challenge until new capabilities are developed and there is the budget to purchase these technologies and services, which are expensive.

Due to the technical challenges of encryption and emerging challenges of 5G, some agencies such as the Australian Commission for Law Enforcement Integrity has noted that law enforcement must better utilise traditional and new ways of investigation, including physical surveillance, human source intelligence, agreements with private and public entities to access collected data for a law-enforcement purpose, better data management and connectivity of internal data sets, and dissemination of information and intelligence to and from other entities (Parliamentary Business Committee Report, 2019). Curiously, private investigation firms do not have access to the same vast troves of rich data held by government agencies; they rely heavily on physical surveillance and human source intelligence both within Australia, but much more importantly for cybercrime, outside of Australia. There is one common feature with the cases explored in this chapter – that cooperation between private industry, including private investigators and law enforcement, will be essential to tackle cybercrime now and into the future (Hunton, 2010).

NOTES

1 Interview with Investigator 2.
2 Interview with Investigator 1.

REFERENCES

60 Minutes. (2019). *Scammers Targeting Australians Busted in Philippines Police Raid*, 2 February. Retrieved from: www.9news.com.au/national/scammers-targeting-australians-busted-in-filipino-police-raid/a7e097ff-f446-4bc2-9b49-820bb9a0e530.

Al-Alosi, Hadeel (2018), *The Criminalisation of Fantasy Material: Law and Sexually Explicit Representations of Fictional Children*, Routledge, New York.

Al-Alosi, Hadeel (2017), "Virtual child pornography can both help and hinder law enforcement", *The Conversation*, 4 September, https://theconversation.com/virtual-child-pornography-could-both-help-and-hinder-law-enforcement-82746.

Aldridge, J., and Decary-Hétu, D. (2016). Cryptomarkets and the future of illicit drug markets. *The Internet and Drug Markets*, 23–32.

Aldridge, J. and Décary-Hétu, D. (2016). Hidden wholesale: The drug diffusing capacity of online drug cryptomarkets. *International Journal of Drug Policy*, 35, 7–15.

Australian Broadcast Corporation 730 New. (2017). *AFP Receives Fresh Intelligence After Darknet Takedown*, 25 July. Retrieved from: www.abc.net.au/7.30/afp-receives-fresh-intelligence-after-dark-net/8743110?nw=0.

Australian Federal Police. (2019). *Annual Report 2018–19*. Retrieved from: www.afp.gov.au/annual-report-2018-19.

Australian Securities and Investment Commission (ASIC), Submission to the Parliamentary Business Committee 2019 (Chapter 3 Going Dark). Retrieved from: https://aph.gov.au/Parliamentary_Business/Committees/Joint/Law_Enforcement/Newanderemerging ICT/Report3.

Bartlett, J. (2015). *The Dark Net*. London: Windmill Books.

Brewster, T. (2019). Discord: The $2 billion gamer's paradise coming to terms with data thieves, child groomers and FBI investigators. *Forbes*, 24 February 2020. Retrieved from: https://www.forbes.com/ sites/thomasbrewster/2019/01/29/discord-the-2-billion-gamers-paradise-coming-to -terms-with-data-thieves-child-groomers-and-fbi-investigators/#c4b26d137416.

Broadhurst, R. (2019). Child sex abuse images and exploitation materials. In Leukfeldt, R. and Thomas, H. (eds), *Cybercrime: The Human Factor*. London: Routledge. Retrieved from: https://ssrn.com/abstract=3384499.

Drew, J. M. (2020). A study of cybercrime victimisation and prevention: Exploring the use of online crime prevention behaviours and strategies. *Journal of Criminological Research, Policy and Practice*.

ECPAT. (2018). Trends in online child sexual abuse material. *ECPAT International*, Bangkok. Retrieved from: www.ecpat.org/wp-content/uploads/2018/07/ECPAT-International-Report-Trends-in-Online-Child-Sexual-Abuse-Material-2018.pdf.

Fairless, D. (2019). What's the best way to fight child pornography? *The Global Mail*, 22 November. Retrieved from: www.theglobeandmail.com/opinion/article-whats-the-best-way-to-fight-child-pornography.

Federal Bureau of Investigation. (2018). *2017 Internet Crime Report*. Internet Crime Complaint Center. Retrieved from: https://pdf.ic3.gov/2017_IC3Report.pdf.

Gillespie, A. (2011). *Child Pornography: Law and Policy*. New York: Routledge.

Greenberg, A. (2017). AlphaBay and Hansa takedowns ensnare thousands of dark web users. *Wired*. Retrieved from: www.wired.com/story/alphabay-hansa-takedown-dark-web-trap/.

Hadlington, L., Lumsden, K., Black, A., and Ferra, F. (2018). A qualitative exploration of police officers' experiences, challenges, and perceptions of cybercrime. *Policing: A Journal of Policy and Practice*. https://doi.org/10.1093/police/pay090.

Hoydal, H. F., Stangvik, E. O. and Hansen, N. R. (2017). Breaking the dark net: Why the police share abuse pics to save children. *VG*, 7 October. Retrieved from: www.vg.no/spesial/2017/undercover-darkweb/?lang=en.

Harkin, D., Whelan, C. and Chang, L. (2018). The challenges facing specialist police cyber-crime units: An empirical analysis. *Police Practice and Research*, 19(6), 519–536.

Huey, L. (2002). Policing the abstract: Some observations on policing cyberspace. *Canadian Journal of Criminology*, 44(3), 243–254.

Hunton, P. (2010). Cyber crime and security: A new model of law enforcement investigation. *Policing: An International Journal of Police Strategies & Management*, 4(4), 385–395. Retrieved from: https://academic-oup-com.ezproxy.uws.edu.au/policing/article/4/4/385/1503754.

Joh, E. E. (2009). Breaking the law to enforce it: Undercover police participation in crime. *Stanford Law Review*, 62(1), 155–199.

Iaccino L. (2017). Operation Artemis: Australian police hijack world's largest paedophile site – and make 1,000 arrests. *International Business Times*, 10 October. Retrieved from: www.ibtimes.co.uk/australian-police-operated-worlds-largest-child-porn-site-dark-web-year-1642367.

Maurushat, A. (2016). Big data use by law enforcement and intelligence in the national security space. *Media and Arts Review*, 21, 229–255.

McInnes, W. (2017). Queensland police take over world's largest child porn forum in sting operation. *Brisbane Times*, 8 October. Retrieved from: www.brisbanetimes.com.au/national/queensland/queensland-police-behind-worlds-largest-child-porn-forum-20171007-gywcps.html.

MIX. (2017). *Dutch Police Secretly Ran a Huge Dark Web Drug Marketplace for a Month*, 21 July. Retrieved from: https://thenextweb.com/insider/2017/07/20/police-fbi-drug-dark-web-market/.

Mountenay, J., Bro, A. and Oteo, A. (2016). *The Internet and Drug Markets, European Monitoring Centre for Drugs and Drug Addiction*. Retrieved from: www.emcdda.europa.eu/system/files/publications/2155/TDXD16001ENN_FINAL.pdf.

Mullin, J. (2015). Ulbricht guilty in silk road online drug-trafficking trial. *Ars Technica*, 4 February. Retrieved from: https://www-emerald-com.ezproxy.uws.edu.au/insight/content/doi/10.1108/13639511211215504/full/html.

Murphy, R. (2010). World's best tax havens. *Forbes*. Retrieved from: www.forbes.com/2010/07/06/tax-havens-delaware-bermuda-markets-singapore-belgium.html#6a3819b825fc.

National Vital Statistics Reports. (2019). *Drug Overdose Deaths Involving Fentanyl 2011–2016*, 21 March. Retrieved from: www.cdc.gov/nchs/data/nvsr/nvsr68/nvsr68_03-508.pdf.

Noyes, J. (2019). Man charged over sexual assault of girl, four others held in online sting. *Sydney Morning Herald*, 10 July. Retrieved from: www.smh.com.au/national/nsw/man-charged-over-sexual-assault-of-girl-four-others-held-in-online-sting-20190710-p525rr.html.

Parliamentary Business Committee. (2019). *Going Dark, ICT/Report3*. Retrieved from: https://aph.gov.au/Parliamentary_Business/Committees/Joint/Law_Enforcement/Newanderemerging.

Powell, M., Cassematis, P., Benson, M., Smallbone, S. and Wortley, R. (2014). Police officers' strategies for coping with the stress of investigating internet child exploitation. *Traumatology: An International Journal*, 20(1), 32–42.

PWC. (2018). *Pulling Fraud Out of the Shadows: Global Economic Crime and Fraud Survey 2018*. Retrieved from: www.digitalpulse.pwc.com.au/report-gecs-global-economic-crime-fraud-survey-2018/.

Queensland Organised Crime Commission of Inquiry. (2015). *Queensland Organised Crime Commission of Inquiry Report*. Retrieved from: www.organisedcrimeinquiry.qld.gov.au/__data/assets/pdf_file/0017/935/QOCCI15287-ORGANISED-CRIME-INQUIRY_Final_Report.pdf.

Queensland Sentencing Advisory Council. (2017). *Classification of Child Exploitation Material for Sentencing Purposes: Final Report*. Brisbane: Queensland Sentencing Advisory Council.

Sharma, T. (2018). *How Does Bitcoin Money Laundering Work?* Retrieved from: www.blockchain-council.org/blockchain/how-bitcoin-money-laundering-works.

Ward, M. (2003). Online dragnet to thwart paedophiles. *BBC* (UK). Retrieved from: http://news.bbc.co.uk/2/hi/technology/3330929.stm.

Wells, M., Finkelhor, D., Wolak, J. and Mitchell, K. J. (2007). Defining child pornography: Law enforcement dilemmas in investigations of internet child pornography possession. *Police Practice and Research*, 8(3), 269–282.

Wortley, R., Smallbone, S., Powell, M. and Cassematis, P. (2014). *Understanding and Managing the Occupational Health Impacts on Investigators of Internet Child Exploitation* (Griffith University and Deakin University). Retrieved from: https://discovery.ucl.ac.uk/id/eprint/1447785/1/Wortley_Understanding%20and%20Managing%20the%20Occupational%20Health%20Impacts%20on%20Investigators%20of%20Internet%20Child%20Exploitation.pdf.

Zabyelina, Y. G. (2017). Can criminals create opportunities for crime? Malvertising and illegal online medicine trade. *Global Crime*, 18(1), 31–48.

CHAPTER 21

Australian police officers and international policing practice

Kelly Moylan, Irena Veljanova, Michael Kennedy, and Philip Birch

INTRODUCTION

Modern day policing has undergone a significant transformation beyond local policing within geographically defined areas, evolving with the age of globalisation and the consequent increased interconnectedness between jurisdictions. While Australia's involvement in international policing extends beyond peace operations, and includes the provision of support to international investigations, hosting liaison roles, and wider international police partnership programmes, this chapter will focus on peacekeeping and capacity building as the most significant and dynamic aspect of international policing in the 21st century. Drawing on the dataset of 41 semi-structured interviews with Australian state and federal police officers between 2013 and 2019 as well as reflecting on the wider literature, this chapter examines the key challenges facing police peacekeeping personnel during deployments to Timor-Leste and the Solomon Islands with the Australian Federal Police (AFP). While these missions have since concluded and have transitioned to partnership programmes, they represent two significant contributions that Australia has made to police peacekeeping and capacity building in the 21st century and reflect the efforts made by Australian governments to engage with policing the Asia-Pacific region. The Australian-led UN missions to Timor-Leste and subsequent Timor-Leste Police Development Program, and the Regional Assistance Mission to the Solomon Islands (RAMSI) intervention in the Solomon Islands, demonstrate the development of international policing practice from conflict cessation to post-conflict rebuilding and long-term overseas partnership initiatives. International policing grew rapidly in the latter half of the 20th century, and as we move through the 21st century, forces of globalisation, movement of people, and technological advancement continue to change the way Australian police engage with their international counterparts. Unpacking the cultural and economic context of these peace operations highlights some of the future challenges and opportunities facing Australian police peacekeepers in an increasingly complex and globalised world.

AUSTRALIAN POLICE AS PEACEKEEPERS AND CAPACITY BUILDERS: THE GLOBALISATION OF CRIME AND INSECURITY TO PEACE OPERATIONS AND POLICE REFORM

Capturing the growth of international policing in the 21st century involves recognising the fundamental shift in the integration of people across the world. Globalisation is the term coined to describe the process and phenomenon where nation states are becoming increasingly interconnected socially, politically, economically, and culturally (McGrew, 2003). The need for a successful international policing agenda is reflected by the consequences of globalisation; matters of police interest now transcend jurisdictional borders as criminal activity benefits from the same opportunities that have allowed capitalism and trade to integrate across international markets (Lemieux, 2010; Findlay, 2000). Consequently, Held and McGrew (2003) argue for the need to think much more broadly about the impact of globalisation on police practice, and how evolving crimes transcend the traditional geopolitical boundaries that have hindered criminal activity in the past. These processes move beyond concerns of local security; for example, sovereign states, particularly developing nations, can struggle to deliver security, order, and peace due to the external and economic pressures triggered by international movements in crime (Casey, 2009). Since policing has historically been constructed within nation-state systems, the prevalence of transnationalisation, or the networks of interconnectedness between individuals and organisations across global borders, is an important facet of the changing face of modern policing (Warren & Palmer, 2015; Palmer, Berlin, & Das, 2012). Such strategies demonstrate the need to recognise that policing and police practice are no longer only localised; as Chan (2005) highlights, "the local and the global have penetrated each other". Indeed, the AFP (2018a) recognise globalisation as one of the key challenges facing the organisation as they move into the future of policing, particularly due to intra-state conflict, mass migration, transnational crime, emergencies, and disasters.

While international policing takes place in a number of ways, one of the key practices engaged by police organisations is through peacekeeping and capacity building, interchangeably titled as peace operations. The term "peace operations" is used to describe a variety of intervention practices that have the goal of preventing, managing, and resolving violence and conflict (UN, 2008). While peacemaking tends to be focused on the cessation of conflict – a task which is usually discharged by the military but can also be conducted by the police – peacekeeping and peacebuilding tend to involve greater participation from civilian police. Peacekeeping typically involves facilitating law and order, the supervision of cease-fire buffer zones, investigatory measures where outside interference is alleged, reconciliation and mediation, and close observational operations where violence is likely to erupt. Beyond peacekeeping, capacity-building practices to re-establish and develop policing are used as a long-term solution once peace has been established (Goldsmith & Harris, 2017). Capacity building measures usually focus on the construction of a functioning body of police in the host nation and involve tasks which are often labelled as "reform, restructuring, and rebuilding" in transitional states (Hughes, Hunt, & Curth-Bibb, 2013; Goldsmith & Harris, 2009). Capacity development represents another facet of international policing, where there is an existing capability to be improved upon, rather than established as is the case in capacity building (McLeod, 2009). These terms are often used interchangeably, but the underlying purpose of these tasks is to facilitate the reconstruction of governance and infrastructure in conflict and post-conflict settings, inclusive of improving the operational standards within their security and criminal justice sectors.

Intra-state conflicts in a number of nations across the world, such as Timor-Leste, have led to the collapse of governance and infrastructure, humanitarian emergencies, destruction of entire communities, and violence against individuals, which all contribute to the need for humanitarian aid, peace operations, and long-term capacity building (Linden, Last, & Murphy, 2007). While peacekeeping and capacity-building operations usually occur in the context of a failed state, particularly where states are unwilling or unable to protect their own citizens, peacekeeping can also occur where there is an invitation to address crime, disorder, or emergencies by the host country in the form of humanitarian aid, such as in the Solomon Islands (Daniel, 2013; Bellamy & Drummond, 2012; Ellison & Pino, 2012; Bellamy & Davies, 2009). The changing nature and role of police peacekeeping operations, depending on the needs of the mission context, has had a significant effect on Australian police peacekeeping practices. Firstly, due to Australia's involvement in the first police peacekeeping operations, and its continued engagement over the past five decades, Australia has contributed extensively to evolving the expectations of international police peacekeeping practices. With over a thousand AFP members engaged in overseas missions throughout that time, Australian police peacekeepers have contributed to setting the standards that are expected of police peacekeepers and capacity builders (Harris, 2010). Since peacekeeping and peacebuilding operations play a significant role in addressing regional insecurity and strengthening human rights and the rule of law (Greener, 2009), it is not surprising that Australia's most prominent and well-known acts of international policing have occurred within the Asia-Pacific region. At the forefront of international policing are the AFP, who have engaged in this space since their inception in 1979.

Prior to the creation of the AFP in 1979, police peacekeepers were deployed internationally with the Commonwealth Police force, commencing with the first contingent to the United Nations Peacekeeping Force in Cyprus in May 1964 in response to an outpouring of intercommunal violence between Greek Cypriots and Turkish Cypriots.

At the time the Australian Prime Minister Robert Menzies called for a swift contribution of Australian police peacekeepers, but the Commonwealth Police Force were too small to provide a contingent of forty officers, so personnel were drawn from each of the eight state and territory police organisations. A total of 37 of the 40 officers were state and territory police, with ten each from NSW and Victoria, five each from QLD and South Australia, three from WA, two from Tasmania, one each from the ACT and the NT, with the remaining three officers employed within the Commonwealth Police Force (Brown, Barker, & Burke, 1984). This diverse construction of police deployed from every police organisation in Australia represented the first of many contributions made by state and territory police to integrate in their efforts towards international peacekeeping and capacity-building missions. In modern times, the AFP have provided a significant number of police personnel for UN missions and to aid in peacekeeping and capacity development in regions including Somalia, Thailand, Cambodia, Mozambique, Haiti, Timor-Leste, the Solomon Islands, Nauru, Papua New Guinea, Vanuatu, Tonga, Samoa, and Afghanistan. From 2004, these missions became the core role of the International Deployment Group (IDG), which as part of its structure, included the secondment of state police officers, in order to provide the "experiences and skills that contribute to the overall effectiveness of the IDG" (Jevtovic, 2005), and in turn, fulfill the staffing requirements of the IDG to engage appropriately with the roles that it has been tasked with performing. Given that most deployments have occurred in the context of an IDG that is not at capacity, seconded state-based police have also been recruited to deploy (Harris, 2010). The decision to include state police in the international peacekeeping space provided a wider complementary skillset, capitalising on the community policing experiences of state police, which many AFP officers do not experience to the same extent based on the nature of their work. In the research conducted between 2013 and 2019, one police participant commended the pooling of resources as a positive experience:

> *In hindsight I think the AFP were probably very smart . . . recruiting state police . . . it meant [we had] a very varied skill set, from homicide detectives to forensic, general duties. . . . I think the AFP probably realised that they didn't have the number but also perhaps the people with the skill sets that they required to work in the Solomons, Papua New Guinea, Timor . . . they were very good with management and doing projects and intel, . . . but just general duty policing . . . relied on state police to perform those duties.*

In 2015, the IDG was integrated into the International Operations function to facilitate flexibility and efficiency in the provision of international functions (AFP, 2016). Beyond peacekeeping and capacity building, the AFP have engaged in partnership programmes within the Pacific, under the regional Pacific Police Development Program, and localised programmes with Nauru, Papua New Guinea, Samoa, Tonga, and Vanuatu. The AFP also contribute personnel to international liaison posts on every continent. As of 2020, the AFP have over 400 personnel within the International Operations portfolio alone, while other portfolios include involvement in counterterrorism, organised crime, emergency management, and other departments requiring levels of international collaboration and engagement for effective management of law enforcement (AFP, 2019a). While the breadth of their foothold in international policing is evident, Australian police have arguably made some of their most significant contributions to international policing within peace operations in Timor-Leste and the Solomon Islands, each spanning much of the 21st century.

MAJOR POLICE PEACEKEEPING MISSIONS IN THE 21ST CENTURY ASIA-PACIFIC: TIMOR-LESTE AND THE SOLOMON ISLANDS

Australia's regional interests have led to two significant missions hosted within the Asia-Pacific context: the UN missions to Timor-Leste commencing at the cusp of the 21st century in 1999 and the RAMSI in 2003. While both contexts were managed differently and served different purposes, they represent major case studies for examining and reflecting on the provision of Australian police to international policing and highlight some of the complex issues facing the international policing agenda in the 21st century.[1]

INTERFET and the UN missions to Timor-Leste

Timor-Leste, formerly known as East Timor, comprises the eastern half of the Island of Timor and a small enclave within West Timor called the Oecusse. East Timor was colonised by Portugal prior to the Japanese occupation during World War II, before the move to independence from Portugal commencing in 1974. This movement culminated in Indonesia invading the nation on December 7, 1975. The next 24 years of conflict between Indonesia and the East Timorese resistance would end the lives of at least 100,000 East Timorese people. While the violence and conflict resulted in the penultimate missions to East Timor, there were further political and economic factors that influenced the final decision by the UN to facilitate an Australian-led mission, INTERFET, in preparation for the first of the five UN missions to take place. In January 1999, the referendum proposed by Indonesia to afford either special autonomy or full independence yielded a majority vote towards full independence from Indonesia, resulting in pro-Indonesia militia initiating violence and destruction of infrastructure within the nation. Economic pressures through the IMF and the World Bank, and diplomatic pressures, led to Indonesia agreeing to INTERFET taking place (Braithwaite, 2013; Strating, 2013; Wheeler & Dunne, 2012; Fernandes,

2010; Lothe & Peake, 2010). In total, there have been five UN missions to Timor-Leste since 1999, with each addressing a different need within the nation for peacekeeping and state-building processes:

1. UNAMET (June to October 1999) was organised to host a referendum to determine whether the people of East Timor would accept special autonomy as a part of Indonesia or separate completely from Indonesian governance;
2. UNTAET (October 1999 to May 2002) involved exercising administrative authority during the transition to independence;
3. UNMISET (May 2002 to May 2005) involved the provision of support to the newly independent nation by enabling it to develop self-sufficiency;
4. UNOTIL (May 2005 to August 2006) involved provisions for facilitating the development of state infrastructure, including developing the police and promoting human rights;
5. UNMIT (August 2006 – December 2012) was established to address the political, humanitarian and security crisis that eventuated towards the end of UNOTIL, which culminated in the 2006 civil disorder where several Timorese defence force members opened fire at unarmed police. Operation Serene eventuated to restore law and order alongside the Australian Defence Force and police from Portugal, New Zealand, and Malaysia. Over 1,500 police personnel, led by the AFP were deployed by the UN during this time to reform the police (PNTL) (den Heyer, 2012; Goldsmith, 2009).

After 2012, police administration was handed back to Timor-Leste, and subsequent engagement from Australian police continued under the Timor-Leste Police Development Program, which is still ongoing in 2020.

The Regional Assistance Mission to the Solomon Islands

RAMSI commenced at the request of the Solomon Islands Prime Minister Sir Allan Kemakeza and with the consent of the majority of the Solomon Islanders through the passing of the *Facilitation of International Assistance Act 2003* by their parliament. The precursor to the culmination of RAMSI can be traced back to tensions resulting from British independence in 1978 and the consequent failure to maintain the nation's economy during the land tensions of the late 1990s, which resulted in inter-ethnic conflict in Honiara. By 2003, the consequences of uneven geographically driven development, mismanagement of resources, lack of infrastructural and technological development, and social and cultural conflict, led to breakdown in governance and law and order resulting in conflict between militia and gangs. The mission was led by the police in the Participating Police Force (PPF), which comprised police from Australia, New Zealand, and many Pacific nations, and consisted of two phases. The first phase required police, with the support of armed forces, to facilitate basic physical security by restoring law and order and disarming the militia. RAMSI then worked towards ending government corruption, establishing a stable economy through rebuilding government institutions and restoring infrastructure for economic, social, educational, transportation, and healthcare development (Whalan, 2010). By the end of the first eight months, Special Coordinator Nick Warner emphasised the achievements made by the PPF towards rebuilding the nation, but by April 2006 riots and civil unrest re-emerged following elections, resulting in criticisms that wider long-term social and economic outcomes had not been unilaterally addressed (McKibbin, 2009; Anderson, 2008). While the mission was widely welcomed, some groups[2] viewed the intervention as a pursuit of "Australian hegemony across the Pacific" and what was perceived as devaluing of local sovereignty (Allen, 2009). RAMSI concluded in 2017, but the AFP continue to provide support through the Solomon Islands Police Development Program, with advisors stationed there to provide specialist support (AFP, 2019b), similar to the capacity development occurring in Timor-Leste.

Timor-Leste and the Solomon Islands missions both offer the opportunity to examine the challenges involved in peacekeeping and potential options for securing sustainable outcomes. The salient themes for improving peacekeeping and capacity-building practices include the promotion of cohesive practices between international and local police, cultural contextualisation of international policing methods, capitalising on informal methods of policing and non-police personnel for police reform through partnerships and collaboration, addressing patriarchal structures to facilitate inclusiveness of women in peacebuilding, and political reform. The next section addresses the main themes that have emerged as crucial to acknowledge to ensure effective international policing in the 21st century.

CHALLENGES AND OPPORTUNITIES FACING AUSTRALIAN POLICE PEACEKEEPERS IN THE 21ST CENTURY

Police peacekeepers face a wide range of challenges throughout peacekeeping and capacity-building missions, which are driven by contextual forces that are frequently outside the control of the personnel engaged in the host context. Politically, international peacekeeping and capacity-building missions are dependent on political motivation by the donor nation to intervene in international conflicts in the first place. For example, Australia did not originally wish to intervene in the Solomon Islands, for several reasons. Culturally, the Solomon Islands experienced considerable levels of inter-ethnic conflict, and Australia did not wish to be viewed as "re-colonisers" of the Asia-Pacific region, instead relying on multilateral agreements to address calls for humanitarian assistance. Economically, the Australian government needed to weigh up the costs and benefits for intervention to justify funding the cause. However, increasing concerns of the impact of state insecurity in the region, particularly regarding terrorism and organised crime, led to the RAMSI agreement (den Heyer, 2010; McDougall, 2010; Goldsmith & Dinnen, 2007; Kabutaulaka, 2005; Wainwright, 2003). On a geopolitical and economic level, the leadership under the Indonesian President Suharto favoured neoliberal economic policies and good diplomatic relations as those which could facilitate trade negotiations between interested nation states, such as Australia, for the oil and gas reserves within Timor. However, the 1999 post-referendum violence led to majority support from the APEC and the UNSC to allow INTERFET. These decisions led to Australian police peacekeepers engaging in international policing within the Asia-Pacific, but many structural challenges beyond the political agenda were evident to the police officers who deployed.

THE RISK OF CULTURAL IMPERIALISM: DO COMMUNITY POLICING AND LIBERAL-DEMOCRATIC MODELS WORK?

A key theme evident in current research into international police reform centres around the challenge of donor police implementing foreign practices in the host context, with particular criticisms on the potential impact of re-colonialism. In this case, donor refers to the nation-state contributors to peace operations, and the host refers the subject recipients of those operations. Foreign police assistance inevitably involves the implementation of foreign policing values and methods, which are often unfamiliar or incongruent within the context in which they are applied (McLeod, 2009). Australian police train and practice within a liberal-democratic society, a system which fundamentally espouses that police operate in a democratic manner. For police, the community-policing based expectations of accountability, representation, trust, and legitimacy are further reinforced by the expectation that broader democratic reforms are taking place in the host context. In areas rebuilding after conflict, transferring democratic and community-based models are more difficult to achieve. In the Solomon Islands, police peacekeepers who arrived after the initial deployments found that policing systems had been implemented that were not properly grasped by the host police. Captured by the following reflection from one of the interviewees of the empirical research conduced between 2013 and 2019, it was noted:

> We were then left with this problem of all these processes and procedures which were forced upon them and they didn't really quite understand it.

Another participant expressed concern that negating local practices that could work in the long term may be just as inappropriate as implementing Australian methods, where those practices do not necessarily sit well:

> [W]e failed to recognise early on that we just thought their standards and everything was just poor and third world and we'll come in and show the way with the you beaut Western ways but there were many things that they had done which were just as good from a methodology point of view . . . it took a lot of time for us to realise well just because we've got new technology doesn't mean it's the right way, there's other ways as well.

This sentiment reflects how critical it is to engage in collaboration as opposed to facilitating the imposition of new methods in a situation where it may not work after the intervention ends. If democratic values are not recognised as authoritative in the host context, then a successful and sustainable system can be difficult to maintain in the long term. One aspect of achieving cultural competency between donor and host is to acknowledge and build upon local cultural values and adapt them for use in capacity-building practices. The Solomon Islands presents one such opportunity to examine collaborative police reform in capacity development through acknowledgement of *wantok* or the social bonds that build connections in local communities and in the wider Melanesian community (Kabutaulaka, 2015), underpinned by common use of pidgin language. In *pijin*, RAMSI was known as Operation Helpem Fren, translated to "Helping Friend", which came to culturally identify the purpose and motivations of the mission. *Wantok* is viewed by practitioners in multiple ways. On one hand, it is viewed as a significant obstacle preventing post-conflict rebuilding, a sentiment reinforced by one participant who reported that "police could be reluctant [to go and arrest] because of wantok". On the other hand, academics such as Brigg (2009) and Nanau (2011) suggest that, if mobilised correctly, wantok systems can enhance relationship-building and encourage a thriving community-based culture, if harnessed in a culturally appropriate way. Kabutaulaka (2015) concludes that positive self-identification can overcome the colonial appropriation of Melanesian terms like wantok, facilitating empowerment for Melanesian communities.

Successful hybridisation of foreign and local police-building practices in the host context requires acknowledgement of local culture, but Australian police peacekeepers have largely experienced local culture as static and difficult to change. Existing research in peacekeeping found that the vast differences between policing in Australia and policing in the host nation were a significant challenge. Police often resorted to undertaking practical policing duties as opposed to mentoring their host counterparts to conduct police activities themselves (Harris, 2010). Our own research conducted between 2013-2019 reinforces this finding, in which one participant explained:

> [O]n one hand we were told to sit back and let them run things their own way, but on the other hand . . . it was like this conflict of well the Solomon Islands would be quite happy to continue going the way they're going . . . they had a different concept, when you apply a western society concept its actually quite different and if we try and then seek to enforce that you start to cross over.

An example of the challenge between facilitating cultural acknowledgement and avoiding cultural imperialism is evident in gender relations. For example, *kastom* law in the Solomon Islands placed significant emphasis on patriarchal structures, while gender-based violence in Timor-Leste and the Solomon Islands received "high levels of social acceptance" in the region (Georgeou & Hawksley, 2016). As one participant noted,

> [G]ender in policing is really important, more women need to be involved and I say that because . . . when you openly challenge sexism across the globe . . . in some regimes because you were born a woman you have no place in the social hierarchy and how wonderful it is to see as you can change hearts and minds . . . champion women being involved in positions of authority and it leads people in societies into a better place I think.

Facilitating cultural change can be a difficult balance between cultural imperialism and encouraging conditions for cultural change from within the host context. Trust is critical here; community members can be suspicious of the donor's motives for intervention (Murney & McFarlane, 2009), and it is crucial for police peacekeepers to engage in genuine communication. However, achieving trust presents difficulties for peacekeeping officers, particularly at the early stages of the mission. In the context of RAMSI, the first PPF members were tasked with working alongside officers who would later be arrested and charged for serious offences during the rising tensions pre-2003 (Putt et al., 2018). Nevertheless, participants from our own research emphasised how important it is for individual donor police officers to demonstrate sincere efforts to understand the host community, as illustrated by the following interviewee:

> [Y]ou're working to develop that rapport with the people, build their confidence back up in policing again and to assist in getting the communications between the local police and the community happening, building up the trust, building the police so that they're working at a level that the community want to work with them and have trust in them.

Seeking police legitimacy with the host police is arguably just as critical for successful police reform as building trust with the local community, suggesting that mutual cooperation towards transparency and understanding is crucial for the changes to stay at the conclusion of the intervention. One such opportunity draws on cultural capital, where

Australian police take opportunities to learn local languages and understand the complex cultural dynamics within the host context.

THE PHYSICAL AND SOCIAL SPACES OF ECONOMIC INEQUALITY

A common thread between the missions to Timor-Leste and the Solomon Islands were the underlying experiences of poverty in both contexts. In the Solomon Islands, police peacekeepers faced the consequences of endemic corruption and resource mismanagement that halted socioeconomic development, while in Timor-Leste, the legacies of violence and displacement were evident. As one participant recounted from their experience in Timor-Lestein Timor-Leste, presented during the gathering of empirical work between 2013–2019:

> *In relation to the public disorder which existed there, . . . it was about poverty, about poor education and about unemployment, and the education and unemployment obviously impacted more on the youth than anyone else and so from a policing perspective what those issues manifest into is the public disorder, the crime and so forth.*

The absence of basic necessities and infrastructure underpinned the mission context in the Solomon Islands as well, where one participant reflected:

> [T]hey weren't getting health support, education support, you know the law and order was just one small part, it was a failed state that had no money, they couldn't afford to buy the most basic of medical support, the things we take for granted like Band-Aids and bandages and simple antiseptics, they had nothing.

Socioeconomic inequality continues to be a consequence of slow and uneven development across both nations, exacerbated by geographically diverse physical landscapes. The Solomon Islands is a nation scattered across six major islands and hundreds of smaller islands spread across thousands of square kilometres, while Timor-Leste is largely mountainous terrain. The aforementioned inequalities in development are impacted by these physical structures, where economic development is focused on urbanised areas as opposed to rural localities. For example, in Timor-Leste, wealth distribution is higher in urban areas, which also have better access to water, sanitation, and electricity, while in the Solomon Islands, government service delivery in rural areas is comparatively poor (Shiosaki, 2017; Putt et al., 2018). The consequences for police peacekeepers are that they face an operational field that is impossible to address without wider systemic infrastructural, economic, and governance developments in place (Harris, 2010). Post-conflict contexts necessitate a humanitarian, community-based response, and one participant from our own research recognised that while police officers are not in a direct position to address the root causes of poverty, education, and unemployment, they can still engage with the demographics most vulnerable to experiencing disadvantage:

> Now from. . . [a] policing perspective we can't do anything about education, it's not our role, we can't employ people and we certainly can't do anything about poverty, so it's about working [with] the kids to . . . minimise what those issues manifest into.

Youths are disproportionately disadvantaged in post-conflict settings, especially where there is little opportunity for employment, and where education is inequitably accessed (Shiosaki, 2017; Goldsmith, 2009). Of those interviewed, it was also recognised that the role of police peacekeepers was critical in the absence of any other infrastructural frameworks for facilitating economic reform. For example, one participant noted:

> [Y]ou're the transport, you're the logistics, you're the everything, there is virtually no other government infrastructure . . . there's very little in comms, transport or anything . . . the only form of government infrastructure there really was the police so you become the de facto answer for everything really.

From our own empirical work, participants offered many examples of their contributions to assisting in humanitarian efforts, including the provision of transport to critically ill individuals and women in labour, the provision of "food, equipment, and technical expertise" where natural disasters had damaged homes and crops, the provision of security for trucks transporting goods, organising sporting equipment and clothing, and engaging the community in topics around equality, human rights, healthcare, and the roles of the criminal justice system. These practices extended the roles performed by police peacekeepers from standard policing and mentoring to performing a wide range of humanitarian functions with the needs of the host communities in mind. Since conflict disproportionately affects developing nations, police peacekeepers are likely to continue to deploy to economically underprivileged parts of the world into the future.

CONCLUSION: THE FUTURE OF AUSTRALIAN POLICE IN THE INTERNATIONAL SPACE

As of January 2020, Australian police are not represented amongst the figures for UN peacekeeping missions, despite higher demands for more police peacekeepers within UN mandated missions (UN, 2020; Sharland, 2016, 2017). However, maintaining involvement in a wide range of international policing initiatives retains significance to Australian police, particularly the AFP. Under the AFP International Engagement Strategy for 2020 and beyond (AFP, 2018b),

Australian involvement in international policing includes engaging in the exchange of criminal intelligence and information sharing, cooperation and collaboration with international police organisations and partners. It further involves targeting transnational offences such as organised crime, terrorism, and child exploitation, through international arrangements, while continuing to undertake peacekeeping and capacity-building measures as required. These measures take several forms in the Asia-Pacific region, such as the Pacific Police Development Programme – Regional (2016) and the newly established Transnational Serious Organised Crime Pacific Taskforce between Australia, Fiji, Tonga, and New Zealand. Such initiatives forge partnerships and information-sharing capabilities between police agencies in addition to building upon existing task forces with other police organisations internationally.

The growing shift towards international engagement is a significant milestone for policing in the 21st century. The AFP identify in their Corporate Plan 2019–2020 that there may be the need to engage "unscheduled evaluations of International Operations" in response to any changes or emerging issues that arise in their operational objectives (p 26). Any future arrangements in international police peacekeeping must continue to be held in a negotiated space which acknowledges that Australian police peacekeepers are well resourced materially and equipped with contextual knowledge to achieve successful and sustainable outcomes towards achieving peace and security.

NOTES

1 The majority of time spent on missions to Timor-Leste and the Solomon Islands occurred concurrently, and the motivations, policies, practices, and outcomes have been subject to much academic interest in the past 20 years. For a comprehensive understanding of the experiences of East Timorese before and during the conflict, read "Chega! The Report of the Commission for Reception, Truth and Reconciliation Timor-Leste Executive Summary", available at http://www.etan.org/etanpdf/2006/CAVR/Chega!-Report-Executive-Summary.pdf. In the Solomon Islands, the United Nations Development Programme released their most recent Summary Report into the National Perceptions Survey on Peacebuilding for Solomon Islands in 2018, available at http://www.undp.org/content/dam/fiji/docs/UN-SOI-PB-perception-survey-summary.pdf. This survey offers insights into the perspectives of Solomon Islanders' current views on the progress of peacebuilding and development in the Solomon Islands, and builds on the previous People's Survey Report conducted collaboratively by the Australian National University and University of the South Pacific in 2013. The 2013 report is available here: http://www.ramsi.org/wp-content/uploads/2014/07/FINAL-Peoples-Survey-2013-1-final-111900c1-79e2-4f41-9801-7f29f6cd2a66-0.pdf.

2 Such as the Malaita Ma'asina Forum Executive (see Allen, M. (2006). "Dissenting Voices: local perspectives on the Regional Assistance Mission to the Solomon Islands." *Pacific Economic Bulletin*, 21(2), 194–201).

REFERENCES

AFP. (2016). A Helping Hand. *AFP Platypus Magazine*. Canberra: Retrieved from http://classic.austlii.edu.au/au/journals/AUFPPlatypus/2016/3.pdf.

AFP. (2018a). *Futures Centre*. Canberra. Retrieved from: www.afp.gov.au/futures.

AFP. (2018b). *International Engagement 2020 and Beyond*. Canberra. Retrieved from: www.afp.gov.au/sites/default/files/PDF/AFPInternationalEngagement2020Strategy.pdf?v=1.

AFP. (2019a). *Annual Report*. Canberra. Retrieved from: www.afp.gov.au/sites/default/files/PDF/Reports/AnnualReport2018-19.pdf.

AFP. (2019b). *AFP Staff Statistics*. Retrieved from: www.afp.gov.au/news-media/facts-and-stats/afp-staff-statistics.

Allen, M. (2009). Resisting RAMSI: Intervention, Identity and Symbolism in the Solomon Islands. *Oceania*, 79(1), 1–16.

Anderson, T. (2008). RAMSI: Intervention, Aid Trauma and Self Governance. *Journal of Australian Political Economy*, 62, 62–93.

Bellamy, A., & Davies, S. (2009). The Responsibility to Protect in the Asia-Pacific Region. *Security Dialogue*, 40(6), 547–574.

Bellamy, A., & Drummond, C. (2012). Southeast Asia: Between Non-Interference and Sovereignty and Responsibility. In W. A. Knight & F. Egerton (Ed.), *The Routledge Handbook of the Responsibility to Protect* (pp. 245–256). Abingdon: Routledge.

Braithwaite, J. (2013). Evaluating the Timor-Leste Peace Operation. In D. Druckman & P. Diehl (Ed.), *Peace Operation Success: A Comparative Analysis*. Leiden: Brill.

Brigg, M. (2009). Wantokism and State Building in the Solomon Islands: A Response to Fukuyama. *Pacific Economic Bulletin*, 24(3), 148–161.

Brown, G., Barker, B., & Burke, T. (1984). *Police as Peace-Keepers: The History of the Australian and New Zealand Police Serving with the United Nations Force in Cyprus 1964–1984*. Melbourne: United Nations Civilian Police Club.

Casey, J. (2009). *Policing the World: The Practice of International and Transnational Policing*. Durham: North Carolina Press.

Chan, J. (2005). Globalisation, Reflexivity, and the Practice of Criminology. In J. Sheptycki & A. Wardak (Ed.), *Transnational and Comparative Criminology*. Abingdon: Routledge.

Daniel, D. (2013). Contemporary Patterns in Peace Operations. In A. Bellamy & P. Williams (Ed.), *Providing Peacekeepers: The Politics, Challenges, and Future of United Nations Peacekeeping Contributions*. Oxford: Oxford University Press.

den Heyer, G. (2010). Measuring Capacity Development and Reform in the Royal Solomon Islands Police Force. *Policing and Society*, 20(3), 298–315.

den Heyer, G. (2012). Post-Conflict Civilian Police Reform: 1999 to 2007. *Police Practice and Research: An International Journal*, (44), 1–35.

Ellison, G., & Pino, N. (Ed.). (2012). *Globalization, Police Reform, and Development*. New York: Palgrave Macmillan.

Fernandes, C. (2010). East Timor and the Struggle for Independence. In L. A. Barria & S. D. Roper (Ed.), *The Development of Institutions of Human Rights*. New York: Palgrave Macmillan.

Findlay, M. (2000). *The Globalisation of Crime: Understanding Transitional Relationships in Context*. Cambridge: Cambridge University Press.

Georgeou, N., & Hawksley, C. (2016). The Responsibility to Protect and the 'Responsibility to Assist': Developing Human Rights Protection Through Police Building. In D. Mayersen (Ed.), *The United Nations and Genocide* (pp. 186–209). Basingstoke, Hampshire: Palgrave Macmillan.

Goldsmith, A. (2009). 'It Wasn't Like Normal Policing': Voices of Australian Police Peacekeepers in Operation Serene, Timor-Leste 2006. *Policing and Society: An International Journal of Research and Policy*, 19(2), 119–133.

Goldsmith, A., & Dinnen, S. (2007). Transnational Police Building: Critical Lessons from Timor-Leste and Solomon Islands. *Third World Quarterly*, 28(6), 1091–1109.

Goldsmith, A., & Harris, V. (2009). Out of Step: Multilateral Police Missions, Culture and Nation-Building in Timor-Leste. *Conflict, Security & Development*, 9(2), 189–211.

Goldsmith, A., & Harris, V. (2017). International Policing Missions: Establishing Trustworthy Policing in Low-Trust Environments. In S. Hufnagel & C. McCartney (Eds.), *Trust in International Police and Justice Cooperation*. Portland, OR: Hart Publishing.

Greener, B. K. (2009). *The New International Policing*. Basingstoke, Hampshire: Palgrave Macmillan.

Harris, V. (2010). Building on San? Australian Police Involvement in International Police Capacity Building. *Policing and Society*, 20(1), 79–98.

Held, D., & McGrew, A. (2003). *The Global Transformations Reader: An Introduction to the Globalization Debate*. Cambridge: Polity Press.

Hughes, B., Hunt, C., & Curth-Bibb, J. (2013). *Forging New Conventional Wisdom Beyond International Policing: Learning from Complex Political Realities*. Boston: Brill.

Jevtovic, P. (2005). *IDG – One Year On*. Retrieved from: http://www5.austlii.edu.au/au/journals/AUFPPlatypus/2005/22.html.

Kabutaulaka, T. (2005). Australian Foreign Policy and the RAMSI Intervention in Solomon Islands. *The Contemporary Pacific*, 17(2), 283–308.

Kabutaulaka, T. (2015). Re-Presenting Melanesia: Ignoble Savages and Melanesian Alter-Narratives. *The Contemporary Pacific*, 27(1), 110–146.

Lemieux, F. (Ed.). (2010). *International Police Cooperation: Emerging Issues, Theory and Practice*. Devon: Willan Publishing.

Linden, R., Last, D., & Murphy, C. (2007). Obstacles on the Road to Peace and Justice: The Role of Civilian Police in Peacekeeping. In A. Goldsmith & J. Sheptycki (Ed.), *Crafting Transnational Policing*. Portland: Hart.

Lothe, E., & Peake, G. (2010). Addressing Symptoms but Not Causes: Stabilisation and Humanitarian Action in Timor-Leste. *Disasters*, 34(3), S427–S443.

McDougall, D. (2010). The Security-Development Nexus: Comparing External Interventions and Development Strategies in East Timor and Solomon Islands. *Asian Security*, 6(2), 170–190.

McGrew, A. (2003). The Globalisation Debate: Putting the Advanced Capitalist State in Place. *Globalization: Critical Concepts in Sociology*, 1, 329–355.

McKibbin, R. (2009). Australian Security and Development in Solomon Islands. *Australian Journal of Political Science*, 44(3), 439–456.

McLeod, A. (2009). Police Capacity Development in the Pacific: The Challenge of Local Context. *Policing and Society: An International Journal of Research and Policy*, 19(2), 147–160.

Murney, T., & McFarlane, J. (2009). Police Development: Confounding Challenges for the International Community. In P. Grabosky (Ed.), *Community Policing and Peacekeeping*. Boca Raton: CRC Press.

Nanau, G. L. (2011). The Wantok System as a Socio-economic and Political Network in Melanesia. *OMNES: The Journal of Multicultural Society*, 2(1), 31–35. http://doi.org/10.15685/omnes.2011.06.2.1.31.

Palmer, D., Berlin, M. M., Das, D. K. (Ed.). (2012). *Global Environment of Policing*. Boca Raton: CRC Press.

Putt, J., Dinnen, S., Keen, M., & Batley, J. (2018). *The RAMSI Legacy for Policing in the Pacific Region*. Australian National University. Retrieved from: http://dpa.bellschool.anu.edu.au/sites/default/files/uploads/2018-02/the_ramsi_legacy_for_policing_in_the_pacific_region_low_res.pdf.

Sharland, L. (2016). *UN Peacekeeping: Time to Build Upon Australia's History*. Retrieved from: www.aspistrategist.org.au/un-peacekeeping-time-build-upon-australias-history-2/.

Sharland, L. (2017). *Australia and UN Peacekeeping at 70: Proud History, Uncertain Future*. Retrieved from: www.aspistrategist.org.au/australia-un-peacekeeping-70-proud-history-uncertain-future/.

Shiosaki, E. (2017). "We Have Resisted, Now We Must Build": Regionalism and Nation-Building in Timor-Leste. *Journal of Southeast Asian Studies*, 48(1), 53–70.

Strating, R. (2013). East Timor's Emerging National Security Agenda: Establishing "Real" Independence. *Asian Security*, 9(3), 185–210.

UN. (2008). *United Nations Peacekeeping Operations Principles and Guidelines*. New York: United Nations. Retrieved from: https://peacekeeping.un.org/sites/default/files/capstone_eng_0.pdf.

UN. (2020). *Contributors to UN Peacekeeping Operations by Country and Post: Police, UN Military Experts on Mission, Staff Officers, and Troops*. Retrieved from: https://peacekeeping.un.org/sites/default/files/1_summary_of_contributions_20.pdf.

Wainwright, E. (2003). Responding to State Failure: The Case of Australia and Solomon Islands. *Australian Journal of International Affairs*, 57(3), 485–498.

Warren, I., & Palmer, D. (2015). *Global Criminology*. Pyrmont, NSW: Thomson Reuters.

Whalan, J. (2010). The Power of Friends: The Regional Assistance Mission to the Solomon Islands. *Journal of Peace Research*, 47(5), 627–637.

SECTION 4
Working with individuals and groups

CHAPTER 22

Mental health and the policing context

Erin Kruger

INTRODUCTION

This chapter examines the question of policing and mental health from two directions. The first section considers mental health among policing professionals. It explains how both the nature of the policing occupation (the stressful and traumatic situations they encounter while fulfilling their duties) and the organisational culture (which includes strenuous workloads, formal inquiries, media scrutiny, and public criticism) leaves them susceptible to stress-related disorders, including depression, anxiety, and PTSD. Research suggests that police have traditionally been disinclined to seek help for such issues for fear of being perceived as weak or unfit for duty. Initiatives to improve mental health among police often operate at the level of the police agency and include fostering supportive workplace cultures and reducing stigma. The second section of the chapter discusses police responses to mental health in the community. By virtue of their occupation, police have relatively frequent contact with individuals suffering from some manifestation of mental illness. Historically, police responses to the mentally ill has been inadequate due to lack of relevant training or understanding. Initiatives designed to rectify this situation include training officers who specialize in the area and having police work closer with their counterparts in the mental health profession. While these two issues – mental health among policing professionals and police responses to mental health in the community – have typically been considered separately, the chapter concludes by arguing for an integrated approach. Here, rather than being compartmentalized as it is now, research, training, and policy would be informed by a larger, more inclusive, and more robust "policing and mental health" framework.

MENTAL HEALTH OF THE POLICE

As part of their work, police are exposed to innumerable stressful situations that may impact their mental health. Statistics show that this occurs at a higher frequency than for those in other occupations. Such stressors can be divided into three categories: stressors "on the job", as part of the policing organisation, and external to the organisation. In the first category are stressors encountered as part of police work. Various critical incidents and potential traumatic events that police encounter during their career put them at high risk for the development of mental health issues (Velden et al., 2013). Police encounter, for example, people who are in danger and distress, threats to officer safety and wellbeing, having to maintain composure when provoked; they carry firearms, are recorded and on camera, and more generally, are responsible for protecting citizen's lives (Purba & Demou, 2019). Other traumatic incidents involve witnessing harms and deaths of children, victims of sexual harassment and sexual assault, serious traffic accidents, suicides, and recurring exposure to violence (Velden et al., 2013). Large-scale, international crimes such as terrorism, cybercrime, organised crime, and the changing nature of crime add to the pressure on officers' mental capacity (Police Federation of Australia [PFA], 2019).

A second group of stressors are related to occupational and organisational culture. These include heavy workload, lack of support, interpersonal conflict with colleagues and supervisors, inadequate resources, time pressure, an overly bureaucratic organisational system, perceived workplace fairness/unfairness, high mental/intellectual demand, job pressure, long working hours, lack of resources and support, ridicule, sexual and language harassment, bias, judgement from peers, lacking influence within the police hierarchy, and over-commitment (Purba & Demou, 2019). Further stressors, as outlined by the PFA (2019), include fear of reporting mental health injuries to the system, perceived lack of leadership, perceived lack of support from politicians and senior management, perceived unfair decision making by managers, perceived insensitivity to personal distress, pressure to achieve fast response times, pressure to clear up crime rates of various types, priorities constantly shifting, economic factors within the workplace, budget constraints, and shift work. In fact, research has found that organisational stressors (which are not specific to police) appear to have more impact on health and wellbeing than daily operational stressors, including exposure to traumatic events (Velden et al., 2013; Beyond Blue [BB], 2018).

In addition to stress on the job and within the police organisation, further stressors exist external to the job itself. These include, for example, the fact that police deal with multiple layers of oversight bodies, various inquiry bodies (including coronial inquires), often unreal community expectations and demands, intense public criticism post-event, criticisms through media/social media, constant news cycle, ongoing changes in police work, and a judicial system that is slow to respond (PFA, 2019)

MENTAL HEALTH ISSUES

Research indicates that police cope with and accept stressful situations as natural requirements of their role, relying on individual coping mechanisms associated with the "police personality" (Purba & Demou, 2019). Resilience, for example, is a positive trait that sustains police through traumatic incidents and allows them to endure in their careers (Velden et al., 2013). In contrast, however, a recent survey of Australian police and emergency services found that many of these employees had substantially higher levels of psychological distress than the average Australian population, with police, in particular, suffering the highest rates. This survey was pronounced by Beyond Blue (BB, 2018) and entitled *Answering the Call*. This is the first national survey in Australia to account for the mental health and wellbeing of Australian police and emergency services personnel. Over 21,014 people took part, and the survey, for the first time, provided some of the key mental health issues faced by police and emergency services personnel. Key protective and risk factors were established. Protective factors included resilience, commitment to service, and sense of community, while risk factors were associated with exposure to traumatic events and the challenges of workplace environments. In all, the survey allows for police and emergency services to benchmark and measure change as it relates to the mental health of their employees.

Key findings from this survey reveal that one in three emergency services employees experience high or very high psychological distress in contrast to just one in eight among all adults in Australia (Australian Bureau of Statistics [ABS], 2015, in BB, 2018). More than one in two-and-a-half employees report having been diagnosed with a mental health condition in their life compared to one in five of all adults in Australia (ABS, 2016; BB, 2018). Employees report having suicidal thoughts over two times higher than adults in the general population and are more than three times more likely to have a suicide plan (ABS, 2016). More than half of all employees indicated that they had experienced a traumatic event that had deeply affected them during the course of their work. Poor workplace practices and culture were found to be as damaging to mental health as occupational trauma. Those who had worked more than ten years were almost twice as likely to experience psychological distress and were six times more likely to experience symptoms of PTSD (BB, 2018). Psychological injuries are often the result or one or more traumatic episodes and can have harmful impacts upon not only the officer but also the officer's family (PFA, 2019). In accordance with the Australian Medical Association's (AMA) (2019) view, then, in performing their jobs, police can pay a "high price" including mental illness, psychological injury, and in the worst cases, suicide. Occupational stress, anxiety, depression, psychological distress, burnout, suicidal ideation, and even suicide are, thus, all detrimental features associated with the mental health conditions of police officers (Purba & Demou, 2019).

POLICE CULTURE AND COPING STRATEGIES

In its traditional formation, policing has been male-dominated, with a culture represented by resilience, endurance, and denial of mental trauma. Police officers have typically refrained from asking for help, due to factors such as autonomy, lack of confidence in mental health providers, and potential stigma associated with "getting help" (Karaffa & Koch, 2016). It has been established that police officers are susceptible to psychological injuries (i.e. depression, anxiety and PTSD) incurred in the line of duty, through the workplace, and in external manifestations (i.e. the impact of media). In conjunction with these stressors, police often face isolation and stigma that accompanies such diagnoses (PFA, 2019). Thus they often refrain from asking for assistance, and their coping strategies are less than ideal. Officers' negative coping strategies (i.e. avoidance, self-criticism) (Knowles & Bull, 2003) and lack of effective stress management in relation to work (Mostert & Rothmann, 2006) contribute to decreased wellbeing. Self-medicating with alcohol is one way officers cope, which often leads to greater levels of anxiety. Sleep disorders are another persistent outcome of psychological injury and chronic stress (Karaffa & Koch, 2016). Adverse coping strategies are linked to shame surrounding such mental health vulnerabilities, the fact that their mental health might burden others, and fear of confessing psychological issues to others (BB, 2018).

While many police officers have good mental health and wellbeing and exhibit high levels of resilience, as discussed, they may not recognise the symptoms of mental trauma, which, in turn, reveals poor mental health literacy amongst police officers. When individuals do not recognise the signs and symptoms of mental health disturbances, they do not realise that they have a mental health condition and are unlikely to seek support (BB, 2018). While this chapter focuses primarily on Australia, a comparison to New York at this point might be of benefit due to its relevance to these issues. Over recent times the New York Police Department (NYPD) has seen a "rash of suicides" by police officers, leading the commissioner to declare a "mental health emergency". These suicides are linked to the larger issue of untreated depression amongst law-enforcement officers throughout the United States (US) (Sisak & Mustian, 2019). In the US, suicides claim more officers' lives annually than violence in the line of duty. According to Rufo (2015), the 12 possible signs of pending suicide by police officers include relationship issues, lack of sleep, financial problems, anxiety and anger, changes and unnecessary risks at work, giving away prized possessions, obvious symptoms of distress, alcohol consumption and other addictive behaviour, noticeable changes in mood, prior suicide attempts in family history, and "cries for help" (pp. 190–191). While many departments offer counselling services (i.e. employee assistance programs), police officers are typically wary of depending on such services for fear that what they say getting back to their supervisors or of being deemed "unfit for duty" (Sisak & Mustian, 2019).

Similar issues exist in the Australian context. Challenges for Australian police forces involve detecting police officers who may be suffering from mental health issues. Assessing mental health issues in officers is difficult when there are low rates of police seeking help for mental health issues or when they refuse to access internal or external support. Other efforts in place include instigating early intervention methods, destigmatising mental health issues, and addressing suicide within ranks. Goals to improve such challenges include education and awareness around mental health, reducing stigma, and supporting those who report mental health issues. Where police do seek mental health services, there is often a delay in accessing appropriate care in a timely manner (PFA, 2019). The AMA (2019) maintains that police continue to need more access to mental health professionals, more dedicated facilities, and more services. These have, to a degree, been provided. In recent years, police and emergency services agencies have noticeably increased activities to support the mental health and wellbeing of their employees and volunteers. Agencies are working to promote mental health and wellbeing, address risk factors, and provide appropriate mental health supports to those who need them (BB, 2018).

RECOMMENDATIONS TO IMPROVE POLICE MENTAL HEALTH

Evidence shows that the police, in particular, are at a higher risk for developing mental health conditions. While police can't remove the risk to exposure to traumatic events, one area to focus on is cultivating workplace culture. Ensuring features such as a balanced workload and supportive relationships by peers and supervisors are in place may reverse the adverse impact of work-related stress on officers' wellbeing (Tomyn et al., 2015; Hesketh et al., 2016) and ensure that employees feel safe and supported (BB, 2018). Improving mental health literacy is another step to assist police personnel in recognising symptoms of anxiety, depression, and PTSD at an earlier stage, so that individuals may seek support and early intervention. Reducing stigma around mental health is vital to police officers seeking support. Australian research around this issue discerned that the majority of police personnel did not hold stigmatising attitudes to their colleagues, with a very low number believing that mental health conditions are the fault of the individual experiencing them or that those with mental health conditions are a burden on others (BB, 2018). Consequently, police officers should feel confident that their colleagues don't blame or resent them, and that they should not blame or resent themselves either (BB, 2018).

A promising example of mental health initiatives in policing can be found in the Queensland Police Service (QPS). The QPS is in the early stages of instilling a rather "holistic" approach to mental health. Their key areas of focus include expanding the knowledge and skills of all employees in managing mental health, both at work and personally. They seek to reduce the incidence of mental illness by viewing mental health as a shared responsibility between affected individuals and the organisation. There is a further emphasis on reducing stigma, supporting individuals through the challenges inherent to the policing profession, and improving training and educational platforms on the topic (Queensland Government [QG], 2019). The QPS approach and similar programs within Australia promote potential solutions to reducing mental health issues at the level of improving workplace cultures, improving mental health literacy, and reducing stigma. Police organisations that provide higher levels of support and inclusiveness, regular discussion about workplace experiences, and effectively manage emotional demands of staff have a better chance of obtaining lower rates of probable PTSD and other forms of psychological distress.

POLICING MENTAL ILLNESS

In this second part of the chapter, how police respond to mental health in the community is considered. Police are simultaneously called to respond to incidents with mentally ill persons on regular and ongoing basis. The issue of policing mentally ill persons across Australia is a familiar one. Police officers in Australia deal with such issues as mental health crises, people battling mental illness, searching for people who have walked away from psychiatric care, and trying to connect the mentally ill with the services they need (White, 2019). The policing of mentally ill persons is, thus, a complicated issue. To begin, the processes of deinstitutionalization and socioeconomic status of many mentally ill persons serve as a background and context with respect to how and why police initially become involved with mentally ill persons.

The process of deinstitutionalization of mentally ill persons occurred several decades ago, in the latter half of the 20th century in Australia. Deinstitutionalisation was characterised by changes in the location, style, and accessibility of treatment and care services for people with mental illnesses. Key features of this political and bureaucratic process included transferring mentally ill persons from psychiatric to community-based settings by increasing the rate of discharges and improving community-based services (Talbott, 1978; Doessel et al., 2009). During this time, mentally ill persons were transferred from psychiatric institutions to community-based settings. Deinstitutionalisation is thought to have overburdened police as front-line responders to mental health crisis incidents (Carroll, 2005). In Australia, as well as internationally, the initial response from police was that of some resentment regarding deinstitutionalization. They claimed that they were not "street-corner psychiatrists" (Lamb et al., 2002, p. 1266; Bartkowiak-Theron & Asquith, 2017). Millions of dollars have been spent in police involvement in mental health crisis incidents or interventions each year. This is in addition to the police management of hospital admissions and assessments, and the often, unnecessary incarceration of mentally disordered and ill individuals (Clifford, 2010). Largely by virtue of the 24/7 nature of their work, police officers are now typically the first, and often the only, responders to mental health crises.

This is not to say there haven't been positives associated with the deinstitutionalization reform (Rosen, 2006). However, there have simultaneously been a number of challenges. For instance, there has arguably not been enough funding for mental health services in the community (i.e. programs, supervision, and services to support the number of mentally ill persons released from institutions) (Clifford, 2010). Consequently, mentally ill persons often come into contact with police and are subsequently criminalised instead of being connected to the psychiatric treatment they require. This trend is evident in Australian prison populations. A relatively recent report, *The Health of Australia's Prisoners, 2015*, reveals the mental health status of those imprisoned. One in four prisoners, for example, received medications for mental health-related issues while in prison. Furthermore, almost half of prison entrants (49%) reported having been told by a health professional that they have a mental health disorder. There is a further gender discrepancy, in that reporting a history of mental health problems was more common among female prisoners (62%) than male (47%) (Australian Government [AG], 2015). As a result, increasing numbers of people with mental illness are coming into contact with both the mental health and criminal justice systems, including both offenders and victims.

At the most extreme and detrimental limits of these interactions are police-involved shootings of mentally ill individuals. The Australian Institute of Criminology's (AIC) National Deaths in Custody Program (NDICP) monitors fatal police shootings and collects detailed information about the nature and circumstances of such incidents. Data collected by the NDICP shows that since 1989–1990 through to 2013, there have been 105 persons fatally shot by police, with available information showing that in 44 (42%) cases, the deceased had been identified as having some sort of mental illness, with psychotic disorders such as schizophrenia being the most common (Australian Institute of Criminology [AIC], 2013). In addition to the tragedy of such events, police shootings of this nature are often highly publicised events. The social and political impacts can be felt across the broader community and influence public perceptions of mental illness as potentially "criminal" and/or "dangerous" (Carroll, 2005). In response to fatal harm or shootings of mentally ill persons, many police officers in Australia have expressed concerns over what they perceive to be a lack of necessary knowledge, skills, and resources to assess and respond appropriately to individuals with mental illness (Clifford, 2010). As previously discussed, shifts in public policy, including the process of deinstitutionalization, have arguably served to increase the likelihood of individuals with a mental health concern coming to the attention of police. Consequently, tragic, high-profile incidents resulting from police interactions with mentally ill persons are subject to internal review, and questions often remain about whether the potential threat posed by the alleged offender was sufficient to warrant police using a firearm (AIC, 2013).

Concerns have therefore been raised regarding police responses to mentally ill persons in these contexts.

Deinstitutionalization is one societal phenomenon that increases contact between police and mentally ill persons. Another socioeconomic factor that deserves attention is income assistance. The Department of Human Services in Australia is responsible for government benefits and support services. In the specific case of income assistance, the Government provides financial assistance for those who have limited ability to earn income because of personal circumstances or disability, including mental health issues. Research done in Canada found that monthly lump-sum welfare payments have been associated with increased illness, mortality, and crime. Pickett et al. (2015) studied whether monthly welfare cheque distribution affects police interactions with mental health patients and any impact this has on emergency department activity. This study found a statistically significant increase in interactions and apprehensions by police and mentally ill persons, and an overall increase in mental health and substance abuse presentations to the emergency department (ED) in the seven-day period following income assistance payments, compared with other days of the month. Apprehended mental health patients seen in the ED are resource intensive, typically requiring urgent assessment, direct supervision, pharmacological and/or physical restraint, seclusion, and treatment in a safe ED environment before being referred to psychiatry services or discharged (Pickett et al., 2015). While the relation of substance abuse to mental health is largely beyond the scope of the current chapter, the study of Pickett and colleagues draws attention to possible links between substance abuse and the deterioration of mental health.

Taken together, the aforementioned study, in conjunction with the historical process of deinstitutionalization, indicate a trend towards police acting as "gatekeepers" to the mental health system (Fisher & Grudzinskas, 2010). The police are, in this instance, a sort of "one stop shop" for complicated social issues, including mental health (Wells & Schafer, 2006). Police have become the default front line in managing people in crisis. This phenomenon is witnessed by the fact that mental health calls are often in the form of medical emergencies as opposed to criminal activity, and police are simply called to facilitate access to medical care. To complicate matters further, police often aren't provided with the right tools for such interventions, and their response is often uninformed and/or inadequate (White, 2019).

RATES OF POLICE CALL-OUTS

Although statistics vary, a general range of the percentage of police call-outs to mental health crises can be estimated. In the Australian Capital Territory (ACT), the Australian Federal Police found that at least 10% of callouts were of this type (White, 2019), with other valuations positing this rate is closer to 20% (White, 2019), and even 30%

in some jurisdictions (Coleman & Cotton, 2010; Herrington & Pole, 2014, p. 501). These Australian results are in line with other studies, including a review by Livingston (2016) that synthesized the call-out rates reported in 85 unique studies of contact between police and people with mental disorders. A summary of these findings saw one in four people with mental disorders having histories of police arrest. The arrest of mentally ill persons is therefore substantially higher than estimated rates among general adult populations in Canada and the United Kingdom (although it corresponds to arrest rates from the general adult population in the US). Livingston's (2016) review also found that about one in ten individuals encountered police in their pathway to mental health care.

With a legal responsibility to respond, police must attend to mental health call-outs. By virtue of their jobs, police are available 24/7, and as such tend to be the first responders to a range of incidents, including those involving people exhibiting signs of a mental illness. Questions remain, however, such as whether police are properly trained to manage such calls. Do they have appropriate mechanisms, capability, and capacity to deal with the mentally ill? Do they have access to the necessary mental health professionals? And why are police sent to mental health calls without access to the tools they need? (White, 2019). The next section considers how, and in what ways, police do respond to mental health call-outs and crises.

MENTAL HEALTH INTERVENTION TEAMS (MHITS)

Police officers have traditionally lacked sufficient mental health training and knowledge of mental illness to manage the risks associated with mentally ill person encounters (Clayfield et al., 2011). A lack of understanding and training may result in police officers making improper decisions when responding to such calls. As such, novel responses in this area have emerged and seek to "mind the gap" – that is, instigate a coordinated approach whereby police and mental health professionals work closely together. On the one hand, police need rapid onsite aid from mental health professionals. On the other hand, mental health professionals might not feel safe in managing some calls without the assistance of police officers. Mental health and police services are, therefore, increasingly working in a synonymous fashion to manage each call appropriately, effectively, and efficiently (White, 2019).

Mental Health Intervention Teams (MHITs) are one example of such a coordinated response that has emanated from the New South Wales Police Force (NSWPF). The program was initiated in 2008 in three local area commands where 111 officers initially received enhanced training. Professed benefits of MHITs are that they increased confidence among police in dealing with mental-health related events, reduced police involvement in transportation of mentally ill persons, and improved handover between police and mental health care services (Herrington & Pole, 2014). That is, improved inter-agency collaboration provides a way to educate officers, improve their understandings of mental health, generally, and improve their handling of cases upon arrival to mental health facilities, specifically. The facilitation of inter-agency cooperation between police and mental health personnel ultimately reduces the amount of time spent by police dealing with these matters (Herrington & Pole, 2014). A further advantage is improved familiarity and proficiency with de-escalation techniques, leaving police more willing and comfortable in interacting with mentally ill persons. MHIT-trained officers recorded a reduction in their reported time spent waiting at hospitals. There was also a noted "bleed effect", wherein MHIT skills were disseminated informally to neighbouring local commands, leading to an overall improvement in dealing with mental health-related events from many police perspectives and avenues (Herrington & Pole, 2014). The general benefits of MHITs, therefore, abound, as witnessed in reduced risk of injury to police and civilians, improved police officers' awareness of mental health issues, and increased collaboration between police and responsible agencies (White, 2019).

The MHIT system, however, is not perfect. There are lingering difficulties, in particular, with inter-agency cooperation. These challenges are largely driven by resourcing concerns, on the one hand, and concern about who might fill the gap left by police in transporting prisoners and providing security, on the other (Herrington & Pole, 2014). These issues point to the fact that a better resourced mental health system is necessary. Alleviating police presence in mental health call-outs would need to be replaced with an adequate alternative such as, perhaps, training and equipping mental health personnel with security capacities. An area for concern that has emerged between police and mental health professionals is in relation to psychiatric emergency care centres (PECCs). PECCs are designed to offer an interim facility for individuals assessed at emergency departments as having a (suspected) mental health concern that requires further observation or supervision in a controlled environment but without necessarily needing admission to a mental health unit. To date, police most frequently cite these "borderline groups" as most problematic as they coast somewhere between community care and mental health treatment facilities, thus making their designation as mentally disordered or ill, criminal or otherwise defined, contingent (Herrington & Pole, 2014).

CONCLUDING THOUGHTS: COMBINING MENTAL HEALTH PERSPECTIVES IN POLICING

The two issues discussed to this point – mental health among policing professionals and police responses to mental health – have typically been considered separately. To conclude, this chapter argues for an integrated approach. Both the mental health of police and that of the communities that they serve are examined to discern if and in what ways police affected with mental health issues might have altered perceptions, judgements, and responses towards mentally ill persons. The literature suggests that police suffer from greater rates of mental health symptoms such as anxiety, depression, and PTSD. To focus on PTSD for a moment, some of the most common symptoms associated with this illness are substance abuse, depression, feelings of hopelessness, suicidal thoughts and feelings, lack of interest in socializing, increased emotional reactions, anxiety, and recurrent flashbacks to the traumatic event (Herman, 2001; Hart, 2015). It might be useful at this stage to parallel PTSD rates in police with PTSD rates experienced by soldiers and war veterans. PTSD theorizing to date has evolved and been applied to soldiers and veterans with great frequency, but less so to police, even though police also experience atrocities, horrific crimes, and death in the line of duty (Papazoglou & Chopko, 2017). For instance, in a study by Komarovskaya et al. (2011), over two-thirds of police officers reported being exposed to at least one event in which they felt a direct threat to their life. With 400 officers being studied, it was found that killing or seriously injuring someone in the line of duty was associated with PTSD symptoms and marginally with depression symptoms (although not with social adjustment or alcohol use) (p. 1335).

With this parallel between police, soldiers, and war veterans in mind, research by Papazoglou and Chopko (2017) on "compassion fatigue" in war veterans may be relevant to police individuals and populations suffering from mental illness. Compassion fatigue, for Figley (2002), is a type of secondary traumatic stress that emanates from front-line professionals caring for those who suffer psychological pain. Police are not necessarily tasked in a "caring" profession as, say, doctors and nurses are, in that police may have to resort to the use of (potentially lethal) force in certain situations and circumstances. However, they may be susceptible to the types of "moral distress" and "moral injury" that is linked to compassion fatigue, all of which is thought to underlie PTSD symptoms. Moral distress is linked to caring professions and is signalled by feelings of frustration, anger, sadness, psychological exhaustion, helplessness, suffering, distress, and physical exhaustion (Wiegand & Funk, 2012). In line with moral distress, the concept of moral injury refers to unprecedented traumatic life events that align with perpetrating, failing to prevent, or bearing witness to actions that "transgress deeply held moral beliefs and expectations" (Litz et al., 2009: 697). Taken together, these processes have been shown to relate to a range of negative mental health outcomes, including PTSD alcohol problems, functional impairment, dissociation, relationship problems, and suicide (Schorr et al., 2018, p. 2204) Similar to moral distress, individuals who suffer from moral injury may experience guilt, frustration, sense of rejection, difficulty forgiving, self-harm, anhedonia, and shame (Shay, 2014; Papazoglou & Chopko, 2017).

Compassion fatigue, and its relation to moral distress and moral injury, are thought to be precursors to PTSD (Nash & Litz, 2013) and are present in PTSD symptoms, such as re-experiencing traumatic incidents, avoidance, and emotional numbing (Papazoglou & Chopko, 2017). With this in mind, one avenue to consider is that police with mental health issues may be "triggered" by mentally ill persons with similar symptoms in the course of their duties. The potential consequences of PTSD in police responses to mentally ill persons are that these symptoms may preclude their ability to perform their duties and make the right decisions, and they may also negatively impact their judgement, decision making, and ability to regulate their negative emotions (i.e. anger, frustration) efficiently. These symptoms may just generally influence their performance negatively. PTSD may surface in police officers in the form of negative or hostile reactions and the unnecessary use of force towards civilians, generally, and in this case, mentally ill persons, specifically (Papazoglou & Chopko, 2017). As it stands, according to a Mental Health Attitude Survey for Police (MHASP) conducted in the US, which sampled 412 police officers, officers tend to view and respond to mentally ill persons in one of four ways. The first is authoritarianism, which assumes mentally ill persons are an inferior class requiring coercive handling. The second is a benevolent approach, which takes more a paternalistic and sympathetic view of mentally ill persons, usually derived from humanistic and religious principles. The third is social restrictiveness, which views mentally ill persons as a threat to society. Lastly, is a community mental health ideology, or a medical model, which purports that mentally ill persons have a health condition like any other (Clayfield et al., 2011). This research is in many ways insightful, but it fails to consider whether the mental health status of the responding police officers influence their perceptions and responses to mentally ill persons. For example, are police officers impacted by depression, anxiety, PTSD, or all of the above, more likely to be empathetic to mentally ill persons? More aggressive? The present chapter does not purport to answer these questions but suggests this relationship as an avenue for further research in policing policy, training, and practice.

Borrowing from Herrington and Pole (2014), a series of "deeper questions" exists in relation to police views and responses to mentally ill persons. That is, should police be involved in dealing with mental ill persons at all? Is addressing the needs of mentally ill persons an effective use of police time and characteristic of their public safety function, or is it an addition that takes them away from their core security role? Are police involved in responding to mentally ill persons because they are the service best suited to this end, or by virtue of their availability 24/7? Does police involvement in dealing with mentally ill persons serve to reduce the risk of harm to all involved, or does it heighten the risk of criminalising those who are in a health crisis? And, perhaps, most significantly, are police with heightened risk of mental health issues themselves best suited to regulate mentally ill persons? With these questions in mind, the scope of future research into mental health and the policing context might benefit from considering an integrated approach. One direction to consider is for police to reframe mental health as an issue "out there" in the community to include mental health issues internal to their organisations as well. This may inform police training and policy in a way that approaches mentally ill persons in the community while simultaneously accounting for the mental health status of police officers. Rather than being compartmentalized as it is now, research, training, and policy would be informed by a larger, more inclusive, and more robust "policing and mental health" framework.

REFERENCES

Australian Bureau of Statistics [ABS]. (2015). *National health survey: First results, 2014–15*. (no. 4364.0.55.001). Retrieved from: www.abs.gov.au/AUSSTATS/abs@.nsf/DetailsPage/4364.0.55.0012014-15?OpenDocument.

Australian Bureau of Statistics. (2016). *Causes of death*. (no. 3303.0). Retrieved from: www.abs.gov.au/AUSSTATS/abs@.nsf/DetailsPage/3303.02016?OpenDocument.

Australian Government [AG], Australian Institute of Health and Welfare. (2015). *The health of Australia's prisoners, 2015*. Retrieved from: www.aihw.gov.au/reports/prisoners/health-of-australias-prisoners-2015/contents/mental-health-of-prison-entrants.

Australian Institute of Criminology [AIC]. (2013). *Police shootings of people with mental illness*. Retrieved from: https://aic.gov.au/publications/rip/rip34.

Australian Medical Association [AMA]. (2019). *Police concern over mental illness*. Retrieved from: https://ama.com.au/ausmed/police-concern-over-mental-illness.

Bartkowiak-Theron, I., & Asquith, N. (2017). Conceptual divides and practice synergies in law enforcement and public health: Some lessons from policing vulnerability in Australia. *Policing and Society*, 27(3), 276–288.

Beyond Blue. (2018). *Answering the call: National survey*. Retrieved from: https://resources.beyondblue.org.au/prism/file?token=BL/1874.

Carroll, M. (2005). Mental-health system overburdening police. *Police Journal*, 86, 18–22.

Clayfield, J., Fletcher, K., & Grudzinskas, A. (2011). Development and validation of the mental health attitude survey for police. *Community Mental Health Journal*, 47(6), 742–751.

Clifford, K. (2010). The thin blue line of mental health in Australia. *Police Practice and Research*, 11(4), 355–370.

Coleman, T., & Cotton, D. (2010). Reducing risk and improving outcomes of police interactions with people with mental illness. *Journal of Police Crisis Negotiations*, 10(1–2), 39–57.

Doessel, D., Williams, R., & Whiteford, H. (2009). Deinstitutionalisation and managerialism in Queensland's public psychiatric institutions: Challenging 'rhetoric' with empirical results. *Australian Journal of Public Administration*, 68(4), 459–483.

Figley, C. (2002). *Treating compassion fatigue*. New York: Brunner-Routledge.

Fisher, W., & Grudzinskas, A. (2010). Crisis intervention teams as the solution to managing crisis involving persons with serious psychiatric illness: Does one size fit all. *Journal of Police Crisis Negotiations*, *10*(1–2), 58–71.

Hart, N. (2015). Veterans battling PTSD. *North Carolina Medical Journal*, *76*(5) 308–309.

Herman, J. (2001). *Trauma and recovery*. London: Pandora.

Herrington, V., & Pole, R. (2014). The impact of police training in mental health: An example from Australia. *Policing and Society*, *24*(5), 501–522.

Hesketh, I., Cooper, C., & Ivy, J. (2016). Wellbeing and engagement in policing: The key to unlocking discretionary effort? *Policing: A Journal of Policy and Practice*, *11*, 62–73.

Karaffa, K., & Koch, J. (2016). Stigma, Pluralistic ignorance, and attitudes toward seeking mental health services among police officers. *Criminal Justice and Behaviour*, *43*, 759–777.

Knowles, S., & Bull, D. (2003). Assessing the impact of shift work and stress on the psychological and physiological wellbeing of police officers. *Canadian Journal of Police and Security Services*, *1*, 337.

Komarovskaya, I., Maguen, S., McCaslin, S., Metzler, T., Madan, A., Brown, A., Galatzer-Levy, I., Henn-Haase, C., & Marmar, C. (2011). The impact of killing and injuring others on mental health symptoms among police officers. *Journal of Psychiatric Research*, *45*, 1332–1336.

Lamb, H., Weinberger, L., & DeCuir, W., (2002). The police and mental health. *Psychiatric Services*, *53*(10), 1266–1271.

Litz, B., Stein, N., Delaney, E., Lebowitz, L., Nash, W., Silva, C. et al. (2009). Moral injury and moral repair in war veterans: A preliminary model and intervention strategy. *Clinical Psychology Review*, *29*, 695–706.

Livingston, J. (2016). *Contact between police and people with mental disorders: A review of rates*. Retrieved from: https://ps.psychiatryonline.org/doi/full/10.1176/appi.ps.201500312.

Mostert, K., & Rothmann, S. (2006). Work-related well-being in the South African police service. *Journal of Criminal Justice*, *34*, 479–491.

Nash, W., & Litz, B. (2013). Moral injury: A mechanism for war-related psychological trauma in military family members. *Clinical Child and Family Psychology Review*, *16*, 365–375.

Papazoglou, K., & Chopko, B. (2017). The role of moral suffering (moral distress and moral injury) in police compassion fatigue and PTSD: An unexplored topic. *Frontiers in Psychology*, *8*, 1999.

Pickett, T., Stenstrom, R., & Abu-Laban, R. (2015). Association between mental health apprehensions by police and monthly income assistance (welfare) payments. *The Canadian Journal of Psychiatry*, *60*(3), 146–150.

Police Federation of Australia (PFA). (2019). *Inquiry into mental health*. Retrieved from: www.pc.gov.au/__data/assets/pdf_file/0003/240699/sub248-mental-health.pdf.

Purba, A., & Demou, E. (2019). The relationship between organisational stressors and mental wellbeing within police officers: A systematic review. *BMC Public Health*, *19*, 1286.

Queensland Government [QT]. (2019). *Improving mental health and wellbeing in Queensland police service.* Retrieved from: www.forgov.qld.gov.au/improving-mental-health-and-wellbeing-queensland-police-service.

Rosen, A. (2006). The Australian experience of deinstitutionalization: Interaction of Australian culture with the development and reform of its mental health services. *Acta Psychiatrica Scandinavica, 429,* 81–89.

Rufo, R. (2015). *Police suicide: Is police culture killing our officers?* Boca Raton: CRC Press.

Schorr, Y., Stein, N., Maguen, S., Barnes, J., Bosch, J. & Litz, B. (2018). Sources of moral injury among war veterans: A qualitative evaluation. *Journal of Clinical Psychology, 74*(12), 2203–2218.

Shay, J. (2014). Moral injury. *Psychoanalytic Psychology, 31,* 182–191.

Sisak, M., & Mustian, J. (2019). *Police departments confront 'epidemic' in officer suicides.* PBS NewsHour. Retrieved from: www.pbs.org/newshour/nation/police-departments-confront-epidemic-in-officer-suicides.

Talbott, J. (1978). *The death of the asylum: A critical study of state hospital management, services and care.* New York: Grune & Stratton.

Tomyn, A., Powell, M., Cassematis, P., Smallbone, S., & Wortley, R. (2015). Examination of the subjective well-being of Australian internet child exploitation investigators. *Australian Journal of Psychology, 50,* 203–211.

Velden, P., Rademaker, A., Vermetten, E., Portengen, M., Yzermans, J., & Grievink, L. (2013). Police officers: A high risk group for the development of mental health disturbances? A cohort study. *BMJ Open, 3,* 1–9.

Wells, W., & Schafer, J. (2006). Officer perceptions of police responses to persons with a mental illness. *Policing: An International Journal of Police Strategies and Management, 29*(4), 23.

White, V. (2019). *Policing on the front line of mental health emergencies: Mind the gap.* Australian Strategic Policy Institute (ASPI). Retrieved from: www.aspistrategist.org.au/policing-on-the-front-line-of-mental-health-emergencies-mind-the-gap/.

Wiegand, D., & Funk, M. (2012). Consequences of clinical situations that cause critical care nurses to experience moral distress. *Nursing Ethics, 19,* 479–487.

CHAPTER 23

Young people, the police, and policing

Philip Birch and Louise A. Sicard

INTRODUCTION

This chapter explores young people and crime within Australia, commencing with a discussion focusing on contextualising the emergence of the contemporary *juvenile delinquent*. Moving forward, this chapter examines the ever-shifting debates on youth governance, including the welfare versus justice debate, actuarial justice, and restorative justice, and considers how such informs contemporary responses to youth offending. Following this, statistics from the Australian Bureau of Statistics [ABS] (2020) and the Australian Institute of Health and Welfare [AIHW] (2019) are presented with regards to the current nature and extent of youth offending in order to contextualise the issue. The chapter is then brought to a close by examining the importance of police-youth relationships as well as the impact of policies and practices used in the policing of young people.

CONTEXTUALISING CONTEMPORARY CONCEPTIONS OF DELINQUENCY

Delinquency is a substitute label for criminal behaviour by a juvenile, where age is the only differentiation. When a young person has committed the offence, this ensures a different label and a different system; they are a juvenile delinquent who will go through the juvenile criminal justice system. Additionally, the term *delinquent* or *juvenile delinquent* implies conduct that does not conform to the legal or moral standards of society and there is often a focus on sexual or moral infringements of society's norms. Significantly, this term can be understood as a relatively modern concept and one that materialised over a particular moment in history (Cunneen, White, & Richards, 2015). The term emerged across Western Europe and North America in the 18th century and gained legal meaning in the 19th century (Shoemaker, 2013), as before this time, youth offenders were not legally separated from the general offending population (Cunneen et al., 2015). However, this is arguably indicative of how "youth" was conceptualised by society prior to the 17th century.

Terms such as childhood, youth, middle age, and elderly are used to denote social categories of age (Fineman, 2011). The behavioural expectations that are attached to each of these categories are culturally produced and sustained through the hegemonic (dominating) order. Social norms work to sustain such age categories, as individuals are socialised through language, school, religion, music, and various other forms of media, including the news, movies, television shows, and social platforms (Fineman, 2011; Lesko, 2012). Additionally, the individual is socialised by their family member and peers, who are themselves influenced and socialised by aforementioned institutional and media structures. It is through this dynamic process of socialisation that individuals form an understanding of certain age categories and what it *means* to be a child, teenager, middle aged, and elderly (Wyn & White, 1997). The term youth, in its modern sense, has developed over the last 300 years, having different cultural meanings since medieval times. This can be identified through the social and economic forces that have produced contemporary ideas about young people (Bernard & Kurlychek, 2010).

From the 14th century to the late 18th century in Western society youth below a certain age were considered to be incapable of reasoning; thus, they were not to be legally held responsible for their actions (Godfrey & Lawrence, 2014). Although this may first appear similar to the contemporary understanding of *doli incapax*, the age at which an individual was viewed as an adult during this time was seven years old (Cunneen et al., 2015). Being granted adult status allowed those aged seven and older the ability to drink alcohol and gamble; however, this status also meant that the individual was to work (Shoemaker, 2013). Apprenticeships and service were a common form of employment for youth and most young people lived in the household of their employer until they could establish an independent household by marriage or inheritance (Hanawalt, 1995). However, due to the rise of industrialisation in the 18th century, this cycle of apprenticeship and service became less common.

The early period of mechanisation in the 18th century mostly required labour-intensive, unskilled work. Thus, this provided work for many children and young people in the factories (Godfrey & Lawrence, 2014). Known as the industrial revolution, this period in history also introduced legislation to regulate the workplace, as a result of abhorrent working conditions. An example of such legislation is the English Factory Act (1833), which dictated that no child below the age of nine was to be employed in cotton mills or factories; hours were to be limited to eight hours a day for those under 13 and 12 hours for those under 18; and further noted that factory owners should provide elementary schooling for their young employees (Muncie, 1999). Additionally, technological advances in manufacturing led to more juveniles being unemployed, as men increasingly took over the position of work that was deemed skilled labour. During this time, most working families needed both parents at work to survive, however, their children were neither at school nor able to work due to the new legislation. This resulted in an increasing number of children from working-class families roaming the streets, becoming vagrants or petty criminals (Muncie, 1999).

As youth unemployment grew, the attendant anxieties about social disorder and juvenile delinquency began to loom larger in the public consciousness. Godfrey and Lawrence (2014) noted that in the UK, as an illustration, there was a rise in the prosecution of juveniles at this time; however, they argued that this does not necessarily equate to youth committing more crime. During the 1800s, there were various legislative changes that impacted the rate of juvenile prosecution. For example, the Juvenile Offenders Act (1847) in the UK, enabled people under the age of 14 to be tried in petty sessions, which significantly increased the rate of juvenile prosecutions. It is further asserted by Godfrey and Lawrence (2014) that before the 1847 Act, statistics of youth crime were not being recorded, therefore the true nature and extent of youth crime at this time is unknown.

It is offered by Cunneen et al. (2015) that the second half of the 19th century is key to understanding the shift in the concept of youth justice, as it birthed the emergence of the "reform movement". Due to the heightened concerns of juvenile delinquency, there were numerous institutional and legal reforms put into place with the underpinning ideals of youth control and reformation (Godfrey & Lawrence, 2014). A core concept behind these changes was the concern for the moral wellbeing of young people, particularly, the view was held that working-class families were ineffective in their parenting (Cunneen et al., 2015). During the second half of the 1800s, reformatories and industrial schools were established to rehabilitate the delinquent and destitute youth (Godfrey & Lawrence, 2014). It is argued that legislation, particularly from the 1870s onwards in Australia, did little to distinguish neglected children from youth offenders, where a child in poverty could be either considered under vagrancy laws and imprisoned or be labelled as destitute and placed within a welfare institution (Cunneen et al., 2015). Thus, this demonstrates the link between the development of the justice and welfare models associated with youth justice, while also highlighting both the marginalisation and criminalisation of the lower classes.

GOVERNANCE AND RISK OF YOUNG PEOPLE

Discussions concerned with the governance of young people will commonly feature the welfare versus justice model debate, where they are presented as opposing approaches (Muncie, 2006). The various governments across the global West are depicted as shifting between two models, where it is generally stated that the welfare model ideologically aligns with political left parties (such as the Australian Labour Party) and the justice model supports conservative right political parties (such as the Australian Liberal Party) (Cunneen et al., 2015; White, Haines, &

Asquith, 2017). Downes and Hansen (2006) asserted that for the first two-thirds of the past century, penal welfarism was "the principal hope of criminologists, penal reformers and most politicians for the reduction of crime and punishment alike" (p. 2). In penal welfarism, behaviour is regarded as arising from a range of factors outside the control of the individual (White et al., 2017). Additionally, the emphasis is placed on the individual's "needs", rather than the "deeds"; thus, rehabilitation is a core goal of the welfare model, where the needs of the young person must be treated through appropriate intervention.

In the mid-to-late 1970s, conservative ideologies had become the dominant voice across the sociopolitical landscapes (White et al., 2017). Accordingly, there was a shift towards justice-orientated approaches, which focused on holding the young person accountable for their offending behaviour (Cunneen et al., 2015). This shift was, at least in part, informed by the decline in the rehabilitative ideal brought about by Martinson's 1974 renown "nothing works" doctrine (Downes & Hansen, 2006). Contrastingly to penal welfarism, the justice approach places the emphasis on the offence rather than on the offender, reinforcing new-right ideologies of responsibilization, where young people are perceived as rational actors and offending is considered a choice (Cunneen et al., 2015; White et al., 2017). Additionally, the justice model promotes "just deserts" in sentencing, with rehabilitation as a secondary goal in sentencing.

Further motivating the shift towards the justice model was both the actual rise and perceived rise in crime during this time. The prevailing attitude was that welfare strategies employed within juvenile justice were "soft" strategies and young people were "getting away" with indiscretions and/or crimes. The media also harnessed this narrative of ineffective lenient sentencing for youth offenders, while simultaneously encouraging of a broader moral panic around the rising rates of crime (Jewkes, 2015; Muncie, 2001). Cunneen et al. (2015) posited that in opposing the "soft" approach of the welfare model, there were unintended consequences, including a net-widening effect, where more young people came into contact with the criminal justice system.

Over the past 30 years Australia has experienced significant changes in the juvenile justice system. It is offered that there have been progressive reforms aiming to reduce the number of youth in institutions as well as an evident resurgence of a "tough on crime" attitude, chiefly seen in punishment-focused sentencing (Cunneen et al., 2015; Gray, 2013: Muncie, 2006). This demonstrates the argument frequently presented by academics; it is not as simple as discussing the shifts between welfare and justice approaches, as contradictory policies and initiatives appear to coexist frequently (Phoenix, 2016; Hannah-Moffat & Maurutto, 2012; Muncie, 2006). Adding to this complexity, in practice, Gray (2013) asserted that youth justice workers often do not fully embrace the official policy directives due to welfare being their priority, commonly using their discretion to "engage in a complex process of resistance, subversion and revision" (p. 524).

Moving on from the debate of welfare versus justice models, scholars considered that, in a postmodern era, penology has changed from reforming individuals into an administrative function of risk; hyper-focused on categorisation, regulating, and managing offenders (Hannah-Moffat & Maurutto, 2012; Muncie, 2006; Pratt, 1989). This postmodern era of administrating the function of risk is symbolised by three current penal practices (Feeley & Simon, 1992). Firstly, the use of incapacitation within this era dictates that current punishment is not concerned with reforming individual offenders but about redistributing the risk away from society into prison. Secondly, sentencing is driven by risk factors rather than the seriousness of the offence. Thirdly, the focus on using risk factors to profile likely offenders and likely criminal situations, which leads to targeted interventions such as intensive supervision programmes and intensive policing practices (O'Malley, 2012). This is known as actuarial justice, where the core concern is the avoidance of future risks/harms. A related core concern, highlighted by Muncie (2006), is that this approach focuses on the quantifiable elements of offending, which results in qualitative elements of offending such as intersecting factors of marginalisation, vulnerability, and discrimination being ignored. Moreover, focusing on young people, it is asserted that "actuarialism denies the essential personal and cultural dynamics of youth justice work" (Muncie, 2006, p. 781).

Alongside welfare, justice, and actuarial approaches, restorative justice is another approach adopted for youth offenders. Based on republican theory, restorative justice places the emphasis on the interactions of the offenders and the victims, with the core goal of repairing the harm caused to the victim by the offender (White et al., 2017). Restorative justice can be implemented throughout various stages of the criminal process and often this encompasses measures such as restitution, compensation, and reparation (Joudo-Larsen, 2014). It is asserted that this approach aids in rectifying the "stolen conflict", as it is argued that the state has removed much of the victim and offender's interaction. Furthermore, another argued strength of this approach is the concentration on diverting young people away from the traditional pathways of the juvenile justice system. This strength is twofold, as it is beneficial to the diverted youth, while also lessening the strain placed on the criminal justice system. Exemplifying this, Webber (2012) offered that in the State of New South Wales (NSW), Australia, youth justice conferencing costs on average 18% less than comparable cases managed through the Children's Court. Yet while Australia is considered a leader in restorative justice, with most states in Australia employing family restorative conferencing (Daly & Hayes, 2001), it is important to acknowledge the mixed results restorative justice practices yield in relation to reoffending (Strang, 2010; Joudo-Larsen, 2014). Following this observation, the chapter turns to explore the nature and extent of youth offending in Australia.

NATURE AND EXTENT OF YOUTH OFFENDING ACROSS AUSTRALIA: INSIGHTS INTO THE CONTEMPORARY LANDSCAPE

Youth offender rate across jurisdictions

To understand the nature and extent of youth offending in Australia, it is beneficial to explore the offender rate across jurisdictions and how this has changed over the past decade, while presenting how this differs to the general offending population. In Australia, 2016 marked the seventh consecutive year of decreased youth offender rates, as from 2009 to 2017, the youth offender rate steadily dropped from 3,339 to 2,330 offenders per 100,000 persons aged 10 to 17 (ABS, 2018). Moreover, the decrease in youth offender rates had happened while there was a 5% raise in general population offending (ABS, 2018). The trend of decreasing rates of youth offending has continued, with Australia experiencing the lowest youth offender rate in the last decade; from 2018 to 2019 the youth offender rate was presented as 2,045 per 100,000 (ABS, 2020).

Within NSW, the rate of youth offending has shown a steady, slight decrease from 2008 to 2019. In 2008 to 2009 the rate of youth offending in NSW was captured at 2,657.2 and, more contemporarily, in 2018 to 2019 the rate was noted as 2,371.9, which is the lowest rate of youth offending in NSW from 2008 to 2019 (ABS, 2020). Upon first glance, this may appear positive, but this is significantly higher than the general offender rate that was 1,736 in 2018 to 2019. Additionally, there has been limited fluctuation in the general offender rates from 2008 to 2019, highlighting that youth offender rates have consistently been higher than the general offender rates in NSW over this time bracket.

Encouragingly, in the State of Western Australia (WA) has experienced a significant decrease in youth offender rates, as in 2008 to 2009 the rate was 4,275.7, whereas in 2018 to 2019 the rate is shown to be almost half that at 2,349.2 (ABS, 2020). Despite this, the youth offender rates in WA have remained consistently higher than the general offender rates, similar to NSW, with a general offender rate of 1,742.9 in 2018 to 2019. Although, the greatest disparity can be seen from 2010 to 2011 where the youth offender rate was noted as 4,809.9, which was over double the general offender rate of 2,008.9. While the State of Victoria has also demonstrated constantly higher youth offender rates than the general offender rates, the gap has steadily started to close. In 2008 to 2009, the youth offender rate was 2,738.3, which was almost double the general offender rate of 1,449. Nevertheless, over the decade the gap gradually closed, with the rate of youth offending in 2018 to 2019 standing at 1,369.1, compared to the general offending rate of 1,330.5. Furthermore, in the State of Queensland has displayed a stable reduction of the gap between youth offender and general offender rates. Illustrating this, the youth offender rate in 2008 to 2009 was 3,575.8 and the general offender rate was 2,451.3, while in 2018 to 2019 the youth offender rate was 2,259, as compared to the general offender rate that was 2,034. The Australian

Capital Terrority (ACT), one of two territories in Australia, continues the trend, through having gradually lowered youth offender rates and closing the gap between youth and general offender rates (ABS, 2020).

Offering some contrast to the previous jurisdictions, Norther Terrority (NT), South Australia (SA), and Tasmania have had higher rates of general offending than youth offender rates. In the territory of NT, there has mostly been a decrease in the youth offender rate over the past decade. Importantly, from 2010 onwards the rate of youth offending has been lower than the general offender rate; in 2010 to 2011 the youth offender rate was 4,045.9, while the general offender rate was 4899.8 (ABS, 2020). In 2018–2019, the NT had a significant gap, with a youth offender rate of 2,963.7 as compared to the general offender rate of 5,191.7. Demonstrating a similar trend, the State of SA has displayed lower youth offender rates that general offender rates since 2012 onward, as in 2012 to 2013 there was a rate of 2,823 youth offenders and a rate of 3,069.2 for general offenders (ABS, 2020). While the State of Tasmania followed suit in 2014 to 2015, with a slightly lower youth offender rate of 2,339.9 than the general offender rate that stood at 2,391.8. Thus, from reviewing these recent statistics, it is presented that the extent of youth offending across Australian jurisdiction is relatively varied.

Types of youth offending

Turning to the types of youth offending in Australia, it is helpful to explore the principal offence type rates for young people. In 2008 to 2009, theft was the highest committed offence by youth in Australia at a rate of 931.9, followed by acts intended to cause injury at 525 and public order offences at 478.8. In contrast to the media representations of young people and crime (Jewkes, 2015), homicide and related offences was the lowest committed offence at 3.3 in 2008 to 2009. Similarly, other high-risk offences such as sexual assault (rate of 49.2) and dangerous acts (rate of 15.2) had low rates. A decade later, the three highest committed offences differ, as in 2018 to 2019 acts intended to cause injury was the highest committed offence at a rate of 392.9, then theft at 311.9, followed by illicit drug offences at 217.3. Significantly, the illicit drug offence rates gradually increased from 2008 to 2014, with the highest rate of 265.7 in 2014 to 2015. Over the past four years this rate has decreased to 217.3 in 2018 to 2019, however, this is still higher than the 2008 to 2009 rate of 174.7. The only other offence type to be higher than its recorded rate in 2008 to 2009 was sexual assault, which was only slightly higher at 56.4. Thus, the changes in offence type rates over the past decade have shown an overall decrease across most offences, with the exception of a slight rise in sexual assault offences and a significant rise in illicit drug offences.

Indigenous youth offending

It is well documented that Indigenous young people come into contact with the criminal justice system at a disproportionally high rate (Cunneen et al., 2015). It has also been nearly 30 years, at the time of writing this chapter, since the Royal Commission into Aboriginal Deaths in Custody that sought to reduce the disproportionate incarceration and deaths in custody rates of Indigenous Australians. Nevertheless, in 2017 to 2018, Indigenous youth were 23 times more likely to be in detention than non-Indigenous youth (AIHW, 2019). Significantly, this demonstrates a higher level of over-representation in Indigenous young people than in Indigenous adults, who were 15 times more likely to be in prison than non-Indigenous adults (AIHW, 2019). This is further highlighted by the ABS (2020), where it is presented that in 2018 to 2019 over a third of Indigenous offenders were under the age of 25 across all jurisdictions. Despite being a brief demonstration of general statistics on Indigenous youth, this evidences the continuing issue of over-representation, chiefly, the over-representation of Indigenous youth in the Australian criminal justice system.

Rates of juvenile detention, supervision, and diversion

This section considers the proportion of youth who were in detention, under community-based supervision, and diverted across Australian jurisdictions. In NSW, 3.4 per 10,000 young people were in detention on an average day in 2017 to 2018, while there were 13.7 per 10,000 in community-based supervision (AIHW, 2019). Victoria had the second-lowest rate of young people in detention at 2.2 and a rate of 9.9 in community-based supervision. In Queensland, there was a rate of 4.1 young people in detention and a comparatively higher rate of 26 youth in community-based supervision. With the second-highest rate of youth in detention, WA had a rate of 5.9 and a rate of 23.7 young people in community-based supervision. In South Australia, there was a low rate of 2.6 young people in detention and 12.6 young people under community-based supervision. Tasmania had the lowest rate of young people in detention with 2 per every 10,000 and a rate of 20 under community-based supervision. The ACT experienced a rate of 3.3 young people in detention and 22.6 in community-based supervision. Lastly, the NT displayed the highest rate of young people in detention, with a rate of 15.2, and the highest rate of young people in community-based supervision, with a rate of 43.1. These statistics demonstrate that there are consistently more youth within community-based supervision than in detention across the jurisdictions in Australia. Despite this, the rate of young people aged 10 to 17 in detention varies quite dramatically, with the lowest rate of detention being 2 per every 10,000 in Tasmania and the highest being 15.7 in the NT.

The ABS (2020) presented the proportion of youth diversion across jurisdiction, noting the percentage for all youth as well as highlighting the differences between Indigenous and non-Indigenous people.[1] From 2009 to 2019, NSW has been the only state to display a significant increase in the overall youth diversion proportion, with 39.5% in 2009 to 2010 and 49.7% in 2018 to 2019. Although reporting a slight increase, the proportions of youth diversion have remained relatively stagnant in WA, with 48% in 2009 to 2010 compared to 49.5% in 2018 to 2019.

This is similar to the NT, where there has only been a minor increase of 41.8% to 42.4% from 2009 to 2019, although in 2012 to 2013 diversion proportions lowered considerably to 27.8%. Other states and territories have shown slight or considerable decreases in youth diversion proportions. For example, Victoria has presented a considerable decrease, where in 2009 to 2010 youth diversion proportions were at 34.8% and have been reduced to 20.7% in 2018 to 2019.

With the exception of the NT, all other states and territories displayed a higher percentage of diversions for non-Indigenous youth than Indigenous youth in 2018 to 2019. The NT presented a 42.5% diversion of Indigenous youth as compared to a slightly lower 40% diversion of non-Indigenous youth in 2018 to 2019. The diversion proportions in WA during this time highlighted a gap, with Indigenous diversion reported at 43.8% and non-Indigenous diversion presented higher at 54.8%. However, other jurisdictions have exhibited greater disparity in diversion proportions in 2018 to 2019. Exemplifying this, NSW captured diversion for Indigenous youth at 22.5%, in comparison to 57.6% for non-Indigenous youth. Arguably, the use of diversion as a means of diverting young people away from the justice system could be better utlised. It is important to note however, that not all young people will be eligible to access diversionary measures. As a consequence this can leave police officers with little option other than to direct a young person into the justice system.

YOUNG PEOPLE AND THE POLICE

Individual perceptions and attitudes of the law and related institutions such as the police are formed through personal experiences as well as the beliefs held by those within a person's close network such as the family and in the person's broader social contexts (Hinds, 2007). It is argued that although perceptions and attitudes are dynamic, positive attitudes towards the police developed during formative years are likely to have a lasting impact for that individual (Hinds, 2007). For young people, their first contact with the justice system is usually a police officer, so in this way, the police can be viewed as the gatekeepers to the justice system (Brunson & Pegram, 2018; Cunneen et al., 2015). Accordingly, research has demonstrated that the first contact between young people and police is crucial to the development of the young person's attitude to authority and the state (Hinds, 2007). Therefore, the role of the police and their approach to young people is of considerable importance in shaping, for life, an individual's attitude towards the law, criminal justice institutions and their processes.

Procedural justice theories consider that individuals who experience fair legal processes will be more likely to view the law as legitimate and that this will positively impact their risk of recidivism and other interactions with the justice system (Penner, Viljoen, Douglas, & Roesch, 2014). Relating specifically to policing, it was asserted that an individual's willingness to cooperate with police is a core factor that impacts police efficacy (Hinds, 2007). Significantly, Hinds' (2007) study found that the perception of police employment of procedural justice was the key element impacting young people's perspectives of police legitimacy.

In Australia and across other countries there have been difficulties in gaining cooperation from youth, chiefly in relation to collaborative crime control efforts (Murphy, 2013). It is suggested that this is related, at least in part, to the notion that youth often hold more negative perceptions of the police than their adult counterparts (Hurst & Frank, 2000; Fagan & Tyler, 2005). Moreover, the work of Thurau (2009) found that police in the United States, United Kingdom, and Australia have disproportionate contact with youth, including high rates of arrest and use of force contact. These findings are further supported by Murphy (2013), who then asserted procedural justice policing should be further employed rather than coercive deterrence-based tactics to respond to this issue of disproportionate contact.

Focusing on Australia, Grossman and Sharples (2010) conducted a study of 500 youth in Victoria, which concentrated on young peoples' perception of the police. A core finding of the research demonstrated that young people felt they would be more likely to contact the police if they thought they were more friendly and respectful towards them. Other research has demonstrated that more informal contact between young people and the police can help to foster beneficial relationships (Hinds, 2009). Exemplifying this, Hinds (2009) examined the Youth Community Alliance (YCA) project, which was an Australian community policing intervention that aimed to build positive youth-police relationships. This project included several activities to increase the formal contact including: three youth-police days to bring youth and police officers together, a competition asking youth to examine how to improve personal safety, a nine-week course of self-defence classes and a movie night with youth and police recruits close to graduation. The findings demonstrated the YCA project as effective in developing beneficial youth-police relationships, which led to increased perceptions of police legitimacy and a higher willingness to assist the police (Hinds, 2009). This demonstrated another approach, besides procedural justice policing, that can positively develop youth perceptions and attitudes towards police.

As presented earlier, the YCA project was a community policing initiative. The approach adopted for policing, commonly referred to as policing style, such as community policing or zero-tolerance policing, can impact on an individual's perception and subsequent attitudes concerning the police. The overall efficacy of police practice has been recognised as being affected by these perceptions and attitudes (Drew & Prenzler, 2015). Cunneen et al. (2015) asserted that how a government responds to crime, including that of the police, is heavily influenced by media depictions of youth crime, particularly the moral panic surrounding such crime. In discussing this, Cunneen et al. (2015) noted the resurgence of zero-tolerance policing that is being used to govern young people, recognising the focus on maintaining public order. This may take the form of "move on" orders, disbanding groups of young people and stopping any undesirable activities, criminal or not (Cunneen et al., 2015).

Zero-tolerance approaches in policy and practice have been embraced across Anglo-American jurisdictions (Tyler, 2011), gained popularity in the UK (particularly during the labour government from 1997 to 2010) and are viewed in high esteem by some politicians and police officers in Australia (Cunneen et al., 2015). Related to zero-tolerance policing, Crawford (2009) explored the impact of dispersal powers used within the UK to control antisocial behaviours in youth. Crawford (2009) noted that, at this time, youth control was a major political focus, so it became a core concern for policy and policing. It was found that the use of dispersal orders could increase the negative perceptions held by youth concerning the police, particularly when used inconsistently (Crawford, 2009). Importantly, due to the discretionary nature of dispersal orders, young people perceived police as unpredictable and unfair, which was found to often provoke defiance (Crawford, 2009). Additionally, Crawford (2009) discussed that, as a result of the dispersal powers escalatory nature, a net-widening effect came into play, with more youth coming into contact with the justice system.

In Australia, although it varies across jurisdiction, the police have been granted powers that align with zero-tolerance policing practices to manage young people. This has included "move on" orders, the casual use of "name-checks", stop and searching powers related to prohibited implements, and enhanced ability to retrieve bodily samples and fingerprints of young offenders (Cunneen et al., 2015). Cunneen et al. (2015) asserted that, despite having only a small body of Australian-focused research on dispersal powers, it is thus far demonstrated that certain groups of people are more negatively impacted than others, chiefly, young people, Indigenous people, and homeless people. For example, similarly to Crawford's (2009) UK-based research, a study in Melbourne, Victoria demonstrated that young people felt unfairly targeted by the stop-and-search policing powers, particularly so if they were a person of colour (Wilson, Rose, & Colvin, 2010). The existing research on zero-tolerance policing approaches and youth has highlighted that such an approach negatively impacts youth-police relationships. Additionally, in some instances, zero-tolerance policing can cause more young people to come into contact with the justice system, chiefly, those with the intersecting factors of race, low socioeconomic status, and sexuality (for research on queer community and policing, see Fileborn, 2019).

The policies that police forces have in place to both guide and inform their work with young people is therefore important. A recent youth strategy released by the NSW police, the NSW Police Force Youth Strategy [PFYS] (2019), illustrates this well. One of the aims presented by this strategy is to increase the overall use of diversion, as this has well-known benefits for young people (PFYS, 2019). Such policy aims and goals are important in terms of informing practice and can be demonstrated in the evidence as making an impact, as the ABS (2020) demonstrated by noting NSW was the only jurisdiction in Australia to have significantly rising diversion proportions over the last decade. Nevertheless, many police youth-based policies across Australian jurisdictions in 2017 to 2018 sought to increase the use of diversion, to less of a success than in NSW, demonstrating that policies in themselves may not effectively filter into practice (AIHW, 2019), and organisational buy-in is essential for ensuring policy converts into practice.

CONCLUSION

The emergence and concept of "young people" over time has shifted, this transition has seen young people finding themselves in vulnerable places and spaces, in particular within the public sphere. As a consequence, there has been a turbulent relationship between the police and young people, with the latter often being conceptualised as needing to be controlled, while simultaneously being viewed as vulnerable and in need of protection. This chapter has reflected on the Australian context which has been shown to share similarities with other countries such as the UK, when exploring the sociopolitical discourse on how young people are and should be governed. While it is encouraging that there are examples across Australia of diverting young people away from the criminal justice system, the media's depiction of young people and their offending is in juxtaposition to the Australian crime statistics. Notwithstanding this, there is the potential to improve young peoples' perceptions, attitudes, and experiences with the police and wider criminal justice system. The police are often the first point of contact for young people with the justice system; ensuring the police have practices that are informed by evidence-based policy in essential in order to ensure an adverse net-widening effect for young people does not emerge.

NOTE

1 There were no statistics recorded for youth diversion in Tasmania over the last decade. South Australia has no recorded statistics for 2018 to 2019 (ABS, 2020).

REFERENCES

Australian Bureau of Statistics (ABS). (2018, February 8). *Youth offender rate falls for seventh consecutive year* [media release]. Retrieved from: www.abs.gov.au/ausstats/abs@.nsf/Lookup/by%20Subject/4519.0~2016-17~Media%20Release~Youth%20 offender%20rate%20falls%20for%20seventh%20consecutive%20year%20(Media%20Release)~17

Australian Bureau of Statistics (ABS). (2020). *Recorded crime – offenders, 2018–19* (No. 4519.0). Canberra: Australian Bureau of Statistics.

Australian Institute of Health and Welfare (AIHW). (2019). *Youth justice in Australia 2017–18*. (No. JUV 129). Canberra: AIHW.

Bernard, T. J., & Kurlychek, M. C. (2010). *The cycle of juvenile justice* (2nd ed.). Oxford: Oxford University Press.

Brunson, R. K., & Pegram, K. (2018). Kids do not so much make trouble, they are trouble: Police-youth relations. *The Future of Children, 28*(1), 83–102.

Crawford, A. (2009). Criminalising sociability through anti-social behaviour legislation: Dispersal powers, young people and the police. *Youth Justice, 9*(1), 5–26.

Cunneen, C., White, R., & Richards, K. (2015). *Juvenile justice: Youth and crime in Australia* (5th ed.). Oxford: Oxford University Press.

Daly, K., & Hayes, H. (2001). *Restorative justice and conferencing in Australia* (pp. 1–6). Canberra: Australian Institute of Criminology.

Downes, D., & Hansen, K. (2006). Welfare and punishment in comparative perspective. *Perspectives on Punishment: The Contours of Control, 2*, 135–154. Retrieved from: www.researchgate.net/profile/Kirstine_Hansen/publication/30527985

Drew, J., & Prenzler, T. (2015). *Contemporary policing practice*. Oxford: Oxford University Press.

Fagan, J., & Tyler, T. R. (2005). Legal socialisation of children and adolescents. *Social Justice Research, 18*(3), 217–242. doi:10.1007/s11211-005-6823-3

Feeley, M. M., & Simon, J. (1992). The new penology: Notes on the emerging strategy of corrections and its implications. *Criminology, 30*(4), 449–474.

Fileborn, B. (2019). Policing youth and queerness: The experiences and perception of young LGBTQ+ people from regional Victoria. *Current Issues in Criminal Justice, 31*(2), 433–451.

Fineman, S. (2011). *Organizing age*. Oxford: Oxford University Press. doi:10.1093/acprof:o sobl/9780199578047.001.0001

Godfrey, B., & Lawrence, P. (2014). *Crime and justice since 1750* (2nd ed.). London: Routledge.

Gray, P. (2013). Assemblages of penal governance, social justice and youth justice partnerships. *Theoretical Criminology, 17*(4), 517–534. doi:10.1177/1362480613 496450

Grossman, M., & Sharples, J. (2010). *Don't go there: Young people's perspectives on community safety and policing: A collaborative research project with Victoria police, region 2 (Westgate)*. Sydney: Victoria University Press.

Hanawalt, B. A. (1995). *Growing up in medieval London: The experience of childhood in history*. New York: Oxford University Press.

Hannah-Moffat, K., & Maurutto, P. (2012). Shifting and targeted forms of penal governance: Bail, punishment and specialized courts. *Theoretical Criminology, 16*(2), 201–219. doi:10.1177/1362480612443302

Hinds, L. (2007). Building policing – youth relationships: The importance of procedural justice. *Youth Justice, 7*(3), 195–209. doi:10.1177/1473225407082510

Hinds, L. (2009). Youth, police legitimacy and informal contact. *Journal of Police and Criminal Psychology, 24*(1), 10–21. doi:10.1007/s11896-008-9031-x

Hurst, Y.G., & Frank, J. (2000). How kids view cops the nature of juvenile attitudes towards the police. *Journal of Criminal Justice, 28*(3), 189–202. doi:10.1016/S0047-2352(00)00035-0

Jewkes, Y. (2015). *Media and crime* (3rd ed.). London: Sage Publications.

Joudo-Larsen, J. (2014). *Restorative justice in the Australian criminal justice system*. Australian Institute of Criminology website. Retrieved from: https://apo.org.au/sites/default/files/resource-files/2014/02/apo-nid38143-1183831.pdf

Lesko, N. (2012). *Act your age! A cultural construction of adolescence* (2nd ed.). New York: Taylor and Francis.

Muncie, J. (1999). *Youth and crime: A critical introduction.* London: Sage Publications.

Muncie, J. (2001). Policy transfers and 'what works': Some reflections on comparative youth justice. *Youth Justice, 1*(3), 27–35. doi.org/10.1177/1473225 40100100304

Muncie, J. (2006). Governing young people: Coherence and contradiction in contemporary youth justice. *Critical Social Policy, 26*(4), 770–793. Retrieved from: http://dx.doi.org/doi:10.1177/0261018306068473

Murphy, K. (2015). Does procedural justice matter to youth? Comparing adults' and youths' willingness to collaborate with police. *Policing and Society, 25*(1), 53–76. doi:10.1080/10439463.2013.802786

New South Wales Police. (2019). *NSW police force youth strategy.* Retrieved from: www.police.nsw.gov.au

O'Malley, P. (2012). Globalising risk? Distinguishing styles of 'neoliberal' criminal justice in Australian and the USA. In T. Newburn & R. Sparks (eds.), *Criminal justice and political cultures: National and international dimensions of crime control* (pp. 30–48). Devon: Willan Publishing.

Penner, E. K., Viljoen, J. L., Douglas, K. S., & Roesch, R. (2014). Procedural justice versus risk factors for offending: Predicting recidivism in youth. *Law and Human Behaviour, 38*(3), 225–259. doi:10.1037/lhb0000055

Phoenix, J. (2016). Against youth justice and youth governance, for youth penalty. *The British Journal of Criminology, 56*(1), 123–140. doi:10. 1093/bjc/azv031

Pratt, J. (1989). Corporatism: The third model of juvenile justice. *The British Journal of Criminology, 29*(3), 236–254.

Shoemaker, D. J. (2013). *Juvenile delinquency* (2nd ed.). London: Rowman & Littlefield.

Strang, H. (2010). Exploring the effects of restorative justice on crime victims of conflict in transitional societies. In S. G. Shoham, P. Knepper, & M. Kett (Eds.), *International handbook of victimology* (pp. 563–582). London: CRC Press, Taylor and Francis Group.

Thurau, L. (2009). Rethinking how we police youth: Incorporating knowledge of adolescence into policing teens. *Children's Legal Rights Journal, 29*, 30–48.

Tyler, T. R. (2011). Trust and legitimacy: Policing in the USA and Europe. *European Journal of Criminology, 8*(4), 254–266. doi:10.1177/1477370811411462

Webber, A. (2012). *Youth justice conferences verses court: A comparison of cost effectiveness* (Report No. 164). Sydney: NSW Bureau of Crime Statistics and Research.

White, R., Haines, F., & Asquith, N. L. (2017). *Crime and criminology* (6th ed.). Oxford: Oxford University Press.

Wilson, D., Rose, J., & Colvin, E. (2010) *Marginalised young people, surveillance and public space report.* Sydney: Youth Affairs Council of Australia.

Wyn, J., & White, R. (1997). *Rethinking youth.* Sydney: Allen and Unwin.

CHAPTER 24

Policing settler colonial societies

Amanda Porter and Chris Cunneen

INTRODUCTION: CHALLENGING THE ORTHODOXY OF "POLICING"

We explore in this chapter the idea and praxis of "policing" within settler colonial societies such as Australia. We do this through consideration of various issues including Aboriginal deaths in police custody and missing and murdered Aboriginal women and children. We conclude with a reflection on strategies of Aboriginal community safety and defence. Our argument in this chapter is informed by various approaches which challenge commonly held ideas and assumptions about policing and legitimacy within settler colonial contexts. The core concepts which support this chapter are decolonial/postcolonialism, abolitionism/ decarceration, settler colonialism, institutional racism and genocide.

Decolonial and postcolonial approaches prioritise reconceptualising Western histories and institutions from the perspectives of the colonised. This is partly a historical task which requires seeing institutions in their colonial context and effect. For example, while popular and mainstream histories of police provide a liberal view of progress from the Peelian model of police in early 19th-century London, a postcolonial approach sees modern policing forged within the context of establishing and maintaining colonial supremacy globally (Brogden, 1987; Cunneen, 2001). The question then arises, "How would we write the history of the development of policing in Australia if our starting point was colonial imperatives of invasion and violence, and of Aboriginal peoples and their resistance to these processes?" We typically see policing within the narrow blinkers of current institutional arrangements of state-based police forces. However, as we argue later in this chapter, it is possible to conceive safety and security in completely different ways that disrupt the conventional paradigm of "policing". Indigenous approaches to supporting social order in communities is distinctive in its foundations, purposes, and rationalities.

Abolitionist and decarceration approaches provide a broad transformative program which is intended to realise social rather than criminal and carceral justice. At their core they provide a way of looking at and thinking about policing and prison as key social problems in themselves rather than crime per se (Langton, 1990, 1992; Porter, 2018; Ruggiero, 2010). Specifically in relation to policing, Vitale (2017) argues that the contemporary rationality of policing is founded in the constant potentiality of state violence and repression. He argues that this needs to be replaced with a very different logic of care, of thoughtfulness and sensitivity to community and individual needs, and is consistent with calls to replace current policing with community empowerment and social justice.

The concept of settler colonialism grounds the concepts of postcolonialism and abolitionism firmly within the Australian context. Settler colonialism is a distinct process of invasion, settlement, and nation-building which radically transformed the lives of those original peoples and tribal nations living in the occupied territories. It is a particular type of colonialism where the primary economic objective is securing permanent access to and control of land and resources. Historically, sovereignty was asserted on the basis of "discovery" and continues to be justified by the primitiveness of Indigenous peoples and their failure to "productively" utilise the land. As Wolfe (2006) has argued, settler colonialism demands that Indigenous peoples had to be either eliminated or contained and controlled in order to make land available as private property for settlers who have come to stay.

The policies and practices of elimination (genocide) and/or containment (institutional racism) became core roles in the developing colonial state and its institutions, including the police. A history of Australian police's involvement in genocide (e.g. the mounted police and native police) and role in implementing policies built on institutional racism (e.g. Aboriginal child removal and protection legislation more generally) is widely recognised (Cunneen, 2001; NISATSIC, 1997; Roberts, 2005; Owen, 2016). It is also essential to recognise that settler colonialism is not a distinct or discrete set of events, it is rather a structural and ongoing relationship. Unlike other forms of colonialism (for example, in Africa, Asia, and the Caribbean) there has never been a decolonial moment where the colonisers left. Settler colonialism has remained a key structural paradigm of Australian policing and the defining characteristics of genocide and institutional racism remain.

PART ONE: COLONIAL LEGACIES AND CONTINUITIES IN POLICING

As the introduction of this chapter acknowledges, the political context of settler colonialsim was the most important factor defining the specific features in Australian policing. Australian police forces today are distinguished by a particular relation to government which can be traced in its legal form to colonial statutes of the mid-19th century, among the earliest examples being the *Police Act 1844* (South Australia) and the *Police Act 1853* (Vic). These colonial statutes required that the police were to be controlled from the central political power, rather than by local political authorities.

Prior to these consolidated acts, policing *within* the colony was locally based and developed specialised and ad hoc functions in places like the gold fields, the water police, and the night watch (Finnane, 1994). Policing *outside* the colony and of the *colonial frontier* took place via three key institutions: the Border Police (established after the Myall Creek Massacre of 1838), the Mounted Police (paid out of British Military appropriations until 1839), and the Native Police. These organisations were reputed for their extreme violence and savage acts of brutality. The war-like police operations which existed were influenced by the level of Aboriginal resistance, which at times could appear to threaten the general prosperity of the colony (Cunneen, 2001; Finnane, 1994). During the period of protectionism that followed in the 20th century, police were given far-reaching powers into the everyday lives of Aboriginal peoples. These included the power to issue rations, to attend school, to see a doctor, to be expelled from a reserve (Cunneen, 2001, pp. 62–72).

While legislative frameworks may have changed over the years, there are continuities in the type of contact between Indigenous people and state police. The concept of "over-policing" is often used to refer to the *degree* of police intervention and the *nature* of police intervention in Indigenous communities. Over-policing draws attention to the continuities in the role of police in the extensive regulation and surveillance of the lives of Aboriginal and Torres Strait Islander people. The degree of intervention can be demonstrated through the number of police stationed in areas with large Aboriginal communities. In addition, over-policing can be seen in the nature of intervention through the use of particular policing *practices* – which we discuss later.

Policies and practices centred on "risk" have become an important contemporary component of policing. The NSW Police Force's Suspect Target Management Plan (STMP) provides an example of how these notions of risk play out and have particular impacts on Aboriginal young people. The STMP "seeks to prevent future offending by targeting repeat offenders and people police believe are likely to commit future crime" – it is "both a police intelligence tool that uses risk assessment to identify suspects and a policing program that guides police interaction with individuals who are subject to the program" (Sentas and Pandolfini, 2017, p. 1). Young people and adults can be subjected to a STMP because of a prior criminal history, friendship or family associations and/or prior interactions with police.[1] STMPs effectively "enables any NSW police officer to place people, including minors, who have never been convicted of an offence but who police suspect to be at risk of committing future crimes as well as recidivist offenders, on a list whereby they are targeted for intensive policing" (Australian Lawyers for Human Rights, 2017). A review of STMP found disproportionate use against children (who comprised just on half of all those subject to a STMP), including some as young as ten. More importantly for our discussion was the fact 44% of the young people subject to a STMP identified as Aboriginal (Sentas and Pandolfini, 2017, p. 11).

Australian Lawyers for Human Rights argued in relation to the STMP that,

> *Intensively policing people who have never been convicted of any offence is inconsistent with fundamental human rights and rule of law principles such as the presumption of innocence. Such people are effectively being punished prospectively via significant police intrusions into their day-to-day life based on an assumption that they might commit a crime at some point in the future* (Australian Lawyers for Human Rights, 2017).

There has also been a substantial growth in police discretionary summary justice in recent years, via the rise of penalty infringement notices, consorting legislation, banning and exclusion orders, alcohol restrictions, paperless arrest laws, and move-on powers (Farmer, 2015; Cunneen et al., 2016; Brown et al., 2017; Behrendt et al., 2019, pp. 89–97). Notably, Aboriginal people are significantly over-represented among the group of people affected through this expansion of police powers. The adverse use of police discretion against Indigenous people was shown recently in a report by the Western Australian Police Service's in-house research unit, which found that Aboriginal drivers received 3.2 times more fines from being pulled over by police than non-Aboriginal drivers. However, when tickets were issued by traffic cameras, Aboriginal drivers received fewer penalties on average than non-Aboriginal drivers. The WA Police research report was based on data collected over five years and acknowledged a "clear ethnic disparity" in police-initiated traffic stops (Wahlquist, 2020).

A significant issue to emerge has been the increasing use of Tasers and OC (Capsicum) spray and their inappropriate and/or excessive use. In Western Australia, the Corruption and Crime Commission investigated the use of Tasers and OC spray after an Indigenous man was tasered seven times in a little over a minute by two police officers. The Commission found the tasering an "undue and excessive use of force which was unreasonable and unjustified" (Corruption and Crime Commission, 2012, p. 1). Two senior police officers were later found guilty of assault and sentenced to suspended gaol terms and fines. In Queensland and NSW, inquiries found that Indigenous people were more likely to be subjected to the use of Tasers and OC spray than other members of the public. In NSW nearly 30% of people tasered were Aboriginal or Torres Strait Islander (NSW Office of the Ombudsman, 2012, p. 99). Indigenous people were also more likely to be subjected to multiple/continued Taser use than other groups. The Queensland Crime and Misconduct Commission (2005, p. x) noted "an unusually high rate of use against people who are

Aboriginal, Torres Strait Islander or Pacific Islander in appearance". Some 33%t of OC spray "subjects" were in this grouping (Crime and Misconduct Commission, 2005, p. 25). Indigenous people comprise around 3% of the state's population.

The violence of policing becomes even more apparent when we examine two of the most polarising issues in relations between Aboriginal and Torres Strait Islander peoples and state police forces: (1) responsibility and accountability in Indigenous deaths in police custody, and (2) the adequacy of police investigations into missing and murdered Indigenous women and children. Both these issues raise broader questions about the role of institutional racism within police services and criminal justice institutions.

Deaths in police custody

River of Tears, Kev Carmody
From the album: Eulogy (For A Black Person) (1991)

They took him out at point blank range
In his home with his small young son
Shot him dead in his Marrickville bed
With a pump action 12 gauge shotgun
Fatherless child and a grieving wife
A black fugitive on the run
On the run from two centuries
Of oppressions loaded gun

Two hundred years in the river of fear
Gunned him down
Terrorists dressed in uniform
Under the protection of their law
Terrorise blacks in dawns of fear
They come smashin' through your door
You're not safe out there on freedom street
You're not safe inside the "can"
For their shotguns and their stunt gas
They're licenced to drop you where you stand
We say oh oh oh oh oooooh
Sad river of tears (Reprinted with Permission of Kobalt Music Publishing)

In 1991 the Royal Commission into Aboriginal Deaths in Custody found that almost two-thirds (63) of the 99 deaths investigated occurred in police custody (rather than adult or juvenile prison). Furthermore, most Aboriginal people at the time of the Royal Commission were in police custody for minor offences, mostly public drunkenness, and to a lesser extent, street offences (Johnston, 1991, vol. 1, pp. 12–13). In particular, Aboriginal women were much more likely to die in police custody compared to other forms of custody – nine of the 11 women who died were in police custody at the time. They were especially likely to be held for minor offences, mostly for the offence of public drunkenness. Others were there for fine default or offensive language. There is evidence over several decades to show that the recommendations of the Royal Commission into Aboriginal Deaths in Custody are often ignored or inadequately implemented in practice (Cunneen and Porter, 2017; Ting, 2011).

Many contemporary Indigenous deaths in police custody arise from people being locked-up for minor offences, and many deaths occur because of a failure to exercise a required duty of care. This failure represents the "violence of neglect". For example, in the case of Ms Dhu, Coroner Fogliani found that the 22- year-old died in police custody in a Western Australian police lock-up after being arrested for unpaid fines relating to public order offences (Fogliani, 2016, para 784). Ms Dhu complained to police about severe pain, vomiting, and partial paralysis and was twice taken to hospital, but on both occasions was sent back to the police lock-up. On the third occasion when she was taken to hospital, she was dying from septicaemia and pneumonia. Police believed her transfer to hospital was not urgent and reportedly told nursing staff she was "faking" her illness. The Coroner described her treatment by police as "appalling" and "unprofessional and inhumane" (Fogliani, 2016, paras 880, 883).

While there has been a long-term change in the location of the majority of deaths in custody from police to prison custody (Gannoni and Bricknell, 2019), many of the core issues remain, including the arrest and detention of people for unpaid fines, for public drunkenness, for their own "welfare", and during police interventions. The following is a summary over the one-year period from December 2017 to December 2018.[2] Cherdeena Wynne, 26, died in a Perth hospital in 2018, after losing consciousness while handcuffed in circumstances that Western Australian police said were related to welfare concerns. In 2018, 16-year-old CD and his 17-year-old friend TS drowned in the Swan River while being pursued by police in response to a report of "teenagers jumping fences". Also in 2018, TK died in police custody in Townsville after his family had called the police because they feared he would self-harm. Police allegedly "spear-tackled" him to the ground. He became unresponsive and could not be revived. In Sydney in 2018, Patrick Fisher fell from a 13th floor balcony while trying to escape police who sought to arrest him for outstanding warrants. In December 2017 Yorta Yorta woman Tanya Day died in hospital after being injured in custody following her arrest on the grounds of protective custody. A train conductor had called police allegedly because she was "unruly", but this was disputed by other passengers. The Coroner has ruled that she will consider evidence on the effects of systemic racism in the matter. At the time of writing none of the coronial investigations for the deaths just mentioned have been completed. At the more extreme level, there were two police fatal shootings of Aboriginal people in late 2019: Joyce Clarke in Geraldton and teenager Jumanji Walker in Yuendumu. In both cases, the police officers have been charged with murder. The problems of the adverse use of police discretion, institutional racism and violence show their most concentrated and disastrous effects in Indigenous deaths in police custody. Many of the deaths noted here have caused significant protest actions across Australia, led by the families of the deceased. Another issue which has been the subject of significant contemporary protest actions, led by bereaved families, has been that of missing and murdered Indigenous women and children.

Missing and murdered women and children

In June 2019 the Final Report of the National Inquiry into Missing and Murdered Indigenous Women and Girls (NIMMIWG, 2019a), "Reclaiming Power and Place", was delivered to the Canadian federal government. It included the testimonies of 2,380 family members, consisting of two volumes and 231 recommendations. The national inquiry revealed a persistent and deliberate pattern of human rights abuses and systemic racism within the provincial police, and it characterised the issue of missing and murdered Aboriginal women and children in terms of "genocide". The report followed a series of inquiries, inquests, and systematic reviews into substandard police investigations into missing persons cases and cold cases. A recent example included the final report into the Thunder Bay police service, which found that the police consistently "devalued Indigenous lives, reflected differential treatment that were based on racist attitudes and stereotypical preconceptions about Indigenous people" (McNeilly, 2018, p. 5).

In Australia, there has been no equivalent national, state, or regional inquiries which have looked at the issue of missing or murdered Indigenous women and children. Instead, Australian inquiries have tended to focus on Aboriginal deaths in police and prison custody, out of home care, and other forms of institutional violence. Many cases of missing and murdered Aboriginal women and children involve inadequate police investigations which are characterised by various failures and shortcomings. These include failure to follow up on crucial leads, the delay in collection of evidence due to racial assumptions made by investigating police officers because of the victim's Aboriginality, political inaction in the decision to prosecute (by the attorney general and public prosecutors within various jurisdictions), and other systemic oversights and shortcomings, including a lack of interest within the mainstream media.

For example, in 2011, a 33-year-old Aboriginal woman, Lynette Daley, was brutally murdered by non-Indigenous men Adrian Attwater and Paul Maris in Maclean, on the far north coast of New South Wales. The investigation and decision to prosecute was initially marred by political inaction and indifference. Although the NSW Director of

Public Prosecutions twice declined to prosecute in relation to Daley's death, an investigation into the circumstances of her death in May 2016 on ABC television promoted public awareness, which eventually led to a review of the decision, a trial, and an eventual conviction. Such an outcome is altogether less than typical.

In 1991, three Aboriginal children – Colleen Walker-Craig, Clinton Speedy-Duroux, and Evelyn Greenup – went missing in the community of Bowraville, also on the far north coast of New South Wales. The initial police investigation in the Bowraville case included the failure to follow up on crucial leads, including witness statements, a delay in the collection of evidence due to racial assumptions made by the investigating police officers due to the victim's Aboriginality, and a delay in the decision to call a homicide team due to the family's Aboriginality, among other issues. In August 2016, then-NSW police commissioner Andrew Scipione delivered a formal apology to the Bowraville families for inadequacies in the initial police investigation. Speaking to families in Bowraville, he stated: "I want to publicly acknowledge that the NSW Police Force could have done more for your families when these crimes first occurred and how this added to your pain, as a grieving community. And for that I am sorry." (ABC News, 2016). The Bowraville families' appeal for special leave was rejected by the High Court of Australia in May 2019.

The stories of Bowraville and Maclean bear similarities to countless other regional and remote townships. These are not isolated cases. They reflect innumerable deaths in which the alleged perpetrator, often a non-Indigenous person, remains at large and for which justice has never been secured. In the community of Borroloola, for example, a young boy was found dead in suspicious circumstances in 2007. A young Aboriginal woman was found dead in 2013 in eerily similar circumstances. In 2018 coroner Greg Cavanagh delivered an inquest with scathing comments about the substandard investigation carried out by the Northern Territory police (Cavanagh, 2018). No one has been charged in relation to either death.

In the township of Bourke, two teenage Aboriginal girls – Mona Smith and Jacinta Smith – died in horrific circumstances – while in the company of a middle-aged non-Indigenous man, who was later acquitted of allegations he had killed the two Aboriginal girls by driving while drunk. A charge of sexual misconduct with a corpse was withdrawn. In 1988 Gomeroi teenager Mark Haines was found dead on a train track in Tamworth in rural New South Wales. It is understood that the coroner determined that Mark died on the railway tracks, however the formal findings of the coroner and the records of the final day of the inquest have apparently been lost. No one was ever arrested or charged in connection with Mark's death. The ABC podcast *Unravel: Blood on the Tracks* examines the circumstances surrounding Mark's death and details a number of the serious shortcomings in the initial police investigation (Clarke, 2018).

The issues of deaths in custody and missing and murdered women and children bring into focus issues such as genocide, institutional racism, institutional sexism, over-policing, under-policing as well as broader social, economic, and intergenerational issues. The Canadian National Inquiry findings support characterising the issue of missing and murdered women and children as genocide (NIMMIWG, 2019a, p. 54). The National Inquiry equally prepared a supplementary report on the Canadian genocide of Indigenous peoples according to the legal definition of "genocide" (NIMMIWG, 2019b). National inquiries and legal definitions aside, the reality of genocide has long been acknowledged by Aboriginal and Torres Strait Islanders. As AJ Whittaker observes, "[T]he settler justice system is nothing but a long queue of First Nations women holding photos of their dead kids" (2019).

PART TWO: RESISTANCE AND DECARCERATION STRATEGIES

So far this chapter has focused on state-centric definitions of policing and security. But what if we were to consider policing much more broadly, from the lens of safety and non-state security governance? This section considers a range of Indigenous safety and security initiatives.

Indigenous security and safety governance

Aboriginal night patrols, streetbeats, and safety governance of self-policing are locally run initiatives with formal agendas that focus on keeping young people safe and on preventing contact between Aboriginal young people and the state police. Patrols operate in a diverse range of urban, rural, and remote settings across some Australian jurisdictions (Porter, 2016, 2018). Blagg (2016) estimates that approximately 130 such patrols operate in Australia, with around two-thirds of these being located in rural and remote parts of Western Australia and the Northern Territory.

The core features of patrol work include independence from state police, a consensual basis of operations, and a connection to the local Indigenous community (Porter, 2016). Indigenous night patrols are distinctive from formal reform efforts that sought to alter the state police, in that a key part of their agenda is to minimise Aboriginal people's contact with the criminal justice system. Importantly, patrols function independently of the state police and, at least in theory, are connected in some way to the local Aboriginal community within which they operate. In practice, they operate with varying levels of community input or involvement from the Aboriginal community. As this implies, patrols do not fall neatly in either the governmental or autonomous reform efforts, and occupy what scholars have termed third or hybrid spaces (Cunneen, 2001; Blagg, 2016).

Despite variation and diversity among initiatives, broad unity can be seen at the level of key functions, which in NSW includes providing transport, maximising safety, the mentoring of Indigenous young people, preventing harmful behaviour, and maximising the safety of young people who "fall through the cracks" of the system (Porter, 2016). Research suggests that the everyday activities of patrols extend beyond Western concepts of policing, crime prevention, and social work; and that they provide a much more encompassing cultural service for Indigenous youth (Porter, 2016). It is perhaps for this reason that – with few exceptions (Langton, 1992; Cunneen, 2001; Blagg, 2016) – the contribution of Indigenous patrols has largely escaped the attention of criminologists.

Custody notification schemes

Indigenous initiated attempts to control interaction with police and increase Aboriginal and Torres Strait Islander wellbeing can take various forms. For example, the Victorian Aboriginal Legal Service (VALS) has been strongly advocating for the introduction of a "Failure to Divert Declaration" which would require police to provide reasons as to why they failed to use diversion for a young person. The Declaration would be submitted to court at the time of filing charges. However, in this section we focus on the use of custody notification schemes (CNS) which are regulatory frameworks that have been developed to minimise Aboriginal and Torres Strait Islander deaths in police custody.

Although the nature of CNS services varies widely across jurisdictions, CNS typically provides a 24 hour, 7 days a week, contact service that compels police – either by legislation, regulations, or formal agreement such as memoranda of understanding – to notify when an Indigenous person is taken into police custody. The key objectives of CNS are to prevent Aboriginal and Torres Strait Islander deaths in police custody, to improve cultural safety while in police custody, and to promote the upholding of the detainees' legal rights and protections while in police custody. At present, it is estimated that 16,000–18,000 Aboriginal and Torres Strait Islander persons in custody use this service each year (Georgatos, 2018; Speakman and Harwin, 2019).

The history of the development of custody notification schemes and other police monitoring bodies is interwoven with Aboriginal activism, particularly the advocacy of families and communities in response to deaths in custody. Particular acknowledgement should be given to the contribution of bereaved families who have lost loved ones in police custody and their supporters, who have been instrumental in establishing CNS as well as lobbying for improvements in their everyday operation. The extended family of Ms Dhu and the Western Australian Deaths in Custody Watch Committee, for example, have been directly involved in the recent establishment of a CNS in Western Australia.

It is useful to consider the example of the CNS model in NSW by way of a case study. The CNS model in NSW is a 24-hour, 7 days a week, phone service provided by the Aboriginal Legal Service (ALS). ALS criminal lawyers operate the phone service, responding to welfare concerns, including threats of self-harm, access to medication, notification of injuries, and ensuring police provide a duty of care. The NSW Police Force (NSWPF) have a statutory duty to notify ALS CNS when an Aboriginal person enters police custody. This statutory requirement was first introduced with the passage of Regulation 28 of *Crimes (Detention After Arrest) Regulation 1998* (NSW). Where the NSWPF fail to adhere to these provisions, any evidence of records of interviews and other evidence may be set aside as inadmissible, as per Hidden J in *Campbell and 4 Ors v Director of Public Prosecutions (NSW)* [2008] NSWSC 1284.

Anecdotal evidence suggests that NSW's regulatory framework has led to a marked decrease in the number of Aboriginal deaths in police custody. However, the recent death of Wiradjuri woman Ms Rebecca Maher raised concerns about the comprehensiveness of NSW's regulatory framework, which did not require NSWPF to contact ALS CNS for people detained in protective custody. The findings of the coronial inquest into Ms Maher's death by the acting NSW state coroner Teresa O'Sullivan led to the statutory duty being expanded to include protective custody, and the Commonwealth Government injecting $1 million to support the expansion in the 2019–2020 financial year (Speakman and Harwin, 2019). Other jurisdictions have not yet amended their respective regulatory frameworks to include protective custody. For example, the *Police Amendment Regulations 2019* (NT) does not include protective custody or the "paperless arrests – legislative regime which provides expansive police powers and is associated with a high rate of Aboriginal incarceration and deaths in custody" (Hunyor, 2014).

Resistance and refusal

These safety and policing accountability mechanisms must not be seen as isolated measures but must be viewed against a broader backdrop of Aboriginal and Torres Strait Islander nation building, language revival, cultural revitalisation practices, and resistance. While resistance can be seen in all these cultural examples – music, art, protest, language – in this section we focus on the example of "no jurisdiction cases" and strategic litigation.

On August 3, 2015, Murrumu Walubara Yidinji ("Murrumu") was arrested in the police watch house in Cairns, Australia, on charges related to driving an unregistered and uninsured car with false plates, and driving without a license while possessing "an article resembling a licence". Murrumu, previously known as Jeremy Geia, was driving in a vehicle using number plates and a driver's license issued by the Sovereign Yidinji Government, known to Crown as "Cairns". The Sovereign Yidinji Government is not recognised by the state of Queensland. At the time of arrest and for the two days he was held in custody, Murrumu repeatedly declared that he is "Murrumu in the appropriate persona", a legal personality that was not recognised by the state of Queensland or the Crown. Two days later, local magistrate Robert

Spencer in the local Cairns Magistrate Court dismissed the case against Jeremy Geia.

Importantly, Indigenous nations globally have organised themselves politically for thousands of years and continue to do so under the radar and without interference from settler court systems, which as the above example demonstrates, have no mechanism for recognising one another. The continuation of these customary rights is reflected in Article 3 of the *United Nations of Declarations of Indigenous Rights*, it equates to a right to freely determine their political, economic, social, and economic development. The issue of non-recognition of Indigenous nationhood and sovereignty was addressed more recently in the *Uluru Statement from the Heart*, which emphasised the need for structural reforms to overcome the economic disenfranchisement and issue of non-recognition which plagues settler colonial legal systems.

There are many other examples of "no jurisdiction" cases. In the late 1980s and early 1990s, Bejam Kunmunara Jarlow Nunukel Kabool ("Denis Walker", 1947–2017), brought a series of cases before the High Court of Australia. Mr Walker was a Nunukul man from Minjerribah-Moorgumpin, or what is known to the Crown as Stradbroke Island, Queensland. He was a famous Aboriginal activist, philosopher, writer, and scholar who committed his entire life to Aboriginal sovereignty and civil rights movements, having co-founded the Brisbane chapter of the Australian Black Panther Party (with the late Sam Watson, in February 1972) and the the Brisbane "Pig Patrol" (a night patrol), known for his central role in the land rights movements in the 1970s, and the establishment of the first Aboriginal Medical Services and Aboriginal Legal Services in Brisbane (also with the late Sam Watson). In the late 1980s, Mr Walker was defending a sacred site on Bundjalung Country, or what is known to the Crown as Nimbin, the far north coast New South Wales. Mr Walker was charged by the police on the grounds of discharging a firearm. Mr Walker challenged the allegations of the grounds on which he was charged and the applicability of statutes and the common law to Aboriginal and Torres Strait Islander Peoples where those laws had been neither requested, nor consented to, by them.

To do this Mr Walker had to ask the High Court to exercise its original jurisdiction to make a determination with respect to two legal issues: firstly, whether Aboriginal customary law survived colonisation, and secondly, whether state statutes and the common law apply to Aboriginal and Torres Strait Islander peoples.[3] The State of New South Wales brought an application that Mr Walker's claim be dismissed on the basis that it did not plead a reasonable cause of action. Mason CJ of the High Court ultimately rejected the matter, stating that Mr Walker was amendable to the jurisdiction of the Crown.

The contrasting examples of Murrumu and the Yidinji Sovereign Government and of Mr Walker and his community defence action are but two examples in a long line of sovereignty activists and counter-colonial protest movements. Despite the rich and vibrant examples of sovereignty initiatives both historically and in the present, Aboriginal sovereignty movements are seldom acknowledged within mainstream policing scholarship. We hope this brief overview goes some way towards correcting this oversight.

CONCLUSION

This chapter discussed the idea and practice of "policing" in settler colonial societies such as Australia. Within the context of settler colonial societies, policing was paramount to securing control of land and resources and extending the frontier of the expanding colonial frontier. This chapter demonstrated the ways in which the development of the state police in settler colonies differed to development of policing for the non-Indigenous civilian population, and was forged in colonial warfare, child removal, genocide and institutional racism – policies which have a continuing legacy and lasting impact today. In addition, contemporary frameworks of risk and the growth in police discretionary justice have furthered the problem of over-policing. This chapter then discussed two key contemporary issues in the policing of settler colonial societies: (1) deaths in police custody, and (2) missing and murdered Indigenous women and children.

The bulk of policing scholarly enquiry and anthologies has been concerned with writings about the "state police". However, as this chapter has demonstrated, it is possible to conceive of safety and security in completely different ways that disrupt the conventional paradigm of "policing". Indigenous approaches to supporting social order in communities is distinctive in its foundations, purposes, and rationalities. The example of Indigenous security initiatives emphasised the key principles of safety, care, community, and critically, independence from the state police. We have also highlighted the importance of resistance and refusal, particularly the "no jurisdiction" cases which challenge the basic right of colonial institutions to police Indigenous people.

NOTES

1. See Law Enforcement Conduct Commission (2000, pp. 19–20) for case studies of Aboriginal children with no prior charge history who were subject to STMP.
2. The discussion of these deaths is drawn from *The Guardian* database, 'Deaths Inside: Indigenous Australian Deaths in Custody', Available at http://www.theguardian.com/australia-news/ng-interactive/2018/aug/28/deaths-inside-indigenous-australian-deaths-in-custody. Accessed 24 Feb 2020.
3. *Walker v the State of New South Wales* [1994] HCA 64.

REFERENCES

ABC News. (2016) 'Bowraville Murders: NSW Police Chief Says Victims' Families Were Let Down'. Available at: www.abc.net.au/news/2016-08-11/andrew-scipione-apologises-to-families-of-bowraville-children/7721492

Australian Lawyers for Human Rights. (2017) 'Human Rights Lawyers Slam Suspect Target Management Scheme'. Available at: https://alhr.org.au/human-rights-lawyers-slam-nsw-pre-emptive-policing-program/.

Behrendt, L., Cunneen, C., Libesman, T. and Watson, N. (2019) *Aboriginal and Torres Strait Islander Legal Relations*. Melbourne: Oxford University Press.

Blagg, H. (2016) *Crime, Aboriginality and the Decolonisation of Justice*, 2nd edition. Annandale: Federation Press.

Brogden, M. (1987) 'The Emergence of the Police: The Colonial Dimension'. *The British Journal of Criminology*, 27(1), 4–14.

Brown, D., Cunneen, C. and Russell, S. (2017) '"It's All About the Benjamins': Infringement Notices and Young People in New South Wales'. *Alternative Law Journal* 42(4), 253–260.

Cavanagh, G. (2018) 'Inquest into the Death of Sasha Loreen Napaljarri Green'. NTLC016. Available at: https://justice.nt.gov.au/__data/assets/pdf_file/0006/525417/A00592013-Sasha-Green.pdf

Clarke, A. (2018) 'Unravel: Blood on the Tracks'. Available at: www.abc.net.au/radio/programs/truecrime/blood-on-the-tracks/

Corruption and Crime Commission, Western Australia. (2012) 'Charges to Be Considered Over Tasering of Kevin Spratt'. Media Release. Perth, Corruption and Crime Commission.

Crime and Misconduct Commission, Queensland. (2005) *Oleoresin Capsicum (OC) Spray Use by Queensland Police*. Brisbane: Crime and Misconduct Commission.

Cunneen, C. (2001) *Conflict, Politics and Crime*. Annandale: Allen and Unwin.

Cunneen, C., Goldson B. and Russell, S. (2016) 'Juvenile Justice, Young People and Human Rights in Australia'. *Current Issues in Criminal Justice*, 28(2), 177–188.

Cunneen, C. and Porter, A. (2017). Indigenous Peoples and Criminal Justice in Australia. In *The Palgrave Handbook of Australian and New Zealand Criminology, Crime and Justice* (pp. 667–682). London: Palgrave Macmillan.

Farmer, C. (2015) '"Is a 24-Hour Ban Such a Bad Thing?" Police-Imposed Banning Notices: Compatible with Human Rights or a Diminution of Due Process?' *Australian Journal of Human Rights*, 20, 29–61.

Finnane, M. (1994) *Police and Government: Histories of Policing in Australia*. Oxford: Oxford University Press.

Fogliani, D. (2016) 'Inquest into the Death of Julieka Ivanna Dhu (11020–14)'. Coroner's Court of Western Australia, Perth, WA.

Gannoni, A. and Bricknell, S. (2019) *Indigenous Deaths in Custody: 25 Years Since the Royal Commission into Aboriginal Deaths in Custody*. Canberra: Australian Institute of Criminology.

Georgatos, G. (2018) 'The Custody Notification System Saves Aboriginal Lives'. *The Guardian*, 15 December. Available at: www.theguardian.com/commentisfree/2016/sep/15/the-custody-notification-system-saves-aboriginal-lives-why-isnt-it-national

Hunyor, J. (2014) 'Imprison Me NT: Paperless Arrests and the Rise of Executive Power in the Northern Territory'. *Indigenous Law Bulletin*, 21(8), 3–9.

Johnston, E. (1991) *Royal Commission into Aboriginal Deaths in Custody. National Report*, 5 Volumes. Canberra: AGSPS, Charles Sturt University.

Langton, M. (1992) 'The Wentworth Lecture: Aborigines and Policing: Aboriginal Solutions from Northern Territory Communities'. *Australian Aboriginal Studies*, 2.

Langton, M. et al. (1990) *Too Much Sorry Business*. Submission of the Northern Territory Aboriginal Issues Unit to Commissioner Elliott Johnston, Royal Commission into Aboriginal Deaths in Custody. Canberra: AGSPS, Charles Sturt University.

Law Enforcement Conduct Commission (LECC). (2000) *An Investigation into the Formulations and Use of the NSW Police Force Suspect Targeting Management Plan on Children and Young People*. Sydney: LECC.

McNeilly, G. (2018) 'Broken Trust: Indigenous People and the Thunder Bay Police Service'. Available at: http://oiprd.on.ca/wp-content/uploads/OIPRD-Broken-Trust-Final-Accessible-E.pdf

National Inquiry into Missing and Murdered Indigenous Women and Girls (Canada). (2019a) 'Reclaiming Power and Place: The Final Report of the National Inquiry into Missing and Murdered Indigenous Women and Girls'. Available at: www.mmiwg-ffada.ca/final-report/

National Inquiry into Missing and Murdered Indigenous Women and Girls (Canada). (2019b) 'Supplementary Report: A Legal Definition of Genocide'. Available at: www.mmiwg-ffada.ca/wp-content/uploads/2019/06/Supplementary-Report_Genocide.pdf

National Inquiry into the Separation of Aboriginal and Torres Strait Islander Children from Their Families (NISATSIC). (1997) *Bringing Them Home*. Sydney: Australian Human Rights Commission.

NSW Office of the Ombudsman. (2012) *How Are Taser Weapons Used by the NSW Police Force?* Sydney: New South Wales Office of the Ombudsman.

Owen, C. (2016) *'Every Mother's Son Is Guilty': Policing the Kimberley Frontier of Western Australia 1882–1905*. Crawley: UWA Publishing.

Porter, A. (2016) 'Decolonizing Policing: Indigenous Patrols, Counter-Policing and Safety'. *Theoretical Criminology*, 24(4), 548–565.

Porter, A. (2018) 'Non-State Policing, Legal Pluralism and the Mundane Governance of "Crime"'. *Sydney Law Review*, 40(4), 445–467.

Roberts, T. (2005) *Frontier Justice: A History of the Gulf Country to 1900*. St Lucia: University of Queensland Press.

Ruggiero, V. (2010) *Penal Abolitionism*. Oxford: Oxford University Press.

Sentas, V. and Pandolfini, C. (2017) *Policing Young People in NSW: A Study of the Suspect Targeting Management Plan*. Sydney: Youth Justice Coalition.

Speakman, M. and Harwin, D. (2019) 'Media Release: Safeguarding Indigenous People in Custody', 15 October. Available at: www.justice.nsw.gov.au/Pages/media-news/media-releases/2019/safeguarding-indigenous-people-in-custody.aspx

Ting, I. (2011) 'Deaths in Custody – An Eleven Part *Crikey* Investigation'. Available at: www.crikey.com.au/deaths-in-custody/

Vitale, A. (2017) *The End of Policing*. London: Verso.

Wahlquist, C. (2020) 'Aboriginal Drivers in WA More Likely to Get Fines from Police Officers That Traffic Cameras'. *The Guardian*, 5 February. Available at: www.theguardian.com/australia-news/2020/feb/05/aboriginal-drivers-in-wa-more-likely-to-get-fines-from-police-officers-than-traffic-cameras

Whittaker, A. (2019) 'Twitter Status', 22 November, 4:56pm. Available at: https://twitter.com/AJ_Whittaker/status/1197755685708021760

Wolfe, P. (2006) 'Settler Colonialism and the Elimination of the Native'. *Journal of Genocide Research*, 8(4), 387–409.

CHAPTER 25

Hate crime
Insights into the context, setting, and prevalence

Philip Birch and Jane L. Ireland

INTRODUCTION

This chapter presents a systematic review conducted as part of a wider empirical study that sought to inform operational police practice in terms of identifying and addressing hate crime. The systematic review was conducted and guided by the PRISMA guidelines (Prisma, 2009), with PsycINFO, Medline, Cochrane Library, and ERIC being used to source existing literature. Analysis of the existing literature generated four themes with a series of subthemes, offering insight into the context, setting, and prevalence of Hate Crime. In doing so, it revealed the complexity of this crime type. The themes presented in this chapter are:

- Theme 1: Nature and Extent of Hate Crime;
- Theme 2: Perpetrators of Hate Crime;
- Theme 3: Victims of Hate Crime;
- Theme 4: Reporting and Recording Hate Crimes/Incidents.

First, the background to this crime type is presented, accounting for the theoretical positions that can be used to understand Hate Crime in a meaningful way for, in particular, practitioners, before moving onto a detailed description of these themes.

BACKGROUND

Globally, there has been a trend in rising levels of hate incidents. In the United States, 7.175 incidents, involving 8,437 offences, were reported in 2017, which was a 5.9% increase from the previous year, according to the Federal Bureau of Investigation (Justice, 2017). In the United Kingdom there were 94,098 hate crime offences recorded by police in England and Wales in 2017/2018, an increase of 17% compared with the previous year (Hambly, Rixom, Singh & WedlakeJames, 2018). In Australia, between the years 2013 and 2016, 1,050 cases were recorded as bias crime, suspected bias crime, or bias incidents in New South Wales, Australia (Mason, 2019). However, these figures may not fully represent the true extent of hate crime, as it is widely acknowledged that hate crime is underreported (Pezzella, Fetzer & Keller, 2019) and that there are problems with identification and categorisation (Mason, 2019). Thus, policing and prosecuting perpetrators, as well as supporting victims of hate crime is an unyielding challenge (Giannasi, 2015). Regardless, scholars have argued the increase in hate crime is reflective of significant social problems within society (Chakraborti, 2018).

Defining and theorising hate crime

There are multiple complexities in defining hate crime. First, definitions vary. A broad definition is that "a hate-motivated crime is one that was motivated in whole or in part, by a bias" (Roberts, 1995, p. 6). However, whilst this definition provides a starting point for defining this crime type, it does not offer any clarification about what types of behaviours constitute hate crimes or who is at risk of hate crime. Indeed, it has been argued that there is no clear consensus about the characteristics of hate crime (Garland, 2012). Adding to the complexity of defining hate crime is whether police forces use an exclusive definition, whereby the crime must be solely based on protected characteristics, or whether a lower threshold is used, as this is likely to impact on hate crime reporting data (Roberts, 1995). Within the UK, the College of Policing (2014, p. 2) define hate crime as any crime or incident where the perpetrator's hostility or prejudice against an identifiable group of people is a factor in determining who is victimised. Five strands of hate crime are identified, including disability, race, religion, sexual orientation, and transgender status. There is some suggestion that this might marginalise other groups, such as the homeless, sex workers, the elderly, and foreign nationals, despite their vulnerability and experiences of hate and prejudice, because of their perceived difference (Chakraborti, 2015a). It could, therefore, be argued that this jeopardises the principle of equality (Mason-Bish, 2015) and creates a victim hierarchy (Walters, Brown & Wiedlitzka, 2016). Marginalising less visible targets, who may not have the means or opportunity to share their experiences, certainly limits any true conceptualisation of this crime.

Intersectionality, which describes the overlap between social correlates such as race, class, and gender, which can create disadvantage and discrimination, also impacts on the way that hate crime is viewed and reported. Hate crime legislation does not consider the fact that a victim may be targeted on the basis of one or more aspect of their identity or lifestyle. Evidencing intersecting prejudices can serve to confuse the recording of hate crime (Walters et al., 2016). The potential diversity in victim experience, as a result of characteristic intersectionality, is also often overlooked (Mason-Bish, 2015). However, discreet categorisation has allowed the law to recognise crimes of hate and prejudice (Mason-Bish, 2015). Without this approach there would be no guidance for the criminal justice system.

There are various theories that attempt to provide an explanation for hate crime. Hierarchy and power dynamics form a common theme within the hate crime literature. For example, Perry (2001, p. 10) defines hate crime as "a mechanism of power, intended to reaffirm the precarious hierarchies that characterise a given social order". However, to view hate crimes in the context of subordination may be an overstatement (Chakraborti, 2015b). It obscures more spontaneous actions and suggests that members of a dominant group can only ever be offenders and members of a minority group can only be victims, which is not reflective of the complexity of hate crime (Hall, 2015). Furthermore, the motivation for hate crime by perpetrators may not solely be about dominance, but may be reflective of other emotions, beliefs, and experiences, such as disconnection, alienation, and feeling abused (Rabrenovic, 2007). Therefore, other theories and approaches should be considered. Individual level explanations of hate crime highlight the concept of the authoritarian personality and how prejudicial attitudes and beliefs towards minority groups develop because these groups are perceived as a challenge to normality (Walters et al., 2016). Similarly, *Social Dominance Theory* (Sidanius & Pratto, 1999, cited in Walters et al., 2016) highlights how those who covet social dominance tend to believe their "in-group" is superior to others and thus they are more prejudiced towards other groups.

It has also been suggested that hate crime may arise from intergroup conflict as a result of competing for resources (Rabrenovic, 2007). *Strain Theory* (Merton, 1968, cited in Walters, 2011) gives support to this, as this theory argues that deviant behaviour occurs as a result of the strain created when culturally prescribed goals cannot be met legitimately (Walters, 2011). Therefore, hate crime can be seen as a product of economic hardship (Anderson, Dyson & Brookes, 2002). Alternatively, a *Symbolic Interactionism* Approach proposes that people in groups communicate orally and via symbols, with personality and behaviour being shaped through communication and interaction with the group. In this context if the group advocates violence towards a particular minority, the members who display such behaviour (e.g. such as engaging in hate crimes) become highly valued (Anderson et al., 2002). In contrast, *Social Learning* perspectives propose that there is a combination of social and psychological factors that influence behaviour. Aggressive behaviour can be learned by observing and imitating the aggressive behaviour of others. Reinforcement can then inform and incentivise this behaviour (Bandura, 1977). Within the context of hate crime, hatred and prejudice thus becomes learnt (Anderson et al., 2002), with factors such as family, religion, economy, government, and education having an impact.

The chapter now moves on to present the findings from a systematic review. The aim of the review was to identify and review published studies examining the causes of hate crime and subsequent risk factors evidenced by the perpetrators and victims associated with this crime type.

A SYSTEMATIC REVIEW: EXPLAINING THE APPROACH AND FRAMEWORK

A systematic literature review was conducted adhering to the relevant sections of the Preferred Reporting Items for Systematic Review (PRISMA, 2009). Searches were completed using the following databases: ERIC, PsycINFO, MEDLINE, and COCHRANE library. These databases were selected because of their relevance to the area of hate crime. The search procedure used the following abstract terms: *Hate Crime OR Prejudice Crime OR Bias Crime AND Triggers AND Causes AND Antecedents OR Risk Factors OR Risk Assessment OR Risk Screening*. Synonyms and Boolean operators were then added. The search was limited to words that were included in the abstract. No date limits were set.

Additional internet searches were undertaken, as was a hand review of the reference lists from identified articles to find additional studies for inclusion. Articles were excluded if they were not full text, if they were not available in the English language or if they were non-empirical (i.e. narrative and review papers). Papers identified from the literature search were initially screened by examining titles and abstracts. Following this, all full text articles that met the inclusion criteria were assessed for eligibility.

A total of 1,222 article hits were returned. Internet searches were conducted which returned 12 article hits. Once duplicates were removed, 1,108 article abstracts were screened for relevance. Abstracts were marked as either relevant, maybe relevant, or not relevant. Those marked as not relevant were given a code based on its reason: (1) abstract only; (2) unrelated topic; (3) secondary source/narrative/review. This resulted in 249 full text articles obtained in full copy formats and reviewed for further screening. A more in-depth inspection of the articles was performed for each of the full text articles. In addition to the reasons for exclusion for the abstract screening, the full text articles were also marked as not being included if they were: (4) not available in the English language. This resulted in 19 articles being identified for the review based on the search criteria. The references of these 19 studies were hand-searched, resulting in a further four studies being identified. As a result, 23 papers were included in the synthesis. Figure 25.1 outlines the process.

Thematic synthesis

A thematic synthesis of the included studies was conducted to identify patterns within the data, following the techniques outlined by Braun and Clarke (2006). Each subtheme is presented with a percentage. This represented the proportion of studies from the systematic review, which related to that issue.

FINDINGS

From the systematic review, four themes emerged. Each theme is presented here containing a series of sub-themes in order to provide

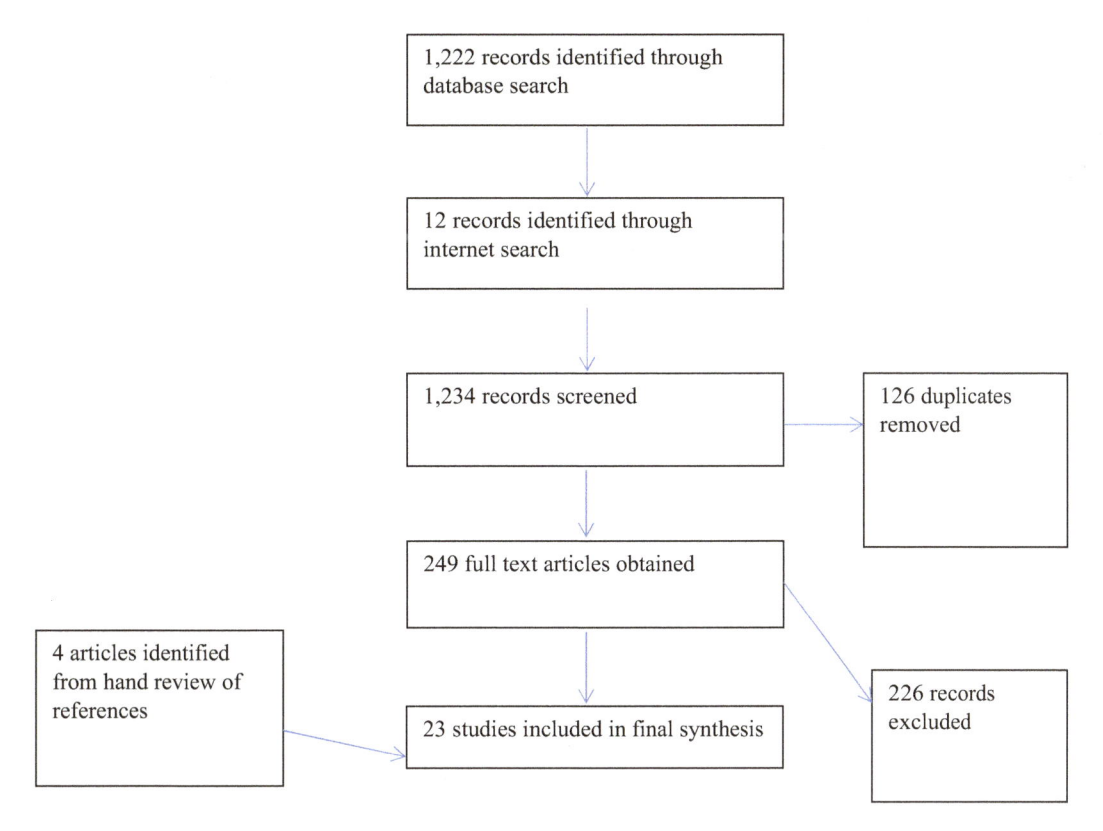

FIGURE 25.1
PRISMA flow chart of included studies

insights into the context, setting, and prevalence of hate crime. As a result, the existing literature can be used to inform police practice with regards to this crime type.

Theme 1: nature and extent of hate crime

Hate crime offences vary in nature (39%)

Several studies highlighted that physical assault, verbal abuse/threats, and property damage were the most frequently reported offences (Czajkoski, 1992; Barnes & Ephross, 1994; Dunbar, 2003; McMahon, West, Lewis, Armstrong & Conway, 2004; Chakraborti, Garland & Hardy, 2014; Paterson, Walters, Brown & Fearn, 2018; Mason, 2019). Within the reviewed studies, it was also reported that racial hate crimes and sexual orientation hate crimes were more likely to be directed against the person, whereas religious hate crimes were more likely to be directed against property (Roberts, 1995; Cheng, Ickes & Kenworthy, 2013).

Hate crime areas are not localised (30%)

The home or public area (e.g. street) were the most common locations for victimisation (McDevitt, Balboni, Garcia & Gu, 2001; McMahon et al.,

2004; Mason, 2005; Tiby, 2007; Chakraborti et al., 2014; Williams & Tregidga, 2014; Walters et al., 2018). It was also reported that victimisation occurred in other areas, such as the workplace, via telephone/internet or SMS text, and on public transport (Mason, 2005; Tiby, 2007; Chakraborti et al., 2014). In one study, it was noted that the location of the hate crime had a significant impact on how the incident affected the victim, particularly if it occurred in or near their home (Chakraborti et al., 2014).

Race informing perpetration and/or victimisation (48%)

Hate crimes/incidents based on race were typically the most common occurrence (McMahon et al., 2004; Iganski et al., 2011; Walters & Krasodomski-Jones, 2018). Several studies showed that ethnicity of hate crime perpetrators was more likely to be white (Czajkoski, 1992; Dunbar, 2003; Dunbar, Quinones & Crevecoeur, 2005; Herek, Cogan & Gillis, 2002; Jolliffe & Farrington, 2019) and that hate crime against black victims was higher than any other race hate crimes (Roberts, 1995; Cheng et al., 2013).

It was also reported that white perpetrators consistently committed more hate crimes against black victims than against any other racial group. Black perpetrators also consistently committed more hate crimes against white victims (Cheng et al., 2013). However, these findings should be interpreted with caution as they may reflect reporting bias.

One study (Dunbar et al., 2005) also identified that racially motivated offenders had more extensive criminal histories than those who committed offences based on religious bias. They also had significantly more severe histories of violence.

Theme 2: perpetrators of hate crime

Men are more likely to be potential hate perpetrators (41%)

Numerous studies showed that men were more likely to commit or be accused of committing hate crime (Czajkoski, 1992; Herek et al., 2002; Dunbar et al., 2005; Mason, 2005; Tiby, 2007; Iganski et al., 2011; Roxell, 2011; Chakraborti et al., 2014; Walters et al., 2018).

Hate perpetrators are more likely to be younger (22%)

Perpetrators were more likely to be teenagers or younger adults below the age of 35 (Herek et al., 2002; Iganski et al., 2011; Roxell, 2011, Chakraborti et al., 2014; Jolliffe & Farrington, 2019). However, there was evidence that when compared to non-hate crime violent offenders, violent hate crime offenders were significantly older (Jolliffe & Farrington, 2019).

Perpetrators may have pre-existing antisocial tendencies and/or mental health/trauma issues (17%)

Antisocial tendencies reflect behaviours that are not in keeping with societal norms, such as unemployment, offending, and substance misuse. Within the literature there was some evidence that perpetrators were likely to have prior criminal convictions (Dunbar, 2003; Dunbar et al., 2005;

Jolliffe & Farrington, 2019) and were unemployed (Dunbar, 2003; Iganski et al., 2011). It was also reported that hate crime offenders who committed offences based on racial hatred had more extensive and violent criminal histories. (Dunbar et al., 2005). One study found that over half of hate crime perpetrators had a history of substance misuse and nearly one in four had had psychiatric treatment (Dunbar, 2003). There was also evidence of maladjustment, specifically parental separation and/or domestic violence within the family history (Dunbar, 2003; Dunbar et al., 2005).

Perpetrators are unlikely to belong to a hate group or be hate crime specialists (18%)

Although only two studies reported on hate groups, there was evidence that only a small number of offenders were part of hate-orientated gangs or groups (Dunbar, 2003; Dunbar et al., 2005). Two studies (Roxell, 2011; Jolliffe & Farrington, 2019) noted that hate crime offenders were unlikely to be specialists who committed only hate-motivated crime.

Hate crime as a uni-or-multiple perpetrator offence (30%)

Although some studies found that hate crimes were generally committed by one suspect/perpetrator (Tiby, 2007; Roxell, 2011; Walters et al., 2018), some studies showed that multiple perpetrators were often involved (McDevitt et al., 2001; Herek et al., 2002, Dunbar, 2003; Chakraborti et al., 2014). Those experiencing sexual violence were more likely than others to state that the offence had been committed by one perpetrator (Chakraborti et al., 2014).

Hate crime as a multifaceted motivated event (9%)

Only two studies made reference to perpetrator motivation. McDevitt, Levin and Bennett (2002), for example, found four primary motivations, which they described as thrill seeking, defensive, mission, and retaliatory. Perpetrators motivated by thrill seeking were described as having a desire to be powerful and committed their crimes for excitement, whereas perpetrators whose motivation was defensive were described as trying to protect their "turf" and protect against perceived threats. Mission perpetrators were reported as being motivated to "rid the world of evil" and retaliatory-motivated perpetrators as attempting to avenge a perceived wrong. In a later study by Dunbar (2003), it was reported that when one or more signifiers of racial bias motivation were present (e.g. membership in a hate group), the nature of aggression was more instrumental and planned, with instrumentally aggressive perpetrators typically seeking social dominance rather than monetary or material gain.

Theme 3: victims of hate crime
Men are more likely to be identified as victims (26%)

According to several studies, men were generally more likely to be the victims of hate crime (Czajkoski, 1992; Herek, Gillis & Cogan, 1999; Tiby, 2007; Chakraborti et al., 2014; Mason, 2019). However, one study

(Mason, 2005) found that although men were more likely to report racial and homophobic incidents as a whole, in their sample, victims of racial incidents were more likely to be women, whereas men were more likely to be victims of homophobic incidents.

Hate crime victims are likely to be adults (17%)

There was little information reported relating to victim age, but one study reported that most hate crimes were committed by adults against adults (Czajkoski, 1992). Another found the mean age of victims was 35 (Walters et al., 2018), with Mason (2019) reporting victims were aged between 30–65 years. It may be that victim age differs depending on the type of hate crime. Although generalisations cannot be made, one study found that those reporting harassment tended to be older than those reporting hate crime as a whole (Mason, 2005).

Hate crime victims identifying as homosexual are most at risk (22%)

Several studies showed that victims identifying as homosexual were more likely to experience hate crime and targeted hostility (Roberts, 1995; Herek et al., 1999; Cheng et al., 2013; Chakraborti et al., 2014, Mahoney, Davies & Scurlock-Evans, 2014). One study reported that hate crimes against male victims, who identified as homosexual victims, were significantly higher than hate crimes against female victims, who identified as homosexual (Cheng et al., 2013).

Victims identifying as Muslim may be more likely to be victims of hate crime (17%)

Although evidence is limited, some studies reported that victims who identified as Muslim were more likely to be targeted (Cheng et al., 2013; Chakraborti, et al., 2014; Walters, et al., 2018; Mason, 2019) and to cite their religion as the reason for their victimisation (Chakraborti et al., 2014).

Pre-existing relationships between victims and perpetrators (35%)

Although some studies found that perpetrators were more likely to be strangers (McDevitt et al., 2001; Herek et al., 2002; Williams et al., 2018), numerous studies found that perpetrators were often known to the victim (Mason, 2005; Tiby, 2007; Roxell, 2011; Chakraborti et al., 2014). In one study it was reported that disabled victims were more likely to know the perpetrator, with neighbour reported as the most common relationship when the perpetrator was known (Walters et al., 2018). Dunbar (2003) further reported that offenders of multiple-perpetrator hate crimes were less likely to have a prior relationship with the victim(s).

Evidence of repeated victimisation (17%)

Several studies reported that there was evidence that repeat or ongoing victimisation was common (Barnes & Ephross, 1994; Mason, 2005; Chakraborti et al., 2014; Paterson et al., 2018).

Negative impacts on victims and the wider community (34%)

Several studies revealed that there was a significant psychological impact for those experiencing hate crimes, including increased anger, fear, and vulnerability (Herek et al., 1999; McDevitt et al., 2001; Chakraborti et al., 2014; Paterson et al., 2018). It was reported that this often led to behavioural changes, such as increasing personal safety, avoiding areas, or changing appearance (Barnes & Ephross, 1994; Simich & Kang-Brown, 2018; Chakraborti et al., 2014). Two studies found that those experiencing transgender or disability crime were significantly more likely to experience both psychological impacts and physical reactions, including depression and suicidality (Chakraborti et al., 2014; Williams et al., 2014). In addition, it was recognised that the effects of hate crime were likely to reach beyond the victim and potentially have a negative impact on other members of society who identify with the victims. A study by Paterson et al. (2018), for example, found that even indirect experience of hate crime victimisation could lead to feelings of anger and vulnerability.

Theme 4: reporting and recording hate crimes/incidents

Reporting differs based on the nature of the hate crime and the experience of the victim(s) (17%)

It was evident that only a small portion of hate crime victims reported the incident to the police (Chakraborti et al., 2014; Simich & Kang-Brown, 2018), although hate crimes deemed serious were more likely reported (Roxell, 2011; Chakraborti et al., 2014). One study also found that older victims were more likely to report the crime, with previous victims less likely to report another hate crime (Paterson et al., 2018). Victims were slightly less likely to report if the perpetrator was known to them in some way (Simich & Kang-Brown, 2018).

Lack of confidence in an official response (17%)

The primary reason for not reporting was a belief that the police would not take action and/or that they would not take the incident seriously (Chakraborti et al., 2014; Simich & Kang-Brown, 2018). While there is evidence that some victims were dissatisfied with the police response, there was also evidence that when victims do engage with the police, they rate their experience positively (Chakraborti et al., 2014). However, misreporting of hate crime by police was identified as an issue in some studies, with hate-crime motivation being neglected or not fully representative of the offence (Czajkoski, 1992; McMahon et al., 2004; Simich & Kang-Brown, 2018).

DISCUSSION

This chapter has examined the context, setting, and prevalence of hate crime. In doing so, it can help inform police practice with regards to the nature and extent of offending along with providing some direction concerning who are involved in such offences. As a result, several themes of interest for the profession have emerged, which will be presented here. These include diversity, definition and reporting practice, a role for race, accounting for perpetrator and victim characteristics and the support required, recognising pre-existing relationships in the perpetrator-victim relationship, and remaining mindful that hate crime can occur anywhere and be motivated by several and sometimes shared reasons, whilst also being attentive to an evolving literature base.

The results from the systematic review reflect the diversity of hate crime and how *hate crime offences vary in nature*, with crimes ranging from physical assault to vandalism of property. There was also evidence highlighting differences in how hate crime is targeted, with racial and sexual orientation hate crimes reported as more likely to be directed against the person and religious hate crimes more likely to be directed against property. Further research is needed to explore these differences to determine whether they are a genuine reflection of victim experiences and, if so, why these differences occur, or whether these differences are more reflective of reporting and recording issues concerning hate crime. In terms of practice, it is important that those working with victims and perpetrators appreciate the subtleties and variety of forms that hate crime can comprise and, in doing so, can properly identify and address it.

Race was reported as a significant factor informing *perpetration and/or victimisation* of hate crime. There are no clear explanations for this, although a range of factors including intolerance, perceived threat, insecurity, and strain, as well as vulnerability, may be relevant. It is likely that the significance of race is multilayered and as more is learned about hate crime perpetration and victimisation, a better understanding may be gained. In the meantime, although the reasons why race is significant may not be fully understood, it is important that this factor is accounted for, since it has implications for the coordination of resources and the development of hate-crime prevention strategies.

Being male, young, and white were clearly highlighted as *perpetrator characteristics* within several studies. There was some evidence that perpetrators were more likely to be unemployed and have a history of offending, substance misuse, psychiatric treatment, and a family history of domestic violence or parental separation. In addition, there was evidence that perpetrators were unlikely to be specialists in hate-crime offences and that only a small number belonged to hate-motivated groups. The age-crime curve is a well-established relationship within the literature, with criminal behaviour typically peaking in adolescence and young adulthood (Roque, Posick & Hoyle, 2016), with the general profile of offenders tending to be young males (Iganski et al., 2011). Many of the characteristics identified in this review are already commonly explored in structured risk assessments for violent offenders (Douglas, Hart, Webster & Belfrage, 2013). It may therefore be useful to consider how resources can be utilised to target those at risk of perpetrating hate crime, to support deterrence and desistance. However, it is also important that in identifying prevalent or typical characteristics, other types of perpetrators, such as women, are not overlooked. Further research is needed with perpetrators to better understand the realities of hate crime in relation to perpetrator characteristics.

From the studies reviewed, the most likely *victim characteristics* were reported as being male, black, homosexual, Muslim, or disabled. Interestingly, victims perceived that they were often targeted based on more than one aspect of their identity or lifestyle. Identifying victim characteristics is undoubtedly important in order to focus resources and support crime-prevention measures by the police. However, further investigation is required, particularly in relation to hidden victims who may not feel or be able to report their experiences and accounting for intersectionality in victim characteristics.

The evidence with regards to *pre-existing relationships between victims and perpetrators* was unclear. Some studies reported that perpetrators of hate crime were likely to have some degree of acquaintance with the victim(s), whilst others reported perpetrators were more likely to be strangers. Problems with the recording and reporting of hate crimes, including misreporting, fear, and mistrust, may provide some explanation for why there is inconclusive evidence about the relationship between victims and perpetrators. Equally, there could just be diversity in the relationship that is not always accounted for. It is important that police are sensitive to this, the potential impact any pre-existing relationship may have on victims, and their willingness to report their experiences to an investigating officer.

Hate crimes areas were not localised, with the studies reviewed reporting offences occurring in a range of places. This would suggest that it would not be effective to try to localise police resources. There was also some evidence that victim impact differs depending on location, with some studies indicating that impact was more significant when incidents took place in or near the home. It may be that if victims perceive the home and the surrounding area as a safe personal space, the violation experienced as a result of an attack in this location intensifies the psychological and emotional trauma following the incident. It may be useful for police to be particularly attuned to this so that they can enhance proactive signposting to victim-support agencies.

The review also identified a relative paucity of research concerning the motivation for hate crime. One study identified four motivations: thrill seeking, defensive, mission, and retaliatory. Another reported that the more planned and aggressive hate-crime perpetrators are typically seeking social dominance. However, this does not explain hate crimes where exploitation is a central motivation (Hamad, 2017). It is therefore likely that hate crime is *a multifaceted motivated event*, particularly as intersecting prejudices may be present. Establishing perpetrator motivation is likely difficult, particularly when the perpetrator(s) is unknown. However, awareness of these different typologies may support police in their questioning of victim(s) and any suspected perpetrator(s) as they seek to support a potential prosecution. It would be useful for future research to explore whether motivation varies for different types of hate crime, as this may support hate-crime detection, interventions, and rehabilitation.

There was evidence in the studies that some victims experienced greater *frequency of victimisation*. This may be because victims are unable or unwilling to seek help, perhaps due to normalisation of hate crime or other factors, such as lack of trust in the police. Alternatively, it may be that the action taken by the police is insufficient in preventing further victimisation. Understanding why frequent victimisation occurs is important if hate-crime incidents are to be reduced. Maintaining awareness that a victim may have experienced victimisation in the past and that the perpetrator may have committed previous offences may assist police in their investigations and help offer some insight into what influences hate-crime re-victimisation.

The *impact of victimisation* was reported within the studies as significant. It involved negative psychological and behavioural effects, sometimes reaching beyond the victim to the wider community. These effects included increased anger, fear, and vulnerability, changes in routine and personal safety, and within the transgender and disabled community, higher rates of depression and suicidality. It is therefore essential that efforts are made to appropriately support victims of hate crime to try to limit the negative impact of their experiences. This should inform the approach the police take when working with victims of hate crime. Indeed, it has been suggested that hate-crime victims should not be subjected to unnecessary or intrusive questioning by the police in order to prevent secondary victimisation (European Commission, 2017). Ensuring that all police consistently refer victims to support agencies, and that there is a commitment to evaluating the effectiveness of such support, could assist with preventing secondary victimisation.

There are clear gaps within the literature around motivations for hate crime, the official response to hate crime, and the treatment of hate-crime perpetrators. Further research into perpetrator and victim characteristics is also needed. Without this, the true picture of hate crime will remain unclear, and it is unlikely that hate-crime policies, initiatives, and procedures will be fully effective, as they are unable to capture the evolving nature of such crime. Utilising other sources of data, such as court judgements, may also prove useful in addressing some of the deficits in the literature.

Problems with *recording and reporting of hate crimes* were evident in the studies we reviewed. Serious hate crimes were more likely to be reported and older victims were more likely to report their experiences. However, victims who had experienced previous hate crimes or hate incidents were less likely to report another hate crime. This remained the case if the perpetrator was known to the victim. Reasons for not reporting included lack of belief in the police and normalisation of hate crime. For some victims who do report, there was evidence of dissatisfaction with the response received, which may reinforce negative beliefs about the police and reduce motivation to report further crimes. Misreporting of hate crime by police was also identified as a problem. This has serious implications, since accurate reporting is crucial to understanding and responding effectively to hate crime (Roberts et al., 2013). It has been recognised that if the police are proactive and focus on delivering services that meet the needs of victims, victims can be supported to disclose (College of Policing, 2014). Working with local communities to build positive relationships and encourage hate-crime reporting, as well as supporting police to recognise and understand the complexities of hate crimes through additional training, may be valuable strategies to use in addressing some of the reporting issues.

Although hate crime is under-reported and under-recorded, it is clear that victim experiences are diverse and that the impact of victimisation has significantly negative consequences. There is some information about who perpetrates hate crime, where they perpetrate it, and why, but further research is needed in relation to both perpetrators and victims to enhance understanding and inform interventions and policy.

What remains clear is that police play a central role in addressing hate crime, in all aspects of prevention, disruption, and reduction. It is important that they are appropriately resourced for dealing with hate crime, perhaps with specific police investigation teams dedicated to dealing with hate crime. Furthermore, ensuring police receive the specialist training needed will be crucial in ensuring they remain confident in recognising hate crime and feel able to effectively support victims. Evidence-informed structured assessments, which highlight risk indicators, may therefore represent an important addition in assisting police to identify suspects and potential victims.

REFERENCES

Anderson, J. F., Dyson, L., & Brookes, W. (2002). Preventing hate crime and profiling hate crime offenders. *The Western Journal of Black Studies*, *26*(3), 140–148.

Bandura, A. (1977). *Social learning theory*. Englewood Cliffs, NJ: Prentice Hall.

Barnes, A., & Ephross, P. H. (1994). The impact of hate violence on victims: Emotional and behavioral responses to attacks. *Social Work*, *39*(3), 247–251.

Braun, V., & Clarke, V. (2006). Using thematic analysis in psychology. *Qualitative Research in Psychology*, *3*, 77–101. http://doi:10.1191/1478088706qp063oa

Chakraborti, N. (2015a). Framing the boundaries of hate crime. In N. Hall, A. Corb, P. Giannasi, & J. G. D. Grieve (Eds.), *The Routledge international handbook on hate crime* (pp. 13–23). London: Routledge.

Chakraborti, N. (2015b). Re-thinking hate crime: Fresh challenges for policy and practice. *Journal of Interpersonal Violence*, *30*(10), 1738–1754.

Chakraborti, N. (2018). Responding to hate crime: Escalating problems, continued failings. *Criminology and Criminal Justice*, *18*(4), 387–404. https://doi.org/10.1177/1748895817736096

Chakraborti, N., Garland, J., & Hardy, S. (2014). *Leicester hate crime project: Findings and conclusions*. Leicester: University of Leicester Press.

Cheng, W., Ickes, W., & Kenworthy, J. B. (2013). The phenomenon of hate crimes in the United States. *Journal of Applied Social Psychology*, *43*(4), 761–794. http://dx.doi.org/10.1111/jasp.12004

College of Policing. (2014). *National policing hate crime strategy*. Retrieved from: www.college.police.uk/What-we-do/Support/Equality/Documents/National-Policing-Hate-Crime-strategy.pdf#search=hate%20crime

Czajkoski, E. H. (1992). Criminalizing hate: An empirical assessment. *Federal Probation*, *56*(3), 36–40.

Department of Justice. (2017). *Hate crime statistics*. Retrieved from: www.justice.gov/hatecrimes/hate-crime-statistics

Douglas, K. S., Hart, S. D., Webster, C. D., & Belfrage, H. (2013). *HCR-20V3: Assessing risk of violence – user guide*. Burnaby, Canada: Mental Health, Law, and Policy Institute, Simon Fraser University.

Dunbar, E. (2003). Symbolic, relational, and ideological signifiers of bias-motivated offenders: Toward a strategy of assessment. *American Journal of Orthopsychiatry*, *73*, 203–211.

Dunbar, E., Quinones, J., & Crevecoeur, D. A. (2005). Assessment of hate crime offenders: The role of bias intent in examining violence risk. *Journal of Forensic Psychology Practice*, *5*(1), 1–19.

European Commission. (2017). *Ensuring justice, protection and support for victims of hate crime and hate speech: 10 key guiding principles*. Retrieved from: www.google.co.uk/url?sa=t&rct=j&q=&esrc=s&source=web&cd=1&ved=2ahUKEwi8wKTQo-DjAhXWXRUIHSfhDXkQFjAAegQIAhAC&url=https%3A%2F%2Fec.europa.eu%2Fnewsroom%2Fjust%2Fdocument.cfm%3Fdoc_id%3D48874&usg=AOvVaw1MMlCbNFLYpCPDpuioDLFK

Garland, J. (2012). Difficulties in defining hate crime victimization. *International Review of Victimology*, *18*(1), 25–37. https://doi.org/10.1177/0269758011422473

Giannasi, P. (2015). Policing and hate crime. In N. Hall, A. Corb, P. Giannasi, & J. Grieve (Eds.), *The Routledge international handbook on hate crime* (pp. 331–342). London: Routledge, Taylor & Francis Group.

Hall, N. (2015). Understanding hate crimes: Sociological and criminological perspectives. In N. Hall, A. Corb, P. Giannasi, & J. Grieve (Eds.), *The international handbook of hate crime*. London: Routledge.

Hamad, R. (2017). *Hate crime: Causes, motivations and effective interventions for criminal justice social work*. Edinburgh: City of Edinburgh Council.

Hambly, O., Rixom, J., Singh, S., & WedlakeJames, T. (2018). *Hate crime: A thematic review of the current evidence*. Home Office. Retrieved from: https://assets.publishing.service.gov.uk/government/uploads/system/uploads/attachment_data/file/748140/hate-crime-a-thematic-review-of-the-current-evidence-oct2018-horr102.pdf

Herek, G. M., Cogan, J. C., & Gillis, J. R. (2002). Victim experiences in hate crimes based on sexual orientation. *Journal of Social Issues*, *58*, 319–339.

Herek, G. M., Gillis, J. R., & Cogan, J. C. (1999). Psychological sequelae of hate crime victimization among lesbian, gay, and bisexual adults. *Journal of Consulting and Clinical Psychology*, *67*, 945–951.

Iganski, P., Dixon, L., Kielinger, V., Mason, G., Jack, M., Perry, B., Stelman, A., Bargen, J., Lagou, S., Pfeffer, R., & Smith, D. (2011). *Rehabilitation of hate crime offenders*.

Scotland: Equality and Human Rights Commission. Retrieved from: www.hate crimescotland.org/wp/wp-content/uploads/2014/08/Rehabilitation-of-Hate-Crime-Offenders-Report-EHRC-Scotland-2011.pdf

Jolliffe, D., & Farrington, D. P. (2019). The criminal careers of those imprisoned for hate crime in the UK. *European Journal of Criminology, 51*, 621–634. https://doi.org/10.1177/1477370819839598

Mahoney, B., Davies, M., & Scurlock-Evans, L. (2014). Victimization among female and male sexual minority status groups: Evidence from the British crime survey 2007–2010. *Journal of Homosexuality, 61*(10), 1435–1461.

Mason, G. (2005). Hate crime and the image of the stranger. *British Journal of Criminology, 45*, 837–859.

Mason, G. (2019). A picture of bias crime in New South Wales. *Cosmopolitan Civil Societies: An Interdisciplinary Journal, 11*(1), 47–66. https://doi.org/10.5130/ccs.v11.i1.6402

Mason-Bish, H. (2015). We need to talk about women. In N. Chakraborti & J. Garland (Eds.), *Responding to hate crime: The case for connecting policy and research*. Bristol: Policy Press.

McDevitt, J., Balboni, J., Garcia, L., & Gu, J. (2001). Consequences for victims: A comparison of bias- and non-bias-motivated assaults. *American Behavioral Scientist, 45*(4), 697–713. https://doi.org/10.1177/0002764201045004010

McDevitt, J., Levin, J., & Bennett, S. (2002). Hate crime offenders: An expanded typology. *Journal of Social Issues, 58*(2), 303–317.

McMahon, B. T., West, S. L., Lewis, A. N., Armstrong, A. J., & Conway, J. P. (2004). Hate crimes and disability in America. *Rehabilitation Counseling Bulletin, 47*(2), 66–75.

Paterson, J., Walters, M. A., Brown, R., & Fearn, H. (2018). *Sussex hate crime project: Final report*. Retrieved from: www.sussex.ac.uk/webteam/gateway/file.php?name=sussex-hate-crime-project-report.pdf&site=430

Perry, B. (2001). *In the name of hate: Understanding hate crimes*. New York: Routledge.

Pezzella, F. S., Fetzer, M. D., & Keller, T. (2019). The dark figure of hate crime underreporting. *American Behavioral Scientist* [Online]. https://doi.org/10.1177/0002764218823844

PRISMA. (2009). *Prisma 2009 checklist*. Retrieved from: http://prisma-statement.org/documents/PRISMA%202009%20checklist.pdf

Rabrenovic, G. (2007). *Addressing hate and violence*. Warsaw: Human Dimension Implementation Meeting.

Roberts, C., Innes, M., Williams, M., Tregidga, J., Gadd, D., & Cook, N. (Eds.). (2013). *Understanding who commits hate crime and why they do it* (Welsh Government Social Research). Cardiff: Welsh Government.

Roberts, J. V. (1995). *Disproportionate harm: Hate crime in Canada – an analysis of recent statistics* (Working Document WD1995-11e). Ottawa: Department of Justice Canada. Retrieved from: www.justice.gc.ca/eng/rp-pr/csj-sjc/crime/wd95_11-dt95_11/wd95_11.pdf

Roque, M., Posick, C., & Hoyle, J. (2015). Age and crime. In *The encyclopedia of crime and punishment* (pp. 1–8). New York: John Wiley & Sons, Inc. Retrieved from: https://onlinelibrary.wiley.com/doi/full/10.1002/9781118519639.wbecpx275

Roxell, L. (2011). Hate, threats, and violence: A register study of persons suspected of hate crime. *Journal of Scandinavian Studies in Criminology and Crime Prevention, 12*(2), 198–215.

Simich, L. and Kang-Brown, J. (2018). *Questioning bias: Validating a bias crime assessment tool in California and New Jersey, summary overview*. Office of Justice Programs' National Criminal Justice Reference Service. Retrieved from: www.ncjrs.gov/pdffiles1/nij/grants/252010.pdf

Tiby, E. (2007). Constructions of homophobic hate crimes: Definitions, decisions, data. *Journal of Scandinavian Studies in Criminology and Crime Prevention, 8*, 114–137.

Walters, M. (2011). A general theories of hate crime? Strain, doing difference and self control. *Critical Criminology, 19*(4), 313–330. Retrieved from: https://papers.ssrn.com/sol3/papers.cfm?abstract_id=2470051

Walters, M., Brown, R., & Wiedlitzka, S. (2016). *Causes and motivations of hate crime*. Manchester: Equality and Human Rights Commission.

Walters, M., & Krasodomski-Jones, A. (2018). *Patterns of hate crime: Who, what, when and where?* Project Report, DEMOS. Retrieved from: www.demos.co.uk/wp-content/uploads/2018/08/PatternsOfHateCrimeReport-.pdf

Williams, M. L., & Tregidga, J. (2014). Hate crime victimization in Wales: Psychological and physical impacts across seven hate crime victim types. *British Journal of Criminology, 54*(5), 946–967.

CHAPTER 26

Policing interpersonal violence

Mark R. Kebbell and Janet M. Evans

INTRODUCTION

The most important job of the police is protecting people from violence. Violence can take many forms. At one extreme are irreversible forms of violence; murder, manslaughter, and violence of such profound impact that the victim is left with life-changing injuries – such as traumatic brain injury. At the other end of the continuum there are punches and slaps that result in little or no physical injury. Fortunately, rates of violence are decreasing broadly (Pinker, 2012). Police have contributed to these reductions. For instance, crimes such as intimate partner violence and sex crime are policed more effectively in developed nations than in the past (Gregory & Lees, 2012; Kebbell, 2019), and to some extent police databases and intelligence systems are identifying violent offenders more efficiently (Ratcliffe, 2016). Nevertheless, violence remains a persistent and significant challenge for police. In this chapter we will outline the ways that police can respond to violence more effectively.

This chapter begins with an outline of how police investigate violence and reviews a body of literature that shows that effective interviewing and investigation by police are critical to the quality of evidence that is obtained and in turn the likelihood that perpetrators will be held accountable for their violence. Nevertheless, a violent offence is rarely an isolated event to be treated on its own. Police need to use what they find out about violence in the community to create intelligence that can be used to reduce violence, bringing this chapter to a close on that point.

INVESTIGATING ALLEGATIONS OF VIOLENCE

Most investigations into violent offending are reactive. This means police respond to a reported crime and start an investigation. The way in which crime is reported varies. For instance, a victim might go to a police station to tell the police of a crime. Alternatively, a member of the public might report a crime; for example, they might report a disturbance. If the police believe a crime has occurred, an investigation may commence if there are resources and a desire to do so. The fact that police have so much discretion, and limited resources, means that few violent crimes are investigated thoroughly unless they are very serious. Even serious crime such as child rape is not necessarily investigated. In one of the most extreme examples of police discretion being exercised poorly, South Yorkshire Police in the UK declined to investigate the rapes and sexual assaults of more than 1,500 white girls and women in Rotherham because they were concerned that to do so might appear racist because the perpetrators were mainly both Muslim and British-Pakistani (Jay, 2014). In contrast, careful and competent policing creates a virtuous circle whereby more is known about what is happening in a community, allowing for an effective response from police and other community organisations. Within the virtuous circle, intelligence is also collected that at the time may not result in a prosecution but later contributes to an understanding by police that enables another course of action, like prevention. The alternative is allowing community offending to occur.

INTERVIEWING WITNESSES AND VICTIMS

If a crime is investigated, this will usually begin with interviewing the victim and other witnesses. In this aspect of the investigation, police can make a big difference to the quality of an investigation by choosing to interview well. A substantial body of research evidence shows that police officers' interviewing can have a substantial impact on how much information is obtained from a person and the accuracy and usefulness of this information. The kind of questions to which people tend to provide the most accurate answers (i.e., where the proportion of correct to incorrect information is greatest) are open, uninterrupted, free recall questions; such as, "What happened?" For these questions, eyewitnesses generally provide very accurate answers. Even eyewitnesses who typically show poorer memories than the general population such as older adults, children, and those with intellectual disabilities, can show high accuracy rates for these types of questions, thus enabling them to report the most important central details of a crime (Kebbell & Wagstaff, 1999: Oxburgh, Myklebust, & Grant, 2010).

Other questioning strategies can reduce the accuracy of answers given by witnesses. Broadly speaking, as statements or questions eliciting information become more specific and closed (for example, from "describe him" to "describe his clothes" to "describe his shirt" to "What colour was his shirt?"), responses become less accurate. This is particularly the case for older adults, children, and people with intellectual disabilities who are particularly vulnerable to violence. Nevertheless, closed questions may have to be used *as a last resort* to elicit information about something the witness may have omitted. The influence of these question types can be understood in terms of the demands of the different questions. For more open questions, the task is to tell the interviewer what the witness *can* remember. For more specific, closed questions, however, the task changes to one of providing the interviewer with what he or she *wants* the witness to remember. One result of this is that witnesses tend to provide less accurate answers to specific questions because they replace gaps in memory with distorted or inaccurate material. In other words, they may become suggestible to the demands of the interviewer (Oxburgh, Myklebust, & Grant, 2010).

Questions of suggestibility also arise in response to leading questions. Leading questions are those that suggest or imply the response required. For instance, a leading question such as "Was his shirt red?" suggests that the man wore a red shirt. The accuracy of answers provided by normal adults can be adversely affected by leading questions. Research shows that police without specific training, practice, and support generally interview poorly, and their interviews are characterised by more closed and leading questions than open questions (Milne & Bull, 1999). The implication is that effective training and practice of police concerning interviewing witnesses will improve the amount of useful information collected and enhance prosecutions. Research varies with regards to how much of an improvement interview training will make and is dependent on how poorly interviewers were initially – improvements are greater for previously poor interviewers. Nevertheless, an interview procedure for police, called the "cognitive interview" can more than double the information obtained from victims and witnesses (Fisher & Geiselman, 1992; Memon, Meissner, & Fraser, 2010; Milne & Bull, 1999). Further, if victim and witness evidence is recorded, this allows for the information to be available for use in the investigation or as intelligence. In comparison, written statements lose most of the account because the officer cannot take notes quickly enough or remember everything that was said (Köhnken, Thürer, & Zoberbier, 1994).

Some further points need to be borne in mind when interviewing witnesses who have experienced violence. Traumatised witnesses often have intrusive thoughts when trying to recall the event immediately after it occurred. For example, a woman might be trying to remember details of the crime when, unknown to the police officer, she might start to think about how she could have been killed or what revenge she would like to exact. These intrusive thoughts can break the witness's concentration, and impair the ability to remember details of the event in question. Again, patient and sensitive interviewing can help to minimise the impact of these difficulties (Fisher & Geiselman, 1992). However, it is useful to make a distinction between intrusive emotions that occur after the event and emotions experienced at the time. Whereas intrusive emotional thoughts can have a detrimental effect on memory if they occur after the event, some research suggests that remembering what was experienced emotionally during an event can help improve memory for the event by providing retrieval cues. If a witness remembers how he or she felt and thought emotionally at the time of a crime, it may help memory for details of the crime.

It is important not to confuse what appears to be poor memory with a simple reluctance to report details of what happened. Testifying in court concerning violence can involve considerable actual or potential costs for witnesses. Witnesses may often be frightened of reprisals against them, or the event may be too painful or embarrassing to report, and being a witness in court is also a time-consuming and unnerving event (for related research, see Maynard, 1994). Many witnesses may, therefore, be reluctant to give accurate testimony, or try to change their testimony, in order to withdraw from the process of testifying in court. The desire to withdraw from the process may be further intensified if, during the interview stage, a police officer communicates to the witness that the case is not important, is rude to the witness, blames the witness, or wastes the witness's time. Problems of this kind can often be overcome if the interviewer is sensitive and takes the time to establish rapport (Fisher & Geiselman, 1992). Alternatively, as discussed later, victim and witness information can be used for intelligence to shed light on what is happening and who is offending rather than only for prosecutions. To summarize, police can interview witnesses more effectively than they do typically and elicit better evidence, which improves responses to violence.

INTERVIEWING SUSPECTS

Victims and witnesses are not the only people who are interviewed by police. Effective interviewing of suspects is also critical to obtaining either incriminating or exonerating accounts and to prevent false confessions. Generally, there are three important advantages associated with a guilty offender confessing to police. Firstly, the likelihood of a conviction being secured is greatly increased. Secondly, if an offender confesses, the likelihood of the victim having to give evidence in court is reduced, as is the negative impact on the victim from testifying about their abuse (Eastwood & Patton, 2002; Lipovsky, 1994). This is particularly pertinent for cases involving violence or vulnerable and intimidated witnesses. For example, testifying in a trial is one of four significant predictors of PTSD symptoms in adult survivors of child rape, and having a civil lawsuit pending is one of three predictors of depression among adult victims (Epstein, Saunders, & Kilpatrick, 1997). Thirdly, an advantage of an offender confessing early in the investigation is that a lengthy trial can be avoided, reducing the resources needed to continue an investigation and prosecution.

One way of shedding light on offenders' reasons for confessing is to ask them. Gudjonsson and Petursson (1991) did this with 74 Icelandic prisoners who had confessed. Respondents were required to respond to questions using a Likert scale that was labeled "not at all" (1 or 2) to "very much so" (6 or 7). The majority (55%) of offenders gave scores of 6 or 7 to the question, "Did you think the police would eventually prove you did it?" and this was the most frequently rated reason for confessing. Gudjonsson and colleagues have replicated this finding (Gudjonsson & Sigurdsson, 1999, 2000). Whilst this approach provides useful information, these data have to be treated with caution. As with all self-report data, participants are likely to be motivated to portray themselves in a good light, and saying they confessed because of evidence may be more desirable for them to say that, for example, the police persuaded them to confess. Another drawback to this approach is that offenders are relying on their memories for what happened, in some instances, many years ago. Nevertheless, a field study conducted by Moston, Stephenson, and Williamson (1992) in England provides additional support for the importance of evidence.

Moston, Stephenson, and Williamson (1992) investigated confession rates for 1,067 suspects who had been interviewed by detectives (although the majority of cases were non-violent). The results showed that when the researchers rated the evidence against the suspect as weak, confessions occurred less than 10% of the time, and denials occurred 77% of the time. When the evidence was rated as strong by the researchers, confessions were frequent, occurring in 67% of cases, while denials were infrequent, occurring in 16% of cases. The most frequent form of evidence against a suspect is an eyewitness account (Kebbell & Milne, 1998), and this reinforces the importance of interviewing eyewitnesses properly that was discussed in the previous section.

A survey of 83 men convicted of murder or sexual offences by Holmberg and Christianson (2002) is relevant here. They found aggression, hostility, and insulting and condemning behavior, which they labeled "dominance", reduced the likelihood of a confession. However, friendliness, the suspect feeling acknowledged and respected as a human being, and a feeling of cooperation, which they labeled "humanity", were associated with increases in the number of confessions. Perhaps the lack of effectiveness of dominance may be due to "psychological reactance" (Brehm, 1966). Brehm showed that when individuals perceive an unfair restriction on their actions, in this case their ability to deny an offence or give their own account of an event, an intense motivational state is produced that means the individual attempts to challenge the restriction and obtain the denied item, choice, or behaviour. Put simply, we want what we can't have. In an interview characterised by dominance and pressure to confess, reactance will take the form of a decision to deny the alleged offence and terminate the interview.

Conversely, the fact that the humanistic approach can be successful could be explicable in terms of offenders feeling more comfortable with the officer and thus more able to reduce their guilt and to get things off their chest, particularly compared to an officer who displays dominance. Again, however, there is a problem with the correlational nature of this study, which makes it impossible to determine a causal relationship between these variables and outcomes. For example, offenders could be more likely to confess because officers responded positively to them, or alternatively, officers could have responded more positively to the offenders *because* they were confessing; at this stage we do not know for sure.

Further support for the idea that displaying positive attitudes to offenders may increase confessions whilst displaying negative attitudes may decrease confessions is shown by Kebbell, Hurren, and Mazerolle (2006), who questioned 19 convicted sex offenders concerning their beliefs about how the police can increase or decrease the likelihood of a sex offender confessing. Participants suggested that interviewers were most likely to secure confessions if they were compassionate, neutral, and fair, while aggressive and biased interviewers were reported as being less likely to be successful. Though this study is limited by the small sample size, and the fact that there may be differences between how sex offenders say they react to an interviewer and how they *do* react to an interviewer, the results suggest some form of cause and effect relationship. The implication is that police interviewers should be encouraged to have, or at least display, more positive attitudes to suspects, which may increase the likelihood of obtaining a confession.

Baldwin (1993) conducted a field study in the UK in which he evaluated 600 video and audio-taped suspect interviews. Importantly, Baldwin (1993) studied suspects' admissions and denials, as well as when they occurred. Full confessions, or confessions to some part of the allegation, occurred immediately in 51.9% of interviews, while 32.7% denied immediately and continued that denial throughout the interview. Baldwin (1993) found that 2.3% denied at first but subsequently admitted some part of the allegation, 4.2% denied but did shift their position during the interview, and 3.3% completely changed their account and confessed. This could be taken to suggest that police interviewing has little impact on suspects' decisions to confess or deny, and that the suspect has usually decided beforehand whether they will confess to or deny the allegation.

Alternatively, however, Kebbell, Hurren, and Mazerolle (2006) found that half of their sample of convicted sex offenders had not made a decision to confess or deny prior to their police interview. Potentially, this can be interpreted as indicating that suspects make up their mind to confess or deny early in the interview and then subsequently rarely deviate from this decision. This seems plausible. An extensive social psychological literature shows a "commitment bias", whereby people remain committed to an initial position even when extensive evidence suggests they should change their position (e.g. Edwards & Smith, 1996). For criminal suspects in particular, changing an account is even more difficult than usual, as they must not only change their position but also admit that their previous account was false and that they lied to the police. One technique that police can use is to ask the suspect not to comment immediately and to advise them to listen to the evidence before speaking.

The Baldwin (1993) study is also relevant here, because of his assertions concerning the quality of police interviews. Baldwin identified a discrepancy between how the police *say* they interview and how they *actually* interview. He found that the police officers in their sample often spoke of high-level psychological concepts that they applied in their interviewing, but in reality their interviewing was more closely characterised by ineptitude and limited social skills. This finding has been found in other research (for comprehensive review, see Griffiths & Milne, 2018). The fact that some offenders (particularly sex offenders) have personality deficits (e.g. Fisher, Beech, & Browne, 1999) may make interviewing more difficult because of the suspect's poor interpersonal skills.

Police seem motivated to improve their interviewing; for instance, a survey of 2,679 Australian police officers revealed that officers showed a positive attitude to receiving interview training (Milne et al., 2011). To summarize, police can interview suspects effectively, and this improves the quality of evidence available and sheds additional light on how to respond to violence.

INVESTIGATIVE SKILLS

While police should interview effectively, they also need to make sense of what they find. Evidence concerning police officers' decision making is sparse. Indeed, literature searches show that there are more studies concerning the investigative skills of fictional detective Sherlock Holmes than there are of real detectives. A rare exception is the work of Fahsing and Ask (2016). They compared the quality of detectives' decision making between novice and experienced detectives in England and Norway. Participants were presented with two semi-fictitious cases and were asked to report all relevant investigative hypotheses and necessary investigative actions in each case. Training and experience influenced the quality of investigative actions, suggesting that police investigation can be a factor in successful outcomes. The implication is that police officers' ability to make sense of crimes is not static but can be enhanced with training and experience.

Similarly, the complexity of police investigations means that some police officers perform better than others. For example, Westera et al. (2016) interviewed 30 qualified detectives from different police services in Australia and New Zealand to tease out what made the difference between an effective detective and a less-effective detective. The data gained from each interview method were content-analysed for themes, using a bottom-up approach, to derive skill categories from participants' responses rather than existing frameworks. The most critical skill was communication, which was cited by all detectives at some stage during the interview and was the most frequently cited skill. Of course, this is a skill that is critical to being an effective interviewer – the importance of which is explained in the previous sections. Motivation was the second most frequently cited skill. The trying conditions of the work mean that an absence of motivation contributed to poor performance.

Completing the top five skills were factors that are likely foundations for how effective investigations are conducted – thoroughness, decision making, and management. Detectives described the importance of applying these skills across all aspects of the investigation, from planning an investigation to examining a scene, interviewing, or preparing a prosecution file – all required at the same time one is dealing with a high investigative workload.

Experience and knowledge were perceived as important requirements for effective performance. Teamwork and leadership were also seen as vital, suggesting that an ability to work with others is a core component of detective work. In contrast, the more individual characteristics of tenacity and resilience were identified and often cited as leading to high levels of investigative performance. Taken as whole, this suggests that police responses to violence at an investigative level can be improved by selecting, training, and creating a work environment in which police can investigate violence effectively. If reducing violence is considered to be important, then the most effective police (both sworn and unsworn) should be deployed in response.

IDENTIFYING HIGH-RISK VIOLENT OFFENDERS

Identifying the most dangerous violent offenders is essential. As mentioned earlier, resources are limited and not all offences are investigated thoroughly. However, the offences of the most dangerous, *known*, violent offenders should be investigated thoroughly. Risk assessment allows limited resources to be focused on those who are most in need of police investigation. This is consistent with Risk-Needs-Responsivity theory (Andrews, Bonta, & Hoge, 1990), a theory that has a strong evidence base for the effective management of offenders within correctional environments (Bonta & Andrews, 2017; Ogloff & Davis, 2004). The basic premise of this approach is targeting the most resources to those who are at highest "risk".

Various factors help identify high-risk offenders. There are factors for generally violent offenders (see Rice, Harris, & Lang, 2013), sex offenders (see Hanson, 1998), and intimate partner violence offenders (see Kebbell, 2019) – many of which overlap. To a large extent these risk assessments rely on previous behaviour predicting future behaviour. Put simply, people who have committed a great deal of violent crime in the past are more likely to commit violent crime in the future (Bonta & Andrews, 2017). Of course, there are caveats to this – some offenders may simply be more likely to be caught and intelligent offenders may be under-represented, and many offenders will reduce their level of risk as they age (Kebbell, 2019). Nevertheless, as a "rule-of-thumb", someone who has been extremely, and frequently, violent in the past is more likely to be violent in the future than someone who has no history of violence. However, as mentioned at the very beginning, most violent crime is not investigated and prosecuted. Therefore, to have a greater understanding of what is happening in a community, and who is doing what, to whom, police need to use their intelligence holdings effectively and prioritise their investigations with an intelligence-led approach; this intelligence holding includes acts of violence that may not have resulted in a conviction, such as when multiple allegations are made.

An example of how this might work illustrates the point. Leonard Fraser was a man who was convicted of the abduction, rape, and murder of a nine-year-old girl, Keyra Steinhardt. He was also convicted of the murder of Beverley Leggo and Sylvia Benedetti, and the manslaughter of Julie Turner (Doneman, 2006). While the killings might not have been predictable, specifically, the likelihood of Fraser committing serious violent offences was clear extremely high. He had been diagnosed as a psychopath more than a decade before the murders, after being convicted of the rape and attempted rape of several women. In addition, he had been convicted of multiple other serious offences since the rapes, and police were aware of multiple allegations of Fraser's offending in the community in the run-up to the killings. Some of his alleged offences that he was not prosecuted for, included grooming children sexually, selling drugs, the rape of a terminally ill woman in a hospital chapel and having sex with a blue-heeler dog (while sex offending against dogs may not seem particularly harmful compared with the other offences, what it does show is sexual deviation that in turn indicates high risk of sex offending; Hanson, 1998). The implication of this is clear: all the offences that Fraser was alleged to have been committing should have been investigated thoroughly and by the best, most competent police available to prevent his future offending. To reiterate, when there are very high-risk, violent offenders in the community, police need to investigate any allegations against them as thoroughly as possible.

INTELLIGENCE-LED POLICING

Intelligence-led policing began to appear in Australia and New Zealand in the late 1990s. Implementing intelligence-led policing in Australia and New Zealand has not been easy or without backwards steps. Intelligence-led policing can be defined as "the application of criminal intelligence analysis as an objective decision-making tool in order to facilitate crime reduction and prevention through effective policing strategies and external partnership projects drawn from an evidential base" (Ratcliffe, 2003, p. 3). A core principle is the fact that crime is not randomly distributed and that all people are not equally likely to commit crime; the highest risk criminals are active and committing a disproportionate amount of crime, including violent crime.

Police are adept at collecting information, the many systems and databases attest to this, and the collection of information about violence is no exception. There are already many sources of data that, when collated and analysed, provide insights about the perpetration of violence; the gap often is in dedicating resources to the analysis of the information. Information that is collected through witness, suspect, and victim interviews is seldom easily accessible to analysts who are tasked with considering crime problems and attention to their intelligence value. For effective intelligence, an analyst needs to use all these information sources discussed here (see Evans & Kebbell, 2012). This intelligence assessment can then be used by police to make changes to resource allocation that in turn will impact on violent offenders (Ratcliffe, 2003).

In the case of violence, the analyst may be using crime pattern analysis to establish hotspots, trends, and patterns to influence police deployment. Comparative Case Analysis may be deployed to establish a connection to one offender(s) for a number of similar offences, to connect different types of offences through establishing similar facts, as well as developing a target-specific or location-specific analysis to identify vulnerabilities in victims, offenders, and locations. Using these analytical tools, the analyst can identify some of the most high-risk offenders and in turn the most vulnerable victims and locations that, through design or geography, bring together victims and offenders. Intelligence can also be used to identify situational factors that may facilitate offending (this is important; see Wortley [2012] for more details). The evidence from interviews is likely to be critical here. A vast array of information is collected during a skilled interview, compared with a poor interview, that may provide insight into the psychology of offending. At an intelligence level, well-executed interviews with witnesses and suspects can collectively establish underlying behaviours of those who perpetrate violence and can identify offenders (Kebbell, 2019). A caveat to any intelligence is the adage "rubbish in, rubbish out". As mentioned, better interviewing and investigation will lead to better material for intelligence analysis.

Intelligence can be both proactive and reactive in the policing of violence. Proactively, analysts can use formal risk assessment tools, such as those mentioned previously, to determine priority targets and then use psychological indicators to anticipate which offenders will most likely change their pattern of behaviour. This is starting to happen, as demonstrated in the shift in language from policing by consent to harm reduction and risk management (Harfield & Kleiven 2008). Proactively intelligence units are able to provide analysis to identify and understand high-risk victim groups and provide tailored prevention advice. For instance, Capellan and Lewandowski (2019) provide an example with their study of how to use intelligence-led policing to identify and prevent mass public shootings. Reactively, analysts can monitor environmental changes when interventions are trialled or implemented as well as provide hotspot analysis to determine the best localities for prevention activities. Summers and Rossmo (2019) demonstrate how hotspot analyses were used to deter offenders from offending in identified hotspots, and they note that repeated thwarted attempts at committing a criminal act in the hotspot was the most successful strategy.

CONCLUSION

There is a great deal that police can do to improve their response to reduce violence. The first is to interview victims and witnesses more effectively, which will yield more evidence. The second is to interview suspects more effectively, which will improve the evidence collected, including evidence that may exonerate the suspect. The third is to integrate the evidence to gather an intelligence picture concerning who is doing what, to whom, and how. The final component is to actively target who and what is responsible for the most violence. This is an evidence-based approach that protects victims and holds violent offenders accountable.

REFERENCES

Andrews, D. A., Bonta, J., & Hoge, R. D. (1990). Classification for effective rehabilitation: Rediscovering psychology. *Criminal justice and Behavior*, *17*(1), 19–52.

Baldwin, J. (1993). Police interview techniques: Establishing truth or proof? *The British Journal of Criminology*, *33*, 325–352.

Bonta, J., & Andrews, D. A. (2017). *The Psychology of Criminal Behavior*. New York: Routledge.

Brehm, J. W. (1966). *A Theory of Psychological Reactance*. New York: Academic Press.

Capellan, J. A., & Lewandowski, C. (2019). Can threat assessment help police prevent mass public shootings? Testing an intelligence-led policing tool. *Policing: An International Journal*, *4*(1).

Doneman, P. (2006). *Things a Killer Would Know: The True Story of Leonard Fraser*. Canberra: Allen & Unwin.

Eastwood, C., & Patton, W. (2002). *The Experiences of Child Complainants of Sexual Abuse in the Criminal Justice System* (p. 156). Canberra: Criminology Research Council.

Edwards, K., & Smith, E. E. (1996). A disconfirmation bias in the evaluation of arguments. *Journal of Personality and Social Psychology*, *71*(1), 5–24.

Epstein, J. N., Saunders, B. E., & Kilpatrick, D. G. (1997). Predicting PTSD in women with a history of childhood rape. *Journal of Traumatic Stress*, *10*(4), 573–588.

Evans, J. M., & Kebbell, M. R. (2012). The effective analyst: A study of what makes an effective crime and intelligence analyst. *Policing and Society*, *22*(2), 204–219.

Fahsing, I., & Ask, K. (2016). The making of an expert detective: The role of experience in English and Norwegian police officers' investigative decision-making. *Psychology, Crime & Law*, *22*(3), 203–223.

Fisher, D., Beech, A., & Browne, K. (1999). Comparison of sex offenders to nonoffenders on selected psychological measures. *International Journal of Offender Therapy and Comparative Criminology*, *43*(4), 473–491.

Fisher, R. P., & Geiselman, R. E. (1992). *Memory Enhancing Techniques for Investigative Interviewing: The Cognitive Interview*. Springfield, IL: Charles C. Thomas Publisher.

Gregory, J., & Lees, S. (2012). *Policing Sexual Assault*. London: Routledge.

Griffiths, A., & Milne, R. (Eds.). (2018). *The Psychology of Criminal Investigation: From Theory to Practice*. London: Routledge.

Gudjonsson, G. H., & Petursson, H. (1991). Custodial interrogation: Why do suspects confess and how does it relate to their crime, attitude and personality? *Personality and Individual Differences*, *12*(3), 295–306.

Gudjonsson, G. H., & Sigurdsson, J. F. (1999). The Gudjonsson confession questionnaire-revised (GCQ-R) factor structure and its relationship with personality. *Personality and Individual Differences*, *27*(5), 953–968.

Gudjonsson, G. H., & Sigurdsson, J. F. (2000). Differences and similarities between violent offenders and sex offenders. *Child Abuse & Neglect*, *24*(3), 363–372.

Hanson, R. K. (1998). What do we know about sex offender risk assessment? *Psychology, Public Policy, and Law*, *4*(1–2), 50–72.

Harfield, C., & Kleiven, M. (2008). Intelligence, knowledge and the reconfiguration of policing. In C. Harfield, A. MacVean, J. Grieve, & D. Phillips (Eds.), *The Handbook of Intelligent Policing. Consilience, Crime Control and Community Safety* (pp. 239–254). Oxford: Oxford University Press.

Holmberg, U., & Christianson, S. Å. (2002). Murderers' and sexual offenders' experiences of police interviews and their inclination to admit or deny crimes. *Behavioral Sciences & the Law*, *20*(1–2), 31–45.

Jay, A. (2014). *Independent Inquiry into Child Sexual Exploitation in Rotherham: 1997–2013*. Rotherham: Rotherham Metropolitan Borough Council: *Factors That Influence Eyewitness Accuracy*. London: Home Office.

Kebbell, M. R., Hurren, E. J., & Mazerolle, P. (2006). Sex offenders' perceptions of how they were interviewed. *Canadian Journal of Police & Security Services*, *4*, 67–75.

Köhnken, G., Thürer, C., & Zoberbier, D. (1994). The cognitive interview: Are the interviewers' memories enhanced, too? *Applied Cognitive Psychology*, *8*(1), 13–24.

Lipovsky, J. A. (1994). The impact of court on children: Research findings and practical recommendations. *Journal of Interpersonal Violence*, *9*(2), 238–257.

Maynard, W. (1994). *Witness Intimidation: Strategies for Prevention*. London: Home Office.

Memon, A., Meissner, C. A., & Fraser, J. (2010). The cognitive interview: A meta-analytic review and study space analysis of the past 25 years. *Psychology, Public Policy, and Law*, *16*(4), 340–372.

Milne, B., & Bull, R. (1999). *Investigative Interviewing: Psychology and Practice*. Chichester: Wiley.

Milne, B., Roberts, K. A., Hill, J. A., & Moston, S. (2011). Police perceptions of investigative interviewing: Training needs and operational practices in Australia. *The British Journal of Forensic Practice*, *13*, 72–83.

Moston, S., Stephenson, G. M., & Williamson, T. M. (1992). The effects of case characteristics on suspect behaviour during police questioning. *The British Journal of Criminology*, *32*(1), 23–40.

Ogloff, J. R., & Davis, M. R. (2004). Advances in offender assessment and rehabilitation: Contributions of the risk – needs – responsivity approach. *Psychology, Crime & Law*, *10*(3), 229–242.

Oxburgh, G. E., Myklebust, T., & Grant, T. (2010). The question of question types in police interviews: a review of the literature from a psychological and linguistic perspective. *International Journal of Speech, Language & the Law, 17*, 45–66.

Pinker, S. (2012). *The Better Angels of Our Nature: Why Violence Has Declined*. New York: Penguin Books.

Ratcliffe, J. H. (2003). Intelligence-led policing. In *Trends & Issues in Crime and Criminal Justice* (p. 248). Canberra: Australian Institute of Criminology. https://aic.gov.au/publications/tandi/tandi248

Ratcliffe, J. H. (2016). *Intelligence-Led Policing* (2nd ed.). London: Routledge.

Rice, M. E., Harris, G. T., & Lang, C. (2013). Validation of and revision to the VRAG and SORAG: The violence risk appraisal guide – revised (VRAG-R). *Psychological Assessment, 25*(3), 951–965.

Summers, L., & Rossmo, D. K. (2019). Offender interviews: Implications for intelligence-led policing. *Policing: An International Journal, 42*(1).

Westera, N. J., Kebbell, M. R., Milne, B., & Green, T. (2016). Towards a more effective detective. *Policing and Society, 26*, 1–17.

Wortley, R. (2012). Exploring the person-situation interaction in situational crime prevention. In N. Tilley & G. Farrell (Eds.), *The Reasoning Criminologist: Essays in Honour of Ronald V. Clarke* (pp. 184–193). London: Routledge.

CHAPTER 27

Policing domestic and family violence

Christopher Dowling, Hayley Boxall, and Anthony Morgan

INTRODUCTION

Police have a unique and important role in responding to domestic and family violence in Australia. As frontline responders and gatekeepers to the criminal justice system, the police response has a major influence on the outcomes for victim/survivors and offenders. Although the majority of domestic and family violence incidents are not reported to the police (Australian Bureau of Statistics [ABS], 2017), it is estimated that the police respond to a domestic violence incident every two minutes (Blumer, 2016). Domestic and family violence incidents account for a significant proportion of homicides (Bricknell, 2020), reported incidents of assault (Bureau of Crime Statistics and Research, 2020; Crime Statistics Agency Victoria, 2020), and offenders proceeded against by police (ABS, 2020), and because they are more time-consuming than non-family violence incidents (Crime and Misconduct Commission, 2005; Victorian Auditor-General, 2009), a disproportionate amount of police time.

Police have contact with some of the most high-risk and prolific offenders in the community. Domestic and family violence offenders are often repeat offenders. A systematic review of Australian domestic violence studies from 1990–2018 found that approximately one in two offenders reported to the police will go on to reoffend within five years (Hulme, Morgan & Boxall, 2019). Police often have multiple contacts with individual offenders for domestic violence behaviours (Morgan, Boxall & Brown, 2018). Certainly, evidence suggests that reoffending is concentrated within a small group of offenders who account for a disproportionate number of domestic violence offences (Millsteed & Coghlan, 2016) and associated harms (Kerr, Whyte & Strang, 2017; Sherman et al., 2016).

Relatedly, in their role as first-responders, police have contact with the most vulnerable victim/survivors of domestic and family violence – vulnerable to experiencing repeat violence, being negatively impacted by further abuse, and experiencing multiple barriers to help-seeking and support. For example, repeat violence is more likely to be experienced by victims in disadvantaged communities, living in remote areas, with low educational attainment, who have a disability or are pregnant or have new children (Dowling & Morgan, 2019; Rahman, 2018). Meanwhile, victim/survivors who report to the police are more likely than not to have histories of abuse and physical injury (Voce & Boxall, 2018), which means police frequently respond to incidents involving ongoing abuse, often where there is risk of physical harm and escalating violence.

The police have a particularly important role in addressing the risk of short-term repeat violence. Two recent studies – one focused on domestic violence involving adult offenders, the other focused on adolescent family violence offenders – found one in four offenders reoffended within six months of contact with the police, with risk of repeat violence peaking at around four weeks (Boxall & Morgan, 2020; Morgan, Boxall & Brown, 2018). These studies also found that risk of reoffending is dynamic and cumulative, increasing with every reoffence. Morgan, Boxall, and Brown (2018) found that 14% of adult domestic violence offenders were involved in another incident within 60 days of the index offence, that 28% of these offenders reoffended again within the next 60 days, and that nearly half – 43% – of this relatively small cohort committed a third reoffence within another 60-day period. Certainly, then, the police may have a role in interrupting or disrupting emerging or established patterns of domestic and family violence.

Encouragingly, evidence shows that the police response to domestic and family violence can reduce repeat offending and victimisation, and improve criminal justice outcomes (Dowling et al., 2018; Mazerolle et al., 2018). At the same time, there have undoubtedly been cases in which the response by police has not met the expectations of victims and the wider community (Douglas, 2019), highlighted in inquiries such as the Victorian Royal Commission into Family Violence (State of Victoria, 2016), which led to extensive reform. This chapter examines the evidence around common policing responses, highlights some recent innovations in Australian policing, and explores emerging challenges for law enforcement.

HOW DO POLICE RESPOND TO DOMESTIC AND FAMILY VIOLENCE IN AUSTRALIA?

Police in Australia respond to domestic and family violence in a number of ways. These responses centre on achieving three different yet equally important objectives:

- Prevention: ensuring that offenders do not perpetrate further violence;

- Investigation and prosecution: clearing domestic and family violence cases and ensuring criminal justice outcomes; and,
- Supporting victims: improving victims' safety, wellbeing, and confidence in the police.

There is considerable overlap in these objectives, yet achieving one can also sometimes come at the expense of others. Further, the effectiveness of police responses in achieving these objectives is often contingent on the nature and characteristics of the offenders, victims, and incidents concerned. A critical challenge for police in Australia is balancing these objectives when responding to domestic and family violence, and appropriately targeting and tailoring responses to ensure that their effectiveness is optimised.

Arrest

Police have the power to arrest and detain an individual when they are suspected of having committed an offence. This is an important first step in the criminal justice process, but it can also have immediate benefits in terms of ensuring the safety of victims. Importantly, police in Australia are strongly encouraged to arrest suspected perpetrators of domestic and family violence (under pro-arrest or positive action policies), with legislation in all states and territories now making it easier for them to do so. The introduction of these policies reflects a growing recognition within police – and the broader community – of the seriousness of domestic and family violence. This mirrors international trends towards pro- or mandatory arrest policies, although the latter have not been adopted by Australian police (Celik, 2013).

A number of early international studies demonstrated the deterrent effect of arrest in preventing further violence. The earliest of these, Sherman and Berk's (1984) seminal arrest experiment, found that offenders who were arrested were significantly less likely to reoffend than those who were subjected to mediation and temporary removal. That this difference held regardless of the length of time it took for perpetrators to be reunited with their victims further led the authors to conclude that the effectiveness of arrest is due to deterrence rather than incapacitation. However, many later studies, including a number of replication experiments, have found a modest overall impact of arrest on reoffending, pointing out that arrest seems to be most effective in reducing repeat offending with first-time offenders and offenders that have a stronger connection to certain social controls (i.e. married, employed), and ineffective or even counterproductive with repeat offenders and those who have weaker connections to these controls (Vigurs et al., 2016). Mandatory arrest policies have been shown to increase harm to victims, rather than reduce violence, particularly among ethnic minorities (Mazerolle et al., 2018).

Importantly, this research focuses on the effectiveness of arrest in reducing *reoffending*. Less research has examined the impact of arrest on *revictimisation*. The few studies that do, drawing on victimisation survey data in the US, have found that arrest does not reduce the likelihood of revictimisation over and above the mere reporting of domestic violence incidents to the police (Felson, Ackerman & Gallagher, 2005; Xie & Lynch, 2017). In other words, police may, in some cases, deter further domestic and family violence by simply attending the scene of an incident, regardless of whether or not they arrest anyone.

While a number of studies have shown that victims of domestic and family violence are generally more satisfied with police when offenders are arrested, and report an increased willingness to engage with the criminal justice system (Robinson & Chandek, 2000; Stephens & Sinden, 2000; Wilson & Jasinski, 2004), this is not always the case. Many victims who call the police do not want the offender arrested; they simply want immediate protection from the offender. Those who do not want offenders arrested are, unsurprisingly, less satisfied with police if arrest does occur and are unlikely to cooperate with police investigations (Hirschel & Hutchison, 2003; Smith, 2000). A disregard for victim/survivor opposition to arrest can also lead to increased police distrust and can discourage future reporting (Dugan, 2003).

Protection orders

Protection orders (also known as domestic violence orders, apprehended violence orders, family violence orders, and intervention orders) are one of the most common responses to domestic and family violence, and their use has grown significantly in recent years. While protection orders are typically issued through civil proceedings, police are responsible for their enforcement, giving them their intended deterrent effect, and breaches of them are investigated and charged as criminal offences. Police may also apply to courts for an order on behalf of the victim/survivor and, in some jurisdictions, issue short-term interim orders directly, although victims are also free to lodge order applications themselves. Importantly, while protection orders are issued, applied, and enforced under state and territory legislation, the recently introduced National Domestic Violence Order Scheme provides the legislative and technical framework for protection orders issued in one jurisdiction to automatically apply nationally.

Protection orders do have a modest effect on the prevalence of domestic violence revictimisation while they are in place, although evidence is currently unclear on whether they prevent escalation in the severity or frequency of further violence (see Benitez, McNiel & Binder, 2010; Cordier et al., 2019; Dowling et al., 2018 for reviews). Importantly, these studies have often relied on official data and data on more serious breaches (i.e. those involving physical violence). Self-report data reveal a higher frequency of lower-level breaches involving phone/internet contact and stalking (Holt et al., 2003; Ragusa, 2012; Tam et al., 2016; Trimboli & Bonney, 1997). These lower-level breaches present police with a number of investigative challenges, namely, a lack of evidence that makes arresting and charging offenders harder to justify and increases the difficulty of securing prosecutions and convictions (Crime and Misconduct Commission, 2005; Trimboli & Bonney, 1997). However, around a half to three-quarters of victims feel safer and experience increased levels of wellbeing as a result of having a protection order granted, although this depends heavily on whether these orders are seen to be enforced and how often or severely they are breached (Home Office, 2016; Lewis et al., 2000; Trimboli & Bonney, 1997).

Similar to arrest, the effectiveness of protection orders in preventing further violence hinges on a number of contextual factors. They appear to be more effective where victims are employed and of a higher socioeconomic status (Burgess-Proctor, 2003; Carlson, Harris & Holden, 1999), and when victims are no longer in a relationship with their perpetrator (Carlson, Harris & Holden, 1999; Logan & Walker, 2009), while having little to no impact where perpetrators have a prior official history of criminal and/or domestic violence offending (Keilitz, Hannaford & Efkeman, 1996; Logan & Walker, 2009, 2010; Meloy et al., 1997) and mental health issues (Meloy et al., 1997). In short, they work best when there is no financial or legal reason for ongoing contact between victim/survivors and offenders, and when offenders have not shown a history of violent or unpredictable behaviour (Dowling et al., 2018).

Investigation and charging

Police investigations of domestic and family violence play a critical role in substantiating whether a crime occurred, identifying perpetrators, and ensuring appropriate criminal justice outcomes. The investigation of a domestic violence matter begins at the scene of an incident or upon the receipt of a report. These preliminary investigative activities are often used to determine whether there are sufficient grounds for the police responses already discussed (i.e. arrest and protection orders). Further subsequent investigation is undertaken to support the laying of charges and, ultimately, the prosecution of offenders. Like arrest, police in Australia are now encouraged to investigate domestic and family violence and, where supported by evidence, to lay charges, even in cases where victims do not want charges laid.

However, increased investigative effort, as measured by police decisions to undertake further investigations, time spent investigating, and the variety of different types of evidence collected, does not necessarily improve the likelihood of criminal justice outcomes (Belknap & Graham, 2000; Hartley & Frohmann, 2003; Nelson, 2013; Pennell & Burke, 2002; Smithey, Green & Giacomazzi, 2004; Whetstone, 2001). Force-wide increases in investigative effort, and in the proportion of matters for which charges are laid, can just as easily lead to rising costs and criminal justice system bottlenecks, with no associated increase in the rate of successful prosecutions (Belknap & Graham, 2000; Rodwell & Smith, 2008; Victorian Auditor-General, 2009).

Critically, while investigative effort may only marginally improve the viability of a domestic and family violence case for further criminal justice action, it can play a critical role in improving victim/survivor wellbeing and confidence in the police. More intensive investigations let victims see that their cases are being taken seriously, increasing their trust in the police to handle future incidents and encouraging future reporting (Hartley & Frohmann, 2003; Robinson & Stroshine, 2005). However, like arrest, victims' attitudes towards investigations depend on why they called the police in the first place (Belknap & Sullivan, 2002; Fleury-Steiner et al., 2006). Among those who do not want offenders charged, investigative effort and aggressive charging can reduce victim/survivor satisfaction, along with their likelihood of calling the police again.

Investigative success in domestic and family violence cases often hinges on the availability of certain types of evidence to collect rather than the time or effort police spend trying to collect it. Victim/survivor testimony is the most commonly used form of evidence and appears to be the most important to securing criminal justice outcomes. Victim/survivor testimony, and general victim/survivor cooperation with police, has been found to significantly increase the chances of charges being laid and successful prosecutions (Bechtel et al., 2012; Dawson & Dinovitzer, 2001; Kingsnorth et al., 2001). Photographic evidence has also been found to increase the chances of successful prosecution (Garcia, 2003; Kingsnorth et al., 2001). Witness testimony appears to be less important to achieving these criminal justice outcomes (Bechtel et al., 2012; Dawson & Dinovitzer, 2001; Kingsnorth et al., 2001; Nelson, 2013), while other forms of evidence, including medical/forensic evidence and emergency call recordings/transcripts, appear to have little impact (Cook et al., 2004; Dawson & Dinovitzer, 2001; Kingsnorth et al., 2001; Nelson, 2013). However, since research has not examined whether these forms of evidence are typically collected alongside, or instead of, the testimony of victims, it is difficult to determine exactly how useful this evidence is and under what circumstances it can be useful.

INNOVATIONS IN POLICE RESPONSES TO DOMESTIC AND FAMILY VIOLENCE

Mounting public and political pressure to better address domestic and family violence has led to various innovations. Front-line police in Australia now typically undergo specialised training in responding to domestic and family violence (Douglas, 2019). Specialised training has been shown to improve officers' confidence in and ability to respond to domestic and family violence when its severity and harm are emphasised, and when the focus is on teaching tangible skills (e.g. conflict resolution, investigative techniques) as opposed to changing broader attitudes regarding violence, gender, and sexuality (Blaney, 2010; Luna-Firebaugh et al., 2002; Toon et al., 2005). Relatedly, specialist investigative teams with more advanced training have been established in most states and territories to take on particularly difficult or serious cases of domestic and family violence. Evaluations have shown that these units enhance trust and encourage the reporting of domestic and family violence, encourage more thorough investigations and the collection of more evidence, and can improve criminal justice outcomes (Friday et al., 2006; Harrell et al., 2006; Holder & Caruana, 2006; Whetstone, 2001). They are, however, not universally effective (Mazerolle et al., 2018).

Given the limitations in police time and resources, and the differences between cases in the likelihood of further violence, police in Australia are increasingly relying on formal risk assessment tools. These tools are designed to help prioritise cases and ensure police focus on those victims who most need protection. Many tools now used by police in Australia demonstrate acceptable levels of accuracy in predicting further violence (Dowling & Morgan, 2019; Mason & Julian, 2009; Millsteed & Coghlan, 2016), but there is little evidence of whether their use helps police prevent further violence. There is evidence they encourage police to conduct more thorough investigations (Cook et al., 2004), and they almost certainly facilitate greater accountability through the oversight mechanisms in place to review assessments.

There have also been advances in proactive policing and multi-agency responses. Several police agencies have implemented high-risk offender targeting teams with proactive checks and intensive responses to prolific and serious offenders. Inter-agency working between police, child protection services, correctional services, and victim/survivor support services is common and, in many respects, Australia has been a leader in this area (Breckenridge et al., 2016). This usually involves participation in multi-agency case management and safety planning for victims and offenders. Recently, attention has shifted to the potential of new policing strategies, including focused deterrence models (Morgan et al., 2020) and women's police stations (Carrington et al., 2020), based on promising evidence from overseas, although these models are yet to be implemented.

Technology-based responses are also an increasingly important component of the policing response, particularly in relation to investigations and offender management. Body-worn cameras have also been rolled out by policing agencies across Australia. These cameras aid in the investigation of domestic and family violence incidents, and the laying of charges, by recording critical crime scene details, including injuries, property damage, and victim/offender interactions and behaviours. While expensive, and at times subject to technical faults and human error (Drover & Ariel, 2015; Miller, Toliver & Police Executive Research Forum, 2014), international evaluations of body-worn cameras have nevertheless found that they increase the rate of successful prosecutions, including for family violence cases (Mazerolle et al., 2018; Morrow, Katz & Choate, 2016; Owens, Mann & Mckenna, 2014). Domestic violence evidence-in-chief, which allows victims to provide video or audio recorded evidence immediately following a reported incident of violence, has also been introduced, with strong evidence that it contributes to improved prosecution outcomes (Yeong & Poynton, 2019).

Finally, a number of surveillance-based responses to domestic and family violence have been trialled across Australia, including GPS tracking of perpetrators and rapid alert technologies (i.e. panic buttons) that allow victims to quickly alert police. Victims have reported feeling safer with these measures in place (Carter & Grommon, 2016; Natarajan, 2016), although findings are mixed as to whether they actually reduce the likelihood of further violence (Brame et al., 2015; Hester & Westmarland, 2005; Taylor & MacKay, 2011). Importantly, studies have noted the technical faults that emerge recurrently with these technologies, along with the practical difficulties police face implementing comprehensive surveillance schemes, and responding quickly to breaches (Nancarrow & Modini, 2018; Queensland Police Service, 2019).

EMERGING CHALLENGES FOR POLICE

Importantly, community understanding of domestic and family violence is changing. There is growing recognition that, in many situations, the violence is ongoing, comprising a pattern of behaviour that evolves over the life of a relationship. This is certainly supported by the analysis of police administrative data, with rates of reoffending against the same partner being very high (Boxall & Morgan, 2020; Hulme, Morgan & Boxall, 2019; Morgan, Boxall & Brown, 2018). However, when responding to domestic violence calls for service, the police are focused primarily on the reported *incident* of violence or abuse. When they attend a scene, their primary responsibility is to investigate the circumstances of the incident, determine whether an offence has occurred (Walklate & Fitz-Gibbon, 2019), and gather evidence to support subsequent criminal justice decision-making processes. Stark (2012) calls this the "violent incident model" (200).

However, there is growing pressure on police to investigate and understand the contextual factors surrounding the violence, including situating incidents within the history of abuse in the relationship (New South Wales Police Force, 2018; Wangmann, Laing & Stubbs, 2020). It has been argued that by investigating patterns of violence, rather than individual acts of abuse, criminal justice processes better reflect the lived experiences of victim/survivors of domestic violence (Bishop & Bettinson, 2018; Stark, 2012) and help police to make more appropriate decisions regarding the response to the violence (e.g. the identification of primary perpetrators; Boxall & Morgan, 2020; Wangmann, Laing & Stubbs, 2020).

Nowhere is the tension between the violent incident model for responding to domestic violence and current understandings of domestic violence more apparent than the policing of coercive controlling behaviours. In recent years there has been a growing pressure in Australia for states and territories to criminalise coercive controlling behaviours (McGorrery & McMahon, 2020). Rather than being experienced as a series of events or acts of abuse, coercive controlling behaviours are a "liberty crime" (Stark, 2007), whereby offenders micro-regulate the lives of victim/survivors, creating environments of dread and anxiety. This may involve the offender constantly belittling and insulting the victim/survivor, creating rules about what the victim/survivor can and cannot do, monitoring their whereabouts and stalking them, interfering with their relationships with family, friends, and the children, as well as threats and physical violence (McMahon & McGorrery, 2016; Stark, 2007).

Taking the criminal offence of coercive and controlling behaviours implemented in England and Wales in 2015 and Scotland in 2019 as examples, criminalising coercive control would require the police to investigate and provide evidence of patterns of behaviour that had a detrimental impact on the victim/survivor, including isolation, dependence or subordination to the offender, controlling or regulating everyday activities, depriving them of their freedom, frightening, or humiliating them. Without engaging here in the ongoing debate around the potential positive and negative impacts of specific laws criminalising coercive controlling behaviours on social understanding of domestic violence as well as victim/survivors (see, for example, Bishop & Bettinson, 2018; McMahon & McGorrery, 2016; Stark, 2012; Walklate & Fitz-Gibbon, 2019), it can still be stated that such laws would present a significant challenge to police. Their primary responsibility is to respond to incidents, and they have little experience and capacity to investigate historical incidents of abuse, particularly non-physical forms of violence where there may be little evidence (Bishop & Bettinson, 2018). As noted by Walklate and Fitz-Gibbon: "For criminal justice professionals, it moves the focus away from responding to victims in an incident-led approach to process-led manner that is concerned with addressing the cumulative effect of the minutiae of everyday behaviours" (2019, p. 95).

Nevertheless, even without this legislation, there is growing pressure on police to recognise and respond to signs of coercive controlling behaviour in abusive relationships, especially as evidence mounts regarding the presence of coercive controlling behaviour in abuse that ends in homicide (Monckton Smith, 2019). This includes coercive controlling behaviour that manifests in technology-based abuse, another area of growing concern because of the impact it can have on the physical and psychological wellbeing of victims/survivors, and because it is not bound by geography and requires no physical contact between victim/survivor and offender (Douglas, Harris & Dragiewicz, 2019; Harris & Woodlock, 2019). Importantly, many of the behaviours that characterise coercive control are already criminalised. The challenge, with or without new legislation, is changing a police culture that prioritises acts of physical violence and views those incidents as being more serious and harmful to victims (Douglas, 2019).

A related issue is the misidentification of victim/survivors as primary perpetrators of domestic violence. This is not a new concern, having been raised by feminist and legal scholars and victim/survivor advocates for decades as an unintended consequence of mandatory arrest policies in jurisdictions like the United States (Goodmark, 2018; Martin, 1997). While Australian police have not followed the United States in adopting mandatory arrest, pro-arrest policies or codes of practice encourage police to make an arrest in incidents involving domestic violence (Wangmann, Laing & Stubbs, 2020; Victoria Police, 2019). The benefit of this is obvious – it encourages police to take action to protect victims and to treat domestic violence seriously – but it can also lead to the misidentification of victim/survivors as perpetrators. For example, research has clearly shown the use of violence within relationships is gendered and men and women use violence for different reasons. Women are more likely than men to use violence for self-defensive and retaliatory purposes (Dasgupta, 2002; Hamberger, 1997; Kernsmith, 2005; Mackay et al., 2018; Miller & Meloy, 2006). In a recent Australian study, female persons of interest were found to be responding to the immediate abusive behaviours of their partner, or in the context of prior violence perpetrated by their partner, in as many as half of all incidents (Boxall & Morgan, 2020). Moving beyond an incident focus can help to mitigate the risk that this wider context is overlooked but would constitute a major shift in how police – and the wider criminal justice system – responds to domestic and family violence.

CONCLUSION

There are few areas of contemporary policing as closely scrutinised or as challenging as the response to domestic and family violence. Police are, understandably, under enormous pressure to ensure the safety of victim/survivors and to hold offenders accountable. They perform a vital role; they can influence the likelihood of further violence, victim/survivor safety and satisfaction, and criminal justice outcomes. And few would argue that Australian policing agencies have not made substantial gains with respect to how they approach domestic and family violence. Major inquiries have acted as a significant catalyst for change, and these changes have been informed by a growing body of evidence. That said, there remains much more to be done. Rates of domestic homicide may have declined to their lowest levels on record (Bricknell, 2020), but there is little evidence of improvements in self-reported victimisation and violence (ABS, 2017, 2020). And, while there is a body of Australian research on the drivers and dynamics of domestic and family violence, recent large-scale reviews have highlighted the lack of rigorous evidence from Australia on effective policing responses (Dowling et al., 2018; Mazerolle et al., 2018). Police must therefore look to build on the progress that has been made, to innovate, and to continue the process of organisational reform in this area but also monitor, evaluate, and reflect on their performance.

REFERENCES

Australian Bureau of Statistics. (2017). *Personal safety, Australia, 2016 (4906.0)*. Australian Bureau of Statistics. Accessed at: www.abs.gov.au/ausstats/abs@.nsf/mf/4906.0

Australian Bureau of Statistics. (2020). *Recorded crime – offenders, 2018–19* (Cat. no. 4519.0). Australian Bureau of Statistics. Accessed at: www.abs.gov.au/ausstats/abs@.nsf/Lookup/by%20Subject/4519.0~2018-19~Main%20Features~Experimental%20Family%20and%20Domestic%20Violence%20Statistics~16

Bechtel, K. A., Alarid, L. F., Holsinger. A., & Holsinger, K. (2012). Predictors of domestic violence prosecution in a state court. *Victims and Offenders*, 7(2), 143–160.

Belknap, J., & Graham, D. L. R. (2000). *Factors related to domestic violence court dispositions in a large urban area: The role of victim/witness reluctance and other variables: Final report*. Accessed at: www.ncjrs.gov/App/Publications/abstract.aspx?ID=184232

Belknap, J., & Sullivan, C. M. (2002). *Longitudinal study of battered women in the system: The victims' and decision-makers perceptions, final report*. Rockville, MD: National Institute of Justice/NCJRS Paper Reproduction Sales.

Benitez, C. T., McNiel, D. E., & Binder, R. L. (2010). Do protection orders protect? *Journal of the American Academy of Psychiatry and the Law*, 38(3), 376–385.

Bishop, C., & Bettinson, V. (2018). Evidencing domestic violence*, including behaviour that falls under the new offence of 'controlling or coercive behaviour'. *The International Journal of Evidence & Proof*, 22(1), 3–29.

Blaney, E. (2010). Police officers' views of specialized intimate partner violence training. *Policing: An International Journal of Police Strategies and Management*, 33(2), 354–375.

Blumer, C. (2016). Australian police deal with domestic violence every two minutes. *ABC News*, 21 April. Accessed at: http://www.abc.net.au/news/2016-04-21/domestic-violence/7341716

Boxall, H., & Morgan, A. (2020). Repeat domestic and family violence among young people. *Trends & Issues in Crime and Criminal Justice*, 591. Australian Institute of Criminology. Accessed at: https://aic.gov.au/publications/tandi/tandi591.

Brame, R., Kaukinen, C., Gover, A. R., & Lattimore, P. K. (2015). No-contact orders, victim safety, and offender recidivism in cases of misdemeanour criminal domestic violence: A randomized experiment. *American Journal of Criminal Justice*, 40, 225–249.

Breckenridge, J., Chung, D., Spinney, A., & Zufferey, C. (2016). *National mapping and meta-evaluation outlining key features of effective "safe at home" programs that enhance safety and prevent homelessness for women and their children who have experienced domestic and family violence: Final report* (Horizons Research Report no. 1). Sydney: Australia's National Research Organisation for Women's Safety.

Bricknell, S. (2020). *Homicide in Australia 2017–18* (No. 23; Statistical Report). Australian Institute of Criminology. Accessed at: https://aic.gov.au/publications/sr/sr23

Bureau of Crime Statistics and Research. (2020). *Recorded crime reports*. NSW Bureau of Crime Statistics and Research. Accessed at: www.bocsar.nsw.gov.au:443/Pages/bocsar_crime_stats/bocsar_latest_quarterly_and_annual_reports.aspx

Burgess-Proctor, A. (2003). Evaluating the efficacy of protection orders for victims of domestic violence. *Women and Criminal Justice*, 15(1), 33–54.

Carlson, M. J., Harris, S. D., & Holden, G. W. (1999). Protective orders and domestic violence: Risk factors for re-abuse. *Journal of Family Violence*, 14(2), 205–226.

Carrington, K., Guala, N., Puyol, M. V., & Sozzo, M. (2020). How women's police stations empower women, widen access to justice and prevent gender violence. *International Journal for Crime, Justice and Social Democracy*, 9(1), 42–67.

Carter, J. G., & Grommon, E. (2016). Police as alert responders? Lessons learned about perceived roles and responses from pretrial GPS supervision of domestic violence defendants. *Policing: A Journal of Policy and Practice*, 10(4), 361–377.

Celik, A. (2013). An analysis of mandatory arrest policy on domestic violence. *International Journal of Human Sciences*, 10(1), 1503–1523.

Cook, D., Burton, M., Robinson, A., & Vallely, C. (2004). *Evaluation of specialist domestic violence courts/fast track systems*. Crown Prosecution Service and Department for Constitutional Affairs. Accessed at: https://wlv.openrepository.com/handle/2436/22612

Cordier, R., Chung, D., Wilkes-Gillan, S., & Speyer, R. (2019). The effectiveness of protection orders in reducing recidivism in domestic violence: A systematic review and meta-analysis. *Trauma, Violence and Abuse*. Accessed at: https://journals.sagepub.com/doi/full/10.1177/1524838019882361?casa_token=rRYeqbJZ-T88AAAAA%3AcZ3s0lDgiUkEot0argotrCLun3pwxKcyraiYoYxoc8Iyrko5-w6iZk2_sdu3wlCLfPlpRBCFZImCJA

Crime and Misconduct Commission. (2005). *Policing domestic violence in Queensland: Meeting the challenges*. Crime and Misconduct Commission. Accessed at: www.ccc.qld.gov.au/publications/policing-domestic-violence-queensland-meeting-challenges

Crime Statistics Agency Victoria. (2020). *Recorded criminal incidents* [Publication]. Crime Statistics Agency. Accessed at: www.crimestatistics.vic.gov.au/crime-statistics/latest-crime-data/recorded-criminal-incidents

Dasgupta, S. D. (2002). A framework for understanding women's use of nonlethal violence in intimate heterosexual relationships. *Violence Against Women*, 8(11), 1364–1389.

Dawson, M., & Dinovitzer, R. (2001). Victim cooperation and the prosecution of domestic violence in a specialized court. *Justice Quarterly*, 18(3), 593–622.

Douglas, H. (2019). Policing domestic and family violence. *International Journal for Crime, Justice and Social Democracy*, 8(2), 31–49. https://doi.org/10.5204/ijcjsd.v8i2.1122

Douglas, H., Harris, B. A., & Dragiewicz, M. (2019). Technology-facilitated domestic and family violence: Women's experiences. *The British Journal of Criminology*, 59(3), 551–570.

Dowling, C., & Morgan, A. (2019). Predicting repeat domestic violence: Improving police risk assessment. *Trends & Issues in Crime and Criminal Justice*, 581. Accessed at: https://aic.gov.au/publications/tandi/tandi581

Dowling, C., Morgan, A., Hulme, S., Manning, M., & Wong, G. (2018). Protection orders for domestic violence: A systematic review. *Trends & Issues in Crime and Criminal Justice*, 551. Australian Institute of Criminology. Accessed at: https://aic.gov.au/publications/tandi/tandi551

Drover, P., & Ariel, B. (2015). Leading an experiment in police body-worn video cameras. *International Criminal Justice Review*, 25(1), 80–97.

Dugan, L. (2003). Domestic violence legislation: Exploring its impact on the likelihood of domestic violence, police involvement, and arrest. *Criminology & Public Policy*, 2(2), 283–312.

Felson, R. B., Ackerman, J. M., & Gallagher, C. A. (2005). Police intervention and the repeat of domestic assault. *Criminology*, 43(3), 563–588.

Fleury-Steiner, R. E., Bybee, D., Sullivan, C. M., & Belknap, J. (2006). Contextual factors impacting battered women's intentions to reuse the criminal legal system. *Journal of Community Psychology*, 34(3), 327–342.

Friday, P. C., Lord, V. B., Exum, M. L., & Hartman, J. L. (2006). *Evaluating the impact of a specialised domestic violence police unit: Final report.* University of North Carolina. Accessed at: https://nij.ojp.gov/library/publications/evaluating-impact-specialized-domestic-violence-police-unit-final-report

Garcia, C. A. (2003). Digital photographic evidence and the adjudication of domestic violence cases. *Journal of Criminal Justice*, 31, 579–587.

Goodmark, L. (2018). *Decriminalizing domestic violence: A balanced policy approach to intimate partner violence.* Oakland: University of California Press.

Hamberger, L. K. (1997). Female offenders in domestic violence: A look at actions in their context. *Journal of Aggression, Maltreatment & Trauma*, 1(1), 117–129.

Harrell, A., Schaffer, M., DeStefano, C., & Castro, J. (2006). *The evaluation of Milwaukee's judicial oversight demonstration.* Urban Institute. Accessed at: www.urban.org/research/publication/evaluation-milwaukees-judicial-oversight-demonstration

Harris, B. A., & Woodlock, D. (2019). Digital coercive control: Insights from two landmark domestic violence studies. *The British Journal of Criminology*, 59(3), 530–550.

Hartley, C. H., & Frohmann, L. (2003). *Cook county target abuser call (TAC): An evaluation of a specialized domestic violence court.* University of Iowa. Accessed at: www.ncjrs.gov/App/abstractdb/AbstractDBDetails.aspx?id=202944

Hester, M., & Westmarland, N. (2005). *Tackling domestic violence: Effective interventions and approaches.* London: Home Office.

Hirschel, D., & Hutchison, I. W. (2003). The voices of domestic violence victims: Predictors of victim preference for arrest and the relationship between preference for arrest and revictimization. *Crime & Delinquency*, 49(2), 313–336.

Holder, R., & Caruana, J. (2006). *Criminal justice intervention in family violence in the ACT: The family violence intervention program 1998–2006.* Office of the Victims of Crime Coordinator. Accessed at: www.academia.edu/29679209/Criminal_Justice_Intervention_in_Family_Violence_in_the_ACT_The_Family_Violence_Intervention_Program_1998-2006

Holt, V. L., Kernic, M. A., Wolf, M. E., & Rivara, F. P. (2003). Do protection orders affect the likelihood of future partner violence and injury? *American Journal of Preventative Medicine*, 24(1), 16–21.

Home Office. (2016). *Domestic violence protection orders (DPVO) one year on: Home office assessment of national roll-out.* Home Office. Accessed at: www.gov.uk/government/publications/domestic-violence-protection-orders-assessment-of-national-roll-out

Hulme, S., Morgan, A., & Boxall, H. (2019). Domestic violence offenders, prior offending and reoffending in Australia. *Trends & Issues in Crime and Criminal Justice*, 580. Canberra: Australian Institute of Criminology.

Keilitz, S. L., Hannaford, P. L., & Efkeman, H. S. (1996). *Civil protection orders: The benefits and limitations for victims of domestic violence.* Washington, DC: National Centre for State Courts.

Kernsmith, P. (2005). Exerting power or striking back: A gendered comparison of motivations for domestic violence perpetration. *Violence and Victims*, 20(2), 173–185.

Kerr, J., Whyte, C., & Strang, H. (2017). Targeting escalation and harm in intimate partner violence: Evidence from Northern Territory police, Australia. *Cambridge Journal of Evidence-Based Policing*, 1(2–3), 143–159.

Kingsnorth, R. F., MacIntosh, R. C., Berdahl, T., Blades, C., & Rossi, S, (2001). Domestic violence: The role of interracial/ethnic dyads in criminal court processing. *Journal of Contemporary Criminal Justice*, 17(2), 123–141.

Lewis, R., Dobash, R. P., Dobash, R. E., & Cavanagh, K. (2000). Protection, prevention, rehabilitation or justice? Women's use of the law to challenge domestic violence. *Domestic Violence: Global Responses*, 7(1), 179–205.

Logan, T. K., & Walker, R. (2009). Civil protective order outcomes: Violations and perceptions of effectiveness. *Journal of Interpersonal Violence*, 24(4), 675–692.

Logan, T. K., & Walker, R. (2010). Civil protective order effectiveness: Justice or just a piece of paper? *Violence and Victims*, 25(3), 332–348.

Luna-Firebaugh, E. M., Lobo, S., Hailer, J., Barragan, D., Mortensen M., & Pearson D. (2002). *Impact evaluation of STOP Grant Programs for reducing violence against women among Indian tribes*. University of Arizona. Accessed at: www.ncjrs.gov/App/Publications/abstract.aspx?ID=195174

Mackay, J., Bowen, E., Walker, K., & O'Doherty, L. (2018). Risk factors for female perpetrators of intimate partner violence within criminal justice settings: A systematic review. *Aggression and Violent Behavior*, 41, 128–146.

Martin, M. E. (1997). Double your trouble: Dual arrest in family violence. *Journal of Family Violence*, 12(2), 139–157.

Mason, R., & Julian, R. (2009). *Analysis of the Tasmania police risk assessment screening tool (RAST): Final report*. Tasmanian Institute of Law Enforcement Studies. Accessed at: www.safeathome.tas.gov.au/publications

Mazerolle, L., Eggins, E., Sydes, M., Hine, L., McEwan, J., Norrie, G. & Somerville, A. (2018). *Criminal justice responses to domestic and family violence: A rapid review of the evaluation literature*. Brisbane: The University of Queensland. Accessed at: www.courts.qld.gov.au/__data/assets/pdf_file/0006/586185/systematic-review-of-criminal-justice-responses-to-domestic-and-family-violence.pdf

McGorrery, P., & McMahon, M. (2020). Coercive control is a key part of domestic violence: So why isn't it a crime across Australia? *The Conversation*, 27 February. Accessed at: https://theconversation.com/coercive-control-is-a-key-part-of-domestic-violence-so-why-isnt-it-a-crime-across-australia-132444

McMahon, M., & McGorrery, P. (2016). Criminalising emotional abuse, intimidation and economic abuse in the context of family violence: The Tasmanian experience. *University of Tasmania Law Review*, 35(2), 1–22.

Meloy, J. R., Cowett, P. Y., Parker, S. B., Hofland, B., & Friedland, A. (1997). Domestic protection orders and the prediction of subsequent criminality and violence toward protectees. *Psychotherapy*, 34(4), 447–458.

Miller, S. L., & Meloy, M. L. (2006). Women's use of force: Voices of women arrested for domestic violence. *Violence Against Women*, 12(1), 89–115.

Miller, S. L., Toliver, J., & Police Executive Research Forum (2014). *Implementing a body-worn camera program: Recommendations and lessons learned*. Office of Community Oriented Policing Services. Accessed at: www.policeforum.org/assets/docs/Free_Online_Documents/Technology/implementing%20a%20body-worn%20camera%20program.pdf

Millsteed, M., & Coghlan, S. (2016). Predictors of recidivism amongst police recorded family violence perpetrators. *In Brief*, 4. Accessed at: www.crimestatistics.vic.gov.

au/research-and-evaluation/predictors-of-recidivism-amongst-police-recorded-family-violence

Monckton Smith, J. (2019). Intimate partner femicide: Using Foucauldian analysis to track an eight stage progression to homicide. *Violence Against Women*. Accessed at: https://journals.sagepub.com/doi/full/10.1177/1077801219863876?casa_token=zuEmay9nh_YAAAAA%3A1lFBrVuI4vC_LLReTg_X6XGCsybmg_RLwYNc4EQ8PkscnFaOS17vl4X49K_v7fhM4xFUPQ8hC9Jy5g

Morgan, A., Boxall, H. & Brown, R. (2018). Targeting repeat domestic violence: Assessing short-term risk of reoffending. *Trends & Issues in Crime and Criminal Justice*, 552. Australian Institute of Criminology. Accessed at: https://aic.gov.au/publications/tandi/tandi552

Morgan, A., Boxall, H., Dowling, C., & Brown, R. (2020). Policing repeat domestic violence: Would focused deterrence work in Australia? *Trends & Issues in Crime and Criminal Justice*, 593, 1–20.

Morrow, W. J., Katz, C. M., & Choate, D. E. (2016). Assessing the impact of police body-worn cameras on arresting, prosecuting, and convicting suspects of intimate partner violence. *Police Quarterly*, 19(3), 303–325.

Nancarrow, H., & Modini, T. (2018). *Electronic monitoring in the context of domestic and family violence*. Report for the Queensland Department of Justice and Attorney-General. Australia's National Research Organisation for Women's Safety. Accessed at: www.anrows.org.au/project/electronic-monitoring-in-the-context-of-domestic-and-family-violence/

Natarajan, M. (2016). Police responses to domestic violence: A case study of TecSOS mobile phone use in the London metropolitan police service. *Policing: A Journal of Policy and Practice*, 10(4), 378–390.

Nelson, E. L. (2013). The relationship between individual police officer work habits and the stated reasons prosecutors reject their domestic violence investigations. *Sage Open*, 3(4). Accessed at: https://journals.sagepub.com/doi/full/10.1177/2158244013511826

New South Wales Police Force. (2018). *Code of practice for the NSW Police Force response to domestic and family violence*. NSW Police Force. Accessed at: www.police.nsw.gov.au/__data/assets/pdf_file/0016/165202/Code_of_Practice_for_the_NSWPF_response_to_Domestic_and_Family_Violence.pdf

Owens, C., Mann, D., & Mckenna, R. (2014). *The Essex body worn video trial: The impact of body worn video on criminal outcomes of domestic abuse incidents*. UK College of Policing. Accessed at: https://whatworks.college.police.uk/Research/Research-Map/Pages/ResearchProject.aspx?projectid=313

Pennell, S., & Burke, C. (2002). *A centralized response to domestic violence: San Diego county Sheriff*. San Diego's Regional Planning Agency. Accessed at: www.sandag.org/index.asp?classid=14&subclassid=18&projectid=139&fuseaction=projects.detail

Queensland Police Service. (2019). *Domestic and family violence GPS-enabled electronic monitoring technology: Evaluation report*. State of Queensland. Accessed at: www.police.qld.gov.au/initiatives/electronic-monitoring-gps-tracking-of-bailees/about-electronic-monitoring

Ragusa, A. T. (2012). Rural Australian women's legal help seeking for intimate partner violence: women intimate partner violence victim survivors' perceptions of criminal justice support services. *Journal of Interpersonal Violence*, 28(4), 685–717.

Rahman, S. (2018). Assessing the risk of repeat intimate partner assault. *Crime and Justice Bulletin*, 220, 1–20.

Robinson, A. L., & Chandek, M. S. (2000). Philosophy into practice? Community policing units and domestic violence victim participation. *Policing: An International Journal of Police Strategies and Management, 23*(3), 280–302.

Robinson, A. L., & Stroshine, M. S. (2005). The importance of expectation fulfilment on domestic violence victims' satisfaction with the police in the UK. *Policing: An International Journal of Police Strategies and Management, 28*(2), 301–320.

Rodwell, L., & Smith, N. (2008). *An evaluation of the NSW domestic violence intervention court model.* State of New South Wales. Accessed at: www.bocsar.nsw.gov.au/Pages/bocsar_media_releases/2012/bocsar_mr_cjb155.aspx

Sherman, L. W., & Berk, R. A. (1984). The specific deterrent effects of arrest for domestic assault. *American Sociological Review, 49,* 261–272.

Sherman, L. W., Bland, M., House, P., & Strang, H. (2016). *The felonious few vs. the miscreant many.* Cambridge: Cambridge Centre for Evidence Based Policing.

Smith, A. (2000). It's my decision, isn't it? A research note on battered women's perceptions of mandatory intervention laws. *Violence Against Women, 6*(12), 1384–1402.

Smithey, M., Green, S. E., & Giacomazzi, A. L. (2004). The ineffectiveness of training on increasing time at the scene, acceptance for prosecution, and convictions of domestic violence cases. *The Police Journal, 77,* 309–326.

Stark, E. (2007). *Interpersonal violence. Coercive control: How men entrap women in personal life.* Oxford: Oxford University Press.

Stark, E. (2012). Looking beyond domestic violence: Policing coercive control. *Journal of Police Crisis Negotiations, 12,* 199–217.

State of Victoria. (2016). *Royal commission into family violence: Summary and recommendations.* State of Victoria. Accessed at: www.rcfv.com.au/Report-Recommendations

Stephens, B. J., & Sinden, P. G. (2000). Victims' voices: Domestic assault victims' perceptions of police demeanor. *Journal of Interpersonal Violence, 15*(5), 534–547.

Tam, D. M. Y., Tutty, L. M., Zhuang, Z. H., & Paz, E. (2016). Racial minority women and criminal justice responses to domestic violence. *Journal of Family Violence, 31,* 527–538.

Taylor, E., & Mackay, R. (2011). *BSAFE pilot project 2007–2010.* Goulburn: Women's Health Goulburn North East.

Toon, R., Hart, B., Welch, N., Coronado, N., & Hunting, D. (2005). *Layers of meaning: Domestic violence and law enforcement attitudes in Arizona.* Arizona: Arizona State University.

Trimboli, L., & Bonney, R., (1997). *An evaluation of the NSW apprehended violence order scheme.* State of New South Wales. Accessed at: www.austlii.edu.au/au/journals/NSWBOCSARLES/1997/11.pdf

Victoria Police. (2019). *Code of practice for the investigation of family violence.* Melbourne: Victoria Police. Accessed at: www.police.vic.gov.au/code-practice-investigation-family-violence

Victorian Auditor-General. (2009). *Implementing Victoria Police's code of practice for the investigation of family violence.* Victorian Auditor-General's Office. Accessed at: www.parliament.vic.gov.au/papers/govpub/VPARL2006-10No205.pdf

Vigurs, C., Wire, J., Myhill, A., & Gough, D. (2016). *Police initial responses to domestic abuse: A systematic review.* UK College of Policing. Accessed at: https://whatworks.college.police.uk/Research/Documents/Police_initial_responses_domestic_abuse.pdf

Voce, I., & Boxall, H. (2018). Who reports domestic violence to police? A review of the evidence. *Trends and Issues in Crime and Criminal Justice*, 559. Australian Institute of Criminology. Accessed at: https://aic.gov.au/publications/tandi/tandi559

Walklate, S., & Fitz-Gibbon, K. (2019). The criminalisation of coercive control: The power of law? *International Journal for Crime, Justice and Social Democracy*, 8(4), 94–108.

Wangmann, J., Laing, L., & Stubbs, J. (2020). Exploring gender differences in domestic violence reported to the NSW police force. *Current Issues in Criminal Justice*, 1–22.

Whetstone, T. S. (2001). Measuring the impact of a domestic violence coordinated response team. *Policing: An International Journal of Police Strategies and Management*, 24(3), 371–398.

Wilson, S., & Jasinski, J. L. (2004). Public satisfaction with the police in domestic violence cases: The importance of arrest, expectations, and involuntary contact. *American Journal of Criminal Justice*, 28(2), 235–254.

Xie, M., & Lynch, J. P. (2017). The effects of arrest, reporting to the police, and victim services on intimate partner violence. *Journal of Research in Crime and Delinquency*, 54(3), 338–378.

Yeong, S., & Poynton, S. (2019). *A follow-up analysis on the 2015 domestic violence evidence-in-chief (DVEC) reforms*. Applied Research in Crime and Justice Conference, Sydney. Accessed at: www.bocsar.nsw.gov.au/Documents/2019_Conference/0214_1530_ARCJ19_C4.04_B402_Steve_Yeong.pdf

CHAPTER 28

Police interaction with vulnerable victims

Amber McKinley

INTRODUCTION

Police are usually the first point of contact victims have within the Criminal Justice System (CJS), and that interaction may determine whether the victim will proceed to an investigation or elect to only report and leave the CJS. The significance of the victim leaving the CJS is that no one is held to account for the crime, there is no closure for the victim, and there is little deterrent effect for future perpetrators. This is the reason that a strong and trusting relationship between police and the wider community is fundamental to public safety and order and that this bond endures, allowing police to carry out their function with public consent.

The role of police includes law enforcement, public order and safety, security, and justice (Australian Government Police Services, 2018). Whilst police are legally obligated to act with integrity, maintain confidentiality, and work to maintain the right of fair process for all (NSW Police Annual Report 2018–19, 2020); they also have the ability to use discretion in certain circumstances. Discretion is:

> *a key feature of policing in Australia . . . premised on the principle that '[s]trict adherence to the letter of the law in many cases would be too harsh and justice may be better served by not introducing an offender into the criminal justice process* (Australian Law Reform Commission, 2020, pp. 14–21).

The use of police discretion has significant impact on both offenders and victims of crime, and the interaction between police and victims are often complex, unequal, and can be conducted in situations where danger, confusion, and trauma are present. Police may not initially be able to identify and clearly label the participants in the event as either a victim, an offender, or a witness/bystander, and personal circumstances of those involved may eventually see them treated as both offender and victim, further deepening the complex nature of the situation.

Some of these circumstances will be examined later in this chapter, and to illustrate the complexities faced by police and victims, case studies will be used, examining the following themes:

1. Investigating missing persons, (the matter of Peter English);
2. Working to reduce Family and Domestic Violence (FDV), including sexual assault, (the matters of Hannah Clarke and 'Mia');
3. Interacting with the Indigenous community, (the matter of 'Kirra'); and
4. Concerns for welfare, public disturbances, or serious crime related to mental illness, (the matter of Michael Furlong).

This chapter will examine the role of police in society, review the positive aspects of their interactions with victims, and examine the negative outcomes of police contact. These examples will be highlighted using the case studies just mentioned. In all matters presented in this chapter, the victims have displayed a number of vulnerabilities.

For the purposes of this chapter, a victim of crime is defined as "someone who suffers . . . any harm or loss attributable to the action of an individual, group, or organization that can affect a person" (Petherick & Sinnamon, 2014, cited in Petherick & Sinnamon, 2016, p. 80). Many victims can be described as vulnerable. A vulnerable person is anyone who lacks social capital and is described by the Australia Department of Social Services (2019) as:

a. a child or children;
b. an individual aged 18 years and above who is or may be unable to take care of themselves, or is unable to protect themselves against harm or exploitation by reason of age, illness, trauma or disability, or any other reason;
c. Australian Defence Force families;[1]
d. disabled;
e. elderly;
f. previously incarcerated;
g. a homeless person;
h. Indigenous;
i. an itinerant worker;
j. mentally ill;
k. a migrant, asylum seeker, refugee, or trafficked person;
l. an out of home care child or young adult; and
m. a previous victim.

Police play a vital role in responding to and providing support for vulnerable victims in the aftermath of crime. Each victim is unique, and this is a constant and significant challenge for police because it is their job to resolve the problem legally whilst meeting the individual's needs and doing no further harm. In addition to the previous llustrations of vulnerability, further layers of vulnerability can be added when the victim is, for example, a member of culturally and linguistically diverse communities (CALD) or identifies as LGBTQI+.[2]

Given the specific needs of these diverse groups, significant challenges are faced by police when victimisation occurs. The role of police extends to guiding people on how to report crime and managing their expectations throughout the process whilst being sensitive to the individual's needs. The police also must provide advice on support services and potentially attending court. All of these factors are critical to victim recovery, especially in relation to serious interpersonal crimes, such as Family and Domestic Violence (FDV) or sexual offences, especially given the enormous cost to the individual, their community, and the nation.

Each year crime in Australia costs the country billions of dollars. The most recent Australian research indicates that the cost to the population is over $48 billion in 2017 (Steering Committee for the Review of Government Service Provision, Report on Government Services, 2016, p. 15). Given that many interpersonal crimes, such as sexual offences, FDV, and "scamming" or phishing crime have very low reporting rates, it is likely that these figures are only a small indication of the true extent of monetary losses incurred (Domestic Violence Resource Centre Victoria, 2017). Police are the conduit for victims to not only seek recompense for the crime committed against them, but for the community at large to feel safe and secure.

ROLE OF POLICE

As stated earlier, the function of police is to uphold the law; apply due process, reduce and investigate crime; and apprehend and prosecute suspects (Davies, Francis & Greer, 2007). Police are required to do this with integrity, whilst using discretion and proportionality. However, on occasions when the needs of victims are not met, there is a danger that the relationship between police and the victim will become fractious and break down to the point that the victim will elect to withdraw from the process. It is at this point that some victims will seek support and acknowledgement through social and news media, which can become difficult for police to control and respond to. (Turvey, 2013). Whilst such an event is the worst case scenario for the police and victim relationship, it is accepted that the majority of police are professional in their conduct and follow policies and procedures that they have been educated and trained in.

By way of an example, the New South Wales Charter of Victim's Rights (Charter of Victim's Rights, *Victim's Rights and Support Act 2013*) states that police will treat the victim with empathy, respect, and fairness and will investigate criminal matters on their behalf. Victims of crime may need specialised help and support, and police can advise on how to access this help. Police will strive to be professional, show commitment, lead by example, and be accountable to both internal and external stakeholders; maintain high personal standards, taking pride in their conduct; openly communicate and deal with the victim honestly and consistently; and be transparent in the delivery of their service (Charter of Victim's Rights, Victim's Rights and Support Act, 2013). However, if these principles are not adhered to, severe consequences can arise for all parties involved. Doerner and Lab state:

> *First, they suffer at the hands of their criminals. Then, by participating in the criminal justice system, they risk even more damage. By making a choice to void the system, victims are able to minimize their losses* (Doerner & Lab, 2017, p. 55).

This "damage" can occur when victims feel ignored, pressured, or disbelieved by police, or when "making a statement" is the only important consideration. It can happen when police see themselves as investigators, not psychologists, and feel that their role is to obtain evidence from the victim, at which point their relationship effectively ends. This is not a cynical move on the part of the police; instead, they believe that other agencies are better equipped to deal with the ongoing complex nature of the victim's trauma. (Papazoglou & Tuttle, 2018; Stenross & Kleinman, 1989). Some police have very little interaction with the victims other than to take a statement or process their remains in the case of a homicide (McKinley, 2015). When police have tunnel vision and are emotionally removed from their work and a victim's needs, investigative failures can occur.

Rossmo (2008) suggests that there are significant issues such as cognitive bias, including perception; intuition; tunnel vision; organisational traps; groupthink; rumour; ego; and probability errors, that can be made by veteran investigators, along with analytical errors and the absence of specific strategies to minimise the risk of criminal investigative failures (2008, pp. 9–54). Victims approach police in an emotional context, where they are looking to satisfy needs related to their harm and loss. Law enforcement comes from an objective and professional context, where in the worst instances, behaviour can border on dismissive and even apathetic (Goodrum, 2007, p. 753). However, Henry (2004) found that police used emotional distance to survive their frontline duties and disassociate from their emotions.

Henry's (2004) work on police trauma and the psychology of survival implies that what victims notice is the emotional detachment that officers develop to buffer and protect themselves from becoming scarred by the trauma and anguish they are often immersed in when dealing with serious crimes against victims. The following case studies identify some of the major issues discussed in this section and highlight the difficulties for police investigators when dealing with victims of serious crime

MISSING PERSONS

Australian Federal Police (AFP) statistics indicate that about 38,000 people are reported missing in Australia every year (2020). Of these, about 64% of reports are resolved within 24 hours, 86% are resolved within a week, and 99% are resolved within a year (Australian Federal Police Missing Persons National Dataset, 2020, p. 1). Missing persons demographics are made up of 51% males and 49% females, with almost half (49%) of missing persons being teenagers aged between 13 and 17 years. Other vulnerable groups include children or persons with mental health issues, intellectual or physical disabilities, or chronic drug (ab)use, (AFP Missing Persons National Dataset, 2020).

Although police have a great deal of success in finding and returning missing persons back to their homes, complaints from missing persons' families include that the disappearance of their loved one does not appear to generate any immediate concern from police, despite the reporting party's insistence on the victim's absence being out of character. In many cases that have been reviewed, the reporters of the missing person indicated that police perceived the missing person as an adult, capable of taking care of themselves, and sometimes suggesting that the missing person will return home soon of their own volition (National Missing Persons Advocacy Network, 2018).

The point of balance between the commencement of a police investigation, and the missing person's family's expectation that police will treat the report as a cause for concern is often many days after the person has gone missing, especially if they are an adult with no known, or obvious, vulnerabilities. The expectation of the person reporting is that police will always establish the location of the missing person using all police resources available and that the individual will be returned to them unharmed.

Case 1 – disappeared without a trace

Peter English is a 37-year-old male, who was a resident of Caboolture, Queensland, who was last seen at Mount Isa on February 11, 2019. The Queensland Police Force initially believed Peter travelled north to Mackay or alternatively back to south-east Queensland. However, the Northern Territory Police allege that his car was seen in Tennant Creek, Northern Territory, which is 661 kilometres west of Mount Isa on the Barkly Highway. Consequently, the search for Peter was shifted to a remote corner of the Northern Territory two months after he was last seen. He was last seen driving alone in his Ford FG Falcon sedan, and he last made contact with family on February 11, 2019. Police state that it is out of character for Peter not to remain in regular contact with family. He was unemployed at the time of his disappearance.

This case example highlights that in many cases missing persons are never found and the lack of information about their current location, or even whether they are alive or deceased, places a huge burden on the people left behind, on the community from which they disappeared, and on police resources. In the eyes of the community and the close family of the missing person, the police should have the capacity to locate the missing person without delay.

SEXUAL, FAMILY, AND DOMESTIC VIOLENCE

Family and Domestic Violence (FDV) is the leading cause of death of women aged 15–44 years (Domestic Violence Resource Centre Victoria, DVRCV, 2017), and violence against women is estimated to cost the Australian economy $22 billion each year (KPMG, 2016). Most women leaving a violent relationship move out of their home. Domestic and family violence is the leading cause of homelessness for women and their children. Intimate partner violence is a leading contributor to illness, disability, and premature death for women aged 18–44 (Ayre et al., 2016).

Across Australia, police respond to one family violence incident every two minutes, and women are three times more likely than men to experience violence from their partner (Walton, 2020). According to Our Watch, a non-governmental organisation that campaigns against violence against women and families, one woman a week is killed by a current or former partner (Walton, 2020). Nine women have been murdered by men in Australia since January 1, 2020. The support group "Australian Women Against Violence Alliance" (AWAVA) called for "urgent and immediate changes to improve women's safety" in response to the murders of Hannah Clarke and her three children in February 2020.

Case 2 – chronic and fatal family violence

Hannah Clarke and her three children, daughters Laianah, six; Aaliyah, four; and a three-year-old son, Trey, were allegedly murdered by her former partner, Rowan Baxter, on February 19, 2020. Clarke had a police-issued protection order against her ex-partner, and there was a history of violence in the relationship. Media statements suggest that Hannah and her children burned to death when Rowan Baxter poured petrol on their vehicle and set it alight. He then committed suicide at the scene. To date, the investigation is ongoing.

Notwithstanding the significant complexities surrounding FDV, there can also be co-committed sexual offending. This serious and debilitating crime affects a considerable number of people, and one which is increasing in prominence and awareness internationally. The next case study is less complex than that of Hannah and her family. Mia's[3] case is far more likely to occur in Australia; in fact, it is tragically a very common scenario for sexual assault.

Case 3 – interpersonal violence

Mia, 20 years old, moved from the country to the city to start university and soon after was invited to a party which was for her friend who was turning 21. The party was at a mutual friend's parent's house in the inner city. One of the first people Mia met at the party was a man who told her he was friends with Mia's new university friends. Over the course of the evening they moved out to the veranda and found a couch to share. They had a few more drinks, although they didn't eat anything.

Mia's friends saw them together, and based upon the way that the two were interacting, believed that they were attracted to each other, so they purposefully left them alone. What they did not know was that Mia had no experience with boys, was a virgin, and had never drank as much as she had that evening. In the early hours of the morning Mai and the man left the party in a shared taxi.

Partygoers had said Mia was flirty, so when she and the man left the party, no one intervened. A few girlfriends texted her the next day, tormenting her about being so drunk and leaving with a stranger. Mia awoke the next morning, partially naked, feeling sick, with no idea where she was.

Sexual offending has high impact and prevalence in Australia. Sexual assault is the fourth most serious crime by volume of victims, with 24,957 individuals affected in 2017 – it is the most serious offence against the person by victim volume (Australian Institute of Criminology, 2017).

In the category of Non-Assaultive Sexual Offences, 53% of women and 25% of men surveyed in a 2016 study had experienced sexual offending in their lifetime (Australian Bureau of Statistics, 2017a). According to ABS statistics, between 2016 and 2017 there was an 8% increase in the number of victims recorded for sexual assault – this can be contrasted with most other forms of serious crime against the person, which all fell at significant rates (Australian Bureau of Statistics, 2017b). This demonstrates the high, and increasing, reported rates of sexual crime in Australia.

Reporting of sexual crime persistently increased in Australia for the previous decade, reaching record highs by number of victims, with an estimated annual economic cost of $21.7 billion dollars a year to the Australian economy as well as untold costs in mental illness, personal suffering, early mortality, and physical harm for victims (PwC, 2015). Research suggests that worldwide, sexual offences are one of the most under-reported crimes, along with domestic violence, malicious property damage, and gang crimes (Australia Crime Victimisation, 2019; Gotsis & Dobson, 2018). In countries that publish crime data, most show increased reporting of sexual offences (World Health Organisation, 2018). This could be due to one or more of the following:

1. Increased use of social media impacting the way witness reporting occurs;
2. There has been a cultural shift emphasising the role of the bystander in crimes by such statements as "the standard you walk past is the standard you accept[4]" (Salter, 2013);
3. More sexual offences are occurring;
4. New laws and policies, requiring mandatory reporting and recording have come into use (Mathews & Kenny, 2008); or
5. Victims are more comfortable coming forward to law enforcement, medical specialists, psychologists, or women's outreach centres (Green, 2015).

The rise in reporting means that police are involved to a much greater degree than previously and despite the trend within Australia for police forces to maintain bespoke sexual offence investigation teams, the volume of such crime means that there is usually less time for investigators to build a meaningful rapport with victims and to advise them appropriately on how the investigation is progressing and where to seek support. This can lead to a situation where the victim does not feel believed, is disappointed with police interaction, or feels that they have not had their expectations managed appropriately. This can culminate in a decision to withdraw from the process and the inevitable cessation of investigations, leading to a perpetrator who is free to continue with their criminal behaviour (Karmen, 2001).

In the next section of this chapter the relationship between Indigenous people and police is discussed and analysed.

INDIGENOUS PEOPLE AND POLICE

Shepherd (2014) posited that migrants from non-English-speaking backgrounds had an innate fear of police, often due to previous experiences with authorities in their countries of origin, intergenerational trauma, and high levels of corruption within government-run agencies. The challenges for police in engaging with Indigenous communities do not appear too much different than that of ethnic minority groups.

The relationship between police and the Indigenous community is complex, unequal, and often based upon prejudice (Cunneen, 2001). Dwyer (2018, p. 160) states "Indigenous people have had a history of mistrusting police due to their role in colonisation, paternal government strategies and racist and coercive practices such as over-policing and overt biases when applying the law." Both historic and contemporary complaints of harsh, prejudicial treatment, racism, inappropriate behaviour, and seemingly excessive sentences are the most common issues. From the perspective of the police, the high levels of violence and abuse seen in some Indigenous communities are closely linked to a wide range of other problems such as community dysfunction, marginalisation, disempowerment, poverty, alcohol/substance (ab)use, antisocial behaviours, and chronic health problems (Meuleners, Hendrie & Lee, 2008; Murphy & Cherney, 2012; Paradies, 2016).

Case 4 – a lifetime of mistreatment

Kirra[5] was 17 years old and a victim of sexual assault, domestic violence, and theft by her on-again, off-again 21-year-old boyfriend, Yarren. They lived in a shared household with his family in a remote community where at least another nine people live. Kirra's parents were frequently away drinking and drug taking in a nearby town, and her life was characterised by malnutrition, developmental delays, a lack of education, and a lack of stability.

She met and started sexual relations with Yarren when she was 14 years old. He had an outstanding warrant for violence against previous partners. Kirra had no family support in the community and very little formal support after her mother was killed by her father. Yarren's parents were also absent for the majority of his formative years. His father, a drug user and alcoholic with co-morbid health issues, was jailed for violent assaults.

Kirra had just got her first job, but Yarren and his brother controlled her money, frequently stealing it to buy drugs. He attacked her, wielding a metal fry pan and caused serious injury to her face and scalp, and no one assisted her to report the assault to police. Yarren regularly used illicit drugs and sexually and physically abused her. When she attempted to leave, he threatened to self-harm or to kill her. Some of the women Kirra knew helped her access a health clinic once, but she was reluctant to disclose and left soon after meeting the doctor. When the clinic tried to follow up, Yarren threatened violence to the medic. Kirra refused to discuss her issues with anyone else, including the police.

Kirra's case study identifies both static and dynamic risks, chronic mistreatment, and intergenerational fear and trauma that directly affected her ability to engage with medical staff and police agencies. Continuous efforts made by police officers will benefit both police and society, ensuring better engagment and rapport building with Indigenous populations, resulting in an increase in reporting of interpersonal violence. By jointly participating in collaborative crime control efforts and creating more Indigenous liaison specialists the gap between culture, law and communities can be closed creating better interactions with police. Best practice would seem to have police officers adopt and adapt cultural and societal norms from within the communities they serve; using police discretion, the law and Indigenous lore to best serve, secure and protect communities.

The final section of this chapter is one of the largest groups of vulnerable victims that police frequently deal with, people living with mental illness.

MENTAL ILLNESS

One of the unintended consequences that occurred after the Richmond Report (1983) into Health Services for the Psychiatrically Ill and Developmentally Disabled was to shift those people who lived in institutionalised care to community-based care homes with the intention of a more positive lifestyle, stability, and a chance to interact within a functional community. Instead, due to many reasons, including a lack of government funding, some people living with mental illness ended up in the community with little to no safeguards. Community-based networks and systems did not receive sufficient funding and were unable to fully engage with all clients. Emergency departments, medical centres, crisis lines, mental health teams, and other agencies are limited in what they can offer and achieve, and many work as silos and are not well integrated with each other to support their clients. Reductions in hospital admissions, specialist psychiatric beds, and services are now only available for those persons in acute crisis, and even then for limited periods. These are the factors that can lead those people living with mental illness to come into contact with police.

When police reach a scene, they may not be aware that the individual they have been called to deal with has a mental illness (Forsythe & Gaffney, 2012; Romanucci, 2016). However, when it becomes apparent, it is critical that police ignore prejudice, commonly accepted myths, and stereotypes popularised by the media linking violent behaviour and mental illness (Ogloff et al., 2007; Slate, Buffington-Vollum & Johnson, 2013). Irrational behaviour displayed by a person with mental illness is often misunderstood and judged to be antagonistic, belligerent, or as resisting arrest (Forsythe & Gaffney, 2012; Ogloff et al., 2007). Police education and training has changed and has been enhanced considerably over the past decade, especially after the Coroner's enquiries into deaths in custody, "suicide by cop", and the mistreatment of mentally ill inmates.

Case 5 – not guilty by reason of mental illness

In June 2002, Michael Furlong (the victim) and his brother went shopping. Present within a store they visited was Mr Sorrell. The brothers left the store and were followed by Sorrell to another store. Upon leaving this second store, the brothers were approached by Sorrell. After speaking to Michael, Sorrell killed him with a knife and chased the victim's brother, who escaped. The next day police apprehended Sorrell while he slept in his vehicle. Police found a large hunting knife as well as the victim's wallet. Sorrell was subsequently charged with the murder of Michael.

At his trial Sorrell pleaded not guilty and raised the defence of insanity. In a trial before a judge alone, three psychiatrists gave evidence that at the time of the commission of the offence Sorrell was suffering from a mental illness and that he satisfied the criteria for the M'Naghten Rule.[6] Evidence presented showed that Sorrell had a history of paranoid schizophrenia and had been previously detained in forensic psychiatric hospitals in Australia and in the United Kingdom. It appeared that at the time of killing Michael, Sorrell was suffering from a delusion that Michael was a federal police officer who was persecuting him using secret technology and that a drug had been administered to him in his toothpaste to enable vibrations of his larynx to be detected and recorded at a distance, that his private thoughts thereby became able to be discussed, and that the police were going to kill him.

The trial judge, Justice James, found Sorrell not guilty of the murder charge on the grounds of his mental illness and ordered his immediate detention in a secure psychiatric facility. He expressed his sympathy for the family and loved ones of Michael, noting the enormity of the tragedy they had suffered, as had the community at large, as a result of the actions of a person suffering from a mental illness (Chappell, 2010, pp. 42–43; *R v Sorrell*, 2003).

CONCLUSION

This chapter has provided a broad overview of the interaction of police and vulnerable victims within society. Considering that the police are usually the first point of contact victims have within the Criminal Justice System (CJS), the relationship that is built by police in the initial meetings is critical, and in the main the meetings with victims are conducted professionally and in the best interests of the victims. A strong and trusting relationship between police and the wider community is vital to public order and safety and allows police to carry out their function with public consent. Although the primary functions of police include law enforcement, keeping the peace, and serving the community, it is critical that they use discretion, especially when encountering vulnerable people and victims.

This chapter analysed the role of police in society, reviewed both the positive and negative aspects of their interactions with vulnerable victims, and illustrated some of the high-volume crime types using examples. In all of the case studies, the victims, as well as some perpetrators, displayed multidimensional vulnerabilities. Extant research shows that victims of crime play an essential and critical role in the CJS, as once they have reported the alleged crime against them, they have to participate in the investigation and then, if the investigation process is successful, they will most probably be required to testify in court. The interaction between police and victims is so significant, some would say, that without successful court outcomes, there is little to no deterrent to potential and current perpetrators of crime, which would ultimately lead to chaos, anarchy, and the downfall of civil society.

Over the past decades, after external reviews, Coroner enquiries and high-profile court cases, police have begun to recognise that to successfully accomplish their objectives they must acknowledge that they must increase the attention paid to the needs of vulnerable victims. As first responders to an immense assortment of traumatic events, police are the victim's key to justice, safety, peace, support, and information. In order to achieve this mission, they have to understand and offer vital elements to vulnerable victims for their recovery. For many victims, the trauma they experience from the crime(s) against them leaves lasting scars and negative impressions in their lives. Traumatised victims, especially those without family or support networks, find it more difficult to navigate legal, medical, or psychological support at the time of the incident or upon reporting the crime(s). Mistreatment, abuse, and neglect are highly interrelated and complex problems; many of the vulnerable victims that police encounter have unfavourable behaviours, adverse health consequences, and high levels of homelessness and risk-taking behaviours. A substantial proportion of the vulnerable people known to police live with mental illness, drug and alcohol misuse, homelessness, and intentional self-harm. The impact of crime increases risk factors in the burden of disease to these already defenceless people.

Many crime victims experience anxiety, are continually vulnerable to additional danger and trauma, and frequently require an urgent response. The behaviour that police witness from vulnerable people in distress can be on a continuum from confused disorientation to fear and aggression and on to rage and shame. The reactions to these behaviours will be expressed through fight, flight, freeze, or fawn (Walker's trauma typology). Police officers have a vital role to play to use their powers to protect, responding to, and supporting, victims of crime. To appropriately assist these people, it is critical that the police remain calm, objective, act with sensitivity, and are proportionate in their response. Whilst responding to the needs of the person who called for their assistance, they must also establish safety for the victim, effectively communicate their intentions, and ultimately assist the vulnerable person in getting help and support whilst upholding the law.

Education and training are required to institute and sustain this change. Whilst the specific needs of individual victims remain constant, the way in which police are able to successfully effect positive response will change over time as education and training programs evolve, technology advances, crime analysis and intelligence develops, and investigation techniques are enhanced. Responding appropriately to all victims is not only in line with community expectations but also within the police forces' duty of care and mission. Improving the police response to victims of any crime type, but especially to those who are vulnerable, will require adjusting some of the behaviours, protocols, responses, and values that are at the core of law enforcement.

NOTES

1. Due to the transient nature of their work and lack of support network for victims of interpersonal violence.
2. Lesbian, Gay, Bi-sexual, Transsexual, Queer, Intersex, plus.
3. Name changed to protect the victim's identity.
4. Extract from speech on unacceptable behaviour delivered by LTGEN D Morrison AO, former Chief of Army on 13 Jun 2013, which he later attributed to the former CDF – General DJ Hurley AC, DSC.
5. Names changed to protect parties involved.
6. A rule for defining insanity that focuses on the cognitive state of the defendant at the time of committing the act with which he or she is charged. It states that to plead insanity, the accused must be "laboring under such a defect of reason, from disease of the mind, as not to know the nature and quality of the act he was doing, or if he did know it, he did not know that what he was doing was wrong." The rule was established in 1843 by judges in England after the trial of Daniel M'Naghten (Quote from American Psychological Association).

REFERENCES

Australian Bureau of Statistics. (2017a). *Personal safety 2016*. Retrieved from: https://www.abs.gov.au/ausstats/abs@.nsf/mf/4906.0

Australian Bureau of Statistics. (2017b). *Recorded crime – Victims, Australian 2017*. Retrieved from: https://www.abs.gov.au/ausstats/abs@.nsf/Lookup/by%20Subject/4510.0~2017~Media%20Release~Recording%20of%20sexual%20assaults%20reaches%20eight-year%20high%20(Media%20Release)~16

Australia Crime Victimisation. (2019). *Reporting of crime to the police*. Retrieved from: www.abs.gov.au/ausstats/abs@.nsf/Lookup/by%20Subject/4530.0~2016-17~Main%20Features~Reporting%20of%20crime%20to%20police~7

Australia Department of Social Services. (2019). *About the department*. Retrieved from: https://www.dss.gov.au/about-the-department/doing-business-with-dss/vulnerable-persons-police-checks-and-criminal-offences

Australian Federal Police Missing Persons National Dataset. (2020). *Commonwealth of Australia (2017) Australian federal police missing persons*. Retrieved from: https://missingpersons.gov.au/search/qld/peter-english

Australian Government Services. (2018). *Police services*. Retrieved from: www.australia.gov.au/information-and-services/public-safety-and-law/police-and-crime-prevention/police-services-states

Australian Institute of Criminology. (2017). *Australian crime: Facts and figures – victims of crime*. Retrieved from: https://crimestats.aic.gov.au/facts_figures/1_victims/

Australian Law Reform Commission. (2020). *Section 14.21 police discretion*. Retrieved from: www.alrc.gov.au/publication/pathways-to-justice-inquiry-into-the-incarceration-rate-of-aboriginal-and-torres-strait-islander-peoples-alrc-report-133/14-police-accountability/improving-police-practices-and-procedures/

Ayre, J., Lum On, M., Webster, K., Gourley, M., & Moon, L. (2016). *Examination of the burden of disease of intimate partner violence against women in 2011: Final report (ANROWS Horizons, 6)*. Sydney: ANROWS.

Chappell, D. (2010). Victimisation and the insanity defence: Coping with confusion, conflict and conciliation. *Psychiatry, Psychology and Law, 17*(1), 39–51.

Charter of Victim's Rights. (2013). *Victim's rights and support act*. Retrieved from: www.victimsservices.justice.nsw.gov.au/Documents/fs10_charter.pdf

Cunneen, C. (2001). *Conflict, politics and crime: Aboriginal communities and the police*. Sydney: Allen & Unwin.

Davies, P., Francis, P., & Greer, C. (2007). *Victims, crime and society*. Chapter 1, 5, pp. 2–8. London: Sage Publications.

Doerner, W. G., & Lab, S. P. (2017). *Victimology*. Eighth Edition, Chapter 6, pp. 133–167; Chapter 7, pp. 168–200. London: Routledge, Taylor and Francis.

Domestic Violence Resource Centre Victoria (DVRCV). (2017). *Family and domestic violence in Australia*. Retrieved from: www.dvrcv.org.au/about/what-domestic-violence

Dwyer, A. I. (2018). *Understanding police-Indigenous relations in remote and rural Australia: Police perspectives*. Queensland University of Technology. Doctoral dissertation.

Forsythe, L., & Gaffney, A. (2012). Mental disorder prevalence at the gateway to the criminal justice system. *Trends and Issues in Crime and Criminal Justice, 438*(1).

Goodrum, S. (2007). Victims' rights, victims' expectations, and law enforcement workers' constraints in cases of murder. *Law & Social Inquiry, 32*(3), 725–757.

Gotsis, T., & Dobson, M. (2018). *A statistical snapshot of crime and justice in New South Wales EE5/18*. NSW Parliamentary Research Service. Retrieved from: www.parliament.nsw.gov.au/researchpapers/Documents/A%20statistical%20snapshot%20of%20crime%20and%20justice%20in%20NSW.pdf

Green, E. (2015). *Consent isn't enough: The troubling sex of fifty shades*. Retrieved from: www.theatlantic.com/culture/archive/2015/02/consent-isnt-enough-in-fifty-shades-of-grey/385267/

Henry, V. E. (2004). *Death work: Police, trauma, and the psychology of survival*. Oxford: Oxford University Press.

Karmen, A. (2001). *Crime victims: An introduction to victimology*. Fourth Edition, Chapter 3, pp. 87–94; Chapter 4, pp. 148–161. London: Wadsworth Thomson Learning.

KPMG. (2016). *The cost of violence against women and their children in Australia*. Final Report. Retrieved from: www.dss.gov.au/sites/default/files/documents/08_2016/the_cost_of_violence_against_women_and_their_children_in_australia_-_summary_report_may_2016.pdf

Mathews, B., & Kenny, M. C. (2008). Mandatory reporting legislation in the United States, Canada, and Australia: A cross-jurisdictional review of key features, differences, and issues. *Child Maltreatment*, *13*(1), 50–63.

McKinley, A. (2015). *Homicide solvability and applied victimology in New South Wales, 1994–2013*. Criminology Department, Faculty of Social Science, Bond University, Gold Coast. Ph.D. Thesis.

Meuleners, L., Hendrie, D., & Lee, A. H. (2008). Measuring the burden of interpersonal violence victimisation in Western Australia. *Trends & Issues in Crime & Criminal Justice*, *352*.

Murphy, K., & Cherney, A. (2012). Understanding cooperation with police in a diverse society. *The British Journal of Criminology*, *52*(1), 181–201.

National Missing Persons Advocacy Network. 2018. *SOS: Search options and support: A guide for the families and friends of missing people*. Canberra: Australian Federal Police.

NSW Police Force. (2020). *NSW police annual report 2018–19*. Retrieved from: www.police.nsw.gov.au/__data/assets/pdf_file/0010/658513/NSWPF_2018-19_Annual_Report.pdf

Ogloff, J. R. P., Davis, M. R., Rivers, G., & Ross, S. (2007). *The identification of mental disorders in the criminal justice system*. Canberra: Australian Institute of Criminology.

Papazoglou, K., & Tuttle, B. M. (2018). Fighting police trauma: Practical approaches to addressing psychological needs of officers. *Sage Open*. https://doi.org/10.1177/2158244018794794

Paradies, Y. (2016). Colonisation, racism and indigenous health. *Journal of Population Research*, *33*(1), 83–96.

Petherick, W., & Sinnamon, G. (2016). *The psychology of criminal and antisocial behavior: Victim and offender perspectives*. First Edition, p. 80. New York: Academic Press.

PwC Australia. (2015). *A high price to pay: The economic case for preventing violence against women*. Retrieved from: www.pwc.com.au/pdf/a-high-price-to-pay.pdf

Regina v Sorrell [2003] NSWSC 30 (February 7) [Sorrell].

Richmond, D. (1983). *The report of the inquiry into health services for the psychiatrically ill and developmentally disabled*. NSW Ministry of Health. Retrieved from: https://

nswmentalhealthcommission.com.au/sites/default/files/Inquriy%20into%20 Health%20Services%20for%20the%20Psychiatrically%20Ill%20and%20Developmentally%20Disabled%20-%20Richmond%20Report%20-%201983.pdf

Romanucci, A. M. (2016). *Excessive police force against the emotionally disturbed: 52 Trial 10*. American Association for Justice. Retrieved from: https://rblaw.net/personalinjurylawyers/wp-content/uploads/2014/05/TRIAL-Oct-2016.pdf

Rossmo, D. K. (2008). *Criminal investigative failures*. London: CRC Press.

Salter, M. (2013). Justice and revenge in online counter-publics: Emerging responses to sexual violence in the age of social media. *Crime, Media, Culture*, 9(3), 225–242.

Shepherd, S. M. (2014). Why diversity may not mend adversity – an Australian commentary on multicultural affirmative action strategies in law enforcement. *Current Issues in Criminal Justice*, 26(2), 241–248.

Slate, R. N., Buffington-Vollum, J. K., & Johnson, W. W. (2013). *The criminalization of mental illness: Crisis and opportunity for the justice system*. North Carolina: Carolina Academic Press.

Steering Committee for the Review of Government Service Provision, Report on Government Services. (2016). *Commonwealth of Australia. Report on Government Services*. C19. Retrieved from: www.pc.gov.au/research/ongoing/report-on-government-services/2016/justice/rogs-2016-volumec-justice.pdf

Stenross, B., & Kleinman, S. (1989). The highs and lows of emotional labor: Detectives' encounters with criminals and victims. *Journal of Contemporary Ethnography*, 17, 435–452.

Turvey, B. E. (2013). *Forensic victimology: Examining violent crime victims in investigative and legal contexts*. Second Edition, Chapter 2, 5, pp. 33–71, 165–203. New York: Elsevier Science Publishing Co.

Walton, K. (2020). *Australia urged to take action amid rising violence against women*. Retrieved from https://www.aljazeera.com/news/2020/03/australia-urged-action-rising-violence-women-200306022709312.html

World Health Organisation (WHO). (2018). *Guidelines for medico-legal care for victims of sexual violence*. Retrieved from www.who.int/violence_injury_prevention/publications/violence/med_leg_guidelines/en/

Index

9/11 terrorist attacks 271
70/20/10 theoretical approach 30
1967 Tasmanian Bushfires 268

Aboriginals: challenged by social disadvantage 44; deaths in police custody 397; identity, historical racism in policing 125–126; and police, relationship between 44; sovereignty movements 407–408; women and children, missing and murdered 397, 403–405
Abrahamson, Douglas E. 199
ABS *see* Australian Bureau of Statistics
ACCC *see* Australian Competition and Consumer Commission
accountability 97, 102, 206; mechanisms for policing 41; notions of 40; safety and policing 407
ACDC *see* Australian Counter Disaster College
ACIC *see* Australian Criminal Intelligence Commission
ACORN *see* Australian Cybercrime Online Reporting Network
ACT *see* Australian Capital Territory
Action Research model 294
adaptation 23

adapting predictive analysis 131–132
adaptive nature of police work 28
ADPP *see* Associate Degree in Policing Practice
AFP *see* Australian Federal Police
"African gang crime" 242
aggressive tactics 58
aging society and police leaders 44
AI-assisted information technologies 114
AICD *see* Australian Institute of Company Directors
AI policing tools: bias distortion concerns 123; mapping operational and cultural biases 123–124; opportunities and challenges 125; predictive and proactive 122; risks associated with 124–125; for routine policing 124; through smart technology devices 123
air travel, efforts for protecting 303
Al-Alosi, Hadeel 333
alcohol consumption and wellbeing 84, 88
Alcohol Use Disorders Identification Test 84
AlphaBay (darknet marketplace) 338
Al Qaeda 301
alt-right crime 307
anti-colonial struggles 300

ANZCoPP *see* Association for Australia New Zealand Council of Police Professionalization
ANZEMC *see* Australia-New Zealand Emergency Management Committee
ANZFSS *see* Australian and New Zealand Forensic Science Society
ANZPAA *see* Australian and New Zealand Policing Advisory Agency
APMC *see* Australian Police Ministers Council
apprenticeship model of education 11, 16
artificial intelligence 23, 125, 333; *see also* AI policing tools
ASIAL *see* Australian Security Industry Association Limited
ASIC *see* Australian Securities and Investment Commission
ASIO *see* Australian Security Intelligence Organisation
Associate Degree in Policing Practice 12, 19
Association for Australia New Zealand Council of Police Professionalization 105
Atkins, Paul 71
attitudes towards police 57
AUDIT *see* Alcohol Use Disorders Identification Test

INDEX

AUSTRAC *see* Australian Transaction Reports and Analysis Centre
Australia and New Zealand Counter Terrorism Committee 303
Australian and New Zealand Forensic Science Society 178
Australian and New Zealand Policing Advisory Agency: education and training framework 1; guidelines for police use of force 186–187
Australian Border Force (ABF) 147, 319
Australian Bureau of Statistics 383, 467; 2016 Census conducted by 43; Crime Victimisation Survey 291
Australian Capital Territory 147, 272, 352; human rights legislation 100; Operation Anchorage 290; police call-outs to mental health crises 374; police education and training in 17, 18; police "Use of Force Report" 187; Policing Emergency Management and Planning Team 270; state police emergency-management units 270
Australian Commonwealth Law Enforcement Integrity Commission 320
Australian Competition and Consumer Commission 291
Australian Counter Disaster College 269
Australian Crime Commission Act 2002 315
Australian Crime Commission and CrimTRAC, merging of 135
Australian Criminal Intelligence Commission: Australian Priority Organisation Target list 135; education and training continuum 131; intelligence-led policing 134; tackling transnational and organised crime 320; tertiary recognised qualifications 131

Australian Criminal Intelligence Model 131, 133–134
Australian Criminal Intelligence Strategy 135–136
Australian Criminal Justice 113
Australian Cybercrime Online Reporting Network 325
Australia-New Zealand Emergency Management Committee 272
Australian Federal Police 203–205, 213, 336, 351; engagement with international partners 309, 310; future of 360; for international liaison posts 353; for partnership programmes 352–353; peacekeeping mission of Solomon Islands with 349, 354–355; peacekeeping mission of Timor-Leste with 349, 353–354; police personnel for UN missions 351, 352; rates of police call-outs 374–375; stable funding within 213; tackling organised online fraud 336; transnational and organised crime tackling 319–320, 322
Australian Institute of Company Directors 51
Australian Institute of Police Management (AIPM) 47, 49
Australian National Counter Terrorism Committee 271
Australian Police Leadership Academy 47
Australian Police Ministers Council 11
Australian police peacekeepers: AFP members 351; challenges and opportunities faced by 355–356; Commonwealth Police force 351–352; in Cyprus 351–352; future of 360–361; for peacekeeping and capacity-building missions 352; RAMSI to Solomon Islands 354–355; state police deployments as 352; UN missions to Timor-Leste 353–354; *see also* Australian Federal Police

Australian Priority Organisation Target list 135
Australian Royal Commission 202
Australian Securities and Investment Commission 291, 320, 336
Australian Security Industry Association Limited 226
Australian Security Intelligence Organisation 300
Australian Signals Directorate 320
Australian Strategy for Protecting Crowded Places from Terrorism 223
Australian Transaction Reports and Analysis Centre 320
Australia Open Colleges 31
authenticity concerns, communication role plays 61–62
authoritarianism 378
authority 45, 116, 249; discretionary 119; exercising 41; notions of 40–41
automatic teller machine (ATM) ram raids, strategy to stop outbreak of 225
autonomy 74; and career stage 80–81; contexts supporting 78–79; and wellbeing 75
autonomy-supporting contexts of SDT 73

Baader-Meinhoff gang 300
basic intelligence 129
Beckley, Alan 93
behaviour management of children, teacher training in 65
benevolent approach 378
Bertillonage 168
Birch, Philip 1, 23, 71, 349, 383, 413
Black Saturday Bushfires of 2009 273
body-worn cameras 97
Boursnell, Melanie 23
Boxall, Hayley 443
brand management 49
Brown, Rick 315

Bsafe (personal security program) 287–288
Budapest Convention 325
bullying in workplace 72
burglaries, crime prevention initiatives for 290–291
burnout and wellbeing 88, 89

camaraderie 94
capability-based system of professional development 27, 29
capacity building 349–352, 355, 357
capitalist labour ordering 116
card fraud 292
career stage and wellbeing indicators 87–88
Cazes, Alexandre 338
Centrelink 225
change fatigue, concept of 48
change interventions 77
change management: driven by crisis 48; fundamental to 47; guidebooks on 106; leadership through 47–49
change manager 47
Charles Sturt University (CSU) and NSWPF, partnership between 12
Chief Officers 46–47
child sexual abuse investigations 202
child sexual abuse material, online *see* online child sexual abuse material
"Chip and PIN" technology 292
chronic and fatal family violence 466
CITDC *see* Criminal Intel Training and Development Continuum
citizen encounters, power dispersal in 114
citizen journalism 239–240, 245–248
civil defence, to emergency management 268–269
Civil Defence School 268–270
civilian complaints 59
civilian educators 12, 23–24
clinical communication skills 62

closed occupational culture of police 11
CNS *see* custody notification schemes
COAG *see* Council of Australian Governments
cognitive and motor skills 28
cognitive processes, motor learning 28
collaboration preconditions 206
collaborative partnerships 210, 211, 213, 215–216; desirability of 202; operational mechanisms for 208
Collaborative Policing Framework 208, *209*
command type and needs satisfaction 86–87
"common clientele" 253
communication 48, 75; *see also* communication skills
communication role plays: authenticity issue in 61–62; benefits of 62–63
communication skills: for building relationships 63–65; need for enhancement of 55; strategies to enhance 61; student-centred learning of 61; trainee teachers' 61–62; *see also* effective communication skills
communistic wave 300
community diversity, influences on police leaders 43–44
community engagement: countering radicalisation 308–310; via social media 244
community mental health ideology 378
community policing 289–290; concept of 10; and liberal-democratic models 356–359
comparative analysis 173
competence: and career stage 81; contexts supporting 79
competence-supporting contexts of SDT 73–74
complaints against police 101; *see also* customer service complaints
consumerist society, expansion of 8

"contain and negotiate" policy 308
contemporary policing 1, 27, 114; core requirement of 34; labour market and 29; models 205, 211
contingency planning 48
Conversation Management (CM) framework of investigative interviewing 149–151, 154–158
coping mechanisms: employed by police organisation members 76; and police culture 369–371
corrections intelligence 138–140
corruption risk, organised and transnational crime 322–323
Council of Australian Governments 229, 271
counter-colonial protest movements 407–408
counterterrorism: challenges 305–308; engagement with business sector and private security 311; engagement with international partners 309; engagement with vulnerable communities 308, 310; funding 271; interoperability 310–311; issues for police leaders 309; national exercises 307; policing leadership 311–312
Courtesy, Professionalism and Respect Policy 59
covert surveillance 225
COVID-19 pandemic 47–48, 259–261, 277, 311, 327
CPR *see* Courtesy, Professionalism and Respect Policy
craftsmen/women 13–14
Craven, Rhonda 71
crime 27; detection analysis, AI-information tool for 123; policy evolution 283; prevention activities 9, 284; *see also* cybercrime; hate crime; organised and transnational crime; transnational crime
Crime and Corruption Commission 321

Crime and Misconduct Commission 59
"crime containment" model 283, 293
crime news production 239; audience assumptions for 240; news values 240–241; sources of crime news 241–242; systemic journalistic practices 240
crime prevention case studies: Bsafe (personal security program) 287–288; Geelong Venues against Violence Accord 285–287; random breath testing (RBT), reducing crashes through 285; Strike Force Piccadilly (problem-solving initiative) 288–289
crime prevention reforms, failure of: community policing 289–290; fraud 291–292; Operation Anchorage 290–291; random breath testing 292–293
crime reduction 203; partnerships in 224; problem-solving models 203
crime reduction strategies 55, 56; and effective communication skills 58–60; problematic issue concerning 58–59
Crime Statistics Agency 255
criminal intelligence 2; challenge for 131; changes in 129; corrections system and 138–140; cultural problems in 130–132; definition of 129
Criminal Intel Training and Development Continuum 134
criminalistics 176
crisis in policing: community policing 289–290; Community Policing movement 284; with explosion of crime 283–284; fraud 291–292; intelligence-led policing 284; Operation Anchorage 290–291; problem-oriented policing 284; Project Sunbird 292; random breath testing 292–293; third-party policing 284

critical reflection and analysis abilities 25
critical reflective practice 30
cross-disciplinary engagement 201
cross-sector collaboration 200–201
cryptocurrencies 324
cryptocurrency service providers, regulation of 326
"CSI effect" 164
Cubitt, Timothy 315
cultural imperialism 356–359
culturally diverse nation 43
cultures of secrecy 210–211
Cunneen, Chris 397
custody notification schemes 406–407
customer service 57
customer service complaints: contributing factors to 55; against NSWP officers 60–61
customer service obligations, communication relationship with 56–58; Corporate Plan and Annual Reports 56–57; "customer service speak" 57; NSWPF Customer Service Charter 56; NSWPF Customer Service Guidelines 56; public support and police misconduct 56–57
customer service practices, for building relationships 63–65
customer service strategies 55, 56
cybercrime 2, 318; investigation challenges 333, 344–345; online child sexual abuse material 341–344; online drug markets, darknet forums 337–340; organised online fraud 334–337; remedy sought by victim 333
cyber-intrusion 333
cybersecurity 333

darknet markets 324–325; *see also* online drug markets, darknet forums
Data Retention regime 326
Daubert v Merrell Dow Pharmaceuticals case 179

DDC *see* District Disaster Controller
decolonial approaches 397
defence forces 47
degree-holder entry 16
delinquency, contemporary conceptions of 383–385
democratic policing: definition 93–94; key principles of 94; reliance on community trust 95
democratisation 8
"detective" 27
developed countries, population decline in 8
Dicke, Theresa 71
digital media 2; *see also* media and policing organisations, relationship between
digital news outlets 239
Disaster Management Act 2003 (Qld) 273, 274, 275
disaster management/emergency-management legislation 269, 272
discretion 113, 114, 461; behind exercise of policing power 116; context-specific 119–120; enabling potential of 114; exercised by police 115; impact measurement 120–122; policing power and 118–119; predeterminants for 119; routine policing 124; with and without moderation 117; *see also* AI policing tools
dissent trigger 115–116
distance education 19
"distinctly separate systems" 254
District Disaster Controller 274
diversified policing 221–222
DNA identification 169
domestic and family violence, Australian police response to 444; arrest 445; emerging challenges for 450–452; influence on outcomes 443; innovations in 448–450; investigation and charging 447–448; objectives of 444–445; protection orders 446–447

domestic violence 44; police leaders focus on 44–45
Dowling, Christopher 443
Dror, Itiel 179–180
drug crypto markets 339–340

early-career training 75–76
economic inequality, physical and social spaces of 359–360
education *see* police education
effective communication skills 55; and crime reduction strategies 58–60; and customer service obligations 56–58; importance in policing 55; strategies to enhance 61
Emergencies Act 2004 (ACT) 272
emergency/disaster controller of states and territories 272–274
emergency management, state police agencies in 267; civil defence units 268; community recovery plan 277–278; disaster events 268; education and training for 270; emergency/disaster response 275–277; future for 278–279; history of 267–268; legislation for 269; local/municipal roles and responsibilities 275; national emergency-management relationships 271–272; NDO 268–269; regional/district roles and responsibilities 274–275; state-level roles and responsibilities 272–274; state police emergency-management units 270; terrorist attacks 271
Emergency Management Act 2005 (SA) 272
Emergency Management Act 2005 (WA) 273
Emergency Management Act 2006 (Tas) 273, 274, 275
Emergency Management Act 2013 (NT) 273
Emergency Management Act 2013 (Vic) 273, 274
Emergency Management Commissioner 274

emergency services leaders *vs.* police leaders 52
emotional intelligence 46
empathy with victims 103
empirical analysis 172–173
employment opportunities and formal education 31
England and Wales, police training in: consistent approach to 15–16; PEQF routes of entry 16
Enlightenment period and scientific reasoning 163
environmental and climate change 9
ethical decisions 99
ethical dilemmas 98–100
ethical practice 93
Evans, Janet M. 429
evidence-based policing 10, 284
expert witnesses 167
extremist groups 302
Eyes on the Street initiative 225

family and domestic violence 466–468
family and intimate partner violence 255; homicides 256; policing-public health interface for 256–257; *see also* violence
Family Violence Command 256
FDV *see* family and domestic violence
fentanyl overdoses 339
Findlay, Mark 113
fingerprint identification 168–169
fingerprint laboratories, accuracy testing of 180
Fire Services Commissioner Act 2010 (Vic) 273
Fitzgerald vision for community policing 289–290
force and partnership working, use of 2
foreign police assistance 356
forensic identification: Bertillonage 168; cameras 169; database system 168; DNA identification 169; facial identification 169–170; fingerprint identification 168–169; Peel's work for 167; working principle in 176
forensic intelligence: eliminating suspects from perspective of 170–171; need to develop 166
forensic medicine 166
Forensic Procedures Act (2000) 166
forensic psychiatrists 166–167
forensic science 2; conceptual development of 175–176; divisions and disciplines 164–167, 170; forensic intelligence and 167; in intelligence-led policing practices 167; practice in policing 170–175; questioning reliability of 177–180; theoretical foundations 175–177
forensic science practices 164, 166; comparative analysis 173; empirical analysis 172–173; examination findings 173–174; interpretative analysis 173; methodological approaches 171–173; non-identification 170–171; observation 173; person of interest's (POI) height, photogrammetric examination of 174–175; sequence of scientific investigation 171; staff expertise 170; theoretical model of 171–172
formal education 30–31
fraud 291–292; Australian research on 291; enforcement and prevention 291; as fastest growing crime 291
Free Recall (FR) framework of investigative interviewing 149–154
funding for collaborative policing policy 212–213
future police leaders 51–52

Gaffey, John 239
Gallagher, Peter 71
Gangs Intelligence Hub 135
Geelong Venues against Violence Accord 285–287

gender: equality and police integrity 102–104; and needs satisfaction 86; and wellbeing outcomes 86
General Life Satisfaction 84
German police, four-tier career system of 16
global economy 7
globalisation 7, 350
good governance practices 206
Goodman-Delahunty, Jane 199
good partnership 201; mechanisms of 205–208; problem-solving partnerships 203–204; research partnerships 202–203; training partnerships 204–205
Guo, Jiesi 71

Hansa (darknet marketplace) 338–339
hate crime 307, 421–425; defining and theorising 414–415, 422; incidents 413–414; nature and extent of 417–418, 422; perpetrators of 418–419, 422; reporting and recording 421–422, 424–425; systematic review 416; victims of 419–421, 424
health, social determinants of 253
health inequalities 253
higher education and police education, partnership between 16
higher-education qualifications 16–17
high-risk violent offenders, identifying 436–437
historical racism, in policing aboriginal identity 125–126
hostage-taking in Brighton community of Melbourne 202
human rights, in policing 100
human rights, travesties of 114
human trafficking 201

ICT-enabled offences 323–325
IDG see International Deployment Group
illicit drug use 258–259, 316–317
ILT see instructor-led teaching
"image work" and police media units 242–245
Independent Broad-Based Anti-Corruption Commission 321
Indigenous people 95, 125, 398–400, 468–469
Indigenous security and safety governance 405–406
individualisation, concept of 176
information and knowledge acquisition, barriers to 211–212
information and knowledge sharing, impediments to 212, 213
information-heavy products 131
ingenious card database system 168
institutional barriers to partnership 210–212; barriers to information and knowledge acquisition 211–212; cultures of secrecy 210–211; inadequate funding 212–213
institutional governance 95
instructor-led teaching 26, 30
intelligence 129–130; see also criminal intelligence
intelligence-led police 166
intelligence-led policing 131, 437–439; Australian Criminal Intelligence Model 133–134; Australian Criminal Intelligence Strategy 135–136; forensic intelligence and 166–167; interpretations 132; lack of uniformity with respect to 132–133; origin in United Kingdom 132; violence 437–439
intelligence products 131–132
interactions with people 7, 13, 57–59; see also victims, police interaction with
internal and external change within societies 8
International Deployment Group 352
international partners, engagement with 309
international policing 349; capacity building 351; cultural imperialism risk with 356–359; globalisation impact on 350; peacekeeping 350
International Positive Psychology Association 72
interoperability 310–311
inter-organisational relationships 201
interpersonal violence 466–467
interpretative analysis 173
interviewing suspects 432–435
intimate samples, collection of 166
intra-state conflicts 351
investigative interviewing 2; background of 145–147; CM framework for 149–151, 154–158; Free Recall (FR) for 149–154; interviewee-centered approach 149–150; interviewing protocols 149; need for development and reform in 148; plan execution 158; planning methodologies 149; policing landscape issues in 147–148; research involving police agencies 147
Investigative Interviewing Force Champion 147
investigative skills 435–436
IPPA see International Positive Psychology Association
Ireland, Jane L. 413
ISIS see Islamic State in Iraq and the Sham
Islamic fundamentalist terror 300
Islamic State in Iraq and the Sham: ambition of 301; extreme fundamentalist regime 302; fighting force of 301; forces fighting against 302; military defeat 302; origin of 301; recruiting videos 301–302; self-promotion using social media 301; threat posed by 302–303

Jay, Daren 145
jihad 302

Kaldas, Nick 299
Kebbell, Mark R. 429
Kennedy, Michael 1, 71, 93, 349

Kesic, Dragana 183
Kirk, Paul 176
Koehler, Jonathan 176–177
Kruger, Erin 1, 367

laboratory-based forensic science 165–166
labour market, fluidity of 29
law enforcement and public health *see* public health and policing
law enforcement model of policing 8
LDMG *see* Local Disaster Management Group
"Leaderless Jihad" 301
leadership *see* police leadership
leadership changes: conditions influencing need for 40; correlation with organisational changes 39; impact of 39
leadership in crisis *vs.* leadership through crisis 45–47
leadership through change 47–49
leadership through crisis *vs.* leadership in crisis 45–47
learner-centric models *see* student-centred learning
learning: concepts associated with 24; focus in policing 25; levels of 26; with police organisations 25
learning organisation: in police contexts 31–32; theory of 30
legislative framework, changing ICT environment 325–326
legislative knowledge-based side of policing 26
legitimacy, police 40–41, 52, 114, 206
Leibniz, Gottfried 176
Leibniz's Law 176
Lesbian, Gay, Bisexual, Transsexual, Queer, Intersex, and Asexual (LGBTQIA+) community 43–44
liberal-democratic models and community policing 356–359
liberal education, method of 10
lifelong career option, policing as 27
lifelong learner 29, 31

lifelong learning 27; definition of 30; essential characteristics of 31; need for 29–31; reasons for 31
Lindt café siege 305
Local Disaster Management Group 275
Locard, Edmond 175
Locard's Exchange Principle 175–176
London Metropolitan Police 40
Luxemburg, Rosa 113
Lysons-Smith, Shane 129

management and leadership, difference between 42
Manock, Ian 267
Marsh, Herbert W. 71
Maurushat, Alana 333
McKinley, Amber 461
MCPEM *see* Ministerial Council for Police and Emergency Management
media and policing organisations, relationship between: citizen journalism 245–248; police-media engagement online 243–245; police media units and "image work" 242–243; power struggles 241; sousveillance 248–250; substantial changes in 239; technological accountability 245–250
media engagement goals of policing organisations 242–243
media-related technological developments 239
medical division of forensic science 166
medical students 62
mental health 3
Mental Health Attitude Survey for Police 378
Mental Health Intervention Teams 375–376
mental health issues: lack of support to prevent 97; police call-outs to 374–375; police responses to 367, 372–374, 378–379; and wellbeing 76
mental health literacy 371–372

mental health of police: compassion fatigue 377–378; initiatives to improve 367; organisational culture impact on 367, 368; policing occupation impact on 367–368; PTSD rates 369, 377–378; recommendations to improve 371–372; stress-related disorders 367–369, 377
mental-ill health, factors associated with 74, 75
methamphetamine use 316–317
methodological approaches of forensic science 171, **172**; comparative analysis 173; empirical analysis 172–173; interpretative analysis 173; observation 173
MHASP *see* Mental Health Attitude Survey for Police
MHITs *see* Mental Health Intervention Teams
migration and immigration 8
militarisation 96
military leaders *vs.* police leaders 52
mindfulness 63, 88
Ministerial Council for Police and Emergency Management 271–272
misconduct and corruption, in police forces: external oversight of investigations into 101–102; vulnerable areas of police work 101; ways to address 104–105
missing person 464–465
MLA *see* mutual legal assistance
Model for Real World Enquiry to criminal investigations 204
modern-day police force 2
Modern policing 47
money laundering 317–318
Moore, Mark 48
moral values 12
Morgan, Anthony 315, 443
mosque attack 202
motor learning, in weapons training 28
Moylan, Kelly 349

multi-jurisdictional development 49
Munich Olympic attack 305
Municipal Emergency Management Coordinator 275
mutual legal assistance 321

National Anti-Gangs Squad 320
National Criminal Intelligence Capability Committee 135
National Criminal Intelligence System 129, 135, 325
National Drug Strategy 258
national emergency-management relationships 271–272
National Intelligence Model 133
National Motor Vehicle Theft Reduction Council 224–225
National Police Professional Implementation Advisory Committee 11
National Police Reference System 135–136
National Research Council (NRC) inquiries 177–178
National Strategy to Fight Transnational, Serious and Organized Crime Model 214
National Target System 135
natural disasters 9
Natural Disasters Organisation 268–269
NCICC *see* National Criminal Intelligence Capability Committee
NDO *see* Natural Disasters Organisation
needs fulfillment and mental health 82–83
need support, circumstances of 78, **79**
"neighbourhood policing" 254
New South Wales: police education and training in 17; Police Media Unit (PMU) 241–243
New South Wales Crime Commission 321
New South Wales Police Force: *Annual Report* for 2018/19 284; commitment to enhance customer service 56; crime news production 241–242;
Customer Service Charter 56; customer service complaints concerning 60–61; Customer Service Guidelines 56; general duties police officers 59; need support in **79**
New South Wales Police Force 267; Code of Conduct and Ethics 98; Corporate Plan 57; Customer Service Charter 100; wellbeing programs, satisfaction and engagement with 85
New South Wales Police Force Academy 12, 19
news stories, newsworthiness of 240
news values 240
New Zealand 303
Night Watch 267
NMVTRC *see* National Motor Vehicle Theft Reduction Council
noble cause corruption 99–100
non-judgemental approach 63
Northern Territory 191, 273, 465; police education and training in 17, **18**, police force history 267
NPPIAC *see* National Police Professional Implementation Advisory Committee
NPRS *see* National Police Reference System
NSWPF *see* New South Wales Police
NSWPF Corporate Plan 58
NSWPF *see* New South Wales Police Force
NSWPF Academy *see* New South Wales Police Force Academy
nursing 28–29

occupational stress and wellbeing 77
officer 23
OMCG *see* outlaw motorcycle gangs
online assessments 23
online child sexual abuse material 341–344; case study of 342; challenges for law enforcement 342–344; key issues of 342–344; market of 341; "sexting" 342–343
online drug markets, darknet forums 337–340; advantages for stakeholders 339–340; case study of 339; cryptocurrencies use 338; darknet markets, takedown of 338–339; drug crypto markets 339; encrypted communications 337–338; harm reduction forums 340; key issues and challenges of 339–340; Silk Road 1 339; TOR browser and TAILS 338
online fraud 333
online news 241
online news delivery 241
on-the job-training 23, 30
operational intelligence: changes in 137–138; definition of 130
operational policing 28
Operation Anchorage 290–291
Operation Helpem Fren 357
Operation Pendennis 310
organisational diversity 29
organisational ethics 95
organisational justice theory 97
organisational planning 42
organisational police culture 95–97, 210; institutional governance 95; media and citizen support 96; militarisation 96; police legitimacy 95; practitioner's ethics 95–96; procedural justice and 96–97; rank-and-file police 96; support for mental health issues 97
organisational resilience 48
organisational units, restructuring of 48
organised and transnational crime: corruption risk from 322–323; cost to Australia 316; cryptocurrencies 324; cybercrime 318; darknet markets 324–325; emerging trends in 326–327; encryption challenges 324; ICT-enabled offences 323–325; illicit drug activity 316–317; international cooperation to

tackle 321–322, 325–326; investigations 321–322; money laundering 317–318; outlaw motorcycle gangs 317; policing at Commonwealth level 319–320; policing at state and territory level 320–321

organised crime: definition of 315; transnational *vs.* 316

organised online fraud 334–337; boiler room fraud 334; case studies 335–336; cryptocurrency 334; key issues and challenges 334, 336; tackling 336–337; types of 334

outlaw motorcycle gangs 317

pandemics 259–261; *see also* COVID-19 pandemic

Pankhurst, Gary 145

paramilitary model of policing 9

partnership approach to policing 10–11; *see also* strategic partnerships

peacekeeping mission of Solomon Islands with AFP 349, 354–355

peacekeeping mission of Timor-Leste with AFP 349, 353–354

peacekeeping operations *see* peace operations

PEACE model framework: CM framework 149–151, 154–158; Free Recall (FR) 149–154; plan execution 158

peace operations: capacity-building practices and 351; changing nature and role of 351; in context of failed state 351; definition of 350; focus on conflict cessation 350; as humanitarian aid 351

Pearls Program 49

Peelian model of police 397

"Peelian Principles" and modern policing 40–41

Peel Police in London 116

PEQF *see* Policing Education Qualifications Framework

perception, enslaving role of 115

personal development 31; definition 32; in policing context 32–33

Philip, Arthur 267

physical activity and wellbeing 88

physical wellbeing promotion 76

"places of mass gatherings" 308

"pluralised policing" 221

police call-outs, rates of 374–375

police communication training: perceived gaps in knowledge 63; role plays 61–63

police-community continuum of interaction 206, *207*

police counterterrorism teams 271

"police/crime" television programs 46

police culture 50; and associated issues 94–95; and coping strategies 369–371; incompatibility with criminal intelligence 130; intelligence incompatibility with 130; negative aspects of 94–95; organisational 95–97

police custody, deaths in 401–403

police discretion, application of 2

police education 1, 2, 10, 23; classroom-based learning 25–26; defining 25–29; earliest stages of 10; flexibility 19; insularity concerns 11; models of 10–11; phases of 26; "sage on the stage" education 26; traditional approach to 11, 25–26, 30; and training, differences between 26–29; training syllabus 11; university education 11

police education and training: adapting 28; in Australia **17–18**; for emergency management 270; professional practice-based education 25; tactical element of practice 25

police ethics 97–100; definition of 97; enhancing 104–105; ethical codes for practitioners 97–98; ethical decisions 99; ethical dilemmas 98–100;
noble cause corruption 99–100; NSWPF Code of Conduct and Ethics 98; Police Service of Northern Ireland (PSNI) Code of Ethics 2008 98

police force, modern-day issues faced by 2–3

police-health-research partnership 256

police higher education 10, 11

police integrity 102–104; gender equality affecting 102–104; in NSW and Croatia 102

police intelligence *see* criminal intelligence

police leaders 2, 39; accountability of 41; adapting to changes 47–48; aging society related challenges to 44; appointment of 50; community diversity influencing 43–44; counterterrorism issues for 309; critical factor in "success" of 45; focus on domestic violence 44–45; fundamental competency of 39; with high level of emotional intelligence 46; key attributes of 45, 48; legitimacy of 40–41; responsibilities of 47, 48; social disadvantage within community challenging 44; technology impact on 45; *vs.* emergency services leaders 52; *vs.* military leaders 52

police leadership 39; appointment process 39; associated with Chief Officers 46; assumptions about 40; broadening capabilities 27; building 25; community members' expectation of 51; counterterrorism 311–312; decision making 47; development 49–51; and management, difference between 42; models 50; of organisation 30; as position 46; proactive 42; quality and wellbeing 77; stakeholders 49; uniqueness concept of 52; visible 49–50

police legitimacy 95; aggressive tactics and 58; factors contributing towards 16; and procedural justice, link between 57
police management 294
police media units and "image work" 242–245
police misconduct and public support, link between 57, 58
police officer wellbeing *see* police psychological wellbeing
police organisations 19, 23; education requirements 28; movement from craft to profession 13–14; personal development within 32–33; professional "Education and Training" service 26–27, 30; professional standards department 101; as standalone agencies 10
police policy and practice 199, 200; collaborative policing framework 208–209; cross-disciplinary engagement 201; cross-sector collaboration 200–201; cultures of secrecy within 210–211; development of 199; implications for 214–215; inadequate funding for 212–213; inter-organisational relationships 201; methods to develop 208–210; policy capability knowledge barriers 211–212; problem-solving partnerships 203–204; research partnerships 202–203; shared value creation 201–202; training partnerships 204–205; transdisciplinary partnerships 213–214
police policy documents 284
police practice 2; *see also* police education; police psychological wellbeing; police training
police problems 203
police profession, career pathways and options in 27
police psychological wellbeing 71, 90; costs of 72; differences across career stage and position 75; positive psychology approach to 72–73; psychosocial factors crucial for 72; self-determination theory and 73–74; *see also* wellbeing
police psychological wellbeing, factors associated with: alcohol consumption 84, 88; alcohol use 84; autonomy 75; burnout 88, 89; career stage and wellbeing indicators 87–88; command type and needs satisfaction 86–87; communication 75; coping mechanisms 76; early-career training 75–76; gender and needs satisfaction 86; gender and wellbeing outcomes 86; leadership quality 77; mental health difficulties 76; mindfulness 88; occupational stress 77; physical activity 88; physical wellbeing promotion 76; psychological distress 84, 88, 89; psychological inflexibility 88, 89; psychological needs satisfaction and wellbeing 85–86; PTSD symptoms 88, 89; rank 87; restricted duties and long-term sick leave 88–89; satisfaction and engagement 85; screening processes 75; staff roles and needs satisfaction 86; support for injured officers 75; wellbeing and life satisfaction 84; wellbeing initiatives 85; workload 77; years in police force 87
police public relations activities 239
police recruits, in Germany 16
police-research partnership agenda 202
police service, PEQF routes of entry into 16
Police Service of Northern Ireland (PSNI) Code of Ethics 2008 98
police training 2, 7; accreditation of 16; annual mandatory training 25; mandatory training 17, 18; partnerships 204–205; practitioner-focused skills-based 18–19; probationary period 18; review of 11; at state level 12
police use of force 194; in Australia 186–187; fatal force use 183–184, 187–188; non-fatal force use 184, 188–191; persons with mental health issues 184–186, 191–193; and race, link between 184
policing 1, 2, 13, 24; changes impacting 7; definition 7; evolution alongside societal technological advancement 28; as profession 12–13
policing agencies 9; future challenges of 7–9, 23; organisational challenges of 9–10; origins and structures of 9
"policing by consent" model 40–41
Policing Education Qualifications Framework 16
policing organisation professional development *see* professional development
policing power: abusive phenomenon 114; AI policing tools for 122; defensive role for 116; and discretion 118–120; as discretionary decision-making 113, 114; in lawless ecosystems 114; substantive context of 113; as uncivilising force 115
policing power abuse 113; in citizen encounters 114–115; efforts to constrain 114; by Hong Kong Police 114, 115, 116; impact measurement 120–122
policing-public health interface *see* police-health-research partnership
policy capacity 206
political landscape, in future 8
political protest 9
politics and police using data 140–141
POP *see* problem-oriented policing

INDEX

POPP *see* Problem-Oriented and Partnership Policing
population shift 8
Porter, Amanda 397
Porter, Glenn 163
portfolio approach to career 29
positive psychology 72–73
postcolonial approaches 397
Post-Traumatic Stress Disorder 71, 88, 89
Pracademic 33
pracademic: creating space for 29; notion of 24; potential in policing professions 35
practice-based learning enabling 29
practitioner's ethics 95
predictive and proactive algorithms 122
predictive policing 131
Preferred Reporting Items for Systematic Review 416
pre-join degree 16
Prenzler, Tim 221, 283
PRISMA *see* Preferred Reporting Items for Systematic Review
private policing/security sector: business drivers of 223; characterisation of 221–222; engagement with 311; and public security, ties between 225–227; regulation of 228–229; size of 223–224
private security 232; common form of engagement of 224; definition of 222; engaged in policing roles 222; firms 221; powers and immunities 229–231; training 229
proactive leadership 42
Problem-Oriented and Partnership Policing 284
problem-oriented policing 203, 294
Problem Oriented Policing approach 10
problem-solving methodology 294
problem-solving model 203–204
problem-solving partnerships 203–204
procedural justice: definition 57; elements in police interactions for RBT 59–60; and organisational justice 96–97; and police legitimacy, link between 57
profession 105
professional approach 12–13
professional career, discursive shift to 27
professional development 1, 23, 31; definition 31; engagement in 31–32; need for 32; and police practice 31–32
professional discretion 15
professionalism 65
professionalisation of policing 1, **15**, 19, 24, 28–29, 98, 204; characteristics of 105; craftsmen/women 13–14; criminal intelligence units 130; debate on 52; development of 106; diversity of 27; senior professionals 14; shift to 14–15; young professionals 14
professionalised policing model 28
professional practice-based education 25
professional standards department 101, 104–105
project management 42
protection orders 446–447
psychological distress and wellbeing 72, 84, 88, 89
psychological inflexibility and wellbeing 88, 89
psychological needs across career 80
psychological needs satisfaction and wellbeing 85–86
psychological need support, officer experiences of 89–90; autonomy, contexts supporting 78–79; autonomy and career stage 80–81; competence, contexts supporting 79; competence and career stage 81; needs fulfillment and mental health 82–83; need support, circumstances of 78, **79**; psychological needs across career 80; relatedness and career stage 81–82; relatedness satisfaction, contexts supporting 79–80
PTSD *see* Post-Traumatic Stress Disorder
public disorder, incidents of 96
public dissent 116
public health and policing 2, 253; "distinctly separate systems" towards 254; evidence-based practice for 254, 256–257; illicit drug use 258–259; opportunities challenging 261–262; pandemics 259–261; purpose of 254; road safety 257–258; violence reduction 255–257
public health crisis 253–254
public policy and policing *see* police policy and practice
public policy collaboration 199, 200; collaborative approaches 201; collaborative policing framework 208–209; cross-disciplinary engagement 201; cross-sector collaboration 200–201; institutional barriers to 210–212; inter-organisational relationships 201; methods to develop 208–210; problem-solving partnerships 203–204; research partnerships 202–203; shared value creation 201–202; strategic partnerships 200–201; training partnerships 204–205; transdisciplinary partnerships 213–214
public relations practices of police 243
public safety and security issues 23, 199; complexity and pluralistic nature of 200; human trafficking 201
public value 48

QCET *see* Queensland Community Engagement Trial
Queensland 17, 273, 274
Queensland Community Engagement Trial 257–258
Queensland Police Service (QPS) 284, 289–290, 294, 371–372

racial stereotyping 123
RAMSI intervention in Solomon Islands 349
random breath testing 292–293; encounters with police 59–60; reducing crashes through 285; and traffic crashes, link between 293
rank and wellbeing 87
Rapoport, David 300
rapport, building and maintenance of 149
RBT *see* random breath testing
real-time intelligence sharing system 135
reflective practice: impact of 34–35; skill of 33–34
reflective practitioner, ethos of 65–66
reflexivity 206
Regional Assistance Mission to Solomon Islands 354–355
Regional Emergency Management Committee 274
Regional Emergency Management Controller 274
relatedness: and career stage 81–82; satisfaction, contexts supporting 79–80
relatedness-supporting contexts of SDT 74
relationship-building practices, communication skills for 63–65
relationship management 46
REMC *see* Regional Emergency Management Committee
renaissance period and scientific reasoning 163
research partnerships 202–203
"response policing" 254
responsibility, notions of 40
restricted duties and long-term sick leave 88–89
retention of officers, factors associated with 74
returning fighters, debate on 305–306
right-wing extremism, re-emergence of 307
road fatalities 293
road safety initiatives 257–258, 292–293

Robinson, Simon 267
Rogers, Colin 7
role plays: authenticity concerns in 61–62; benefits of 62–63
rote-based learning system 29
Royal Commission into Aged Care Quality and Safety in Australia 44
Royal Marines 267
rule of law 93–94
Ryan, Richard M. 71

Saks, Michael 176–177
SAPol *see* South Australian Police
SARA *see* "Scan, Analyse, Respond, Assess"
Sarre, Rick 221, 283
satisfaction and engagement 85
"Scan, Analyse, Respond, Assess" 294
scientific method 163–164
scientific reasoning: advantages of 163; development of 163–164; philosophical challenges and complexities 164
scientific revolution 163
screening processes 75
SDT *see* self-determination theory
SEC *see* State Emergency Coordinator
secrecy within policing 210–211
security officers, safety of 227–228
security "quilt" *see* "pluralised policing"
self-awareness 46
self-determination theory 78; basic psychological needs of 73–74; needs frustration and poorer wellbeing 75; needs satisfaction and positive wellbeing 75
self-policing 8
self-reflection 206
self-regulation 46
senior officer ranks, shift in 27
senior police leaders: international development 49; roles of 51
senior police officer 46
senior professionals 14

Serious Financial Crime Taskforce 320
settler colonial societies: concept of 398; policing 397–401
"sexting" 342–343
sexual crime 467
shared value creation 201–202
shoplifter, dealing with 14
Short Warwick Edinburgh Mental Well-Being Scale 84
Sicard, Louise A. 383
siege scenario 307–308
skill acquisition 31
social awareness 46
social cohesiveness and urbanisation, link between 8
social contract 93
social control 7
social disadvantage, within community 44
social media 239; community engagement via 244, 245; information sharing 244; news distribution through 241; police image management with 243–245; as source of news 241
social movements, governance difficulties with 8
social restrictiveness 378
Social Science Research and Intelligence in Australia (report) 202
solvability analysis 122
sousveillance 248–250
South Australia 17, **18**, 272–273, 276, 352
South Australian Police 270
sovereignty activists 407–408
Sports Integrity Australia 320
staff roles and needs satisfaction 86
state and citizens, relationship between 7
state and territory police: role in countering terrorism 303–304; role in emergency management 270, 272–275
State Emergency and Rescue Management Act 1989 (NSW) 272
State Emergency Coordinator 275

state emergency/disaster controller 272
state police emergency-management units 270
Stenning, Philip 222
Stewart, Ian 39
STMP *see* Suspect Targeting Management Plan
strategic intelligence: changes in 136–137; definition of 131
strategic leaders 42
strategic partnerships: collaborative policing framework 208–209; cross-disciplinary engagement 201; cross-sector collaboration 200–201; five-stage life cycle of 208, *209*; institutional barriers to 210–212; methods to develop 208–210; problem-solving partnerships 203–204; research partnerships 202–203; shared value creation 201–202; training partnerships 204–205
strategic vision 206
Strike Force Piccadilly (problem-solving initiative) 225, 288–289
structural racism 95
student-centred learning 27
student police officer 14
Sub-Saharan Africa and South Asia, population rise in 8
succession planning 51
suicide attacks, motivation for 303
Sunbird (project) 292
Sunderland, Graham 39
support for injured officers 75
surveillance and situational crime prevention techniques 9
Suspect Targeting Management Plan 58
sustainable crime reduction 283
sustainable multisectoral analysis 199

tactical element of practice 25
tactical intelligence 129–130
tactical operations space 310
talent management 51
"tap-and-go" ("contactless" or "pay wave") card payment systems 292
Tasmania 267, 274, 275, 352, 389, 390; emergency-management in 274, 275; police education and training in 17, **18**; Port Arthur Massacre 276
Tasmania Police 19, 147, 274, 277
Tasmania Police Academy 19
teaching 28–29
technical training 25
technological accountability: citizen journalism 245–248; sousveillance 248–250
technology: benefits 9; challenges for police 9; developments in 9; impact on policing 45; influence on police leaders 45
technology gap 9
technology use 8–9; adapting to 23, 28; in problem solving 30
telecommunications metadata 326
territory emergency/disaster controller 272
terrorism 9; accountability and scrutiny challenges 305; 9/11 attacks 301; as disaster threat 271; four modern waves of 300; history of 301; Islamic fundamentalist phase 300–301; motivation for 303; opportunities to counter 308–309; paradigm shift in dealing with 304–305; police weapon and training debate 308; returning fighters 305–306; right-wing extremism 307; siege scenario challenges 307–308; state and territory police in countering 303–304; threat of 300; ubiquitous incidence of 299
tertiary education partnerships 204
tertiary qualifications 52
Thomas, Stuart D.M. 183, 253
Timor-Leste: INTERFET mission to 353; UN mission to 354

Timor-Leste Police Development Program 349
Torres Strait Islander community 44
Tracy, Cyclone 268, 269
traditional crime and new technologies 9
traditional cultural approach to policing 130–131
trainee teacher education 61–62
training: craftsmen 14; partnerships 204–205; professional framework for 15–16; syllabus 11
transnational crime: definition of 315–316; organised *vs.* 316
transnationalisation 350
transnational nature of CAM 342

uniqueness, concept of 176
United Kingdom 133, 324; hate crime offences 413; intelligence-led policing in 132; investigative interviewing structure in 147; National Crime Squad 341; National Intelligence Model 133
urbanisation 8
US city policing 116
US President's Council of Advisors on Science and Technology (PCAST) report 177–179

value-adding to intelligence products 131–132
Van Zanden, Brooke 71
Veljanova, Irena 349
victims, police interaction with 462; family and domestic violence (FDV) 466–468; importance of 461; indigenous people 468–469; missing person 464–465; people living with mental illness 469–471
victims of crime 3, 462
Victorian Bushfires Royal Commission 273
Victoria Police model 186
Victoria Police Screening Assessment for Family Violence Risk 256–257

Victoria Police's Use of Force Register 186–187
violence: costs to health systems 255; evidence-based practice for 254, 256–257; family and intimate partner violence 255, 256; forms of 429; front-line police role in 255–256; high-risk violent offenders, identifying 436–437; intelligence-led policing 437–439; investigating allegations of 429–430; investigative skills for policing 435–436; suspects, interviewing 432–433; witnesses and victims, interviewing 430–432
visible leadership 49–50
vocational framework for education 27
vocational sectors, relevance of policing capabilities in 27
Voce, Isabella 315
Vollmer, August 10
VP-SAFvR *see* Victoria Police Screening Assessment for Family Violence Risk
vulnerable areas of police work 101
vulnerable person 462

Wales *see* England and Wales, police training in
wellbeing 2; and autonomy 75; and communication 75; initiatives 85; and life satisfaction 84; *see also* police psychological wellbeing
Western Australia 187, 190, 273, 275; Eyes on the Street initiative 225; police education and training in 17; RBT and traffic crashes, link between 293
Whitford, Troy 129
Wintle, Emma 7
Wood Commission, positive changes from 94–95
Wooden, Ken 55

Wood Royal Commission 12, 19, 106
work-based learning 24
"workers" and professionals, divisions existing between 13
workload and wellbeing 77
workplace learning 24
workplace simulations 23
workplace stressors 71–72, 74

young people: governance and risk of 385–387; interactions with 59; and police, relationships between 58–59, 63, 391–394
young professionals 14
youth offenders: across jurisdiction 388–389; under community-based supervision 390–391; in detention 390–391; diverted across jurisdiction 390–391; indigenous 389–390; types of 389

Zedner, Lucia 222

Lightning Source UK Ltd.
Milton Keynes UK
UKHW050155051121
393416UK00004B/9